Kesselring's Last Battle

Kesselring's Last Battle

War Crimes Trials and Cold War Politics, 1945–1960

Kerstin von Lingen

Translated by Alexandra Klemm

UNIVERSITY PRESS OF KANSAS

All photographs are from Albert Kesselring's collection, now in possession of Dr. Rainer Kesselring.

Originally published in German by Verlag Ferdinand Schöningh GmbH, 2004

Published by the University Press of Kansas (Lawrence, Kansas 66045), which was organized by the Kansas Board of Regents and is operated and funded by Emporia State University, Fort Hays State University, Kansas State University, Pittsburg State University, the University of Kansas, and Wichita State University.

Library of Congress Cataloging-in-Publication Data
Lingen, Kerstin von, 1971–
Kesselring's Last battle : war crimes trials and Cold War politics, 1945–1960 / Kerstin von Lingen ; translated by Alexandra Klemm.
p. cm. — (Modern war studies)
Includes bibliographical references and index.
ISBN 978-0-7006-1641-1 (cloth : alk. paper)
1. Kesselring, Albert, 1885-1960—Trials, litigation, etc. 2. Trials (Genocide)—Germany—Nuremberg. 3. War crimes trials. 4. Cold War. 5. International War Crimes Tribunal. I. Title.

KK73.5.K47L56 2009
341.6′90268—dc22

2008045734

British Library Cataloguing-in-Publication Data is available.

Printed in the United States of America
10 9 8 7 6 5 4 3 2 1

The paper used in this publication is acid free and meets the minimum requirements of the American National Standard for Perma-nence of Paper for Printed Library Materials Z39.48-1992.

CONTENTS

ACKNOWLEDGMENTS

This book was written primarily during 1999–2001 while I was working in Tübingen University's Special Research Section 437, which deals with "Experiences of War—War and Society in the Modern Era." The book was based on the theoretical groundwork laid by fellow researchers in the section.[1] As well as being afforded the opportunity to participate in this research, I was able to enjoy a superbly equipped working environment. This was of both psychological and practical benefit: as a mother, I simply would not have been able to complete the work without these facilities. Therefore, particular thanks must go to the Special Research Section and to the German Research Foundation for sponsoring young academics in research sections throughout Germany.

The progress of the manuscript through a labyrinth of reviewing and other editorial procedures would not have been as smooth—or, indeed, possible—without the tireless support of Michael Briggs, editor-in-chief of the University Press of Kansas. I would also like to thank Susan McRory, Susan Schott, Joan Sherman, and Cathy Evans of the press. Finally, a translation is always only as good as the translator's abilities: I was lucky to find the Dublin-based translator Alexandra Klemm.

This work actually had four "progenitors." My academic advisers were Professor Dieter Langewiesche of Tübingen University and Professor Hans-Peter Ullmann of Cologne University. Not only did they offer me a position in the Special Research Section "Experience at War" in Tübingen, they also encouraged me during the various phases of the work's evolution and offered many valuable suggestions. In addition, I consider myself fortunate to have had Dr. Gerhard Schreiber and Dr. Georg Meyer, of Freiburg University, as mentors. Both men—who are now retired—are known for their expertise, Dr. Schreiber on the issue of war crimes in Italy and Dr. Meyer on the rearmament debate. During the 1990s, they were also both active on behalf of the German Institute of Military History, which has since moved from Freiburg to Potsdam. Although these two historians' research areas and approaches are very different, it was precisely the dynamic interaction between their findings that influenced and advanced this work on Albert Kesselring.

Thanks to my time studying at the University of Freiburg in Breisgau (which was then located close to the German Institute of Military History) and the University of Milan in Italy, I benefited from an academic dialogue with a range of interested colleagues in both Germany and Italy at an early point in my research. During my studies at Freiburg University, my interest in the Wehrmacht as an area of research was initially awakened by Professor Wilhelm Deist, Professor Bernd Martin, Professor Manfred Messerschmidt, and Dr. Wolfram Wette. In addition, my work for the Professor Wolfgang Reinhardt Chair at the Department of Modern History at Freiburg University taught me a meticulous approach to academic research, training I have always found of great benefit. The proximity to the German Institute of Military History in Freiburg was extremely helpful when it came to the genesis of this book. I owe particular thanks to Professor Hans-Erich Volkmann, Professor Rolf-Dieter Müller, and Dr. Winfried Heinemann, and I am grateful for the contributions made by other colleagues as well. Professor Gerhard Weinberg of the University of North Carolina at Chapel Hill, Professor Richard Breitman of the American University in Washington, Professor Gerhard Hirschfeld of Stuttgart University, and Professor Dietrich Beyrau of Tübingen University all showed unusual interest in my work, and I would like to thank them. My gratitude also goes to Professor Norbert Frei of Jena University for giving me the opportunity to discuss my theories in his colloquium.

As a result of my master's thesis on German foreign propaganda in Italy from 1943 to 1945, I was offered a course bursary for the German Historical Institute in Rome. This experience provided me with my first Italian academic contacts, and at this point, I would like to thank Professor Arnold Esch, Dr. Jens Petersen, and Dr. Lutz Klinkhammer. I always benefited from my contact with Italian colleagues, especially my academic supervisor, Professor Ivano Granata of the University of Milan. I am particularly indebted to Professor Paolo Pezzino and Professor Michele Battini of the University of Pisa. They welcomed me into their academic circle, and once I had completed my work, they did all in their power to promote it by offering me lecture and publication opportunities.

I am often asked why I chose precisely this subject. During my time studying in Milan, I became aware that the period of German occupation in northern Italy, toward the end of World War II, was one of the pivotal moments in the sometimes turbulent history that Germany and Italy share. Many aspects of the current relations between the two countries can only be explained by referring to this past. I found that the image of Albert Kesselring, whose name is almost universally known in Italy, was far more positive in Italy than in Germany. I was particularly interested in tracking down the origins of this incongruity.

I received significant and varied assistance during the many years I spent researching this work in various archives. Freiburg Archive Director Dr. Manfred Kehrig, together with his head of department, Dr. Günter Fetzer, as well as Lutz Möser in Berlin, displayed great commitment to my research into the Kesselring case. Various veterans' associations—including the Verband deutscher Soldaten (VdS), the Luftwaffenring, the Verband deutsches Afrikakorps, and the Ordensgemeinschaft der Ritterkreuzträger des Eisernen Kreuzes e. V.—were willing to open their private archives for the first time in the interests of research, which allowed me to document Kesselring's work for their organizations. I am also very grateful to the Kesselring family and other private individuals who spoke with me and offered their personal perspectives on the Kesselring trial and the World War II period on the southern front. Many of them did not hesitate to provide me with private documents and records for my research, despite the fact that they viewed my work with some skepticism. Even though I may not have succeeded in winning them over to my theories, I am greatly honored by having at least won their trust during the course of what were sometimes fierce disagreements.

My acknowledgments would not be complete if I failed to mention the help provided by my colleagues and friends, who supported me and offered constructive criticism. In particular, the English version of this work has benefited from the valuable suggestions offered by Bryan Mark Rigg (American Military University), Alaric Searle (Salford University, Manchester), Gerhard Weinberg (Chapel Hill), Richard Breitman (Washington), and Judi O'Brien.

I would like to offer a special word of thanks to the Holocaust scholar Stephen Tyas for his constant support and advice, not to mention his trips to Britain's National Archives during the final stages of this translation.

I could not have written this book without the support of my family and in particular my husband, David. I am especially indebted to my parents, Heidemarie and Hans-Heinrich Schmelzer, and my in-laws, Gabriele and Dr. Michael von Lingen, as well as my grandparents. This book is dedicated with all my love to my children, Anastassia and Constantin, who have had to share their mom with Mr. Kesselring during the past few years.

Kerstin von Lingen

Tübingen, February 2008

Introduction

Nearly fifty years elapsed between the establishment of the International Military Tribunal (IMT) in Nuremberg—the first court charged with prosecuting war crimes after 1945—and the establishment of the International Criminal Tribunal in The Hague following the Yugoslav conflict in the 1990s. Yet even today, there is some dispute concerning the interpretation of fundamental legal issues.[1] Controversy continues to surround the topic of war crimes trials. The unusually constant level of interest in such crimes and their prosecution reflects not only the unsolved issues of history but also the emotional dimension of such issues. Since World War II, the general public has remained ambivalent about the purpose of war crimes trials. The demand for "justice" is considered by many as synonymous with the demand for "punishment." Yet the limits to such proceedings are repeatedly illustrated by the clash between prosecution options and the inflated expectations of victims or their relatives. Even a cursory examination of the media reaction to convictions and acquittals demonstrates this ambivalence.

When searching for the reasons that war crimes trials fail, we must look at the interplay between political and personal relationships—an interplay that may determine the course of a trial and also influence any subsequent decision to grant clemency. It quickly becomes clear that the planning framework and guidelines governing such proceedings may be amended to meet the political requirements of the day. The war crimes trials following World War II—in particular, the Allied proceedings in the wake of the Nuremberg IMT process—were intertwined with the political environment at the start of the Cold War. When laying down war crimes guidelines, the Allies were heavily influenced by concepts underpinning the law of occupation, as well as by foreign policy considerations. After 1949, the West German government also had to take domestic political concerns into account. Nevertheless, ever since the Nuremberg trials, there have been those who glibly condemn what they term "victors' justice"—a justice that, such people claim, serves merely to satisfy the victors' thirst for vengeance. In the postwar years, that argument allowed the defendants (and their former comrades-in-arms) to champion a legalistic approach that probed individual guilt and responsibility while failing to pay due attention to the multifaceted forms of involvement in war crimes. The same argument helped drive the formation of various interest groups that in the early 1950s came together in an informal yet powerful "war criminals' lobby."

Since the mid-1990s, historians have placed particular emphasis on researching the Wehrmacht's participation in war crimes against the civilian populations in occupied territories during World War II. The clearer the evidence of such complicity on the eastern front, the more searching the questions became regarding Wehrmacht behavior on other fronts.[2] The debate surrounding the use of legal means to confront war crimes, which was reignited with the Italian trials of Erich Priebke (in 1996) and Friedrich Engel (in 2002), has focused increased public attention on the Italian theater of war. Italy has long been deemed a forgotten theater devoid of notable incidents, let alone crimes against the civilian population. This perception is particularly surprising because, after the war, the British conducted a series of trials on war crimes committed by the Wehrmacht in Italy. An examination of these trials has been long overdue. The Venice trial of Field Marshal Albert Kesselring, in particular, illustrates the manner in which a punishable action—an action condemned during a war crimes trial—can disappear from the collective memory, while the trial itself can be retrospectively reinterpreted as an exercise in victors' justice that had not been preceded by any crime. Such misinterpretation and reinterpretation can be explained by considerations of *Vergangenheitspolitik*—the politics of memory—that accompanied the war crimes trials after 1945.

The treatment of German war criminals had the potential to affect public opinion strongly, and it therefore attained political significance, not least with regard to the planned rearmament of Germany. Today, it is generally accepted that German rearmament was more or less bought in exchange for the release of prominent war criminals in Allied custody.[3] But exactly how this was accomplished remains largely unexplored. An examination of the Kesselring case allows us, for the first time, to show precisely how a network of veterans, lawyers, and groups of German sympathizers, primarily in the United Kingdom and United States, achieved their goal—securing Kesselring's release. Kesselring's case is more than an example of post-1945 war crimes policy: it is a major component of our critical engagement with the Wehrmacht. Thus, the campaign to have Kesselring released was not merely an event in one man's biography; rather, it was an episode that influenced public discourse, marked by the attempt to have a representative of the old elite rehabilitated at the expense of historical truth.

Addressing this issue under the rubric of *Vergangenheitsbewältigung* (coming to terms with the past) does not do it justice, since this term takes insufficient account of the political environment surrounding the rearmament debate at the beginning of the 1950s. In addition, there can be no question of a legally feasible "coming to terms" with war crimes. The word coined by Norbert Frei—*Vergangenheitspolitik* (politics of memory)—appears more suitable, referring as it does to a political process involving the amnesty and integration of tainted National Socialist functionaries.[4] The terminology of Frei's study, which examined the early years of the Federal Republic of Germany, can be applied to the Allied policy vis-à-vis tainted Nazi elites. After all, the German General Treaty was also supposed to represent a "symbolic line drawn under the era of direct occupation."[5] The present study attempts to assign phases to these social processes, while also illuminating the constraints and mechanisms that informed British policy when it came to the treatment of war criminals. If, as Frei contended, German Vergangenheitspolitik started with the establishment of the Federal Republic, British Vergangenheitspolitik can be divided into three phases. Following preliminary consideration of the issue during the war, National Socialist perpetrators and officers were actively prosecuted between 1945 and 1949. The war crimes trials were held in three main waves: from 1945 to 1946, 1946 to 1947, and 1947 to 1949. From 1949 until around 1952, under pressure from broad-based campaigns in Germany, the UK, and the United States, a shift in the Anglo-American politics of memory became apparent.

One characteristic of Vergangenheitspolitik posited by Frei involves the active, co-constructing role played by published opinion,[6] as was apparent in the Kesselring case. The occupying powers gradually appropriated, and in some cases accommodated, the expectations and aspirations contained in German demands. As a result, Allied policy shifted, moving to a new position dominated by considerations of security policy. During the 1950s, the British and Americans deliberately reinforced the image of a "clean Wehrmacht" and a fair fight on all fronts in order to increase their own military prestige as the victors over an initially superior opponent while also forestalling questions concerning Allied participation in war crimes. A reversal of the British politics of memory, resulting in Kesselring's rehabilitation, became possible in the wake of the debate surrounding German rearmament. From 1952, the Allies acted as partners in the Adenauerian policy, and the psychological effects attendant on the process of re-creating a narrative became evident. During this period, Germans had sole jurisdiction over an increasing number of war crimes trials, including the trials of prominent senior Wehrmacht officers such as Field Marshal Ferdinand Schörner and Generals Hasso von Manteuffel and Theodor Tolsdorff. Alaric Searle's pioneering research in this area complements the present study.[7]

The Kesselring Case

From February to May 1947, the former commander-in-chief of both Army Group C and the South-Western Command, Generalfeldmarschall Albert Kesselring, stood trial before a British military court in Venice. As commander-in-chief of German troops, he was accused of having killed around 9,000 women, children, and old people in the course of so-called punishment actions during the German retreat through Italy between 1943 and 1945. These actions took place in the context of the battle against partisans being waged by the Wehrmacht and Schutzstaffel (SS) troops.[8] The British charges against Kesselring related, first, to the implementing of a reprisal operation in the Fosse Ardeatine in Rome, during which 335 people were murdered in retribution for an attack, and, second, to the inciting of his troops to wage war against Italian civilians by issuing so-called *Bandenbefehle* (partisan orders). It was precisely the illegality of reprisals that defined this particular war crime and that formed the pivotal point of the indictment.

The Allied prosecutors set great store by proving Kesselring's personal responsibility for facilitating the illegal (in terms of international law) behavior of his troops in a court of law, thus enabling them to legally pin down one of the individuals responsible for events as a whole.[9] With particular regard to the rejection of a futile victors' justice that became evident following the main Nuremberg war crimes trials (the IMT), it was especially important to Allied prosecutors that the German population be educated regarding the criminal nature of Adolf Hitler's Wehrmacht. In this context, emphasis was placed on a conceptual link between the political facilitation of the crimes and the barbarities carried out by others.[10]

During the defense preparations, it became clear that the old hierarchical military patterns of behavior still held sway. Thus, Kesselring's former General Staff formed the nucleus of these defense efforts,[11] illustrating the symbolic value of the trial for all "Italy fighters." For many veterans, the trial represented a "final Italian battle"—a battle that had to be won so that the Wehrmacht could at least register a moral victory in the wake of the lost war. In 1946, in a letter to his lawyer, Albert Kesselring wrote that he would "defend himself vehemently in the interests of the Wehrmacht's reputation."[12] He saw the trial as his final historical mission. Thus, Kesselring himself molded the image of the "final battle"—the ultimate battle in which, as former commander-in-chief of Wehrmacht forces in Italy, he had to prevail. The extent to which this view was common currency among veterans of the Italian campaign was illustrated by the remarks of military judge Hans Keller, who privately stated that Kesselring "owed it to the decent German soldiers who fought and bled under his command to speak one last time, for only thus could the foundations be laid for a just verdict when truth emerges victorious in the future. I am firmly convinced that that time will come. We may not live to see it, but at least we will have worked for it."[13]

The death sentence imposed on Kesselring was immediately commuted by the British commander of Allied forces in the Mediterranean. During the course of his imprisonment, Kesselring became a figurehead for the veterans' associations, which made their consent to the creation of a new German army contingent on the prior release of the most important war criminals. Kesselring was released for health reasons in October 1952. As a result, Konrad Adenauer's security policy received the requisite endorsement from political parties and civic organizations within Germany. The way was now clear for the Federal Republic to make a military contribution to West European security.

Kesselring's release, in turn, helped frame the discussions in the Bundestag regarding ratification of the General Treaty, by making it easier for many delegates to give their consent. And beyond that, it had a normative impact in the context of the debate on German war guilt that had been taking place since 1945. In practical terms, the general's release was tantamount to rehabilitation at the highest level. As far as the veterans were concerned, the war criminals issue provided a fertile breeding ground for generating a new narrative of the past. Millions of former soldiers, believing that "the allied war crimes policy had denied them the certainty of having gone to war in a just cause," now linked their own expectations to the fate of their former commander-in-chief.[14] By creating a quasi-official war memory, it appeared possible to ascribe retrospective meaning to years of service for the homeland, thus relieving individual soldiers—and the Wehrmacht as a whole—of responsibility for war crimes.[15]

The Kesselring case illustrates the different dimensions of the public's memory of the war they had just survived. The arguments advanced in favor of pardoning the former field marshal reflected a resurgent German self-confidence, a confidence that consistently blanked out the involvement of the Wehrmacht and the SS in war crimes in Italy and that later, aided by Kesselring's memoirs, fervently denied any such involvement. At the beginning of the 1950s, in the "no-man's land between demilitarization and rearmament" and in the absence of any close scrutiny of the charges against him (or perhaps in deliberate ignorance of them),[16] Kesselring became a martyr. It could be said that, for the last time, he assumed the role of a "leading comrade" whose fate could become the spark igniting criticism of an allegedly antiveteran policy. Former Wehrmacht members seized on Albert Kesselring's fate as a case in point for the construction of a new identity. The fight to have him pardoned and released was considered a matter of honor, for he embodied the manner in which the new state dealt with its predecessor's old servants. This fact prompts one to probe the argumentation strategies "with the help of which one's own war experiences and the role of the Wehrmacht were given meaning and integrated into the German cultural memory during the first decade following the war."[17] Former comrades, as well as lawyers,[18] politicians, and church representatives in Germany, the UK, and the United States, were actively involved in the process of creating and informing a new narrative by establishing a positive image of the Italian campaign. It is noteworthy that the arguments advanced in the various petitions on Kesselring's behalf were also seized on and put forward by groups that were not primarily interested in his release but had, rather, chosen him as a symbol for their own causes.

All of them, coordinated by Kesselring's defense counsel, Hans Laternser, and accompanied by a barrage of publicity, combined to exert pressure for Kesselring's release—pressure to which British Vergangenheitspolitik had to react. In the context of the escalating Cold War and given the security policy aim of incorporating West Germany into a military alliance such as the European Defense Community (EDC) or the North Atlantic Treaty Organization (NATO), London considered that releasing a relatively small number of German military icons from the last war was a lesser evil than having to dispense with the whole of West Germany as an ally in a future war.

The themes addressed by this work have thus been flagged: the precedent-setting nature of the trial in the context of Allied policy, the manner in which one defendant stood proxy for the entire Wehrmacht, and the image of the "decent German soldier in Italy" that was created by the defense during Kesselring's trial and maintained throughout the campaign to have him pardoned. During the 1950s, this image flowed into the "legend of the clean Wehrmacht," according to which only SS troops or "asocial elements" were responsible for shooting hostages and murdering Jews.[19]

Current Status of Historical Research

In this volume, I attempt to synthesize the research by German and Italian contemporary historians into Vergangenheitsbewältigung and the war in

Italy, combining this with my own extensive study of primary sources and placing it in the context of research into German rearmament. One explanation for the earlier reluctance to address this issue is that such an effort necessarily involves relating the Kesselring case to the crimes of World War II, coming to terms with war crimes following Nuremberg, considering the rearmament debate and its link with solving the war criminals issue, and exploring the politics of the veterans' associations. Since the mid-1990s, however, the debate surrounding the triangle formed by war crimes, the politics of memory, and the rearmament debate has advanced significantly, and it is now possible to build on this advance.

Despite extensive scholarly research, it is apparent that the public had remained largely unaware of the killing of civilians in territories occupied by Germany during World War II. This fact was made clear by the debate surrounding the (first) exhibition *Vernichtungskrieg: Verbrechen der Wehrmacht 1941–1944* (War of Annihilation: Crimes of the Wehrmacht 1941–1944), mounted by the Hamburger Institut für Sozialforschung (Hamburg Institute for Social Research) from 1995 to 1999.[20] Although this exhibition focused on war crimes in the Balkans and the East, thus addressing an issue that had long been researched by historians,[21] only since the beginning of the 1990s has the issue of war crimes against prisoners of war (POWs), including crimes committed by the Allies, been debated,[22] prompting an engagement or confrontation with the notion of a "fair war" that persists today.

For decades, both German and Italian historians paid little attention to the German occupation of Italy. For Italians, the foundation myth of the democratic postwar Italy surrounding the liberation struggle of the *Resistenza* (Resistance) offered a smoke screen that concealed the Italian wartime experience of their German allies. For many years, this attitude prevented a critical examination not only of the Italian position during the final two years of the war but also of German war crimes. Thus, for example, Italian historical research consistently denied a link between partisan actions and German repression.[23] However, the Resistenza myth has been questioned in Italy since the beginning of the 1990s.[24] Once the prominent Italian scholar Claudio Pavone had broken the taboo in 1991, citing the Resistenza as part of an intra-Italian civil war,[25] the focus also widened to include other issues.[26] Examples include the research conducted into war crimes committed by Italian soldiers, especially in the Balkans[27] and North Africa,[28] which prompted questions in the Italian parliament in 2001 as to whether such crimes had in fact occurred and if so why the criminals had not been punished.[29]

In Germany, scholarly interest in the Italian theater of war can be traced back to 1982 when writer and journalist Ernst Kuby published a polemic that for the first time stated the Germans bore the blame for the Appenine escalation—contrary to the notion, endorsed by Kesselring, that the Italians "betrayed" their German allies in 1943.[30] In 1990, Kuby's work was followed by Gerhard Schreiber's extensive study of the systematic humiliation of Italian military internees in *Italienischen Militärinternierte im Deutschen Machtbereich* (Italian Military Internees in the German Sphere of Authority).[31] From a research perspective, this publication ignited the debate on the Italian theater of war. In 1993, Lutz Klinkhammer presented the first study of German occupation policy in Italy.[32]

Three years later, Schreiber published a further detailed examination on the subject, *Deutsche Kriegsverbrechen in Italien* (German War Crimes in Italy), which, probably also due to the enormous media interest in the War of Annihilation exhibition,[33] heralded a large number of other studies on individual aspects of these issues by both German[34] and Italian[35] historians. Schreiber's study, together with the study by Friedrich Andrae that was published almost simultaneously,[36] not only illuminated the individual war crimes but also offered theses on the genesis of these crimes in Italy. Schreiber found that, in some cases, the partisan orders that had originally been issued on the eastern front were also replicated word for word in Italy.[37] In addition, he provided the first overview of all acts of violence committed by German troops (not only by the Wehrmacht) against Italian citizens. Even though not all Wehrmacht units in Italy were involved in war crimes, Schreiber pointed to the "value system of National Socialism rooted in racial ideology,"[38] which led him to conclude that there was no reason to assume that "most of the troops, if confronted with such instructions, would not have carried them out."[39] In 1998, however, Klinkhammer posited the thesis that Italy nevertheless represented "an exceptional case among the occupied countries," involving a quasi-"Western" model of occupation that did not fundamentally challenge the collaboration policy and therefore placed relatively little reliance on repression as a tool for maintaining authority.[40] This so-called exceptional case thesis has been contradicted not only by Schreiber but also by Wolfram Wette and Gerd R. Ueberschär and, most recently, by Raymond Ruch.[41]

Despite the important studies by Schreiber, Andrae, and Klinkhammer, a great deal of research remains to be done on war crimes in Italy. There is still a lack of some fundamental data. The number of victims claimed by the various massacres has not yet been reliably determined. The identity of the perpetrator units is unknown. Light is yet to be shed on the background to, and detailed conduct of, the war crimes themselves. In particular, research into the collaboration of Fascist units in German war crimes is only in its early stages even now. Since 2001, several Italian universities have been collaborating on research intended to fill these gaps.[42]

With regard to the thematic complex relating to rearmament and the Vergangenheitsbewältigung of German war crimes,[43] recent years have seen a growing focus on the German officer corps.[44] There is heightened interest in the Allied trials in the context of historical engagement.[45] Recent legal assessments of the war crimes trials, which also examine the Kesselring trial, have been provided by Robert Herde[46] and Jörn Axel Kämmerer.[47] Studies published in England have highlighted the Allied preparations for the trials,[48] as well as the domestic political intrigues that ultimately led to the collapse of the war crimes policy.

Popular history has dominated the literature on Kesselring to date,[49] but the number of academic studies has increased, especially in recent times.[50] Nevertheless, even the most current biographical works have not satisfactorily elucidated Kesselring's impact on postwar German politics. Schreiber has initiated a historical examination of Kesselring's role in fighting the Italian partisans,[51] and Italian scholars have supplemented this effort by issuing a volume of documents.[52] In a hotly debated essay on the fatal shooting of an American commando troop on March 23, 1944, in northern Italy,[53] Richard Raiber addressed the Kesselring trial strategy. It is noteworthy that the Anglo-American publications remain wedded to Kesselring's tactical and operational skill and his soldierly myth whereas, due to a preoccupation with war crimes in Italy, some German publications take the opposite view, focusing on Kesselring's metamorphosis into a commander who acted culpably during the final months of the war. It sometimes seems that the actual facts surrounding war crimes in Italy, and the perpetrators, are obscured by the focus on one man, both by those who seek to exonerate Kesselring and by those who seek to render him culpable. The present study synthesizes the work already done while also using primary sources to verify Kesselring's significance in the triangular construct comprising the war crimes trials, the politics of memory, and the rearmament debate.

Questions Addressed

In this study, I have traced the shift in British Vergangenheitspolitik using the Kesselring case. For this purpose, the trial of Field Marshal Kesselring was examined (1) in the context of how it affected the image of the war and of the Wehrmacht in the Italian arena, and (2) in the context of the publicity methods used to make the images embodied in the trial the basis for the "legend of the clean Wehrmacht" in Italy—a legend that then legitimized Kesselring's release in conjunction with German rearmament. My aim was to examine the Kesselring case in the context of its symptomatic effect on British Vergangenheitspolitik and its German counterpart, in particular Adenauer's security policy goals.

There were two main aspects to the trial of Albert Kesselring. The initial task was to clarify the correct legal attribution of individual responsibility for war crimes and to ascertain the position of each individual in the chain of command. However, this effort did not provide answers about the actual conduct of the Italian campaign. At issue was a legal attribution of guilt, rather than a historical or political assessment. At the Moscow Conference of Foreign Ministers, held in October 1943, it was decided that, although the Allies would try the main culprits for war crimes, the countries affected would also carry out their own war crimes trials. Since the Allied occupation of Italy was under British command, a British military court would bear formal responsibility for the planned war crimes trials. In legal terms, therefore, the British war crimes trial of Kesselring, the former supreme commander, was a precondition for the Italian courts' power to convict individual culprits.

At the same time, the legal process unwittingly bolstered the myth of Kesselring's innocence. To provoke general doubt regarding the field marshal's culpability, his counsel, Hans Laternser, exploited legal deficiencies (such as the failure to swear witnesses) in the prosecution's attempt to prove his client's legal responsibility for specific cases. Thus, Laternser coupled the dual aspects of the trial in order to add weight to his argument in favor of the "decent" Wehrmacht in Italy. It appeared that he could dispel the negative image rooted in actual war events by overemphasizing the legal deficiencies of the prosecution's case, while simultaneously anchoring a positive image in the collective memory, where it could function as a mitigating factor. Theoretically, a commander-in-chief who was acquitted on this basis could have been given a new military command. In the 1950s, against the background of deliberations on German rearmament, this was not an unrealistic scenario.

Although it ended with his conviction, the Kesselring trial propagated the myth of the former field marshal's innocence, and it was thus a major component in the subsequent rehabilitation strategy pursued during the debate on German rearmament. Because of the rehabilitation of the image of the Wehrmacht in Italy, the crimes committed by the SS (Schutzstaffel) and the SD (Sicherheitsdienst, or Security Service) remained unacknowledged or only reluctantly acknowledged. Since there was not one trial of senior SS police officers or SD leaders for war crimes in Italy,[54] even the SS massacres—of which there were around 214 in Tuscany alone[55]—failed to enter the

German public consciousness.[56] This situation has only changed in recent years: thanks to the 1996 Priebke trial, as well as the 2002 trial of Friedrich Engel and the trial regarding the killings at Sant'Anna di Stazzema, the war crimes committed in Italy have been brought back into the collective German memory to form a new war narrative.[57]

Sources

In the absence of a fully reliable biographical study of Albert Kesselring, my first task in preparing the present study was to trace his career. Historian Reinhard Stumpf has developed a model for analyzing the military elite of the Wehrmacht, and this seemed a suitable tool to use when considering Kesselring. The model investigates a subject's rank, career, origins, and patterns of political-social behavior.[58] Unfortunately, it was not possible to address all four aspects exhaustively due to a dearth of source material on Kesselring. The origins of his family are fairly well documented because his certificate of Aryan origin has been preserved.[59] To analyze Kesselring's career, I first consulted his personnel file in the Munich-based Bavarian War Archives.[60] This source detailed his early career in the Royal Bavarian Army (which was demobilized in 1918) but only contained official entries until 1919; luckily, there were also a few subsequent random inclusions, particularly from the time of the Reichswehr. The Wehrmacht personnel file created during the Third Reich was apparently purged after the war and therefore merely contained a brief summary of Kesselring's career.[61] In addition, files were also available documenting his various military positions. However, the depredations of war resulted in a glaring gap between 1919 and 1938. Chance finds in the files of the U.S. Office of Strategic Services (OSS) could not compensate for the absence of Kesselring's personnel evaluations for the war years until 1945, but they did illustrate his opponents' contemporaneous assessment of him, providing not only impressions but also an American military evaluation of Kesselring's operational and tactical skills.

After 1946, like many of his comrades, Kesselring wrote studies for the Operational History (German) Section, generally referred to as the Historical Division. His expert studies of military operations during World War II constituted another interesting body of source material, providing insight into his military self-image. The Historical Division was a German working group within the U.S. Army's Army History Department. Its aim was to enhance the American army's historiography of its World War II operations by contrasting and comparing it with reports by Wehrmacht generals.[62] Historian Bernd Wegner has noted that the authors of those reports had a self-justifying aim:

they hoped their writings would constitute a final historiographic victory, securing them "a place in history."[63] They were offered an opportunity to paint a picture of warriors pursuing their craft while holding aloft the banner of soldierly virtues.[64]

Few of Kesselring's wartime letters or diary entries have survived; those in his papers relate almost exclusively to the period after 1945. Therefore, his handwritten "Londoner Tagebuch," ("London Diary"), which is not a contemporary diary but was written in 1946 while he was in custody in London, was a valuable source for my research. In it, Kesselring attempted, even before the trial, to reflect on the Italian campaign a year after the end of the war and account to himself for his own actions. In the diary, one can already detect the exculpatory lines of reasoning that he later developed in his memoirs.

Thanks to these sources, it was possible to reconstruct Kesselring's career and family background reasonably well, albeit with gaps. However, the issue of his patterns of social-political behavior was more problematic, since I had to rely solely on his memoirs for a reconstruction of his "interior life"—and those memoirs constituted a justification rather than an explanation of his actions and motivations. Nonetheless, research on autobiographical literature has shown that the memories of participants in events can be used as a source if they are viewed in the context of the author's aims and self-image.[65] Kesselring wrote his memoirs while he was in custody,[66] prompting one to assume that his intention was further circumscribed by the desire to offer mitigating evidence that might also be of legal benefit.[67] In addition, Wegner has pointed to the manner in which officers' memoirs influenced public discourse in the 1950s: until the files "plundered" by the Allies were returned in the 1960s, such memoirs were often the only source for research into World War II.[68]

To cast light on the political backdrops to the war crimes trials, in this study—for the first time—extensive source material from various provenances was scrutinized and analyzed in both public and private archives in Germany, the UK, the United States, and Italy. In addition to the British trial files, the prime minister's correspondence, the War Office files, the records of the War Crimes Group/South East Europe in the UK National Archives–London (formerly known as the Public Record Office),[69] and the trial transcripts in London's Imperial War Museum,[70] I found the papers of Kesselring's counsel, Hans Laternser, in the Freiburg Military Archives particularly useful.[71] The Laternser papers documented the preparation and conduct of the trial, providing insights into behind-the-scenes linkages and into the decisive role Laternser himself played in the campaign for Kesselring's release. His correspondence with the defendant and with other witnesses drawn from the leadership of the South-Western Command offered a glimpse into the mentality of the German officer corps after 1945, a group that felt defamed both by the Allies and by German politicians. The officer corps was perceived externally as a coherent group, despite the internal struggles that took place between its members as they tried to come up with a valid version of their official war memory.[72] To verify and consolidate discernible lines of reasoning, I consulted the papers of Kesselring and his fellow officers Dietrich Beelitz, Hans Röttiger, and Eberhard von Mackensen. In addition, I studied the papers of German ambassador Rudolf Rahn, as well as those of ordinary soldiers such as Fritz Pfrommer, who kept the South-Western Command's war journal, and August Lindner. Certain documents from Erwin Rommel's and Heinrich von Vietinghoff's papers (some of which remain in family ownership) were examined, as were the papers of the lawyer Rudolf Aschenauer, who represented Kesselring during his denazification case. With the help of eyewitnesses living abroad, it was also possible to reconstruct the manner in which the trial was financed by donations from Brazil. Research in the Jesuit archives in Munich uncovered the key role played by the Jesuit priest Alfons Hiemer in the defense team.[73] Archival research in Washington, where I consulted intelligence files,[74] and in Rome[75] provided information on the roles played by the United States and Italy in preparing and conducting the trial, as well as information on the domestic reactions to the British verdict. The holdings of the Italian State Archives in Rome included protests against Kesselring's release in 1952.

As indicated earlier, the OSS continued to maintain intelligence files on Kesselring following his release, and the field marshal was also featured in other intelligence material of secondary importance. Thus, the German Verfassungsschutz (Office of Constitutional Protection) started a "Kesselring file" after his speeches to veterans' associations and his expert testimony in the so-called Generals' trials conducted before German courts,[76] and the East German Ministry of State Security (known as the Stasi) collected references to Kesselring's war crimes in order to "use them in a press campaign should the opportunity arise."[77] For the first time, the files of various *Traditionsverbände* (veterans' associations) have been examined, including the Verband deutscher Soldaten (German Soldiers' Association, VdS), the Luftwaffenring (Luftwaffe Circle), the Verband deutsches Afrikakorps (German Africa Corps), and the Ordensgemeinschaft der Ritterkreuzträger des Eisernen Kreuzes e. V. (Order of the Knight's Cross). These papers are retained in closed collections.

My analysis of various collections of press cuttings on Kesselring held in the Koblenz Federal Archives, together with the Laternser papers illustrating the full extent of the lawyer's press contacts, provided a picture of a cleverly engineered campaign that ultimately resulted in Kesselring's release in 1952. Laternser was in contact with the editorial offices of periodicals such as *Christ und Welt, Stern, Spiegel,* and *ZEIT,* and reports in these publications were taken up by other media outlets, contributing to the fundamentally positive attitude already mentioned. Although press reportage had readily accommodated Kesselring's interests until 1952, the situation changed dramatically when he was released and assumed the honorary presidency of three military Traditionsverbände, in particular the Stahlhelm. The *Frankfurter Allgemeine Zeitung, Frankfurter Rundschau, Die Welt,* and the *Süddeutsche Zeitung* were extremely critical in their coverage of Kesselring's activities as a veterans' leader, and letters from readers indicated that such criticism struck a chord with the German public. As my study demonstrates (in contrast to the thrust of other research in recent years), the positive image of Albert Kesselring that had been fostered prior to his release was turned around and destroyed by his own behavior after he was freed.

Chapter 1

On the Italian Stage: Albert Kesselring

There is no doubt that Albert Kesselring influenced perceptions of the war in Italy. It therefore makes sense to examine his career in the context of his involvement in the Italian theater. The first issue to be addressed is precisely the nature of the war crimes committed under Kesselring's command. Beyond reconstructing individual massacres, it is vital to examine the chain of command when it came to antipartisan warfare, taking into account the overall military and operational situation, clarifying Kesselring's role in that chain of command, and investigating the possible reasons for the ruthless approach adopted by the Wehrmacht.

By analyzing Kesselring's origins and career, we can also examine whether his actions as an officer were typical of the National Socialists or whether he simply continued to uncritically espouse those concepts of loyalty and honor acquired during the Wilhelmine era. Kesselring's military career was defined by his position on the General Staff of the Luftwaffe from 1933 to 1937 (the period of National Socialist entrenchment) and by his command postings, ranging from the Battle of Britain to service in Africa and Italy up to 1943. Given the myth that Kesselring himself fostered—not least in the title of his memoirs, *Soldat bis zum letzten Tag* (A Soldier to the End), published by the former field marshal and convicted war criminal in 1953—it seems useful to examine Kesselring's soldierly image in light of military concepts of honor. Such an examination also requires us to probe Kesselring's view of the war in Italy. During his career, Kesselring's concept of soldierly behavior underwent a change, acquiring a certain ambivalence that enabled him to downplay the war crimes committed in Italy. Finally, when examining Kesselring's military career, one must ask to what extent his internment as a POW in 1945 affected his self-image. What external influences hardened the sense among Wehrmacht generals that they had been defamed by the Allies? And how did this individual sense of defamation lead to a general denial of the massacres in Italy?

Because the trial of Albert Kesselring focused on the issue of his participation in the Fosse Ardeatine massacre, his role in escalating the antipartisan war faded into the background. It therefore is useful to devote a second section in this chapter to the war in Italy, concentrating on Kesselring's role as commander-in-chief and on the issue of the antipartisan war.

Military Career, 1904–1945

If only due to his rank, Generalfeldmarschall Albert Kesselring was a prime representative of the Wehrmacht elite. Yet up to now, little has been known about him, and much of what is known is anecdotal. The man called "Uncle Albert" by his troops and "Smiling Al" by the Allies was one of the most popular military leaders of World War II among the rank and file. He was considered a great tactician and manager but without the strategic brilliance of men such as Erich von Manstein or Erwin Rommel. Kesselring's colleagues were irritated by his optimism about improving relations with the Italians, and Hitler considered him too soft. His soldiers, however, revered him as a general with the common touch, whose sense of responsibility toward his troops was underlined by regular, and often unannounced, visits to the front. Italian churchmen praised his attempts to preserve Italy's art treasures from war damage. During the 1950s, this picture of Kesselring, which had been presented at his trial, was seized on and embellished by a range of memoirists. Yet when one considers the bloody assaults on whole villages during the Wehrmacht retreat in the summer of 1944, the picture of the "good general" painted during his trial seems like a travesty.

Albert Kesselring was born in 1885 in the town of Marktsteft, in the Lower Franconia region of Bavaria. His father, Carl Adolf, was a teacher, and his mother, Rosina, had been born a Kesselring, marrying her second cousin. The spelling of their surname is disputed. The form Keßelring is used in the Registry Office, but Albert Kesselring himself used a double "s," and I have retained this spelling.

"I do not come from a military family."[1] That opening sentence in Albert Kesselring's memoirs hints at his latent inferiority complex in regard to army comrades with stronger military backgrounds. This feeling of inferiority may also explain his attempt to trace his name back to an aristocratic family.[2] Kesselring's early years were spent in rural surroundings in Marktsteft, where his relatives had operated the family brewery since 1688 (the brewery still exists today) and owned various agricultural enterprises. Kesselring's father had already risen from this modest environment by training as a primary school teacher.[3] After a brief stint as seminar director at the Royal Bavarian Teacher Training Institute in Wunsidel, Carl Kesselring was promoted to the position of schools director in Bayreuth, a senior civil service position. The family had thus succeeded in rising socially to join the middle class.[4]

In Bayreuth, Albert Kesselring attended the Christian Ernestinum secondary school, obtaining his university matriculation certificate in 1904. Historian Peter Herde has speculated that Kesselring came under the sway of the "national spirit" prevalent in Bayreuth and that he combined loyalty to the empire with Bavarian patriotism, since this topic formed the subject of his matriculation essay.[5] Scholar Kenneth Macksey has also pointed out that Kesselring was influenced by the atmosphere prevailing in Bayreuth. He probably viewed himself as a subject of the German emperor first and a Bavarian second.[6] An evaluation of his school reports shows that, except for sports, Kesselring was a pupil of average talent. Though he displayed no gift for ancient languages,[7] his teacher considered him to be "very diligent" in studying English and Italian. His matriculation certificate gives us a mixed picture: "His performance is moderate, his judgment unsure and his thinking sluggish. He is also easily unnerved and rattled. His character is good-tempered and upright, but still insufficiently developed; his behavior is composed and decent."[8] Kesselring did display the "characteristics typical of schoolteachers' families . . . diligence, discipline and striving for advancement." He had the "mentality of one rising from the lower classes" who sought to battle his way to the top through "above-average performance."[9]

Kesselring's father was anxious to consolidate his newly achieved middle-class status and provide his sons with a good education. Unlike his two older brothers, Albert did not seem particularly suited to university studies.[10] Therefore, with his family's agreement, he sought a commission in the Bavarian Army—and the social standing that went with membership in the officer class.[11] "I wanted to be a soldier, was hell-bent on this profession and—I can say this looking back—put my heart and soul into being a soldier," wrote Kesselring in his memoirs.[12] He joined the Royal Bavarian Army in 1904. Six years later, he married Pauline Anna Keyssler, a rich apothecary's daughter from Bayreuth, and they honeymooned in Italy.[13] The marriage remained childless. Although subsequently revered by many of his soldiers as a father figure, Albert Kesselring was not a family man; rather, he devoted himself completely to his job as an army officer.

Kesselring's career proceeded along lines that were quite common at the time. He belonged to the age cohort of officers born between 1881 and 1900, who filled over half of all senior Wehrmacht positions during World War II. In 1904, he began his military career as a *Fahnenjunker* (corporal cadet). His involvement with the Royal Bavarian Army, with its proud insistence on independence, should be particularly emphasized. The criteria for acceptance as an officer cadet in Bavaria were more stringent than those, for example, in Prussia.[14] A matriculation certificate was required for acceptance into the Bavarian Army, whereas a simple intermediate certificate and attendance at war college sufficed in Prussia. Further, the Prussian War College was home to a disproportionate number of scions of the rural aristocracy, but in Bavaria, over 80 percent of the officers came from the educated and propertied upper classes. A smaller proportion (15–18 percent) came from the middle classes, of whom around 7 percent were from teachers' families. The aristocracy accounted for less than 9 percent. The Bavarian Army already displayed a trend toward bourgeoisification, and this—combined with policies such as according prominence to young squad leaders—encouraged elite recruitment. Such methods were later refined by the National Socialists in their efforts to recruit an officer elite.[15] The heavily bourgeois nature of the Bavarian Army left its mark on Kesselring.[16] However, Bavaria also witnessed the emergence of a "new aristocracy" in the officer corps, and there is no doubt that he was proud of his advancement to the officer class.

Kesselring served in the 2nd Bavarian Heavy Artillery Regiment, stationed in Metz, and received outstanding reports from the start. Regimental commander Otto Mayer added the following note to a routine assessment dated January 1, 1909: "Among the younger officers, Lieutenant Kesselring is by far the best; all indications are that he promises to distinguish himself far above the average."[17] As early as 1911, a "qualification report" noted his military leadership qualities.[18] Kesselring was allowed to attend the School of Artillery and Engineering in Munich from 1908 to 1910. Army life clearly suited Kesselring more than scholarship: freed from academic studies, he now received very positive assessments.[19] His superiors found that he had "a positive intellectual inclination," a "superb sense of duty," a "reliable and stable character," and a "quick understanding," and he was described as "resolute and lively." They also considered him to have "authority over subordinates," to whom his attitude was "decisive, just and benevolent," whereas his behavior toward superiors was "tactful and modest."[20] Kesselring's "good nature" and "polished social deportment" were also mentioned.

It was felt that Kesselring was both temperamentally suited to and technically interested in new forms of weaponry. In 1912, he completed a training course as a balloon observer in the dirigible section—his first contact with what was later to be the Luftwaffe. Historian Reinhard Stumpf has noted that it was the primarily middle-class officers in the technically demanding artillery regiments who were most open to modern aviation, unlike infantry or cavalry officers, who tended to be more focused on tradition. Thus, as happened with many soldiers, Kesselring's early inclination and experience foreshadowed his subsequent career development as a Luftwaffe officer.[21] Kesselring's superiors also considered posting him as an instructor to the School of Artillery and Engineering in Munich because he had developed into an "expert with an understanding of the interplay between tactics and technology."[22] But this was not to be: Kesselring was appointed to the General Staff and therefore already occupied a senior position during World War I. This career path was not unusual for members of heavy artillery regiments, whose reputation had been enhanced by the fact that that war was dominated by artillery to an almost unprecedented degree.[23] Many officers with a heavy artillery background subsequently occupied leading positions in World War II.[24] Kesselring was thus part of that group of successful young officers who advanced in their military careers during World War I, achieved promotion in the years following 1919, and then formed part of the military elite after the end of the 1920s, especially following Hitler's rearmament.[25] During his lifetime, Kesselring was aware of being an arriviste, and he took pains to continue consolidating his newly achieved social position. This attitude may also help to explain his tendency to use submissiveness as a tool with which to secure his achievements.[26]

The years of World War I left their mark on what was to become the Wehrmacht elite.[27] Before moving to the General Staff, Kesselring experienced the war on the front lines. For eight months, he served with the troops in Flanders and Vogesen, and he was promoted to captain in 1915. As early as January 2, 1917, the increasingly difficult situation on the western front prompted Lieutenant General Hans Kreppel to note that Kesselring should be transferred to the General Staff "even though he did not attend the War Academy," for he was an "alert and persistent observer with very strong nerves."[28] This assessment was an accolade for Kesselring who, during the battles for Arras in 1917, had distinguished himself "by his tireless and assiduous work, and by the preparation of clear and carefully constructed orders" despite the fact that, on occasion, he "had been on duty for over 20 hours."[29] In those battles, Kesselring had succeeded in repelling a British bridgehead by means of a tactical dodge with operational consequences, subsequently closing the impending gaps in the line of defense and thus avoiding the threatening retreat[30]—a gambit for which he was to find renewed use in Italy thirty years later. Since Kesselring had "proven himself in battle," there was no longer anything to prevent his transfer to the General Staff.[31] In fact, given the difficult war situation, he was not even required to undergo the so-called Sedan course prescribed for aspiring General Staff officers.[32] In the autumn of 1917, Kesselring's political views were influenced by his transfer, pending his appointment to the General Staff, to the 2nd Territorial Army Division on the eastern front, where his anti-Bolshevism was hardened by his contact with Soviet soldiers' councils during the peace negotiations on the Düna. Kesselring was to retain this attitude for the rest of his life.[33]

On November 10, 1918, Kesselring was tasked with demobilizing the III Bavarian Army Corps in Nuremberg. There, he demonstrated unusual insubordination for an ambitious officer. He had an argument with the leader of the Freikorps (Free Corps) and refused to execute commands he believed were nonsensical: as a result of this insubordination, which he thought was his duty, Kesselring was "led off into a greasy cell."[34] His superior, Major Hans Seyler—chief of the General Staff with the General Command of the III Bavarian Army Corps—censured Kesselring for having been too "stubborn" in this particular case and for having "failed to display the requisite discretion." Seyler stated, "His dogged insistence on sticking to a view, once formed, resulted in a lack of flexibility which quite often had a negative impact on his work."[35] The brigade commander, Major General Eugen Ritter von Zoellner, observed that "due to his long service in senior staff positions," Kesselring had probably "become accustomed to overestimating himself from a young age." This tendency caused Kesselring "to sometimes fail to recognize the difficulties encountered by the troops when executing commands from above, especially in difficult times."[36] Von Zoellner had, in the past, gotten Kesselring transferred because of the "particular cause," and he felt that a prolonged deployment on troop service "as a battery commander was not only appropriate but also in Kesselring's interest." Von Zoellner believed Kesselring should only be proposed "for re-deployment to the General Staff after proving himself." It was the worst assessment Kesselring had ever received, and his career seemed to be in grave danger.

During the next few years, he deliberately reined in his tendency to overrate himself and instead seized on this challenge as an opportunity to prove himself through performance. He apparently completed his two-year stint as a battery commander with the 24th Artillery Regiment to the satisfaction of his superiors, although his assessments have unfortunately not been preserved. In 1922, his transfer to Berlin and the Reichswehr was approved.[37]

There, Kesselring served as an administrative expert, a deployment that suited his personal abilities. It was purely because of career calculations that he repeatedly returned to troop service as a means to achieve promotion to the next rank. His military advancement was steady, and it accelerated markedly after 1925.[38] Thus, in 1926, he was posted as a major to the staff of the army command; he was transferred to the army office, or Wehramt, in 1927 and then, on February 1, 1927, was posted to the General Staff of the 7th

Division in Munich. In 1930, he was promoted to lieutenant colonel. As a battalion commander in the 4th Artillery Regiment of the III Army Corps, Kesselring fulfilled the criteria for promotion to colonel in 1932. He then resumed his work in the Reichswehr personnel section, a position he first occupied in 1931.

A passage from Kesselring's subsequent memoirs shows how he internalized the self-image of the army that prevailed during the Weimar Republic and how he used the putatively nonpolitical nature of the army as a retrospective legitimating tool: "We had become nonpolitical, outside all party politics. We had been deliberately trained by Colonel General Hans von Seeckt to be nonpolitical soldiers who, in the confusion of the times, facilitated the expectation of a bloodless outcome to all crises merely because of their 'existence' and their attitude. Germany's apolitical Wehrmacht had, unconsciously and invisibly, become the retaining political pillar of the government elected by the people."[39]

It is noteworthy that, in this passage, Kesselring cited Seeckt by name as something of a role model, thus indicating the latter's special significance for Kesselring's own worldview. After all, it was Seeckt himself who—fully aware of his political responsibility—made nonpartisanship a tenet of the new army. This nonpartisanship was intended to ensure that the army "was kept out of the social and revolutionary unrest of the 1920s and internally strengthened."[40] In this regard, there were close ties between the new republic and the old elites, for both had an interest in maintaining order to protect themselves and the Reich and thus found themselves acting as equal partners. In Seeckt's view, this pact posed a dual challenge: to reestablish order and thus to gain the freedom of action needed to pursue his actual goal of creating a new army—the Reichswehr—out of the old Imperial army. Achieving these goals required complete parity between the interests of the republic and those of the army. After all, as Seeckt put it, "order is a prerequisite, not only for the preservation of the Reich sought by both sides, but also for the consolidation of the Reich and for the development of the army itself."[41] In his view, loyalty to the state meant "loyalty to a state which currently assumes the form of a republic" and to which there was no alternative.[42] It is characteristic of Seeckt's approach that he always collaborated loyally and unquestioningly with the elected government of the Reich and its president, Paul von Hindenburg, and that he always acted in accordance with the constitution.[43] Seeckt demanded discipline and unconditional obedience in order to cement the authority of the military leadership, thus reestablishing control over the army and guaranteeing its operational readiness.[44] The fact that Kesselring endorsed this idea of strengthening military command authority in times of crisis can be seen, for example, in the controversial *Bandenbefehle* (partisan orders) he issued in the summer of 1944. In light of his subsequent career, it is reasonable to assume that Kesselring adopted Seeckt's creed of absolute loyalty, loyalty that was viewed as "nonpartisan." This ethic is also reflected in Kesselring's memoirs, in which he adamantly refused to retrospectively criticize Hitler.[45]

However, Kesselring learned more than philosophy from Seeckt. As one of the army chief of staff's closest subordinates, he spent years dealing with training, organization, and technology involving all types of weaponry. He also dealt with budgetary, administrative, and legal matters, as well as questions of international law. In addition, Kesselring helped address problems arising with the International Military Control Commission (IMCC), which was tasked with monitoring the arms restrictions imposed by the Versailles Treaty. Thanks to a clever circumvention of these restrictions, it was possible to build up an effective new army,[46] and his contribution to this covert rearmament earned him the appreciative nickname "Commissioner for Savings" in Berlin. And as Seeckt's first general chief of staff, Kesselring carried out the preliminary clandestine tests that were part of the plan to develop an air force. These tests were conducted together with the Soviet Union in the city of Lips during 1923 and 1924, in contravention of the arms restrictions. Kesselring confirmed this for the record in 1946 in Nuremberg.[47] He was also centrally involved in the so-called Great Plan for a 102-division army, which was also prepared covertly during 1923 and 1924.[48] Like so many of his colleagues, Kesselring viewed this deliberate breach of the provisions of the Versailles Treaty as a patriotic duty.

The Weimar Republic represented a relatively quiet phase of Kesselring's career, during which he developed his military reputation as a technocrat, viewing himself as a servant of the state. In the 1930s, he experienced the "new era" as an observer. Like many others, he was repelled by the aggressive tone and manner of the National Socialists. This reaction may also have been due to the poor impression made on Kesselring by Munich National Socialists (later known as the *alten Kämpfer* [old fighters]) during his time with the Munich Wehrkreiskommando VII (Military District Command VII) at the end of the 1920s.[49] Nevertheless, his attitude to the rise of the National Socialists was fundamentally positive, even though he did not overtly agree with the party's political goals.[50] The year 1933 was decisive for Kesselring's career: on October 1, 1933, he was appointed head of the administrative office in the newly created Ministry of Aviation, where he began his career with the rank of commodore. Since the Luftwaffe—then being covertly developed—still lacked firm structures, it offered far better promotional opportunities than the army.[51]

As early as 1934, Hermann Göring promoted Kesselring to *Generalmajor* (major general), and promotion to the rank of *Generalleutnant* (lieutenant general) followed in 1936. At the age of forty-eight, he learned to fly, an achievement that earned him the respect of his men. Kesselring was flattered by the social advancement associated with a position in the new air force, and the regime's pomp and ceremony, as he subsequently wrote in his memoirs, made an "extraordinary impression" on him.[52] Even after the passage of years, his self-image was still based on vainglory, as indicated in his own words: "As members of the Luftwaffe, under the umbrella of the commander-in-chief and his then powerful personality, we enjoyed the agreeable respect of all social circles, including the National Socialist party."[53] Gaining such respect, particularly among the ranks of the new rulers, was the personal motivation behind Kesselring's extraordinary commitment, satisfying his desire to be part of the elite. This voluntary bond was accompanied by a much stronger military bond. Kesselring felt unconditionally bound to Hitler by the personal oath of loyalty that members of the German military swore to their leader (known colloquially as the Hitler oath).[54]

Albert Kesselring was also among the recipients of Hitler's grants, the so-called compensation payments of RM 6,000—at that time a huge sum.[55] When later interrogated in Nuremberg, he tried to downplay this connection between personal corruption and the "military entanglement" represented by the oath by emphasizing the accidental nature of his meteoric rise. He claimed that he was merely a "serviceable soldier"—a sort of skilled technician—whom the regime had made use of: "We soldiers of the General Staff and the Führerkorps were proud to be the technicians of our calling."[56]

Like many of his comrades, the officer Albert Kesselring also averted his gaze from things that discomforted him, knowing that his position would have suffered had he protested. Thus, he retrospectively justified his deliberate silence when Jewish comrades were ejected from the Wehrmacht.[57] The claim made in his memoirs to the effect that a senior officer in the army was able to remain apolitical is simply not credible in such a context.

Kesselring was one of those capable officers who ensured that the officer corps in the new air force benefited from a remarkable professional background developed in the former Imperial armed forces. And as a result, the Luftwaffe was transformed into a world-class air force in just a few years.[58] As head of the air force administrative office, Kesselring, together with the Finance Ministry, was responsible for the Luftwaffe's budget (amounting to millions of reichsmarks). He prepared financial plans, established airfields and training sites, and promoted contact with businesses—especially aircraft factories—since he was responsible for aircraft production.[59] Rearmament was thus part of his job description, and he was punctilious in meeting his obligations. Thanks to his own commitment to developing the Luftwaffe, which was considered a specifically National Socialist section of the armed forces, Kesselring also changed his view of Hitler. During the first five years of the Third Reich, he became a supporter of Hitler's policies. In this regard, he found himself sucked into the maelstrom of National Socialist ideology, which skillfully used military virtues as guiding principles—principles with which Kesselring could identify. He quite naturally was drawn to concepts of loyalty, comradeship, and dutifulness, not to mention the idea of war as a *Kulturkampf* (cultural battle).[60]

Kesselring was promoted again in 1936. Following the death of the head of the Luftwaffe Command Office, Walter Wever, in a flying accident, he was made chief of the General Staff of the Luftwaffe for one year.[61] He was thus in overall charge of pilot training, organization of the antiaircraft artillery, and air force signals and communications. In his capacity as chief of the General Staff, one of Kesselring's most controversial decisions was to halt the plans made by his predecessor, Wever, for constructing a strategic long-range bomber (known as the Urals bomber),[62] while simultaneously neglecting the expansion of the fighter aircraft fleet and developing a uniform air *defense* organization.[63] The fact is that, like most senior Luftwaffe officers, Kesselring came from an army background, and that experience permeated his thinking.[64] In his view, the Luftwaffe's primary task was to provide attack support for the army. He adamantly rejected the notion of strategic bombing.[65]

Kesselring was involved in the decision to provide assistance to Francisco Franco by offering him a few units (the so-called Condor Legion); it was intended that these troops would gather initial combat experience in Spain. Kesselring gave remarkably short shrift to this period in his memoirs. It is perhaps not surprising that there was not even one mention of the city of Guernica, destroyed by German bombs on April 26, 1934.[66] Instead, he confined himself to a general comment that German troops had "made Franco's victory possible."[67] Yet Guernica played an important role in the German air force's strategic planning. And despite the fact that, during the 1930s, the members of the Luftwaffe General Staff officially confirmed their opposition to the use of bombing as an instrument of terror by ratifying the Hague Land War Regulations, they viewed the Spanish civil war as a test battleground, demonstrating the effects on morale and material of, for example, bombing raids.[68] During the course of the twentieth century, the idea of waging an air war on a civilian population became integral to modern warfare. Indeed, although it was occasionally decried for propaganda purposes, aerial warfare against civilians was not viewed as a war crime by the planning bodies of any country.[69]

Given this background, it is easy to understand why, years later, the Allies declined to bring those in command of the German air war to trial.

Kesselring was bothered by the uncooperative leadership style that existed under Göring and the lack of information provided to the Luftwaffe chief of General Staff.[70] After just one year, he requested a transfer to field duty;[71] his reasons also included differences between himself and his superior, Undersecretary of State in the Air Force Ministry (and later Generalfeldmarschall) Erhard Milch.[72] Kesselring's request was granted: he was promoted to the rank of *General der Flieger* (Luftwaffe [air force] general) and entrusted with command of Luftwaffe District III. In 1938, he was appointed head of Air Group One, and in contrast to most other officers, he provided his subordinates with strong leadership.[73] In the same year, his air group was involved in occupying the Sudetenland, and it took part in the bombing of Warsaw in 1939. Kesselring was awarded the Iron Cross for his military service during these operations.[74] Following successful Luftwaffe operations during the French campaign, Hitler awarded Kesselring (now head of Air Group Two) a field marshal's baton: Kesselring thus skipped a rank. This accelerated promotion underscored Hitler's personal appreciation of the Bavarian "people's general," who might not have achieved such a high rank in the Bavarian Army;[75] such quick advancement was also a function of the improved promotion opportunities for officers in wartime. If only for reasons of proportionality, Luftwaffe officers could anticipate that their ranks would be adjusted to senior ranks in other branches of the armed forces.[76]

In November 1941, in view of the joint war being waged by Germany and its Italian allies against Allied troops in North Africa, Kesselring was appointed commander-in-chief of Army Group South, but he did not bear this title for long. In 1943, following the fall of Benito Mussolini and the German occupation of upper Italy, he was given sole command in Italy, along with the title of commander-in-chief, South-Western Command. In this capacity, he led Army Group C in its fighting retreat, accompanied by heavy casualties, from Naples along the Po River, until March 1945.

On the one hand, Kesselring saw himself as "the senior man in Italy," a perception that gave rise to an autocratic leadership style. He attempted to make all decisions personally and to maintain constant contact with the front-line troops by means of unremitting inspection tours. On the other hand, Kesselring the soldier always attempted to meet the expectations of his superiors, and until the end, he strove to perform his duties to his superiors' satisfaction. During the course of the war, he was one of the few senior Wehrmacht officers who were never relieved of their duties by Hitler. In September 1942, he was briefly considered as a successor to Wilhelm Keitel,[77] indicating the high regard in which he was held by the Führer. Like other senior commanders, Kesselring sent a telegram of loyalty to the Führer's headquarters after news emerged about the attempted assassination of Hitler on July 20, 1944.[78] When questioned as a witness in 1946 in Nuremberg, he emphasized his close ties to Hitler. Kesselring proudly stated that he enjoyed "a certain confidential relationship with the Führer," never presented himself as an "eternal know-it-all and quibbler," and otherwise "fully confined himself to his field of work."[79]

He defined his personal worldview as a soldier and commander-in-chief in a witness statement made in Nuremberg:

> I demand a high degree of political insight from every senior officer, ensuring that he has an accurate understanding of all events in political life at home and abroad. I demand that he act as an adviser to the country's leaders, that he think ahead while simultaneously reconciling military imperatives with political circumstances. . . . Under no circumstances, however, can I accept a political soldier who pursues *his* own politics based on *his* particular views, thus misconstruing the essence of what it is to be a soldier.[80]

However, following the Allied march into Rome in June 1944, Kesselring did, on at least some occasions, fail to maintain the perspective one would expect of the commander-in-chief in Italy; this lapse occurred when the Wehrmacht found itself forced into a disorganized, hasty retreat across the Apennines. That retreat was also hindered by a significant increase in partisan activity. On July 7, 1944, the British commander-in-chief, Harold Alexander, called on the Italian Resistenza to support the Allied advance "with all the means" at its disposal and to "ambush" German soldiers.[81] There is no doubt that the Bandenbefehle that Kesselring then personally drafted and issued on June 17 and July 1, 1944, in which he promised to "cover every officer," increased the hatred felt by German soldiers for "the Italians." The antipartisan orders radicalized both Wehrmacht and partisan units and thus contributed to the escalation of the war in Italy during the summer of 1944.

For the final eight weeks of the war, Kesselring was commander-in-chief, Western Command, tasked with halting the advance of the Allies after they crossed the Rhine at Remagen. Officer Ulrich de Maizière described a scene during which Kesselring informed Hitler of the hopeless situation on the western front: "And Kesselring took his leave with the words: 'Mein Führer! I will try again!'"[82] Scholar Manfred Messerschmidt has noted that these "Führer presentations" demonstrated the "remains of a well-rehearsed procedure carried out against the backdrop of military senselessness," thus helping explain

Kesselring's demeanor in the situation.[83] According to his subordinates, Kesselring always emerged from meetings with Hitler "as though in a trance" and then felt that "anything was possible": "Each time, he was convinced of the prospects for final victory—at least to the outside."[84] Kesselring himself confirmed this in a 1946 diary entry, stating, "We still had men and material. Even today, the fact that these were being saved for subsequent re-formations is a puzzle to which I do not have the answer."[85]

Kesselring's political-military illusions included the notion that will and determination, together with fanaticism and hatred, could force a turn in events.[86] Historian Wolfram Wette has pointed out that, toward the end of the war, an increasing detachment from reality could be observed among the Wehrmacht generals as a whole. At the time, professional military thinking was distinguished by ignorance of the social, economic, and political realities, and this "was particularly reflected in the inadequate analysis of economic opportunities, and in the disproportionate weight given to the brilliance of commanders in the field."[87] This attitude was also expressed in the daily order issued by Kesselring on April 3, 1945. Addressing an army that only had ammunition and fuel reserves for a few weeks, he appealed to the battle-weary soldiers: "To fail now means to betray Germany. Those who fell while holding to a victorious belief in Germany's future expect that their sacrifice shall not have been in vain. I am appealing to every one of you: be part of a committed battle community which values honor more than life."[88] Here, Kesselring clearly revealed the trauma of World War I rooted in the allegedly ignoble betrayal of the troops by the home front.[89] It was quite clear that to fight until the last bullet was deemed "not a politically and morally reprehensible end, but rather an honorable process in which the strong simply overcame the weak."[90]

Kesselring also endorsed Hitler's order that deserters and stragglers should be hanged from the nearest tree,[91] and he complained to one of the headquarters (HQ) liaison officers, Rudolf-Christoph von Gersdorff, telling Gersdorff (who sought to make Kesselring aware of the hopeless war situation) that he had "driven through the entire rear army area" and had not "seen one man hanged." Gersdorff recalled that "he left me with the request that his orders be better executed in the future."[92] There can be no doubt that Kesselring's rigid stance during the final days of the war claimed countless victims among his own soldiers. He was not part of the relatively isolated "common-sense alliance" that, during the last days of the fighting, attempted, despite the threat of court-martial, to prevent drastic orders from being executed. Rather, Kesselring pursued a "strategy of self-destruction" that clearly reflected Hitler's input.[93] This course indicated a high degree of loyalty—if only personal loyalty to the Führer. After the war, other officers accused Kesselring of taking his Wagnerian loyalty to Hitler too far by refusing to surrender, instead urging his soldiers to fight until the end. Even in an "obviously hopeless situation, he was unable to re-establish a rational political approach."[94]

Hitler rewarded this loyalty, promoting Kesselring one last time. In his will, written on April 29, 1945, he appointed Grand Admiral Karl Dönitz *Reichskanzler* (chancellor of the Reich) and head of state and, in military terms, commander-in-chief of northern Germany (commander-in-chief, Northern Command).[95] Kesselring was to perform the same function for southern Germany and the "Alpine Fortress" as commander-in-chief, Southern Command. He was thus one of the two last senior military figures in the Wehrmacht with powers of command.

Although Kesselring realized that the military resistance was about to collapse, he felt bound to defend the homeland on the Führer's orders. In contrast to the situation in 1918, senior generals now gradually realized that the war was lost. However, fear of the reaction of the Schutzstaffel (SS) rendered them "unable to even initiate the preliminaries required to end the senseless fighting."[96] The unconditional surrender that the Allies, meeting in Casablanca, had formulated as a war aim transformed the hopeless struggle into a patriotic duty, even in the eyes of those who had distanced themselves from the regime by that point.[97] Kesselring thus believed, following the decisions made at Casablanca, that exploratory peace talks were futile at best and criminal at worst.[98] It should be noted, however, that fear of reprisals by the SS against the Wehrmacht leadership were they to seize the initiative may also have played a role in Kesselring's attitude.

When news of the long-planned surrender in Italy was broadcast on the radio on May 2, 1945, Kesselring ordered that the two officers bearing military responsibility—Generaloberst Heinrich von Vietinghoff-Scheel and his chief of General Staff, Hans Röttiger—be arrested pending possible courts-martial. Kesselring's hesitation to confirm surrender indicated his fear of SS sanctions. The two Wehrmacht officers were released only when the supreme SS and police commander in Italy, Karl Wolff, who had led the surrender negotiations, intervened and disclosed his involvement.[99] On May 6, Kesselring signed the truce agreement on behalf of Army Group C (*Alpenfestung*, or Alpine Fortress, Germany's "national redoubt") in Berchtesgaden.

Even years after the war, Kesselring still defended his maxim of "persevere until the end" and rejected charges that he had made the wrong decision when interpreting his oath as binding him to the person of the commander-in-chief,[100] rather than, as Vietinghoff demanded, interpreting it as an oath of loyalty to the German people.[101] It was only in the immediate aftermath of the war, while in detention in London during 1946, that Kesselring allowed himself some rather more critical conclusions—conclusions that indicate some reflection. He wrote in his journal:

> Certainly, one could have put an end to it earlier; but no one fighting on the front could do that since stepping out of line could pose a risk to one's neighbor or the soldier to one's rear. . . . Nevertheless, one can empathize with the fact that it was not my military ambition to have my true place in history associated for all time with the collapse of the German Wehrmacht.[102]

However, unlike Hitler, Kesselring believed suicide was the wrong course:

> I did not want to issue a confession of guilt by taking such a course, since I had no guilt to confess. I came increasingly to the conclusion that a leader—regardless of what happens—cannot abandon his men in times of crisis.[103]

For Kesselring, the time of crisis arrived during his 1947 trial for war crimes in Venice. Following the verdict, the defendant wrote in his diary:

> Pronounced guilty and sentenced to death by firing squad. Thus will an end be put to a long life full of work, responsibility and blessings. God only knows why?[104]

Kesselring clearly did not know. He saw himself as a "nonpartisan soldier" who had "only done his duty." In view of his own impending trial, he subsumed the war crimes committed in Italy, which he initially certainly regretted personally,[105] in one sentence fragment: "Guerrilla warfare, in violation of international law and in its immoral manifestations which are unfortunately unavoidable!"[106]

Kesselring thus turned himself into a "small cog" in the machine—what one could term a victim of the military calling. He created a myth focused on himself (a myth that resonated during the 1950s) and saw himself as a victim. In this regard, scholar Thomas Kühne has coined the term *victimization trap*.[107] Once caught in this trap, "duty and an overarching, almost internalized obedience, exempts one from individual responsibility and from the need to reflect on the place of the individual in grand politics."[108] Killing is legitimized and substituted by the principle of command and obedience and the reference to the "soldier's service ethos," which defines the individual's position in the chain of command as insignificant and obscures one's own responsibility through repeated recourse to the "duty" one is bound to fulfill.[109] Only by overemphasizing soldierly values was it possible "to reach beyond the immediate past and the charges resulting from that past, to subordinate the extraordinary nature of war crimes to normality, and thus to relativize the specifics of the Second World War for the bulk of the Wehrmacht."[110] To facilitate the moral justification of the soldierly existence, the "contrast between killing and being killed is dismantled, with the aid of a catalogue of soldierly virtues rooted in Christian tradition," in favor of selfless values such as duty, service to the homeland, and a myth of victimhood.[111]

War in Italy, 1943–1945

There is no doubt that Kesselring was the Wehrmacht's expert on Italy, with an in-depth knowledge of local conditions. Since November 25, 1941, he had been commander-in-chief, Southern Command, with a command post in Rome. In 1941, in the context of the Africa campaign, Kesselring's primary duty was "to establish a center of power for the Axis in the central Mediterranean" and to observe enemy sea movements.[112] His task was to maintain contact with Germany's Italian allies and secure the supply chain to Africa. To avoid irritating the Italians by imposing yet another German commander-in-chief, Kesselring's place in the chain of command was extremely complicated. On the one hand, in terms of matters pertaining to the air force, he reported to the German commander-in-chief of the Luftwaffe, Hermann Göring. On the other hand, however, when it came to his "primary duty" relating to the Africa campaign, he reported to Mussolini and received Il Duce's directives through the Comando Supremo, the supreme command of the Italian armed forces in Rome under General Ugo Cavallero. Consequently, Kesselring had no powers of command over German army or navy units—and certainly no say over Italian forces.[113] He mediated between the militarily weaker but very sensitive Italian allies (to whom he was ostensibly subordinated) and the often temperamental Erwin Rommel, who was not always inclined to obey the instructions issued by the Italian Comando Supremo. Kesselring's diplomatic skills were thus tested. Surviving pictures from this era illustrate his position: for example, we are familiar with images of an eternally "smiling Kesselring" from the *Wochenschau*, the weekly newsreel shown in German cinemas.[114]

From 1943 on, the situation in the Italian theater of war was extremely complex, reaching a crisis point in the summer of that year.[115] Militarily, the Wehrmacht had been on the retreat in Italy since the Allied landing in Sicily on July 10, 1943. It was clear to all involved that the attack on "Fortress

Europe" had started, and it soon became apparent that the Allied advance had been slowed down but could not be halted. From a political point of view, the overthrow of Mussolini on July 25 naturally helped destabilize the country, and the Wehrmacht occupation, which also involved Fascist formations, triggered a civil war in Italy. Among the Italian public, the willingness to resist the occupation was encouraged by Communist and Socialist party functionaries returning from exile and logistically assisted by the Allies. Thus, as commander-in-chief in Italy, Kesselring had to deal with a wide range of military and administrative problems of a complexity he was simply not equipped to handle. However, he was able to slow Allied progress, earning him Hitler's respect. Italy thus represented a major opportunity for Kesselring to advance his career.

The German Period of Occupation

After Mussolini was toppled on July 25, 1943, and his successor, Marshal Pietro Badoglio, concluded the September 3 truce with the Allies, announced five days later (despite repeated assurances by the marshal that he would continue the war on Germany's side), Italy declared war on the German Wehrmacht on September 11.[116] The German leadership was not wholly unprepared for this crisis: plans for German countermeasures in the event of a change of government in Rome had been in place for some months.[117] Immediately after the overthrow of Mussolini, Hitler started deploying as many German divisions as possible to Italy and Yugoslavia in order to maintain control over Germany's former allies.[118]

As far as Kesselring was concerned, the Italian exit from the war was the key event enabling him to once again portray himself as a military expert in the eyes of Hitler, following his deployment in the 1940 air war on Britain. For this purpose, he first had to assert himself vis-à-vis his rival Rommel. When the truce was declared on September 8, 1943, there were still two German commanders-in-chief in Italy: Generalfeldmarschall Erwin Rommel, commander-in-chief of Army Group B, and Generalfeldmarschall Albert Kesselring, commander-in-chief of the Southern Command. Following an order issued by Hitler, they were joined by the supreme SS and police commander in Italy, in the person of SS Obergruppenführer and General of the Waffen SS Karl Wolff.[119]

As well as being considered ideologically equal, Italy was viewed by the Germans as perhaps the "only true ally of the German Reich" in World War II.[120] It is therefore not surprising that the Italian decision to declare a truce hit German soldiers serving in Italy hard, even though insiders on both sides had been aware since the end of spring 1943 that the alliance was coming to an end.[121] Those in military circles reacted to the truce with expressions of fury, generally culminating in the remark that Italy had now "betrayed the Reich for a second time." Kesselring himself is reported to have said that he "only had hatred left for the Italians."[122] Even on the day the truce was announced, he issued daily orders to his troops indicating the accepted form of words to be used by the military—a formulation that was subsequently adopted and further disseminated by Hitler: "The Italian Government has committed the most dastardly treachery by agreeing [to] a truce with the enemy behind our backs. . . . In an appeal to their honor, the Italian troops must be called on to continue the fight at our side; otherwise they must be ruthlessly disarmed. For the rest, no quarter can be given to turncoats!"[123]

Rommel appeared to accept the Italian exit from the war with rather more equanimity—after all, it merely confirmed what he had long anticipated.[124] Rommel's attitude to the Italians was one of "deep, imperious and uncompromising mistrust."[125] Indeed, Italian observers viewed him as an "Italy hater."[126] In his radio address on September 10, Hitler adopted the terminology that had already been sanctioned by the military. In an allusion to what were overblown National Socialist concepts of allegiance, he quite deliberately spoke of the "clique of traitors" surrounding the new government around Badoglio. This remark was primarily a reference to the betrayal of Il Duce—a reference designed to heighten sentiment against the new Italian government within the Reich. As scholar Gerhard Schreiber put it, "A whole nation had been carelessly branded as traitors, and the 'deep hatred' felt by many Germans for Italy at that time may—together with a sense of revenge—have made it easier for military circles to accept criminal orders."[127]

However, the personal disappointment felt by many generals was of relatively little importance in view of the military threat posed by the new posttruce situation. Although the Allies had landed in Sicily back in July 1943, there were still no Allied soldiers on the Italian mainland. Hitler now had to bear two goals in mind. On the one hand, the war had to be kept as far away from the Reich's borders as possible. Italy therefore had to be retained as a buffer zone that could be used to absorb the impact of the Allied offensive. On the other hand, it was vital to prevent Italian soldiers from joining the Allies as promised. Thus, following the Italian truce on September 8, 1943, the Wehrmacht was ordered to disarm the Italian army and occupy the country.[128] The Italian soldiers were faced with a choice: they could either continue fighting at Germany's side or surrender their weapons. In the event of "resistance"—and, in particular, if Italian weapons were passed on to "rebels"—Italian officers were to be shot as "insurgents," subject to certain conditions.[129]

In many areas, the military leadership seized on the disarmament order as an opportunity to seek revenge and raise the flagging morale of the German troops. In large swathes of the country, the erstwhile allies still found themselves side by side, resulting in some bizarre scenes within certain barracks. A lack of control meant that the German soldiers entrusted with disarming their former Italian allies were given the freedom to obtain personal redress for what they viewed as the humiliating termination of the alliance.[130] There were instances of spontaneous mistreatment of Italians by members of the Wehrmacht. Indeed, Schreiber surmised that the German soldiers viewed Italy as an "El Dorado of unlimited licentiousness and plunder," especially since any inhibitions had been dissipated by the criminal orders issued by Hitler and the Wehrmacht High Command.[131]

As a consequence, members of the Italian armed forces resisted disarmament, contributing to a significant escalation in brutality.[132] One explanation for the increasing harshness of the measures taken could be that the German leaders wanted to lose no time in focusing on their primary task: repelling the Allied advance. To do so, they had to gain control of the situation in Italy. And in some cases, the Germans' former comrades-in-arms fell victim to full-blown massacres, primarily in Cephalonia where, under the general commanding the *Gebirgsjäger* (mountain troopers), Hubert Lanz, 5,000 Italian officers and men in the "Acqui" Division were shot—despite having already surrendered.[133] There can be no doubt that any German soldier who had read the "10 commandments" in his military manual knew that it was prohibited to kill an enemy who had surrendered; such actions were outlawed by Article 23 of the Hague Land War Regulations.[134] However, by embracing the rallying cry of "Betrayal!" the German soldiers had taken the first disinhibiting step on a path that was to lead to a radicalization of warfare on the Apennine Peninsula. In his area of command in southern Italy, Kesselring initially sent home the soldiers from divisions that had surrendered, after first disarming them.[135] But once resistance started to develop (for example, on Corsica), he, too, ordered that Italian "rebels" in hiding should be "mowed down" without due process.[136]

The balance sheet of these disarmament actions is well established: fatalities totaled 6,094,[137] and around 620,000 Italian soldiers, the so-called military internees, found themselves in the hands of German forces after September 8. It is obvious even from the nomenclature used (*military internees*) that a deliberate decision had been made not to treat these soldiers as prisoners of war subject to the rules of the Geneva Convention. In many cases, they were used for forced labor, and at least 45,000 never returned home.[138]

On September 9, 1943, amid the confusion following the Italian exit from the war, Hitler received news that Allied troops had landed at Salerno, south of Naples. The fear was that the Allies would use the element of surprise and the disarray among the Germans to immediately push forward to Rome. The lines of defense in southern Italy—that is, in Kesselring's area of command—were reinforced. Kesselring now had an opportunity to exhibit his military skills.

His task was unexpectedly made easier when the rapid Allied advance fizzled out, for several reasons. In Italy, for the first time, the disunity among the Allies was revealed when it came to strategic matters (later, their inability to reconcile their different positions reemerged in respect to war crimes issues).[139] However, Italy was of secondary importance to the Allies in terms of their military planning of World War II.[140] For a long time, there was no common strategy, which became strikingly obvious following the successful landing at Salerno.[141] It was at this point that the fundamental difficulties entailed by the coalition war became evident. Although the British hoped to pry open Fortress Europe by launching an attack on what Winston Churchill termed the "soft underbelly of Europe," the Americans favored landing a direct blow on the German wall of defense along the Atlantic front in northern France.[142] The British tended toward caution, favoring a tactic of slow attrition, in the hope that the enemy forces would more or less wear themselves down during retreat battles. For their part, the American planners pursued a tactic of "massive attack" that promised maximum success in the shortest possible time.[143] Given the situation in the autumn of 1943, the American planners' take on the massive attack strategy was to use the element of surprise in the Salerno landing in order to push forward to Rome, whereas the British were inclined to wait for a while. The British view initially prevailed, partly because it was Field Marshal Alexander's turn to exercise overall command.[144]

Meanwhile, Kesselring was able to gather the Wehrmacht troops in southern Italy and regroup them in quickly fortified positions along the lines of defense right across Italy. The Wehrmacht did not retreat to northern Italy, as the Allied staffs had anticipated, but only moved back to the Salerno-Foggia line. In terms of the Italian campaign, the Allied war aim had been to tie up German troops and thus keep them away from the second front in northern France, where the invasion was scheduled for 1944. This aim was achieved but at a greater cost to the Allies in terms of manpower and material than anticipated. After a few days, Kesselring succeeded in halting the advance and establishing the battle lines at the level of the Gustav Berhard Post military line of defense. In addition to tying up a large number of the Allied troops earmarked for the invasion, Kesselring thereby gained the room for maneuver required to implement the German occupation of northern Italy. Alexander would compare Kesselring's tactics to the operation of a "hydraulic buffer,"[145] and no doubt the respect enjoyed by Kesselring in Anglo-American military circles dated back to this period and his "elastic defense" strategy:[146] it was the respect owed to an enemy of equal standing.[147]

By holding the fortified line, Kesselring certainly also enhanced his reputation with Hitler, who until then had viewed him as an administrative expert with diplomatic skills. On November 21, 1943, Kesselring assumed overall command of the Italian theater from Rommel, who had been ordered to France to intercept the pending invasion.[148] Kesselring's title was now commander-in-chief, South-Western Command, and commander-in-chief, Army Group C. Overnight, he had become the most powerful man in the Mediterranean region.

To avoid being distracted from the primary task of repelling the enemy, it was necessary to establish control of the domestic political situation as quickly as possible.[149] In order to obtain Italian consent to the planned German measures, Hitler insisted that the continuity of the Fascist state be secured and that a government be installed in northern Italy with Mussolini at its head.[150] Since his overthrow on July 25, Mussolini had been held by the Badoglio government at an unknown location. The occupation of Italy finally made it possible to liberate Mussolini in a spectacular operation. On September 12, 1943, German paratroopers released Il Duce from a hotel at the top of the Gran Sasso in the Abruzzi Mountains in a propaganda coup that helped demonstrate Hitler's power to all of occupied Europe.[151] But the "magic bond" between the two dictators had been broken. Hitler now viewed his former tutor with skepticism, as someone with a doubtful future who would continue to depend on the goodwill of his German friends.[152] For his part, Mussolini no longer had freedom of choice when it came to his dealings with Hitler.[153] Though Il Duce's liberation was presented as a great victory to German soldiers—and to the home front—those in military circles were rather more dubious about its significance.[154]

Losing no time, Mussolini proclaimed the Stato Repubblicano d'Italia on September 8, 1943. On December 1, the title of the new state was changed to Repubblica Sociale Italiana (RSI). Its provisional capital was in Salò on Lake Garda because, as the Germans made clear to Mussolini, Rome was "too dangerous." In fact, both Kesselring (in his capacity as military commander of Rome) and the pope had spoken out against allowing fascism back into the Eternal City.[155] An SS detachment kept Mussolini under close surveillance at his headquarters at Fasano, near Salò. This was the most visible indication that the new Fascist government remained a puppet regime dependent on Hitler's good graces.

Thanks to Italy's status as a former ally, the German occupation of the country was fundamentally different from the Wehrmacht's usual occupation practice. According to scholar Lutz Klinkhammer, the occupation of Italy adhered to what one could call the "Western Model," rather than primarily amounting to a "war of destruction." Although the Germans did pursue "a policy of destruction towards partisans and civilians living in partisan areas," this was only "implemented in respect of a minority" and did not result in a "general questioning of the policy of collaboration applied to Italy."[156] The occupation was associated with enormous administrative costs, which the German authorities could not fund alone. Reichsminister and head of the Police and SS Heinrich Himmler did not always have enough police personnel at his disposal to establish a regime of terror,[157] and so the German authorities often selected their henchmen from a large number of local applicants, as is evident from the records maintained by Organization Todt (a civil and military engineering group in the Third Reich, named after its founder, Fritz Todt) and the Wehrmacht.[158] Such posts were sought after because the work was of a civilian nature and because deportation into the Reich could be avoided if one could verify employment by a German authority in Italy. It is also conceivable that many Italians believed the distorted picture of the Allies that had been presented through years of propaganda and therefore felt they were better off in German hands. What is certain is that by the end of 1944, the behavior of the Axis partner had thoroughly smashed this illusion.[159]

Economic reasons also favored the occupation of Italy. Northern Italy—especially the fertile Po Valley and the major armaments factories—was vital to the German Reich. Following the loss of the Ukraine, Berlin intended for Italy to secure Germany's grain supply and for the Italian war machine to be put at Hitler's disposal.[160] As far as the military authorities were concerned, the liberation of Mussolini and the subsequent reestablishment of his government limited their freedom of action, since consultation with any local officials often slowed them down.[161] In central Italy, however, day-to-day life continued under the German administration even after the RSI was established, and the Reichsmark was used as a parallel currency. There, the Wehrmacht established military commandants' headquarters, which were to perform administrative duties and, in particular, control food rations until the liberation of Rome in June 1944. This military administration was developed and controlled by German civilian experts.[162]

Kesselring had a special interest in a subdepartment of the military administration, which enjoyed his personal protection and was subsequently used in the attempt to exonerate him during his trial—the Arts and Monuments Protection Squad. This department was specially created under the management of Dr. Bernhard von Tieschowitz, who was succeeded by Professor Gerhard Evers in November 1943. Kesselring was particularly interested in protecting

Italy's art treasures, and he devoted far greater attention to supervising measures to that end than he did to, for example, supervising the manner in which his troops treated the Italian civilian population. As an organization, the German art protection squad—known as the Kunstschutz—was part of the rear echelon. Thus, although its staffers reported to the plenipotentiary Wehrmacht general in Italy, Rudolf Toussaint,[163] they received their orders from Supreme SS and Police Commander Karl Wolff, who was responsible for the rear echelon. Many Italian art treasures and archives were saved from the fighting. Some treasures that were considered of particular value were stored in the Vatican, which was considered a safe location.[164] However, even when the occupying forces were working to protect cultural assets, a fundamental mistrust of the Italian authorities and their efficiency was evident. All the German authorities involved avoided giving Italians control over the art depots because, in addition to worries about "inappropriate transport or storage," they feared that "entire collections would be sold to Switzerland."[165] For that reason, the German Kunstschutz depot was handed over only to Allied counterparts in 1945, rather than to the Italian transitional government.[166] After the war, the Italians repeatedly claimed that the Kunstschutz was one of Germany's best-disguised "art theft organizations."[167] Researchers have been unable to confirm this allegation,[168] although there were certain instances when SS authorities "substantially plundered private collections."[169]

Certainly, the advancing Allies felt that the Kunstschutz had performed its duties very efficiently. A 1945 Allied investigation report emphasized that Italian cultural treasures had suffered relatively little war damage,[170] and it attributed this primarily to the large-scale allocation of Wehrmacht conveyances, as well as generous gasoline rations.[171] The report stated that, in the battle zone, German soldiers even rescued art treasures from buildings under fire.[172] Certainly, the personal interest evinced by the commander-in-chief contributed to the relatively high proportion of art treasures that were saved: Kesselring was regularly updated on the operations to evacuate cultural assets.[173] There can also be no doubt that he did at least attempt to have Italy's urban heritage sites declared "open cities," thus ensuring that they would not be involved in the fighting.[174] However, he was only successful in a few cases, such as in Siena and Assisi. Moreover, Rome and Florence were drawn into the fighting by both sides, which meant that their open city status was rendered meaningless in practice.[175]

The German occupation resulted in significant internal political tensions in Italy. In addition to the external devastation wreaked by Allied air raids and the battles along the front line, Italy had to cope with an internal conflict that assumed the proportions of a civil war. Italy's population seemed to split into two camps. One camp maintained its loyalty to Mussolini and his German allies to the end. The other camp joined the resistance, in a radical break with both the Fascist state and its own past.[176] Most Italians, clearly tired of the war, apparently adopted a wait-and-see attitude.[177] The mood of resignation evident in the Italian population after September 9 was summed up by the writer Curzio Malaparte. He wrote: "The fun was now over. Once again we joined columns and—with no weapons or flags—marched to the next battlefield to join the Allies and together win this war, which we had just lost together with the Germans."[178] Ordinary Italians generally only decided to resist once the measures adopted by the occupiers affected their own lives.[179] Thus, the numbers of people joining the Resistenza troops in the mountains rose disproportionately as German terror against the rural population increased.[180]

By the autumn of 1943, resistance against the German occupation was already organized and sponsored by various political groups that—despite other ideological differences—were united in their battle aims against the Germans. So-called political committees maintained contact with (initially small) armed groups in the mountains. By September 18, 1943, the Resistenza had 1,500 armed members—1,000 in northern Italy and a further 500 around Rome and in the Marken and Abruzzi regions.[181] Socialist and Communist politicians returned from exile.[182] In Rome, opposition groups formed the Comitato di Liberazione Nazionale (Committee of National Liberation, CLN). The founding members included representatives from across the political spectrum, from Christian Democrats to Socialists.[183] The founding preamble noted that the anti-Fascist groups would call the Italian people to arms at the point when National Socialism attempted to reinstall its Fascist allies in government.[184] In practical terms, this amounted to a declaration of war against the German occupation forces—a war that, from the start, received logistical and financial assistance from the Allies.[185]

Several reasons motivated the Allied intelligence services to assist the Resistenza. It was hoped that a "patriotic liberation" of the occupied countries would strengthen the national and political self-esteem of the peoples concerned and that this, in turn, would ideally result in the development of new democratic forms of government after the war.[186] These calculations were certainly rewarded in the case of Italy. The first postwar governments were formed by the political representatives of the partisan formations.[187] Especially in the context of the nascent Cold War, the Allies were concerned to ensure that the military Resistenza formations were dissolved immediately after victory so that they could not be deployed against the Allies. It was also always made clear that the partisan movement was a "spin-off" of the actual victors, dependent on Allied goodwill and assistance. Thus, despite the personal impetus and heroism of individuals, the war conducted by the Resistenza was, in the final analysis, a "dependent war assuming dependent forms within a Grand Strategy pursued by the Allied backing powers."[188]

All these factors meant that as far as the German troops were concerned, the war in Italy was transformed not only into the feared "second front" in Italy but also into a "second war"—one war being conducted against the Allies and one against the partisans who, of course, were part of the occupied population. Thanks to the participation of Fascist auxiliary troops, this German antipartisan war was enduringly radicalized, developing into a civil war over which the Germans lost control.[189] Given that this civil war was taking place in a zone of operations vital to the Reich, it naturally ran counter to Hitler's calculations. Therefore, in northern Italy, the SS took command of strong military divisions and also assumed police duties to secure German rule.[190] One result of this was that the *Reichsfürer SS* and head of the police and SS, Heinrich Himmler, had a personal representative in Italy in the form of Karl Wolff. Together with the presence in Italy of the Wehrmacht, the German Foreign Office, and Albert Speer's ministry (armaments and war production), this generated confusion and blurred the lines of command when it came to military and occupation matters.[191] The foreign propaganda section, a division within the German Foreign Office, had the difficult task of promoting a consensual attitute toward the German occupation regime.[192]

But Italy was militarily lost to Germany. In January 1944, the Allies succeeded in landing at Anzio and Nettuno, to the north of the front (the Gustav Line), and extending a stable bridgehead. Yet despite Allied air superiority, the Italian fronts remained steady for another few months, albeit with heavy casualties on both sides. The Battle of Monte Cassino was emblematic of this situation. Lasting for almost five months, it resulted in the near-complete destruction of the old Benedictine abbey by Allied bombing raids.[193] Hitler himself gave the order to halt operations, and he decorated his field commanders after the battle. On July 19, 1944, Kesselring's fortieth anniversary as a soldier, Hitler awarded him the brilliants to the Knight's Cross with Oak Leaf and Swords, which he had received in 1942. This was the Wehrmacht's highest decoration, and Kesselring was only the twenty-seventh recipient. His position as a member of the Wehrmacht elite was thus established beyond dispute.

The Antipartisan War and the Bandenbefehle Issued by Kesselring, Summer 1944

When examining the Italian theater of war, one cannot help asking how—given that Italy had been a former German ally—it was there that antipartisan warfare mutated into deliberate terror aimed at the rural population. Lutz Klinkhammer has correctly noted that in view of the suffering of the survivors and the relatives of the victims, any attempts to analyze and historically classify the massacres committed during the German occupation must remain unsatisfactory. Nevertheless, making such an attempt is necessary in order to identify those bearing both individual and institutional responsibility.[194]

In 1946, giving evidence at Nuremburg, Albert Kesselring justified the Wehrmacht's ruthless approach to the antipartisan war by claiming that, at the time, he had been informed there were areas and zones in Italy where "everyone—man, woman and child—was associated with the partisans, whether as fighters or fellow-travelers."[195] In respect to the countermeasures adopted, it was a matter of "indifference" to him whether these people "were involved of their own volition or as a result of gentle pressure" because "such distinctions were not drawn by the bullet finding a German soldier; therefore, this situation could only be viewed militarily rather than emotionally."[196]

From 1943 to 1945, the Wehrmacht conducted a war of retreat in Italy, which was hindered by sabotage operations carried out by the Resistenza; this resistance was perceived by the Wehrmacht as equivalent to a war conducted by the entire Italian population against the German military. Notions of the enemy thus became blurred, and German soldiers no longer differentiated between the civilian population and their paramilitary enemies in the Resistenza troops. A peasant seeking to prevent his cattle from being requisitioned was fought with the same implacable determination as a Communist sabotage unit, which meant that, in practical terms, the two were equated.

From the very beginning, the Resistenza's war-by-ambush strategy presented the Wehrmacht with significant problems.[197] The "punishment actions" carried out by the Wehrmacht with incredible brutality give an indication of the scale of the threats emanating from the war behind the front. Schreiber has pointed out that "the Resistenza achieved a military effect if only because of the sense of threat which its mere existence instilled in the German military": "It generated a permanent sense of insecurity, forcing a constant state of defense readiness or making monitoring steps necessary."[198] Klinkhammer, too, has observed that the reasons for the striking brutality used against the partisans included the weakening of the Wehrmacht from the spring of 1944, a demoralizing sense of defeat, and—for example, in the case of the Fourteenth Army after surrendering Rome—the stresses and pressures of a disorderly retreat that entailed the loss of major items of equipment and weapons.[199] By issuing strict orders and guidelines for dealing with a partisan attack, Kesselring attempted to return some sense of security to the German soldiers, thus restoring order within the Wehrmacht and the reputation of the German army, both of which, together with internal discipline, had been severely damaged by excessive looting and other abuses. In this situation, his orders had the effect of a carte blanche issued to the troops. In particular, they helped reinforce the fear felt by soldiers who had already been physically weakened by constant retreats, thereby radicalizing and further disinhibiting them.

The escalation of the war against the partisans was also aided by the confused lines of demarcation between the Wehrmacht and the SS. In accordance with Hitler's instruction dated August 18, 1942, the army was responsible for antipartisan warfare in the operational areas.[200] In Italy, the Army High Command was responsible for combating partisans in the operational areas and within the approximately thirty-kilometer-wide coastal strip, with the exception of the operational zone in northern Italy. The SS bore sole responsibility for those territories that had officially been declared partisan areas. The various authorities repeatedly got in each other's way. There was the commander-in-chief, South-Western Command, who was responsible for the operational areas. There was the plenipotentiary general of the German Wehrmacht, as territorial commander (from 1943 to summer 1944, this was infantry general Rudolf Toussaint, and from summer 1944 on, it was Waffen SS General Karl Wolff). And there was the supreme SS and police commander (from summer 1944 on, Wolff had additional power, acting simultaneously as plentipotentiary general of the Wehrmacht.) "Together, and also in a certain rivalry with the plenipotentiary general," Schreiber noted, these commanders "secured those occupied territories which did not form part of the operational areas." [201] Therefore, on January 19, 1944, Hitler decided that Kesselring should "if required by the situation, have full authority over all Wehrmacht and SS troops located within Italian borders and suited to ground fighting."[202]

By the 1943–1944 winter, extensive areas were already controlled by partisan groups operating locally. The partisan formations were increasingly free to operate behind the front, and in certain areas, they completely paralyzed supply lines and communication. The relevant military command posts did not feel able to gain control of the situation. To develop a German defense position, such as the planned Gothic Line (later known as the Green Line), it seemed expedient to ensure that a sole body had responsibility for all antipartisan warfare, which could then be better coordinated. Accordingly, on April 1, 1944, Kesselring attempted to obtain authority over the "supreme SS and police commander," within whose jurisdiction the Apennines, as a partisan area, lay. Unsurprisingly, this move provoked a stormy protest from Himmler. On April 26, the Wehrmacht High Command issued a compromise proposal: the commander-in-chief, South-Western Command, would have "supreme command of all antipartisan operations in Italy," but the supreme SS and police commander would retain "responsibility for implementation" outside the operational area and the coastal strip; he would "report personally" to Kesselring in this capacity and was to act according to "Kesselring's directives."[203] Daily reports regarding the operations carried out would be sent to the commander-in-chief, South-Western Command. Kesselring, Himmler, and Wolff finally agreed to the proposal, but it was clear to Kesselring that this solution carried a "slight political aftertaste" and could "not be militarily satisfactory."[204]

For the Wehrmacht, the April 1944 agreement meant that the Army High Command would retain responsibility for antipartisan warfare in the operational areas and the coastal strip, even if the SS was tasked with actually carrying out the operations.[205] This separation of duties and command powers resulted in certain problems, since Kesselring was only officially informed about the actual manner of implementation via casualty reports, ammunition consumption logs, and brief daily reports. This situation afforded the SS an opportunity for independent action, and it created a favorable climate for the perpetration of massacres.[206] An examination of the relevant files has shown that in several cases, the daily reports only briefly referenced the actual events, or they used wording ("partisans put down") that gave little indication of the savage nature of the operations being carried out or the people who were affected, including women and children.[207]

However, the military leadership did not show any interest in receiving more precise information. It should also be noted that it was already the practice of German troops to enter imprecise reports in their official war journals. Thus, a retrospective reconstruction of events is difficult. Albert Kesselring was aware of this practice, and he occasionally joked that "the distortion of war history starts when the ordnance officer puts pen to paper in the war journal."[208] It therefore seems possible that the Wehrmacht leadership, by tolerating the war journal distortions, sanctioned and accepted the failure to pursue German perpetrators when excesses occurred. The "clean maintenance" or retrospective cleansing of the war logs was due, on the one hand, to fear of Allied prosecutions (which had already been announced) and, on the other hand, to moral scruples, since there can be no doubt that many commanders retained a sense of justice and injustice.[209] However, the distortions did make it easier to claim after the war that such raids had not taken place.

Wolff received his directives on how to proceed against the partisans directly from Himmler. He simply had to comply with Kesselring's basic orders, which were formulated so as to allow plenty of room for maneuver. For his part, Kesselring was guided by the instructions issued by the Führer's headquarters. The "directives for fighting the partisan movement," issued by the Wehrmacht High Command on April 6, 1944, were implemented by Kesselring using language such as "fire immediately and without question in the event of a raid" and "in the current situation, an excessively hard clampdown will never be grounds for punishment." On April 13, he ratcheted up the language still further: "Flaccid and indecisive leaders," he warned, would be "brought to book, because they endanger the troops under their command and the respect enjoyed by the German Wehrmacht."[210] In an order governing "responsibility for antipartisan warfare in Italy," dated May 1, 1944, the specific regulations were reissued.[211] This order unambiguously defined the responsibilities of Wehrmacht officers. Thus, Kesselring announced that responsibility for "reconnaissance and execution of the operations" should remain "in the hands of the Ic officers (3rd General Staff Officers, chief intelligence officers) attached to the army groups and the Army High Command."[212]

Following the fall of Rome on June 4, 1944, and Field Marshal Alexander's appeal to the Italians to kill Germans "wherever you encounter them"—adding the rider that they should be attacked "from the rear, so that you can kill again"—the partisan war entered its most acute phase.[213] All attempts to prevent the escalation of the terror and its extension to the civilian population were abandoned as militarily infeasible. As commander-in chief, Albert Kesselring played a direct part in the further escalation of the war conducted against the civilian population by issuing two so-called Bandenbefehle. These antipartisan orders show how the pressure exerted by the Allied front radicalized Kesselring's view of conditions in Italy.

On June 17, 1944, Kesselring issued a Bandenbefehl that tightened up the general Wehrmacht High Command directives issued in April.[214] In this order, "everyone" was assured of absolute indemnity if they "exceed our normal restraint."[215] In other words, any prosecution by the Wehrmacht courts was ruled out from the very beginning. Admittedly, Kesselring was not the author of the wording "even against women and children" that appeared in his order: this language can be traced back to an order issued by the Wehrmacht High Command on December 16, 1942, and it referred to antipartisan warfare in Russia.[216] In this High Command order, Hitler had declared that taking a ruthless approach to partisans and "partisan collaborators" was every soldier's "duty." To avoid any misunderstanding, he added that "consideration" of any kind was a "crime against the German people and against the soldiers at the front." Hitler thus ruled out any concern with reservations or scruples, not to mention fear of prosecution, from the start, effectively criminalizing the observance of international legal standards (e.g., courts-martial).[217] Kesselring adopted this formula.[218]

Schreiber has pointed out that the instructions issued by German commanders in respect to antipartisan warfare had a consistently normative effect, representing a carte blanche for many troop commanders,[219] all of whom received the Bandenbefehl signed by Kesselring. It should, however, be noted that these orders were probably not always passed verbatim down the ranks.[220] Since the danger posed by the partisans was viewed as particularly serious following the fall of Rome on June 4, 1944, regular troops were generally deployed in antipartisan operations. It was initially proposed to use elite infantry units for this purpose, but as the extent and severity of the antipartisan war increased, Kesselring ordered the "massive deployment of artillery, grenade and mine throwers, armored cars, flame throwers and other technical combat equipment."[221] On July 1, he again enjoined his soldiers to take a hard line,[222] but he simultaneously ordered that German soldiers who looted and raped were to be shot on the spot. This second order was primarily based on military considerations: only a disciplined army could survive the defensive battles in Italy.[223]

The Italian public was notified of the Bandenbefehle by means of wall posters.[224] Reprisals generally occurred after a German soldier had been killed or injured by partisans.[225] To heighten the deterrent effect, the posters were used to establish the link between the reprisals and the killing or injury of German soldiers and to warn of further reprisals if such events were repeated. The British Commission of Enquiry subsequently found that the reprisals had been well planned and that detachments from a range of units were transported to the locations in order to carry out the operations.[226] The units involved always proceeded in the same manner. If Wehrmacht soldiers were murdered in the immediate vicinity of a village, the inhabitants would be mowed down with machine guns, and any homes still inhabited would be torched.

We know that, in certain cases, Wehrmacht commanders complained about the approach adopted by SS troops and lodged protests with Kesselring. In 1946, for example, Panzertruppen General Joachim Lemelsen, commander-in-chief of the Fourteenth Army, stated for the record that such reprisals had been the subject of preliminary investigations but without results.[227] This statement is one example of commanders' reservations about and investigations of the effect of Kesselring's orders on their troops. However, these investigations often failed to produce tangible results, since Hitler himself had forbidden prosecution and few soldiers had the courage to testify against their superiors. This fact was illustrated by the internal investigation of the 1944 massacre perpetrated by the Wehrmacht under General Eduard Crasemann in the swamps of Fuccecchio.[228] Not one German soldier was held accountable for cruelties associated with an antipartisan operation.[229]

Panzertruppen General Traugott Herr, commander of the LXXVI Panzer Corps in Italy, testified in court that Kesselring had sentenced German soldiers to death in cases of theft and rape. However, Herr also stated that Kesselring had only been informed "in isolated cases"—sometimes by Herr himself—of excesses committed during the course of antipartisan operations, and Herr had complained about the troops' behavior at San Polo. One can thus only conclude with historian Schreiber that "what happened in Italy was no secret, even if there were varying degrees of knowledge, and was certainly not a secret among high-ranking German officers."[230] In this regard, historian Omer Bartov has noted that "the legalization of authorized, and the tolerance of unauthorized, crime contributed significantly to the remarkable resolve demonstrated by the Wehrmacht in battle, quite apart from the fact that many soldiers already felt that they had to stick together precisely because they had encumbered themselves with joint guilt."[231]

Certainly, there were unequivocal reports of German terror operations elsewhere, for example, in Tuscany. In August, the German ambassador to the RSI, Rudolf Rahn, notified Kesselring that Mussolini had complained of Italian citizens being gunned down by German army units within RSI borders.[232] On August 21, 1944, Kesselring reacted by issuing an edict to his troops, acknowledging that "in the context of the antipartisan warfare and the major antipartisan operations, incidents have occurred during recent weeks which have damaged the German Wehrmacht's reputation and discipline, and which no longer have anything to do with reprisal operations."[233]

The reason for Kesselring's edict was the collapse of discipline within his own troops, which put an overall military victory at risk. The massacres drove many previously quiescent Italians into the partisans' arms; it was now highly unlikely that they would provide any tangible assistance during the difficult defensive battles being fought by the Germans. Bartov has pointed out that this vicious circle—disciplinary measures against German troops, which resulted in increasing barbarity by the soldiers, in turn resulting in further disciplinary measures—simply recruited new fighters to the ranks of the partisans.[234] These considerations can also be detected in the edict issued by Kesselring. It may be that Allied threats had an effect as well. For instance, Field Marshal Alexander, speaking in a radio broadcast, had already announced that German commanders would be held to account for their ruthless methods after the war.[235]

However, during the four weeks following Alexander's radio broadcast, nothing changed in the approach adopted by German troops to antipartisan warfare. Only at the end of September, after increased political pressure resulted from a forceful complaint by Mussolini, did Kesselring issue another order to his troops. He stated that the massacres of civilians, "the manner of which causes outrage, and is even driving those decent elements in the population, who are prepared to fight, into the enemy camp or towards the partisans," had to stop. At the same time, in view of "deceitful ambushes" by partisans, the commander-in-chief expressed understanding of the fact that innocent people had also been killed in the heat of battle.[236] Kesselring promised that the "most blatant cases" Il Duce complained of would be the subject of courts-martial.In the end, some incidents were, in fact, investigated, but the proceedings were halted inconclusively.[237] Kesselring threatened that he was "no longer prepared to stand by and watch this." He thus admitted that his "pacification policy" had not only failed but also caused a further escalation, radicalizing all elements in Italy. In addition, he implicitly admitted that he had stood by in silence for some time while the killing continued.[238]

It was only after Kesselring's edict that the Germans made a real effort to stay within the boundaries of legality in conducting the war. In essence, there was a change of policy toward the partisans. The change may have been due to two factors: Kesselring's personal absence from the front and the hopeless military situation that resulted in separate, local truce agreements with the partisans. Following a serious car accident in October 1944, Kesselring was out of action for three months, and leadership in this issue was assumed by Generaloberst Heinrich von Vietinghoff-Scheel, who was rather more moderate.[239] Then, after just four weeks back in his old position, Kesselring was appointed commander-in-chief, Western Command, and at that point, he left Italy for good.

In summary, the Germans' anticipated successes in quelling the partisan fighting never materialized. Although partisan activity was crushed in some areas, the massacres of Italian civilians rendered collaboration between civilian and military authorities impossible in practice, and sabotage was the order of the day. Kesselring's Bandenbefehle did not achieve the intended "pacification"; rather, they achieved the exact opposite. The partisans significantly increased their recruitment, and the general public, which had initially been wary of or downright hostile to the Resistenza troops, offered them growing support.[240]

The connection between the brutal approach adopted by the Germans and the heavy losses suffered by the Wehrmacht as a result of partisan activity has been repeatedly highlighted in historical studies. However, it remains difficult to determine the precise number of casualties inflicted on the Germans as a result of partisan attacks. Using the reports filed each morning by the chief of operations for Army Group C, Schreiber has calculated that from July 21 to September 25, 1944, 624 Germans died, 993 were wounded, and 872 were missing or taken hostage.[241] During the same period, German records show there were 9,520 partisan deaths.[242] It would thus be a gross exaggeration to speak of enormous German losses. On the German side—for instance, in the Wehrmacht files—some duplication occurred when German losses were counted, as was shown by Carlo Gentile's comparison with the casualty reports issued by the Deutsche Dienststelle in Berlin.[243] However, the ambiguous counting method itself was also problematic: for example, did the term *partisans* refer to all the casualties recorded, including women and children? Indeed, the numbers of civilian casualties claimed by the partisan war in Italy are still debated today. For many years, resistance historiography was based on exaggerated figures. It is only in recent years that these figures have been adjusted downward—often quite significantly.[244] Current estimates put the number of civilian casualties during the occupation period (1943–1945) at a minimum of 9,200 women, children, and old people.[245]

It is unlikely that the figures available are sufficient for a clear conclusion on the partisan war. However, the function that was performed by the figures at the time is apparent. The constant focus on the high level of German losses served to justify the actions taken by the Wehrmacht, whose leaders—after the war—felt constrained to explain how this "bloodthirsty frenzy" had occurred.[246] However, reading the statements made after the war, one could also conclude that the sense of threat felt by the Germans was so strong (even as early as the spring of 1944, when they were only aware of isolated partisan attacks) that it became the motor driving the antipartisan war. And in the course of that war, old prejudices were reinforced, and both sides allowed themselves to be driven to excesses.

Starting with Klinkhammer's thesis that "95 out of 100 soldiers in the German forces stationed in Italy were neither directly nor indirectly involved in murders of civilians,"[247] there has been a heated debate among historians regarding whether Italy was a special case in terms of occupied territories in Europe.[248] An investigation of precisely why there was a particularly high number of massacres in certain areas of the front and low numbers in others would seem to be more profitable, as would an investigation of why earlier ideological indoctrination or membership in the SS did not automatically lead to involvement in these massacres. Matta has concluded that most incidents occurred in the front area of the occupation zone and were perpetrated by troops deployed at the front. This situation contrasted with that on the eastern front, where antipartisan warfare tended to take place in the hinterland or in the context of special operations.[249] If one traces the movements of particular units and correlates those movements with the number of war crimes in specific zones, certain units regularly appear as perpetrators of war crimes.[250] In Italy, the 1st Paratrooper Division, the Hermann Göring Division, and the 16th SS Panzer Grenadier Division were deployed particularly frequently in antipartisan operations, and they were therefore disproportionately involved in massacres. Isolated Wehrmacht units have also been accused of excesses, as in Civitella, Fuccecchio, and Pietransieri. Klinkhammer has noted that these actions apparently "tended to involve reprisals during retreat."[251] There is some dispute regarding whether there was, in all cases, a direct connection between Kesselring's orders and the atrocities committed. Klinkhammer has assumed that many of the SS units involved paid no attention to the carte blanche issued by their commander-in-chief: rather, they equated the order already received from Berlin to cleanse an area of partisans to an instruction to conduct a large-scale liquidation of the civilian population.[252]

However, given that not all SS units deployed in Italy were involved in war crimes, we must seek a more comprehensive explanation. To that end, it is instructive to examine the involvement of individual officers. According to Gentile, following the promulgation of Kesselring's orders, there was a marked increase in personal disinhibition among SS detachments whose leaders had served in the Russian campaign[253] or in the so-called *Totenkopf* (death's head) concentration camp guard units.[254] These *SS Unterführer* (subcommanders), who had already been radicalized by their early individual political conditioning, helped influence German recruits in Italy, most of whom were very young and poorly trained. The result was that the number of war crimes spiraled during the summer of 1944 in areas where these formations operated. The crucial factor here, according to Gentile, was a "highly explosive combination of political conditioning, experience and convictions, which could metamorphose into deadly action at any time."[255] Klinkhammer emphasized that criminal instructions issued by the leadership always had to be combined with an individual predisposition in order to set in train the deadly mechanism of the so-called punishment operations.[256] And Thomas Kühne observed that the "National Socialist war blurred the boundaries between regular and criminal wartime killing; boundaries which are important to the military system of standards."[257] At this point, it should also be noted as well that the constant willingness of soldiers to kill fostered the development of a deadening mechanism that, in turn, created a sense of indifference toward the lives of civilians.[258]

During recent years, historians and sociologists have increasingly focused on the antipartisan war as a deviation from military norms of warfare.[259] The present work only offers some general reflections on the genesis of the perpetrators. In contrast to the frontline battle against the Allies, antipartisan warfare was not governed by any ethical standards. One can only speculate on the impact that knowledge of such murder operations (or direct involvement in them) had on Wehrmacht soldiers. Kühne has posited that these factors clearly resulted in a perversion of the soldierly *ideal of chivalry*. The longstanding principle in international humanitarian law regarding *comradeship with the enemy*—whom one fought in a chivalrous manner and to whom one showed mercy when taking him as a prisoner of war—and the general principle that one protects the civilian population from fighting were both superseded during World War II.[260] Thus, back in March 30, 1941, when Hitler gave a private speech to a group of Wehrmacht generals, he demanded that they "move on from the concept of soldierly comradeship in this war."[261] The decree on military jurisdiction (*Kriegsgerichtsbarkeitserlass*), which—with particular regard to the war in the East—exempted soldiers from prosecution for committing crimes against the civilian population,[262] was the final nail in the coffin of the chivalrous ideal of earlier times. The propaganda used to indoctrinate the soldiers played a significant role. The official wording adopted by Hitler and the Wehrmacht High Command in their orders (which, as a matter of principle, referred to Italians as "common traitors" and criminalized the partisan movement as a collection of lawless bandits) helped lessen the respect for life.[263]

In National Socialist warfare, the boundaries separating comrades from noncomrades and combatants from noncombatants were replaced by a new boundary that separated the "master race" from the "inferior races."[264] The more successful a "hard line" was, the better. The fear coursing through German soldiers, combined with the bitterness sparked by the death of comrades and a sense of insecurity when moving around the country, often caused individual detachments to overreact, which, in turn, quickly escalated the antipartisan war. One explanatory factor is the thesis of Thomas Kühne of the collective of *comradeship as a normative force*.[265] Military sociologists have found that "the closer troops are to the enemy, the less the influence of the formal control system, and the more decisive the norm and control system exercised by the primary group for the soldiers' behavior."[266] Excesses are committed under cover of the group, and the individual soldier can be confident that his comrades will not betray him. As Kühne saw it, the myth of comradeship thus acted as an "engine barbarizing this war."[267] The mixture of prejudices and fear resulted in a brutalization among individual troop detachments that was difficult to control and that, as Bartov showed, was the result of a prolonged process: "Filled with fear of their superiors and unable to conquer the enemy, the soldiers increasingly took out their frustration on the civilians and POWs in the occupied territories."[268]

For the commander-in-chief of the Italian theater, the psychosocial factors disinhibiting the Wehrmacht were a dual challenge. Although Kesselring wanted to address the risk posed by the partisans militarily, he found it more and more difficult to maintain control over his troops[269] and to punish solo runs by local commanders.[270] He thus failed to satisfactorily fulfill his leadership role. Schreiber has correctly noted that the commander-in-chief alone had control over the "direct military reaction and the extent and brutality of reprisals," and in connection with the Bandenbefehle, he has written of a "terrorist reckoning" on the part of the German political and military leadership.[271] When one remembers that Kesselring had already, in advance of the unrest, had considerable problems with certain units that failed to comply with his orders and were seen as undisciplined, it is clear he should have considered the effect that an order promising indemnity for "each individual" would have on the morale of troop units that had already been disinhibited. This fact was also acknowledged by his subordinate officers. Once again, it was General Lemelsen who, when reviewing the "antipartisan warfare weeks" in October 1944, ventured to conclude that the operations had failed. The fight against the "bands" had, he said, been "wrongly" conducted and had "forced the mass of the Italian population into the arms of the partisans," while the German troops had been "roughened and barbarized by this method of fighting."[272]

One may therefore conclude that Albert Kesselring, through the orders he issued, played a direct role in radicalizing warfare in Italy, that he tacitly tolerated (if not encouraged) the excesses against the civilian population, and that on Hitler's orders, he would not let the perpetrators be prosecuted by German military courts. At best, he merely initiated routine investigations that generally ended inconclusively.

Kesselring's View of the War in Italy

Using Kesselring's own statements regarding the antipartisan war in Italy, one can trace the development and reinterpretation of his view of the Italian war. Three phases can be distinguished. The first phase began with the statements he made in July 1946, when he was a witness in the International Military Tribunal (IMT) trial of the General Staff in Nuremberg. The second was marked by his statements—after he had been charged—to British interrogation officers in London during October 1946. The third phase involved his trial testimony in Venice from February to April 1947.

During his testimony before the IMT, Kesselring had already had two opportunities to address the antipartisan war in Italy. The specific cases involved actions in Civitella and Stia, which had been cited as war crimes in the flyer issued by Field Marshal Alexander in June 1944. On July 3, 1946, Kesselring was questioned about these cases by Dr. Robert Kempner in Nuremberg. He testified that, due to the escalation of the "guerrilla war" and the "equally unpleasant self-help remedies adopted by the troops," he had felt constrained to issue the Bandenbefehle in order "to avoid chaos."[273] He pointed out that he was bearing "heavy burdens" at that time and was therefore unable to have a military judge assess the compliance of his orders with international law; rather, he allowed "his own conscience to decide that they were acceptable."[274] He showed great understanding for his soldiers in the situation because "this atmosphere of hatred and revenge" was, in the final analysis, due to "the behavior of the people" for whom "German soldiers had sacrificed much blood."[275] However, he said he had always remained in control and, "like a doctor," had "kept his hand on the pulse of this whole movement" so that he could "issue both alleviating and aggravating orders."[276] He repudiated the charge that "insufficient supervision" had allowed such incidents to take place behind his back. Kesselring thus not only admitted that appalling incidents had occurred but also acknowledged that these were actually the result of an atmosphere of hatred and revenge together with his orders, which were intended to contain the excesses.

Kesselring noted retrospectively that much was now "no longer comprehensible" to him, but he said he had intended to "stave off" this "atmosphere . . . where soldiers only saw blood before their eyes, this wave."[277] Testifying in Nuremberg, where he had been transferred from his detention cage in London when the IMT trial started, he was still able to find explicit words of sympathy for the Italians: "I regret every one of these incidents, I used every means to ensure that this illegal antipartisan warfare situation could not occur, precisely because I knew that barbarities and atrocities on both sides cannot be avoided." Kempner probed further: "In other words, it is certain that the things mentioned did occur?" Kesselring responded: "Yes, of course, but it is a very regrettable matter."[278] During the first period of detention in London, Kesselring had been more frank. He stated that he had decided "because of self-defense considerations in respect of myself and my troops" to place himself "in front of his soldiers"; however, he said that he ruled out assuming liability for "common crimes committed by our soldiers where these were not committed in the heat of the moment."[279]

The picture of the war in Italy painted by Kesselring while he was in London during this first detention period came closer to reality than any others he was to draw—but only for a short while. Even before he was constrained to defend his own actions, he described antipartisan warfare as a military operation in the course of which one had to accept the death of innocent victims in order to avoid risking the overall success of the operation, defined in this case as a peaceful hinterland for the German frontline troops. Kesselring was able to be self-critical and to condemn the excesses as intemperate. According to his assessment, however, the blame for the escalation of violence, which he personally appeared to regret, lay with the war waged by the partisans, which he rejected as "unmilitary" and "underhand" and which he said had been logistically supported by the Allies. Because of his countless trips to the front, Kesselring was, if only from hearsay, aware of the "assaults" he had thus described.[280]

Once he himself was brought to trial by the Allies, his empathetic view of the victims' suffering was superseded by a discourse on guilt. Kesselring's perception of Italy became noticeably dimmer. It appeared to him that the entire population was infiltrated by partisans and that the German Wehrmacht in Italy was the victim rather than aggressor. This picture was further refined during the course of Kesselring's trial testimony in Venice, and he enlarged on it even further in later years, especially during the 1950s. While in London during October 1946, Kesselring remarked that when it came to Italy, "everyone was in cahoots in the guerrilla areas" and that the public itself was therefore to blame for the attacks.[281] He saw no connection between his orders and the massacres in the summer of 1944.[282] Rather, he stated that his orders were intended to provide young, inexperienced officers, who were no longer able to rein in their troops, with a directive so that "spontaneous outbreaks of hatred" could be avoided. According to Kesselring's London statement, his orders were always within the linguistic confines of the Wehrmacht High Command instructions. "I ordered that the fight be conducted with 'maximum severity'—not with 'the most brutal means' as defined by the Wehr-macht High Command—and, in my order issued on July 1st 1944, I added that I would give cover to any commander who—in the heat of battle or as a result of understandable over-enthusiasm or inability—exceeded what would be considered normal goals."[283] He "regretted the attacks" but believed that "only a few commanders can have adopted an incorrect approach."[284] He specified in detail those troop units that could have committed the individual massacres, and he attempted to recollect each specific case.[285] However, Kesselring was already inserting handwritten annotations on his attorney's materials to the effect that the Italians had exaggerated slightly in their depictions of events: "The facts of the matter extrapolated from the files make an implausible impression in respect of many points; some have already been refuted."[286] He assumed that "the more senior troop commanders were unaware of most of the incidents, or had received an innocuous battle report which did not appear to render intervention justified or necessary." Despite the fact that he himself had already admitted to the "hard" German conduct of the war, Kesselring's self-justification mechanism prevailed once again: "For the rest: Guerrilla warfare, in violation of international law and in its immoral manifestations which are unfortunately unavoidable!"[287]

Finally, when on trial in Venice during February 1947, Kesselring showed himself to be incorrigible. He stressed his inability to understand how he could be charged with inciting war crimes and fundamentally doubted the deeds described: "Rahn described the incidents as 'understandable' to Il Duce. I went beyond this and ordered the most stringent intervention. When I received the letter, I had to assume the veracity of these events, despite the fact that, at first glance, some appeared to be implausible and false. I wanted to calm Il Duce down."[288]

Kesselring doggedly stuck to a version of events that depicted barbarities as an unavoidable side effect of any war. Atrocities had occurred "under the influence of wild passion, the rage of war or merely for reasons of revenge."[289] Believing himself covered by international law, he was able to dispel any (merely rhetorical) self-doubt regarding the legality of his orders:

> I do sometimes find myself shaking my head when I remember this or that action or order, but then when I put myself into the situation, into the overall atmosphere and think back, it becomes immediately and compellingly clear that the decision I took was inescapable and no other decision would have been possible. I believe that nobody in Nuremberg was able to imagine themselves in the Italian atmosphere of the guerrilla war.[290]

For the purpose of his trial strategy, he developed a purely military picture of the war in Italy, which had been a "campaign like any other." Although there were, regrettably, victims among the civilian population, these casualties had ultimately been caused by the "partisans' manner of fighting, which was contrary to international law." Such comments marked the final transformative phase in Kesselring's view of Italy: deaths among the civilian population had to be accepted in the context of the overall fight, especially if the civilians had more or less gambled away protection by German troops as a result of their own behavior. There were no longer any words of compunction in Kesselring's narrative.

Kesselring's Involvement in War Crimes

During his trial, Kesselring was accused not only of issuing the Bandenbefehle but also of having been involved in the shootings in the Fosse Ardeatine, which constituted a punishment action in the wake of a partisan bomb attack on a German police unit on Rasella Street in Rome on March 23, 1944, resulting in heavy German losses. As will be shown later in this volume, he probably did not bear any responsibility for the events that unfolded in Rome following the attack. Yet by focusing on events in Rome during his trial, his hope was to distract from his knowledge of the shooting of an American commando unit in northern Italy, which used the code name Ginny Mission. The Ginny Mission shooting has been uncovered by the American historian Richard Raiber only in 1997.[291]

The Allied courts were consistent in inflicting strict penalties for the shooting of POWs. Raiber has concluded that Kesselring therefore decided to exaggerate his responsibility for the Fosse Ardeatine shootings in order to divert attention from his complicity in the Ginny Mission affair.[292] Kesselring had hoped to escape conviction, since military law experts viewed the Fosse Ardeatine case as a reprisal covered by the laws of war. This observation leads to a further conclusion, namely, that the Wehrmacht officers needed to look back on a "clean Italian theater of war," in which any atrocities that had occurred were deemed justified. In this regard, it appears plausible that agreements had been made at an early stage to ensure that the myth of a clean war would be passed on "accurately" following defeat. This theory is buttressed by the fact that direct orders were issued to destroy files; furthermore, the results of investigations were suppressed or simply not distributed to the military justice authorities.[293]

What is certain is that although Kesselring did not participate in either of the two events, he did bear formal responsibility for them as commander-in-chief. Raiber claimed that Kesselring preferred to be tried for the shootings in the Fosse Ardeatine caves, hoping that this would result in either a custodial sentence or an acquittal. By contrast, in cases involving murdered Allied soldiers, convictions as a matter of principle resulted in death sentences that were executed immediately; such was the case with the Ginny Mission affair, for which General Anton Dostler was sentenced to death.[294]

The Ginny Mission case was crucial to Kesselring's trial strategy, if one assumes that part of that strategy involved a possible ruse. For this reason, the attack of March 23 and the 335 shootings in Rome's Fosse Ardeatine that ensued, on the one hand, and the shooting of the 15 American Ginny Mission soldiers, on the other, were, for the first time, counterpoised: the intention was to assess Kesselring's possible involvement in these events.

Despite being the subject of four major trials, the attack in the Via Rasella and the actions that were subsequently taken—and especially the chain of orders that resulted in the shooting of 335 Italians—have not yet been conclusively reconstructed.[295] Since contemporary sources are few and far between and all relevant war journals are believed lost,[296] we can only reconstruct events by using Wehrmacht files and the British files covering the trials of Kesselring, Mackensen, and Mältzer. An accurate reconstruction also requires correlating such material with the range of relevant autobiographical literature.[297] Considerable problems are posed by the witness statements in this regard. These statements were designed to minimize the the witness's own role, to incriminate the High Command, or to either assist or damage the defendant. During the Kesselring trial, for instance, there was a striking discrepancy between the testimony of General Staff officers Dietrich Beelitz and Siegfried Westphal and the statement by Herbert Kappler, the main witness for the prosecution. This discrepancy could explain why, later in the trial, the British prosecutors assumed that there had been collusion between the witnesses.[298] The different times given for the crucial agreements provoked particular misgivings.[299]

The Communist attack had been carefully planned for March 23, 1944, because the twenty-fifth anniversary of the birth of the Fascist movement—the Fasci—was approaching. It therefore appears that those who perpetrated the attack may have taken the possibility of a harsh reaction by the German occupation forces into account. On that date, shortly after 3:00 P.M. in Rome's Via Rasella, an attack was launched on the German police unit "Bozen," which, as it did every day, was marching through the Via Rasella, traveling from Foro Mussolini across the Piazza del Popolo and Largo del Tritone to its barracks in the Castro Pretorio. When the company passed a street-sweeper's cart, the bomb hidden there was detonated by Rosario Bentivegna, a student and member of the Communist partisan group known as Gruppo d'Azione Pattriotica (Partisan Mobile Squad, GAP) in Rome.[300] In all, 28 policemen died on the spot, 5 more succumbed to their injuries during the next few hours, and a further 68 were wounded, some of them seriously.[301] At least 3 Italian civilians were killed,[302] but it is unclear whether some of the deaths occurred in the shoot-out that followed the explosion.[303] Little is known about the German unit involved, the 11th Company of the Bozen police regiment's 3rd Battalion. This police detachment was assigned a range of duties in Rome, and like all other police regiments, it bore the title "SS Police Regiment" following Himmler's decree of February 1944. However, this fact should certainly not be used to justify the use of descriptions such as "brutal SS hordes or infamous partisan hunters," which can sometimes be found in the relevant literature.[304]

Contemporary witnesses have provided conflicting accounts of the chain of command that came into play following the attack, and it is still not certain precisely how the SD (Sicherheitsdienst, or Security Service) was tasked with carrying out the reprisal shootings that followed in the Fosse Ardeatine. Usual official procedure prescribed an inspection of the scene and notification of the relevant military authorities, including Kesselring's headquarters, followed by a decision on how to respond to the attack.

At first, everything proceeded according to regulations. The German *Stadtkommandant* (meaning "city commandant," referring to the military governor of Rome), Generalleutnant Kurt Mältzer, together with the head of the SiPo (Security Police) and the SD's Rome field office, Obersturmbannführer Herbert Kappler, went to the Via Rasella, where they found a scene of confusion. Wounded soldiers lay among their dead comrades, while others shot aimlessly at the surrounding houses; yet other police soldiers had already arrested several passing pedestrians and put them up against a wall. Mältzer demanded that the whole quarter be razed to the ground.[305] It has been claimed that Kappler then asked to be put in charge of the affair, although witness statements provide the only evidence for this asssertion.[306]

In his capacity as Stadtkommandant, Mältzer had already contacted Army Group C at around 3:45 P.M.: the army group was the supreme military authority for the operational zone, which had included Rome since the landing at Nettuno. In the headquarters of the South-Western Command, at Monte Soratte near Rome, Kesselring's chief of operations, Colonel Dietrich Beelitz, took Mältzer's call, since Kesselring was on leave and the chief of the General Staff, Siegfried Westphal, was on an inspection tour with the Reconnaissance Division 400. Beelitz forbade the demolition of the quarter, and he referred Mältzer to the Fourteenth Army, which had jurisdiction over the Stadtkommandant. Mältzer was thus referred to Eberhard von Mackensen, who immediately recalled Westphal to headquarters. He then reported the attack to General Horst Freiherr Treusch von Buttlar-Brandenfels in the Wehrmacht High Command, which was located in Hitler's Berchtesgaden headquarters on the Obersalzberg at that time.

At around 4:30 P.M., the Wehrmacht High Command came back with Hitler's response. In a rage, he had apparently demanded that the entire neighborhood be razed; at a minimum, thirty or fifty Italians should be killed for each police fatality.[307] Beelitz protested against this extreme demand and was instructed to report back with a counterproposal as soon as possible. In view of the difficult military situation following the landing at Anzio and the Allied advance on Rome, the Wehrmacht High Command clearly wanted to give Kesselring a free hand.[308] Beelitz contacted the Fourteenth Army again and discovered that Mältzer and Mackensen had agreed on the reprisal: ten Italians were to be shot for every German fatality. This German reaction was not surprising, since Mackensen had previously adopted this approach in similar cases.[309] Witness statements confirm that he delegated responsibility for executing the reprisal to the SD. In a telephone conversation between 6:00 P.M. and 7:00 P.M., he agreed with Kappler that only "those [already] sentenced to death" could be included in the reprisal. If an insufficient number of people had been sentenced to death, Kappler spontaneously suggested shooting fewer persons but reporting a higher figure to the top.[310] Klinkhammer's theory thus appears plausible: he has suggested that the decision to carry out the shooting using a one-to-ten ratio was made in the Fourteenth Army headquarters or may even have been made by Mackensen himself.

There is no written evidence in the records for the conclusions that follow on Kesselring's involvement in the decision-making process regarding the shooting. However, the witness statements did play a significant role in subsequent court proceedings. During his trial, Kesselring obviously tried to conceal the fact that he was absent from headquarters when the incident occurred. He got into a muddle several times, making contradictory statements regarding alleged meetings or telephone conversations.

Raiber has painstakingly proven that, at the time, Kesselring was actually on an inspection tour of northern Italy in order to assess coastal defense facilities. I have succeeded in tracking down the flight log kept by Kesselring's pilot, and I can thus confirm Raiber's theory beyond doubt.[311] The version promulgated during the trial, by contrast, was merely based on statements by General Staff officers Beelitz and Westphal, who were assisted by the fact that all relevant war journals from the Army Group C area were considered lost; as a result, no written documentation was available during the trial. According to this version, Kesselring returned "from a trip to the front" at around 7:00 P.M. and was immediately briefed by Westphal and Beelitz.[312] Shortly thereafter, Kappler telephoned Kesselring to confirm that there were enough people sentenced to death to meet the Germans' need. The first order from the Führer's headquarters was received in Monte Soratte at around 8:00 P.M., with instructions from Hitler to shoot ten Italian hostages for every police fatality. Kesselring is said to have substituted the word *Italians* for *hostages*, since no hostages had previously been taken who would thus be available for shooting; the Germans therefore did not have any hostages in the literal sense of the word. Thus amended, the order was transmitted for execution to the Fourteenth Army under Mackensen's command.

Allegedly, however, Hitler then issued a second order assigning responsibility for the execution of the shootings to the SD. In the testimony about this alleged second order, the statements of those involved—especially Westphal—tailed off in nebulous language and became implausible. Thus, Generaloberst Alfred Jodl himself had apparently instructed an "astounded" Westphal that the SD was to be assigned responsibility for conducting the reprisal and had to report on the execution by the following evening.[313] Westphal had then notified Kesselring of this "happy turn of events," and he personally passed the order on to the Fourteenth Army. He consulted with the army group's chief of intelligence, Major Josef Zolling, who agreed with the chief of General Staff that the Wehrmacht was now "absolved of all responsibility."

General Wolf-Rüdiger Hauser, chief of Staff of the Fourteenth Army, had reported the latest Führer order to his superior, Mackensen, who, in turn, claimed—at around midnight—to have called Generalleutnant Mältzer to notify him that he was no longer involved in the issue and that the SD would dispose of the matter. Major Helmut Böhm—Mältzer's chief of operations—then passed the second Führer order verbatim to Kappler, who thus officially received the order to carry out the execution from Hitler himself.

There is some speculation that this second Führer order never existed but was instead part of a retrospective cover story devised by the Wehrmacht authorities. Klinkhammer has emphasized that Hitler often gave his generals free rein in such matters, and moreover, he had lost interest in events in Rome after his initial fury.[314] The responsibility for the shootings therefore probably lay with the Wehrmacht, even if opinions differ on whether the order was personally issued by Mackensen or, as seems more probable, by Westphal. Given his position as chief of the General Staff and thus Kesselring's deputy, it seems quite likely that Westphal would have issued such an order. My thesis is buttressed by a chance discovery in the relevant files. In a telephone conversation that, like all conversations, was minuted (the minutes only having been preserved by accident), Westphal stated that he felt a shooting operation using the one-to-ten ratio was "expedient," since this approach had been adopted "recently in Rome."[315] Westphal explicitly stressed that "the decision rests with the army in such cases."

What is certain, however, is that it was not the army but rather the SD under Herbert Kappler that launched preparations for the shootings. According to his own statements,[316] Kappler had at first released the passersby who had been arrested in the vicinity of the Via Rasella (except for four wanted individuals), but now he lost no time: he started preparing a hostage list during the night of March 23, 1944.[317] By that point, 28 German police soldiers had died, so Kappler asked his superior, Dr. Wilhelm Harster, for permission to include 57 Jews on the list so that the requisite number of 280 could be achieved more quickly. The next morning, Kappler was notified that more policemen had died, and thereupon, he requested the Italian police to provide him with a further 50 people for execution.[318]

In the early afternoon of March 24, Kappler, together with his officers and an SD group, executed the Italians in the Fosse Ardeatine caves. Subsequent exhumations and investigations have confirmed that the hostages were led into the caves in groups of 5, each killed by a shot in the neck.[319] The executions took several hours. In all, 335 Italians, rather than the 330 originally planned, were shot. The 5-person error occurred because the Italian police had provided more people than requested. The mistake was noticed too late, and probably because they would have been eyewitnesses, the "extra" 5 people were also shot. After the execution, Kappler ordered that the caves be blown up to obliterate any traces of the event. The fact that some of the victims were still alive at that point is confirmed by the messages to their families that were found beside the bodies.[320]

Kappler reported the executions to the head of the SD in Italy, Waffen SS General Wilhelm Harster, providing him with the names of the victims and not concealing that "five too many" had been shot. The report to Harster indicated that, by then, an order to execute the shootings had been received through official SS channels, requiring a subsequent report. In addition, Karl Wolff—in his capacity as supreme SS and police commander in Italy and thus the supreme commander of the unit in question—was notified. Like Mackensen, he had traveled to Rome to speak at the memorial service for the murdered soldiers.[321] Mältzer, as senior officer, also received notice of execution from Kappler; this was then passed to the South-Western Command through the usual channels, and the executions were reported to the Führer's headquarters that evening, together with the reports for the day.

When it came to the shootings in the Fosse Ardeatine, German Wehrmacht officers felt a retrospective sense of injustice. After the war, an army judge, Dr. Georg Steigerthal, stated for the record that the shootings had "taken place in an outrageous manner." He himself claims to have drawn Colonel Hauser's attention to the fact that "this gave an operation which was compliant with international law the appearance of mass murder."[322] In the wake of persistent rumors in the foreign media regarding war crimes in Italy, the case was referred for clarification to the Wehrmacht Investigation Office. The aim was to find a culprit who could be brought before the German courts. Then came an inquiry[323] from the Wehrmacht leadership (Wehrmacht Führungsstab, WFst) to the head of the SD and SS Reichsführer Himmler regarding events in the Fosse Ardeatine.[324] Himmler replied that he did not feel an investigation would be "expedient." He justified his response by stating that, because the incident had been dealt with extensively by "enemy propaganda," the best course was to let the dust settle, "since our side raising the matter again would trigger a new wave of propaganda."[325] This decision spelled an end to the investigations.

Kesselring's credibility—and that of the officers testifying on his behalf—was shattered by another incident. The Wehrmacht was also involved in a war crime in northern Italy, which took place almost simultaneously with the Rome attack and subsequent massacre. On March 24, 1944, one day after the Rome shootings, the American commando unit code-named the Ginny Mission landed on the Ligurian coast in the La Spezia area. The unit, comprising fifteen American soldiers of Italian descent, was caught while preparing sabotage operations. The men were summarily shot on March 26. Since the Americans wore regular uniforms and had surrendered without a fight, these shootings constituted a war crime. According to the rules of the Geneva Convention, the men should have been sent to a POW camp. The general commanding the LXXV Army Corps of the Liguria Army Group, Anton Dostler, ordered the execution shortly after showing Kesselring the coastal defense facilities. One may therefore conjecture that Kesselring was either involved in the decision or that his approval was sought. In terms of martial law, the basis for these executions was a secret order issued by Hitler (the so-called Command Order) that was unknown even to some senior command authorities, as became apparent from subsequent witness statements.[326] On October 18, 1942, Hitler issued Decree No. 46. According to this order, members of enemy sabotage units were to be "ruthlessly mown down in battle," and under no circumstances were they to be sent to POW camps.[327]

Since any documentation regarding the shootings was deliberately removed from all relevant war diaries as early as the summer of 1944, arousing suspicions of collusion among all participants,[328] the details of the chain of command involved in the execution of fifteen men remain unclear. Prince Alexander of Dohna-Schlobitten, Dostler's chief intelligence officer, was the only one of those involved to have described these events in his memoirs. According to his recollections, he received a report that the members of the commando unit had been taken prisoner on March 24, 1944, and were initially ordered to be sent to a POW camp.[329] However, Dostler's chief of staff, Colonel Wilhelm Krähe, referred him verbally to the existing secret order issued by Hitler, which required that the men be shot. Plans to send them to a POW camp were then aborted. Since Dohna refused to shoot the Americans,[330] they remained with the troops until General Dostler returned and decided the matter. Two days after the American sabotage troops were taken prisoner, he ordered that they be shot. He thus committed what could be termed a double war crime because—as the American investigators found—he breached both the Geneva Convention and Hitler's Command Order, which, after all, required "immediate transfer to the SS."[331]

It remains debatable whether and to what extent Kesselring was actually aware of the commandos having landed and the order to shoot them; we also do not know whether he became aware of these events only after the shooting. It seems unlikely that Dostler would not have discussed the urgent issue of what to do with the American sabotage troops with the visiting field marshal. But Kesselring may have deliberately decided not to get involved, and perhaps he told Dostler that it was "up to him" to deal with the Americans.

One report has survived that placed Kesselring at the scene of the crime at La Spezia, but only after the Ginny Mission men had been shot. A German POW held by the Americans recalled that Kesselring had passed the freshly dug grave of the fifteen Americans together with the commander-in-chief of the army, Infantry General Gustav-Adolf von Zangen, and inquired about the incident.[332]

Nevertheless, in a witness statement issued by Kesselring in 1945, he denied any knowledge of the Ginny Mission shootings.[333] He claimed to be unaware of the Command Order, which in any event had not been applied in Italy.[334] Other sources, however, clearly show that headquarters was aware of events. Westphal contradicted his commander-in-chief by stating that the Command Order was "only applied once" in Italy.[335] He gave direct witness testimony on the Ginny Mission case,[336] in which he said that the army group had learned of the planned executions "at the last minute" and that the teleprinter message he had signed prohibiting the executions had been received a few minutes too late by Dostler. He also repeated this version in his memoirs.[337] Lieutenant Hans-Georg Schultz, chief of operations of the 135th Fortification Brigade commanded by Colonel Kurt Almers, confirmed Westphal's intervention. He had personally seen a telegram from Field Marshal Kesselring's headquarters ordering that the executions not be carried out under any circumstances. However, at that point, the men were already dead.[338]

The role played by Dostler, who knew that he would face the death penalty if convicted, remains unclear. Yet he never mentioned Kesselring when questioned during his own trial. Since contemporary sources repeatedly referred to the strained relationship between Kesselring and Dostler,[339] it seems unlikely that Dostler would have covered for Kesselring simply because of esprit de corps. It is possible, though, that Dostler was prepared to sacrifice himself as the "sole culprit" in order to preserve the positive reputation of the Wehrmacht in Italy and avoid damaging the aura surrounding Kesselring. The destruction of the relevant documentation in the war journals certainly indicates that a decision was made relatively early on to suppress the matter and, therefore, that Dostler may also have been instructed to assume full responsibility.

Raiber's theory positing collusion between the officers to protect Kesselring cannot be satisfactorily substantiated. Nor is it possible to rule out collusion among witnesses aimed at concealing another war crime. However, Raiber's thesis does help explain many contradictions in Kesselring's statements, and it also explains why he appeared unable to recollect the precise sequence of events surrounding the Via Rasella attack during the Rome trial or when cross-examined during his own trial. Given that Kesselring never mentioned the clearly exculpatory fact that he was not in Rome on the day of the attack, one must ask what could have motivated him to nevertheless assume responsibility. There are some indications that he may have taken the blame for the massacre because of loyalty to his chief of General Staff, Siegfried Westphal, perhaps in order to assist the younger man in starting afresh after the war. This hypothesis could help explain Westphal's striking commitment to Kesselring's clemency campaign: Westphal may, in return, have promised to do all in his power to secure Kesselring's release following the latter's conviction. If so, he kept his side of the bargain.

Kesselring as a POW, 1945–1947

Kesselring spent some time in a number of American POW camps, including Mondorf, Oberursel, Königstein, and Allendorf, before being transferred to British custody in 1946. Looking back, he described that period as the bleakest of his life.[340] It is possible that this period of internment fundamentally altered Kesselring's self-image and worldview. One must therefore ask why his views changed or remained the same. Although tentative guilt reflexes can, for example, still be discerned in letters he wrote to his wife, Liny, during May 1945, he abandoned these as early as the summer of 1945 in the face of his treatment by the Allies, which he had not anticipated and which he felt he had not deserved. Instead, he now adopted the widespread view that the generals were being collectively defamed.

The threat of prosecution against both the General Staff and the Wehrmacht High Command led to the development of justification strategies at the expense of a genuine examination of the officers' consciences. As Georg Meyer has pointed out, "The military, whose primary representatives formed part of the state order since 1933, not only—like almost all state and social institutions—subjected itself to the rule of injustice and inhumanity, but also helped facilitate this system, welcoming it and supporting it until the end through unquestioning, dutiful obedience."[341] The suffering experienced in the Allied camps prevented individuals from critically reviewing their own roles in the Third Reich; it also hindered reflection on the culpability of the individual and the officer corps as a whole and, indeed, even obstructed a more general reflection on the reasons for individual and collective failure.

Kesselring's diary allows us to draw precise conclusions regarding his view of the capitulation formalities and his subsequent odyssey through several camps, ending at Nuremberg. Through the Kesselring case, we can better understand the rallying cry of defamation, which played a particularly significant role during the 1950s rearmament debate. Initially, Kesselring still hoped to get off lightly. However, on May 9, 1945—as he noted with a certain pride in his diary—an American major advised him of the "visit" by General Maxwell Taylor of the 101st Airborne Division. Kesselring was taken to the Berchtesgadener Hof hotel in Berchtesgaden. He was allowed to retain his sidearms, decorations, and field marshal's baton. There, he drank tea with General Taylor—an incident recorded in photographs, giving rise to an immediate storm of public criticism in the United States focusing on the cozy atmosphere of this "meeting between gentlemen." The Americans treated Kesselring with distant courtesy. He was allowed to travel unaccompanied to the headquarters of those army groups still fighting in Zeltweg and Graz to finalize arrangements for the capitulation—or, as Kesselring put it, to "supply them with my orders."[342] The fact that he was frequently sought out for interviews with Allied (mainly American) reporters is likely to have boosted his self-image and personal vanity. Thus, the "myth of Kesselring the gentleman" was born just a few hours after his defeat.

On May 15, 1945, after a detour to Augsburg, where he had to surrender his decorations and field marshal's baton,[343] he was taken to the "Ashcan" interrogation center in the Palace-Hotel Mondorf in Luxembourg.[344] A large part of the Third Reich's military and political leadership was gathered there. Kesselring was initially deeply shattered by his experiences in Mondorf, not least because of the marked contrast to his previous life. His social downfall was striking. He recorded in his diary: "At the airport I could see from the security measures how a field marshal had now been transformed into a 'big criminal of war.' There were nearly too many men and weapons deployed both against me and for my protection! Had I not always had my stalwart driver by my side, I would almost have been afraid!"[345]

Once the public became aware of the concentration camp atrocities, security was heavily stepped up, and Kesselring's comfort was severely restricted. Regulations dictated that doors be left open. Glass was removed from the windows and replaced with wire grilling. All furniture was removed and replaced by camp beds, with two blankets apiece. Mirrors were removed, and each room was furnished with just one chair.[346] The camp routine set in during the first few weeks: "Many gentlemen gave lectures which we all found demanding; English lessons were also held," Kesselring noted. Although the generals were allowed to move freely around the grounds, especially in the Grand Hotel's garden, they felt they were under observation and being stared at wherever they went: "We were frequently inspected as though in a zoo. Vile; the first interrogations and forensic discussions began."[347]

Kesselring's next station was the Oberursel camp, where he spent some days in the barracks appraisal center. Even as an experienced officer, Kesselring had a sense of "unease, ranging to fear and terror" when confronted by the Counter-intelligence Corps (CIC) officials interrogating him. In October 1945, as a witness due to testify on Göring's behalf, he was finally transferred to the prison in Nuremberg. Beginning on December 23, 1945, Kesselring spent five months in solitary confinement in the "criminal wing." As part of his "special treatment," he was deprived first of a chair and then of a table.[348] This deprivation was clearly related to the fact that Kesselring testified on Göring's behalf with regard to the bombing raids on the Polish fleet at Warsaw.

In Nuremberg, the generals were able to correspond with their families for the first time. There is no indication in any of the surviving documents that Kesselring used his internment to systematically examine his conscience. Indeed, there are some tenuous indications that he continued to view himself as a loyal servant of Hitler:

> There are certainly some people who felt more or less constrained to serve the Third Reich. But it was not the mass of people! There were also soldiers who repudiated the party from 1934, 1936, hated Hitler, "that fellow," but still went along with everything, allowed themselves to be promoted and pocketed medals. One really needs to find a strong term to sum all this up calmly: Hogwash! When were we actually true to our convictions? Then or now? Can a man with any self-respect deny such a past?[349]

Despite their differences, the generals closed ranks against other senior Nazi figures early on in their imprisonment, hoping to avoid being sentenced to death at Nuremberg. But despite the generals' apparent determination to stick together, strenuous efforts were required behind the scenes to establish a united front vis-à-vis the Allies. In his diary, Kesselring lamented the crumbling esprit de corps:

> I gazed into the abyss during the long months. I felt an inner compulsion to resist; I jumped every hurdle to promote the idea of unity. If the whole world is against us, it is our damned duty to form an indestructible unit. These minor human differences—which, after all, merely express a certain vanity—must be suppressed, just as in every battle aimed at a successful outcome only one will can prevail, and only one road can be traveled—the road to "Victory"![350]

It became apparent that a truthful witness statement could damage other defendants, and therefore—often as a result of pressure exerted by comrades—loyalty and solidarity with the others became the yardstick against which all things were measured.[351] Deliberate lies were told in Nuremberg, and the prison community developed quite effective sanctions to bring witnesses to reason. This fact was illustrated by a chance discovery. After previously stating that the Wehrmacht on the eastern front had been complicit in shooting Jews, General Röttiger revoked his statement in court following long conversations with Manstein and a cross-examination by the attorney Dr. Hans Laternser—a cross-examination that proved uncomfortable for Röttiger.[352]

After their experiences in Nuremberg, the generals were painfully aware that they could not expect any preferential treatment in the pending trials. The self-esteem of these former elites suffered not only as a result of the constant supervision and mocking remarks by the guards but also as a result of the cramped conditions they lived in, with six men squeezed into one cell. This effect was apparent in the deep sense of trauma recorded by Kesselring in his diary when he was contemplating suicide: "Immense inner strength is needed to see beyond all this as though it did not affect one, and thus to get over this bit of life—this bit of life which has lost its value and which—during all those months of prison life—it would have been a release to give up."[353]

From April 3 to April 17, 1946, in the so-called pilots' trial regarding the murder of surrendered pilots, Kesselring testified as a Luftwaffe commander on the orders about how to treat enemy personnel. For this purpose, he was taken to the former concentration camp, where, together with five other generals, he spent ten days in darkness confined in the so-called bunker.[354] Following his stay in Dachau, Kesselring was granted the privilege of a convalescent break in the Nuremberg-Langwasser hospital. His planned testimony in the so-called Malmédy trial was canceled, probably due to his poor health. (The trial was held at Dachau in 1946 and involved Waffen-SS personnel who had killed surrendered U.S. soldiers near Malmédy, Belgium, during the Battle of the Bulge.) He wrote to his wife: "You will have heard on the radio that we are now accommodated in accordance with international regulations. It was high time; our health would not have borne it for much longer."[355] While in the hospital, he heard rumors that he himself would also shortly be tried for incidents relating to the antipartisan war during his tenure as commander-in-chief in Italy.[356]

Were war crimes committed in Italy under Kesselring's command? The answer is yes, even if it is difficult to understand the court's judgment in this matter. In Venice, Kesselring was found to have issued the commands that led to the execution of 335 Italians in the Fosse Ardeatine caves, but in practical terms, he was acquitted when it came to antipartisan warfare. Yet the exact opposite was actually the case.

Albert Kesselring probably did know of the shooting of the American Ginny Mission commando unit but did not issue the order to execute the 335 Italians in Rome. The likely reasons underpinning his decision to more or less switch responsibility for the events, thus obscuring the true circumstances, exemplify the retrospective construction of war memory by the former Wehrmacht generals, who wanted to preserve the Wehrmacht's "clean reputation" in Italy. They also illustrate the esprit de corps among Kesselring's officers in the Italian theater, none of whom betrayed him.

There is no doubt that Kesselring played a major role in radicalizing antipartisan warfare in Italy, even if he was not directly involved in the individual operations. This assessment also holds true when one remembers that the continuous retreat and the escalating number of partisan attacks undermined the troops' discipline and morale. Under pressure from this external threat, Kesselring failed to gain control of developments and to rein in the violent excesses committed against the rural Italian population. Rather, he legitimized these excesses through his orders, and thus, he bore responsibility for them as commander-in-chief in Italy. It was therefore reasonable for Albert Kesselring to be charged with war crimes against Italian civilians following the war.

Chapter 2

Allied Politics of Memory: The War Crimes Trials

As tensions between the Allies mounted in the immediate postwar years, the Allied approach to the war crimes issue itself was transformed. With national interests increasingly accorded priority over what had originally been jointly decided, that approach became more and more focused on the politics of memory. The rigid penal policy evident during the first three postwar years was followed by a phase of indecision that finally culminated in abandoning the entire program of trials.

The configuration among the Western Allies was, from the very beginning, disparate and thus problematic. Following their experience with the Nuremberg International Military Tribunal trials of those deemed to be the major war criminals, and faced with the pressure of Italian demands for control over prosecutions, the British adopted a significantly more easygoing attitude to their own war crimes trials. As a consequence, the date of conviction would play a key role in individual outcomes.

To assess the divergent instructions governing war crimes policy issued by the War Office and the Foreign Office—and the practical implementation of those instructions—it is vital to clarify the original intentions behind, and content of, the Allied agreements that were binding on British military courts. The British change of tack was due to legal arraignment problems, as well as objections to the penal policy raised by military circles and, in particular, by Allied Mediterranean Headquarters in Caserta. These objections reached their zenith in politically motivated demands for clemency to be shown to potential future allies.

With regard to the Italian war crimes trials of German officers, it is apparent that the accused were treated differently depending on when they were convicted. The 1946 Rome trial of Generals Eberhard von Mackensen and Kurt Mältzer was seen as a dry run for the planned trial of the major culprits, and it was conducted in full compliance with the original guidelines governing Allied courts. As early as 1947, however, when Kesselring was put on trial, numerous local British functionaries hindered the court by pursuing a policy of obstruction vis-à-vis the instructions issued by London and by openly displaying sympathy with the accused. This support—which was wholly unexpected—benefited the defense team led by Kesselring's counsel, Dr. Hans Laternser. (An examination of Laternser's defense strategy will also be discussed below.) While Kesselring was undoubtedly guilty, Mackensen and Mältzer had merely obeyed the field marshal's orders. However, despite the principle—codified in military law—that officers obeying superior orders should be safe from prosecution, Kesselring's subordinates ultimately paid a higher price for their actions than did their commanding officer.

In the following section, I will first analyze the Allied planning process, measuring the plans that evolved against the conduct of the first war crimes trial in Italy. The Rome trial can be used to demonstrate how the British believed a trial of German war criminals should ideally have been carried out. The Kesselring trial illustrates the different forces at play behind the scenes that influenced this most important of all British trials. One can also see how, in the final analysis, this trial was a legal failure due to the immediate commutation of the sentence.

Preliminary Allied Considerations

Early on, during their advance through Italy in the summer of 1944, the Allies knew of the attacks launched by German occupation forces on the civilian population of northern Italy in so-called partisan operations. As the front advanced, the killings increased, and the Allies broadcast their intention to prosecute German officers as war criminals, citing the names of villages and units involved. Nonetheless, only a few German officers were tried by British military courts in Italy. The reason for this had to do with domestic political conflicts in the UK in the context of the nascent Cold War—conflicts that resulted in the British adopting a new line in terms of *Vergangenheitspolitik*, the politics of memory.

On October 20, 1944, the British commander-in-chief, Field Marshal Harold Alexander, issued a warning to German troops in Italy. Speaking on the radio, he summarized the guidelines governing the Allied approach to German war crimes. He stated that the way in which German troops were treating the Italian population amounted to a war crime,[1] and he assured all involved that they would be held accountable for their actions following the war. Alexander stated: "The fact that, for example, patriots wearing uniforms, armbands or other insignia could attack German soldiers does not—in terms of international law or any other legal or moral code—justify collective retribution against the population of the village in question, nor does it justify killing people who have not been legally tried and sentenced."[2] Referring to the Moscow Declaration issued by Allied foreign ministers in 1943, relating to the prosecution of war criminals, Alexander announced that his headquarters was already gathering material about the massacres and collecting the names of German officers accused of war crimes.

Since 1940, governments in exile based in London had been providing the British with relatively precise reports concerning German abuses in the countries of occupied Europe.[3] Although the United Nations War Crimes Commission (UNWCC) was established as early as October 1942 by the United States, the UK, China, and the governments in exile,[4] this body only started gathering evidence concerning war crimes and perpetrators one year later.[5] In addition, there were deep divisions among the Allies regarding the manner in which war crimes should be prosecuted and about who should be brought to trial.[6] They had three options: a general amnesty effected by waiving charges, trials in German courts based on German military or criminal law, or trials in Allied courts, the legitimation of which had yet to be defined.[7] It was agreed to conduct trials in Allied courts. Most politicians in the West argued "for a quick and uncomplicated enforcement of sentences based on a resolution adopted by the United Nations."[8] Joseph Stalin, however, appeared to prefer summary sentences and/or mass executions of German officers rather than long, drawn-out court proceedings,[9] and even Winston Churchill and Franklin Roosevelt were initially inclined to this view.[10]

Today, we know that the prospect of punishment neither prevented nor restrained the perpetration of war crimes. On the contrary, from the summer of 1944, an unprecedented wave of violence was launched not only in occupied Europe but also in the concentration camps. It is not inconceivable that the possibility of one day facing criminal charges actually exacerbated the brutality of the perpetrators.[11]

The UNWCC was politically weak, and its resolutions were nonbinding, since they had not been ratified by the Soviet Union.[12] Collection of evidence was uncoordinated—reports of war crimes were not even filed in a card index—which later made it difficult to ensure that charges conformed to systematic criteria. In the final analysis, this lack of organization benefited the accused.[13] In 1942, British intelligence agencies had started gathering material relating to war crimes, compiling a list with over 100,000 names of Germans (primarily concentration camp personnel) involved in such crimes.[14] However, this work did not help the UNWCC because (like its American counterpart) the British secret service was not permitted to disclose such material.[15] But especially after the liberation of Majdanek concentration camp in the autumn of 1944, major media campaigns ensured that preparations for subsequent war crimes trials were put on a rather more serious footing. Similar media campaigns also resulted in the establishment of Allied investigation commissions, such as the British Special Investigative Branch (SIB).[16]

The "Moscow Statement on Atrocities" issued on October 30, 1943, was the first attempt to establish a mandatory framework that would be binding on all three Allies. In the statement, the foreign ministers of Great Britain, the Soviet Union, and the United States reaffirmed their intention to pursue the perpetrators "to the uttermost ends of the earth" in order "that justice may be done."[17] They agreed that war criminals would be sent back to the countries in which the crimes were committed, so that they could be tried according to the laws of the country in question. The major culprits, who could not be assigned to a specific geographic area, would be tried by an Allied court. Churchill hoped to have thus delegated the trials to the countries in question, avoiding Allied involvement.[18] The Allies—and in particular the Americans—felt that the trials were necessary for political reasons. However, these initial attitudes started to waver as a result of the domestic political constraints within the individual Allied states.

The Nuremberg trial of major war criminals (the IMT trial) started on November 20, 1945. There were 20 defendants, selected from a list of 130 named individuals who had "at some point between February 1938 and the end of the war in 1945 served in the Wehrmacht High Command, the Army, Navy or Luftwaffe High Commands, or as commanders-in-chief of troops within the Wehrmacht divisions."[19] The IMT trial ended on October 1, 1946, and resulted in twelve death sentences, seven custodial sentences, and three acquittals. It was of immense historical and legal significance for all sides. The approach taken was unique, punishing the entire leadership elite of a state for its policies and the orders issued.[20] The constitution of the Nuremberg Tribunal reinforced the principle of individual responsibility for state crimes.[21] The trial proceeded according to plan. It was primarily a trial conducted by so-called pencil pushers, and, as intended by the Allies, it provided a historical lesson regarding the climate in which such crimes could occur.[22] The fact that acting under orders was explicitly considered to be a mitigating factor in the London Charter issued on August 8, 1945, was significant for subsequent trials. The charter stated: "The fact that the Defendant acted pursuant to order of his Government or of a superior shall not free him from responsibility, but may be considered in mitigation of punishment if the Tribunal considers that justice so requires."[23] This principle was seized on by defense counsel for the defendants and reinterpreted as an alleged "requirement to obey orders."[24]

Hans Laternser, who subsequently acted as Kesselring's attorney, represented the Wehrmacht General Staff in Nuremberg and played a major role in getting one particular charge dropped for lack of evidence: namely, the allegation that the senior Wehrmacht leadership constituted a criminal organization. But there could be no question of an acquittal. The Nuremberg judgment represented a devastating critique of Hitler's Wehrmacht, and it was clear that further trials could be anticipated.[25] The judges described the German generals as a "disgrace to the honorable profession of arms" and held that the officers were "responsible in large measure for the miseries and suffering that have fallen on millions of men, women and children." Furthermore, their unwillingness to assume command responsibility was bitterly criticized: "When it suits their defense they say they had to obey; when confronted with Hitler's brutal crimes, which are shown to have been within their general knowledge, they say they disobeyed. The truth is they actively participated in all these crimes, or sat silent and acquiescent, witnessing the commission of crimes on a scale larger and more shocking than the world has ever had the misfortune to know." The chief U.S. prosecutor, Robert H. Jackson, made it clear that he would have preferred broadening the IMT indictment to include the generals in question; failing this, however, he announced that there would be further trials "where the facts warrant it, . . . so that those among them who are guilty of these crimes should not escape punishment."[26]

The larger part of the war crimes program took place away from the cameras in the Nuremberg court, which focused on the trial of major war criminals.[27] The Americans demanded that the criminal nature of the National Socialist regime be underlined by trying those senior military figures responsible for events.[28] The aim was to educate the German public regarding the atrocities committed during the war.[29] In particular, the Americans hoped to combat the development of myths surrounding once-celebrated military figures and to destroy the aura surrounding such individuals.[30]

The whole war crimes issue was already moving from the legal to the political level, since the Americans bracketed punishment of war criminals together with the aims of their reeducation policy. They were particularly concerned that the trials be carried out legally and properly. Only by presenting solid evidence would it be possible to counter the view (which was gaining public currency) that Hitler's senior army commanders had merely been soldiers mechanically executing orders. Rather, it was vital to move the focus to the personal role played by the individual generals in the war crimes that were the subject of the trials.[31]

The British War Crimes Trials

Following the promulgation of the Allied Control Council Law No. 10, issued on December 20, 1945, the four military governors appointed by the occupying powers were authorized to establish military courts to try war crimes.[32] Each of the four powers then assumed responsibility for conducting trials of German civilians and military figures. In all, the Allies planned to charge up to 60,000 war criminals.[33] In the four Western zones, charges were brought in 4,864 cases,[34] and around 37,000 individuals were convicted by Soviet courts.[35]

Even in purely formal terms, the Allied military court proceedings would differ from the major Nuremberg trials, for they would not be presided over by representatives of all the Allies. Rather, the trials were to be held in the military courts of one Allied power, sitting in another country affected by the war crime in question and trying members of the armed forces of a third country—in this case, Germany. The military tribunals attempted to ascertain the share of guilt borne by individual German officers. But who was culpable and to what extent? How culpable was a commander-in-chief in respect to acts committed ahead of or behind the front? These moral and ethical issues were raised not only by defense counsel but also by the Allied prosecutors, illustrating the fundamental problem inherent in the trials: were criminal prosecutions even possible for such crimes?

The British shared these reservations, which is why they signed up late (and reluctantly) to the program of trials involving the German military leadership, a program championed primarily by the Americans. The British government—led first by Winston Churchill and then, from August 1945, by Clement Attlee—would have preferred a tacit amnesty implemented by a simple failure to bring charges against the culprits. However, it was clear that such arguments would not prevail within the alliance in the face of demands being made by the countries involved—not to mention the domestic pressure being exerted on U.S. president Harry Truman.[36] The British were not infrequently suspected of being too "pro-German."[37]

However, the British felt that there were plausible arguments militating against the use of legal means to address war crimes. In 1945, the view of Churchill's foreign minister, Anthony Eden, was that long, drawn-out legal proceedings would significantly delay the peace process in Europe.[38] The British feared complications, since there were no clear-cut legal rules governing the punishment of senior decision makers for the actions of military units. Consequently, the British viewed with some trepidation the prospect of prolonged trials with uncertain outcomes—trials that might tie up Allied resources for an extended period while generating in the German public an undesirable sense of solidarity with the defendants.[39] Eden's successor, Ernest Bevin, also shared this skepticism because he personally believed the trials were inimical to British interests. Yet in the face of public outrage in England following revelations of German war crimes together with calls for the guilty to be punished, he was prepared to continue the planned program of trials.[40]

British policy was based on the following considerations. Any juridical approach had to focus on the correct legal attribution of individual responsibility for war crimes. By investigating issues of personal responsibility, such legal proceedings would seek to establish the place of the individual in the chain of command. Thus, in Kesselring's particular case, in order to legally define his responsibility for events as a whole in Italy, the British had to prove in court that he had been personally responsible for facilitating the illegal behavior of his subordinates. At issue was a legal assignment of guilt, rather than a historical or political assessment of the conduct of the war. Summarizing the situation with regard to the German army commanders, the trial report published subsequently noted that "the prosecution maintained that these orders on the one hand and the atrocities alleged to have been committed by the German troops in Italy on the other were cause and effect and that the accused must therefore be held responsible for the actions of the troops under his command."[41]

According to this view, all senior commanders bore criminal responsibility for the disciplinary defects that were the primary cause of many atrocities. What was at issue was a fundamental decision of a precedent nature: a model trial, rather than a question of "the guilt or otherwise of those who actually carried out the atrocities."[42] The Royal Warrant issued on June 14, 1945, established military courts and laid down the rules of procedure.[43] But it proved more difficult than anticipated to legitimize the jurisdiction of Allied courts,[44] for the legal basis for trying military commanders and commanders-in-chief was also the subject of dispute. Which military penal code should apply—the German one in force at the time the crimes were committed, that of the country where the crimes took place, or the British one? The UNWCC initially envisaged basing proceedings on the German military penal code—especially §47—because most of the crimes in question could be classified as murder, manslaughter, battery, or robbery.[45] However, application of this paragraph presupposed the existence of evidence showing that a soldier had *premeditatedly* participated in the execution of illegal acts of war. As had already been shown by the Allied war crimes trials following World War I, it was impossible to prove such premeditation.[46] For this reason, the Allies resorted to their own military penal codes.

Both in the United States and in the UK, there were significant doubts regarding whether—on the basis of the American or British military penal codes—national military courts would be in a position to ascertain the responsibility of individual links in the chain of command, a responsibility that was difficult to define in legal terms.[47] One problem was that both the British and American military penal codes provided for exemption from prosecution if the recipient of an order breached the laws of war because of having received an illegal official order from a military superior.[48] International law was patchy in this regard, leaving room for interpretation. Therefore, the British *Manual of Military Law*—in particular §443, regarding actions committed pursuant to orders from a superior—was amended in April 1944 in anticipation of the planned trials of German and Japanese war criminals.[49] The amendments to both the British and the American military penal codes—which were not publicly disclosed—indicate that the two governments were concerned to ensure that senior German commanders were legally convicted.[50] In 1951, against the backdrop of the Korean War, the British and American military penal codes were restored to their original wording in order to provide optimal cover for British or American soldiers in any future conflict.

There were three consecutive trial phases. The first phase began in 1945 and lasted until 1946, the second lasted from November 1946 to the end of 1948, and the third started in 1949 and ended with the German General Treaty of 1952. During the first phase—between 1945 and 1946—the Allied military courts quickly reached relatively harsh verdicts. Most of these trials involved the shooting of captured Allied soldiers or were directed against concentration camp guard units.[51] During this first phase, most of the defendants—including General Dostler, to whom reference was made earlier—did not have the benefit of a German attorney representing them. Death sentences were generally carried out immediately.

The end of 1946—after the Nuremberg trial—saw the beginning of the second phase of Allied jurisprudence. The trial of the "South-East Generals" and the Wehrmacht High Command trial held in 1947 and 1948 in Nuremberg represented attempts by the Americans to hold selected senior Wehrmacht commanders to account for war crimes by bringing collective charges.[52] The British, by contrast, chose to demonstrate the responsibility of senior commanders for war crimes by holding individual trials of high-ranking officers. Those tried in this fashion included Generalleutnants Eberhard von Mackensen and Kurt Mältzer (1946), Waffen SS Generalleutnant Max

Simon (1947), Generalleutnant Eduard Crasemann (1947), Field Marshal Albert Kesselring (1947), and Field Marshal Erich von Manstein (1949). The custodial sentences imposed were served in Werl, a British military prison in Westphalia. By 1949, British military tribunals had sentenced a total of 230 Germans to death. In addition, 447 defendants received custodial sentences, and a further 260 were acquitted.[53] But none of the death sentences imposed between the end of 1946 and 1948 were actually carried out.[54] The Allied authorities charged with confirming the verdicts increasingly refused to do so, tending instead to display solidarity with the defendants. The prevailing view was that, although one could prove a senior commander had failed in his supervisory duties, one could not prove incitement to murder.[55]

In this context, political considerations regarding the postwar order in Europe surfaced for the first time. It seems that from around the middle of 1946, the fear of communism was greater than the fear of a resurgent German militarism.[56] Planning for the trials was closely intertwined with occupation policy concepts.[57] From the spring of 1947, the Joint Chiefs of Staff 1779 guideline for organizing the occupation and installing a military government assumed the character of a political imperative according to which a stable Germany was made a priority of Anglo-American policy in order to counter the growing threat from the East. In the final analysis, this development meant that the focus was on ending the program of trials being held by the Western Allies.[58] Judges thus found themselves working on a process that was already doomed: their task was to hold trials, yet their orders were to end them.

The third phase began in 1949 and was primarily characterized by appeals: no death sentences were imposed during this period. This third and final phase was exemplified by the last British war crimes trial, that of Field Marshal Erich von Manstein. The Manstein trial—which was highly controversial from the start—was finally held in a British military court in Hamburg: a chivalrous sense of solidarity with an admired former enemy led to a reluctance to deport Manstein to the Soviet Union. The reasons given for the judgment on Manstein illustrate the shift in British politics of memory. Thus, the court actually accepted the defense arguments, justifying the imposition of a relatively lenient eighteen-year prison term by stating (somewhat circuitously) that Manstein had neglected his supervisory duties.[59] The 1949 Manstein trial was the concluding act in the British program of war crimes trials. Following the execution of the last "real war criminal"—a term used by Konrad Adenauer in 1951 to describe Otto Ohlendorf, the heavily incriminated leader of the SD Einsatzgruppen (special SS troops operating in the hinterland of the eastern front)—the Americans also officially ended their involvement in the war crimes issue. They were the last to do so.[60]

British Military Courts in Italy

Following an order issued on February 7, 1944, by the commander-in-chief of Allied forces in the Mediterranean, General Sir John Harding, British military courts were established in those areas of Italy under Allied military control. The formal precondition for obtaining convictions of German officers had thus been met.[61] The first lists of war criminals compiled by the War Crimes Group were circulated as early as June 1945,[62] and in October 1945, the basis for the subsequent indictment was finalized[63]: this was a compilation of German command structures and specific antipartisan operations, together with precise victim numbers.

The existence of three contradictory views within the London government meant that British war crimes policy in Italy veered from one position to another. The British war crimes trials were held in accordance with the political instructions issued by the War Office in London; these, in turn, were based on proposals issued by the judge advocate general (JAG), the British military prosecutor. However, the trials were repeatedly compromised by conflicting views disseminated by officials in the Foreign Office, who attributed a foreign policy dimension to the trials in Italy—and who would have liked to make concessions to Rome. As already indicated, Foreign Secretary Bevin, in particular, felt that trying German generals in the context of the nascent Cold War was a step in the wrong direction.[64] However, even Bevin took pains to maintain appearances, ostensibly stipulating a hard-line approach. It was also thought that the conviction of Kesselring or Karl Wolff might alleviate the difficult domestic political situation in British-occupied Italy.[65]

On principle, the British had undertaken to conduct a trial on the massacre in the Fosse Ardeatine, only charging the highest-ranking German officers who, because of the orders they had issued, bore responsibility for German policy in Italy and for the oppression of the Italian civilian population: "It is proposed to hand over the remaining cases of War Crimes against Italians covered in the Report to the Italian Government who would become responsible for completing the investigations and for trial of those responsible."[66] The British believed that the Italians would require "the fullest possible assistance" from general headquarters (GHQ), for that would be "the only satisfactory way of bringing a number of those cases to trial within a reasonable time." Furthermore, "such a course would do much to reinforce Italian public opinion that these minor German War Criminals would not be allowed to escape unpunished." However, investigators from the War Office primarily associated the British willingness to carry out these trials with a hope that the legality of the proceedings could be controlled—and that, under certain circumstances, erstwhile adversaries could be spared. Thus, the list of German war criminals "from Kesselring to Wolff" whom the British refused, under any circumstances, to surrender to the Italians could be viewed as something of an internal "list of merit."[67]

At the beginning of 1946, the JAG laid down the guidelines governing British policy.[68] Since the officers due to be charged with the massacre in the Fosse Ardeatine would also be tried for reprisals against Italian civilians, the JAG felt that it was expedient to try all defendants together in a single trial addressing all counts of the indictment. However, such a trial would only involve officers up to the rank of major general.[69] It had originally been planned to hold the trials in London; Wolff was already in a British POW camp, and Kesselring had been transported for interrogation to the "District Cage" in London, the prison for high-ranking German officers.[70] However, because it was hoped that the trials would be exemplary proceedings, it was decided to hold them in Nuremberg.[71] And due to occupation policy considerations, the British decided to hold those trials relating to Italy in Italy—a decision enthusiastically welcomed by the Italian media.[72] Once this decision had been made, one of the interpreters' cabins used in Nuremberg was moved to Italy.[73]

By February 1945, a commission had been formed in Italy to investigate German war crimes; this commission worked closely with British and American investigators.[74] The results of the Allied investigations were the subject of a rather acerbic remark by an Italian Foreign Ministry official liaising with Allied headquarters who had no illusions about Allied intentions.[75] As early as July 1945, Italy contacted the chairperson of the UNWCC, Lord Cecil Wright, through its London ambassador, requesting that the British accept a list of the war criminals being sought by Italy.[76] On September 13, 1945, this list was submitted to the UN by the provisional Italian government.[77] It was then sent on to Allied headquarters in Europe, in an attempt to lend further weight to the Italians' demands that they be permitted to try German officers themselves.[78] The Italians were also aware that the British approach to the war crimes trials was dominated by national interests—a point emphasized by Foreign Minister Count Vittorio Zoppi: "For the Allies, the significance of the trials is more political than military."[79]

In a memorandum from the Allied Control Commission dated April 9, 1946, Italy's Supreme Military Tribunal was once again requested to compile counts for an indictment in the Fosse Ardeatine case and to seek extradition of the three accused individuals: Albert Kesselring, Herbert Kappler, and Eugen Dollmann.[80] The requisite applications were then filed.[81] An internal report indicated the Italian Foreign Ministry was confident that the British would surrender their jurisdiction with regard to German war criminals, since it made little sense for the Italians to be restricted to trying insignificant cases while the Allies tried the major cases. After all, the war crimes involved had been committed against Italian citizens.[82] On principle, the War Office agreed that the Italians should try all war crimes committed against Italians in their own country, but high-ranking German officers[83]—specifically, Field Marshal Kesselring—were explicitly excluded from this provision.[84] Thus, the conviction of the commander-in-chief was a legal *prerequisite* if perpetrators of war crimes were to be found guilty by Italian courts.

It quickly became clear to British investigators that the number of individual war crimes was too great for a single trial, and they therefore decided to conduct two British trials in Italy: one relating to the massacre in the Fosse Ardeatine and another focusing on incitement to wage war against the civilian population. The first was to be held in Rome, trying Kesselring, Mackensen (and possibly his chief of staff, Hauser), and Mältzer (and possibly his chief of staff, Böhm), together with Police Chief Harster, Wolff in his capacity as supreme SS and police commander, and Herbert Kappler as the "executing body."[85] It was intended that a second trial would try all German commanders-in-chief and commanding generals. The British thus planned to charge Kesselring; the army commanders-in-chief Generaloberst Lemelsen (Fourteenth Army) and Generaloberst von Vietinghoff-Scheel (Tenth Army); the supreme SS and police commander in Italy and Waffen SS general, Karl Wolff; General Schlemm as the commanding general of the I Paratrooper Corps; General Herr as the commanding general of the LXXVI Panzer Corps; Generalleutnant Paul Conradt as commander of the Hermann Göring Division; Generalleutnant Richard Heidrich as commander of the 1st Paratrooper Division; and Waffen SS Generalleutnant and SS Gruppenführer Max Simon, commander of "Das Reich," the 16th Panzer Grenadier Division. There was still some dispute regarding the manner in which members of the General Staff were to be dealt with.[86] British legal opinion held that they could not be considered responsible for atrocities, since they prepared orders but did not actively execute them.[87] This position also corresponded with the American view.[88]

The British investigators made it quite clear that the trials of the commanders-in-chief were being planned as a matter of duty, rather than in pursuit of British interests. Thus, the Allied War Crimes Commission found that it was "not British policy to bring the actual perpetrators of the atrocities to trial, except in cases where the victims were Allied soldiers."[89] The military solidarity with former foes was remarkable. It was only on the basis of "careful consideration" that the British would agree to put General Staff officers on trial—and in that event, the trial would be "before a British military court."[90]

Although the Allies cooperated fairly well, they did not conceal their mistrust of the Italian authorities—a mistrust of which the Italians were painfully aware.[91] The British were prepared to provide the Italians with the incriminating evidence at a later date. However, Germans would only be extradited if "there was clarity regarding the agreement that the death penalty could not be imposed on them, and that they could only be released with the written consent of Allied Headquarters."[92] British and American officers were openly dubious of the efficiency of the Italian authorities, and some even questioned the (already agreed-upon) handover of records to the Italians to enable them to prepare for the lesser trials of the actual culprits: Colonel Robert Bradshaw, for example, noted the "danger of handing over any but the smallest fry to the Italians."[93] Ways and means were clearly found to thwart the Italian investigations; otherwise, it is hard to explain the gross negligence with which seized files were handled and the sloppy manner in which they were passed on to the Italian authorities.[94] American investigation files that should have been given to the Italian authorities in the spring of 1946 apparently never reached Rome.[95] Recent research has shown that there were also powerful interests in Italy working to prevent any prosecutions,[96] and work is ongoing to discover the whereabouts of these investigation files between 1946 and 1994.[97] Obviously, inquiries either were not made at the time or were foiled, since these files only resurfaced in 1994.[98] Since 1996, there have been several trials in Italy; among the best known are the trials of Erich Priebke in 1996, Karl Hass in 1997, and Friedrich Engel in 2002 as well as the trial focusing on the massacre in Sant'Anna di Stazzema in La Spezia, which lasted from 2004 to 2006. In Germany, the Stuttgart and Dortmund public prosecutors are still conducting preliminary investigations into massacres in Tuscany. However, apart from the 2000 Engel trial in Hamburg, no court proceedings have yet been initiated.

Three factions within the British camp—the JAG Office, the War Office, and the Foreign Office—struggled for supremacy in the war crimes issue. Although the JAG clearly stipulated that the actual perpetrators should be surrendered for trial to the Italian authorities, his superiors in the War Office had reservations and wanted the culprits to be tried by the British. One of the demands was phrased this way: "Formation commanders who construed his [Kesselring's] orders as a license to murder the innocent could in no circumstances evade responsibility."[99] They were to be tried by British military courts "for their offences against the Italian population." The real reason for this British offer was rooted in a mistrust of the Italian government, which, according to the War Office, could not be trusted to prosecute the accused efficiently and in accordance with the rule of law: "That Government has not the machinery nor the energy to carry through trials of such complication and there may be reason to fear that where the question of responsibility was one of real difficulty the accused might not receive a fair trial at the hands of the Italians."[100]

The Foreign Office pursued quite a different strategy—a strategy determined by foreign policy considerations, resulting in a far more sympathetic attitude toward the Italians. Whitehall officials had absolutely no objection to handing all cases over to the Italians. Indeed, they encouraged the Italians to plan their own Fosse Ardeatine trial: after all, this war crime was an "Italian matter." A Foreign Office memo suggested that "the Italians would expect to handle this case and should be given the opportunity of doing so."[101] Whitehall also suggested handing the second planned British trial over to the Italians; that proceeding was intended to try those responsible for the "campaign of reprisals."[102] Indeed, Whitehall even felt that Rome's request for one of the judges to be Italian was worthy of consideration. The Italians had pointed out that the Fosse Ardeatine massacre was a special case with national symbolic significance. Therefore, the inclusion of an Italian judge in the tribunal would help diffuse political tensions "in view of the quite particular nature of the crimes in question and of the impression it would leave on the Italians and especially the Rome population."[103] Participation in the trials was not merely symbolic for the Italians: it was also a matter of prestige because it would signal Italy's place among the victors to the world,[104] indicating that fascism had merely been "a footnote in Italian history."[105] The treatment of those responsible for the crimes committed in the Fosse Ardeatine would reflect the Italian government's ability to assert itself, and it was thus of great domestic political importance.[106]

The Foreign Office initially seemed to agree and proposed wording that stated cases should, for political reasons, "be handed over to the Italian Government for trial in Italian courts" unless the "Commander-in-Chief [of Mediterranean forces] felt that there were special reasons for making such a course undesirable."[107] However, given the initial attitude of mistrust, it seems doubtful that this was a genuine attempt at accommodation. After all, the War Office was in complete agreement with the judge advocate general in refusing to countenance the participation of Italian judges. Colonel Halse finally came up with the wording that saved the day. He pointed out that, in accordance with section 5, paragraph 3 of the 1945 Royal Warrant legitimizing the war crimes trials, the Italians were not entitled to have a judge participate in the proceedings. This option was only open to the Allies, and "Italy can never, of course, be called an Ally"—that was Halse's verdict.[108]

In purely legalistic terms, this finding cannot be disputed. After the Italians declared war on the German Reich on October 13, 1943, Italy was accorded the status of a "co-belligerent," but it was explicitly designated a "non-Ally"; thus, in a formal sense, it did not enjoy military parity with the Allied powers.[109] Now this distinction assumed a new significance with regard to the courts trying war crimes. However, Halse's statement—intended for internal consumption—said a good deal more than other Allied authorities would have dared say directly to the Italians: Halse indicated that Italy was not considered a full ally, even though the Resistenza liberation movement had paved the way for Allied troops. The Allies felt that, after Mussolini's twenty-two-year rule, Italy was itself too deeply immersed in criminality for Italians to be allowed to judge their former German allies. One should also not underestimate the deep contempt felt, especially in military quarters, for Italy's decision to "change sides" in the autumn of 1943. The Italian protests therefore fell on deaf ears.[110]

Some elements in Italy also harbored reservations about launching a criminal prosecution. Foreign Minister Count Vittorio Zoppi considered whether the Italian state, together with survivors, should file a civil suit against the accused Germans in order to obtain a place for Italy on the judges' bench.[111] But this move would have left Italian defendants open to such civil suits abroad—not a pleasant prospect in view of the various pending extradition requests lodged by Yugoslavia. Because many Italians were being sought as war criminals by Yugoslavia and the Soviet Union (some were the subject of extradition proceedings, and others were already in custody in the countries in question), the provisional Italian government—which was not yet the government of a sovereign state—refrained from making formal requests for German officers to be tried.[112] The Italians' official line was that they would not extradite their own citizens. They also wanted to retain the right to try their citizens themselves.[113] As a result, the German war criminals found themselves in an unexpectedly favorable situation.

The British ambassador to Rome, Ward, attempted in vain to strengthen the position of the Foreign Office and to convince headquarters in Caserta that Mackensen and Mältzer should be handed over to the Italians for trial.[114] But the military view prevailed, and Ward was informed that the trial would be handled by the British to avoid any "lynching or other undesirable incidents" during the proceedings.[115] Ward complained to his superiors, pointing out that a "particularly revolting crime by Germans against Italian citizens" was involved, and he went on to state, "I do not see the logic of trial being a purely Allied affair still less a purely British one."[116] Ward asked that the Italians be somehow accommodated.[117] The Foreign Office therefore proposed a compromise to Allied HQ in Caserta: the Italians could send nonvoting observers to the trial. The matter was thus resolved by sending Colonel Salvatore D'Agate and his interpreter, Captain Alessandro Fioretti, to act as official Italians observers monitoring the British trials of German officers who had served in the Italian theater.[118]

Although internal cooperation in London proved difficult, the smooth collaboration between American and British authorities attracted praise at an official level. Officers in American custody were (as pointed out by the judge advocate general) dispatched without ceremony to England for interrogation.[119] Yet it should be noted that—by emphasizing a certain matter-of-factness—this remark generated some doubts about whether the collaboration was actually as smooth as stated. In reality, the Americans deliberately obstructed British investigators. Thus, for example, while in U.S. custody, Albert Kesselring enjoyed the special protection of American military authorities—not least because his involvement in the Historical Division was important to those same authorities. In fact, Colonel Potter, the head of the Historical Division, was repeatedly successful in delaying Kesselring's extradition to the UK by citing "ongoing historical studies."[120] Although the British asked Potter to cease thwarting their requests and to surrender Kesselring immediately to stand trial as planned,[121] they were only successful in January 1947—after several approaches had been made.

The Americans also protected Kesselring by failing to disclose their information on the evidence of war crimes in Italy. In the case of Italy, it could be said that Allied collaboration was heavily circumscribed and that investigation results were viewed as national property. Knowledge, after all, is power—and in this instance, it was deliberately withheld. Many cases therefore remained unresolved as far as the British were concerned, despite the fact that they had been the subject of prolonged and extensive American investigations. As a result, trials were launched with incomplete evidence. This situation was particularly striking in the Kesselring case, especially with regard to the issue of antipartisan warfare. Charges were not brought in respect to any of the incidents that had taken place within the subsequent American operational (and interrogation) territory. Such incidents included the Marzabotto[122] and Sant'Anna di Stazzema cases.[123] Some of the details remain uninvestigated today, and in many instances, it is no longer possible to bring a prosecution because those responsible have since died.[124] Whether this withholding of information occurred for security reasons or because the Americans hoped to bring a spectacular case to court themselves must remain a matter for speculation.[125]

To meet the preconditions for bringing charges in accordance with the accepted precepts of criminal law, British jurisprudence required the existence of a prima facie case. Accordingly, evidence must have been gathered and verified in advance in order to justify bringing the charges. The rule of thumb was that as much evidence as possible must have been gathered and that involvement in at least two incidents could be proven.[126] The investigators in Italy warned their political masters in the War Office that precipitate action could trigger a fiasco: "It is strongly represented that this case should not be brought to trial unless we are certain of securing a majority of convictions, as otherwise the effort will not be worthwhile."[127]

Within eighteen months, British investigators working for the War Crimes Group/South-East Europe, together with the interrogation officers from the judge advocate general's office, had pieced together a picture of the war in Italy by questioning German officers in British custody.[128] The British investigators complained that, in many cases, the "highly coloured and exaggerated" descriptions provided by Italian sources would not withstand examination, and they noted that it had proven necessary to dispatch many of those working for the 78th Special Investigation Department to the areas in question to find out if "atrocities on the lines reported had in fact taken place."[129] The investigators believed that a military reaction to a group of partisans, regardless of the uniforms they wore, did not constitute a war crime, since such partisans had sought a fight:[130] rather, war crimes consisted of disproportionate "punishment operations" aimed at civilians. It was precisely the illegality of reprisals that defined this particular war crime and formed the pivotal point of the indictment.

Prosecutors accused the German units in question of deliberately using terror against noncombatants in order to hit the partisans where they were vulnerable—possibly in a very personal manner by killing their relatives. For this reason, interrogators attempted to discover whether atrocities were connected with previous partisan activities, as well as the extent to which the German military leaders intended to set an example. The planning of such reprisals (specific date, place, and time) had to be concretely proven.[131] There was also an evenhanded reference to British support for the partisan war: the German war against the Italian people was seen as a result of the partisan war, and it was noted that "it is beyond dispute that the Partisans in Italy were, from early 1944, acting in conjunction with Allied Forces."[132]

The interrogations addressed three principal questions: (1) were the Bandenbefehle, or antipartisan orders, issued on Kesselring's own initiative or were they issued per instructions from the Führer's headquarters? (2) was there an explanation for the frequent involvement of specific divisions in the crimes? and (3) who issued the order to carry out the reprisal in the Fosse Ardeatine?[133] With regard to the first question, all witnesses agreed that Kesselring had worded these orders particularly harshly following instructions from the Wehrmacht High Command. Similarly, all witnesses concurred—sometimes providing extensive details—that it was the partisans' horrific methods of combating the Wehrmacht that had provoked such a reaction in the first place.

It should be noted that when reference is made to German war crimes in Italy, Kesselring's name is generally linked with that of Karl Wolff, the supreme SS and police commander in Italy, because the Wehrmacht and SS shared a complicated competency when it came to antipartisan warfare. However, as will be described briefly in the pages ahead, Wolff enjoyed a degree of protection—especially from the American intelligence establishment—that was not available to Kesselring.

The American military prosecutors did seem to be determined to bring Karl Wolff to trial in Nuremberg. To that end, the prosecutor Edward G. Rigney, who was preparing to try SS personnel in Nuremberg, provided investigators from the British War Crimes Group with incriminating material relating to Wolff and even met with investigators to discuss the case.[134] However, in August 1946, the chief British prosecutor, Telford Taylor, invited the head of the British judge advocate general's office in Naples, Major Field-Fisher, to Nuremberg in order to discuss fundamental issues relating to the prosecution of German war criminals.[135] It seems, though, that the primary purpose of this meeting may have been to protect Wolff, whose name was subsequently effectively deleted from the British lists. Until then, Wolff had always been mentioned in the same breath as the planned trial of Field Marshal Kesselring.[136] There are strong indications that powerful American forces—especially in the ranks of the Office of Strategic Services (OSS)—were protecting Wolff, even though no concrete evidence to this effect has been found in the records.

It is noteworthy that even though Wehrmacht commanders repeatedly referred to SS responsibility for the massacres under interrogation,[137] the SS leadership was largely spared prosecution. Preparations were made to try Karl Wolff and Himmler's personal representative in Italy, SS Standartenführer Dollmann,[138] but these trials never took place. Notwithstanding this, the judge advocate general was aware—and was able to show with the aid of several documents—that Supreme SS and Police Commander Karl Wolff bore responsibility for several war crimes.[139]

As already indicated, it would appear that the SS officers were being shielded from prosecution by Allied authorities—especially by the American secret service.[140] The SS officers, in particular, seemed to have been given more favorable conditions by disclosing insider knowledge,[141] although this was repeatedly denied by the military authorities.[142] Statements made by several of those involved indicate that the protection afforded to Wolff, Harster, and Kappler could have been due to secret agreements made with Wolff during the surrender negotiations.[143] Thus, in 1946, SS Sturmbannführer Heinrich Andergassen, who was sentenced to death by a British military court, stated for the record that Wolff had reached an agreement with Allen Dulles according to which, in return for Wolff's efforts to achieve a partial surrender on the southern front, the Allied courts would not try any war crimes committed by the SS.[144] Putting SS men on trial was described as a "matter of policy" on which "HQ is not competent to pronounce."[145] This policy still needs to be more fully researched.[146]

It is not clear when the British abandoned their original intention to hold two major war crimes trials in Italy in favor of individual trials.[147] The deciding factors may, however, have related to organizational and formal problems, since preparatory investigations for the trials were at quite different stages. Trial preparations proved extremely difficult. Investigators had to search for suitable evidence and question witnesses, and beyond that, the investigations were hampered by a personnel shortage, postal and transport difficulties, and acute time pressures.[148] Nonetheless, by January 1946, the British investigations had progressed to the point where the parties could consider setting trial dates in respect to the highest-ranking German generals. When Kesselring's trial started on February 10, 1947, the plan was that it would last no longer than two weeks and would be following by the start of Wolff's trial.[149]

But London had decided otherwise. Between September and December 1947, the British authorities clearly changed their approach to the Karl Wolff case, abandoning their plan to try him for war crimes committed by SS troops in Italy. However, an absence of sources means that this change in tack cannot be fully documented. Halse summarized the situation in a secret memorandum written in January 1947. According to this memorandum, it seemed highly probable that Wolff would never come to trial, unless the Italians filed another request seeking his extradition.[150] Regardless of the agreements relating to Belgian and Czech extradition requests, Halse recommended surrendering Wolff to the Americans until a final decision had been reached.[151] What this meant was clear: Wolff was safe from the British program of trials in Italy and would also probably not be extradited.

Some Allied authorities themselves paid the price for the degree to which decisions relevant to the politics of memory were kept secret. While the decision was being made in London to end the trials, individual JAG investigation groups in the Mediterranean region were kept in the dark. The final attempts by the War Crimes Commission to obtain evidence against Wolff by questioning subordinates such as SS Gruppenführer Harro With[152] did not bear fruit.[153]

The Allied War Crimes Groups in Italy thus, until the end, continued to pursue a comparatively idealistic approach: they were determined to ensure that all war criminals received their just punishment, and they tirelessly collected evidence, even when—in political terms—it was clear that the end of the trials was already in sight. By September 1947, investigators had finally gathered sufficient evidence against Harster and Wolff in connection with the death of political prisoners at Fossoli concentration camp near Modena,[154] which had been under Wolff's personal control.[155] Between November 1943 and the end of 1944, Fossoli had served as a transit point for at least 3,198 Jews and political prisoners on their way to Auschwitz.[156] However, London halted the preparations for the Fossoli trial because it was not possible to be "completely sure" of a conviction.[157] The judge advocate general nonetheless encouraged the Dutch authorities to resubmit their request for Harster's extradition. London's strategy was clear: SS men were not to be tried in British courts if there was even a scintilla of doubt regarding the likelihood of obtaining a conviction. In Holland, Harster was accused of participating in the murder of Dutch Jews. A trial on this charge appeared to have a far greater prospect of success than a trial involving the crimes committed in Fossoli.

In conclusion, it is evident that—despite official assurances from the Foreign Office that war criminals were being relentlessly pursued—a more pragmatic approach to the war crimes issue was being adopted in London, especially by the War Office. This view was transmitted to the judge advocate general (who was subordinate to the War Office) in the form of what could be termed a "feasibility directive." Due to political considerations, the work of the War Crimes Commission's investigation groups was halted, and personnel were gradually withdrawn.

In the final analysis, the pragmatic approach—which dictated that the Wehrmacht trials (considered "simpler") should be prepared first—prevented SS members from being tried for war crimes. The shortage of personnel in the British War Crimes Groups significantly delayed preparations for the trials of SS Generals Harster and Wolff. Consequently, preparations were not sufficiently advanced by a specific date to guarantee a conviction—which, in turn, meant that the planned trials no longer met the political preconditions for charges to be brought.

Italy was also vacillating. In domestic political terms, the Italian public's desire for Germans to be punished had an immense legitimating significance. The foreign policy maneuvers undertaken to spare Italian POWs in the Balkans had to, conversely, also apply to German war criminals imprisoned in Italy. In respect to the trials of German war criminals, Italy's lack of national sovereignty and the need to meet the expectations of its own citizens, when juxtaposed with its interest in obtaining convictions, resulted in a compromise that benefited the German defendants while completely failing to obtain justice for the victims of war crimes.

Due to a political shift in the context of the Cold War, the British war crimes program thus ended in disappointment both for the British investigators and for the Italians.[158] The Italians felt that their desire for war crimes to be expiated was not taken seriously—never mind advocated—either at the state level or at a provincial or regional level, and this, in turn, was bound to foster anti-British resentment in Italy.

Dress Rehearsal for the Kesselring Trial: The 1946 Trial of Mackensen and Mältzer in Rome

The crimes at Fosse Ardeatine had quickly become a national Italian symbol for German brutality. A trial was thus anticipated with some eagerness in Italy.[159] Indeed, from the beginning, the proceedings were associated with high expectations.[160] Once it had been decided to hold two separate trials, the British saw the Rome trial as a dry run for the main event—the trial of Field Marshal Kesselring. Preparations for the Rome trial were therefore meticulous. At the request of the Italians, who wanted to satisfy public interest, the trial took place in Rome and not, as originally intended, in Naples, near Allied headquarters in Caserta.[161] The conflict between British and Italian expectations was thus already apparent: London expected an exemplary verdict, whereas Rome hoped for punishment. It was clear that there was no de facto possibility of the accused being acquitted.

The trial of Generaloberst Eberhard von Mackensen, commander-in-chief of the Fourteenth Army, and Generalleutnant Kurt Mältzer, military commander of Rome, started on October 18, 1946. The case was heard by a British military court sitting at Rome's La Sapienza University.[162] The presiding judge was Major Ian Playfair, and the prosecutors were Colonel Richard Halse and Judge Advocate General C. L. Stirling. As in the subsequent Kesselring trial, Colonel James Notestein was dispatched by the Americans to observe proceedings in Rome.[163]

The British trial strategy in Rome was divided into four stages, starting with a reconstruction of events and culminating in a careful determination of guilt. First, it had to be proven that 335 Italian civilians had been shot in Rome on March 23, 1944. Second, it had to be proven that this incident did not involve the execution of legally imposed death sentences but rather was a reprisal carried out by the German authorities. Third, the judge advocate general had to prove that the shootings constituted a breach of the laws of war. And fourth, he had to prove that, as commanders-in-chief, the accused could be held liable for the massacre.

The defendants did not dispute having passed on the order to kill the civilians, which they had received from Kesselring's headquarters. For its part, the court accepted that a ratio of ten to one was reasonable and emphasized the illegality of the partisan attack in the Via Rasella. The main bones of contention in the Rome trial were whether the reprisal was conducted in accordance with the laws of war and who bore responsibility for it—in particular, for selecting the victims.[164] Both Mackensen and Mältzer stated that they had left this matter to Kappler's sole discretion. Mackensen testified that he had agreed with Kappler that only people who had already been sentenced to death would be selected for execution and that, if necessary, a higher figure than the number actually shot would be reported to headquarters. Kappler confirmed this agreement.[165] However, the prosecution, represented by Halse, criticized the fact that neither Mackensen nor Mältzer had paid attention to Kappler's selection of persons for execution and therefore had to that extent accepted the possibility of innocent people being killed. Thus, there was no doubt that the five people executed over and above the prescribed number of hostages were victims of Mackensen's and Mältzer's "insufficient supervision."[166]

The defense tried to plead extenuating circumstances—or even obtain an acquittal—by arguing that the accused had done everything possible to mitigate the executions. The aim of this defense strategy was to shift all blame onto Kappler, who had compiled the so-called death list and carried out the executions. The goal was to prove that the executions were solely a matter for the SD, over which—as was well known—the Wehrmacht had no influence. Kappler himself vehemently denied the existence of a Führer order mandating the SD to carry out the shootings.[167] Scholar Robert Herde has concluded that the "Wehrmacht's military authority in respect of the SD" had been "fully maintained" when it came to matters of "hostage shootings" and that one therefore had to assume "Wehrmacht culpability" in regard to the execution order being issued.[168] The defense itself, at another point in the trial, had accepted the supreme authority of the Wehrmacht.[169]

The court found Eberhard von Mackensen and Kurt Mältzer guilty of causing the death of 335 Italians, and it sentenced them to death by firing squad.

As was the convention in British military court proceedings, there was no written statement of the grounds for this judgment. Therefore, it is impossible to determine conclusively whether the men were convicted because they had carried out a reprisal, because of the high number of those killed, or because of the brutal nature of the executions.[170] The judge advocate general upheld the conviction and recommended confirming the death sentences.[171]Italian reactions to the verdict were carefully analyzed by the British.[172] The Roman public, which had been "primed to expect a national event" by the media and politicians,[173] celebrated the convictions. According to the American magazine *Time*, the widows present in the gallery of the court called "*Grazie*" down into the hall.[174] In his official trial report sent to Prime Minister Attlee, Ambassador Ward described the Rome trial as "dignified" and "fair" to the accused. There was no "disorder" except for a few "angry cries and hisses against the accused" by the relatives of the victims.[175] The "death sentences in the trial" had "satisfied the Italian public platform and the press has ceased asking why Dollmann was not present."[176]

The mood among German officers, in contrast, was one of dismay. Even Kesselring's optimism had dissipated following the conviction of his two subordinates. He recorded in his diary: "The verdict against Mackensen and Mältzer can only be viewed as a political verdict."[177] Kesselring was also upset by the "lynch atmosphere" in the courtroom. The court had not succeeded in preventing Mackensen and Mältzer from being subjected to heckling and other incidents in the courtroom, and the Italian policemen posted in the hall had failed to intervene. Presiding Judge Ian Playfair, writing to the British commander-in-chief of Mediterranean forces, General Sir John Harding, demanded some improvements to ensure the safety of the accused and to prevent any interruptions to court proceedings. Otherwise, he felt that no further trials should be held in the venue.[178]

Shortly after the verdict was announced, several officers—including Kesselring—petitioned the War Office on behalf of Mackensen and Mältzer.[179] Kesselring also wrote to King George VI and to his two military counterparts, Field Marshals Harold Alexander and Bernard Montgomery, as well as to General John Harding, since the verdict had not yet been confirmed.[180] Pope Pius XII ordered a review of the options for intervention,[181] but he was assured that an intervention with the commander-in-chief in the Mediterranean on behalf of the two men would not have the "slightest effect."[182] The main point of criticism was that Eberhard von Mackensen had not been allowed to retain civilian counsel. He and Mältzer had to accept the former army judge Hans Keller—who, as a POW, was also prohibited from practicing his profession—as their court-appointed defense counsel, despite the fact that Mackensen had chosen a different attorney.[183] The British took the criticism on board and allowed Kesselring to select a competent attorney in the form of Hans Laternser. The Rome trial thus marked the end of the first trial phase in British Vergangenheitspolitik.

However, the hope that the conviction of German officers would eliminate tensions between the British military government and Italian authorities was not fulfilled. On December 5, 1946, the Rome liaison officer deployed by GHQ in Caserta noted that the local mood remained very tense and that the press was constantly inquiring about Mackensen's and Mältzer's whereabouts. He felt that it would be unwise to shoot the two men in Rome or to announce the result of the review while they remained in the city. The liaison officer concluded by suggesting that the condemned men be accommodated elsewhere.[184]

Accordingly, Mackensen and Mältzer were first taken to the German "Generals' Camp" at Rimini-Bellaria, and from there, they were transferred to Wolfsberg POW camp in Austria.[185]

Officials in the Foreign Office felt vindicated in their policy of withdrawing from war crimes trials in Italy. One official noted that now that the two "big fish" had been sentenced, the Italians could be left to deal with the small fry, provided they conducted proceedings in a "proper manner."[186] The official word from the Foreign Office officials was that they would "allow the Italians to try the remainder," as long as the Italians prevented any "lynching or other undesirable incidents."[187] On Christmas Eve 1946, the British embassy notified the Foreign Office that the British mission to prosecute war crimes in Italy could be terminated: "On political grounds, we certainly do not want any more British trials in respect of the Ardeatine murders. Anything to do with this atrocity rouses dangerous effervescence at Rome and if the two generals had not been sentenced to death, there would have been a real risk of anti-British demonstrations and even of riots."[188]

The Foreign Office thus adopted the line espoused by the new Anglo-American policy, which (in July 1947) was to seek an end to the Allied trial program pursuant to Directive JCS 1779—even though official confirmation of this new policy only followed some time later.[189]

The dilemma facing British trial policy was again revealed when it came to executing the sentences passed on Mackensen and Mältzer. In this regard, three different British groupings jostled for position. The military authorities under General Harding—who vehemently opposed the death penalty because of military-political considerations such as the possibility of later alliances with the erstwhile enemy—sought to assert their position. The London War Crimes Group endorsed (and prepared) the proposed executions, viewing them as the logical implementation of a judicial decision. And the political instructions issued by the Judge Advocate Department in London changed almost daily. While Judge Advocate General C. L. Stirling argued that the executions should be carried out so as not to damage the credibility of British courts, others were already seeking a political exit route. Thus, a memo from the JAG office to Harding, dated January 7, 1947, already suggested that the death sentence could be commuted to a term of imprisonment, given the fact that Hitler had proposed the reprisal and that Mackensen's army had found itself in a militarily critical position.[190] Harding ordered that Stirling be contacted to discover whether the Kesselring trial would have an impact on the planned executions of Mackensen and Mältzer.[191] He was concerned to ensure that the executions—if they did take place—were not delayed until sentence was pronounced on Kesselring.

A commutation of the sentence did not seem impossible. On April 7, an interim report was received from headquarters stating that, in the case of Mackensen, there were "real doubts" about his guilt.[192] The London War Crimes Group, in a last-ditch attempt to preserve the credibility of the British war crimes trials, proposed that "at least Mältzer" should be executed.[193] However, Colonel Brian Robertson, commander of the British Rhine Army and military governor–designate of the British zone, agreed with the presiding judge in the ongoing Kesselring trial, Major General Ian Hakewell-Smith, that due consideration was required at that point and that there could be a risk of a negative press reaction if Mältzer was executed with unwarranted haste.[194] On April 19, Robertson decided that the execution should be postponed indefinitely.[195] In the end, on July 4, 1947, the sentences imposed on Mackensen and Mältzer were commuted by General Harding to life imprisonment, as was the sentence imposed on Kesselring.[196] Harding's military advisers in Allied headquarters had once again prevailed over the judge advocate general in London and the War Crimes Group.

The 1947 Kesselring Trial

The trial of Albert Kesselring was an exemplary war crimes trial. As already shown, this success as a legal proceeding was due to the manner in which the trial was prepared and conducted by the British, since it formed the nucleus of the British trial program and served as the benchmark for all others. Its significance for British policy is comparable to that of the Nuremberg subsequent trials for American war crimes policy. Consequently, the Italian press certainly did not exaggerate when describing the Kesselring trial as "our own little Nuremberg."[197] The trial was also seen as symbolic of the hoped-for new and improved relations between Britain and Italy. The Italian Peace Treaty was signed in Paris on the day the trial began.

The defense also viewed the proceedings as an exemplary trial. The defense team hoped to present the court with a picture of fair and decent warfare in Italy—a picture that the media would disseminate throughout the world. Of course, the aim was also to destroy the credibility of prosecution witnesses. And at times, this strategy was so successful that an acquittal seemed in the cards.[198] The trial offered both the accused and his witnesses a platform from which to tell a story of soldierly solidarity in the wake of defeat. Like Kesselring[199] and many of his witnesses,[200] his attorneys also viewed the pending trial as an investment in the future—they considered themselves duty-bound to "line up" for this "final battle in Italy" to save the "honor" of Kesselring and of the "decent German soldiers in the Italian theatre" and to vindicate the "truth."[201] Such formulations were common in the trial preparations.[202]

In terms of future appeal proceedings, the Kesselring trial demonstrated the importance of presenting to the court a particular picture of the accused and his actions. What was at stake in Venice in 1947 was nothing less than a public rehabilitation of the reputation of German military leadership as a whole and the justification of Kesselring's military actions in particular. The appointment of a distinguished defense team showed that the German side understood the symbolic nature of the Kesselring trial and used it to draw a positive picture of the war in Italy—a picture that, in turn, could be used to construct an official war memory. Significantly, the defendant himself,[203] as well as his legal counsel,[204] repeatedly used the metaphor of the "final Italian battle" in private correspondence—a battle that had to be won in order to ensure that the Wehrmacht could at least look back on one last moral victory in the wake of the lost war.

Kesselring's Defense Team

Kesselring's defense attorney was crucial to the success of the "innocence campaign" waged during Kesselring's trial. Dr. Hans Laternser, a Wiesbaden attorney born on August 3, 1908, in the Alsace town of Diedenhofen, was one of the best-known defense lawyers in the Nuremberg trials. He defended the General Staff during the trial of major war criminals in 1945 and 1946, and he was one of the leading spokespeople for the defense in the subsequent trials.[205] After the British trial of Albert Kesselring, Laternser acted as defense counsel for Generalfeldmarschall Erich von Manstein during the latter's trial in Hamburg. He was considered an outstandingly successful attorney, specializing particularly in Anglo-Saxon trial law.[206] The issue of antipartisan warfare as the primary charge ran like a common thread through all the trials in which Laternser participated. Only the venues—Italy, the Crimea, the Balkans—changed.

Laternser's career had advanced steadily, if unspectacularly, under Hitler. He had been a member of the National Socialist German Workers Party (Nationalsozialistische Deutsche Arbeiterpartei, NSDAP)[207] and the National Socialist Lawyers' Association since 1933.[208] He took his first state legal examinations in 1930 at the Higher Regional Court in Kassel and obtained his doctorate in 1931 at Marburg University. In 1933, he took a position as a legal trainee at Cologne Higher Regional Court, and in 1934, he sat for his second state legal examinations in Berlin.[209] Since 1934, Laternser had worked as an attorney in Wiesbaden, and he was admitted to plead before the District and Regional Courts. Kesselring's defense attorney could also look back on a military career, albeit a modest one.[210] In 1943, Laternser served at the front when he was transferred to the Luftwaffe Fighter Regiment 29, posted in southern Russia.[211] He moved to Schlangenbad in 1957 and died on July 21, 1969, in Frankfurt.[212]

Laternser's line of argument was similar in all the trials. He was familiar with Anglo-Saxon trial law from the IMT proceedings, and he was particularly skilled in cross-examination, which he used to good effect when seeking to discredit hostile witness statements. The Nuremberg verdict, as he said himself, gave "great satisfaction" to Laternser and the General Staff officers he had defended.[213] Kesselring greatly respected and trusted his attorney.[214] During the IMT proceedings during 1945 and 1946, Kesselring had been involved in the working group led by Laternser, which prepared a defense brief on the duties of the Wehrmacht High Command.[215] Apparently, he had asked Laternser in Nuremberg to start gathering material in his favor.[216]

Laternser looked favorably on the Wehrmacht generals because of his own conservative ethos; beyond that, he felt a kind of group affiliation with the Wehrmacht and its honor code, since he himself had served in the Luftwaffe.[217] His overall approach to his clients was that of a deferential former subordinate, and he never neglected to use full military titles when addressing both clients and witnesses. As far as Laternser was concerned, Kesselring remained the "Esteemed Field Marshal." In each case he was involved in, Laternser seems to have viewed (and accepted) the indictment as a personal challenge. He considered himself particularly duty-bound to defend the senior ranks.[218] He was certainly not driven by financial considerations: Laternser's commitment to the generals did not make him a rich man. Rather, he seems to have been motivated by having the opportunity to influence the historical view of the Wehrmacht's war, even going so far as to disseminate a picture of a better soldiers' Germany not involved in war crimes. He was also interested in enhancing his own prestige as a capable lawyer, and there is no doubt that these trials represented a particular challenge for him.

When the first announcement of his impending trial was broadcast on August 12, 1946, Kesselring—ever loyal to the old hierarchical structures—made contact with Laternser through his former chief of General Staff, Siegfried Westphal.[219] Laternser did not hesitate to accept the brief, despite the fact that—like all internees—Kesselring had had his assets frozen by the Allies. Under the circumstances, Laternser could scarcely hope to receive prompt payment for his services. Hans von Hoermann, who had served with Kesselring in the Royal Bavarian Army and emigrated to Brazil in 1936, offered to guarantee Laternser's fees. Eventually, plans were made to finance the Kesselring trial through donations from Brazil that were to be routed through the Vatican,[220] but the plans collapsed due to an indiscretion.[221] As a result, the defense team in Venice had no funds at its disposal.[222] Laternser later contacted Kesselring offering to "draw a line under my work to date" and waive the fee—a generous offer—but in the same letter, he also wrote that his newly established Wiesbaden practice was developing very slowly.[223] Ultimately, after the trial, the attorneys received significant donations from abroad, in particular South America, so it seems that their costs were covered.[224] Outstanding fees were finally paid by Kesselring's relatives in Franconia.[225]

The appointment of a defense attorney proved problematic at the start. It is not clear whether this was because of faulty communication by the Allied staffs or because of deliberate obstruction of the defense interests. What is certain is that the British first appointed the army judges in Italy—Generalrichter Hans Keller and Oberstrichter Dr. Wolfgang Christ—and then named Keller (who was known from the Rome trial) as Kesselring's court-appointed attorney, without considering the defendant's request that Laternser be appointed.[226] Since Keller had been sought by the prosecutor as a prosecution witness, the British decision was surprising.[227] In fact, Keller was ambivalent about his role, and after the legal defense debacle during the Rome trial, he was unhappy with this latest mandate. However, he told the Jesuit father Alfons Hiemer that he would naturally do his duty and would "fulfill this last obligation to the Fatherland and do my best for this man."[228]

The correspondence between Laternser and Kesselring provides insight into Kesselring's view of the trial. He felt that he had been condemned in advance and noted in his diary that "in the final analysis, after Nuremberg perhaps every country will want to have its own trial with its own field marshal."[229] In addition, he became increasingly pessimistic as the start of the trial approached.[230] He was alarmed by the crumbling comradeship between his fellow prisoners, and from the beginning, he ruled out any clemency petitions on his behalf.[231] He felt particularly threatened by the decision to move the court from Rome to Venice,[232] although the reason for moving the trial turned out to be quite trivial. Colonel Halse's unpublished memoirs suggest that Venice was chosen as the trial venue largely for tourism purposes.[233]

Laternser had to repeatedly restrain Kesselring from acting on his own initiative. The former field marshal drafted numerous letters to potential witnesses as well as round-robins to German "camp elders," who were asked to seek out specific people in the camps they helped administer. Kesselring was thus actively involved in preparing his own defense.[234] For his part, Laternser even absorbed the military vocabulary, using it when writing to important witnesses.[235] In the letters requesting affidavits, which I have examined, it is striking that either Laternser or Kesselring included the following draft wording: "Field Marshal Kesselring has already testified in Nuremberg that . . ."[236] Obviously, inserting this language amounted to an indirect manipulation of witness statements by the defense. By the end of September 1946, Laternser had already collected fifty affidavits on Kesselring's behalf in this manner.[237]

However, the attorney failed to protect his client from the latter's own zealousness. Colonel Alexander Scotland had already noted that Kesselring was not inclined to take the charges against him seriously, for he believed he had done nothing deserving reproach. Even while being questioned in London, he had stated that he was "the leading man in Italy" and bore full responsibility for all that had occurred. He thus displayed not only plenty of injured pride but also boundless naïveté: "If ever a man's exaggerated sense of his own importance was leading him to his doom, that man was Kesselring," concluded Scotland in his memoirs.[238] The statement made by Kesselring on November 13, 1946, to a British officer of the War Crimes Commission in Allendorf demonstrated the same naïveté.[239] And in fact, Kesselring's statements under interrogation in November were later included in the prosecution's evidence. In his account given on March 23 and 24, 1944, he failed to mention either a second Hitler Order or any decision to transfer execution of the order to the SD. Rather, he incriminated himself by remarking that had Kappler not offered to procure candidates for execution, "[I would] not have known how I could have arranged for the Führer's order to be carried out on a fully legal basis."[240]

With regard to his soldiers, Kesselring always remained the loyal commander-in-chief standing in front of his men. Rather than viewing his own actions as incriminating (the issuing of antipartisan orders, in this particular case), he felt incriminated by his subordinates, whom he believed had acted in an "uncomradely" manner.[241] Because of his almost theatrical tendency to overplay his own importance, he tended to put himself to the fore—even when others were actually culpable. Even in retrospect, he could not bear having his performance as "the leading man in Italy" perceived as anything but flawless. He thus portrayed himself to his subordinates as the lead soldier until the end. For example, Kesselring made the following observation during the prosecution's opening address: "The prosecutor's demands are too great: should I verify all my orders? This goes beyond the power of an individual and a military staff charged with conducting a war, who wanted nothing to do with such pettiness and degradation."[242] This spontaneous note revealed Kesselring's attitude—an attitude that utilized military categories of "good" and "bad" soldiers and left it to the SD and SS troops to wage war on the general population, thus meeting Kesselring's demands for a "pacified hinterland." In contrast, his view of the Wehrmacht soldier was a positive one: "Soldiers will understand that one cannot do everything, that criminal activity takes place behind the lines of honest warfare, that one cannot intervene in the command areas of others."[243] Perhaps, as a fellow officer, Dietrich Beelitz, observed, personal vanity was a motivating factor for Kesselring: the former field marshal would "probably never have given up this final opportunity to enjoy the limelight."[244]

In addition to Hans Laternser, who led the team, the defense squad (as Kesselring called it) incorporated several other attorneys. These included the author of the 1936 military penal code, Dr. Erich Schwinge,[245] as well as the young attorney Friedrich Frohwein.[246] They were joined by Dr. Albrecht Schütze, who had served as an army judge in Italy under Kesselring.[247] Laternser attached great importance to academic backup, and this function was performed by Professor Schwinge.[248] Schwinge had served as judge in the South-Western Command during the final phase of the war, from March to April 1945,[249] and was thus personally familiar with the Italian theater. He helped propagate the view of the Wehrmacht as a fair and clean-fighting force, indirectly contributing to the Kesselring myth of the innocent field marshal. Not that his motivations were entirely unselfish: he coauthored the first (and somewhat self-justifying) study of National Socialist military justice.[250] In advance of the Kesselring trial, Laternser submitted to the court his own curriculum vitae (CV) and those of Schwinge, Frohwein, and Schütze. These CVs reveal some interesting cross-connections between the players, going back to the National Socialist era.[251] The Jesuit priest Alfons Hiemer and the former consul general in Rome, Eitel-Friedrich Moellhausen, were appointed to liaise with the Italian authorities.[252] Thanks to these men, the Kesselring trial acquired both its legal and its historical significance. The picture of war in Italy that emerged during the trial—which, in many critical aspects, did not correspond to reality—was largely the fruit of their efforts.

German Defense Strategy

Wolfram Wette has contended that the German officers had already prepared a stylized and distorted image of the Wehrmacht in the first few months after the war.[253] Even during the Nuremberg trials, one can trace the development of what can only be called legal syndicates preparing joint strategies for the war crimes trials. Later, using the cover of an academic colloquium in the form of a circle of lawyers, later named the Heidelberg Circle, these lawyers pooled their experience in order to obtain clemency for those in prison.[254]

The former field marshal was not himself the driving force behind the evolution of the "Kesselring legend," which developed in tandem with the defense strategy. Others wrote the legend on his behalf, primarily his former chief of General Staff, Siegfried Westphal, and his attorney, Hans Laternser. Wette's thesis can thus be further elaborated: a few leading figures among the German officer corps succeeded in constructing an interpretive model that was then adopted by most of their comrades and in particular by the attorneys who seized on this model as a trial strategy.[255]

The defense attorneys believed they would succeed with a strategy built around several defined focal points: (1) Kesselring's integrity and positive attitude toward Italy; (2) the partisans' manner of fighting, which was illegal according to international law; and (3) the "positive factors accompanying the occupation," such as the decision to spare certain cities and evacuate museums and cultural treasures.[256] These points continue to be the primary arguments advanced in defense of Kesselring's honor.[257]

There were three phases in the witness selection process. During the first phase, Kesselring and Laternser primarily concentrated on gathering accurate information regarding Kesselring's service in Italy, since they did not yet have access to the precise wording of the indictment. The second phase started in October 1946 following Kesselring's witness statement to the British interrogation officer Alexander Scotland in the so-called London District Cage, in Kensington. Kesselring had clearly heard hints regarding the content of the indictment, and now the defense team started seeking more concrete affidavits. In particular, they needed witnesses to testify on the whole issue of antipartisan warfare, and they also sought detailed reports on the shootings in the Fosse Ardeatine. The third phase was dominated by shock at the conviction of Mackensen and Mältzer. During this phase, which started in the 1946–1947 winter, Laternser conducted a targeted search for witnesses who could provide testimony to fill the gaps in what was already known about the chain of command following the Rome attack and testify on the origins of the Bandenbefehle. Much of this work was centered on Laternser's attempts to verify the second so-called Hitler Order transferring responsibility for executing the massacre to the SD.

Many members of the officer corps were still interned in the autumn of 1946, which greatly facilitated the collection of affidavits on Kesselring's behalf during the first phase. All that was needed was to write to the German camp commandants, visit the camps where witness statements could be gathered relatively freely, and then have the documents certified by the supervisory authorities. Laternser's first round-robin to the camp commandants, written in September 1946, was still quite vague.[258] It is noteworthy that this letter did not mention the shootings in the Fosse Ardeatine. To exonerate Kesselring, Laternser asked that material be gathered on the "treatment and feeding of the civilian population" and the "recovery and protection of art treasures and sites of cultural interest." The German camp commandants replied by return mail.[259] Some of them had already seized the initiative and were working on behalf of the accused,[260] probably in reaction to the radio announcement of the trial. It is thus clear that the Wehrmacht generals were determined to ensure that none of their own was left to battle victors' justice unaided.

The trial preparations were based in the American Allendorf camp, where a working group of the Historical Division—the section analyzing events during the war—was accommodated. The camp offered access to typewriters, paper, and postal connections,[261] as well as (after the summer of 1947) original documentation that could be of significance in the trial. Kesselring's former chief of General Staff, Hans Röttiger, when writing to Laternser, enclosed a detailed list of the evidentiary documents and statements submitted in Nuremberg[262] that he believed might facilitate Kesselring's defense.[263] He had also prepared a list of possible witnesses to whom Laternser should write.[264] In this regard, Röttiger suggested the indictment might include counts relating to Rotterdam[265] and Coventry,[266] as well as Italy.[267] Witness statements were also sought from the ranks of the Wehrmacht High Command in order to reconstruct the chain of command following the attack in the Via Rasella. Following Jodl's execution in Nuremberg, his senior General Staff officer, Horst Freiherr Treusch von Buttlar-Brandenfels,[268] was the only person who could state unequivocally whether Hitler had himself transferred responsibility for carrying out the shootings to the SD.

The collective interest of the Wehrmacht becomes apparent when one examines the defense preparations. The old military rank structures still held sway, and the General Staff coordinated the witness statements.[269] The erstwhile brothers-in-arms interned in Allendorf worked together to prepare affidavits for their revered field marshal. Kesselring's former chief of operations,

Colonel Dietrich Beelitz, was particularly diligent in this regard.[270] In a letter dated October 22, 1946, Beelitz—writing from Bellaria camp near Rimini—provided Laternser with initial material for Kesselring's defense,[271] whereupon Laternser officially confirmed that Beelitz would be involved in the trial as a "military expert advising the defense."[272] The veterans' statements corresponded with each other to such an extent that they were almost interchangeable. This observation was borne out, for example, in regard to Colonel Ludwig Graf Ingelheim, who had served under Kesselring as aide to the first General Staff officer on the staff of the South-Western Command from April to September 1944; in this post, his responsibilities included antipartisan warfare. Ingelheim revoked his first affidavit and asked that it be "destroyed."[273] The reason he gave was that he had streamlined his statement. General Lemelsen was also asked to "review" his statements: Laternser requested that certain phrases that could incriminate Kesselring be deleted. This commitment to Kesselring personally—a commitment that came to be viewed as part of the "final battle"—exacted a price. Some even found that they had to conceal any reservations or criticisms about Kesselring to avoid being considered "uncomradely." One of these loyal witnesses was the former head of the military administration in Italy, Dr. Friedrich-Constans Seifarth, who testified on Kesselring's behalf despite having differences with him. His statement carried particular weight in court when mention was made of his work on behalf of the Resistanza.[274]

Few could withstand this peer pressure. It is noteworthy that the only incriminating statements regarding orders issued by Kesselring were made by Colonel Klaus von dem Knesebeck.[275] As deputy to Josef Moll, Kesselring's chief of operations and successor to Beelitz, Knesebeck was also responsible for antipartisan warfare during the final phase of the war from autumn 1944, and he himself stood trial in a British military court. Knesebeck, who was charged with transmitting the Command Order, could only communicate with Laternser through his own attorney, Hasche. He provided some information "intended primarily as suggestions" for Kesselring's defense, but he was not available as a witness.[276] To make matters worse, Hasche made it clear to Laternser that he should not call Knesebeck as a witness, since "in the event of cross-examination, [Knesebeck] would be constrained to admit incriminating details, the knowledge of which he would be unable to deny."[277] However, no outright accusation was lodged against Kesselring. One soldier, Eduard Spitzeder, had contacted Laternser to give him "material relating to the Kesselring trial"; he was, he said, "only able to prepare incriminating material regarding K." and wanted to know to whom he should address "such an incriminatory record."[278] Since Laternser did not react further to this "offer" and thus never received the soldier's statement, we do not know what incriminating details Spitzeder wanted to put on the record.[279]

During the initial preparation phase, Laternser placed particular emphasis on Italian defense witnesses, whom he hoped to use to buttress the picture of a "pro-Italian field marshal." But given the prevailing anti-German political climate, it was inadvisable for Italian witnesses to testify on Kesselring's behalf. Most of them refused to appear in court, for this would have entailed running a media gauntlet and could subsequently have made their daily lives significantly more difficult. Certain friends of Kesselring—such as the former German ambassador in Rome, Hans Georg von Mackensen (a brother of the general on trial), and his successor in Salò, Rudolf Rahn—did offer to try to "specify other Italian witnesses and persuade them to testify."[280] But Kesselring was under no illusions: "The Italian witnesses are falling by the wayside; they fear the mob—this is significantly hindering the defense."[281] In the end, there were only a few Italian affidavits, and only one (from the Italian bishop of Velatri) was read into the court record.

In his letters, Laternser painted a picture of the war in Italy that was subsequently to become internalized in the postwar memory. For instance, he wrote that the "illegal behavior of the partisans" was "fully proven"; that shootings had only taken place following "prior judicial review"; and that captured Allied soldiers had also been treated as POWs, even when they were picked up with the partisans (or, in his terminology, *Banden*, or "gangs").[282] Unfortunately, according to Laternser, there were insufficient "numbers of specific probative cases" to prove these facts.[283] He went so far as to claim that the Italian reports he had to date were exaggerated, if not downright untrue. He knew the charge that "senior commanders" had "allowed innocents to be shot without any review" had to be "rebutted."[284]

The requests for affidavits from specific commanders were strikingly detailed and precise in regard to locations and other information. Looking at the list of Italian place-names, it seems that the German side knew precisely where the Wehrmacht might have been involved in war crimes.[285] In fact, the prosecution did not list all the massacre locations specified by German officers—indicating that the British either were not yet aware of all the incidents or had not yet concluded their investigations in this regard.

Neither the defendant himself nor his attorney had any doubt of Kesselring's complicity in radicalizing the antipartisan war in Italy. Regarding the antipartisan orders, or Bandenbefehle, Kesselring wrote to Laternser: "With my signature, I bear sole responsibility for X as well."[286] And he went on: "I was responsible for discipline, and therefore I had sole authority to lay down the path I wished to take, or could take, to achieve the goal. I can only restate that I had as little concrete knowledge as my masters. The rumors were enough for me!"[287] Regarding the statement made by his former army judge, Hans Keller, who had complained that an order as important as the Bandenbefehl should have been discussed with the army judges before being issued by the Operations Department, Kesselring countered:

> I think [the antipartisan order] was certainly dictated by me, written personally or written into the record. Therefore I can only say what I thought at the time. Certainly not taking over the Wehrmacht High Command order; after all, if that were the case I would have promulgated it. I certainly spoke to my officers about it, and let them know my thoughts, as I and Beelitz have already informed the court. I vehemently reject any other insinuation, which is either untrue or construed.[288]

What did Kesselring know of the massacres that took place in Italy during the summer of 1944?[289] He noted that his order of August 21, 1944, did not constitute a "restriction": it was merely a criticism of the incidents, of which he had had no "concrete knowledge," though he needed to have them verified. The order had been primarily directed at junior officers, young men who did not yet have his experience. He added, "Shortcomings always occur; experience showed that corrections are necessary and certainly do not constitute an indictable offence."[290]

Privately, Kesselring wrote that he was also aware of other punishment operations that had not been included in the indictment.[291] But he said he was not aware of reports relating to events at Padulivo that cost thirteen civilians their lives. Shocked, he wrote, "If true, an appalling crime!"[292] Yet after making this declaration, his exculpatory mechanism immediately kicked in, and Kesselring excused those involved by stating that the responsible officer "had no time to go into the mountains, and therefore killed the people in the village." He thus gave an insight into the casual mentality that allowed the Germans to treat Italian lives so carelessly.

Concrete British preparations for the Kesselring trial started when the former field marshal was transferred from Nuremberg to the Kensington District Cage in London, where he was to be questioned about war crimes in Italy committed on the basis of his orders.[293] He was interrogated in London by Colonel Alexander Scotland. Although his treatment in the District Cage was initially extremely poor,[294] Kesselring won the friendship of his interrogation officers over time.[295] Consequently, he enjoyed more freedoms, was treated like a "gentlemen," and was allowed to see the sights of London in the company of British officers. He took careful note of positive coverage in the British and Allied media regarding himself and the Wehrmacht in general.[296]

Thanks to his knowledge of German and his extensive secret service experience, Scotland was a particularly competent member of the British War Crimes Commission. From the start, he bluntly told his superiors that he believed Kesselring was wrongly accused in respect to antipartisan warfare. In his view, the German was being scapegoated for "crimes which, to say the least, were no proper concern of Britain's."[297] Scotland even provided Kesselring with deliberate assistance by openly informing the former field marshal of the current situation and disclosing his own reservations: Kesselring wrote that Scotland "hopes and wishes that the trial will not take place."[298] According to Scotland, the trial, if it did occur, could only be a formality under these circumstances. Scotland was also quite open when discussing the pending trial in the context of the British politics of memory. To quote Kesselring again, citing Scotland: "The trial was not so much an historical trial as a kind of Nuremberg spectacle, in which my obligation might be not only to address my own concerns, but to speak and fight for the military as a whole. He [Scotland] does not believe that the Army generals will be charged in respect of the anti-partisan war, but he does think it is possible that I will have to justify my orders."[299]

Scotland was thus more than a friend to Kesselring: he was an invaluable—if covert—adviser to the defense. The change in the German defense strategy that occurred after Kesselring's London interrogation was clearly due to external advice, and it is obvious that the amended line of defense was based on information provided by Scotland to Kesselring while the latter was being questioned in London's Kensington Cage.[300]

Scotland provided the impetus for the development of the Kesselring myth in Britain. He also recommended approaching senior officers from the enemy camp and appealing to their sense of honor and the international esprit de corps among senior high-ranking military men. Kesselring thereupon pled his case in writing to Field Marshal Bernard Montgomery, Field Marshal Harold Alexander, and Allen W. Dulles, who had been in charge of the Berlin office of the American secret service (the OSS) during the war. Montgomery did not respond at all, and Dulles remained cautious.[301] He merely stated that he had ordered negotiations to be conducted with Generaloberst von Vietinghoff-Scheel and Karl Wolff regarding the surrender in Italy.[302] Dulles could therefore only confirm that Wolff and von Vietinghoff had done all in their power to prevent destruction. Given this wording, his statement was useless to Kesselring; reading between the lines, Dulles was indicating that Kesselring had, in fact, done his utmost to prevent the surrender in northern Italy at the last minute. Field Marshal Alexander, who had earlier given a newspaper interview saying that Kesselring had fought "fairly,"[303] had since been appointed governor-general of Canada and was therefore also required to be politically circumspect: he declined to reply.[304] Through official channels, however, he certainly did bring influence to bear on the Kesselring trial, which will be discussed in more detail later in this volume. In terms of trial strategy, Alexander's statement on the Italian theater was articulated in court by Scotland.

Laternser wrote to thank Scotland for his help and said he would pursue Scotland's "suggestions." The matter at hand related to details of civilian massacres in Italy. Now, during the second preparation phase, Laternser began systematically gathering witness statements on the antipartisan war, or *Bandenkrieg*.[305] This is the area in which the change in defense strategy was manifested. During the earlier Nuremberg proceedings, defense counsel had decided to deny any knowledge of excesses committed by the German forces. Now, following Scotland's advice, it was decided to plead that the accused had been completely unaware of the true extent of the atrocities.

Back from London, Kesselring also embarked on a second phase of trial preparations in Allendorf camp, where he was carrying out research for the Historical Division: he was seeking specific witness statements. Together with his former chief of General Staff, Siegfried Westphal, who was also interned in Allendorf, Kesselring drafted a set of guidelines for his trial. Working with his attorneys Hans Laternser, Friedrich Frohwein, and Albrecht Schütze, he then developed these into what seemed to be a promising strategy.[306] He felt it was particularly important to "familiarize the gentlemen with my trains of thought," with the aid of his London statements. Although this approach did not directly influence any witnesses, one can assume that, when visiting Rimini, the attorneys only recorded those statements that corresponded with Kesselring's own. In Kesselring's words, they "made my statements available so that Mr. . . . can respond."[307]

During the third preparation phase, following the Rome trial, defense counsel were convinced that the documentation showing the chain of command following the attack was sufficient and that the primary focus should now switch to gathering mitigating evidence relating to the antipartisan warfare charge. Laternser more or less told witnesses how to formulate their statements on the antipartisan war, thus firmly laying down the course to be navigated. Given that the generals were largely inexperienced in legal matters, one can assume that they were quite relieved to be provided with a statement template they could fall back on.[308] Not surprisingly, some of the testimony given during the trial was repeated verbatim by several witnesses.

On January 7, 1947, Laternser sent a final circular to the German POW camp commandants, requesting "that all commanding generals and divisional commanders who served in Italy during the war lose no time in responding to the following items."[309] Despite the cool and unemotional legalese with which Laternser wrote about the list of crime locations, the document still reveals quite a lot about his picture of Italy and about the disdain with which he personally viewed the credibility of Italian witness statements: "With regard to the above-mentioned events, excesses were allegedly committed by German troops, for which Field Marshal Kesselring is being held to account because these excesses were allegedly based on orders issued by him." Laternser also asked the generals whether "shootings of partisans, civilians and Allied soldiers ever occurred without a judicial or court martial review" and whether "the above-mentioned gentlemen had initiated court martial proceedings in respect of the troops' misconduct towards the civilian population."[310] Only Generaloberst von Vietinghoff addressed all the questions.[311]

In the end, Laternser—who had initially avoided calling witnesses from the ranks of the SS—decided to ask them for help,[312] and he requested statements from Waffen SS General Max Simon and SS Obergruppenführers Willy Tensfeld and Karl Brunner.[313] The men approached by Laternser clearly used the opportunity to exonerate themselves of any suspected involvement in antipartisan warfare. Slightly annoyed, Laternser confirmed receipt of several affidavits "of a general nature." However, Hans Röttiger succeeded in obtaining a statement from SS Obersturmbannführer Ekkehardt Albert, chief of operations of the 16th Panzer Grenadier Division,[314] the only affidavit issued by an SS member on Kesselring's behalf dealing with the issue of antipartisan warfare. Albert stated that he was unaware of Kesselring's orders. Since it was the 16th SS Panzer Grenadier Division that had carried out numerous punishment operations directed at the civilian population, Albert's statement was particularly valuable to the defense, buttressing the idea that the troops had committed atrocities on their own initiative rather than as a result of Kesselring's order. However, Laternser did not use Albert's affidavit, possibly because the second count of the indictment—relating to antipartisan warfare—was not the focus of the proceedings. This issue did not really play a role until the trial of General Simon. However, there may have been another reason for Laternser's failure to use Albert's affidavit. In a telegram following the operation in Marzabotto, Kesselring congratulated the commander of the 16th Panzer Grenadier Division on his "success in combating partisans," and he put him forward for promotion. There can therefore be no doubt that Kesselring was aware of the 16th Panzer Grenadier Division's activities behind the lines.[315]

Laternser also attempted to obtain clerical affidavits confirming Kesselring's pro-Italian stance. In this regard, the Jesuit priest Alfons Hiemer was primarily responsible for selecting witnesses and meeting with them to discuss their affidavits. Hiemer had been in Rome since 1936 and had met Kesselring in 1944 while acting as spokesperson for the Italian bishops in the matter of protecting church property.[316] Laternser asked the archbishops of Milan, Bologna, and Florence to provide a response to prepared questions mainly concentrating on Kesselring's "greatness of character" and Christian virtue.[317] The attorney calculated that church confirmation of Kesselring's humanitarian outlook would work in the defendant's favor during the trial. However, Laternser also indicated to the archbishop of Florence that he had his own motives relating to the politics of memory: "During the trial all will depend—perhaps decisively—on presenting the court with a true picture of Field Marshal Kesselring's positive attributes." He said, "The Bishops under your sway, who are well-known to Your Eminence, should also be asked to provide statements on these issues."[318] Writing to the archbishop of Cologne's private secretary, Laternser described the role he felt the Catholic hierarchy should play in this trial: "I would ask for a positive reply, especially as such a step by the Church in a trial of historical significance, on behalf of a general who, to the best of my knowledge, has done nothing dishonorable, would help shine a new light on the Catholic church's interest in German affairs, and its willingness to aid all those who seek its help, even if they belong to other denominations."[319]

Laternser was also hopeful that the Vatican would intervene, since rumors were circulating to the effect that it had secretly approved of German reprisals following Communist attacks. However, because Vatican files on the Fosse Ardeatine case are not only patchy but also difficult to access, it is impossible to fully assess the extent to which the Holy See in 1944 was able to, or did, intervene in German retaliatory measures.[320] Certainly, the Vatican policy was ambivalent: although the pope had granted Allied soldiers sanctuary in the Vatican until 1944, it was the Germans who enjoyed his protection after June of that year—from the ambassador down to escaped soldiers.[321] After the war, he remained true to his principle of covert partisanship. While prohibiting church affidavits, he facilitated indirect assistance to the Germans by allowing the church to transmit letters and sometimes even donations (for example, in the context of the papal aid organization helping German POWs).[322]

Hiemer sought assistance directly from the Holy See, clearly specifying the kind of statements required in addition to general information on German measures taken to protect Italian cultural treasures:

> It would be of truly decisive value if the Holy See could provide us with a certified copy of the field marshal's letter in which (in accordance with his belief at the time) he stresses that the Fosse Ardeatine did not (as was indicated by the *Osservatore Romano*, and as was actually the case) involve the shootings of innocent people, but rather only involved the shooting of people who had already been sentenced to death by the courts.[323]

The Vatican refused Hiemer's request for affidavits regarding events in Rome, as it was official church policy not to make public statements on the matter.[324] However, church bodies did offer logistical assistance. Thus, Kesselring's defense team stayed with the German Franciscan sisters in Venice, and it was offered church lodgings while visiting Rome to obtain documentation and affidavits. Laternser was also provided with legal texts from the church's extensive library holdings—material that would have been difficult or impossible to obtain elsewhere.[325]

The bishops of Alatri, Ferentino, and Veroli responded with a benevolent but meaningless statement.[326] In contrast, the archbishops of Florence and Siena took the opportunity to remind Kesselring of his crimes. The archbishop of Florence wrote that he could "not offer anything in your favor," but he did have "much to say against the Field Marshal, since he is charged with the terror under which my diocese also suffered."[327] The archbishop of Siena referred to the looting of the city by German troops during their retreat on July 2, 1944, and asked, "How can I believe that German troops dared rape, loot and rob on their own initiative, rather than because of an order issued by their commander-in-chief?"[328] The testimony offered by Archbishop Venturi of Chieti was the only positive response Laternser received from clerical circles,[329] and even that was merely offered in the form of a telegram. Venturi attested to Kesselring's efforts to surrender the city of Chieti without a fight, thus saving it from destruction, and this message was submitted and read in court on April 26.[330] However, as a whole, the church statements received did not meet Laternser's expectations; instead, they tended to incriminate Kesselring and his conduct of the war.

In general, the defense team was well prepared for the trial. The Allies did not obstruct Laternser's efforts on behalf of his client. He was able to meet with Kesselring several times in order to develop the defense.[331] He was also allowed to use Allied postal channels, for example, when writing to request affidavits.[332] By the time the trial started in February 1947, Laternser had 1,002 affidavits on Kesselring's behalf.[333] In Venice, he and his staff were accommodated at the British Army's expense, and Laternser also benefited from other forms of unofficial assistance, not to mention the unconcealed sympathy of the British guards,[334] who admired Kesselring as a great strategist. Sympathetic journalists also supplied Laternser with additional information, material he would not have been able to obtain otherwise. Most witnesses were still interned in Rimini, a massive camp holding German POWs, and were brought each day to a British camp in Venice—and given the good food they had there, many would have enjoyed longer visits.[335]

Kesselring arrived in Italy on January 18, 1947, having been transferred from Allendorf camp.[336] The trial started at 10 A.M. on the morning of February 10, 1947.[337] In an effective public relations move, the cars that had been provided were left standing empty, and Kesselring instead traveled by boat to the courthouse, where international journalists were already gathered.[338] Kesselring abhorred "all the photography."[339] But for one last time, he was able to bask in the glow of being the leading man in Italy: all traffic on land and on water was halted to ensure that the field marshal was safely transported to court via the Grand Canal.[340]

Trial in Venice

Any trial analysis must trace the various lines of argument, thus allowing one to extrapolate the prosecution and defense strategies. In the following pages, I will also identify some of the trial's weaknesses, while counterpoising the narratives presented in court.

The British were represented by Major General I. Hakewell-Smith as presiding judge, assisted by four lieutenant colonels: P. M. Marjoribanks-Egerton, A. W. Gibbon, W. H. Medlam, and W. Turner-Coles.[341] C. L. Stirling acted as judge advocate general, just as he did during the Rome trial, and the prosecution was represented by Colonel Richard C. Halse. On behalf of the Americans, Colonel James Notestein, of the 92nd Infantry Division, and Colonel Preston J. C. Murphy, of the Adjutant General's Office (AGO), were dispatched to observe the trial. Both men were attached to the War Crimes Group of the Allied Mediterranean Forces. Surprisingly, the Americans remained completely uninvolved in both the trial preparations and the proceedings themselves.[342] Although Laternser had briefly planned to call American witnesses to testify to Kesselring's "chivalrous manner of fighting" in Italy, he quickly abandoned the idea.[343] But during the proceedings, the American observers apparently sympathized relatively openly with the German field marshal—and this, in itself, was of help to Laternser.[344]

British military court proceedings are largely based on common-law principles, except that the presiding judge is assisted by officers acting as members of the court rather than by a lay jury. In contrast to continental European rules of procedure, the public prosecutor—or, in military courts, the judge advocate general—is not obliged to gather exculpatory as well as incriminating evidence.[345]

The case against Kesselring was based on the voluntary statements made by the former field marshal in October 1946 to Colonel Scotland.[346] The charges brought against him by the British prosecutor were admirably clear. It was alleged that with the so-called Bandenbefehle he issued on June 17 and July 1, 1944, which had resulted in the massacres of Italian villagers, most of whom were women and children, he had rendered himself the "principal or accessory" and had not taken "reasonable steps" in order to "maintain discipline among the troops under this command." It was also alleged that he had failed to personally ensure that discipline was reestablished during retreat.[347] Only in September 1944, following Mussolini's protests, did Kesselring criticize the attacks and threaten the troop commanders responsible with court-martial proceedings: "The reasonable and probable result of the orders issued by him in June 1944 was that the gravest atrocities would occur. He cannot escape the consequences of this issue of illegal orders by canceling them some months later."[348] Evidence of "Kesselring's negligence" with regard to the three issues mentioned was to be provided by showing that he was aware of his troops' criminal actions and had previously failed to take legal action against them:

> With the knowledge certainly of what had been ordered in the *Ardeatine* Caves case, and possibly of what had happened during the first partisan drive, he nevertheless issued his order of 17 June 44, giving his protection to any commander who exceeded "our usual restraint in the choice and severity of the methods he adopts against partisans." . . . The majority of the atrocities investigated or reliably reported occurred during the period from the middle of June to the end of September and were no doubt the direct result of the orders which were issued.[349]

Consequently, the main charge against Kesselring was that he had "reasonable grounds" to suspect that "atrocities were being committed" and failed either to investigate or to issue orders with a view to prevent further occurrences.[350] Colonel Halse—in accordance with the political imperative that the illegality of the war crimes be proven—proclaimed a verdict of moral guilt, concluding that the German command leadership was aware not only of the repressive acts taking place but also of their illegality.[351]

The Kesselring trial lasted from February 17 until May 6, 1947. The prosecution wrapped up its case after seven days, following which the defense began its presentation. Indeed, the defense case accounted for most of the trial. At first glance, this may appear to imply a striking imbalance between the parties, since the defense took forty-four days to present its arguments, compared to the scant seven days used by the prosecution. However, during those forty-four days, the prosecution had the opportunity to cross-examine defense witnesses, thus significantly prolonging the proceedings. The judge advocate general presided over the trial, intervening in the proceedings with apposite questions and summing up at the end with his recommendations to the court. After each party—prosecution and defense—rested its case with a final plea, the members of the court then withdrew for several days to deliberate on the verdict, which had to be unanimous. Once the verdict was announced, the court again withdrew to consider the sentence, which was delivered during the next session. As it turned out, Kesselring's was the longest war crimes trial of a German officer held after the war. And in no other British war crimes trial was the defense given so much latitude in presenting its case.

During the Kesselring trial, the prosecution called nine witnesses and entered fifty-seven exhibits into evidence. The main prosecution witness was SS Obersturmbannführer Herbert Kappler. The defense called twenty-one witnesses and entered fifty-five exhibits into evidence. The main defense witnesses were Kesselring himself and his General Staff officers, especially Beelitz and Westphal. From the beginning, the trial was dogged by translation difficulties resulting from the fact that witnesses were questioned in German and the language of the court was English. Translation errors were particularly frequent when it came to analyzing Kesselring's Bandenbefehle, and these errors militated against an accurate reconstruction of the facts. The British legal team was aware of the language problem: Richard Halse noted in his reminiscences that he had ordered two different translators to work on Kesselring's orders in order to catch any parts that could pose a problem.[352] In the final analysis, the language difficulties unexpectedly worked in Kesselring's favor. For example, the British court interpreter, Major Forrest, a German Jewish émigré who was shunned by the British officers,[353] repeatedly translated entire passages so that they sounded "smoother" than the original German. Italian journalists were therefore under the impression that he was sympathetic to Kesselring.[354]

From the outset, Kesselring enjoyed the sympathy of most of the British team, and over the course of the trial, the prosecutor Colonel Halse proved particularly friendly. Italian newspapers noted with some annoyance that Halse always addressed Kesselring by the German courtesy title "Herr Feldmarschall"[355] and that he lost no opportunity during the proceedings to refer to Laternser as "my learned friend."[356] For his part, Kesselring felt almost at ease in Venice. In his diary, he happily noted the "many friendly gestures made by officers," and he was able to hold court with his former subordinates.[357] Colonel Halse, like other officers of the court, often gave Kesselring tobacco,[358] and he found his courtroom encounters with the defendant intellectually stimulating; he later referred to Kesselring's sense of wit and irony.[359] Halse was also glad that he had found a legal equal in the person of Laternser, who had successfully defended the German General Staff at Nuremberg.[360] During the trial, Halse invited the defense team to a dinner party in the luxurious Hotel Danieli, where the British were staying.[361]

The court had to address two main issues. First, was Kesselring or the SD responsible for the shootings? And second, did the execution of 335 Italians constitute a legally permissible reprisal or a war crime?[362] The prosecution team, and therefore also the defense, worked around two fixed points. On the one hand, they had to address the proportionality of the reprisal killings in the Fosse Ardeatine, and, on the other hand, they had to address the issue of whether Kesselring's Bandenbefehle had been deliberately couched in such a manner that they could be interpreted as giving license to murder.

The indictment was read out to Kesselring, and he pleaded not guilty to the shootings in the Fosse Ardeatine and to inciting his troops to wage war on the civilian population.[363] At that point, Laternser requested a two-week adjournment, reminding the court that when his client was in London during September 1946, he had been promised "this trial would be conducted fairly."[364] Thus, the recurring "fair trial" theme had already surfaced during the first few minutes of the proceedings. Subsequently, especially following Kesselring's conviction, this theme was reworked to underpin the myth of the unfairly convicted field marshal. In the early going, Laternser also skillfully seized on the opportunity to note that this was a "historic trial"—the first mention in court of a term that would become a catchphrase.[365] Kesselring's attorney had thus already brought into play the two basic themes of the defense: doubts relating to the fairness of the opposing side and the goal of, once and for all, clearing the names of German generals in the course of a symbolic trial. An important factor in Laternser's legal strategy was his reference to the legal principle of *nulla poena sine lege*: one cannot be punished for doing something that was not prohibited by law at the time the act was committed. According to the defense argument, the events in Italy had at no time been censured by the international law section of the Wehrmacht High Command. Kesselring was therefore unaware that he had breached international law by issuing the orders, as was now being alleged by the Allies. This claim, however, was not substantiated by any of the witness testimony.[366]

In his opening speech, counsel for the prosecution made it clear at once that the British court would only address the charges submitted in the indictment; it would not allow itself to be forced by "the press or others" to expand the indictment to include other counts.[367] Although this remark was undoubtedly aimed at the Italian authorities, it also showed that the British were aware they had not gathered all the evidence they needed against Kesselring. He then reiterated the charges. The first count alleged involvement in the Fosse Ardeatine reprisals in Rome, which resulted in the death of 335 Italians. The second count alleged incitement to wage war on the civilian population—and in this regard, Halse described the Bandenbefehle issued by Kesselring on June 17 and July 1, 1944, pointing out that they had been drafted by the field marshal himself.[368] Halse noted rather acerbically that, if the usual German practice was to shoot innocent victims in a ratio of ten to one or to have a field marshal offer indemnity to troop commanders for such attacks, the troops had basically been offered carte blanche to rampage through Italy, killing as they saw fit.[369] According to Halse, the second charge against Kesselring resulted from the extraordinarily brutal means adopted by the German Wehrmacht—means that could not be tolerated.[370] The British prosecutor thus again reflected the general political approach embodied in British war crimes policy.

Kesselring's defense misjudged the core of the British prosecution—which was to bring the former field marshal to account for a generally misguided policy—and attempted to prove Kesselring's personal innocence. This line of argument would subsequently form the basis of the Kesselring myth.

Kesselring listened carefully to the prosecutor's opening speech, and he wrote in his diary that "he had been strangely affected by some points."[371] He admitted to Laternser that "none of us thought that the Rome case would, somehow and at some time, be termed a war crime."[372] He was quite open to the hearing of evidence, and he showed signs of genuine remorse and shock when the prosecution displayed photos of the massacre in the Fuccecchio swamps and of the exhumation of bodies in the Fosse Ardeatine caves.[373]

From a British perspective, the primary charge against Kesselring in the Fosse Ardeatine case was that he had "ordered reprisals at the rate of ten to one, which was excessive, and that as he had passed the orders to subordinate army formations, he was responsible for the way in which they were carried out."[374] In his opening speech, Halse noted that, as he saw it, Kesselring's participation in the Rome massacre happened by chance because of the involvement of a police battalion; the British view was that the real responsibility lay with the supreme SS and police commander in Italy, Karl Wolff. Therefore, Halse evinced little surprise that the execution of the reprisal was finally transferred to the SD, which he termed Germany's "black sheep," doing the dirty work on behalf of everyone else.[375] He doubted whether Hitler himself had tasked the SD with the executions, and he tended to believe that Kesselring had allowed a subordinate body—in this case, the Fourteenth Army—to assign responsibility for carrying out the order. Kesselring was thus guilty of culpable negligence and carelessness.[376] Halse's view was that the former field marshal had acted irresponsibly.[377] According to the British military penal code, a reprisal such as that in the Fosse Ardeatine was illegal because it involved the shooting of noncombatants.[378] Proportionality could only have been ensured—according to Halse's argument, formulated on the basis of military law—if the block of houses directly surrounding the scene of the crime had been blown up. The court's task was to assess, first, whether the act constituted a war crime in and of itself and, second, whether ordering a reprisal and allowing innocent victims to be killed constituted a war crime.[379]

Initially, Laternser exhausted all the legal means at his disposal in an attempt to have the evidence excluded. An opportunity to deploy such legal tactics arose when the prosecution presented several exhibits relating to the charge that Kesselring had incited the troops to wage war on the civilian population through his Bandenbefehle;[380] the exhibits were intended to document the massacre. Laternser criticized specific affidavits as "irrelevant," "untrue," or "falsified."[381] These exhibits could be challenged on purely technical grounds, since they had not been affirmed under oath. English military police had visited the villages in question and talked to survivors. They were then able to summarize the probable course of events. "Based on experience," said Laternser, "memories of stirring events such as these can be particularly heavily influenced by the lively temperament of Italian witnesses,"[382] and he requested that the so-called sergeant affidavits be excluded from evidence.[383] His request was granted.

In the British judges' view, the fact that Kesselring (after being notified of the bomb attack) had once again confirmed that sufficient persons sentenced to death were available "to carry out the reprisal without killing innocents" was a mitigating factor.[384] Laternser used this finding as putative proof that, when transmitting Hitler's first order (according to which hostages should be shot using a ten-to-one ratio), Kesselring had deliberately omitted the word *hostages* precisely to prevent innocent people being killed.[385] Hitler's second order, tasking the SD with execution of the punishment operation, had, according to Laternser's argument, exonerated Kesselring from all responsibility for the nature of the massacre. However, the defense never managed to prove the existence of this second order in court.

The proceedings were uneventful. The judge advocate general and counsel for the prosecution repeatedly questioned witnesses regarding their statements during the Rome trial in an attempt to rattle them and—where they deviated from those statements—prove that they must have discussed their remarks in the interim.[386] If there really was retrospective collusion among all the witnesses, as alleged by prosecutor Halse when Beelitz was being cross-examined on March 21, 1947, it worked like a dream. During the Kesselring trial, all Wehrmacht officers testified that after Hitler's first order, there was a second order transferring execution of the reprisal to the SD—thus removing responsibility from the army and assigning it to the SD.[387] The main witnesses had already testified in the Rome trial, where they may have prepared a standardized version of events, but any collusion probably went back to their days in Allendorf camp.

Kesselring did not make it easy for military witnesses to take his part, since he contradicted certain decisive passages in his Rome testimony. In Rome, he had described himself as the "sole guilty party" because he was the one who had been ordered by Hitler to carry out the reprisal—a version of events that even the court felt was a downright lie intended to protect his subordinates.[388] Kesselring's Rome testimony, in particular, was repeatedly cited in subsequent reports on the former field marshal: "I assume full responsibility. I do not understand why Generalleutnant von Mackensen has been sentenced to death for this, for if there is any guilt it is mine and mine alone."[389] Since Kesselring was reluctant to reveal that he had stayed in La Spezia, which could have linked him with knowledge of the shooting of an American commando unit there, his statements on the command sequence following the attack in the Via Rasella were inevitably unsatisfactory.[390] He thus found himself contradicting his chief witness, Siegfried Westphal. Westphal initially testified that Kesselring had not been contacted by his General Staff officers at all to get orders on how to deal with the partisan assault on the police company,[391] but a few days later, he remembered "with certainty" that he had handed his superior "the second order issued by Hitler, providing for execution by the SD, on the evening of March 23rd."[392] When confronted with this statement in court, Kesselring was adamant that he did not remember the events described by Westphal. Thereafter, Westphal explained this "painful difference with Kesselring" by referring to the "severe skull injuries suffered by the Field Marshal" in October 1944, following which such details may well have disappeared from his memory. This "medical maneuver" was used to brush aside any discrepancies in the testimony. The German witnesses, understanding that Westphal's version was to prevail, kept silent. Only the witness immediately following Westphal, Kesselring's intelligence officer Zolling, clearly remained in the dark regarding Westphal's statement. Zolling testified that Westphal "had only informed him verbally of the second Führer order."[393]

The prosecution seems to have largely fallen in with this version of events, and even Halse surprisingly opted not to probe Kesselring's precise whereabouts—despite the fact that he himself was dubious. Instead, he challenged Kesselring: "If one of your General Staff officers transmitted the order to the 14th Army while you were at the front and unaware of what was happening, then you would not now be charged with responsibility for the shooting of 335 Italians."[394] But Kesselring did not respond, and Halse did the defense a favor by maintaining a complicit silence. He later wrote in his memoirs that he had "always had a sneaking feeling that Kesselring was not at his headquarters at the time the order came through" and that he had only assumed responsibility for the order because of loyalty to his subordinates.[395] However, he was unable to resolve the contradictions. He assumed that Kesselring's intention was to shield Beelitz, whom he considered the real culprit,[396] yet all the available sources indicate that only the chief of General Staff, Siegfried Westphal, could have authorized such an order instead of Kesselring himself, since he acted as deputy in the commander's absence from headquarters.

There are two possible reasons why Kesselring may have shielded Westphal. Military sociologists have found that covering for errors made by one's subordinates is a basic element of the "code of comradeship" and serves to promote unconditional group cohesion.[397] Hitler had laid down this line, emphasizing that soldiers had to be sure of "absolute backing" from their senior commanders so that the "poor devils" did not have to fear being subsequently held to account.[398] In similar fashion, Kesselring always stressed a commander's duty to look after his soldiers' welfare. His creed was that he would always place himself in front of his men. However, Kesselring also had an egocentric motivation for his self-sacrifice: as the supposed leading man in Italy, his self-image was dominated by vainglory. In his court testimony, Zolling noted that Kesselring "always wanted to assume sole responsibility for German interests in Italy."[399] Elsewhere, Kesselring wrote that he still felt responsible for his men "even if I am myself accused of war crimes," and he wanted to prevent them from being at the mercy of a "vengeful justice."[400]

With regard to the second charge—inciting the troops to wage war on the civilian population by issuing more ruthless antipartisan orders—the prosecution's initial strategy was to analyze the wording of these orders, prove their effect by describing various massacres, and conclude that Kesselring had been fully aware of events. The prosecution's primary concern was to ensure that the very act of issuing orders that resulted in war crimes was itself defined as a war crime.[401] In contrast, Laternser argued that, by issuing the orders, Kesselring's intention was to prevent "worse events." However, the testimony by Franciscan priest Lino delle Piane regarding the massacre at Bardine San Terenzo, where over 100 women and children were murdered and then burned beyond recognition, rendered Kesselring's persistent self-delusion apparent—even to the defendant. He cried out in court, "This is such a barbarity that no-one could believe it to be the work of German soldiers."[402] Writing in his diary, he noted that "an Italian witness brought along horrible photos, and a Franciscan priest made a similar statement."[403] It sounds as though, until that moment, Kesselring had really not considered the specific barbaric consequences of his orders.

Nevertheless, his defense mechanism proved resilient, enabling him to resist the growing suspicion of his moral guilt. Kesselring's statement that the atrocities "had not taken place in that way"[404] and that the few antipartisan operations he could recall had merely served "military imperatives" caused a stir both in the court and especially in the media.[405] Kesselring also stated that he had ordered certain incidents investigated and generally demanded tighter supervision of the troops. He felt that no proof had been offered showing that the excesses were "intrinsically linked to my orders," let alone "chronologically associated" with them.[406] Some of the incidents had clearly taken place before he issued the orders. Kesselring claimed in court that "Fascist units" were responsible for the Bardine massacre.[407] His conclusion was clear: this was the hidden face of war, and the atrocities described would probably have taken place in the absence of his orders.

During cross-examination, some witnesses gave substance to the charge that the Wehrmacht failed to ensure what Halse termed the "humane" execution of the shootings. Kesselring's former intelligence officer, Zolling, stated that they "paid no further attention to the reprisal" once the execution order had been transferred to the SD.[408] His testimony lent weight to the prosecution view that it made no difference to the Germans how the Italians died. Kesselring considered Zolling a "difficult case."[409]

The affidavit by General Joachim Lemelsen—whose last posting was as commander-in-chief of the Fourteenth Army in Italy—was also unambiguous. Lemelsen's affidavit regarding his time in Italy was dated June 1946 in Bridgend—an English camp beyond the control of Kesselring's close associates. As a long-serving officer, Lemelsen felt that Kesselring's order "posed a grave risk to discipline and order, given the critical situation at the time and the fact that emotions were running high among the troops. It would have been futile to withhold the order, since it reached the troops through various channels, and the Field Marshal—during his frequent visits to the front—always checked personally to ensure that his orders had been successfully transmitted."[410]

Lemelsen displayed a remarkable spirit of resistance: as early as 1941, when commanding the Central Army Group in Russia, he had protested against the "senseless shooting of civilians."[411] His moral criticism intuitively found the weak spot in the defense. Lemelsen grasped the basis of the charges against Kesselring earlier than his colleagues: he understood that Kesselring was charged with issuing orders that could be viewed as a license to kill—and given the military and political tensions prevailing at the time, they were so viewed, at least by the SS troops. He thus demonstrated that the Wehrmacht had by no means completely forfeited its sense of justice. It appears quite plausible that generals at the front protested against Kesselring's Bandenbefehle. However, such objections could only have been made verbally, since no officer could openly criticize a superior's orders.

In court, Laternser confronted Lemelsen with his London affidavit. Under the scrutiny of former comrades, the general tried to take his words back. He said his London affidavit had been "a major error."[412] After all, Lemelsen continued, he was aware of Kesselring's pro-Italian attitude and knew that he wanted to spare the civilian population. He himself had transmitted the orders "without reservations."[413] And that statement was certainly true: on July 3, 1944, Lemelsen issued an order of his own, which fully mirrored the severity of Kesselring's wording.[414] However, Lemelsen's order was not available to the Allies. In any event, the fact that he raised objections to Kesselring's order while he was a prisoner of war aroused suspicions among his comrades, who felt he was trying to distract attention from himself. His courtroom avowals of solidarity with Kesselring came too late. General Lemelsen's reputation among his fellow soldiers seems to have suffered heavily as a result of his Venice testimony.[415]

Kesselring's normal restraint was supplanted by real anger: "He should have spoken with me, rather than making some sort of statements while a prisoner of war!"[416] Kesselring felt that Lemelsen's statements were the result of "cage psychosis"[417]: "If, because of shame at his behavior, a general reveals this emotional collapse to the world, that alone is proof of its existence. Quite apart from that, as I testified in the witness box, every sentence was wrong because a) it was *Desordre*, b) orders were only sent to him, c) I was never deaf to sensible counterarguments and d) the troops and various commanders demanded more."[418]

In court, however, Kesselring tried to downplay any disunity among

German officers, instead stressing the loyalty that existed within the military. He acknowledged Lemelsen's affidavit had left him with a "bitter aftertaste," and he was "extremely sorry that he now had to once again raise this matter between two officers in public."[419] The *Times* carried these references to the military honor code and the "imperative of silence" in full, thus stressing military solidarity more than Lemelsen's noble attempt to find the truth.[420]

Laternser gave the closing speech for the defense on April 30, 1947, once again summarizing the case for his client's innocence. In his seventy-page closing statement, he developed a novel view of the events surrounding the Rome attack. In the process, he showed himself to be remarkably skilled at eliding important details in such a manner that his omissions were scarcely noticed, thus painting a completely new picture of events.[421] With regard to the first charge, he stressed that the SD bore sole blame, and Kesselring had never been notified of the events comprising the second charge. Laternser attached particular weight to the second order issued by Hitler, transferring responsibility for execution to the SD, and he conspicuously ignored the fact that, although the SD was tactically subordinate to Himmler, an exceptional provision meant that it was operationally subject to the Army High Command in respect to the battle zone surrounding Rome. The reference to the consistency of the statements issued by Kesselring's staff officers, all of whom attested to the second Führer order, was also risky, since Kesselring himself had been unable to clearly recall this order during his testimony (of course, this was because he was not in Rome at the time). Laternser made one throwaway remark that not only was noteworthy in itself but also was to contribute significantly to the Kesselring myth: he stated that the crimes with which Kesselring was charged were acts that "must be of secondary importance in the thinking and planning of any field commander, and can only be of minor significance when the verdict of history is pronounced on the personality of a field commander."[422]

Kesselring, who had initially been unhappy with some of the points Laternser planned to make,[423] was fully reconciled following his attorney's rhetorically impressive courtroom performance. A delighted Kesselring wrote to Laternser's wife, Hilde, that the closing speech "could not have been more effectively constructed." However, they still did not know if they could dare hope: "Whether the verdict, which we expect on Monday, will reflect our efforts, expectations and spirit, is another story altogether."[424]

The trial ended on May 1 with the closing speech for the prosecution. Halse rejected the claim made by Kesselring and his staff that a second Führer order had been issued. He gave equally little credence to the alleged telephone conversation between Kappler and Kesselring regarding the fact that enough people with pending death sentences had been located for purposes of the reprisal action. Rather, Halse asserted, Kesselring had paid no attention to the selection of candidates for execution,[425] despite the fact that this was within the formal remit of the Fourteenth Army, whose battle zone included Rome.[426] Regarding the second count, Halse concluded that Kesselring had breached the accepted rules of international law by allowing civilians to fall victim to German reprisals without investigation or summary (military) court proceedings.

The judge advocate general then gave his summing up. In his remarks to the court, Stirling made it clear that international law was ambiguous when it came to the legality of reprisals.[427] Therefore, there were only two issues before the court. First, did responsibility for the shootings lie with Kesselring or with the SD? And second, did the shooting of 335 Italians constitute a legally admissible reprisal or a war crime? As the "UNWCC Law Report on the Kesselring Trial" pointed out, Stirling believed the Fosse Ardeatine massacre constituted a war crime rather than a legally admissible reprisal. He felt that the ten-to-one ratio was excessive, and he was particularly disquieted by the fact that 335 people, rather than 330, had actually been killed: "Whatever you may think about International Law and reprisals, clearly five of these 335 Italians were murdered. That was a war crime and you cannot get away from it. There was no Führer order to cover it and it was quite outside the reprisal."[428] This action—the murder of the 5 "extra" Italians—was not covered by any order issued by Hitler, nor did it have anything to do with reprisals. Nevertheless, Stirling concluded that Kesselring would have to be acquitted if, in the view of the court, it had been proven that the SD bore responsibility for the shootings.

In terms of the second charge—incitement to wage war on the civilian population—the judge advocate general stated that Kesselring had issued his orders "deliberately and knowingly" at a time when tension among the troops was already running high; he should therefore have predicted the consequences of these orders. Indeed, Stirling went further: "By bringing these orders into existence, [Kesselring had intended] to bring about those results."[429] Nonetheless, the court had not succeeded in clarifying whether the shootings in Italy constituted "reprisals" or "shootings of hostages." As the report on the Kesselring trial elaborated:

> It is usual to speak of "hostage" in occupied territories when the occupying forces imprison members of the community of the occupied territory announcing at the same time that they will be treated as hostages if the community does not refrain from certain activities against the occupying

> forces. The term "reprisal" is used in this connection for measures taken by the occupying forces in retaliation for the unlawful conduct of unidentified members of the community of the occupied territory. Thus hostages are taken *before* the act of illegitimate warfare committed by the enemy whereas reprisals are inflicted *after* such an act.

It proved impossible to arrive at a definition during the trial: "The Prosecution described both parts of the order as reprisals; Defense Counsel treated the taking of hostages as the first step towards inflicting reprisals. The Judge Advocate did not refer to the distinction in his summing up."[430] The definition would have penal implications, and the problem was solved only at a later trial at Nuremberg, in 1948.[431] The decisive factor, according to Stirling, was whether Kesselring had issued his orders knowing and intending that Italian civilians would be killed by units under his command, contrary to international law.[432] This question remained unresolved, and the American trial observer Colonel Murphy reported as much to Washington.[433]

On May 4 and 5, 1947, the court withdrew to the Lido coast outside Venice to deliberate. The verdict was pronounced on May 6: "Guilty on both counts." Murphy noted that the prosecution waived its right to make a speech at that point.[434] As is usual in British trials, the sentence was not announced until the afternoon. Kesselring was to be shot. The sentence was actually an unusual concession by the British to the field marshal, for death by firing squad was considered an honorable end for a soldier, in contrast to death by hanging, as was called for in sentences meted out in Nuremberg and Rome. The Kesselring sentence also indicated the difficulties experienced by the court in dealing with their highly esteemed former enemy.

Contrary to British fears, there was no public reaction to the verdict in the courtroom. Even those who heard the announcement outside the court building remained calm.[435] Only *Avanti!* expressed the public sentiment: the verdict had been "anticipated by Italy."[436]

Both Kesselring and his counsel were taken aback by the outcome of the trial. A stunned Kesselring wrote in his diary: "Pronounced guilty and sentenced to death by firing squad. Thus will an end be put to a long life full of work, responsibility and blessings. God only knows why?"[437] The points that Kesselring himself jotted down toward the end of the trial as an *aide-mémoire* for Laternser when drafting his closing speech give us some insight into the former field marshal's own view of proceedings.[438] Specifically, looking back on the trial, Kesselring felt that the court had not taken the trouble to assess the subjective circumstances (for example, in the Rome case) and reconstruct the situation that obtained before the 335 hostages were shot. "Biased"—that was Kesselring's view of the prosecutor, Richard Halse, and the judge advocate general, C. L. Stirling, since they had previously performed the same functions in the Rome trial of Mackensen and Mältzer. "A man cannot shed his own past, and must therefore be viewed as biased," pronounced Kesselring.[439] Ironically, he was reflecting on the earlier roles played by Halse and Stirling, rather than on his own destiny. Kesselring expressed doubts about the competency of the court, saying that "lower ranks simply could not empathize with the atmosphere." And knowing that the German military penal code was in agreement with him on this issue, he demanded to be tried according to German law; he argued that he should not be disadvantaged "by customary law which, in turn, depends on the fragmentary nature of international law," especially since it was "unjust to expect a German commander to recognize another country's legal concepts."[440] Kesselring therefore believed that he had been pronounced guilty not because of German violations but solely on the basis of victor's justice: "Given the facts of the matter, it is difficult to explain the trial. Such an explanation may be contained in the remark of a senior English officer who told me: 'Your greatest crime is simply that you lost the war'!"[441]

Kesselring's defense mechanism immediately kicked in: he felt that the political dimension of his "show trial" had been quite obvious: "The verdict had to go against me since (1) it had been preceded by the Rome trial, acceptance of which the Judge Advocate General was desperately seeking; (2) the partisan activity which continues today could not go down in history as a crime, and (3) the intention was to cut German officers, and thus German soldierhood, to the quick."[442]

Writing to his wife, Liny, Kesselring noted that the prosecutor's closing speech had "had the intended effect," successfully portraying him as a monster.[443] He said that the prosecutor had "done his duty" and presented the defendant as a "beast," which Kesselring considered "rather primitive": "I was amazed to discover that the findings of the trial had completely passed him by. He sought a guilty verdict!" Kesselring had expected to be acquitted, but now, he stated he would "accept the death sentence" because his travails could have an "inspirational historical significance."[444]

In the absence of a written statement about the grounds for the court's findings, Laternser produced a precise analysis of the judge advocate general's summation. He concluded that there were two primary reasons for Kesselring's conviction. First, the British judges believed it had been proven that Kesselring had ordered the 335 hostages to be shot in Rome and, second, they considered that the massacres in Italy were due to Kesselring's Bandenbefehle and that the field marshal was therefore also guilty of "inciting war against the civilian population." The second count offered no grounds for appeal, but Laternser likely would have been justified in seeking to have the guilty verdict quashed if he could show that the hostage shootings were committed by the SS and thus did not fall within Kesselring's area of responsibility. Therefore, any petition would have to focus on demonstrating that the SS or SD bore responsibility for the massacre.

To substantiate the claim that the SD was responsible for the Rome massacre, the primary task was to find the second Hitler Order attested to by defense witnesses, as well as the war journal that was thought to have disappeared after 1945.[445] Whatever efforts were made in this respect were rather halfhearted, as can be seen from circumstances described in the following brief digression. In February 1948, after completing his trial duties at Nuremberg, Laternser attempted to find out more on the whereabouts of the war journal through General Westphal.[446] Westphal recalled rumors that circulated after the war, and Laternser noted: "Most of the war journal was not destroyed. Buried near Bozen. Pfrommer knows the location and the name of the person who did it." However, he made no attempt to discover the hiding place.[447] There is still no trace of the original South-Western Command war journal files, although one can hazard a guess regarding their whereabouts,[448] and the carbon copies of the war journal maintained by Army Group C, which were stored in a depot in Potsdam, may have been destroyed during a bombing raid in the spring of 1945.[449] So it remains unclear whether the war journals were destroyed or captured by the advancing Allies. Unless they are discovered in some secret American depot,[450] we will have to continue relying on conjecture when reconstructing the events of March 23, 1944.

Laternser came to the conclusion that, in the (intentional or otherwise) absence of the original documentation, the only option was to use affidavits *testifying* to the existence of a second Führer order for the purposes of any appeal. However, the former war diarists Fritz Pfrommer, Klaus Kunkel, and Hans Eberhardt proved less than helpful in this endeavor.[451] Although Pfrommer clearly remembered the two orders that "were probably even available in writing"[452] and offered to personally testify to this on Kesselring's behalf,[453] Dr. Hans Eberhardt was clearly quite unaware of this second order.[454] But he was prepared to testify in court that "in the early morning of March 24th 1944, he had been informed by Major Böhm that General Mältzer had received a 'Führer order' from Generaloberst von Mackensen which was to be passed on to the SD."[455] Laternser then wrote to the former war diarist Kunkel seeking confirmation of this information. As usual, Laternser had already drafted the required statement,[456] but Kunkel did not use Laternser's wording. In his affidavit, he explained that, though he "remembered with certainty that responsibility for executing the massacre had been transferred to the SD" and that a ratio of ten to one had been laid down, he had only entered Mältzer's instruction in the war journal: "I never saw the order itself." Rather, at the time, he had been informed by his superior officer, Eberhardt, that the order "went above our office."[457]

Laternser's new petition emphasized the statement made by Jodl's first General Staff officer in the Wehrmacht, Horst Freiherr Treusch von Buttlar-Brandenfels. Buttlar deviated substantially from his affidavits that were read out during the trial. Now, suddenly, he confirmed telephone conversations with Westphal—conversations he had failed to mention in his 1947 written statement. He also confirmed having had a telephone conversation with Colonel Beelitz.[458] Laternser probably hoped to use Buttlar's statement to draw legal attention to the witnesses Beelitz and Westphal, whose testimony had been rock-solid on Kesselring's behalf; unlike Buttlar, they were prepared to repeat their statements in the event of an appeal.[459] Beelitz was not the only one to be surprised that "Buttlar only now remembers something of such importance to the field marshal."[460] One can only surmise that Laternser's influence on Buttlar's new statements actually amounted to witness manipulation. After studying all the relevant records and statements, it seems highly probable that the second Führer order never existed but rather was concocted to facilitate Laternser's trial strategy.[461]

After the verdict was announced, it became apparent that the fight would continue at another level during the years to come. The outcome of Kesselring's "final battle" was certainly not decided by the verdict of the court. The Reuters office asked Kesselring to write a personal statement as part of the bureau's trial coverage,[462] thus offering the former field marshal an invaluable forum. Kesselring's so-called closing words illustrated the progress of the battle.[463] Two versions of the document have been preserved, including Kesselring's own draft. Though he superficially reflected on the charges and his own possible guilt in this document, the main thrust was to stress his innocence. It was all "very simple," as far as he was concerned. He had performed the duties with which he was entrusted "in a military fashion," even "taking into account significant disadvantages for the German conduct of the war"; "even today, this is acknowledged to a remarkably high degree by historians."[464] Italy, its cultural treasures, and even its people "had suffered less in their own country than most of the other warring nations." This statement indicates that, after his trial, Kesselring was no longer prepared to bear any share of the moral blame for the deaths of civilian victims as a result of his orders. Rather, he immediately returned to his favorite theme: the "illegal partisan war" that threatened to result in a "battle of unbridled passions." The ambiguous status of the Resistenza troops in terms of international law also provided Kesselring with an opening for criticism: "I can simply no longer consider it right for an illegal band to commit serious gratuitous and provocative crimes with impunity, and for those bands then even to be glorified, while opposing soldiers fighting for their very lives are branded as criminals and brought before court."[465]

Similar wordings can also be found in a letter dated May 6, 1947, which Kesselring included in his memoirs.[466] The letter expressed his views on the death penalty: although he had sought an acquittal, he said he would "welcome" the execution. An acquittal would have "demonstrated to world opinion that there were and are millions of decent Germans," but the death sentence imposed would also be of public benefit "because it would create a martyr for the German people, whose memory and continued presence could provide an impetus to the youth." Kesselring's sense of self-worth was clearly sufficient for him to seek such a mythic conclusion to his career. Because of the exemplary function he saw himself performing, he had decided to "continue fighting until the end for justice for myself and my soldiers."[467]

But Laternser had other plans. He drafted a new "closing statement"—which was still attributed to Kesselring—and arranged for the Reuters office to publish it. There is no doubt that this marked the birth of the Kesselring myth.[468] With an obvious acknowledgment of the pending death sentence, Laternser ended the revised closing statement for his client with these words: "Whatever the outcome, I will be able to bear it. In times of deep humiliation, I have learnt to raise myself higher by standing on my misery."[469] The growth of a "veterans' Italy" legend, which had started during the trial, now continued with Laternser's fictitious closing statement by the former field marshal—a statement that was geared to the media. Kesselring's image until the trial was that of the upstanding general who assumed responsibility for his subordinates' errors and would, if necessary, pay for them with his life, but Laternser's closing statement reinvented that image. Kesselring was now presented as a general suffering the insult of a wrongful conviction, who now—tried in combat—demanded justice. This image of the soldier on duty was also presented to the outside world. Expressions of personal regret or reflections on the trial would merely get in the way of this newly sculpted image. Therefore, just one sentence from Kesselring's own draft was included in Laternser's closing statement.

Kesselring's cause received an unexpected boost from the Americans. American trial observer Colonel Murphy prepared a report on the Venice proceedings for Washington, and his conclusion was surprisingly favorable to the former field marshal. Quite apart from the question of reasonable doubt, the evidence was insufficient to convince Murphy that Kesselring was guilty on either of the two counts.[470] Murphy criticized the composition of the court, which, in his view, hardly corresponded to the field marshal's military rank: he doubted the ability of the officers composing the court to either visualize or correctly assess Kesselring's problems, military actions, or orders in the field.[471]

The Americans clearly had little interest in trying senior German military personnel. They were far more interested in the information they could obtain from their erstwhile opponents regarding the course of operations during the recent war—and regarding their future enemies in the East. As a member of the U.S.-led Historical Division, Kesselring had long proven his willingness to cooperate with the Americans. Thus, the American observer's report on the Kesselring trial concluded with a historical footnote: Murphy recorded Zolling's statement that Kesselring and his staff had known nothing of the impending Allied landings at Anzio and Nettuno until the morning of January 21, 1944, when a coast guard officer reported to headquarters that the Allies were advancing before his eyes.[472] This was the only point seized on by the American War Department Special Staff. Lieutenant Colonel William O'Perry encouraged Colonel Murphy—his divisional colleague—to sound out Kesselring on the Anzio landings.[473] In view of what were apparently flattering remarks made by Kesselring, he suggested writing an article about the landings or publishing a Festschrift in praise of the division. O'Perry's letter helps explain the striking restraint exhibited by the United States when it came to the Kesselring trial. The field marshal—who was almost affectionately known as "the old boy"[474]—had accorded respect to his former enemies, and now, in turn, he could expect the Americans to return the favor. After all, the Americans' own division enjoyed an aura of invincibility thanks to their victory over Kesselring's brave troops—troops whose reputation was legendary. Thus, any damage done to the reputation of Kesselring's troops would inevitably lower the standing of the Americans' own troops.

In the legal arena, the Americans did not share their British colleagues' assessment of Kesselring's guilt. Thus, as early as November 1947, just six months after Kesselring was sentenced to death, the American prosecutor Theodore Fenstermacher, speaking during the Case 7 trial of Field Marshal Wilhelm List in Nuremberg, voiced criticism of his British colleagues. He remarked that the Kesselring case had by no means been as clear-cut as that of List because Kesselring had not been proven to be directly responsible for ordering reprisals. And yet, he pointed out, a British court had sentenced Kesselring to death (although the sentence had subsequently been "*corrected*" to life imprisonment).[475]

For a society that had for years been subjected to propaganda reports, press coverage of the trial had an educational effect in Germany.[476] The newspapers generally refrained from editorial comment and allowed the grisly facts to speak for themselves.[477] As a result, readers were able to draw their own conclusions regarding the involvement of the Wehrmacht in war crimes. British press coverage of the proceedings primarily comprised relatively brief reports without verbatim quotes. German press coverage was short on specifics,[478] preferring to highlight Kesselring's knowledge of the crimes,[479] but Italian media reports tended to be very detailed.[480]

Meanwhile, especially in Germany, the focus had clearly shifted to a different and higher level. The concept of "war as a crime" was stressed, together with the alleged betrayal of the German people by the country's generals, who—as vassals of Hitler—were complicit in the downfall of the Reich.[481] And in the United States, the press was, virtually without exception, either neutral or positive toward Kesselring: long excerpts from his testimony were cited verbatim, ensuring that his arguments reached a broad audience.[482] The moral aspects—the lessons learned from the trial—were also touched upon.[483] The Frankfurt-based *Neue Zeitung*, which was subject to American influence, editorialized:

> The end of Kesselring should also be the end of a disastrous intellectual philosophy. The end of Kesselring must be a rebirth of the philosophy of a clearly liberal, humane and Christian morality, which once allowed Germany's name to resound positively throughout the world. If Kesselring's end results in such a new beginning, then Germany may justifiably hope to have learnt a new morality based on the experience of pain which it not only inflicted on others, but also suffered itself, and may thus hope to reap a new respect.[484]

Italian newspapers noted with some satisfaction that the Kesselring trial had provided them with a "little Nuremberg" in terms of the rank and renown of both the defendant and the German and British legal teams.[485] The basic tenor of the coverage was that Italy had demanded this trial and Italy had now obtained satisfaction.

At the same time, the Italian attitude toward the Kesselring trial was also heavily marked by disenchantment, if not outright disappointment. Initially, the local communities affected had expected justice to be done and the guilty to be punished. At the beginning of the trial, the Italian press described individual massacres in detail in an effort to bring the crimes back into focus.[486] Some observers viewed this tactic as "malicious," claiming that the intention was "clearly to prepare the public for a guilty verdict."[487] However, the hope that these crimes would be expiated was disappointed—either because the indictment failed to include most of the cases or because it turned out that Kesselring could not be held to account for them. Many small communities felt (not without reason) that their cases would disappear into oblivion unless they were tagged onto a major British trial.

In addition to the dashed hope that numerous civilian deaths would somehow be expiated, another problem arose. Public opinion in Italy was by no means as homogeneous as a quick reading of the critical press would suggest. The country was split between "good Resistenza fighters" (the partisans) and evil "*Traditori*" (the traitors or collaborators who stayed with Mussolini). Laternser's private papers included a folder of letters received from Italians. Most correspondents had a positive attitude to Kesselring, illustrating a noteworthy aspect of the whole affair: the Kesselring trial attracted controversy even in Italy. Regardless of their authors' personal motivations, these letters reflected the extent to which Italian society was divided at the time. Disapproval of the former commander-in-chief's trial permeated all levels of society, although letters with a military focus predominated. One letter, for example, was from "an Italian soldier, not a Fascist, whose uniform still bears traces of German and Italian blood which was shed together while combating the red barbarism"; the author greeted "the man of courage whom you have the honor of defending."[488] Other military letters concerning this "unjust victor's trial" were signed in full—entailing a degree of risk for the signatories.[489] Laternser also received letters from local partisans' associations, criticizing the trial as "redundant" and stating that they would happily have dealt "summarily" with Kesselring as he had dealt with their dead comrades.[490]

The case of Albert Kesselring is symbolic of a war crimes policy that had already become detached from the initial guidelines issued by London and that—regardless of the verdict—resulted in the defendant enjoying the sympathy of the court, thus laying the foundations for eventual clemency and for countless campaigns for Kesselring's release. Some aspects of the trial are of particular interest. One is the fact that Laternser's defense strategy proved quite unsuccessful, for (in contrast to the IMT trial strategy) the focus was not on the defendant's complicity in the acts committed by a criminal state but rather on the issuing of specific orders—charges that proved far more difficult to refute. Unlike the situation in Nuremberg, it was insufficient merely to claim ignorance of the regime's criminal nature or to claim that one had not intended the regime's criminal policies to be implemented in a particular fashion.

Kesselring did benefit from the fact that the prosecution was subject to diverse—and sometimes contradictory—political guidelines. Three points stand out today: the trial's legal and moral dimension, its political implications and significance in making Kesselring both a martyr and a mythical figure, and the general implications of the Wehrmacht's behavior in Italy for the postwar debate. Since there was no written statement about the grounds for the judgment in the Kesselring trial and given the secret nature of the deliberations leading to the verdict, it is difficult today to arrive at an unambiguous legal assessment of the guilty verdicts imposed on Kesselring, Mackensen, and Mältzer. However, when one examines the course of the Kesselring trial—in particular, the closing defense and prosecution speeches, the judge advocate general's summing up, and the focus of witness questioning—it is clear that the whole issue of command responsibility (in the context of the commander's negligence) played only a fringe role in the proceedings.[491] The difficulties inherent in trying to separate moral and legal responsibility were revealed during the trial—despite the fact that the British had confined themselves to two charges in respect to which they believed they could demonstrate the defendant's concrete complicity. Nevertheless, the prosecution failed to prove that Kesselring had ordered force (at least beyond what was, unfortunately, normal at the time) to be used against innocent civilians rather than partisans or even that he had knowingly tolerated such violence. In addition, the fact that the commander-in-chief's conviction was required before the Italian program of trials could commence illustrated the enormous implications of the British trial program in terms of the politics of memory.

The war crimes trials also had repercussions beyond the purely legal evaluation of the crimes. Thanks to the manner in which the Kesselring trial was conducted and the pictures of the crimes that were drawn in the courtroom, the proceedings helped to mold Kesselring's image—an image that was to survive well into the postwar era. Historian Donald Bloxham stressed that trials had the potential to "re-shape the subject matter."[492] In the case of Kesselring, the image crafted during the trial was that of a "clean war on the southern front" in Italy, and the trial offered Laternser an opportunity to enhance and refine this image. He was assisted in this endeavor by the recurring theme of horror tales allegedly invented by the Italians. The myth of a "clean Wehrmacht" in Italy can thus be traced back to Laternser's trial strategy. This myth was to accompany Kesselring through all phases of his clemency campaign, and it was then incorporated into the collective war memory within German postwar society. Even today, it is repeatedly said that "it had been impossible to prove" Kesselring's involvement in war crimes.[493] This objection was taken on trust for many years. Until the 1990s, at least in Germany, it was thought that the evidence produced during the Kesselring trial put an end to the issue of war crimes in Italy. Yet at the same time, the public has rarely questioned the war crimes committed in the East.

Chapter 3

In Search of a New British Politics of Memory

The announcement of the Kesselring verdict in May 1947 was followed by the formation of pressure groups not only in Germany but also in the UK and Italy. These groups—which emerged simultaneously and spontaneously in the aftermath of the verdict—devised strategies to obtain Kesselring's freedom, and they initially operated quite independently of each other. The collective pressure exerted by such groups forced the British government to change tack on the war crimes issue, reshaping Britain's politics of memory. Thus, the change in Britain's policy on war criminals must first be examined in light of the various pressure groups lobbying for Kesselring's release. For that purpose, their arguments will be presented in the pages ahead, followed by an examination of how—once legal remedies had been exhausted in 1949—Kesselring's counsel, Hans Laternser, identified and consolidated the isolated efforts being made on Kesselring's behalf into a promising campaign that also incorporated the press. That campaign will be examined in more detail in the following chapter; the present chapter focuses on the change of course in Britain's Vergangenheitspolitik that was triggered by a shift in the balance of political forces relating to the war crimes issue. That shift ultimately resulted in Kesselring's reprieve.

The Domestic Political Debate Following the Verdict

To the British government's surprise, Kesselring's sentence caused outrage in England. It became apparent that the German field marshal enjoyed the sympathy of many of his former British foes. If, as already outlined, domestic political positions had been laboriously woven into an official British politics of memory in terms of the war crimes issue when the trials were being planned, that policy changed again after the verdict was announced—and after the emergence of open opposition in England. In this regard, the Italian position following Kesselring's sentence played an important role. The most obvious sign of this transformation was the decision made on July 4, 1947, by Lieutenant General Sir John Harding, British commander of Allied forces in the Mediterranean, to commute the death sentences imposed on Kesselring and Generals Mackensen and Mältzer to life imprisonment.

The repeal of Kesselring's death sentence was solely due to domestic pressure exerted in the UK. Opposition politicians—primarily Winston Churchill—used parliamentary questions to drum up political pressure for action on behalf of the German war criminals. Their campaign was taken up by the press, and the pressure increased to the point that the British government finally had to react. Numerous English politicians deplored "British victors' justice," church leaders preached reconciliation, and senior British officers raised their voices to praise Kesselring's military skill. They were all given plenty of media coverage, thus creating the British version of the "upright and fair Italian theater of war" image. In addition, they triggered a debate on the very purpose of war crimes trials—a bitter debate that continued to rage in England until Kesselring's release in 1952.

The Commutation of the Death Sentence

The different English positions can be assigned to distinct groups of individuals. The judge advocate general and his advisers in the War Office argued for the death sentence to be carried out, just as they had previously argued for the trials to be held. Foreign Secretary Ernest Bevin, however, had reservations rooted in the occupation policy toward Germany. Bevin's position thus coincided with that of the Opposition under Churchill. In the House of Lords, there was a broad front opposed to the Kesselring verdict and, indeed, to the war crimes trials themselves, and many church leaders, senior military figures, and war veterans went out on a limb, going so far as to call for an end to the trials.

The prime minister's files contain internal correspondence on the efforts to avert a death sentence for Kesselring. That correspondence clearly illustrates the turning point in the British policy on war criminals. There were two opposing camps. One camp included the leader of the Opposition, Winston Churchill, supported by Field Marshal Alexander. This camp was opposed by government offices represented by the prime minister's permanent secretaries, Foreign Secretary Ernest Bevin and Secretary of State for War Frederick Bellenger.[1] The government representatives argued that it was necessary to convict Kesselring in order to exact retribution for the war crimes that had been committed. In the Opposition, by contrast, there was a prevailing view that a military opponent who had fought "honestly" or "cleanly" on the battlefield could not be convicted of war crimes by the victors. Kesselring sympathizers in the military establishment were united in their criticism of the verdict from the very beginning.

Churchill performed a bridging function between the military and political establishments. He forcefully championed Kesselring's cause. On the day the sentence was announced, he telephoned Prime Minister Attlee to state that he was "much worried" about the sentence, which was "too much," especially when one considered "that Field Marshall Alexander said that on the whole Kesselring had fought fairly."[2] Churchill asked that the government explain its position again in Parliament. Church representatives also came to Churchill's aid, speaking out on Kesselring's behalf: in a letter to the editor published in both the *Times* and the *Daily Telegraph*, Bishop Golding-Bird asked, "Have we not had enough bloodshed?"[3] Further, he said that the "death penalty for war criminals, however heinous their crimes, should cease to be exacted." The bishop's plea clearly also referred to Kesselring.

As a former commander-in-chief himself, Churchill was familiar with military imperatives and did not wish to judge his former German opponents—whom he respected greatly—in purely legal terms. He saw the risk of turning martyrs into heroes and wanted to avoid encumbering British politics with a legacy of war crimes trials. This attitude accorded with his belief that "grass grows over the battlefield, but over the scaffold never."[4] He indirectly questioned the trials when he told Prime Minister Attlee: "It is in my opinion a matter of public policy whether the process of killing the leaders of the defeated enemy has not now exhausted any usefulness it may have had."[5] Referring to the protests in army circles against Kesselring's conviction, Churchill added the rider that "perhaps you will have noted Sir Oliver Leese's view." He thus indicated to Attlee that they were witnessing merely the early formation of a broad front of opposition.

In an interview given by General Leese on May 11, 1947, the commander of the British Eighth Army in Italy had said he was "very sad" to learn of the death sentence imposed on Kesselring, whom he described as a "gallant soldier." Leese went on to echo Field Marshal Alexander, who said that Kesselring had been an "extremely gallant soldier who fought his battles fairly and squarely."[6] Leese also referred to what he considered British victors' justice and warned that in a future war, legal opinion could be turned against the victors of today—a view that may have reflected a sense of unease regarding the Allied air war waged on German cities.[7]

Following this initial spontaneous reaction, Churchill—as illustrated by his correspondence—assumed leadership of the pro-Kesselring faction and developed a strategy to save the German field marshal.[8] Thus, for example, he turned to the former commander-in-chief in Italy, Field Marshal Alexander (then governor-general of Canada) and asked him to intervene on Kesselring's behalf.[9] In response, Earl Alexander appealed to Attlee, requesting that he pardon Kesselring.[10] Churchill also persuaded members of the House of Lords to vigorously defend Kesselring.[11] Their efforts, led by Viscount William de L'Isle and Dudley as the chief advocate of a pardon,[12] resulted in the House of Lords debating the Kesselring case on May 13, 1947. Lord de L'Isle noted that Kesselring's fate would have significance for both domestic policy and foreign policy in England: "Apart from purely judicial considerations, matters of high and important public interest are involved."[13]

Following Churchill's intervention, coupled with Field Marshal Alexander's telegram and the question raised in the House of Lords, a sense of unease started to spread within government circles. War Office personnel contacted the Foreign Office to ask how matters should proceed.[14] In an internal memorandum, the War Office expressed concerns that the verdict could have a negative impact on Britain's international reputation: "If the sentence of death is confirmed, and if Kesselring has to be shot, it is, of course, undesirable from the point of view of the law and from the point of view of humanity that there should be a political discussion about it. In the circumstances, however, it is probably unavoidable."[15]

The Italian position also had a direct influence on British war crimes policy when it came to deciding on a venue: as it transpired, it would actually be impossible to sentence Kesselring to death in Italy. Pursuant to an inquiry from the Foreign Ministry in Rome, the Italian military prosecutor stated that Italian law would preclude "imposing the death penalty on Kesselring in view of the evidence submitted," and this finding would also apply to Mackensen and Mältzer. The death penalty could only be imposed for "premeditated crimes," such as those with which Herbert Kappler was charged, since such crimes had been explicitly exempted when the death penalty was abolished.[16] It also appeared that Italy was unwilling to assume any responsibility for the verdict of the British military tribunal and, further, that it wanted the British to bear sole responsibility for enforcement of that verdict. The Italian government refused to execute Kesselring because the death penalty was considered a "Fascist practice" and had been abolished in Italy in 1944.

The British were extremely vexed by the attitude of the Italians,[17] for the sentences had partly been imposed to meet the expectations of the Italian public and to make the Allied occupation of Italy easier. British officials now faced a dilemma. To maintain their credibility, they had to devise a feasible course of action that would unite the three disparate positions. They had to succeed in bringing together the Italian public's demand for punishment of German war criminals, the Italian government's refusal to carry out the execution, and the British public's reluctance to see the death sentence executed.

The shift in policy was also due to the pressure exerted by British public opinion. The *New York Times* took note of the movement in the British press to come to Kesselring's aid.[18] The sympathetic British media campaign on the former field marshal's behalf, which started with news reports on his mental and physical state,[19] inadvertently metamorphosed into a debate on the purpose of war crimes trials in general. Thus, for example, the *Continental Daily Mail* provocatively asked, "Will it help to shoot Kesselring?" and it commented on the whole issue of "soldiers and obedience." For the first time, victors were charged with sitting in judgment: "If we are to be consistent, i.e., if the rule of law is really to be brought in, it is absurd to confine accusations, as now, to ex-enemy officers. Were there no reprisals, no breaches of the laws of war on the Allied side?"[20]

In the *Sunday Chronicle*, Milton Shulman addressed the concept of delayed punishment and argued strongly that German officers did not have a "moral choice" between obedience and disobedience during the war. He contended that in view of what was then known about Kesselring's conduct of the Italian campaign, one could assert he had not played an active part on his own initiative in planning the crimes of which he was convicted; Shulman pointed out that Kesselring had neither drafted nor drawn up the order that resulted in the Fosse Ardeatine massacre.[21] Shulman called for the death penalty to be commuted to imprisonment, and he concluded: "The problem which Nuremberg and the subsequent war crimes trials has still left confused and unsolved is the determination of exactly what rules and standards a soldier must conform to in order to avoid being branded as a war criminal internationally or as a traitor nationally."

The letters-to-the-editor pages of British newspapers were dominated by contributions questioning the purpose of such trials and demanding that Britain cease its support for such proceedings. For instance, Denis Johnston, former British war correspondent in Italy, wrote to the *Times* warning that "at the end of the next war, this fatal principle of common responsibility may be applied to us."[22] Another writer argued that an end should be put to the trials in view of Britain's own war crimes.[23] Letter writers charged British policy not only with pursuing victor's justice but also with arbitrariness. One reader, writing to the *Daily Telegraph*, surmised that "Göring, Ribbentrop and the other star felons had the worst possible luck, because if their trials could have been deferred until now they might have been gaoled for life." The same writer also noted that "in the Continental countries, where the memories of the war years are still very grim, there will be little support for such a queer notion that the calendar should get the better of justice."[24]

Randolph Churchill, a member of Parliament (MP) and son of the former prime minister, came to his father's aid, adding fuel to the debate with a letter to the *Daily Telegraph*. Published under the provocative heading "Need Mercy Be Denied?" the letter borrowed from Christian rhetoric and concepts of forgiveness and stated, "It is shameful that two years after Germany unconditionally surrendered we should still be hounding down our defeated and defenseless foes."[25] Churchill concluded his letter with a vehement demand for the churches to take a position on the issue from the perspective of "the Christian ethic."[26]

But not all were content to forget the past. Thus, a letter published in the *Daily Telegraph* on May 16 asked whether Field Marshal Alexander's view that Kesselring had fought fairly excused the fact that he "murdered 336 people."[27] Another reader criticized the military's loyalty to Kesselring, arguing that solidarity among soldiers had gone too far in this case: "By their protests they are condoning the attitude that, no matter how brutal an order is, it must be carried out."[28] A writer to the *Times* questioned whether "crimes should go unpunished if committed by generals in wartime" and remarked that the "real question is: are we to have legal precedents for punishing international crime?"[29] It is noteworthy that the private opinions expressed in these readers' letters were neither taken up nor developed by any public figures. It was therefore easy for Randolph Churchill to dismiss the criticism of his stance, countering it with the argument that the question of excusing monstrous acts was "not the issue" and that one should rather consider whether it was desirable "as a Christian people [to continue] in cold blood a policy of vengeance."[30] He thereby tossed the ball back into the political court.

How was the British politics of memory to be reshaped in terms of the war crimes issue? The legal advice from the office of the judge advocate general was clear: the verdict was final and the sentence justified because Kesselring was guilty of the crimes with which he had been charged.[31] The Royal Warrant issued in August 1945 severely limited the legal remedies open to Kesselring in appealing the verdict. Sir Hartley Shawcross, British chief prosecutor at Nuremberg, was known for his incorruptible and uncompromising attitude toward suspected war criminals. Although Shawcross believed that the only avenue open in the Kesselring case was a royal pardon, he noted that only British subjects could petition the king for mercy.[32] In this regard, he felt that intervention on Kesselring's behalf by Alexander and Churchill would carry particular weight with Attlee. Shawcross pleaded with Bellenger, as secretary of state for war, to use his power to intervene in the decision and, if necessary, oppose the Mediterranean commander-in-chief in respect to the death sentence. Shawcross argued that a decision to grant a pardon could only represent a political—rather than a legal—solution to the Kesselring problem and that such a responsibility "should not be laid wholly on the shoulders of the Commander-in-Chief."[33]

However, regardless of the judge advocate general's view, the government had decided to change its policy on the war crimes issue. There was a tinge of bitterness in Bellenger's comment to Bevin: "If we must accept that it is quite definite that the death sentence will not be carried out in the case of any war criminals we hand over to the Italians for trial it is clearly a matter for serious and urgent consideration whether any of the death sentences awarded by our Courts in Italy should be carried out."[34]

Bellenger advocated a severe punishment policy, and as secretary of state for war, he had the power to grant pardons in controversial cases.[35] Although he stressed he was "most reluctant" to intervene further to influence the decision of General Harding or to use his own power to commute the sentences, he made it clear that he understood the demands of the changed political environment.[36] Writing to Foreign Secretary Ernest Bevin, Bellenger mentioned the option of commuting the death sentences imposed on Mackensen and Mältzer to life imprisonment and handing Generals Crasemann and Simon over for trial by the Italian courts. In a telling phrase indicating his appreciation of the new situation, he wrote: "I assume that you would also advocate commutation of the death sentence just passed on Field Marshal Kesselring." The War Office then notified General Harding's Mediterranean headquarters that there would be no more British death sentences and that those already imposed would be commuted to life imprisonment.[37] Consequently, there was a conflict between the judge advocate general's position—which held that Kesselring was guilty—and the government's political decision to exercise clemency.

In effect, Harding had been authorized by two separate government departments pursuing conflicting interests to either execute or revoke the sentences. His decision was worthy of Solomon: he confirmed the guilty verdicts but commuted the death sentences to life imprisonment.[38] Harding justified his decision by stating that, based on his "own personal knowledge" and on Field Marshal Alexander's statement, he felt certain Kesselring had fought cleanly and fairly and displayed a sense of responsibility to the Italian civilian population and Italian culture "except for the two instances forming the subject of the charges." Making no bones about his military perspective, Harding also argued that, in view of the Rome attacks and the order issued by Hitler, Kesselring was compelled to take countermeasures so as not to put his troops' safety at risk. In addition, Harding noted that the legal basis for reprisals was not even clearly defined in the British military manual.[39] Although these extenuating circumstances also applied to Mackensen and Mältzer, Harding stressed his personal view that, as military commander of Rome, Mältzer would have been involved in supervising the massacre. However, Harding did not feel that any greater blame could be attached to the three accused in light of the fact that the person directly responsible—Herbert Kappler—had not yet been put on trial. "I cannot reconcile it with my conscience," he stated, "to confirm the sentence of death on Kesselring, Mackensen and Mältzer while there is the slightest possibility that Kappler may be awarded a lesser penalty, and I believe that possibility exists."[40]

At the same time, Harding noted that it would be not only legally impossible but also "contrary to the dictates of humanity" to defer a final decision on the Kesselring, Mackensen, and Mältzer cases until judgment had been passed on Kappler. Commutation was thus the only way out of Harding's—and the government's—dilemma.[41] The reasons given by Harding when arguing for the death penalty to be set aside laid the foundation for the myth of the innocent Field Marshal Kesselring who was unjustly condemned—a myth that quickly gained currency in the Anglo-Saxon world.[42]

The Final British Trial: The Manstein Case

Shortly after the verdict was announced, Kesselring was already considered innocent by large sections of the British political establishment, media, and public. In view of the fact that the British military tribunal had produced comprehensive evidence of his guilt just a few months earlier, this shift in public opinion was remarkable. That shift forced the British government to change tack in terms of its Vergangenheitspolitik.

The London government was extremely relieved to find that Harding's decision attracted relatively little criticism in Italy. Admittedly, members of the local Brescia group of the Associazione Nazionale Partigiani d'Italia (National Partisan's Association) made their anger at the commutation of Kesselring's sentence known to the Allied headquarters in Padua, but that was the only objection to reach London, indicating that there was no organized campaign of protest in Italy.[43] There were merely a few isolated angry comments in the Italian press. For example, *Il Tempo* noted that the Italian general Nicola Bellomo had been "executed for shooting a single Briton," whereas Kesselring—who had "hundreds of Italians" on his conscience—was now being spared.[44] The charge was that the government was using a double standard that placed less value on Italian lives. Citing this article and referring to Kesselring, the *New York Times* observed that the number of Italian victims "was apparently not sufficient to have him executed."[45]

The validity of the British war crimes trials at home was shattered by the tenor of domestic discourse as well as by the debates in the House of Lords.

On January 26, 1948, the office of the judge advocate general sent a telegram to the War Crimes Group/South East Europe, which was still busy gathering evidence. In an attempt to mollify the War Crimes Group, the telegram stated that the Foreign Office was "still" addressing the basic issue of "war crimes trials for German generals who committed crimes against Italians."[46] However, by February 19, 1948—one year after the public furor of the Kesselring trial—a resigned judge advocate general had capitulated. Pointing out that the matter of a continuation of the trials had been raised with the Foreign Office on December 10, 1947 (and that his office had been pressing for a reply ever since), he noted the decision was "that no Germans will in future be tried by British Military Courts for war crimes committed against Italian victims."[47] The rug had been pulled out from under British prosecutors' feet. The moral purpose of these trials had been diluted by protests at home, and the country felt it could no longer tie up the administrative manpower required to gather evidence and conduct the trials.

In view of these circumstances, all of which signaled a clear switch in the war crimes policy being pursued by London, the final British war crimes trial against Erich von Manstein degenerated into farce. From the autumn of 1947, the controversy surrounding the last planned trial ensured that the whole matter of war crimes once again dominated the front pages. It was evident that the issue of British war crimes policy was no closer to a resolution. Domestic British conflicts of interest, as well as tensions within the alliance relating to the politics of memory, were brought to the fore again during the public discourse in advance of this trial.

Thanks to American preparations for the planned trial of senior Wehrmacht High Command officers, including Field Marshal Ritter von Leeb and others (known as Case 12), evidence had surfaced in 1947 incriminating high-ranking German military figures who had been in British custody since 1945.[48] The officers concerned were Erich von Manstein, Walter von Brauchitsch, Gerd von Rundstedt, and Adolf Strauss. Justice Telford Taylor suggested to Hartley Shawcross that the British should send their four prisoners to be included in the trial being conducted by the Americans. He also pointed to the "moral obligation" the Allies had to exact retribution for German crimes, specifically those committed on the eastern front. This demand forced the hand of the British government. The imperative for solidarity among the Allies placed a question mark over London's decision to cease holding war crimes trials. Foreign Secretary Bevin insisted that Britain would conduct the final scheduled trial and then terminate the trial program. Once War Secretary Bellenger had seen the documentary evidence, which he was persuaded provided ample justification for legal proceedings, he too reluctantly agreed. However, he predicted that this move would entail a political loss of face at home and that it would be difficult to explain the trial to the British public: "We were all hoping that there would be no more of these trials of German Generals."[49] Bellenger felt that the best solution would be to hand the four men over to the Americans to be dealt with during the Case 12 trial.

The decision met with unexpected opposition from the British military governor in Germany, Sir Sholto Douglas, whose position was decidedly pro-German. He did not equivocate when arguing for the planned trial to be abandoned:

> We know that the Americans will make use of a lot of evidence of a very dubious character. Yet we are apparently prepared to send these men, including one who is seventy-three, to trial by the Americans. I frankly do not like this. I feel that if the Americans wish to be critical about our inaction in trying war criminals, I should prefer that they should continue to criticize rather than that we should commit an injustice in order to avoid their criticism.[50]

Internal soundings of the American military by General Lucius Clay, the military governor in Germany, produced surprising results: it appeared that the U.S. military establishment was also reluctant to hold the Wehrmacht High Command trials. Clay bluntly informed the British representative, Sir Brian Robertson, that he did not believe the generals should be put on trial and said he hoped "we [the Americans] would come to the conclusion that we would not try them either."[51] Robertson then confidentially informed the Foreign Office that he thought one could safely put the planned Manstein trial on ice without running the risk of any serious criticism from the Americans. However, Taylor—the most prominent of that group of Nuremberg lawyers who were determined to see their moral obligation to prosecute war crimes through to the end—continued to exert pressure on Shawcross. Shawcross, in turn, pressed Foreign Secretary Bevin to reach a decision. Britain's moral responsibility was also emphasized in Parliament. MPs felt that too many ordinary German soldiers had been punished for senior commanders at the eastern front to be allowed to get off scot-free. Bevin also could not expect any help from the cabinet in reaching a decision: indeed, cabinet members expressed reservations about the trial and the anticipated difficulties in presenting it to the public. Bevin's legal advisers counseled caution as well, since there was no guarantee that the German generals would actually be convicted.[52] Bevin was forced to take a political decision. In the event, his decision that the trial should go ahead ran counter to the recommendations of his military and legal advisers.

Unexpected difficulties arose once it became obvious that three of the accused might be released to go home for health reasons, in which case, the fourth general—Manstein—would also be released, on the grounds of equal treatment ("all four or none"). The Soviet authorities had filed an extradition request for Manstein and Rundstedt, and the Americans wanted them—together with Brauchitsch—to testify as witnesses at Nuremberg. Therefore, the only means of protecting the generals was to put them on trial in a British court. The British judge advocate general advanced a similar argument with regard to having the generals testify: there would be a credibility gap if the British canceled their own trial "for medical reasons" and then sent the three generals to testify at Nuremberg, where they would "probably incriminate themselves." The government decided to schedule the official end of the British war crimes trials for September 1, 1948, and to commence preparations for the final trial. However, it was agreed privately that those preparations should be dragged out until September,[53] after which there would be no more trials.

Even though the reasons given by the Foreign Office were rather more circumspect, Shawcross was extremely critical of the decision, feeling that military interests dominated British policy and had prevailed on this occasion. He noted bitterly that the victims were not "simply Russians and Poles" and that a different conclusion would have been reached if Britain's own interests were at stake. He issued a vehement appeal in which he argued that British credibility had to be at the center of the war crimes policy.[54] The cabinet took the side of the German generals, rejecting Shawcross's charge of delay out of hand. The accused officers were taken to the British POW camp in Munsterlager, and the order was given to start preparing for the trial.

The British military governor, Sir Brian Robertson, was furious that the decision to hold the trial had, after all, been made without consulting him, especially in view of the current difficult situation, for the Cold War had been brought to a new level of intensity by the Berlin blockade. He pointed out that it was not in Britain's interest "for the occupying power to be identified with war crimes trials over three years after the German capitulation."[55] The press became aware of Robertson's criticism, and the "trial of the generals" became the subject of an increasing number of parliamentary questions. In view of the mounting pressure, Bevin felt constrained to resubmit the issue to the cabinet for a decision.[56] Although the cabinet reaffirmed its decision to hold the trial in view of its significance for Britain's political credibility, it proved impossible to silence the criticism at home. Matters were complicated by the deteriorating health of two of the accused, Rundstedt and Strauss, who were certified as unfit to stand trial by military doctors in Munsterlager. Bellenger's successor in the War Office, Emanuel Shinwell, felt that the doctors' decision "was extremely embarrassing from [a] political and international point of view."[57]

It became increasingly obvious that the military lobby seeking an end to the war crimes trials would win the argument. With the enthusiastic support of sections of the press, Winston Churchill—as leader of the Opposition—spearheaded the political criticism of the government's war crimes trials. He fulminated that "revenge is, of all satisfactions, the most costly and long drawn out; retributive persecution is, of all policies, the most pernicious. Our policy, subject to the exceptional cases I have mentioned, should henceforward be to draw the sponge across the crimes and horrors of the past—hard as that might be—and look for the sake of all our salvation toward the future."[58]

In a phrase that caught the media's attention, Churchill termed the planned trial an "act of administrative and political stupidity,"[59] and he noted that German concurrence in the nascent Cold War was of a certain significance. He ostentatiously joined a public drive for donations to help pay for a lawyer for Erich von Manstein. This move caused particular outrage in the Soviet Union, given that the Soviets had hoped to try Manstein themselves.[60]

On May 5, 1949, during a House of Lords debate on the war crimes issue, the bishop of Chichester, George Bell, argued for the unconditional release of the German officers: "After all this time, at this distance from the Moscow Declaration, after four years of imprisonment, let them go."[61] He was supported by Lord Maurice Hankey.[62] Even the former lord chancellor, Viscount John Simon, pointed to the educational effect of the British war crimes trials—an effect that he claimed had already been achieved. He asked what advantage could be gained by making an example of Manstein yet again.[63] The tenor of the House of Lords debate clearly reflected Hankey's view that justice was being confused with revenge. The debate caused Bevin to revisit the war crimes issues with his American and French colleagues, with whom he devised a common position. It was decided that, with the exception of the Manstein case, Britain would not hold any further war crimes trials. In future, they agreed, crimes against humanity would be tried solely before German courts, and extradition requests would be dealt with on a case-by-case basis.[64]

The Manstein trial, which finally took place from August to December 1949, was neither a legal nor a political success.[65] Although the accused was sentenced to eighteen years of imprisonment, his British defense counsel, Reginald Paget, was able to refute several of the counts in the indictment.

Manstein was cleared of eight of the original seventeen counts due to insufficient evidence, and just two of the counts were upheld in their original form. The entire trial was held against a background of unremitting criticism back in Britain, and it became clear that there was now a united front of British opposition to the war crimes trials more broadly. British politicians had never been able to muster much enthusiasm for punishing their wartime foes,[66] and many felt that justice had already been served by the Nuremberg trials. Major Colin Dalrymple, a Venice-based liaison officer sympathetic to Kesselring, accurately described the public mood. Dalrymple asserted that the Manstein trial was extremely unpopular in England because it had been severely delayed, and he noted that there had even been reservations concerning the Venice trial.[67] This assessment presaged the subsequent link drawn between Kesselring's fate and that of Manstein. Press coverage of the "Werl Generals" also tended to focus on the two "innocent" military icons, Kesselring and Manstein.[68]

The political reservations expressed by Churchill when arguing against convicting Manstein even appear to have struck a chord with the judges: immediately before pronouncing judgment, the British presiding officer, Lieutenant General Frank Simpson, was quoted as saying that, for the first time in his life, he had been constrained to act contrary to his conviction. He went on to say that had he been in Kesselring's situation, he could only have acted the same way. Nonetheless, he continued, he had had no choice but to convict Kesselring given prevailing circumstances.[69] Such a statement by a British jurist would have been unthinkable during any of the previous trials. In making his remarks, Simpson was not only criticizing the British politics of memory but also implying that the trial had not been fair.

The fact that the final British war crimes trial took place at all is due to the personal commitment of the foreign secretary, Ernest Bevin.[70] He was convinced that Manstein was a genuine war criminal, and he hoped that General Robertson would not reduce his sentence.[71] Sir Hartley Shawcross was also appalled at the very idea that sentences could be reviewed as a result of the changed political environment.[72] Nevertheless, in his capacity as commander-in-chief of the British Army of the Rhine (BAOR), Sir Brian Robertson reduced Manstein's sentence to twelve years. He justified his decision by referring to the unique nature of conditions on the eastern front and stating that Russian crimes remained unpunished. He also criticized the fact that none of the jury members had served in the field, which meant they were unable to understand the dilemmas facing a commander-in-chief.[73]

The decision that Britain would no longer try those accused of committing crimes against nationals of other countries was not reached in isolation:

rather, the decision was part of an Allied consensus. In 1949, the Americans also decided that the so-called Case 11 would be the last of those held in the aftermath of Nuremberg.[74] (Also known as the Ministries Case, this omnibus trial included senior diplomats and others.) Occupation policy considerations formed the basis for the decision.

This shift in policy could also be detected in the utterances of individual British officials. For example, as he left Germany after many years as military governor, Sir Brian Robertson's verdict on those war criminals still in custody was significantly more restrained than the views he expressed at the start of his governorship. Comments Robertson made to Sir Ivone Kirkpatrick clearly illustrated the shift in British policy. He emphasized the educational aspect of the war crimes trials:

> I quite agree that Manstein is probably a very bad man and deserves no special consideration. However, punishment is not awarded in order to take revenge on a criminal but in order to create an impression on the rest of the population and thereby to prevent crimes of a similar nature in the future. The question, therefore, is not so much whether Manstein deserves a life sentence as whether such a sentence will create a beneficial impression on the Germans. My own view is that it will tend to make Manstein a martyr to German eyes. I believe, on the contrary, that we could create a good impression by a reduction of sentence coupled with a public statement of Manstein's crimes.[75]

"Reeducation" was to be the guiding principle behind the new British line. Victors' justice, with its attendant stigma, was to be a thing of the past. Revenge was to be replaced by deterrence. And the public was to be educated about crimes that, if they were the subject of purely academic debate rather than of criminal prosecution, would (it was feared) leave the victims without the satisfaction of having their day in court. Yet times had changed. The reeducation line might have played well with the public in 1945, when the overriding concern was to prevent a repeat of the past, but by 1949, the educational value of the trials carried less weight than concerns about the potential domestic and international damage the British government might suffer as a result of protests and demonstrations of solidarity with the accused.

The shift in the British politics of memory was felt immediately. The doubts were reflected in the Review Board convened to examine the British war crimes trials. Chaired by General Wade, it delivered its report at the end of 1949, recommending that—on principle—the verdicts should not be questioned and advising against reviewing the trial files.[76] General Wade had privately advocated a review of Kesselring's sentence, since "Kesselring was innocent of the charge on which he was convicted."[77] He felt that there was a particular lack of clarity surrounding the former field marshal's involvement in the Fosse Ardeatine massacre. The Review Board's report prompted misgivings in the British legal department in Germany: in view of the report's conclusions, how could the high commissioner's legal advisers, Brown and Moller, formulate a rejection of Laternser's 1949 petition? Writing to the chief legal officer of the British land commissioner's office in Düsseldorf, Moller confirmed that officials "intended to commence a comprehensive review of the sentences by way of clemency later in the year when the present review of long term sentences is completed."[78] In light of the edict that British trials should not be questioned under any circumstances, this position represented an initial concession.

Manstein's defense counsel, Reginald Paget, was quick to recognize and take advantage of the new mood. In a book recounting his experiences during the Manstein trial, he was one of the first to publicly link the victors' justice argument with a possible German contribution to Allied defenses—something that was already being discussed behind closed doors: "If Western Europe is to be defensible, these decent soldiers must be our comrades. It is not within the power of conquerors to condemn the vanquished."[79]

In conclusion, it should be noted that the conviction of German war criminals was never a priority in terms of the British politics of memory.[80] Those advocating convictions were based in the Foreign Office, whereas most of those opposing convictions could be found in the War Office. Solidarity with the erstwhile German enemy was thus most apparent in military circles.[81] It is not surprising, then, that the critics of Britain's former Vergangenheitspolitik included the British military governor of Germany, Sir Brian Robertson. The Attlee government, despite being a partner in initiating the war crimes trials and zealously defending the concept of retribution, adopted a conciliatory approach not only with regard to the Kesselring case but also during the subsequent debate surrounding the Manstein trial. This fact can be explained by the shift in British public opinion in favor of the German generals—a shift to which the British government could not remain indifferent.

In terms of domestic policy, any debate surrounding a convicted German war criminal was regarded as potentially dangerous and undesirable.[82] It was important to ensure that those potential voters who had fought against Kesselring in the war and formed their own (positive) view of him were not dismissed as a minority and neglected. For the veterans, what was at stake was not simply Kesselring's life but the reputation of the Allied armies that had fought the Wehrmacht in Italy, particularly the British Eighth Army. There was also a risk that any close examination of Kesselring's conduct of the Italian campaign would also shine a spotlight on British conduct in the Italian theater—on Britain's provision of weapons and ammunition to the partisans and on its dealings with the Italian civilian population. Even in England, there was no real interest in seriously probing the history of the Italian campaign. Thus, the British narrative of a clean and fair Italian theater of war came to be written.

Marching Separately, Attacking Jointly: German Efforts to Secure Kesselring's Release, 1947–1949

The domestic policy factors that triggered a policy shift in the UK were aggravated by the efforts of various interest groups in Germany. While Laternser was pursuing Kesselring's case through legal channels, various private individuals—primarily Kesselring's former subordinates—attempted to petition the British authorities on his behalf; at the same time, they were also taking advantage of personal contacts with the Allies to secure favors for the former field marshal. Press reports of the poor prison conditions sometimes endured by Kesselring generated public sympathy. Thanks to the constant repetition of such reports, that sympathy, in turn, helped rework the image of a war criminal. The impression generated was that of a "military gentleman" languishing behind bars. The impression was reinforced by Kesselring's own self-portrayal in his contributions to the American Historical Division, preparing the ground for an organized campaign that could no longer be ignored by the British political establishment.

The attorney Hans Laternser played a pivotal role in the clemency campaign. By advancing new and legally persuasive evidence, he hoped to have his client's case reopened. In pursuit of this aim, he submitted a petition on Kesselring's behalf immediately after the sentence was pronounced, in 1947, and again in 1948. Kesselring was transferred to Werl Prison in October 1947, and on October 23, Laternser was officially instructed to represent further the interests of all three men convicted of war crimes in Italy: Kesselring, Mackensen, and Mältzer.[83] Laternser started preparing his second petition, gathering extensive material in the process.[84] The petition included a request for the case to be reopened, and it was submitted to the British War Office on March 26, 1949. Laternser also maintained close contact with other attorneys who had been involved in war crimes trials, hoping to develop a joint strategy to have the case reopened.[85]

Kesselring had prepared a draft of the petition seeking to have his case reopened.[86] Wholly caught up in his historical mission, he wrote to Laternser,

"In this regard I have focused not only on our own proceedings, but on the war crimes trials in general. I have spoken with many convicted prisoners in Wolfsberg and Werl,[87] and have discussed their individual cases, yet common sense makes it impossible to understand these verdicts."[88] Once again resorting to military terminology and refining the notion of a "final battle," Kesselring concluded that, in his view, war crimes trials constituted a form of "illegal warfare."[89] He had discussed and agreed on the wording of his brief with Mackensen and Mältzer (who were also being held in Wolfsberg and were later jointly transferred to Werl Prison in Westphalia), and they had added their own comments. Mackensen and Mältzer had also enclosed handwritten statements protesting their innocence,[90] and they insisted that Judge Advocate General C. L. Stirling should be barred from presiding over any retrial on the grounds of bias.[91]

In January 1948, Laternser visited Werl for the first time, where (unusually) he met all three of his clients.[92] They spent three hours drafting the second petition and discussing it in minute detail. As in the first petition, their strategy focused on Laternser's thesis that, because responsibility for shooting the hostages had been transferred to the SD, the Wehrmacht had no further involvement in the matter. The attorney also hoped to integrate into the second petition his opening and closing speeches on behalf of Field Marshal von List (one of the defendants in the subsequent 1948 Nuremberg proceedings against the "South-Eastern Generals," known as Case 7), since that case had also involved hostage shootings.[93] He received a forty-page draft from Kesselring. Mackensen had written six pages, and Mältzer contributed a further ten to the effort. Kesselring's strategy was to obtain the immediate release of Mackensen and Mältzer on the grounds of "insufficient competency."[94] As far as his own case was concerned, he was seeking mitigation of his sentence on the grounds outlined by Laternser. Kesselring hoped that the controversial case of General Fritz Hildemann—a fellow inmate in Werl—would lead to his own case being reopened.[95]

Private Interventions on Kesselring's Behalf before His Imprisonment in Werl

Quite apart from Dr. Laternser's legal efforts to secure a review of Kesselring's case, various private individuals were attempting to intervene on the former field marshal's behalf. These interventions were initially spontaneous, but they were subsequently coordinated by Laternser as part of a major campaign. Kesselring's General Staff officers, mainly Beelitz, Westphal, and other former comrades-in-arms,[96] who were then being held in various POW camps, were determined to "fight on" and "save the field marshal's life."[97] Both through letters[98] and in person following their release,[99] these officers disseminated not only their personal view of their revered commander but also their view of what they regarded as the discriminatory treatment Kesselring received at the hands of the British in Venice. In this way, they helped to lay the foundations for the Kesselring myth in Germany.

Immediately following the verdict, former Wehrmacht officers submitted a wave of clemency petitions on Kesselring's behalf; this approach was in line with the reaction following other verdicts in Nuremberg. Beelitz and Westphal petitioned King George VI, asking that the verdict not be confirmed.[100] Their document was signed by the last two officers commanding the Tenth and Fourteenth Armies, Generals Lemelsen and Herr, and it had been translated into English by Heinrich Melzer, a military interpreter who had also acted for the defense during the Venice trial.[101] An identical petition was submitted to the Vatican.[102] The Historical Division in London received clemency petitions on Kesselring's behalf from former Luftwaffe officers,[103] and the former field marshal's German colleagues working for the Historical Division in Garmisch also raised their voices.[104] A telegram was received from the American POW camp in Allendorf,[105] signed by Field Marshal von Leeb—the oldest officer interned in the camp—and Generaloberst Johannes Blaskowitz, the camp supervisor.

Siegfried Westphal was particularly committed to Kesselring's cause. Both the meticulous preparation and the trial strategy itself can be attributed, in part, to his thorough planning—planning that was always carefully coordinated with Kesselring's attorney, Hans Laternser. Westphal had good reason to do all in his power to assist his former commander-in-chief: after all, the British had originally planned to bring the relevant General Staff chiefs to trial as well. With what we know today, it is clear that Westphal—as chief of General Staff, South-Western Command—was the officer who transmitted the order to carry out the massacre in the Fosse Ardeatine. And it is possible that Kesselring's primary objective in generously assuming responsibility for the Fosse Ardeatine massacre was to shield Westphal. In return, it is likely that Westphal made every conceivable effort to save Kesselring.

Liny Kesselring, the field marshal's wife, also submitted an appeal. Writing "as a woman," she addressed her plea directly to Queen Elizabeth, wife of George VI. As well as stressing the high regard in which her husband was held by British officers, she noted that the verdict had not been universally well received in Italy, "even though it was Italians who were affected by my husband's measures."[106]

From the beginning, Kesselring's attorney, Hans Laternser, tried to coordinate any clemency appeals submitted on behalf of his client. By ensuring that such appeals were submitted simultaneously with his own initial petition, he hoped that a coordinated campaign would develop. This strategy was strikingly illustrated by the appeal submitted by the Jesuit priest Alfons Hiemer (who had been part of Kesselring's defense team) to Pope Pius XII. Father Hiemer asked the pope to intervene because Kesselring's trial had never been about the former field marshal himself but rather involved "the fate of many other generals, the honor of the German officer corps as a whole and, indeed, the honor of all officers who loyally performed their soldierly duty."[107] Surviving correspondence indicates that Laternser completely reworded Hiemer's letter, enclosing his own closing speech from the Venice trial, which "clearly shows Kesselring's innocence."[108] He also stressed that the petition he would be submitting during the next few days to protest against "the legally unsafe verdict" was "well-founded."

Thus, just a few days after sentence had been pronounced on Kesselring, Laternser had introduced what was to become a recurring theme: that of victors' justice. Explaining the purpose of his letter, he wrote that the pope's intervention would "help set aside a verdict which many people consider unjust, and would also be of great value to many other German generals who appear to be facing a similar fate in the courts of various countries because of actions which, as soldiers, they were duty-bound to perform."[109] Here, Laternser was touching on another recurring theme: soldiers who, in carrying out criminal orders, were merely doing their duty. In this way, he thus ensured that crime was isolated from context and reduced to nothing more than the performance of a soldierly duty. By stressing the significance of a papal intervention in this case—an intervention that would set a precedent—Laternser hoped to persuade Pope Pius of the matter's magnitude.

His strategy bore fruit. The pope is thought to have appealed to George VI and General Harding seeking clemency for Kesselring,[110] and he would advocate on the former field marshal's behalf again.[111] Clearly, the Vatican was on Kesselring's side.

Media Coverage of Kesselring's Imprisonment

A selective analysis of press coverage indicates that once Kesselring's sentence had been pronounced, the German and English papers ceased reporting on war crimes committed in Italy. Instead, articles on Kesselring's imprisonment tended to depict the former field marshal as a pitiable figure languishing in jail. This media strategy proved successful—and it was a considerable annoyance to the British authorities. This fact is illustrated, for example, by the Christmas campaigns mounted by some major daily newspapers, whereby readers offered to spend Christmas behind bars so that the "innocent men of Werl" could spend the festive season in freedom. Thus, in December 1950, a "former German officer" offered to take Kesselring's place over the holiday,[112] and similar offers were made during subsequent years, primarily by veterans.[113] The British officials were taken aback by this proposal,[114] which they refused to entertain.[115]

Initially, there was little reason to feel sorry for Kesselring. On May 12, 1947, he was transferred to the British POW camp at Wolfsberg in Carinthia. The considerate treatment he enjoyed, both en route to Wolfsberg and in the camp itself,[116] encouraged him to believe that his sentence would not be confirmed: perhaps the whole trial had simply been a huge mistake.[117] He had a cell to himself, was allowed to read newspapers, and took frequent strolls.[118] He remarked gratefully on the "excellent English food," and he attended the regular theater performances staged in Wolfsberg camp to entertain the prisoners.[119] Writing about the camp, he noted that he was met everywhere with "gratifying understanding."[120] He also resumed his work on the history of the war for the Historical Division, which he found fulfilling.[121] Although escape plans were discussed in the camp, these were quickly dismissed,[122] but the recurring escape rumors certainly enhanced Kesselring's image. As the highest-ranking Wehrmacht officer convicted of war crimes, there was a perception that he was to be saved from victors' justice.

On October 22, 1947, Kesselring, Mackensen, and Mältzer were transferred to the British military prison in the Westphalian town of Werl. The former field marshal was humiliated by the initial examination and prisoner registration procedure, which included fingerprinting.[123] His social downfall was now plain for all to see. During his first meeting with Laternser after the trial, Kesselring complained that he had ended up in prison and was being treated as a criminal like all the others. As Laternser put it, "He feels that the manner of his imprisonment does not in any way correspond with the position and respect which he has hitherto enjoyed."[124]

Yet there is no doubt that Kesselring received preferential treatment in Werl when compared with those convicted of "ordinary" crimes. He did not have to wear prison garb, he was accommodated in a single cell, and he had contact with his fellow prisoners; cell doors remained open during the day. Twice a day, prisoners were allowed to walk in the yard for three-quarters of an hour, and the prison authorities made it clear that the generals were free to occupy themselves by "writing historical works or otherwise, for example in the garden."[125] Kesselring received regular, albeit infrequent, visits from his wife,[126] and at the start of his sentence, he was examined by his former military physician, Professor Hans Bürkle de la Camp.[127] He had no difficulty meeting Liny in Bavaria when he was traveling to give testimony in Nuremberg, for example, during the Wehrmacht High Command trial during the autumn of 1948.[128] He was also granted five-day temporary release orders on several occasions, in 1948 and 1950 and twice during 1952. Like all the other inmates, he was able to attend prison concerts.

Kesselring's self-confidence was renewed in prison. Having appointed himself spokesperson for the other generals, he organized English lessons for the prisoners as early as May 1948.[129] In addition, he regularly attended Mass and maintained close contact with the prison chaplain, Father Victor Kleyer. However, he was not necessarily turning to religion, for Father Kleyer also played a secular role for the inmates of Werl. In fact, Kesselring's attorney, Dr. Hans Laternser, used Father Kleyer to circumvent censorship rules, sending him prohibited items such as newspaper cuttings or books[130] as well as money[131] and gifts intended for the prisoners: the chaplain's mail was not censored, and he had free access to the Werl inmates. Kesselring marked certain letters to Laternser with the note "only via our friend," especially when the letters dealt with press contacts, which were prohibited for prisoners.[132] For instance, in May 1950,[133] November 1950,[134] and February 1951, Kesselring received letters from the British interrogation officer Colonel Scotland through Father Kleyer.[135] These letters included information on Scotland's efforts to exert pressure on politicians and public opinion, with the aim of having Kesselring's case reopened.

Kesselring also attempted to generate press coverage of Werl Prison in order to increase the pressure on British authorities.[136] Initially, he arranged for Laternser to complain to Colonel Halse that Kesselring and his two subordinates were occupied in "glueing paper bags, counting needles and locksmithing."[137] In May 1948, Siegfried Westphal contacted the British military governor of North Rhine–Westphalia, General Sir Alec Bishop, on Kesselring's behalf, seeking an improvement in prison conditions.[138] Writing to the British military historian Sir Basil Liddell Hart, Westphal noted that Kesselring was suffering under the poor conditions at Werl: "I have heard that food is scarce, the cell damp and mail limited to receiving three letters a month, and his state of health is not good."[139] The hope was that Liddell Hart, on receiving this letter, would be moved to champion Kesselring's cause in the media.

The prison authorities realized that the prisoners' self-aggrandizement strategy—pursued by describing their situation in the most pitiable terms—could pose a problem. Accordingly, they attempted to improve prison conditions so as to avoid giving any grounds for complaint. Daily prison life entered a new phase following the report of the 1948 Commission of Enquiry chaired by Alec Bishop. Kesselring discovered with pleasure that the bars in the visiting room had been removed and that each prisoner was allowed to read one of the four approved daily newspapers.[140] In addition, with the arrival of their "seventh companion in misery,"[141] they were transferred from their damp cells into another wing of the prison.[142] There, they were allowed to move freely around the section, which was dubbed the "generals' wing." However, the new prison commander, Lieutenant Colonel E. R. Vickers,[143] replaced the German prison staffers guarding the generals (some of these guards were former Waffen SS members and POWs themselves) with English guards.[144] There is no doubt that very close ties had developed between the German guards and the imprisoned generals, as was illustrated, for example, by a birthday card the guards sent to Kesselring in November 1948.[145] From the end of 1949, the Red Cross—under the auspices of Elise Weecks, head of the organization's North Rhine–Westphalia section—was allowed to conduct regular inspections in Werl, leading to "noticeable improvements" in prison conditions, as Kesselring recorded with some satisfaction in January 1950.[146]

From 1950, the British decided to facilitate regular press coverage of Werl in order to silence criticism in Germany about the reputedly inhumane prison conditions obtaining there. On June 24, 1950, the *Dithmarscher Landeszeitung* carried a report entitled "First Visit to Manstein and Kesselring." The paper described Werl as a "comfortable retirement home." The prisoners were "not locked in cells" but spent their time in a "cozy recreation room"; they had "comfortable chairs," and "each prisoner has his own garden plot where he can raise whatever he wants."[147] Five years after the war's end, such conditions were, in fact, far better than those being endured by most Germans. But the imprisoned officers still found cause for complaint: they believed their convictions to be "unjust" and "illegal." Remarkably, the paper concluded that they had been "found guilty of war crimes." By Christmas 1948, *Der Spiegel* was able to report that "the days of glueing paper bags" were over for Kesselring. He was now writing the "history of his military campaigns" on behalf of "the American Army's Historical Division."[148] Indeed, prison conditions improved to such an extent that, at the beginning of 1952, the *Deutsche Woche* found that officers imprisoned in Werl were enjoying conditions akin to those in an officers' mess.[149]

But along with the improved prison conditions came criticism in Britain about the benevolent treatment allegedly being enjoyed by the inmates.[150] The prison authorities found themselves facing a dilemma. On the one hand, the British wanted to forestall the defendants' "victim strategy," but on the other hand, London was confronting domestic political demands that the prison conditions reflect the gravity of the war crimes committed.

Kesselring's Work for the Historical Division

Kesselring's work for the American Historical Division helped generate a positive image of the former field marshal in the Anglo-Saxon world, and it played an important role in recruiting Allied advocates (generally military) to his cause.[151]

Initially, the U.S. Army merely planned to carry out surveys documenting the German adversaries' views of World War II campaigns.[152] In January 1946, these unsystematic surveys conducted by the Shuster Commission (named after its director)[153] gave rise to the Operational History (German) Section under the direction of the former German army chief of General Staff, Generaloberst Franz Halder.[154] From the autumn of 1946, the German generals were treated as freelance contributors and provided with relatively comfortable accommodations in Allendorf. They had substantial freedom of movement and were able to talk to each other without supervision.[155] Inducements also included more generous calorie rations and monthly wages of between RM 400 and RM 700.[156]

In the summer of 1946, while the Nuremberg trial was still in progress, Kesselring started working for the newly established Historical Division in Allendorf. He found the work of great interest. His involvement in the Americans' studies of World War II enhanced his self-image and the notion of his own "historical significance," which he repeatedly stressed in his journals.[157] He received a further boost from Mother Alfonsa, prioress of the German Franciscan sisters in Venice's Casa Fontana. In their correspondence, Mother Alfonsa—who had taken care of him during his trial[158]—confirmed his own view that the outcome of the "final battle" had by no means been decided and that the aim must now be to ensure that his reputation was beyond reproach when it came to the overall memory of the war: "I see from your letters that you are still the same great and courageous warrior and victor as before, even though the battlefield has changed. God will one day decide which were the greatest victories of your life: those on the battlefields of Italy, or those behind dungeon walls. In my eyes, silent heroism demands far more greatness of spirit."[159]

Kesselring's work for the Historical Division offered him a forum in which to achieve this aim. The studies offer a telling indication of Kesselring's early efforts to erect a monument to himself and to memorialize not only the "Italy fighters" but also the Afrikakorps and "his" Luftwaffe.[160] In January 1948, he was working simultaneously on studies of the "Mediterranean theater of war" and the "problem facing the German leadership," a report on the "relations between the different fronts," and a manuscript on the "continuation of the war in Italy."[161] The makeup of the work group largely corresponded to the composition of the staffs during the period being examined.[162] In this way, the Historical Division offered senior officers opportunities for maintaining contact with former comrades, while also preparing the ground for the development of networks later on.

Franz Halder had a significant influence on the Allied politics of memory, thanks to his battle to secure recognition for Wehrmacht achievements. He conducted this battle with the aid of his operational-strategic study group, which comprised several thousand officers.[163] It was Halder who laid down the explanatory line to be adopted in the Historical Division: it had been "Hitler's war," a war in which militarily justified objections lodged by senior officers were swept aside. The outcome of the war could therefore be attributed to Hitler's incorrigibility and dilettantism.[164] Finally, Halder was also the first to promulgate the idea of making a sharp distinction between the atrocities committed by the SS and the purportedly clean conduct of the war by the Wehrmacht. This approach was later adopted by defense attorneys in Nuremberg, and it was subsequently expanded on in the memoirs written by former Wehrmacht officers (including Kesselring) during the 1950s. Admittedly, the Nuremberg verdicts, as well as the impending prospect that more officers would be brought to trial,[165] dampened the readiness of German officers to cooperate with the Americans. However, like Kesselring, Halder hoped that cooperation would improve the American attitude toward the German officer corps.[166] Older officers, in particular, were sharply critical of this type of cooperation, which—led by Erich von Manstein—they viewed as collaboration.[167] It should be noted that Halder's Historical Division was one of the first gatherings of German officers who, after 1945, carried on the "fight against Bolshevism" on the ideological front, clearing the "path towards a national legitimation of 're-armament' and a military loyalty which was re-defined in terms of alliance policy."[168]

American military officials did not seem particularly interested in prosecuting their former adversaries: indeed, they actively helped cover their tracks. During the years following the IMT and subsequent U.S. trials at Nuremberg, original German documents were, with American assistance, destroyed in the German section of the Historical Division in Allendorf camp for the sake of expediency, so that they could not be used as evidence in a war crimes trial. This destruction was confirmed by General Leo Geyr von Schweppenburg.[169] Friendships were also forged with American officers, despite the fact that such relationships could interfere with the stated Allied goal of collecting material for postwar trials and sitting in judgment during such trials. For example, General William Donovan of the American secret service (the OSS), who briefly served in 1945 as deputy to the chief prosecutor,

Robert H. Jackson,[170] formed a close relationship with the German defense attorney Paul Leverkuehn, whom he provided with private advice and information.[171] Kesselring also enjoyed the protection of American officers, as was shown early on by Colonel Notestein's obstructionist attitude toward the British in Venice. With some gratification, Kesselring noted each compliment paid to him by American soldiers and officers.[172] He even received a letter of thanks from the chief historian of the U.S. Army's military history sector, Major General Orlando Ward, who expressed his gratitude to the "Dear Field Marshal" for his "extraordinary cooperation" in the study of the Italian campaigns.[173] For his part, Colonel Potter—commanding officer of the Historical Division—did all in his power to delay handing Kesselring over to the British to stand trial in Venice, in violation of specific Allied agreements regarding immediately turning over suspected war criminals when requested to do so by Allied authorities.

Kesselring's trial interrupted, but did not end, his work on the Americans' history of World War II. From May 1947, immediately after his verdict was announced, he resumed work on the studies in Wolfsberg.[174] As soon as he was transferred to Werl, he asked the prison commander, Colonel H. C. Morgan, to "be allowed to work more extensively than before on examining events in the Mediterranean theatre of war."[175] Officials in the Historical Division asserted themselves and instructed the British prison authorities to relieve Kesselring of some of his prison tasks.[176] From then on, every four weeks, he received visits (and new material) from Colonel Potter, who was based in the American camp at Neustadt.[177] It may be that differences arose between the American and British Allies regarding the involvement of, and thus the protection granted to, legally convicted war criminals. At this remove, however, such differences are only hinted at when reading between the lines of the surviving documents.

In summary, all these factors—the legal arguments advanced by Dr. Laternser in the clemency petition, the various submissions made to the British authorities by former subordinates, the increasingly positive media coverage of the "pitiable prisoners in Werl," and the highly prized contribution made by senior German officers to the work of the Historical Division—helped chip away at London's consensual determination to see that war criminals were severely punished.

Public Pressure, 1947–1949

The general church criticism of the Allied punishment policy as well as dissenting verdicts reached by Italian military courts had a direct effect on the British politics of memory, for these factors helped lay the groundwork for the subsequent clemency campaigns. The demand that Kesselring be pardoned was endorsed by German church representatives as well as private individuals.

The verdicts rendered in the Italian military courts had a substantial bearing on Laternser's strategy. The trial in October 1948 of SS Obersturmbannführer Herbert Kappler was particularly significant. In addition, the trial of Waffen SS Major Walter Reder,[178] together with the preliminary investigations for the trial of General Wilhelm Schmalz,[179] had shown that the accused units were unaware of Kesselring's orders.[180] Thus, in the Reder case, the Italian military court found there "was no evidence that a superior authority had issued an order to carry out reprisals, or had issued an order which could have resulted in any excesses against the civilian population."[181] This finding formally exonerated Kesselring of charges that he had pursued a reprisal policy. But only now can we prove that, as early as 1942, an order from Hitler himself had indemnified all perpetrators accused of killing civilians during antipartisan measures.[182]

In September 1950, General Schmalz was acquitted because evidence heard during his trial indicated the perpetrators of the alleged crime could have been Italians disguised in German uniforms.[183] With a note of resignation, Kesselring remarked that virtually everybody else would be acquitted—perhaps even Reder and Kappler—while he, Mackensen, and Mältzer, "having fallen victim to a misguided justice, remained in custody."[184] However, Laternser hoped, with some justification, that the Italian verdicts would have repercussions in London.[185] The next chapter will show how the British authorities interpreted the Italian verdicts, incorporating them into their own position.

Thanks to the dissenting verdicts reached by Italian military courts, as well as the growth in Kesselring's support, the London government found itself under mounting pressure to consider reviewing Kesselring's case. In this regard, it should be noted that those championing the former field marshal's cause were often motivated by self-interest.

Church Intervention on Kesselring's Behalf

Since 1945, elements within both the Catholic Church and the Lutheran Church had voiced their objections to the Allied war crimes trials, especially the main tribunal at Nuremberg and the Allied military court proceedings. The churches' general criticism of the Allies benefited those who had been convicted. The churches had their own reasons for seeking a review of the sentences, but these coincided with the interests of those being held behind bars, and as a result, church officials increasingly found themselves acting as unofficial spokespeople for the officers in custody.

Church intervention was rooted not only in humanitarian considerations but also in a critical approach—adopted early on—to the alleged victors' justice dispensed by the Allies.[186] The churches were also critical of the participation of Soviet prosecutors in the Nuremberg trials. The subsequent Nuremberg trials of Wehrmacht officers triggered principled objections from the churches, centered on the issue of the duty to obey orders and the required obedience to Hitler as commander-in-chief of the army. The officers' defense attorneys quickly realized that the churches offered them a platform, and they developed their appeal strategy with an eye to the possibility of church intervention. After the defendants were convicted, the defense teams provided information not only to the officers' friends and relatives but also to individual bishops in the hope that they could exert political pressure.[187] Initially, however, church representatives confined themselves to general criticism, stressing the humanitarian grounds for releasing the prisoners.[188] The churchmen also initiated contact with the defense teams,[189] and a true collaboration started to develop. Even the American secret service had noticed the interplay between churchmen and the war criminals' defense teams.[190]

Within the Catholic Church, the most vocal protestors were Cardinal Josef Frings of Cologne and the Munich suffragan bishop Johann Neuhäusler:[191] both men were ardent advocates for the defendants and their families. When considering the advocacy of the Catholic Church, it is worth noting that the bishops' work for specific war criminals always followed requests made by private individuals.[192] For example, the archbishop of Paderborn, Lorenz Cardinal Jäger, received—through Bishop Neuhäusler—clemency appeals on Kesselring's behalf from Hanns Freiherr von Freytag-Loringhoven and Irmgard Horn-Kesselring. He thereupon took up Kesselring's cause himself. An examination of the accompanying letter written by Bishop Jäger illustrates the nature of the episcopal network acting in support of those convicted of war crimes. Jäger wrote that, though he was not personally acquainted with either the former field marshal or any of the petitioners, he had sought information in Rome regarding Kesselring's conduct during the war.[193] He had been told that "the salvation of the city of Rome and its irreplaceable art treasures was largely due to Field Marshal Kesselring."[194] Further, the views of other Catholic dignitaries campaigning for Kesselring apparently served as character references. These dignitaries included Bishop Alois Hudal,[195] rector of the German Catholic church in Rome, Santa Maria dell'Anima, who had "championed Kesselring's cause in a letter written as early as 1948."[196]

The two German churches, Catholic and Lutheran, played a pivotal role in the clemency debate, especially during the immediate postwar era. However, the Lutherans' criticism had the greatest political impact. Immediately after the war, the Americans accurately read the situation, concluding that even though the Lutheran Church had opposed the Nazis, it nevertheless incorporated tendencies ranging from "extremely conservative to nationalist and Junker-monarchist."[197] Lutheran advocacy for the country's former military elite should be viewed against this background. From 1947 and 1948 on, the Lutheran regional bishops were particularly active in drafting clemency appeals directed at the Allied control authorities. The Lutheran churchmen were even at one with the imprisoned Wehrmacht officers when it came to the wording used: on May 7, 1945, for example, in a circular addressed to Bavarian pastors, the head of the powerful Protestant Landeskirche Bavaria, Landesbischof (Regional Bishop) Hans Meiser, referred to Germany's defeat as the "consummation of the German tragedy."[198] The commitment displayed by individual Lutheran Church figures becomes more understandable if one considers that Protestantism—with its ideals of loyalty to authority and national conservatism—had been more severely shattered by the complete collapse of the German state than other social groupings and was now seeking a new conservative orientation.[199] By issuing the so-called Stuttgart Confession (*Stuttgarter Schuldbekenntnis*) on October 18, 1945, Protestant churchmen, led by Martin Niemöller, Hans Asmussen, Hans Meiser, and Otto Dibelius, confessed in an open declaration their guilt as bystanders. Although the confession was given to ease the acceptance of the German church in the World Church Congress in 1945, it is remarkable that guilt was expressed but collective measures openly rejected. On these grounds, the engagement for the convicted generals also became a crusade for German national innocence. The churchmen who supported the clemency campaigns were members of the old elites but also men of the ecclesiastical resistance movement. The generational change—which also gave rise to increased criticism—only became noticeable at the start of the 1950s.

Those championing the imprisoned war criminals' cause on behalf of the Lutheran Church included the Württemberg regional bishop Theophil Wurm, the Berlin bishop Otto Dibelius,[200] the Hanover-based bishop Hans Lilje, the regional bishop Hans Meiser (mentioned earlier),[201] Consistory President Martin Niemöller,[202] and Prelate Karl Hartenstein.[203] Bishop Wurm had presided over the Evangelical (Lutheran) Church in Germany since its establishment in 1945; his deputy was Martin Niemöller, who also directed the church's external affairs office.[204] Niemöller's commitment to the officers convicted of war crimes was focused on rejecting the Allied justice measures but not on reestablishing German militarism: just five years later, he was among the most vocal critics of rearmament. In 1946, the head of the influential Church Chancellery, Hans Asmussen, achieved prominence as a critic of the Allies. In the spring of that year, he prepared a "list of Allied sins," which was more or less intended to nullify the guilt of the German people. His list included the displacement of ethnic Germans from the East, the unknown fate of German POWs, the denazification and internment of National Socialist functionaries, and the economic impoverishment of the German people. Asmussen announced that all could expect "forgiveness of any sins which resulted in complicity in National Socialism and all its works." This assurance also applied to those "who have yet to be held to account by earthly judges," that is, those "senior officers who wait month by month for their trials to be over."[205]

The Lutheran deacon Hans Schmidt brokered the contact between Laternser and Asmussen[206] because it was known that Asmussen paid regular visits to the bishop of Chichester, George Bell. Asmussen had repeatedly warned Bell that a "new path" had to be pursued, and he demanded that the trials be halted.[207] Even while he was still interned in Wolfsberg, Kesselring himself had suggested presenting his case to the Anglican bishop,[208] who was known to be very pro-German and an outspoken critic of the British war crimes trials.[209] Schmidt wrote to Laternser that he had sent the "Kesselring file, together with a letter of recommendation and explanation, to Victor Gollancz," since Bell was currently away.[210] The intervention by the Lutheran Church thus also helped ensure that the petition reached British publicists—who then picked up the issue. This exposure, in turn, was of great benefit to Kesselring.

Even later, it was primarily the Lutheran Church that championed Kesselring's cause. Under the umbrella of the Hilfswerk der Evangelischen Kirchen in Deutschland (German Lutheran Church's Aid Organization), a Lutheran aid organization, the Lutheran Central Office's Legal Defense Section, headed up by Dr. von Lukowicz, made contact with a legal adviser to the British high commissioner in July 1950.[211] The intent was to demand that the "legal situation" in the British zone be harmonized with the "American situation." This language was code for releasing the prisoners.

In conclusion, the Lutheran Church's intervention played a major role in the Kesselring case. Admittedly, neither the Lutheran Church nor the Catholic Church, as an institution, protested against Albert Kesselring's trial or conviction. But both subsequently sought clemency for the former field marshal. As well as establishing initial contacts with prominent individuals in England (and subsequently with the British occupation authorities in Germany), Lutheran Church leaders personally intervened on Kesselring's behalf by writing letters of recommendation—letters that lent the petition for Kesselring additional weight.

Laternser's Search for Allies

The mobilization of powerful groups in Germany, the UK, and the United States, described previously, generated interest in Kesselring's case, which, in turn, gave rise to a campaign on his behalf and forced the British political establishment to intervene. Laternser hoped to reignite the public debate on war criminals in general, and Kesselring in particular, in order to ramp up the pressure on Allied decision makers. He was confident that, with his assistance, Kesselring would succeed in "having this unjust sentence set aside."[212] Following on from the concept of the trial representing Kesselring's final battle, Laternser believed that, though the first skirmish may have been lost, the outcome of the battle itself had by no means been decided.

As early as autumn 1947, in a memorandum to Laternser discussing future strategy, Kesselring noted the need to inform the public regarding "the circumstances in question" and, through public opinion, to "appeal to the world." For this purpose, prominent individuals were to be used to help shape opinion abroad.[213] Accordingly, the first petition on Kesselring's behalf was sent to a small but influential group of people, most of whom were personally known to Laternser or Kesselring.[214] In addition to Kesselring's own former comrades, the recipients included Catholic and Lutheran church leaders,[215] as well as unofficial Wehrmacht spokesmen such as Generaloberst Franz Halder and Oberstleutnant Viktor von Schweinitz.[216]

One of the most important recipients was Dr. Hans Speidel, whose brother Wilhelm, as former commander-in-chief in the Balkans, had himself been convicted of war crimes and was interned in Landsberg.[217] Hans Speidel (who would become a military adviser to the West German government on matters relating to rearmament) coupled the war criminals issue with possible German rearmament, and he stressed the "historical significance" of the petition for all other defendants in similar cases.[218] Using his contacts with high-ranking American politicians, Speidel hoped to submit the Kesselring petition to a "Mr. M."[219] He indicated to Laternser that the Americans had asked him to "provide documentation regarding the attempt during proceedings to date to shift the responsibility of the SS or SD onto the army, and the attempt by the SD to exert influence on the prosecuting authorities." Speidel was the first to propose the theory that there had been a "final conspiracy by the SS" or the SD. According to this theory, senior SS figures—primarily intelligence officers—had made their extensive expertise available to the Allies following the war on the condition that, in return, they would be exempted from prosecution.[220] Today, we know that Speidel was correct in his surmise. However, such secret agreements remained the exception, and they were largely dependent on good prewar contacts with Allied authorities, the position of the SS officer in question, and the nature of the anticipated charges.[221] Laternser gratefully seized on this theory, and—in the second petition—he was careful to stress that the SS bore the sole blame.[222]

Another goal was to disseminate a petition through trusted Italian contacts.[223] Laternser believed that the benefits of such a move would be twofold. For one thing, such an intervention would come not from Germany but from the country of the victims. For another, Italy could thus make a kind of "restitution" to "the misunderstood benefactor, Kesselring." As he put it, "I am certain that official Italian quarters would make such an intervention on behalf of a man who, as you yourself know, did a great deal for Italy."[224] Laternser's informant, Count Ugo Cavallero, pointed out that "the current Italian situation does not yet favor such a move." In his view, given the political situation at the time, an intercession through the Vatican would be more promising,[225] and he offered to help work for such an intervention. Colonel Peterpaul von Donat, a former section head on Kesselring's staff, had already submitted an appeal to the Italian Ministry of Aviation. The response was ambivalent. He was told that, "despite his regard for Kesselring," the aviation minister was currently not in a position to do anything for him.[226]

The first petition only reached members of the press by chance. Those who did receive it included the American William Hamsher of the Reuters bureau—whom Laternser knew from Nuremberg IMT trial days—and a member of the *Zeit* weekly's editorial team,[227] who received a copy of the petition after the paper published a report critical of Kesselring's sentence.[228] As early as September, Laternser was sending out an appeal written in English, for several individuals, such as Viktor von Schweinitz, had offered to approach friends and journalists in the United States and the UK.[229] There is no evidence to indicate there was any reaction to this appeal.

Laternser proceeded rather more strategically when distributing the second petition in 1948. Many copies were made and distributed in influential quarters as a first move toward mobilizing public opinion.[230] Petitions were sent to the Lutheran bishops Wurm, Lilje, and Dibelius; to the Cologne-based Cardinal Frings; to Pope Pius XII;[231] and to selected German journalists.[232] The list of recipients demonstrates the targeted manner in which critics of the Allied war crimes policy were being approached, especially in the UK. Such British critics included Winston Churchill (leader of the Opposition); the bishop of Chichester, Dr. George Bell (a leading voice in the parliamentary debates surrounding the war crimes trials); and Labour MP Richard

Stokes, with whom Laternser had met on the fringes of the Kappler trial in Rome: the two men had discussed Kesselring's case. Copies were also sent to the writer and publisher Victor Gollancz; J. F. C. Fuller; the historian Basil Liddell Hart; the British military governor in Germany, General Robertson; and Field Marshal Sir Harold Alexander.[233] The campaign to secure Kesselring's release had thus spread beyond Germany.

If one compares the coverage of Kappler's trial and sentencing to life imprisonment with the coverage of the 1947 Kesselring trial, it is obvious that a positive shift had occurred in media opinion. The newsmagazine *Der Spiegel* laid down the new interpretative line, stressing that the attack in the Via Rasella had been intended as a "deliberate provocation by the partisans" with the aim of encouraging the local population to hold fast.[234] In contrast, Kesselring's name was no longer mentioned in connection with the massacre in the Fosse Ardeatine. This fact, in itself, indicates that—instead of being depicted as the "butcher of Italy"—Kesselring was now being painted in a more positive light. Regardless of their veracity or otherwise, such arguments benefited Kesselring—especially since no record can be found of any agreement between Laternser and the journalists in this particular case.

The German press had taken up significant elements of Laternser's exoneration strategy from the second petition, stressing that the reprisal had been in self-defense and that Kesselring's conduct was "otherwise flawless." These arguments were then further disseminated. Consequently, what started as isolated initiatives by individual social groupings, together with initial media contacts, ultimately combined with the results of the Italian court proceedings to generate a campaign calling for a review of Kesselring's case. The British government could not remain indifferent to this pressure.

Thwarted Retribution: Political Intervention in Britain and the United States on Kesselring's Behalf

The initial phase of activity following Kesselring's conviction involved a legal tug-of-war on the issue of permission to appeal, and the second phase involved an attempt to have private individuals intervene. But once the petition was refused in 1949, Kesselring's final battle entered its third and last phase. The aim was to keep the matter in the public eye, for public opinion was the new battleground. The post-1949 period saw the establishment of individual, highly efficient pressure groups in both Britain and the United States. These groups coordinated their political and media interventions and developed organized campaigns with one aim: to achieve Kesselring's release by exerting pressure on the British government.

A close look at some of the British and American actors in this drama will help to explain the circumstances surrounding Kesselring's 1952 release. Alexander Scotland made ostensibly private representations on Kesselring's behalf, and the British military historian Basil Liddell Hart was also active in the efforts to secure the German field marshal's release. Both men were part of Lord Maurice Hankey's circle. The U.S. campaign to have the German generals released was spearheaded by a few influential senators close to the National Council for Prevention of War (NCPW) and its chairman, Frederick J. Libby.[235] The American anticommunist polemicist Freda Utley, a friend of Hankey's, had taken on the task of lobbying senators as well as using her journalistic skills to enhance public awareness of the issue.[236]

Even during the war, the treatment of German war crimes had been the subject of public discourse in both the United States and Britain. Following the war crimes trials, in the debates on the war crimes issue that took place in both the British Parliament and the U.S. Congress after 1948, it once again became clear that there were two opposing camps on the Allied side. Indeed, two completely different Allied groupings existed. The first camp—influenced by the thinking of the U.S. Treasury secretary Henry Morgenthau[237] and by so-called Vansittartism, a movement that took its name from Sir Robert Vansittart, a Foreign Office adviser until 1941[238]—had a significant input into the Allies' initial plans for the postwar period. Morgenthau and Vansittart were in agreement that Germany had to be prevented from ever again attaining economic or political dominance. The second camp was composed of powerful lobbies in both Britain and the United States. Especially after the Federal Republic of Germany was established in 1949, the Morgenthau-Vansittart approach was opposed by these lobbies, which instead sought reconciliation with Germany and the release of all "so-called" war criminals. In this connection, it should be noted that the lobbyists quickly realized terms such as *so-called* could function as valuable shorthand tools with which to express not only their support for individuals convicted of war crimes but also their dissatisfaction with the process as a whole. The Kesselring case allows us, for the first time, to reconstruct the network of major public figures who stepped up the pressure on their respective governments to secure the release of German war criminals. Unpublished documents and interviews with eyewitnesses show that these lobbies were closely intertwined, even if it is not possible today to conclusively verify the linkages in each case.

The British Hankey Group

In Britain, Lord Maurice Hankey was at the heart of a group bringing pressure to bear on the political establishment in respect to the war crimes issue. Although Hankey was the ideological mastermind of a reconciliatory, pro-German policy, he took great care to stay in the background. For that reason, in part, his private intervention on behalf of German war criminals, in particular Kesselring and Manstein, remains largely unknown today.[239] With regard to the British post-1945 war crimes policy, Hankey's aim was to secure an amnesty for those already convicted in order to promote international reconciliation. He repeatedly referred to the crimes committed by the victors and criticized the inadequacy of judicial retribution when dealing with crimes against humanity.[240]

Hankey was one of Britain's most influential politicians, having served in government from 1908 to 1938. Whether as secretary to the War Cabinet, as secretary to the Committee of Imperial Defence, or as clerk of the Privy Council, Hankey occupied key administrative posts where he had a crucial influence on British policy and also became intimately acquainted with the machinery of government.[241] As a British representative, he had led his country's delegation to the Paris Peace Conference after World War I, and he represented Britain in many of the subsequent negotiations addressing postwar issues and the matter of reparations. After retiring in 1938, Hankey returned to the cabinet in 1941 before finally retiring from public life following differences of opinion with Churchill.[242] Having been involved for so many years with war and its consequences, especially for Germany, it is not surprising that Hankey revisited this issue after 1945. His influence on members of government was significant, based not only on personal contacts but also on his ostensible impartiality. He scrupulously avoided being associated with the war crimes issue in public, ensuring that Vansittart and his adherents were unable to dismiss him as a "friend of the Nazis" and isolate him politically. However, Hankey was extremely active in the background. After 1950, he appeared in print as the theoretician behind the amnesty movement for German and Japanese war criminals.[243]

Hankey's circle included influential members of both Houses of Parliament, high-ranking military officers, churchmen, and writers, whose collective motto was "Justice for the Vanquished."[244] The political actors in the group included Lord William de L'Isle and Dudley (House of Lords), Lord Winstor (House of Lords), Lord Francis Pakenham (parliamentary secretary at the War Office, where he worked as a minister at the Control Office for Germany and Austria), and Lord Frederic Maugham,[245] former lord chancellor. There were also links with Labour MP Richard Stokes, who had already attracted attention for his vehement opposition to the policy of dismantlement.[246] Hankey's friends also included E. R. Vickers, the governor of the Werl military prison. Military associates included Field Marshal Alexander,

Colonel Russell Grenfell,[247] and Admiral the Earl of Cork and Orrery. These men supported a general amnesty and kick-started the British debate on the imperative of obeying orders. Although not a member of their inner circle, Winston Churchill was close to Hankey's military associates. But Hankey's correspondents included Anthony Eden, General Douglas MacArthur, and Konrad Adenauer. Indeed, Hankey had a personal meeting with the German chancellor during Adenauer's 1951 visit to London, in which the war criminals issue was the main topic of conversation.[248] Hankey's group's forays into print were led by well-known writers and polemicists such as Victor Gollancz,[249] Basil Liddell Hart, and Manstein's defense counsel, Reginald Paget. The interrelationships among these players are illustrated in the acknowledgment to Paget's book on General Manstein: "The author is most grateful to Lord Hankey for writing a foreword to this book [and] to Captain Liddell Hart for his help with the military section."[250] These individuals were joined by writers on military affairs such as F. J. P. Veale[251] and J. F. C. Fuller.[252] In the context of his 1946–1947 "Save Europe Now" aid drive, Gollancz had already worked with the former U.S. president Herbert Hoover.[253] Dr. George Bell, the bishop of Chichester and an indefatigable campaigner for an end to the war crimes trials, was in close contact with Hankey, whom he consulted about his speeches in the House of Lords.[254]

Thanks to his many years in Whitehall, Hankey had access to the centers of power. This fact becomes apparent when one examines, for example, Hankey's intervention on behalf of Japanese war criminals, which also involved three high-ranking British diplomats.[255] Friends whom Hankey could call upon when special interventions were required (for radio interviews and the like) included Lord Marquess James Edward of Salisbury and Sir W. Strang of the Foreign Office, General Hastings Ismay (Hankey's former deputy in the prime minister's office and subsequently the first NATO secretary-general),[256] General Sir J. Edmonds (author of the *Manual of Military Law*), Major General Robert Clive Bridgeman (Home Guard and Territorial Army), and the Oxford legal scholar Professor A. L. Goodhart. Hankey himself maintained close contact with the editor of the *Times*, who happened to be his brother-in-law. This web of links among the political, media, and business establishments was the most effective network to be formed in respect to the war crimes issue. And Hankey sat in the center of this web, personally coordinating all initiatives taken.

Interventions by Alexander Scotland, British Interrogation Officer

In 1950, Colonel Alexander Scotland was one of the first to publicly call for Kesselring's release. The political significance of his intervention cannot be overstated. It was the first petition to the relevant authorities made by a British subject, and beyond that, it was presented by a former participant in the Kesselring trial, a man who had interrogated Kesselring for the prosecution. In the eyes of the British public, such a man had the right to have his doubts heard, especially since those doubts stemmed from personal knowledge. The main difference between Scotland's efforts and subsequent campaigns was that, rather than seeking a pardon, he sought a review of the verdict and on principle confined himself to legal arguments. Scotland was the first to provoke interest in the case among British military circles and the first to instigate a letter-writing campaign in the *Times*.[257]

In 1946, Scotland had interrogated Kesselring in London. Although he initially felt that the field marshal deserved to go to the gallows, a personal friendship had evolved during long conversations between the two men. Scotland came to believe that Kesselring was innocent, and he was critical of the proceedings throughout the trial.[258] He maintained an intermittent correspondence with Kesselring after the latter's conviction, and in 1949, he contacted Laternser to offer his assistance.[259] Scotland hoped that a presentation of the case would result not only in Kesselring's release but also in a full repeal of the verdicts issued against Kesselring, Mackensen, and Mältzer. He started a second intervention following the acquittal of General Schmalz at the end of 1950.[260]

After Laternser had informed him of the failure of his own petition in April 1950,[261] Scotland wrote that he was "personally very disappointed"[262] to learn that Laternser's effort had not borne fruit and that the "gentlemen involved" were not open to new arguments.[263] He himself intended to write a memorandum on the Kesselring case, which he would distribute to the press and to friends who might "raise the matter politically." Scotland's averred aim was to "create a public demand for a re-hearing or review of the whole position of these three ill-used men." The rejection of Laternser's petition provided Scotland with an opportunity to write to the Foreign Office himself on May 8 (it was surely no coincidence that he chose the anniversary of VE Day).

Laternser had provided him in advance with original German documents, some of which had been annotated and commented on by Kesselring himself.[264] Scotland felt that the German High Command's ambiguous allocation of responsibility for combating the partisans would prove particularly useful in the efforts to intervene on Kesselring's behalf. An order issued in May 1944 by the Wehrmacht High Command OKW, signed by Keitel, had specified the competencies of the Wehrmacht and the SS—that is, of Kesselring and Wolff. This order, which marked the beginning of a correspondence with

SS Reichsführer Heinrich Himmler concerning issues of competency, addressed questions of responsibility for combating partisans. Thus, on March 29, 1944, Kesselring initially ordered that the Wehrmacht and SS should cooperate on this issue, led by the senior officer of the division in question. Himmler, however, succeeded in imposing a binding directive to the effect that responsibility for combating partisans would be divided into specific sections. The order underpinned Kesselring's formal command when it came to fighting partisans in Italy, while also underpinning the effective independence of the SS and police troops under Karl Wolff. Scotland believed that this order would be especially helpful: "It is such a fantastic document that it must be produced and analyzed word for word."[265]

In his sixteen-point submission, Scotland made it clear that he was speaking as an officer who had previously interrogated the three defendants. Moreover, he said that, based on the knowledge he acquired at that time, he found it surprising that the guilty verdicts imposed on the three men were being upheld without a closer examination of the role played by the SS and SD.[266] It remains unclear even today just who gave the execution order in the Fosse Ardeatine.

Scotland was the first to refer to one particular circumstance: the possibility that Kesselring was not present at the planning and execution of the crime.[267] Indeed, the question was whether Kesselring *could* have been present when the decision was made either in Rome or at headquarters and thus whether he bore responsibility for the massacre.[268] In addition, Scotland pointed out that information on the scope for independent action enjoyed by the SS and SD was only then coming to light.[269] He also emphasized the dissenting verdicts issued by Italian military courts in similar cases, such as those against Crasemann, Krummhaar, Tensfeld, Simon, and Kappler. Scotland even wove the argument against victors' justice into his petition.[270] He concluded by noting that Kesselring had spent years providing a "priceless (!) service" to the American Historical Division. "In view of this co-operation," wrote Scotland, "it would be difficult to find a more brutal way of telling a prisoner, a man of high culture and advanced in years, that no matter what he did, he would spend the remainder of his life in a prison cell." Scotland's request was audacious. He demanded that Kesselring, Mackensen, and Mältzer be released; further, he called for their cases to be revisited and for the three men to be pardoned—and consequently rehabilitated. He had thus adopted Kesselring's position, viewing a mere release from prison as inappropriate and instead demanding a full review of the cases. Scotland sent copies of his petition to Prime Minister Anthony Eden, Labour MP Richard Stokes, and the director of Legal Services at the War Office in London.[271]

Scotland's campaign was disrupted by an article by Sefton Delmer on the British war crimes trials, which appeared in the *Daily Express*. Scotland viewed the article as a reaction to his petition to the Foreign Office.[272] Delmer, former head of British war propaganda, had made contact with Kesselring through Laternser, and he had written an article on the war crimes issue that appeared in the regional *Dithmarscher Landeszeitung*, probably as a translation of the *Daily Express* piece.[273] Delmer portrayed Kesselring as the spokesman of the so-called Generals' Group, and he attributed to the former field marshal a clever remark that was even repeated by the respected German weekly newsmagazine *Der Spiegel*: "During the next war we will have to employ lawyers instead of soldiers as officers."[274] According to Delmer's report, the prison authorities imposed stringent restrictions on prison visits for members of the press. Writing to Laternser, Kesselring complained that "Delmer's article certainly did more harm than good."[275]

The shift in Britain's clemency policy was reflected in the internal memos accompanying the progress of Scotland's petition through the various offices involved. It proved difficult to formulate an answer—and thus to react quickly[276]—for it was not clear how Scotland should be countered. After all, one could deduce from his letter that he disapproved of the court verdict and held a "prejudiced view" of the case, in the disparaging words of Douglas Passmore in Wahnerheide (headquarters of the British legal department in Lower Saxony).[277] Nevertheless, in a handwritten annotation to Passmore's memorandum objecting to Scotland's petition, the man who headed up the British high commissioner's legal office and was tasked with advising the governor on applications for clemency, Sir Alfred Brown, wrote, "I rather agree with Scotland generally!"[278] At the same time, he tempered this declaration by writing that "it would be unprofitable to encourage Lt. Col. Scotland to pursue his arguments," since "nothing can now be done by way of appeal or otherwise to alter the decision."[279] Brown also requested a summary of the other "Italian cases"—including the verdicts reached by Italian courts—so that he could assess the proportionality of the verdicts himself. His willingness to revisit the legal arguments marked an internal turning point in British policy toward German war criminals. Indeed, London did start reviewing the Italian cases.[280] Following Scotland's intervention and with the favorable attitude adopted by Brown, Kesselring's prospects for release seemed quite good.

Brown's willingness to revisit the case was not an isolated phenomenon. The British military governor of North Rhine–Westphalia, General Sir Alec Bishop, had already formed a positive view of the Kesselring case when he went to Werl with a British visiting committee from February 17 to 22, 1949.

Kesselring was summoned to meet the visitors for fifteen minutes and was allowed to submit requests;[281] he found that Bishop was "as courteous as he was understanding."[282] Bishop's visit to Werl was only reported by the East Berlin *Der Abend* newspaper, which speculated that Kesselring and Manstein would soon "have their sentences largely commuted."[283] The paper claimed that Bishop had spoken with Kesselring about "the use of his expertise." It is noteworthy that this first reference to a role for Kesselring during a potential rearmament appeared in the communist press.

Encouraged by Scotland's activities, Laternser inquired about the possibility of publishing a letter to the *Times* from the point of view of the defense counsel.[284] He and Kesselring agreed that such a move was "bound to have a good effect."[285] However, Scotland, who wanted to manage the British press campaign himself, rejected the proposal. While reassuring Laternser that the "release of these good men of Werl" was very important to him and that he was "hopeful" that "our hopes and efforts will soon reach a happy conclusion," Scotland cautioned against impatience and precipitate action. In this regard, he warned that the intervention by Princess Elisabeth von Isenburg, who was very active in Germany as the patron of the right-wing aid organization for internees and POWs, would be substantively counterproductive and could endanger the efforts to secure Kesselring's release.[286]

Scotland gave Laternser an indication of the network agitating on Kesselring's behalf in England when he wrote that he was already collaborating with friends in the governor's legal office to prepare the "next strike" so that this "shocking case" could finally be resolved.[287] He noted that his memorandum on the Kesselring case had grown to such an extent that he was considering publishing a book. Prior to any publication, however, Scotland felt that the Foreign Office should have the opportunity to read and respond to his findings. Even before Kesselring was released, Scotland's observations of the trial, as well as his criticism of British military justice in general and the trials of German war criminals in particular, were published in German.[288] After reading Scotland's book, Kesselring felt vindicated in his attitude of denial: "It is quite astounding to see how flimsy the allegedly crucial grounds really were."[289]

Scotland's efforts soon bore their first fruit. The Kesselring issue was kept alive not only by the publication of his book but also by readers' letters and other interventions in the print and broadcast media. Thus, in October 1950, the BBC broadcast a radio program addressing the current mood and problems in Germany. The German-based journalist Saul Friedländer attracted considerable attention when he noted that the continuing imprisonment of Kesselring—"whom many Germans consider innocent"—was currently a major issue in Germany.[290] General Sir Frederick Morgan, who fully concurred in Friedländer's analysis, participated in the program as a British representative. His views were subsequently bolstered by correspondence from Scotland.

In summary, Scotland's ostensibly private interest in Kesselring's fate was reinforced, and finally supplanted, by his political interest (as a member of Hankey's circle) in reconciliation with Germany. He represented the politics of Western integration and therefore espoused a politics of memory that included a demand for the release of all German officers prior to West Germany becoming integrated in the Atlantic Alliance. His personal acquaintance with Kesselring allowed him to illustrate his arguments with a case about which he had personal knowledge. Scotland's political interest thus facilitated Kesselring's own aims while also possibly accelerating the process of political change in Britain.

Sir Basil Liddell Hart

Lord Hankey's circle of friends also included the military historian Sir Basil Liddell Hart, who had been considered a Kesselring supporter since his 1948 plea for prison conditions to be improved in Werl. Hankey had prompted him to take up Kesselring's case and make contact with him in prison.

Liddell Hart had experienced World War I as a British officer at the front, where he was seriously injured. The resulting chronic illness led to his retirement from active service in 1927.[291] He managed to make the transition to civilian life as a lecturer in military theory, and his manual *Strategy—The Indirect Approach* went through six editions between 1929 and 1967, becoming required reading for generations of British officers. Although celebrated and respected at home as a notable theorist, Liddell Hart was pained by the fact that, during World War II, his tactics were only used by the Germans—in particular, Heinz Guderian and Walter von Reichenau. He had a major influence on British public opinion as a correspondent for the *Daily Telegraph* (1925–1935) and the *Times* (1935–1939). Following the collapse of the 1938 military reforms under War Secretary Leslie Hore-Belisha, whom Liddell Hart had served as an adviser, he withdrew from public life. During the war, he made a name for himself as a critic of British war policy and a thorn in the side of the establishment, advocating a compromise peace with Germany. In view of his earlier works, this was seen as nothing less than treason. Consequently, there was little demand for his advice as a private individual and journalist during the war years.

After 1945, his contacts with imprisoned Wehrmacht officers offered him the opportunity to take center stage once again and to carve out a niche for himself as an expert in German World War II strategy.[292] In 1948, he published *The Other Side of the Hill.*[293] Based on interviews with German generals, the book provoked criticism in Britain and admiration in Germany due to its unusual approach: it described the war from the perspective of the defeated generals. It made the best-seller lists in both countries, and a new and expanded edition was published in 1951. Since the publication of his book, if not before, Germans had hoped that Liddell Hart might become a mouthpiece for German interests in England. He was considered a "welcome weapon in the arsenal of those arguing against collective guilt and the 'guilt of the generals.'"[294] But Liddell Hart's interests were not confined to the war that had just been fought. He also was focused on a potential future conflict. His subsequent commitment to German rearmament was revealed in the questions he posed, which were clearly aimed at amassing information that could prove useful in any conflict with the Soviet Union.[295] His privileged access to German military circles enabled him to collaborate with Rommel's widow on the 1953 publication of *The Rommel Papers*, a selection of documents from Rommel's estate.[296] His admiration for German military prowess was evident—though that admiration often clouded his judgment. He was a master at constructing war memories. The positive image of Rommel in the English-speaking world, which owes its origins to Liddell Hart's efforts,[297] is a prime example of this construction of memory.[298] Thanks to Liddell Hart, the German generals were able to convey a view of history to the public (including the public abroad) that would facilitate the rehabilitation of the Wehrmacht.[299]

However, Liddell Hart did not confine his efforts on behalf of the generals to print. He was also one of the earliest critics of the war crimes trials, as illustrated by his correspondence with the judge advocate general, Sir Hartley Shawcross, in September 1945.[300] He intervened behind the scenes for the prisoners, sometimes working closely with the bishop of Chichester in an attempt to utilize church channels.[301] His personal influence was such that all the war criminals still in custody (including Kesselring) hoped that Liddell Hart would take up their cases and ensure they were debated. Liddell Hart, in turn, was greatly interested in securing "fair treatment" for the generals because contact with the officers and the opportunity to engage in free discussion with them would provide valuable material for his military writings.[302] Since Liddell Hart relished his position as an intermediary, it is not surprising that Siegfied Westphal asked him to intercede to secure better prison conditions. Westphal complained that Kesselring was short of food and that his cell was damp; he also claimed that the prisoner was in poor health and only allowed to receive mail three times a month.[303] After receiving information from Laternser about the case, Liddell Hart said that he was "shocked."[304] He agreed with his friends that Kesselring had been unjustly imprisoned, and he promised to do all in his power to help him.[305] He expected the former field marshal's case to be reopened, which, in his view, would result in a significant reduction in the sentence or even an acquittal. Liddell Hart's intervention with Bishop on Kesselring's behalf was successful,[306] resulting in a significant improvement in Kesselring's prison conditions.[307]

But it was only Liddell Hart's links with the Hankey circle that allowed him to work in a wider context, transcending the limits of mere personal intervention. He was hinting at this broader context when he referred to the campaignlike nature of the protest: several of his friends had written to the papers objecting to the verdict, including Field Marshal Alexander.[308] He believed a greater commitment was required. Thus, he told Westphal that even though "there is a growing mood in England regarding a review of the war crimes verdicts," he did not "see any possibility of re-opening the cases, since the German government would not join in the demands."

Following the publication of his book on the German generals, Liddell Hart seemed predestined to play a role in the German rearmament debate.[309] As early as 1948, he had constituted himself the theoretical champion of such rearmament.[310] He succeeded in making the transition to a politically influential stage in the spring of 1952, when Hankey asked him to hold "informal discussions" with Adenauer on a possible amnesty for the war criminals. These discussions were to frame such an amnesty as desirable from a British perspective, representing a package deal linking a German contribution to Western defense with the release of the war criminals. The meeting between Liddell Hart and Adenauer will be examined in more depth later.

In conclusion, it should be noted that, due to his personal connections and his consequent position as an intermediary, Liddell Hart played a key role in molding public opinion on the rearmament issue, especially in Britain, and fostering a positive attitude toward the creation of a new German army. This role earned him the position of an unofficial negotiator, in which capacity he was even granted a personal audience with the German chancellor.

Efforts Made by the "Senators' Circle" and the NCPW in the United States

Many in American circles were also receptive to the German lobbyists' contention that, after preventing the dismantling of Germany's industrial complex, the issues at hand involved addressing "the intellectual and spiritual dismantlement" and the "fundamental defamation of the German soldier" and achieving a "full end to 'victors' justice'" as well as the "release of German soldiers and officers from Allied prisons."[311] German concerns were particularly well received by several U.S. senators: William A. Langer, Republican chairman of the Senate Judiciary Committee; James O. Eastland, a Mississippi Democrat who had already argued trenchantly against the American dismantlement policy;[312] Alexander Wiley, a Wisconsin Republican; Robert Taft, chairman of the Senate Foreign Relations Committee; and Styles Bridges, a New Hampshire Republican.[313] Bridges was a particularly forceful critic of the dismantlement policy, for he believed it could benefit the eastern bloc. This position had earned him the reputation of being "pro-German"—a distinct term of abuse in American politics, at least until 1947. Maine governor Ralph O. Brewster also showed interest in reconciliation with Germany. Together with Taft, he had planned the food deliveries to Germany (in particular, the 1948 delivery of food surpluses that was dubbed the "potato drive").[314] Senator Langer soon became known as the doyen of the American campaign to have the war crimes verdicts reviewed. He was supported in his efforts by former president Herbert Hoover, who demanded an end to the U.S. presence in Europe.[315]

Although a disparate group—Democrat and Republican, southern and northern, ideological conservative and old-style populist—these senators were united by strong anticommunist beliefs coupled with a conviction that the United States should withdraw as much as possible from European affairs.[316] Indeed, back in the 1930s, Senator Styles Bridges had described European politics as an alien mixture of "plots, plans and diseases."[317] Like Bridges, Taft and Hoover had been prominent in the isolationist movement before the war,[318] and they now regrouped in an effort to secure American withdrawal from Germany. Their demands for a shift in occupation policy—accompanied by their intervention in the war criminals debate—represented a logical progression of their isolationist politics. After all, if war was not in the American interest, then it followed that the messy aftermath of war, including occupation and the dispensation of justice through war crimes trials, would be even less in the country's interest.

The war criminals debate provided them with helpful arguments in their efforts to achieve a change at the top in the United States pursuant to the demands for a shift in occupation policy. Their efforts met with success in 1953. As the Cold War became more firmly entrenched, the fear of a resurgent Germany was increasingly overshadowed in the public debate by arguments in favor of a rapid rearmament of Germany, as well as the much-vaunted potential benefits offered by German officers' expertise if a conflict with the Soviet Union should erupt. Thus, the senators' commitment to Kesselring was—in the final analysis—a commitment to German rearmament, which, in turn, was motivated by a fundamentally isolationist approach.

Links among members of the American campaign group were maintained by the National Council for Prevention of War, a pacifist organization that was close to the Quakers both ideologically and in their efforts for the convicted German generals.[319] The NCPW president, Frederick Libby, and the organization's director, James Finucane, maintained contact with the individual senators.[320] The NCPW believed that the primary postwar aim was to supply food to the starving German people.[321] But only in 1947 did President Harry Truman give in to the mounting pressure being exerted by the senators. According to a report by Hoover, who had traveled through the ruins of Germany in 1947 on Truman's behalf,[322] the American food deliveries had started as private initiatives. Truman approved the Marshall Plan, which dispensed reconstruction aid to Europe totaling US$17 billion.[323] The packages sent by the Quakers and the NCPW through the Cooperative for American Relief to Everywhere (CARE packages), beginning in June 1946, were seen as a special gesture toward the Germans.

Deputy Secretary Albion B. Beverage was highly successful in lobbying senators on behalf of the NCPW.[324] In 1947, Beverage was replaced by James Finucane, a change that also initiated a shift in NCPW policy. Finucane believed not only that the industrial dismantlement of Germany should be prevented but also that the country should receive economic aid.[325] If, as was envisaged, the Germans had to pay reparations, they should also be helped to develop a functioning economy in order to earn the money required to pay those reparations.[326] Finucane also addressed the issue of how Germany should be handled politically. The NCPW reconciliation policy included a demand that the Germans "be placed on the same level as other nations" so as to "prevent a third world war." To provide a visible sign of the acceptance of German sovereignty, it was proposed that the war criminals be rehabilitated in a public act. Together with Hanns-Dietrich Ahrens, Finucane personally visited Werl to meet with Albert Kesselring, discuss his options for a pardon or amnesty, and offer American assistance.[327]

From 1947, the NCPW and the Quakers in the United States received support from the primarily charitable American Relief for Germany organization, which collected money throughout the States for displaced persons in Germany, and from the International Christian Leadership, which was led by Dr. Abraham Vereide and based in Seattle, Washington.[328] Well-known American writers such as Christopher Emmet and Dorothy Thompson, who wrote for the *New York Times*, had supported the political and humanitarian efforts of the NCPW and allied organizations since 1947.[329] Press commentators arguing that the United States should be committed to Germany emphasized the financial and political disadvantages the nation would suffer if Germany was dismantled and senior German military figures were imprisoned.

This argument benefited from a shift in American public opinion after 1949, when press reports of unacceptable interrogation methods used by U.S. officers in connection with the Dachau trials caused considerable public concern.[330] A report issued by the NCPW on December 18, 1948, detailing the torture and interrogation methods used in the Malmédy trial,[331] prompted Senator Langer to propose a Senate resolution on January 27, 1949. The title of the resolution was "American Military Justice—America's Shame?"[332] The NCPW was always kept up to date on developments because Langer himself was kept abreast of the situation in Germany through brief memos from individual German confidants such as Dr. Ahrens,[333] as well as German churchmen such as Theophil Wurm, head of the Lutheran Church, and Johann Neuhäusler, suffragan bishop of Munich. The NCPW magazine, *Peace Action*, distinguished itself in the battle for public opinion by publishing particularly pointed articles. At the end of 1954, Libby retired as head of the organization without a successor being appointed, and the NCPW ceased its work: as Libby noted with satisfaction, the organization's main aims had been achieved and the NCPW had rendered itself redundant.[334] In the 1960s, in a congratulatory address on the occasion of his eightieth birthday, Libby was hailed by the Federal Republic of Germany as a fighter for "the livelihood of millions of German workers" and for his "intervention on behalf of German prisoners of war."[335]

Kesselring owed his release to a concerted campaign of intervention by German, British, and American groupings. They, in turn, were supplied with arguments by Germans interested in securing the release of war criminals. In this regard, it was of crucial significance that all the conditions were already in place to facilitate an organized campaign. Those conditions included widespread public interest in the Kesselring case, both in Britain and in the United States, and the existence of organized groups in Germany (especially in North Rhine–Westphalia) that had already successfully opposed the dismantlement policy and now devoted their efforts to securing the release of all war criminals. It is hardly surprising that, in many cases, the same individuals who had previously fought to prevent the dismantlement of German industry now came together to campaign on behalf of another national symbol: the imprisoned Wehrmacht officers.[336] The PR campaign on behalf of Kesselring and Manstein was especially successful in Britain and the United States, thanks to men such as Hankey, Libby, Scotland, and Liddell Hart. The British government now had to act in response to the pressure exerted by these groups and individuals.

Chapter 4

The Politicization of the War Crimes Issue

The year 1949 marked the start of a new era in the occupying powers' approach to Germany,[1] due not only to the establishment of the Federal Republic but also, and primarily, to foreign policy factors. For the first time since 1945, the Western Allies appeared to be facing a real military threat as a result of the Soviet detonation of an atomic bomb in the summer of 1949. This development was accompanied by a reexamination of the American policy of containment toward the Soviet Union, which, in turn, caused the Western Alliance to step up both its conventional and its strategic nuclear armament. Policymakers were investigating ways of wedding all military allies more firmly to the alliance. In this context, plans relating to a remilitarization of Germany started to take shape. The outbreak of the Korean War in June 1950 accelerated the dynamic underlying this process, since it was viewed as a sure sign that the Soviet Union was willing to conjure up a new global conflict. The fear of a Soviet attack on Europe was accompanied by an awareness of the Western Alliance's military inferiority: its only deterrent was in the nuclear arena. In addition, the war in Korea tied up Western troops, further weakening the Western powers. Politicians in the West, warning of the possibility that the Soviets were methodically staging proxy wars,[2] fostered the psychological climate for the political expansion of NATO—and thus also for the admission of a rearmed Germany into a Western defense alliance.

With the establishment of the Federal Republic of Germany in 1949, politicians also turned their attention to the generals in custody. By linking the demand for German sovereignty with integration into the Western defense alliance, the fate of individual war criminals and the issue of their release gained political significance—a significance that put international relations under considerable strain. Therefore, both the Western Allies and the German government authorities had a vested interest in solving the war criminals question as quickly as they could and ensuring that this issue was (as far as possible) decoupled from day-to-day politics.

After describing the different forces at play in the war criminals issue, this chapter will, by making use of previously unpublished documents from the

British National Archives, trace the stormy internal debates both in Germany and in the UK surrounding attempts to resolve the Kesselring case—a case that, in historical terms, was of exemplary significance and highly symbolic for postwar German society. The press campaign mounted to secure Kesselring's release, which accompanied political discourse, illustrated the manner in which the treatment of the war criminals issue was distorted by the debates surrounding German rearmament and integration into the Western Alliance. In the final analysis, Kesselring was the beneficiary of this process.

General Developments in the War Crimes Issue, 1949–1950

Following the end of the Berlin blockade, battle lines were drawn against the Soviet Union, and the North Atlantic Treaty Organization was launched in the wake of the establishment of two German states.[3] The Allies, too, found they were forced to reposition themselves in terms of *Deutschlandpolitik* (policy toward Germany), and this, in turn, led to a repositioning on the war crimes issue. In addition to the foreign policy threat posed by the USSR and the considerations regarding Germany's military potential triggered by that threat, other factors contributed to a sea change in Allied Deutschlandpolitik. Thus, the British were dealing simultaneously with a growing German resistance to industrial dismantlement in the Ruhr region and with a growing self-confidence on the part of the new Bonn government. On the home front, the British government found itself confronting pressure from conservative and liberal circles seeking an end to British involvement in all areas of German public life. It was thus apparent that the future Allied approach to the war crimes issue would be determined not only by Adenauer's security policy but also by the demands posed by former Wehrmacht officers and by the shift in public opinion at home.

Arguments that had originated in Germany were subsequently seized on and disseminated by Allied circles. For the first time, a link between war crimes policy and a future military alliance including German formations was established in the British press, and once again, it was Liddell Hart—writing in July 1948—who (in the eyes of his compatriots) pushed the boat out.[4] Liddell Hart's book *The Other Side of the Hill* should again be mentioned in this context, given the positive image of the Wehrmacht leadership projected there and the book's enormous influence on public opinion regarding the war crimes issue.[5] Writing in the *Daily Express* about the trial of Bochum industrialists resisting the dismantlement process, the journalist James Cameron forged a link between dismantlement and the fate of the war criminals, whom he described as honorable men.[6] Both pieces—Liddell Hart's July 1948 article and Cameron's piece—were written at the urging of Lord Hankey.[7] In his book *Gedanken zur Verteidigung Europas* (Thoughts on European Defense), first published in Germany in 1951, Liddell Hart summarized the debate surrounding a German military contribution to the Alliance and the interplay between that debate and an amnesty for German war criminals.[8]

The establishment of the West German state created a new constellation with regard to the war crimes issue. For the first time, in addition to enjoying the right of free assembly, former Wehrmacht officers were able to organize and campaign for their comrades' release. Although this group had long been thinking about German rearmament, their demands now emerged from back rooms and debating circles into the light of widespread publicity.[9] In this regard, the rehabilitation of convicted war criminals constituted a "preliminary step and pre-condition for re-armament."[10]

Allied and German Plans for Rearmament

Relations between the Western Allies and Germany had to be put on a different footing before Allied war crimes policy could enter a new phase. The Petersberg Agreement, signed on November 22, 1949, in Bonn, was an initial step in this direction. In the agreement, Germany was, for the first time, recognized as a partially sovereign state, and the signals for economic recovery were set. The aim of the Petersberg Agreement was to reintegrate West Germany into the community of nations, while also improving German-Allied relations. Although it included a range of concessions to the Allies, the agreement also provided for the readmission of German representatives into international institutions, thus conferring long-term advantages on Germany. Among other benefits, the Federal Republic was to receive financial aid under the Marshall Plan, and the industrial dismantlement process was halted, especially in the steel and chemical sectors. In return, West Germany undertook to join the International Ruhr Authority, to cooperate with the Allied Control Commission's military security council, and to support the decartelization of German industry.[11] In the opinion of the Allies, these steps represented a minimum in terms of security precautions. Allied security interests were always dominated by two concerns: establishing security *with* Germany while protecting the Allies *from* Germany.[12]

These developments exceeded Adenauer's expectations, enabling him to couple his political demand for German sovereignty with an assurance that his nation would build up its armed forces in the context of a defense alliance—however that alliance was to be configured. These plans were covertly prepared by a staff of military experts, including former OKW staff officers

Hans Speidel and Adolf Heusinger, as well as Infantry General Hermann Foertsch.[13] These officers were free to present Adenauer with their "thoughts on the Federal Republic's external security," and beyond that, they could also be confident that the chancellor would accept and promote their views to Herbert Blank's department. Blank was then engaged in planning what would become the Ministry for Defense, and the coordination office was called the Blank Office after its director.[14] The impending nuclear standoff with the Soviet Union gave rise to Allied calls for West Germany to be included in an arms buildup. Thus, as early as June 1950, the British high commissioner, General Robertson, advocated remilitarization, possibly under the cover of a "Federal police force."[15] However, Adenauer and others feared the time was not yet ripe for domestic political acceptance of German rearmament.

The outbreak of the Korean War on June 25, 1950, is generally regarded as the turning point in the rearmament debate, but in fact, it was simply a catalyst accelerating deliberations that had already been set in motion. In August 1950, Churchill suggested the creation of a European army.[16] In September of the same year, the New York Conference of Foreign Ministers officially endorsed the desirability of German rearmament and proposed that a suitable plan be put in place.[17] However, American deliberations were thwarted by the unhelpful approach adopted by France, which, on October 21, 1950, proposed the creation of a supranational European army including German contingents (called the Pleven Plan).[18] The players in this debate finally agreed on a compromise, according to which plans would be drawn up for the development of a German army before finalizing the political framework conditions.[19] Leaders in the United States, aware of their nation's position as the leading power in the European context and thus also of France's political dependency, decided that West German formations should be established immediately in the NATO framework.[20] The decision to rearm Germany had been made by the autumn of 1950.

Any security concerns the Allies may have had were assuaged by the fact that Adenauer's domestic policy of aligning Germany with the West proved to be an unswerving, core principle of the new German state, making it much easier for the Allies to meet Germany halfway. Negotiations concerning a possible West German defense contribution in NATO were heavily influenced by Adenauer's policy. His hope was that the creation of a new German army would gain him room for maneuver "vis-à-vis the agitation of the right-wing Free Democratic Party (FDP) and DP coalition partners informed by an aggressively nationalist sentiment,"[21] and he planned to integrate the Federal Republic into the western bloc.[22]

Adenauer made no bones about the post-1949 expectations of the German political establishment, which included a protective undertaking and security guarantee on the part of the Allies; a shift to the east in the Western defense line; inclusion of West Germany in the Western security system; a willingness to share responsibility for the security of Western Europe; and deterrence through a military enhancement of the Western Alliance, including the provision of a German contingent.[23] In return, the Federal Republic would refrain from creating a German army independent of any bilateral alliances, although Bonn hoped for political equality and inclusion in a supranational army. Ultimately, rearmament merely served Adenauer as a "vehicle for the earliest possible achievement of full sovereignty for the Federal Republic."[24] He subordinated all other demands to this goal, including, in the final analysis, German reunification.[25]

However, plans to create a new German army just five years after a devastating defeat were still encountering substantial resistance from the German public,[26] and at the same time, there was a growing public interest in the war criminals issue. It did not take long for both concerns to be linked, just as a similar linkage was being forged among military advocates. As early as 1949, the Bundestag debates on the amnesty law caused an initial shift in public opinion, which now sought a more extensive amnesty.[27] Adenauer himself made every effort to ensure that the war criminals issue did not become part of the public discourse.[28] But the "lobbying campaign to preserve the honor of the better Germany"[29]—a campaign conducted by veterans' associations working within various interest groups, on the one hand, and by the media, on the other hand—grew in intensity to such a degree that Adenauer was forced to reluctantly endorse the demand for the war criminals' release in order to preserve domestic peace. In his first government policy statement, issued on September 20, 1949, during the Manstein trial, Chancellor Adenauer stated:

> Those truly guilty of the crimes committed during the National Socialist era and during the war should be punished with all due rigor. . . . Both the war and the chaos of the postwar era represented such a severe test for many, and brought with it such temptation, that one must summon understanding for many lapses. That is why the Federal Government is examining the issue of an amnesty [interjections of "Bravo!"], and is also examining whether the High Commissioners should be petitioned for a corresponding amnesty in respect of sentences imposed by Allied military courts.[30]

However, that was the only occasion during his period in government when Adenauer issued a direct demand for an amnesty. He generally preferred to work behind the scenes on behalf of convicted war criminals.[31] Once an opportunity arose to negotiate for German sovereignty in exchange for the provision of German troops, Adenauer took pains to see that the war criminals issue was not addressed directly. This was the case, for example, in the secret memorandum he addressed to the Allied high commissioners on August 29, 1950, in turn offering a West German defense contribution.[32]

The public debate was reignited following Adenauer's statement on foreign policy principles on November 8, 1950, focusing on the "issue of a contribution by the Federal Republic of Germany to the defense of the West." Hans-Joachim von Merkatz, a Deutsche Partei member of Parliament, quickly seized on this argument and welcomed the idea of a new German army. But he noted that this rendered it "even more unbearable" that former soldiers were still in custody, and he called for solidarity efforts to secure their release. He justified this approach by saying that "men such as Manstein, like Kesselring and others, who are imprisoned in Landsberg and Werl, these men are us, we are all the one. After all, we are also responsible for that with which they, on our behalf, have been accused."[33] The war criminals issue had thus been raised to the status of a national question, and all further political development would depend on the resolution of this issue.

The Attitude of Wehrmacht Officers toward Rearmament

The debate surrounding rearmament and in particular the approach adopted by Wehrmacht officers to their former commanders-in-chief (now convicted war criminals) are crucial to an understanding of why Kesselring was unexpectedly released in 1952. Adenauer had long been aware of the attitude of former Wehrmacht officers, who—since 1946—had issued repeated demands for the release of military prisoners, an umbrella term used to denote both POWs and convicted war criminals.[34] Many of those who had come together after 1949 in a range of semiprivate associations and discussion groups now realized that the proposal to reconstitute a German army presented an opportunity for themselves and their imprisoned comrades. They made it clear that their participation in the development of a new German military would depend on certain demands being met.[35] Representatives of German veterans' associations repeatedly drafted memoranda addressed to the British and American governments in which they expressed their reservations regarding a continuation of the war crimes trial program.[36]

Many former soldiers believed that they had been subjected to a blanket defamation or degradation and felt that, as an entire profession, they had been belittled and reviled by the measures taken by both the occupying powers and the German authorities. The public rejection of everything military—a rejection that grew out of the frustrations attendant upon defeat, not to mention the courtroom revelations regarding war crimes—caused many soldiers to feel they were being persecuted.[37] The denazification process, the war crimes trials, derisory comments about professional soldiers in the media, statements by politicians, and degrading treatment while seeking employment or in the workplace all were felt to be particularly humiliating.[38]

This sensitivity illustrates the extent to which the officer corps, particularly the senior ranks, had been shattered by their military defeat and by the Wehrmacht's inability to extricate itself from entanglement with National Socialism.[39] As a result, all attempts to confront the personal past in an earnest and self-critical manner died at birth. The demand for an end to defamation was "fundamentally [based] on the unspoken desire for rehabilitation and for the German Wehrmacht to be acquitted of complicity in the war."[40] The prevailing belief was not that the German conduct of the war had been dishonorable but rather that the honor and professionalism of German soldiers had been undermined solely by the manner in which they were treated by the victorious powers.[41] This feeling also gave rise at an early stage to demands for the Allies to restore the honor of German soldiers, for example, by issuing some kind of "declaration of honor." Liddell Hart was particularly assiduous in pressing this demand, both through his personal contacts and in his writings.[42]

With the establishment of the Federal Republic in 1949 and the first sessions of the German Bundestag, domestic political demands for sovereignty—even with regard to the war criminals issue—became ever louder.[43] Following the era of occupation, the time had at last come to put an end to "foreign justice."[44] However, the varying motivations underlying these demands should be noted. Although some Wehrmacht officers believed that German courts would be able to determine individual guilt in a "fairer" manner, certain politicians felt otherwise and hoped that collective amnesties would dispose of this vexatious issue once and for all. German public opinion seemed to be shifting in favor of the prisoners. The German soldiers saw their demands as preconditions for cooperating in a German defense contribution, but the Americans viewed them as an attempt to exonerate the German General Staff and officer corps. During conversations with former officers, it became evident to the American high commissioner, John McCloy, that no officer would ever accept the verdicts handed down by Allied courts.

Many asserted that the imprisonment of their comrades weighed intolerably on their consciences, thus rendering cooperation with Allied forces impossible. They questioned whether—in view of the sentences passed on their former comrades—it would be treason to collaborate with erstwhile foes within a defense alliance.[45] Behind the scenes, however, the German generals were deeply divided on whether one could even consider rearmament as long as senior commanders remained in Allied custody. Some felt that the good of the country should take precedence; others advised a boycott. For instance, Generaloberst Hans Reinhardt, a prisoner in Landsberg who had received a fifteen-year custodial sentence in the Nuremberg Case 12, dealing with the Wehrmacht High Command, let his comrades know that "the German and European question, the repulsion of Communism, must be given greater priority than the fate of us few men here."[46] Such an attitude may have made it a great deal easier for some—specifically, those in the Blank Office—to participate in the official plans for a West German defense contribution. However, writing to Kesselring, Laternser criticized the fact that Speidel had "even been prepared to enter discussions" without "first categorically insisting that imprisoned comrades be released."[47]

Advocacy on behalf of those war criminals still in custody became "a seminal moment for an officer corps without an army."[48] In this regard, Generalleutnants Adolf Heusinger[49] and Hans Speidel played a leading role in the war criminals policy adopted by Wehrmacht officers. Indeed, the latter explicitly took Kesselring's part. Speidel, who was considered the unofficial spokesman of the Wehrmacht officers,[50] supported the demands of the Verband deutscher Soldaten (German Soldiers' Association, or VdS), which was seeking common representation of veterans' interests, primarily to pursue pension claims. However, like Heusinger, Speidel preferred to pursue a policy of quiet diplomacy and personal contacts.[51] On New Year's Day 1949, he wrote to Laternser reporting on the various approaches he had made to the Americans regarding retrials for all those in custody. Not least with a view to the fortunes of his own family, he skillfully coupled this issue with the prior release of all prisoners.[52] Working in the background, he held talks with Americans and Germans and advocated a review of the war criminals' sentences—especially since, at an early stage, he had realized that the United States (in particular) was considering rearmament.

Those playing a more or less official role did not have to worry about such scruples. One person in this category was Gerhard von Schwerin, commanding general in Italy in 1945 and, from 1950, Adenauer's first security adviser. Schwerin had paved the way for the Blank Office[53] and had "long advocated the cause of the convicted prisoners in Werl."[54] In June 1950, Schwerin presented two demands to the British military governor of North Rhine–Westphalia. His aim was to harmonize the legal situation in the British zone with that in the American zone. In concrete terms, this meant that the British high commissioner would be granted the right to send cases for retrial to German courts and to issue pardons. In addition, he hoped to secure an improvement in the prison conditions endured by common soldiers in Werl. These demands constituted a daring step forward at the time, and Schwerin offered a realistic assessment of the situation when he noted that the only remaining prospect for success was through the clemency route.[55] He pointed out that vocal criticism of the Allies was counterproductive, since they were trying to address matters. Schwerin therefore sent a confidential message to Laternser: "The brakes must be put on Manstein. He seems to be rather wild, which is damaging the whole affair."

At the beginning of October 1950, when—at the invitation of the Blank Office—ten former generals and admirals, as well as five General Staff officers, met in the Cistercian Monastery at Himmerod in the Eifel Mountains to discuss West Germany's external security, their agenda was dominated by the "so-called war criminals." In a memorandum, they demanded "the cessation of all defamation of German soldiers [including the *Waffen SS*, which at the time was deployed with the Wehrmacht] and measures to shift public opinion at home and abroad."[56] Following a "declaration of honor on behalf of German soldiers" to be issued by the Allies, the Bundestag, and the federal government, those "Germans convicted as 'war criminals'" should be released, the officers stated, as long as they "had only followed orders and did not commit any actions punishable under the old German laws."[57] Only then, according to the memorandum, would it be possible to recruit "really valuable elements who would be indispensable for the development of a reliable and respected force."[58] This assessment was taken very seriously by the Allies. The Americans had no illusions: they knew that Speidel and many of his comrades "would only be available to the new Wehrmacht [*sic!*] once the Bonn government had secured the release of his brothers."[59]

The Allied Approach to the War Crimes Issue

Shortly after the Nuremberg trial of the main war criminals, it became obvious to the Allies that the shock effect of Nuremberg would be short-lived. Rather, "recognition of the Third Reich's unjust character declined with increasing distance," and "during the subsequent Allied trials, [it] was eventually channeled into a perception of a few facts, most of which were also challenged."[60] As scholar Peter Steinbach phrased it, "[The] thorn of National Socialist violence was embedded deep in the flesh of a society which had great difficulty accepting that the facts revealed during the trials represented reality."[61]

Rather than addressing prosecution charges, critics of the war crimes trials tended to make a blanket assertion that those who had, after all, "merely done their duty" were now being held responsible by the *victors*.[62] There was no debate regarding the fact that the military leadership, with its lofty concepts of honor, had sometimes helped draft criminal orders and also been responsible for seeing that those orders were followed. A "derealization" of the National Socialist era set in against the background of denazification and war crimes trials,[63] and as a result, the contemporary historical reality remained concealed behind a "veil of unreality."[64] The unequal implementation of the denazification process, the integration of expelled Germans from the East, the division of Germany, and unease about the alleged victors' justice all combined to promote an internal delimitation on the part of individuals, together with a rejection of Allied policy. The politicization of the war criminals issue meant that undifferentiated demands for a general amnesty were substituted for an objective assessment of individual cases. Such demands had the effect of declaring all soldiers, without distinction, victims of Allied victors' justice. Thus, a distorted esprit de corps transformed all war criminals, including those whose guilt was undisputed, into comrades who were "innocently languishing behind dungeon walls," a complaint that was repeatedly voiced by veterans' associations.[65]

Any Allied decision regarding the war criminals issue would be associated with incalculable risks, since a more benevolent policy toward Germany could easily have created an impression of caprice. In the context of their reeducation policy, it was vital for the Allies to avoid sending a message that, by releasing the war criminals, "miscarriages of justice" were somehow being righted. The shift in the Allied Deutschlandpolitik toward a policy of reintegration was underlined by the appointment of John J. McCloy in July 1949 to succeed General Lucius D. Clay as American high commissioner. McCloy realized that it was impossible to overemphasize the importance of the war criminals issue, which "involved more than punishment or clemency for a handful of criminals."[66] His fear was that the issue could become a "serious impediment to German-American relations" unless the Americans offered the Germans a tangible concession without retrospectively setting the verdicts aside.[67] But how great could that concession be if the goal was to avoid causing public outrage in the United States while simultaneously forestalling German frustration?

The British position on the war criminals issue was not impervious to the new American line of thought. One initial indication of a new British politics of memory was the decision to reduce the custodial sentences imposed on Kesselring, Mackensen, and Mältzer to twenty-one years[68] in an attempt to gauge public reaction in the UK, Germany, and Italy to clemency moves.[69]

The reduction in Kesselring's sentence was a purely political decision, for the painstaking legal assessment of Laternser's petition by the British judge advocate general had revealed that it contained little that was new, and therefore, it was not possible to recommend a sentence reduction.[70] There was no ambiguity regarding the political dimension of the war criminals issue: the judge advocate general, when dismissing the appeal, concluded by declaring that, following a general decision made in London, "the sentences of life imprisonment in all three cases have been commuted to twenty-one years' imprisonment."[71] The decision reflected a complete turnaround in British policy.

The political pressure arising from the external threat and the attendant need to incorporate Germany into a Western defense alliance had smoothed the path toward realignment in the war crimes issue. But decisions had to be substantiated. There was still a need to develop sound arguments relating to a "psychology of the past" that would not only explain the new policy to the British public but also persuade former German Wehrmacht officers to participate in the defense alliance.

Options for Resolving the Kesselring Case

At an international level, the war criminals issue had gained a completely new dimension due to security policy considerations, but this was not yet apparent to the Kesselring lobby. Since neither Laternser's petition nor the review board's report in March 1950 had secured Kesselring's freedom, it seemed advisable to improve coordination of the initiatives aimed at obtaining his release. An attempt had to be made to interest politicians and in particular the media in Kesselring's fate.

Kesselring's counsel, Hans Laternser, played a pivotal role in the campaign to secure his client's release. Laternser ensured that Kesselring's case was taken up by German authorities and church organizations, as well as by the lobbyists campaigning for the release of all those who had been sentenced following the war. Laternser did not conduct his crusade in isolation, as is evident from his involvement in the Heidelberger Juristenkreis (Heidelberg Lawyers' Circle). With the contacts this group had established among church aid organizations and even with government departments in Bonn, all dealing with POW and war criminal issues, "the war criminals' aid cartel had grown to organizational and political dimensions" that quite conceivably could have posed a threat to democracy.[72] The concerted actions of the Kesselring lobby can be traced with the aid of Laternser's papers,[73] which have only now been made publicly available.

The Heidelberg Lawyers' Circle

Initially, those campaigning against the war crimes trials were, by and large, members of the old elites (as already discussed) and in particular the churches. However, opportunities for exerting influence multiplied with the establishment of the Federal Republic. A network of people centered on the Nuremberg defense lawyers used selected actions, underpinned by media assistance, to ensure that the political establishment took note of the war criminals issue.

German lawyers were eager to make amends for the fact that the Allied courts had turned down their appeals. In 1949, the end of the U.S.-led subsequent trials at Nuremberg (a total of twelve cases against the former National Socialist elite) threatened to also put an end to the constant exchange of information among defense attorneys. As a result, in the spring of 1949, the group of Heidelberg lawyers was founded under the auspices of Eduard Wahl, who held the International Law Chair at Heidelberg University. Wahl—who would subsequently be appointed an undersecretary of state in the Federal Justice Ministry—had himself acted as a defense lawyer during the IG Farben trial (Case 6) at Nuremberg.[74] The Heidelberger Juristenkreis acted as a central coordinating body, bundling the interests of the various groups acting on behalf of different war criminals. In this regard, the Lawyers' Circle set priorities and attempted to "prevent activities which appeared to be counterproductive."[75] Members included the following prominent attorneys: Rudolf Aschenauer, who had, inter alia, defended Otto Ohlendorf during the Einsatzgruppen trial (Case 9) and also provided legal representation for almost 700 prisoners in Landsberg, particularly with regard to denazification and pensions issues; Hellmut Becker, Ernst von Weizsäcker's defense counsel during Case 11 against the German Foreign Office; Georg Fröschmann, who had defended, among others, Viktor Brack during the Medical Case (Case 1) as well as Gottlob Berger during Case 11, known as the Ministries Case; Justus Koch, defense counsel in Case 11; Otto Kranzbühler, who acted as defense counsel during Case 5, the trial of Alfred Krupp and Friedrich Flick, and also acted for Karl Dönitz during the IMT trial and for Hermann Röchling when he appeared before a French military court in Rastatt; Hans Laternser; Rudolf Müller; Heinrich von Rospatt; and Helmut Henze.[76] The Heidelberg Lawyers' Circle, which took its name from its meeting venue, also maintained contacts with the judiciary in the form of the *Oberlandesgerichtspräsidenten* (presiding judges), the highest tier of the German legal system at the regional level. The group of presiding judges of the Higher Regional Courts was led by the Celle judge Hodo Freiherr von Hodenberg—an unwavering opponent of Allied jurisprudence. The Heidelberger Juristenkreis also maintained contacts with academics such as Professor Gustav Radbruch and the Munich-based international law expert Professor Erich Kaufmann. Church contacts included Heribert Knott, legal adviser to the Catholic Church, and the secretary of the German Lutheran synod, Hansjürg Ranke. Regular guests attending the Heidelberg Lawyers' Circle's meetings also included former Nuremberg defense counsel Hans Gawlik,[77] as well as Alfons Wahl in his capacity as official representative of the Federal Ministry of Justice.[78] In April 1951, for the first time, Laternser addressed the group, discussing some of the legal problems surrounding the Manstein trial.[79] Although there is no record of Laternser highlighting the Kesselring case during these meetings, we can assume that the case was discussed informally. One of the defense attorneys' duties was to ensure that their views were aired in the media. Thus, Erich Schwinge offered to "demolish" an expert paper on the Kesselring case that had appeared in a legal journal.[80] Schwinge completed his article in November 1950 and planned to publish it anonymously in the journal *Der Fortschritt*, as well as in a legal journal (using his full name). He included a reference to Laternser's book.[81]

The main significance of the Heidelberg Lawyers' Circle lay in its ostensible objectivity. Thus, the "Vergangenheitspolitik of the lawyers' group" was "characterized by an attempt to dispense, as far as possible, with contemporary historical credos." Instead, the idea was to formulate "a legal positivism in respect of Vergangenheitspolitik, which could lay claim to objectivity and which aims to dispose of the war criminals problem once and for all."[82]

The Central Legal Defense Office

In the middle of March 1950, the Central Legal Defense Office, or Rechtsschutz-Stelle, established by the West German government and headed by the attorney Hans Gawlik, took up its duties—duties that its precursor had performed covertly as the Coordinating Office for Aiding the Legal Defense of German Prisoners Abroad. Even the use of the term *Rechtsschutz-Stelle* indicated a growing self-confidence among German government departments. The name assumed that compliance with the law could be assured to those claiming unjust Allied jurisdiction. The office's activities were assisted by individual parliamentarians, among them Herbert Höfler, the head of the Catholic aid agency Caritas who, in 1950, sought to obtain clemency for Germans still imprisoned in Italy.[83] Until the establishment of the Rechtsschutz-Stelle, concrete assistance to prisoners had been provided by the German Red Cross together with the Lutheran and Catholic social aid agencies,[84] and now, these agencies were unwilling to simply relinquish their influence.[85] The Lutheran

Aid Agency for Prisoners of War, in particular, continued to go it alone and play politics with the war criminals issue.[86] However, the groups were eventually integrated into the work of the Rechtsschutz-Stelle. By establishing this office, the Federal Ministry of Justice hoped to provide German prisoners abroad with assistance (primarily financial) when facing trial. In addition, the office considered petitioning for clemency in the event that prisoners were convicted. The Rechtsschutz-Stelle staff kept itself informed of trial issues, and it had a ministerial fund with which to meet costs.

Although the title of the office's precursor indicated that financial aid was to be restricted to Germans imprisoned abroad, Gawlik extended his remit to include the interests of war criminals interned in Germany, together with their attorneys.[87] The financial assistance was of particular benefit to the defense attorneys, who had often worked "on account";[88] for instance, the Rechtsschutz-Stelle paid Laternser's bill for preparing the 1949 Kesselring petition.[89]

But the Rechtsschutz-Stelle provided other types of assistance as well. Office staffers systematically gathered information from defense attorneys so that they could effectively address queries or petitions to the competent occupation authorities. In doing so, they generally took up the defense arguments (often relatively uncritically). They also offered defense attorneys valuable insider advantages as they jostled for position in the clemency debate: thanks to the Rechtsschutz-Stelle, both defense attorneys and their clients were kept informed about any moves made by the federal government. Thus, for example, Laternser knew in 1951 that "the Bonn Rechtsschutz-Stelle [was] currently gathering material on the Werl cases with the aim of approaching the English authorities."[90] A representative of the Federal Ministry for Justice had also been conducting negotiations with the head of the British legal division, Sir Alfred Brown.[91]

The network of informants and information was both tight and effective—and it penetrated to the very top. When it came to options for intervention through the Rechtsschutz-Stelle or the Federal Ministry for Justice, Kesselring seems to have felt that the most appropriate contact person was no less a figure than the German justice minister Thomas Dehler, since the minister was thought to "be open to the issue."[92] Indeed, Dehler had gained some notoriety due to his forthright criticism of the victors' justice dispensed by the occupying powers.[93] Minister Dehler's involvement in advocacy for imprisoned war criminals went beyond the call of duty. Without consulting Adenauer, he presented the Allies with several clemency petitions on behalf of individual defendants, and he made federal funds available to American writers and opinion makers who were seeking to shift U.S. public opinion in favor of the war criminals.[94] Dehler thus posed a potential risk to Adenauer's security policy.

Although the work of the Rechtsschutz-Stelle carried great political weight, the office's involvement sometimes had negative consequences for Adenauer's Deutschlandpolitik. The reputation among the Allies of the office's patron, Justice Minister Dehler, also suffered as a result of his involvement. In Kesselring's case, the official work carried out by the Rechtsschutz-Stelle (which was established toward the end of his imprisonment) was of less importance than Minister Dehler's unofficial advocacy, especially in the United States,[95] which ensured that the former field marshal's fate remained on the public agenda.

The German Soldiers' Association

As already indicated, the German Soldiers' Association, or Verband deutscher Soldaten, played a particularly important role in the nascent rearmament debate, even though its membership constituted a relatively small proportion of the totality of German veterans. Many of those returning from POW camps no longer saw themselves as soldiers: indeed, they were glad to put their war service behind them.[96] They were therefore quite impervious to appeals from veterans' groups such as the VdS.

Nevertheless, the period following 1951 saw the establishment of a growing number of military Traditionsverbände and veterans' organizations.[97] There were three main types of associations.[98] The first type, which encompassed the majority of these groups, had been established shortly after the war in the form of private organizations and were solely concerned with social issues, such as the provision of pensions for former members of the Wehrmacht. The second type of veterans' association comprised politically radical groupings such as the Stahlhelm and the Schutzbund deutscher Soldaten (Protection Committee for German Soldiers). Although their numbers were small, their views ensured that their gatherings and speeches attracted widespread public attention. The third group incorporated a large number of the so-called Traditionsverbände established with the aim of providing veterans from specific units with an opportunity to meet former comrades and exchange reminiscences. The most influential Traditionsverbände included the paratroopers, the Verband deutsches Afrikakorps (German Afrikakorps Association), and the Traditionsverband Grossdeutschland (Greater Germany Veterans' Association), representing former Panzertruppen (armored troops).[99]

Due to the continuing proliferation of new veterans' associations, it seemed expedient to establish an umbrella organization to assert political demands: this new umbrella group was called the Verband deutscher

Soldaten.[100] At its inaugural meeting, former Generaloberst Hans Friessner was elected chairperson, but his term of office was cut short by the furor created by ill-considered media statements he made in December 1951. He was succeeded by a widely respected former admiral, Gottfried Hansen. Public reaction to the establishment of the VdS was negative, due to a perception that career soldiers (as opposed to draftees) were overrepresented in the organization and were seeking a suitable platform for their political activities.[101] But given the disunity among its constituent groups, the VdS did not exercise any real influence. In the end, it was unable to overcome the fragmentary nature of the autonomous Traditionsverbände and become a political force in its own right.[102]

The development of the rearmament debate signaled a shift in relations between political parties and the veterans' associations, since the domestic political resistance encountered by the government parties encouraged them to seek allies in every conceivable quarter.[103] For their part, the veterans' associations had realized that their demands—for example, relating to pensions issues—would only be met if they succeeded in gaining support from the political parties represented in the Bundestag (especially the FDP).[104] The fact that some members of the Bundestag were also members of veterans' associations enabled closer parliamentary contacts to be forged. At the same time, the DP, FDP, and CDU (Christlich Demokratische Union Deutschlands, or Christian Democrats) were also interested in establishing contacts with the veterans' organizations. Fearing that those associations were open to radical influences, they established the Goslaer Kreis (Goslar Group, named after their meeting venue in the town of Goslar, near Hanover), hoping to thus create a veterans' organization that would be more amenable to pressure from the political parties.[105] This initiative failed, however, for membership remained small: most veterans were uninterested in political involvement, and they tended to gravitate toward the Traditionsverbände that focused on maintaining social contacts with former comrades. The beneficiary proved to be the VdS, whose membership numbers rose steadily. From 1952, under the leadership of Admiral Hansen, the VdS pursued a strictly progovernment policy: indeed, many of its activities were first cleared with the West German officials, quickly ensuring that the VdS enjoyed public sympathy and a reputation for dependability.[106] Even by the end of 1951, the VdS was already developing a media presence, having retained the Ahrens public relations firm in Essen, which was asked to address the PR and organizational issues surrounding a release of convicted war criminals.[107] According to Hansen, the new German army's primary task would be to make amends to former Wehrmacht comrades for their sufferings since 1945.[108] The VdS displayed considerable self-confidence in its dealings with the government, as can be seen from its 1952 annual report. Writing in the report, Hansen had demanded that any positions in the new German army be filled solely by professional soldiers, so as to express "soldierly loyalty" to the new government, as opposed to the former officeholders.[109]

The interests of the political parties and the veterans' associations coincided primarily in respect to pension and welfare issues and the impending German defense contribution. As a result, the 1953 Bundestag elections seemed set to turn into a referendum for or against rearmament. However, once rearmament had become a reality and the new German army, the Bundeswehr, had been established, the parties' political interest in the veterans' associations started to wane, and as a result, so did the political influence wielded by those associations.[110]

The general political positioning of the VdS worked in favor of Kesselring. In fact, it is possible that he owed his release—at least partly—to the efforts of VdS chairman Gottfried Hansen, who had for some time been working behind the scenes on the former field marshal's behalf. Once it became clear that the British had decided to release Kesselring, Hansen ostentatiously approached Adenauer (in the autumn of 1952), intervened with the British authorities, and discussed the Kesselring case with Lord Hankey, all in an attempt to gain some public credit for what was already a done deal.

Kesselring's Denazification

Demands from military circles for all war criminals to be released were accompanied by deliberations on how such a step could be officially facilitated. Kesselring's denazification was a formal precondition for his release. At the same time, the denazification verdict on Kesselring—which, as had been anticipated, was positive—became another building block in the campaign to vindicate his honor being waged by those who believed the field marshal had been wrongfully convicted. Kesselring benefited from the timing of his denazification process. After 1948, it became apparent that the civilian courts handling the process (which had been specifically established to deal with denazification proceedings) "based their judgments more on legal than on political criteria"; it seemed, as well, that they had developed "their own exoneration routine," condemning only those who could not somehow prove that they had acted in "good faith."[111] In addition, the Americans in particular had been seeking an end to the denazification process since 1948, for it did not meet their reeducation criteria.

In the autumn of 1950, Dr. Rudolf Aschenauer offered to represent Kesselring in the denazification proceedings together with his Landsberg clients.[112]

Unbidden, he thus became a spokesperson for former Wehrmacht soldiers in respect to pension issues. Although Laternser quickly offered Kesselring his own services for the denazification process,[113] Hans Friessner (as spokesperson for the Landsberg prisoners) asked Kesselring to undergo the process together with the "Landsbergers,"[114] and he emphasized the need to present a united front. Laternser therefore allowed Aschenauer to take the case,[115] whereupon Dr. Aschenauer approached Kesselring in Werl.[116] The symbolic decision by the Landsberg and Werl prisoners to act together in the denazification process shows that the earlier sharp divisions between war criminals and prisoners convicted of crimes against humanity (a distinction established in Nuremberg to differentiate the Wehrmacht, which was presumed to be clean, from SS perpetrators) had started to blur in terms of the debate.[117]

Denazification courts were established in January 1946 following Eisenhower's JCS Directive 1067, designed to cleanse the German administration and identify the involvement in Nazi rule and politics of some 8 million members of the German Nazi Party. The aim of this measure was to reeducate the German people and identify Nazis by distinguishing five categories of culprits: major offenders, offenders, lesser offenders, followers, and exonerated persons.[118] Between 1946 and 1948, 545 civilian courts—the so-called *Spruchkammern*—oversaw around 90,000 cases. All German nationals over eighteen years of age had to be reviewed in order to obtain work permits and food supplies. After the Cold War crisis in Berlin in 1948, however, the whole program was accelerated and later terminated. As denazification was the formal precondition for every bureaucratic action, including the granting of pensions, the retired Wehrmacht generals also had to be reviewed and denazified.

On November 22, 1951, the main chamber of Munich Regional Court filed charges against Albert Kesselring and sought to have him included in Category 1 as a "major culprit."[119] In March 1952, once the indictment had been handed down, Aschenauer visited Kesselring and Mältzer in Werl to clarify certain details of the indictment and his subsequent defense.[120] In this regard, Kesselring was dependent on the statements made by his former comrades. He revealed much of his attitude to the unpleasant formality of denazification in a round-robin, writing that he had been "advised" to have himself "de-nazified to meet the requirements for the granting of a subsistence allowance." Therefore, he said, he was seeking references testifying to "my career, any achievements, defects, my attitude to the state, National Socialism, Jewry, my attitude to my contemporaries, my behavior towards superiors, my character traits."[121] Although the public prosecutor sought to have the former field marshal classified as a "major culprit," all fifty-nine affidavits submitted in his case exonerated Kesselring. The proceedings were therefore discontinued due to a lack of evidence.

Denazification of the former commander-in-chief was a pure formality. As late as 1949, Kesselring had been classified as a "militarist" on the registration form for those released for internment,[122] but he was now classified as a "sympathizer." Those who were so inclined could interpret this as a form of legal absolution, and no one contradicted Aschenauer when he declared that the "British have already come to the realization that Kesselring—the savior of Italy's cultural treasures—has been unjustly imprisoned."[123] Despite the fact that he was unable to attend the proceedings because his application to go on an "official journey" was refused by the Werl authorities,[124] Kesselring had cause for satisfaction.[125] Purging and rehabilitation in the course of denazification had been "merged into one and the same process."[126]

In their coverage of the Kesselring denazification proceedings, the media immediately seized on Aschenauer's interpretation when reporting the verdict. Admittedly, the American-influenced *Neue Zeitung* did stress that the "civilian court proceedings had been discontinued due to the legislation ending the denazification process," since "it was not possible to prove that Kesselring had personally prompted, and could be held responsible for, the shooting of hostages and excesses relating to the anti-partisan war in Italy."[127] Yet only *Die Welt* recalled the war crimes for which Kesselring was imprisoned in Werl, though it also concluded that the "Kesselring prosecution [had] collapsed."[128] *Der Mittag* summarized the verdict as a "moral acquittal."[129] Thanks to the favorable denazification verdict, Laternser now had further ammunition with which to convince the public that his client was innocent and that his release should be viewed as a top priority.

Assault on Public Opinion, 1950–1951

Up to that point, Laternser had placed all his faith in his legal arguments, believing they would lead to a successful appeal; he had only sporadically pursued a private intervention course by attempting to develop personal contacts with influential individuals on Kesselring's behalf. Now, however, he focused his efforts on mobilizing public opinion. Initially, Laternser reverted to a recurring theme: Kesselring had been the victim of a miscarriage of justice. He decried the "field marshal's wrongful conviction" and the "tragic trial" that had landed an "innocent man" in an Allied prison. As he saw it, the inherent duty of any commander to assume responsibility for acts committed within his sphere of command, with or without his knowledge, had to supersede any personal innocence. Even the aspect of moral responsibility remained unaffected by this reality. It thus also became possible to repudiate any guilt in respect to the massacres.

Laternser's interpretation quickly became so widespread that it was no longer necessary to exert direct influence on editorial staffs. Journalists simply gathered their information from Laternser's book. As a result, they were all in agreement: Field Marshal Kesselring had been wrongfully imprisoned. By mobilizing a strong sense of public outrage in favor of the war criminals, the campaign had achieved its first success. The widespread belief that innocent generals were languishing in prison reignited the debate surrounding German rearmament and the possibility that these officers could again assume command.

During a second phase, the campaign was further intensified, and there was a shift in the arguments put forward. "Justice" now took the place of "clemency." Clemency was no longer the issue. What was now at stake was nothing less than the rehabilitation of the war criminals. The groundwork for this was laid in the media, and the issue was subsequently adopted by the political establishment. Uncompromising articles in the German press were accompanied by similar pieces in the British papers, written by correspondents who deplored British victors' justice. And once again, Lord Hankey was at the center of these initiatives. There was a certain media symbiosis at work in the two countries when it came to the war criminals issue, especially during the British general election, and this resulted in the mutual reinforcement of arguments and responses.

The campaign's success was also reflected in the fact that prisoners themselves were able to intervene in the debate. Despite being strictly prohibited from contacting political officeholders about his own case, Kesselring approached Adenauer from prison. That the British prison management was either unable or unwilling to stop him clearly indicates the extent to which there had already been a political paradigm shift due to the success of a relentless media campaign elevating Kesselring to the status of an innocent martyr. It also signaled an impending British policy shift.

Media Campaigns and the Shift in Public Opinion

Laternser realized that exerting influence on the media could open up new opportunities for the Kesselring case. He was thus a striking example of the Nuremberg defense lawyer who sought "with enormous energy . . . to convince both the occupying power and the new German political decision-makers of his own interpretation of the recent past."[130] Initial contacts with journalists often arose through legal colleagues or Kesselring's own friends whom Laternser would ask to meet, and even the federal government's

Rechtsschutz-Stelle sometimes arranged for journalists to meet and interview the defense attorneys. Laternser succeeded in influencing some newspapers directly, and others either adopted the favorable tone of their media brethren or spontaneously decided to embrace a positive approach. An analysis of Laternser's various media contacts is quite illuminating.

His first contact came about by chance. In 1949, during the Manstein trial, a journalist asked him about the current status of the Kesselring case and then wrote that Laternser had filed a petition seeking to have the verdicts in the Kesselring, Mackensen, and Mältzer cases set aside. Although Laternser was initially annoyed that the petition had thus become public knowledge, he also realized that there was a surprising degree of public interest in Kesselring, which could work to the former field marshal's advantage.[131] The report generated a demand for articles on the Kesselring case.[132] Such articles proliferated, and by the summer of 1951—when the German magazine *Stern* published a three-part series on "Freedom for Kesselring and Manstein"—media coverage had assumed the dimensions of a campaign.

The first press campaign on Kesselring's behalf more or less set the tone. In mid-1950, a colleague of Laternser's, Dr. Otto Dix, drew his attention to the American journalist Curt Riess.[133] A "former German" of Jewish descent, Riess was one of the American journalists who had interviewed Kesselring over tea and cookies after his capitulation in Berchtesgaden on May 9, 1945.[134] Kesselring had happy memories of Riess, whom he remembered "very well" and who had introduced himself as a "compatriot" from Lower Franconia.[135] Dix made it clear that he was contacting Laternser at Riess's request, and he urged quick action because Riess had "fantastic connections" in American circles and was "preparing a major campaign."[136] The notion that the press could be interested in Kesselring's fate—perhaps simultaneously in Germany and the United States—was tempting. Laternser agreed to provide Riess with his own legal assessment of the trial,[137] paying particular attention to the approach adopted by Kesselring in occupied Italy and especially the decision to spare Rome.[138] Riess felt that speed was of the essence, since "the time is now psychologically favorable for publication."[139] He urged that no time be lost, claiming, "There is a risk that the press will lose interest in this article, which I have been promising for weeks."[140]

The exoneration strategy pursued by Laternser on Kesselring's behalf once again was detailed in his assessment of the trial. As he had done in the petition, he emphasized Hitler's order that a punishment be imposed, as well as the responsibility of the SD following the second order issued by Hitler. Quite aggressively, Laternser put forward the view that Kesselring had been unjustly accused because "he had nothing to do with the whole affair." Laternser also reinforced his argument with an analysis of international law, in which he claimed that reprisals were "permitted by international law," that the "nature and extent of the punishment [was] a matter of judgment," and that "recourse to innocent people" was covered by international law.[141] Accordingly, he said, it was "absurd" to "assume that [Kesselring] had incited his troops to kill civilians in breach of the laws and customs of war." He concluded: "I do not believe that anything more need be said in this regard."[142] Clearly feeling quite sure of himself, Laternser thought that attestations to Kesselring's honor would lend his report more credibility, and he cited Ernst von Weizsäcker, who, speaking during the Nuremberg IMT trial, had opined that Kesselring would "together with Pope Pius . . . be viewed as the savior of Italian culture."[143] He also cited the statement by Field Marshal Alexander (which was regularly trotted out) to the effect that Kesselring had fought fairly.[144]

Riess rejected Laternser's article because of its "extremely unhappy" formulations,[145] and he decided to take matters into his own hands. On June 26, he sent Laternser his draft article, noting that he had "deliberately omitted the bloodthirsty demands by Allied generals. In the interests of your client, I do not believe it would be beneficial to annoy people." In moving away from Laternser's appeal strategy, he proposed a four-phase campaign on Kesselring's behalf. The first task, he said, was to "distance oneself as far as possible from the atrocities committed by the Third Reich, a large part of the army and the SS." Then, one should argue that "Kesselring cannot be accused of any more or any less than many others who were never brought before court."[146] As a third step, Riess suggested pointing out that Kesselring "was probably not particularly intelligent, certainly not intelligent enough to see through the frightful machinations of the Nazis,"[147] and he proposed stressing Kesselring's "good deeds."[148] In so doing, Riess was primarily concerned with addressing American readers who had been interested in Kesselring ever since the African campaign. In contrast to Laternser's strategy, Riess never tried to argue that Kesselring was innocent; instead, he stressed that since the former field marshal was not a criminal who would commit murder in the future, he should be used to help build a new Germany. Laternser reacted with antagonism to Riess's proposal, and in that reaction, we can detect much about the fundamental differences among those campaigning on Kesselring's behalf.[149] Riess's article, which was entitled "Freedom for Kesselring," appeared in *Quick* magazine on July 23, 1953,[150] and it represented a major publicity push on behalf of both the man and his case. Kesselring himself viewed the article as a "boon" and said that it was "95%" true.[151]

The Riess article triggered heightened interest in German editorial offices and helped underpin the positive image of Kesselring. But the campaign was knocking at an open door, especially in terms of those publications that were already committed to the war criminals issue. Among them was the Stuttgart-based Lutheran weekly *Christ und Welt,* which endorsed the demand issued by the Württemberg diocesan bishop, Theophil Wurm, seeking a general amnesty for war criminals. Just three months later, the editors of the publication approached Laternser in an effort to gather material for a planned series of articles on some "especially tragic war crimes trials,"[152] which "seemed to be increasingly disappearing from public consciousness.[153] *Christ und Welt* intended to publish a set of articles on the Werl prisoners, the first of which would be devoted to Kesselring. The aim was to juxtapose the trial material with the demands made on the Italian state by relatives of the victims, who hoped to sue the Italian government for subsistence pensions.[154]

Although Kesselring attempted to get involved himself, prison guidelines meant that he had to stay in the background. He was only able to provide Laternser with a catalog of items to which journalists' attention should be drawn in the future.[155] This catalog indicated Kesselring's dismissal of the "defective English court proceedings,"[156] and the concluding comment he added made no bones about his views: "unilateral adjudication by the victorious power, based on legal principles which are not generally accepted and which are open to challenge."[157] Obviously, Kesselring was prepared to express harsh—indeed, devastating—criticism of British justice, but given the situation, he was *not* prepared to speak out regarding his conditions of imprisonment: he asked Laternser "not to mention the conditions in Werl." The *Christ und Welt* article appeared on August 2, 1951, below the telling headline "Kesselring, the Italians and the British: An Attack in Rome and Its Bewildering Consequences—Appeal in Werl?"[158] Almost devoid of polemical attacks on the British,[159] the article was completely pro-Kesselring. Laternser had similar contacts with the newsmagazine *Der Spiegel,* which resulted in an article entitled "Enthusiasm for Italy," that portrayed Kesselring as innocent and demanded his release.[160]

The recurring theme of Kesselring's chivalrous conduct of the war in Italy was repeatedly highlighted in the press. *Christ und Welt* found Albert Kesselring's fate particularly bitter because "he was considered a chivalrous officer by almost all soldiers who made his acquaintance in Italy."[161] The *Essener Kurier* saw Kesselring as a "knight in prison garb" and concluded that "seven years in prison is not much when measured against the original death penalty. But they are terrible if the former Luftwaffe marshal and commander-in-chief of German troops in Italy is innocent."[162] Elsewhere, news articles gave weight to the American journalist Curt Riess as a witness on Kesselring's behalf: "After carefully examining all the files and documents relating to the

Kesselring trial," he had come to the conclusion that "the prisoners in Werl were the subjects of a wrongful conviction."[163] Although there was no basis for quoting Riess as a quasi-legal expert, his opinion had the desired effect. And as a result, Riess himself became part of the image campaign being mounted on behalf of the former field marshal.

Other, rather older, civic networks demonstrated that they were on board, too, by joining the Kesselring campaign. In February 1950, the *Hamburger Allgemeine Zeitung* published an article by Will-Werner von Bergen, son of the former German ambassador to Rome. Describing the mood in Italy as the "renaissance of a friendship," he also shone a spotlight on Kesselring's decision to spare the Roman Tiber bridges when leaving the city.[164] Thanks to the increasingly pro-German attitude in Italy that was described by von Bergen, Laternser hoped to place a pro-Kesselring piece in an Italian newspaper through Italian contacts such as Baron Luigi Parilli.[165] However, in the event, no contact was established.

Laternser again fanned the flames of media interest in Kesselring by publishing his own memoirs—*Verteidigung deutscher Soldaten* (Defending German Soldiers)—in the autumn of 1950. He stated, "The main purpose of this publication is to again draw the attention of the Bonn authorities to a problem that remains unresolved."[166] The book set Laternser's arguments down in print—arguments that had already been embraced by the media—and thereby helped lay the foundations for the Kesselring myth. As well as publishing his opening and closing speeches from the field marshal's trial, Laternser reprinted the closing statement attributed to Kesselring, which he had drafted originally.

One of the journalists who responded to Laternser's book and adopted his arguments was Albert Willy Meyer. In a letter to Kesselring, he said he had read Laternser's memoirs with "deep sympathy," adding, "I believe that, particularly in the Kesselring case, the time has come to right a serious wrong."[167] Meyer claimed to be a former member of the Luftwaffe,[168] and he wrote to Kesselring that Laternser's book had shown him "what a serious injustice you have suffered."[169] He endorsed the argument that any German military contribution had to be conditional on Kesselring's release,[170] and in addition to his journalistic advocacy, he directly petitioned British decision makers.[171] Meyer was typical of those whose understanding of the Kesselring case was based solely on Laternser's writings—individuals who disseminated the theme of innocently convicted generals as initially developed by Laternser in aggressively championing Kesselring's cause vis-à-vis the Allied authorities. "In my view," Meyer stated, "Kesselring did no more than any British general would have done, and perhaps done more severely, in order to fulfill the tough duties imposed by anti-partisan warfare."[172] Meyer was emblematic of a certain category of journalist who gravitated toward the Nuremberg defense lawyers, continued to propagate anti-Bolshevik notions of the enemy, and openly advocated using journalistic means to continue the war against the East.[173]

The Media and the British General Election Campaign: Moving toward Rehabilitation Demands

Once Laternser had coordinated the initial shots in the campaign, Kesselring soon found himself making headlines. Even Germany was dominated by the British general election, and the British military prison in Werl was rarely out of the newspapers. But the focus had moved. Given the broad consensus that the generals were wrongfully imprisoned, demands for a pardon were replaced by demands for rehabilitation or retrial. Solidarity with the generals was also apparent in journalists' word choices: they wrote, for example, of the "comrades in misfortune sitting in Werl." To highlight the wrongful nature of the verdicts, the prisoners were always referred to as "so-called war criminals," using quotation marks. The absolute refusal to accept any guilt resulted in the focus being moved from demands for a "general amnesty" to demands for "an injustice to be remedied."[174] Neutral reporting was now a thing of the past; rather, there was a concerted media campaign aimed at exerting pressure on the London and Bonn governments.

The clemency debate launched in the British press during the autumn of 1950 was eagerly seized on by the German media, which coupled it with the rearmament debate. Thus, for example, the *Westdeutsche Tageblatt* criticized the fact that the war criminals enjoyed "neither power nor rights," and it asked in a screaming headline, "When Will the World's Conscience Awake? The Cry for Justice."[175] The newspaper came to the conclusion that the rights of Germans were being trampled underfoot on both sides of the Iron Curtain: "Both here and there, war criminals remain without power or rights. Without an opportunity to appeal, they are dependent on the victors' mercy." The *Dithmarscher Landeszeitung* demanded the release of all prisoners "who had not been convicted because of their own actions, but because they did not prevent the execution of illegal orders."[176] The *Frankfurter Allgemeine Zeitung* (*FAZ*) quoted an anonymous young officer as saying: "I cannot become a soldier to stand guard by the dungeon door of Generalfeldmarschall von Manstein!"[177]

The British media were not impervious to the link forged by their German counterparts between the war criminals' personal integrity, on the one hand, and the intended rearmament of Germany, on the other. The book on the Manstein trial written by Manstein's British defense counsel, Reginald Paget, also caused a stir in the UK.[178] In the book, Paget distanced himself from the war crimes trials, which he termed "England's shame," and stated that he had been deeply shattered by the verdict imposed on Manstein. The preface was written by Lord Hankey, who attacked the British government with unusual severity. He opened by noting that the war crimes trials were among the "shabby episodes" that occasionally marred "the proud story of British justice," and he went on to claim that the "scales were heavily weighted" against Paget's defense of Manstein "before the trial began," since the verdict had already been decided. Not that this surprised Hankey: after all, they were dealing with a "victors' court." Hankey thus intervened directly in the war crimes debate, clearly taking the German side when he demanded nothing less than true rehabilitation of the generals.[179]

Even the *Manchester Guardian* struck a relatively pro-German note.[180] It published a long article indicating that the generals held in Werl considered themselves innocent and therefore rejected any idea of a pardon, let alone escape.[181] For the first time, speculation regarding a future deployment of the generals was voiced. The *Guardian* quoted Erich von Manstein as saying that none of his men would don a uniform while he remained in prison. In addition, Germany had to regain its sovereignty, as defined by Manstein. According to the *Guardian*, the Communist press had long been speculating that the British aim was to ensure that the imprisoned generals were "fat and fit" enough to assume command in the new German army. Nevertheless, the *Manchester Guardian* report ended on a critical note: "War crimes may have been legally proved, but the war criminals are still waiting for their millennium. . . . Under their curious code, then, they must await a retrial which would justify their past acts. In some sense they believe they must re-establish the honor of the German Army. This is the measure of their trust in the system to which they belong."

The *Frankfurter Allgemeine Zeitung* also addressed the link between interned war criminals and possible rearmament in an article beneath the provocative headline "And Werl?" The piece demanded that the "Rome case," which included Kesselring, Mackensen, and Mältzer, be revisited by a nonpartisan court.[182] Soldiers, according to the *FAZ*, were "not criminals" and did not kill "on their own initiative, either for pleasure or because of inclination." Soldiers' actions were based on the "imperative of war" because "an illegal enemy—like the partisans—forced them to be harsh or because, as in all armies throughout the world, responsibility was taken from them by orders from on high." Writing in the *Zeit* weekly newspaper, Countess Marion Dönhoff analyzed the role Werl would play in the British general election and concluded that "the current English Government has not acceded to the numerous petitions and requests seeking a true review. . . . Rather, it remains undeviating in its complacent certainty that its courts adjudicated with infallibility."[183] Dönhoff was the first to refer to the political mechanisms that, in the final analysis, would be decisive in terms of the war criminals issue.

Writing in the *Rheinischen Post*, Manstein's defense counsel, Paul Leverkuehn, criticized British victors' justice and claimed that the verdicts were not persuasive.[184] He demanded a retrial, rather than a "review in an office, where no-one would be heard and which would simply generate renewed confusion as a result of uncontrollable news leaks." The newsmagazine *Der Spiegel* raised its voice on behalf of the "little people who followed orders," and it gave extensive space to the "Trandum case," dealing with the question of obedience to orders as it affected lower ranks.[185] The issue of rearmament and the attitude adopted by former senior Wehrmacht officers bore some strange fruit in the media. In the middle of July, for instance, the *Essener Allgemeine Zeitung* got around the prohibition on interviewing prisoners by publishing an interview with Liny Kesselring in which she stated her husband's view of matters. Kesselring had earlier provided written answers to the questions raised in the article, sending them to his wife as "speaking notes." Ever the statesman, he let it be known through his wife that he demanded "trust" as the basis for a military collaboration informed by equality.[186]

The media campaign reached its zenith with the decision by the illustrated magazine *Stern* to run a series in favor of the two figureheads, Kesselring and Manstein. The series title—"Justice, Not Clemency"—said it all. The articles appeared on August 5, 12, and 19, 1951, and even the title indicates how the focus had shifted. *Stern* was forthright about its intention in publishing this series—there could be no German rearmament without freedom for Manstein and Kesselring.[187] The demand was "not clemency, but justice": "Should clemency be applied where crimes have truly been committed? Where revenge generates injustice, only justice can help us."[188] The arguments in favor of releasing the war criminals had thus reached their climax in the assertion that clemency should only apply to true criminals and that the generals were innocent of any war crimes. Such was the mantra chanted by the press, repeatedly and in different forms. Consequently, *Die Welt* published a resolution adopted by the Werl lawyers, demanding that the verdicts be reviewed because many convictions were due solely to the "intellectual atmosphere of the initial post-war years."[189] The *Hamburger Sonntagsblatt* believed that "one must finally get to the root of the evil," and it reported extensively on Werl, focusing particularly on the "little cases."[190]

By 1952, the generals no longer had any reason to complain of their conditions in Werl. Indeed, the Italian media now took umbrage at how comfortable those conditions had become, criticizing Werl as "the generals' sanatorium" where prisoners awaited their release "in comfortable armchairs."[191] During 1953, Kesselring was twice granted temporary release.[192] He was allowed to remain at large for seven days, although he had to promise not to give any press interviews and to register with the police in Bad Wiessee upon arrival and departure.[193] There was significant media interest in Kesselring's prison leave. For example, a photo report showed him walking along the Tegernsee with his wife and former Generalleutnant Theo Osterkamp; the captions openly speculated about Kesselring's future military deployment.[194] *Der Spiegel* also stressed the civilian tranquility of the scene, publishing a photo of the Kesselrings taking a stroll.[195]

An effort was still being made to observe the rules of the game, yet Kesselring was clearly becoming more and more self-confident. The only opposition to the new hubris of the convicted officers came from the British high commissioner, Sir Ivone Kirkpatrick, as was typified by two examples. In May 1952, Jagdflieger Adolf Galland—a Luftwaffe general who had emigrated to Argentina after the war—asked whether it would be possible to visit Kesselring in Werl. The authorities there were uneasy about his application, since Galland had already caused something of a media storm in Germany, and there were fears that such a visit would generate negative propaganda.[196] Consequently, the Werl officials sought a decision from London,[197] and the response they received was as direct as it was surprising: "There is a greater danger of negative propaganda if we do not allow Galland to see Kesselring."[198] Prohibition was no longer an option. However, Kirkpatrick was annoyed that his advice had been ignored, for a precedent had been set. When General Harry Hoppe submitted a visit application shortly afterward, it too had to be granted.[199]

Hoppe's visit to Kesselring certainly was noteworthy, since it sprang from the linkage between the war criminals issue and the rearmament debate. Hoppe asked Kesselring how he himself would feel if former officers who had thus far refused to participate in a new German army (he was referring to the senior officers in prison) now gave their consent following an explicit request.[200] It seemed that the political aim of securing the war criminals' release in return for German rearmament had almost been achieved. If Kesselring formally authorized recruitment, most officers would make themselves available with a clear conscience. Kirkpatrick found that Kesselring was becoming pivotal as a political "arbitrator."[201] Although the prisoner was therefore forbidden to discuss politics with Hoppe,[202] it is doubtful whether this prohibition was observed.

Reports concerning the life being led by the German generals in Werl were all the rage. The headlines alone often constituted a political program. In November 1951, the *Essener Kurier* published an article under the headline "Panzer-Meyer: I am being treated fairly."[203] False reports to the effect that Kesselring had escaped from Werl triggered a wave of media hysteria.[204] The role being played by Kesselring in the official debate became obvious, and it was also clear that his fate was being closely monitored. Whoever started the rumor could use it to measure the current status of the debate and to assess the potential reaction if Kesselring really was "liberated." Clemency was no longer required: the "injustice" would have to be reversed through rehabilitation.

Kesselring's Appeal to Brown and Adenauer

Following a visit to the Werl prisoners on November 25, 1950, by a sympathetic British Commission of Enquiry led by Sir Alfred Brown—legal adviser to the high commissioner, Sir Ivone Kirkpatrick—Kesselring noted: "One has an indefinable feeling that the atmosphere is now somewhat more favorable to our case."[205] The Werl prisoners were enjoying the increased publicity.

Kesselring then decided to take matters into his own hands. Contrary to prison rules, he addressed an appeal on behalf of himself and his fellow prisoners to Chancellor Adenauer.[206] He wrote that in view of the impending visit by the British foreign secretary Ernest Bevin, Adenauer should take the opportunity to demand that "the same laws be applied even to the so-called war criminals." He proposed providing a statement listing the following reasons for a general review of all sentences and release of all prisoners: (1) the trials had been carried out in an "atmosphere of psychosis" and were therefore procedurally defective; (2) the right to an appeal or review "is customary throughout the civilized world"; (3) new evidence had emerged; (4) the American authorities had already started releasing prisoners in the "Mauthausen" case; and (5) "the defamation, which is also a purely existential matter, can only be eliminated through a trial, rather than through clemency." Obviously, while in Werl, Kesselring was fully informed on the progress of the campaign and the shift in focus toward rehabilitation, with a view to military rearmament. Accordingly, he wrote: "We are not simply speaking on our own behalf! Our appeal to you is also rooted in the political considerations associated with the security issue." Kesselring had presented Adenauer with a list of issues that had to result in his conviction being overturned. The document illustrated his own view of his case, in marked contrast to the opinions he had voiced in 1947.[207] Other sections of the document constituted a plea of justification and did not display any apparent strategy such as that pursued by Laternser.

Kesselring's letter to Adenauer showed quite clearly that, following the acquittal of some of his subordinates, he no longer saw any need for public expressions of regret regarding the killing of Italian civilians.

By the same post, Sir Alfred Brown also received a letter from Kesselring stating reasons why his case should be reviewed.[208] Again contradicting his position during the 1947 Venice trial, Kesselring now admitted that "excesses" had occurred (he had still been casting doubt on this in Venice), but he claimed that they were not due to his orders; rather, they were caused by the frontline troops' retreat maneuvers.[209] According to Kesselring, reversing his previous strategy, an agreement between Kappler and Mackensen meant that the "Wehrmacht [had been] . . . disengaged," which prompted him to issue what could be termed a declaration of honor on Mackensen's behalf: "Any irregularities would have been inconceivable under his responsible command. But—he was disengaged, as was I."[210] Regarding the second count of the indictment (his role in the antipartisan war), Kesselring concluded that "the wording of the orders issued by me did not include any indication—far less an incitement—that Italian civilians should be killed in the context of reprisals."[211] Nor had it been interpreted thus by "any one of my army commanders." That was why the prosecution had been unable to proffer evidence "in a single case." He claimed that "even in those cases where I surmised that the troops' behavior may have breached international law, the Italian laws of war would have prescribed an acquittal. See the case of General Schmalz, commander of the Hermann Göring Panzer division!"[212] Laternser praised the letter, which he described as "very good," and predicted that it would have an effect "in view of Brown's attitude."[213] In regard to other court proceedings in the Italian theater, Kesselring also felt that even "in the other trials conducted by the English and Italians" of German generals Crasemann, Strauch, Tensfeld, and Krummhaar, "no connection had been found between my orders and the offences which occurred."

When considering Kesselring's letter to Brown, it is worth noting that he used a petition on his own behalf to attest to the honor of his subordinates, Mackensen and Simon. What is interesting is that he did not repeat the mantra—established following the Nuremberg proceedings—that the SS troops were solely responsible. Instead, he even praised Waffen SS General Max Simon. Kesselring observed that, "fully aware of the significance of my assessment," he had found Simon to be an "upright soldier" whom he had come to "know and respect" and whose words were always marked by "the highest degree of probity."[214] This rather naive wording suggests that Laternser no longer had influence over his client. By this time, it appears, Kesselring was able to plead his cause relatively autonomously. Although there was no reaction to his letter to Adenauer, Kesselring made Adenauer an offer: he would "personally approach [*sic!*]" the speaker of the British House of Commons in order to ask to have "the actual course of the proceedings"—"[which] with the passage of time, seem to have resulted in incomprehensible verdicts"—reviewed by a commission in Werl.[215] There is no doubt that Kesselring's self-confidence had grown, leading him to overestimate the public opportunities available to war criminals.

The British legal department in Wahnerheide was unsure whether this letter—which had dutifully been intercepted by the prison censors—should even be allowed to leave Werl.[216] After weighing the pros and cons, the Foreign Office decided that it should not be sent and that Kesselring should be rebuked accordingly for having created the impression that he wished "to transfer current responsibility from His Majesty's Government to the German Federal Chancellor."[217] The permanent secretary in the German Foreign Office, Walter Hallstein, was informed, at the request of M. E. Bathurst, Kirkpatrick's secretary, that a letter to Adenauer had been intercepted. Hallstein lodged an official protest following this notification, asserting that he could not see "that Mr. Kesselring acted with the intention of transferring responsibility at any level to the Federal government in respect of those Germans convicted of war crimes."[218] Therefore, he could not concur in the decision to withhold the letter: "The Federal Government regrets this step, particularly since it could awaken in the prisoners the erroneous impression that they are to be prohibited from addressing requests and queries to the supreme German authorities."

The power of the West German government had grown significantly, and by now, the war criminals held in Werl had become bargaining chips deployed by both sides in their ongoing wrangles. The media campaign also helped ensure that the issue remained omnipresent. The focus had shifted from clemency to rehabilitation, but how could this approach be implemented politically?

Paradigm Shift: The Sea Change in British War Crimes Policy

With the backing of Lord Hankey, members of the British government now raised their heads above the parapet, openly advocating a modification of the existing war criminals policy. The opinion-forming processes were accompanied by convoluted formulations from the office of the judge advocate general. Policymakers somehow had to find a balance between avoiding self-criticism, on the one hand, and adapting to new circumstances, on the other hand. Meanwhile, it became evident to all that a point of no return had been reached. The review of the Kesselring case was correspondingly positive—and controversial. It also gave rise to some annoyance, and senior British officials were left with the task of explaining the contradictions. Kirkpatrick, the British high commissioner, was faced with growing criticism, and his fallback position was that since the hard line had been laid down by the Foreign Office, it should be defended by Foreign Office officials.

Although declarations of honor directed at German soldiers were intended to facilitate the ratification debate, they also showed that the Allies had accepted the main arguments put forward by the war criminals lobby, such as the demand for rehabilitation. The war criminals issue ended up being decoupled from the original legal intention underpinning the process, which was to punish crimes while giving victims the satisfaction of seeing justice restored. Instead, the issue had been transformed into a weight that the various parties alternately tossed onto the political scales.

The British Review Report on the Kesselring Case

The British Foreign Office monitored the mood shift in Germany by keeping a close eye on media coverage and German reactions. The legal department of the British High Commission drew London's attention to the fact that the *Stern* series in particular had given rise to the impression that two men of honor, Kesselring and Manstein, were being wrongfully held in Werl.[219] To reinforce this impression, the magazine had no scruples about publishing a facsimile of a private letter from Field Marshal Alexander that described Kesselring as an "able opponent."[220] The German translation of the book written by Manstein's counsel, Reginald Paget, also caused consternation in London. Hankey's foreword to the book was particularly well received by the German press. German public opinion joined with Paget in demanding not only that all verdicts be set aside but also that the generals be rehabilitated as a precondition for future military collaboration.

As a result of the media campaign, there seems to have been growing doubt in London regarding the evidence proffered by the prosecution during the Kesselring trial. This impression arises from the contents of a British dossier on the Kesselring case, compiled in 1951, as well as the report of the Review Board, which summarized the weaknesses of the trial: "The issue which the court had to decide was, therefore, in the words of the Judge Advocate, whether the accused's orders were 'a definite incitement to kill Italians or just badly worded orders which were rather carelessly drafted,' and whether all or any of the instances of indiscriminate killing of Italians by German troops were a 'direct consequence of these orders.'"[221] This statement is particularly remarkable because neither the indictment nor the judge advocate general's recommended verdict granted Kesselring the benefit of extenuating circumstances such as "badly worded orders." Now, these extenuating circumstances appeared to offer a way out for the former field marshal.

Contrary to the views previously held by official experts, the Review Board's report, entitled "Notes on the Case," showed absolute understanding for the hard line taken by Kesselring against the partisans, since, after all, he was dealing with "irresponsible people in the main whom he could not negotiate with." The report cited the remark made by the judge advocate during his summing up to the effect that reprisals were "appropriate" in the circumstances.[222] There was no way to prevent Kesselring from shooting innocent Italians because, in the end, it was impossible to track down the actual culprits, and Kesselring should enjoy the benefit of the doubt—*in dubio pro reo*—given the legal situation.[223] The task of the court had been to adjudicate whether responsibility for the shootings lay with "the German armed forces, represented by the accused, or the Security Service, represented by the head of the SD in Rome," and whether the shooting of 335 Italians constituted a legitimate reprisal or a war crime.[224] With regard to the second count, the judge advocate general had noted that Kesselring "deliberately and knowingly when he produced the relevant orders was having them produced in such form that he knew what the results would be and that he intended by bringing these orders into existence, to bring about those results." According to the earlier interpretation, Kesselring had thus sanctioned the death of numerous innocent victims. The court had left open the question of whether it was permissible to kill innocent people, but that issue now had to be resolved. After all, the American courts—such as that in Nuremberg—had come to a different conclusion, as in Case 7, in respect to hostages and reprisals. Legal experts, represented by Cambridge professor Lauterpacht, pointed out that the taking of hostages "must not be confused with the still existing practice of seizing enemy individuals for the purpose of making them the object of reprisals."[225] The Review Board's report was obviously an attempt to provide an official justification for the shift in British attitudes toward German war criminals. It should be noted that the legal issue at the heart of the matter has still not been definitively resolved.[226]

Affirmative statements by British war veterans, which had a positive effect on opinion in London and Wahnerheide, forced officials to take a further step down the road toward rehabilitation. J. Quentin Hughes, a British Luftwaffe specialist who had been taken prisoner in January 1944 following a sabotage operation behind German lines, was prompted by his friend Colonel D. A. Stirling,[227] assistant to the high commissioner in Germany, to petition Kirkpatrick.[228] Stirling saw to it that the petition quickly became widely known, and he sent Hughes's affidavit directly to the general commanding British troops in Germany, Sir Brian Robertson, for his opinion.[229] Robertson had been involved in the May 1949 decision to halt British war crimes trials; in fact, he had been one of the driving forces behind this policy shift.[230] He felt the Germans should be disabused of the notion that the Allies were pursuing petty revenge if true reeducation—in the sense of learning about the crimes committed and lessening the German tendency to idolize senior military figures—was to be achieved.

Robertson's legal adviser decided to seek advice on this difficult matter, so he asked for an opinion from the legal adviser to the high commissioner, Sir Alfred Brown.[231] Brown's response to T. G. Coverdale, marked "private and confidential," reveals much about the mind-set then prevalent among British authorities. It is particularly revealing of the attitude adopted by British administrators based in Germany, who were closely monitoring local opinion and drawing conclusions in respect to their own policies, which differed from those in London. Brown wrote that a growing number of people were now interested in the fate of senior German officers, and he looked forward to General Bishop—who was intently following the Manstein and Kesselring cases—issuing proposals for their early release. Brown spoke candidly about his views: "Frankly, I have been very unhappy about the trials held before these special military tribunals. Many of the convictions have seemed to me wrong in law or sentences have been very heavy."[232] He hoped that, in the "not too distant future," he himself would have a hand in obtaining a review of the convictions and a reduction in the sentences. However, he cautioned that one should not expect too much, since the body actually empowered to exercise clemency—the Foreign Office—continued to focus on the cases of the former commanders-in-chief. He wrote, "You are probably not unaware that the Secretary of State [Foreign Secretary Bevin] holds rather strong views which made him hesitate for some time in transferring to Germany powers of clemency. He seems to feel that many of the lower ranking criminals were executed and that it is only where the criminals had a high rank that death sentences have been freely commuted."

Brown pointed out that the recommendations by the 1949 Wade Commission, which were then being implemented, had triggered significant protests in England, which led him to fear that he could do no more than "intervene in the small number of cases of little public interest where it is brought to my attention that the court was quite clearly wrong in its decision." The fact that nonmilitary lawyers had presided over the military courts constituted a British failing, according to Brown. In Nuremberg, the Americans had shown how such trials could be successfully conducted, and their conclusions had, in many respects, differed from those reached by the British military courts.[233] Finally, Brown hinted that the High Commission was currently considering the option of a "semiopen" prison, somewhat analogous to a parole procedure.[234] British caution was once again apparent in Brown's conclusion: "An American precedent would clearly be of great use in justifying any action we may ourselves take."

During 1950, opposition to the release from prison in Britain—specifically within the government and in particular the Foreign Office—was significantly greater than in the United States. Nor did it appear that any critical voices were being raised in the United States that could be echoed in London. As far as the British were concerned, the dilemma facing Allied Deutschlandpolitik was that the punishments needed to be explained in Germany whereas clemency needed to be justified abroad without explaining too much of the Cold War policy aims that had justified the clemency debate.[235]

Declarations of Honor

In 1951, the Americans were the first to pursue a new politics of memory: to wit, the politics of rehabilitation. They thus met all the main German preconditions for rearmament, as will be demonstrated in the pages ahead.[236] In addition to the release of prominent war criminals, which had already been proposed, the restoration of German soldiers' honor through so-called declarations of honor was considered particularly important if consent to German rearmament was to be obtained. Officials in German military circles hoped that if the latter demand was met, "a far-reaching social consensus regarding the Wehrmacht's distance from National Socialist crimes" would be achieved.[237] During subsequent years, this consensus was to attain the status of a myth.

On January 21, 1951, following the first official meeting between the American general Dwight D. Eisenhower and the former German generals Adolf Heusinger and Hans Speidel, focusing on the modalities of German rearmament,[238] the American high commissioner, John McCloy, together with the general commanding American forces in Europe, Thomas T. Handy, announced that war criminals held in Landsberg following convictions at Nuremberg and Dachau would have their sentences commuted.[239] Just two pending executions would be carried out; other death sentences would be commuted to prison terms, and some prisoners, including Alfred Krupp, would be granted early release.

It was expected that the German public would react badly to the announcement of two more executions, and the Americans had prepared leaflets designed to counter this. These leaflets described the various crimes of which the prisoners had been convicted in an attempt to refresh the public's memory, which once again illustrated that the motives underlying the American trials were primarily educational. However, though the releases and accompanying explanations had been very well planned in Germany, with most German newspapers expressing approval, the reaction abroad was devastating. When McCloy told his French colleagues that he feared negative German reactions to further executions in Landsberg (at a time when an amnesty was already in the cards), André François-Poncet riposted that "quite different people will be very angry if no one is executed."[240] He continued by stressing that Germany had to "be reminded from time to time that the war crimes were unfortunately not an invention."[241] Even the American high commissioner, McCloy, pointed out that the accused had not been convicted as soldiers but rather for their part in the inhuman National Socialist racial policy, and he stressed that it had not been militarily necessary to "slaughter Jews" or other civilians.[242] McCloy tried in vain to circumvent the rehabilitation demands being issued by the war criminals lobby by emphasizing that the sentence reviews did not affect the honor of German soldiers in general. However, senior Allied military officials were prepared to make further concessions to the Germans even in this regard.

On January 23, 1951, the commander-in-chief of NATO forces in Europe, General Eisenhower, made a statement regarding Wehrmacht rehabilitation and the development of a new German military.[243] This statement was interpreted by many former Wehrmacht members as a declaration of honor, and it was followed on April 5, 1951, by a statement from Konrad Adenauer. Speaking in the Bundestag, Adenauer sought to restore the honor of ordinary soldiers "who had committed no wrongdoing."[244] The chancellor was still pursuing the original distinction between "real war criminals" and senior commanders who had found themselves almost inadvertently in court as a result of the so-called imperative of obeying orders. Thus, he stated that he did not intend to intervene on behalf of "thieves or murderers" or "people like Pohl or Ohlendorf who are acknowledged to have committed terrible crimes."

Domestically, Adenauer was focused not only on gaining votes but also on maintaining social peace. He attempted to secure the latter through the Act to Regularize the Legal Circumstances of Persons Covered by Article 131 of West Germany's constitution, the Basic Law (known as the 131 Act). This measure was enacted to assist persons who had previously been subject to automatic arrest or removal from office as members of the old elites or the National Socialist administration (*Beamten*) by providing for their reemployment or the settlement of their pension claims. The new law helped ensure that former professional soldiers (as well as members of other groups, such as judges and teachers) were put on an economically equal footing with their peers. The only remaining demand of the veterans' interest groups—which had originally been established to secure their members' pension rights and now found themselves robbed of their raison d'être—was the release of those comrades still in custody. The declarations of honor had put in place the framework conditions for German rearmament and the participation of former Wehrmacht officers.

The Attitude of British High Commissioner Ivone Kirkpatrick

Like the Germans, the British too pursued a politics of memory, and they now found themselves constrained to take a clear position—and to measure it against the policy adopted by the Americans. The efforts to integrate West Germany into the Western Alliance and the associated demand for rehabilitation of the war criminals had already delineated tight boundaries within which room for maneuver was limited. This situation posed a dilemma for the British government. Measured in terms of the foreign policy damage associated with the rearmament debate, public opinion in Britain was counterpoised with that in Germany. At the same time, the foreign policy risks had to be weighed against a realistic assessment of the extent to which rearmament would transform Germany into a potential threat.

The new British high commissioner, Sir Ivone Kirkpatrick, who had taken office in 1950, played a pivotal role in the transformation of British war crimes policy. After the establishment of the Federal Republic in 1949, the British foreign secretary had the power to exercise clemency on behalf of the Crown. This power was now delegated to the high commissioner—and he was determined to make use of it. Kirkpatrick displayed a remarkable degree of openness when, speaking at the British Press Club in Berlin on January 16, 1951, he responded to a question from an American journalist regarding the sentences imposed on Admirals Erich Raeder and Karl Dönitz: "If we are agreed in striving for peace, then we should agree that hatred and revenge are bad counselors."[245] This remark created quite a stir, for it appeared that the UK's most senior representative in Germany was confirming that the trials had been governed by hatred and revenge. In response, Prime Minister Clement Attlee vetoed such assumptions, and Parliament revoked the high commissioner's authority to issue pardons.[246] Once again, the foreign secretary became the sole repository of clemency, and any review of the sentences was ruled out as a precaution, since no legal function was involved.

Kirkpatrick, who briefly considered resigning,[247] stressed that, while he was by no means opposed to the war crimes trials, he believed the prisoners remaining in Werl were true criminals.[248] Between December 1949 and February 1951, he had already released 27 individuals, but 200 prisoners were still in custody, of whom 25 were soldiers. These included the most prominent prisoners, Field Marshals Kesselring and von Manstein, as well as 121 concentration camp guards and 83 other individuals (SS, Gestapo, criminal police, prison directors, and civilians). On February 3, 1951, in a damage-control exercise, Kirkpatrick justified himself to the Foreign Office as follows:

> My remarks on hatred and revenge must be read against the German background. It is a regrettable fact that even moderate Germans such as the protestant Bishops and sensible SPD men who have themselves suffered from Nazi persecution resent the war crimes trials and greedily swallow the criticism published in England and elsewhere. The question does poison feeling toward the West and whilst we clearly must not allow ourselves to be deflected from doing what is right, we have an interest in mitigating public resentment. . . . It may be argued that justice should be done without regard to public opinion, but it is surely important also to satisfy public opinion that justice is being done.[249]

The Foreign Office now tried to elucidate the political aspects of the war criminals issue in a memorandum drafted for the cabinet meeting on February 12, 1951. For the first time, a new line was presented in this memorandum, explicitly coupling war crimes policy and the Western integration of Germany.[250]

Sir Hartley Shawcross, the former British chief prosecutor in Nuremberg who had since been appointed home secretary, was the sole dissenting voice: in another memorandum presented to cabinet, he stated that he was not prepared to sacrifice the legality and legitimacy of the war crimes trials to the deteriorating relations with the Soviet Union.[251] He would have no hand, he said, in restoring the honor of Nazis and SS members.[252]

Speaking in the House of Commons, Attlee denied that there was any connection between rearmament and the war criminals issue: he asserted that there had been no material changes that could cast doubt on the verdicts reached by British courts.[253] Nevertheless, in the *Times* and elsewhere, Shawcross tirelessly warned against any attempt to allow political opportunism to muddy the clemency issue.[254]

The British cabinet members found themselves confronting difficult questions. Should they heed the mood in Germany and make political decisions reflecting the link between rearmament and the release of all war criminals? Or should they heed the change in British public opinion, which had now turned decisively against clemency?

This change in British opinion was particularly remarkable given that the 1949 Manstein trial had been extremely unpopular, and there was a general welcome for the decision not to hold any further British war crimes trials. The British criticism of German rearmament and of any softening in terms of the war criminals issue was based on fears of a resurgent German militarism, coupled with a revitalization of German heavy industry.[255] These fears had been reinforced by the release of Alfred Krupp. The cabinet concluded its deliberations on the war criminals issue in May with a clear warning to the foreign secretary that he should not allow himself to be swayed by political considerations. The cabinet minutes noted that the vast majority of war criminals in British custody had been convicted of "normal" war crimes rather than of political transgressions.[256] There would be no blanket review of the cases of convicted German war criminals—then or in the future.

British government officials had laid down a new line: they would neither review sentences nor cave in to German pressure. They thus hoped to gain time while awaiting developments.

The Turning Point: Churchill's 1951 Election Victory

A political paradigm shift, however, meant that this line could no longer be maintained. The shift was determined by two factors: the Tories, under Winston Churchill, won the general election in the autumn of 1951, and negotiations had commenced regarding the Federal Republic's new legal status.

The release of senior German military figures held at Werl Prison was a matter close to the heart of the new British prime minister, Churchill. Upon being reelected, he immediately demanded that his foreign secretary submit a report on those German generals who remained in custody, as well as on Rudolf Hess, Hitler's deputy. Churchill had repeatedly drawn attention to himself through his ambivalent remarks on the trials, and in the late 1940s, he had made it quite clear that he believed the matter should be brought to a close. Admittedly, during the Nuremberg trials he had stressed the legitimacy of the tribunal, which he himself had established, while also emphasizing the gravity of the crimes with which the defendants were charged. However, he had also spoken out against stigmatizing all Germans, underscoring his demand that there should be an end to the affair. This view received a boost from an initiative by Lord Hankey who, in a letter to the *Times*, demanded that senior German military figures be released from prison in order to obtain their consent to German rearmament—which, of course, was a stated aim of British security policy.[257]

For the first time, French defense minister René Pleven's plan for the creation of a European defense alliance seemed to offer an alternative to Germany's inclusion in NATO. German sovereignty, which was a precondition for German rearmament, would mean an end to occupation and would therefore also spell an end to Allied legal jurisdiction. The British dilemma had thus been refigured. Following the issues of "clemency or justice" and "politics and justice," new questions arose. How would the public respond to a rehabilitation of the war criminals? And how would that response impact on the inclusion of Germany in a Western alliance, whatever its nature?

Intervention by Labour MP Richard Stokes and Kurt Schumacher

The domestic political conflicts were reflected in the debate triggered by an intervention by the Labour Party MP Richard Stokes. Stokes—who served briefly as minister of works in Clement Attlee's government—was the most senior political figure to play a pivotal role when it came to clemency petitions on Kesselring's behalf. Even during the war, he had attracted attention as a result of his pro-German attitude and his anti-Semitic statements, and in 1940, he advocated concluding a separate peace with Germany. He later criticized the Allied carpet bombing of Germany, which he did not believe was militarily justified.[258] Stokes was thus the ideal contact person when the German opposition leader—Kurt Schumacher, chairman of the Sozialdemokratische Partei Deutschlands (Social Democratic Party of Germany, SPD)—decided to submit a three-page petition on Kesselring's behalf.

According to Schumacher, he had decided to champion the former field marshal's cause as a result of pressure from SPD colleagues and local associations. However, although he had been told that Kesselring was innocent, he was also aware that a pardon would "inflict pain on the Italian people, who had suffered so terribly while Kesselring was commander-in-chief in Italy"—something that should be avoided. Schumacher had evidently internalized the arguments made by Kesselring's defense team: the version of the case he submitted to Stokes corresponded to that presented by Laternser in his book. With regard to the shootings in the Fosse Ardeatine, Schumacher had come to the conclusion that Kesselring was not involved in this "act of terror which was ordered by Hitler and executed by the SD." He thus deemed the field marshal innocent of the first charge, and he felt that it was "even more unlikely" that Kesselring had incited the troops to wage war on civilians. As he wrote in a letter to Stokes, "There is nothing in Kesselring's conduct of the war in Italy to lend credence to the assertion that he did not fight the war fairly as a soldier, but rather conducted it as a barbaric terrorist."[259] He was therefore of the opinion that, during the "understandable upheaval of the post-war era," a verdict had been reached that "will not survive the judgment of history" and that "threatens to encumber relations between Germany and Great Britain—relations which are particularly close to our hearts—with prejudices." In writing this letter, Schumacher stated, his aim was to identify ways of improving those relations—through Kesselring's release. In conclusion, he said he would be raising the issue publicly in Germany, and he suggested that Stokes follow suit while keeping the correspondence between them confidential.

In a friendly response, Stokes wrote that he was in full agreement with Schumacher. He would do what he could and had passed Schumacher's letter on to Foreign Secretary Eden, with whom he would subsequently discuss the matter in person.[260] In addition, Stokes suggested that there would be an opportunity to raise Kesselring's case at the beginning of December, during a meeting with Kirkpatrick and Adenauer. In a subsequent letter to Eden, Stokes wrote that he supported Schumacher's petition and believed that Kesselring should be released as soon as possible.

Schumacher's petition indicated that Kirkpatrick had assessed the situation correctly. Antagonism to the war crimes trials was not the preserve of the Far Right but rather ran like a thread through all layers of society. In this regard, Schumacher's petition to Stokes was dramatic but not unique. As early as July 11, 1951, Countess Marion Dönhoff of the *Zeit* weekly newspaper had contacted Richard Stokes on Kesselring's behalf.[261] This contact had, in turn, followed an earlier intervention in Kesselring's favor by the Vatican, in 1950.[262] A remarkable alliance had been forged.

Stokes's unambiguous position was not well received in London. The Foreign Office was attempting to come up with more cautious wordings, and Hancock, head of the German Political Department in the Foreign Office, feared that Stokes's unreserved response to Schumacher could be used for propaganda purposes in Germany. His view was that Kirkpatrick should be "prepared" for an impending assault by Stokes.[263] Writing to Bathurst, Hancock enclosed the draft of an official response from the Foreign Office to Stokes. This draft is illuminating, showing as it does that it was quite possible to use interventions at the highest level in order to exert pressure for or against an amnesty. The response drafted by Hancock stated that "Kesselring's case will certainly be considered" in the course of the review then under way: everything possible was being done.[264]

Kirkpatrick complained immediately: "This is a thoroughly dishonest draft to which I object."[265] For one thing, he said, it was not at all clear whether Kesselring's case would be reviewed or what the outcome of such a review would be; for another, it was not Kirkpatrick's fault that Kesselring was languishing in prison: the former field marshal had brought it on himself. In particular, Kirkpatrick repudiated Schumacher's criticism of the manner in which the verdict had been reached. Commenting on Schumacher's claim that the verdict had been one of revenge reached during a period of upheaval, he reminded the Foreign Office that "good Anglo-German relations" could not "constitute a ground for clemency." London had, however, more or less come around to the way of thinking criticized by Kirkpatrick.

Kirkpatrick passed the contentious draft, together with the correspondence between Stokes and Schumacher, to Frank Roberts in the Foreign Office. He complained that he was now being depicted as solely responsible for the fact that high-ranking Germans remained in prison when, the previous February, he had been unable to get his own proposals for a sensible clemency policy heard. In addition, he said, he was informed by a reliable source that Schumacher was "not in the least interested in clemency for war criminals." Kirkpatrick made no bones about his views: "The fact is that I have been given very precise instructions which prohibit me from attaching any weight whatsoever to the sort of considerations which Dr. Schumacher invokes. To put the matter in a nutshell, the responsibility for this whole business has been taken over by the Foreign Office who have elected to adopt a tough attitude."[266]

Consequently, Kirkpatrick felt that it was up to the Foreign Office to justify this unpopular policy publicly. Kirkpatrick's private secretary, Bathurst, wrote to Hancock and noted that the high commissioner wanted to make it clear to Stokes that the foreign secretary was the sole court of appeal when it came to clemency and made such decisions alone.[267]

Lord Hankey intervened in the clemency row with a new proposal. On November 21, 1951, in a widely publicized speech in the House of Lords, he addressed the issue of convicted German war criminals, stating that only a general amnesty could be the basis of peaceful and constructive cooperation between the two peoples.[268] Hankey received backing from George Bell, the bishop of Chichester, who spoke briefly in his support. In view of the pending negotiations on the war criminals issue, Hankey's proposals provided the British government with an option that merited consideration.

Adenauer's Visit to London

Chancellor Adenauer visited London at the beginning of December 1951. The war criminals issue was one of the main topics of discussion during his meeting with the newly appointed foreign secretary, Anthony Eden. On the issue of how war criminals should be treated once the Federal Republic had attained sovereignty, Eden had the "Japanese model" in mind. In September 1951, Japan had accepted the Allied verdicts in the war crimes trials and in return demanded the return of its sovereignty.[269] However, Germany was in a stronger position because it was being asked to set up a new army—and it was precisely for that task that the "experience of prominent prisoners" would be required. Writing on the fringes on the meeting, Herbert Blankenhorn—in his capacity as security adviser to the federal government, involved in mustering a new German army—noted that reservations were expressed only in respect to Eric von Manstein, whose case was on everyone's lips again following the publication of the book by his defense counsel, Paget.[270] Adenauer used his London trip to draw attention to this problem, explicitly demanding the release of Kesselring and Manstein.[271] And Churchill seized the opportunity to tell Adenauer in confidence that he had always hated the belated war crimes trials.

Adenauer also met with Lord Hankey, one of those advocating a general amnesty. Hankey had caused a stir with his remark that the Allies had committed as many crimes during World War II as the Germans.[272] Nevertheless, Adenauer was politically shrewd enough to avoid openly endorsing the demands made by the combative peer: his catalog of requests did not include a general amnesty. But indirectly, the Federal Republic worked hard to ensure that Hankey's views got a public airing. For instance, the German government's press and information office issued a translation of the November 21 speech given by Hankey in the House of Lords, which soon was the subject of extensive commentary in the German media.[273] In view of the tense mood during Adenauer's visit, Hankey resolutely refused to make any media comments on the issue. Writing to a friend, he said: "For my part I mean to avoid coming into the limelight, as I shall be accused of 'egging on the Nazis and putting ideas into their heads.' . . . I can, however, still do a good deal to bring influential people to realize how vital a factor the so-called War Criminal question is."[274]

When it came to the war criminals issue, the main problem was related to Allied clemency law. It was initially decided that a tripartite committee—one American officer, one British officer, and a German representative—would be tasked with processing clemency petitions. But even with a tripartite clemency board, some of those involved would have to remain in custody because they were not innocent. What was to become of them? The first suggestion—to transfer the war criminals to German prisons—was categorically rejected. Meanwhile, the British foreign secretary told Adenauer in confidence that he was considering establishing a three-person clemency commission made up of one Allied representative, one German, and one neutral member.[275] Adenauer agreed to the proposal in principle, provided that the commission was chaired by the neutral member.

However, the other Allies were by no means in agreement.[276] It was still unclear whether it would be possible to obtain American and French consent to the model discussed with Eden, which entailed the acceptance of all sentences applied to German officers by Allied courts in return for sovereignty. The Americans, in particular, feared (not without reason) that public pressure would then quickly cause the prison gates to be opened, and the British pointed to their experience in Italy: Italians convicted by British courts had been released after the Italian authorities were granted jurisdiction and the power to hold trials by the Allied Military Government.[277] At no time had the repugnant nature of the crimes been acknowledged. The United States was reluctant to surrender its clemency powers, and even the people in American military circles remained skeptical, for they feared that any prison releases would result in a further glorification of the war criminals involved. General Handy, who had shared the responsibility for issuing the Landsberg pardons in January 1951, pointed out that the Germans viewed many of the war criminals as political and military martyrs rather than as lawbreakers. The French government felt that the clemency commission should only be accorded an advisory role.[278]

The issue of clemency for the war criminals—now inextricably linked with plans for German rearmament—threatened to rend the Allied coalition asunder. As a result, ratification of the German General Treaty was significantly delayed. Indeed, it appeared doubtful whether it would be ratified at all.[279]

Media Reactions

During Adenauer's London visit, his hosts presented him with a Christmas present: a new provision allowing periods of internment prior to conviction to be offset against sentences. This offsetting provision resulted in the release of 30 of the 200 prisoners remaining in Werl.[280] On March 1, 1952, a further 10 officers were released from the prison.[281] Although Adenauer tried to ensure that the media did not paint these releases as the sole result of his visit, that is precisely the public impression that was created. An analysis of the media coverage following Adenauer's trip to England indicates that the most explosive issue in the clemency debate revolved around acknowledgment of the verdicts. Large sections of the German public hoped that the German General Treaty would be accompanied by a wave of releases, but that would have reinjected the issue of acknowledging guilt into the war criminals debate. To circumvent this contentious topic, the alleged illegality of the British verdicts was stressed instead.

Adenauer's London visit was generally viewed as an affirmation of Germany's standing. Thus, on December 18, 1951, the *Kölnische Rundschau* already felt confident in asserting that "the Werl prison will be empty in two years."[282] The *Hamburger Freie Presse* reported that Waffen SS General Herbert Gille had petitioned Churchill for clemency and sought "the release of Field Marshals Manstein and Kesselring, still held in Werl."[283] However, there is no record of this reported clemency petition. The American *Neue Zeitung* (which was the first newspaper to be reestablished in the U.S. German occupation zone and which still reflected American views) reported that the sentences meted out to the former generals were to be "reduced" and that a "special decision by the British government was anticipated" in the Manstein case, since he had not submitted his case for review.[284] The weekly *Deutsche Woche*, in a story on the "General Staff in Gaol," even portrayed the Allies as the benefactors and friends of the generals.[285] On the same page, the paper carried an advertisement for "comradely aid for Werl and Landsberg," seeking donations. The *Heimkehrer* wanted to finally see "action," and it reported extensively on a debate in the British House of Lords dealing with the war criminals issue.[286]

At the same time, criticism of Allied victors' justice was becoming increasingly vocal. The Frankfurt-based *Deutsche Kurier*, in a story headlined "Ambush Warfare," criticized the British conduct of Kesselring's trial as "unfair" and stressed the illegality of partisan operations: "None of the charges against him coincide with English interests. This would only be the case if the victors were pursuing a specific political plan which rendered a collective conviction of all senior German troop commanders necessary."[287] In Munich, the *Revue* carried a photo essay on "The Last Men of Werl."[288] The accompanying text noted that the original wording of the British *Manual of Military Law*, on the basis of which most of the war criminals in Werler had been convicted, had been reinstated in 1950 with an eye to the Korean War. The *Rheinische Post* newspaper reported that the Moers CVJM (Christlicher Verein Junger Männer, or YMCA) had conducted a fund-raising campaign to bring a "touch of Christmas to those who have foundered and been misused," and it seized on the opportunity to take a swipe at the British authorities by adding, "including those whom no court today would be likely to convict."[289] The shift in focus toward demands for rehabilitation had finally taken hold in the media at large. To quote the *FAZ*, "One cannot issue an amnesty to the innocent."[290]

Nevertheless, criticism of the commission model—as well as each demand for a general amnesty—was yet another hurdle confronting the ratification negotiations for the German General Treaty. The *FAZ* was the first to understand this, with an article headlined "The War Criminals' Gloriole: In Search of a Navigable Path on the Fringes of the Politically Possible and the Humanely Desirable."[291] The writer, Thilo Bode, drew a dividing line: the real murderers should remain in Allied custody, thus more or less shouldering the burden for all Nazi atrocities, and members of the functionary elites (as well as soldiers in general) should "now finally be freed from the stain of co-responsibility, and released from custody."[292] Thus, in a manner similar to Adenauer's (the chancellor liked to refer to "real criminals"), Bode stressed class differences: the culprits often hailed from the working classes, whereas the guilt of the "bourgeois desk perpetrators and sympathizers" was often not apparent to the public.[293]

Not surprisingly, the East German press rejected any link between the war criminals issue and rearmament. The East Berlin *Friedenspost* editorialized that what was taking place could only be termed a "pilgrimage to Werl," and it noted acerbically:

> It should be said at the start that all is well with . . . the ladies and gentlemen serving their "sentences of honor" in Werl, awaiting their new deployment in the service of inhumanity and racial madness. Not that that's any wonder: after all, the prison director Colonel Vickers is a scion of the British-German Vickers and Armstrong family who profited hugely from war in the past, and will therefore—like our Krupp people—do all in their power to start a third world war.[294]

Other left-wing papers were also critical.[295] The Communist *Tat*, published in Frankfurt, claimed that Waffen SS General Kurt Meyer, who was also imprisoned in Werl, was already working on strategic plans for the next war—this time on behalf of a "European Army": "He views Werl prison, where he currently finds himself, as an ideal war academy where—together with Field Marshals Manstein and Kesselring—he can elucidate plans for a war of attack on the East—plans which may go beyond the theoretical."[296] The redeployment of convicted war criminals, or the "reliance on Hitler's murder henchmen," amounted to a "declaration of moral bankruptcy which is almost unparalleled in history."[297] The Italian Communist *L'Unità* scoffed that the release of "concentration camp beasts and murderers" was due solely to the pressure exerted on Adenauer by former "Nazi officers" who had made their consent to the peace treaty and to a "future military alliance" contingent on the releases.[298] *Der Mittag* quoted a correspondent of the *Daily Mail*,

Charles Wighton, as saying that the legal advisers to the Foreign Office were preparing the release of well-known war criminals, including Kesselring and von Manstein; the release of the two field marshals was "part of the price which the British will have to pay for the 12 divisions in West Germany they seek."[299]

Friends of Kesselring, such as Colonel Peterpaul von Donat, detected the public's mood swing and thus felt able to write encouragingly to their former commander in Werl. Von Donat wrote:

> The solution: no military contribution before the prisoners have been released and the true criminals have been handed over to a German court—this solution has gradually become common currency. Ever more prominent voices are joining the debate, such as Admiral Hansen, Ramcke, who seems to be a decent speaker, and the association of soldiers serving at the front during both wars, who want to elect either yourself or Field Marshal von Manstein to their board. I see you sitting in the chair formerly occupied by our old Hindenburg.[300]

Germany's disempowered military elite thus gave voice to its hopes. Kesselring and Manstein had become the figureheads, father figures, and symbols of the rearmament debate.

Positions on the German General Treaty in the Spring of 1952

On both sides, the psychological hurdles in the way of ratification of the German General Treaty grew ever steeper as a solution to the war criminals issue was increasingly coupled with fundamental foreign and security policy decisions.[301] In foreign policy terms, the Federal Republic found itself in a delicate situation during the spring of 1954.[302] Discussions regarding a European Defense Community (EDC) were in full swing, the Saarland issue remained unresolved, and in March Adenauer received Stalin's note proposing reunification of Germany in return for demilitarization.[303] Especially in advance of the military debate due to take place in the Bundestag on February 7 and 8, 1952, Adenauer wanted to be sure that the war criminals issue—which he still tended to view as subordinate—was not accorded excessive public space.

During the Bundestag debate, the spokesperson for the coalition parliamentary grouping and chairperson of the Heidelberg Lawyers' Circle, Eduard Wahl, talked of his work in the Central Legal Defense Office, which operated in the shadows of the official political establishment in lobbying on the war crimes issue. Both the content and the manner of his presentation were moderate.[304] However, the FDP junior coalition partner seized the opportunity to make its position quite clear. (Under its chairman, Friedrich Middelhauve, the FDP was spearheading the campaign for former soldiers to be recompensed—a campaign that reached its unabashed climax in the publication of *The German Program* in the summer of 1952.)[305] August-Martin Euler, who represented the liberal FDP in the Bundestag, gave a new impetus to demands for Kesselring's release by forging a direct link between the field marshal's imprisonment and planned German rearmament. He was clear and candid in expressing his views:

> I cannot imagine that new German troops would march past the windows of Werl prison as long as the prison is home not only to Field Marshal von Manstein and Kesselring, but also to many deserving officers and common people who can be accused of nothing but that they availed of the options offered by warfare—options which must be and are offered under international law—to save their very lives in the face of perfidious and barbarous warfare."[306]

Euler was aware of Hankey's demand for senior German military figures to be rehabilitated and cited him saying, "No Englishman would agree to England entering an alliance with nations still holding English prisoners from a past war in custody."[307] Euler's appeal also included a reference to Paget's speech in the British House of Commons: "If the Allies want honorable German men—rather than mere adventurers and mercenaries—to serve in a European army of their own free will, then they must ensure that Manstein, and those of his fellow-prisoners who were not thrown into prison because of personal transgressions, are released."[308] The Bundestag then adopted a resolution demanding that the remaining war criminals be released from prison following an "objective review of individual cases."[309] The recurring theme of "personal innocence" had now entered political discourse.

Despite the fact that it was in full agreement with the federal government in this matter, the SPD found itself marginalized in the debate. That the Bundestag resolution was coupled with a declaration regarding a new German defense contribution—which the SPD rejected under current conditions—helped give rise to a perception that the SPD was not advocating the war criminals' cause.[310] This was not the case, as was apparent from Schumacher's intervention.

The funeral of Britain's King George VI in February 1952 provided an unscheduled opportunity for all foreign ministers to meet. This opportunity was used to relaunch discussions on a European defense community, which had come to a standstill—and to include Chancellor Adenauer in those discussions. The high commissioners had prepared a paper describing the Bundestag's demand for war criminals to be released as a sticking point and obstacle to the negotiations.[311] It was made quite clear to Adenauer that the three powers intended to hand the prisoners over to the German authorities as soon as they acknowledged the validity of the verdicts and undertook to ensure that they were enforced.[312] Justice Minister Thomas Dehler (FDP) had drafted a memorandum for Adenauer to present in London. In his draft, Dehler rejected any acknowledgment of the verdicts' validity,[313] but Adenauer, hoping to keep the Allies on board, asked Dehler to make some cosmetic amendments, such as using the term Eden had chosen for the commission—"Mixed Board"—instead of the term "Mixed Clemency Board," which Adenauer had earlier rejected. The word *clemency* seemed excessively coupled with the Allied verdicts, which Adenauer (and the German government as a whole) did not want to acknowledge under any circumstances, taking into account the "psychological significance of the war criminals issue" for the German public.[314] He also continuously referred to "remission of sentence."[315] The compromise solution was to ensure that the commission—comprising one representative from each of the Allies and three Germans—only had consultative powers. Once again, no clear resolution had been reached.

Bonn's reaction to the draft treaty was cautious, for it was felt that acknowledgment of the verdicts constituted the greatest problem. Justice Minister Dehler was particularly annoyed that Adenauer had failed to convey his clear-cut demands to the British government.[316] The German Justice Ministry had particular reservations about the proposal to exclude university teachers and judges from participation in the Mixed Board, since this would mean forfeiting the expertise of such professionals. Once again, the preferred option of the Federal Justice Ministry and the Rechtsschutz-Stelle became clear: they hoped that sentences would be reviewed by members of the Heidelberg Lawyers' Circle,[317] which, put bluntly, meant an impressive number of Nuremberg defense attorneys. The lawyers evidently hoped that by consolidating their energies and developing a united strategy, they could help their military clients win their appeals.

On February 20, 1952, attempting to play a mediating role, Lord Hankey gathered his closest allies together in London's United Services Club to discuss how they could assist matters and to consider measures that might facilitate ratification.[318] Those attending the meeting included the bishop of Chichester; Admiral of the Fleet William Boyle, 12th Earl of Cork and Orrery; Reginald Fletcher, 1st Baron Winster; Captain Russell Grenfell; Montgomery Belgion; and F. J. P. Veale.[319] It was decided to dispatch Sir Basil

Liddell Hart as an emissary to Bonn in order to discuss the ratification with Adenauer[320] and once again elucidate Hankey's proposal for a general amnesty—something Adenauer welcomed, while still avoiding nailing his colors to the mast.[321]

Pending signature of the Treaty for Regulating Matters Relating to the War and Period of Occupation (known as the Transition Treaty or General Treaty) on May 26, 1952, in Bonn, Adenauer attempted to maintain total secrecy regarding the document in hopes of ensuring that the war criminals issue did not block ratification.[322] The relevant cabinet members were only notified of the treaty's details on April 25. And as expected, Article 6, Part 1 of the treaty—the war criminals issue and the requisite acknowledgment of Allied verdicts—triggered a storm of protest. Eduard Wahl, who was generally known for his moderation, felt that if Germany accepted the prisoners, public opinion could come to the unfortunate conclusion that they had been found guilty under German law. Walter Strauss, permanent secretary in the Federal Justice Ministry, demanded that if Germany accepted custodial responsibility for the prisoners, it should also be awarded sole powers of clemency.[323] Adolf Heusinger added his voice to the debate, presenting the latest amnesty demands of the VdS and warning that the war criminals issue had to be solved "before the first German soldier dons a uniform." The coalition's position was now clear: it sought "renegotiations with the aim of shedding the obligation to assume custodial responsibility (and thus to acknowledge the verdicts)."[324] Since Adenauer feared that the Bundestag might fail to ratify the General Treaty because of the war criminals issue, he sought further concessions from the high commissioners. The British finally devised a compromise formula, according to which the Allies would retain the war criminals in their prisons until the federal government had passed the requisite legislation and was thus in a position to assume the obligation.

Although the intervening three weeks before the treaty was signed were marked by hectic discussions about details, as well as almost daily cabinet meetings, the text of the document remained largely unchanged.[325] Adenauer traveled to London for further talks. There, the circle around Lord Hankey had expanded the rehabilitation argument to include another aspect. On May 14, 1952, the House of Lords debated the war criminals problem. During the debate, both Lord Cork and Orrery and Lord Hankey addressed the issue of "obedience to orders," demanding that the transmission of orders not render a soldier liable to prosecution. Obviously, if one accepted this argument, senior German military figures convicted of such crimes should be released.[326] Following his return on May 18, Adenauer—in accordance with his weekly ritual—invited selected journalists to tea in the Chancellery. Though the atmosphere of these off-the-record chats was friendly, the sessions were motivated by a political calculation: through them, Adenauer could be certain that his message would get a public airing. On this occasion, the chancellor explained that the British government had paid proper attention to the war criminals issue and was well disposed to the German position.[327]

Action was required, and not only by cabinet members such as Erich Mende (FDP), Hans-Christoph Seebohm (DP), and Heinrich Hellwege (DP), who often formed an unofficial opposition to Adenauer's position, but also by certain church representatives.[328] Adenauer took the opportunity of the "birth of the General Treaty" to ask the high commissioners to offer a sign of goodwill in the form of clemency for specific prisoners. Pointing to concessions that had already been made, the high commissioners refused his request.[329] At that point, the "Generals' wing" in Werl was still home to Kesselring, Manstein, Mackensen, Simon, Wolf, Mältzer, and Gallenkamp.

Nevertheless, the negotiations gave Adenauer cause for satisfaction. His visit in London had resulted in the establishment of a mixed clemency board, and furthermore, he had persuaded the Allies to agree to a clause according to which Germany did not have to again implicitly acknowledge the verdicts—a concession of major domestic political significance. Yet not a single "voice of importance" in the press offered "acknowledgement or respect" to the Allies for their concessions.[330] This was largely due to the fact that such a gesture would have given a boost to the Far Right, which until then had largely expressed itself outside the Bundestag and which was increasingly threatening to pose a domestic political problem.[331]

Heinrich Hellwege, chairman of the Deutsche Partei and minister for Bundesrat affairs, advocated a policy of reintegrating Wehrmacht officers. The DP was one of the first political parties to take up the war criminals' cause and capitalize on it politically. Hellwege liked to boast that he was the first minister to "raise the names of Manstein and Kesselring in public."[332] He planned to visit Werl in order to discuss "the issue of the mixed clemency board" with Kesselring.[333] Naturally, this appeared inadvisable to the high commissioner's legal department. It was decided in London that, though Kesselring should be allowed to receive Hellwege's letter, the planned discussions should be prevented.[334] The British legal adviser, M. F. P. Herchenroder, felt that Kesselring could be attempting "to constitute himself the unofficial spokesman of the war criminals in Werl."[335] According to Herchenroder, Kesselring apparently believed that the relevant authorities were insufficiently informed regarding the war criminals issue and therefore required his enlightenment. The members of the clemency board obviously could not "receive instructions from someone whose petition they were to consider."[336] The Foreign

Office believed that Kirkpatrick should be quite open with Adenauer and should explain the British concerns about a visit to Werl by a German commission headed up by Hellwege.[337] However, Kirkpatrick did not feel that this fell within his remit and coolly informed London that he had no imminent plans to meet with the chancellor.[338]

Prime Minister Winston Churchill urged that a gesture be made. He felt that former German officers should receive separate (and thus more honorable) treatment, and he complained that all opportunities to improve relations between the two countries had been frittered away.[339] Despite the movement that had occurred, the British political establishment was still unable to agree on a clear policy in terms of the war criminals problem. "At a time when we were pursuing unity with much skill and patience over four or five years," Churchill observed, the British had "managed to get the worst of both worlds with the German nation about the release of war criminals." In a stinging criticism of the former foreign secretary, the prime minister went on to note that "at a time when we were pursuing unity in our relations with Germany and in their manufacture of arms and ammunitions Mr. Bevin foolishly embarked on new prosecutions of German commanders." In concrete terms, Churchill said that he had "always hoped that we might make a friendly gesture by the release of several hundred of the so-called war criminals, especially the people in high command who had no more to do with many of the atrocities than President Truman with the atomic bombing of Hiroshima and Nagasaki." He urged that the Germans themselves be allowed to decide who should be released, and he ended by noting that the prisoners would soon be released in any event, regardless of what "we or the Americans say or do."[340]

Eden clearly found it difficult to comprehend Churchill's position and again explained to the prime minister that those in custody were by no means "honorable German officers."[341] Moreover, it would scarcely be possible to release several hundred from Werl, since only 128 prisoners remained, including many concentration camp guards whom Eden considered to be the "real thugs."[342] Of the 603 prisoners held in Landesberg, Werl, and Wittlich, just 88 were former members of the Wehrmacht.[343] Eden felt that he was also speaking on behalf of Adenauer, who had repeatedly stated for the record that his concern was to secure the release of "innocent" men, not criminals. However, during a press conference, Adenauer said that priority should not be given to securing the release of Manstein and Kesselring.[344] An amicable solution to the war criminals issue thus seemed unlikely in the spring of 1952.[345]

The campaign for the prisoners' release was already having an impact on German public opinion. In this regard, Frei has correctly noted that "the fewer war criminals remained in Allied prisons, the more unconditional the solidarity with them."[346] The recurring claim that a high number of innocent soldiers were languishing in prison is disproved by figures from the German Foreign Office. According to these figures, on November 27, 1952, Werl was home to 11 former soldiers, 1 Waffen SS general, 26 policemen or members of the SD, and 49 concentration camp guards.[347] At the end of 1952, the Allensbach Institute polling company found that 65 percent of Germans were convinced of Kesselring's innocence, and 55 percent believed that German soldiers should not face charges because of their behavior in occupied countries during the war.[348]

In conclusion, it should be noted that—given the domestic political hurdles faced by Adenauer in negotiating ratification of the General Treaty—the Allies were increasingly willing to make the chancellor's difficult task easier by displaying an unusual degree of accommodation with regard to the war criminals issue. Thus, the link between rearmament and a prior release of the war criminals had permeated political thinking, and it was endorsed by (in particular) the British and Americans. Nonetheless, they were determined not to be seen as bowing to German pressure.

(above) Carl Kesselring, Albert's father, in 1880, five years before his youngest son was born. The elder Kesselring was a high school teacher, who was promoted to the position of Schools Director in Bayreuth. The family had thus succeeded in rising socially to join the middle class

(right) In 1904 Kesselring began his military career as a *Fahnenjunker*, or corporal cadet, in the Royal Bavarian Army. "I wanted to be a soldier, was hell-bent on this profession and—I can say this looking back—put my heart and soul into being a soldier," wrote Kesselring in his memoirs. In 1906, he attended the Royal Bavarian Parade (Königsparade) and proudly sent this picture home to his sister.

Kesselring, shown here in 1907, served in the 2nd Bavarian Heavy Artillery Regiment, in Metz, and received outstanding reports from the start. Regimental stationed commander Otto Mayer noted in 1909: "Among the younger officers, Lieutenant Kesselring is by far the best . . . he promises to distinguish himself far above the average."

The General Staff of the 2nd Bavarian Heavy Artillery Regiment, regimental headquarters at Lambusard chez Lille, France; from left: Hauptmann Eberhardt, Major Weller, General Kreppel (with beard), Oberleutnant Kesselring (in white gala uniform). Before moving to the General Staff, Kesselring had distinguished himself on the front line. For eight months he served with the troops in Flanders and Vogesen and was promoted to captain in 1915. During the battles for Arras he had succeeded in repelling a British bridgehead by means of a tactical dodge with operational consequences, subsequently closing the impending gaps in the line of defense and avoiding the threatened retreat, a gambit for which he was to find renewed use in Italy thirty years later.

The staff of the 2nd Bavarian Heavy Artillery Regiment in 1916, Lambusard chez Lille, France. From left: Major Weller, Hauptmann Eberhardt, General Kreppel, Oberleutnant Kesselring.

Kesselring (with white map) in a balloon in France, 1917. Kesselring was not only temperamentally suited to, but also technically interested in, new forms of weaponry. In 1912 he completed a training course as a balloon observer in the dirigible section—his first contact with what became the Luftwaffe. The largely middle-class officers in the technically demanding artillery regiments were more open to modern aviation than the infantry or cavalry officers, who tended to be more focused on tradition; Kesselring's subsequent career development as a Luftwaffe officer was thus not unusual.

Kesselring in 1922, soon after his appointment to the Reichswehr ministry at Berlin, where he served as a military expert.

(Top) Kesselring and his father in 1932, shortly before the latter's death, in one of the rare personal pictures of Kesselring. It is no coincidence that it dates from the Weimar Republic years, a relatively quiet phase of Kesselring's career. *(Bottom)* Albert Kesselring and his wife, Pauline Anna Keyssler, take a stroll with Kesselring's aged father at his hometown of Bayreuth in 1932.

Kesselring was flattered by the social advancement associated with a position in the new air force and by the regime's pomp and ceremony. He was involved in the decision to provide assistance to Franco by offering him a few units (the so-called Condor Legion under the command of Generaloberst Wolfram von Richthofen). Its involvement in the Spanish Civil War played an important role in the German air force's strategic planning: the war was viewed as a test battleground demonstrating the effects of bombing raids on morale and matériel. Here Kesselring is shown with Richthofen in 1940.

Kesselring was among the capable officers who transformed the Luftwaffe into a world-class air force in just a few years. This November 1940 photograph shows Kesselring at the flag ceremony at the VIII Fliegerkorps at Mönchen-Gladbach.

Kesselring with Göring at the channel coast, February 1940, explaining his strategy during the air battle against Britain.

Field marshal promotion ceremony at Carinhall, 1940, with Göring (Kesselring is fifth from left). In 1938 Kesselring had been appointed head of Air Group One, which was involved in the occupation of the Sudetenland and then took part in the bombing of Warsaw in 1939 and of Rotterdam in 1940. Following successful Luftwaffe operations during the French campaign, Hitler awarded Kesselring (now head of Air Group Two) a field marshal's baton: Kesselring thus skipped a rank. This accelerated promotion underlined Hitler's personal appreciation of the Bavarian "people's general" as well as the improved promotion opportunities for officers in wartime.

Kesselring was awarded the Iron Cross for his military service during operations at Warsaw, Rotterdam, and in France in 1940. Here, he receives congratulations from Hitler during the ceremony. Thanks to his own commitment to developing the Luftwaffe, which was considered a specifically National Socialist section of the armed forces, Kesselring also changed his view of Hitler and became a supporter of Hitler's policies.

Kesselring portrayed with the Iron Cross in 1940.

Kesselring in Russia in early autumn of 1941 with Air Group One at a staff meeting, planning the advance toward Moscow, which started October 2, 1941. It resulted in a complete German disaster, leading to the German withdrawal in early 1942. The atmosphere of the victorious blitzkrieg of "Operation Barbarossa" during the previous month in Russia is still visible in the faces of those listening to Kesselring's strategic explanations, and few would have anticipated the complete disaster of the German Luftwaffe during the battle of the Russian capital later that year.

Kesselring visiting soldiers at the "Ostwall" trenches in Russia, summer 1941. Revered by many of his soldiers as a father figure, he devoted himself completely to his job as an army officer. From his Reichswehr times, Kesselring had absorbed Seeckt's views of demanding discipline and unconditional obedience in order to solidify the authority of the military leadership, thus ensuring its operational readiness.

In 1933, at the age of forty-eight, Kesselring had learned to fly, an achievement that earned him the respect of his men. He was one of the most popular German officers during the war. Here he is shown with men of the air squadron Wilke after awarding them the Iron Cross in 1941 in Russia.

In November 1941, Kesselring was appointed commander-in-chief of Army Group South. Because of Italian sensitivities, Kesselring's place in the chain of command in Africa was extremely complicated. For air force matters he reported to the German commander-in-chief of the Luftwaffe, Hermann Göring, but when it came to his "primary duty" relating to the Africa campaign, he reported to Mussolini and received the Duce's directives through the "Comando Supremo," the supreme command of the Italian armed forces in Rome. This meant that Kesselring had no powers of command over German army or navy units—and certainly no say over Italian forces. He mediated between the militarily weaker Italian allies and the often temperamental Afrika Korps commander, Erwin Rommel, who was not always inclined to obey the instructions of the Comando Supremo. Here Kesselring prepares to board a plane in Comiso, Sicily, in March 1942.

Kesselring inspecting the former Allied headquarters at Tobruk after the Axis victory in May 1942, when 32,000 Allied soldiers fell into German hands. Kesselring's adversary Erwin Rommel, the victorious general, was promoted to field marshal as a result.

August 21, 1942, meeting at Schloss Klessheim near Salzburg with Hitler and Mussolini, Keitel and Kesselring (from back). Kesselring saw himself as "the senior man in Italy," a perception that gave rise to an autocratic leadership style.

Kesselring in 1942 on a minesweeper in the Mediterranean Sea. Since November 25, 1941, he had been commander-in-chief, Southern Command. In the Africa campaign, Kesselring's primary duty was "to establish a centre of power for the Axis in the central Mediterranean" and to observe enemy sea movements. He had to maintain contact with Germany's Italian allies and secure the supply chain to Africa—a test of his diplomatic skills.

Kesselring was one of the few senior Wehrmacht officers never to be relieved of his duties by Hitler. In September 1942, he was briefly considered as a successor to Keitel, indicating the high regard in which he was held by the Führer. In 1942, he was awarded the Oak Leaf with Swords; here he celebrates the award privately at his headquarters in Sicily. On July 19, 1944, Kesselring received the brilliants to the Iron Cross and was the last officer to meet the Führer before the attempted assassination of Hitler the next day. Like other senior commanders, Kesselring rushed to send a telegram of loyalty to the Führer's headquarters once the news broke.

At Florence near the Arno River, 1944. In 1943, following the fall of Mussolini and the German occupation of Upper Italy, Kesselring was given sole command in Italy. He led Army Group C in its fighting retreat, accompanied by heavy casualties, from Naples along the Po River, until March 1945. The Wehrmacht had been on the retreat in Italy since the Allied landing in Sicily on July 10 and was forced into a hasty retreat across the Apennines, hindered by a significant increase in partisan activity. The *Bandenbefehle*, or antipartisan orders, which Kesselring personally drafted and issued on June 17 and July 1, 1944, increased the hatred felt by German soldiers for the Italians, radicalized both Wehrmacht and partisan units, and contributed to the escalation of the war in Italy during the summer of 1944.

One of Kesselring's first actions shortly after his release from prison in October 1952 was to demand that all German officers in custody be released. He argued that letting some guilty officers go would "never be as great [an] injustice [as that] inflicted on hundreds of other officers who were convicted and imprisoned for years for acts which they did not commit"—a group in which he definitely included himself. His naïve demand for a general amnesty was rooted in the conviction that he was indispensable to the planned rearmament.

Chief Inspector of the Luftwaffe of the Bundeswehr General Joseph Kammhuber speaking at the funeral of Kesselring, his superior during World War II, at Bad Wiessee, Tegernsee (Bavaria), July 1960. The funeral was an informal meeting of the Nazi military elite. SS and police chief of Italy Karl Wolff is in the first row (with white hair, above the hat of the soldier holding the wreath). In 2000, when a memorial event was held to mark the fortieth anniversary of Kesselring's death, only a small group of aging veterans representing the German Montecassino Association and the Association of German Paratroopers attended. The Bundeswehr declined to be present, stating that the former field marshal was "not worthy of being part of our tradition."

Chapter 5

Kesselring's Release

There was a very real danger that the Bundestag would fail to ratify the General Treaty and associated supplementary agreements, as well as the draft treaty establishing a European defense community, because of the focus on the war criminals issue. It was clear that further concessions by London would help Adenauer obtain the requisite consent to the General Treaty. But the British faced a dilemma: how could they release Kesselring without appearing to have caved in to German pressure?

Political developments in the war criminals issue were accompanied by individual initiatives, ensuring that any primarily political decision to release Kesselring would be transformed into a decision with explicit implications for the politics of memory. First, the group around Lord Hankey increased its pressure on the British government. At the same time, Kesselring was elected honorary president of three German veterans' associations, thus elevating him to the status of a soldierly role model. For the former field marshal to receive such recognition was equivalent to both symbolic and moral rehabilitation. But it was not until Kesselring was diagnosed with cancer in the summer of 1952 that an opportunity arose to justify his premature release.

Once a British military doctor had confirmed the cancer diagnosis on behalf of the Foreign Office in September 1952, clemency was just a formality. By the end of October, Kesselring was already able to leave the clinic a free man. London was unperturbed by the storm of protest in Italy, especially since Kesselring's release went almost unnoticed in the rest of the world. The British government had provided Adenauer with the requisite cover, and ratification was now certain. However, the relaxed political atmosphere was shattered by Kesselring himself when, after his own release, he demanded that other prisoners be freed—a demand supported by right-wing and nationalist veterans' associations. Kesselring's demand, which coincided with a widely publicized speech by Bernhard Ramcke to SS veterans, soon caused an unwelcome spotlight to be shone on Britain's clemency policy. The situation demanded maximum diplomatic finesse in order to minimize the political damage. The resolution of the ongoing war criminals issue—an issue that, in the end, even involved senior NATO figures—was now at stake. But the political establishment had already developed a primary principle: war crimes had to be legally expiated. This development, signs of which were already evident in respect to the Kesselring case, continued.

Finally, one must ask whether, given his role as chairperson of various veterans' associations, Kesselring could ever have been an appropriate role model in the effort to invest the new German army, the Bundeswehr, with a fresh sense of tradition. One must also ask how he should be assessed today. There were several reasons why Kesselring was unable to perform the intended role of a figurehead who would help create a new narrative for former Wehrmacht members, thus encouraging them, under his leadership, to offer their unqualified consent to rearmament. In retrospect, Kesselring's ill-considered public appearances—especially during 1954, when he spoke at veterans' meetings and offered himself as an expert witness in court—would seem to have disqualified him from playing a role in moderating (let alone actively participating in) any repositioning of a new German army during what was to be a decisive, and thus difficult, phase. An examination of media reaction to his memoirs and subsequent public appearances shows that Kesselring himself frittered away the goodwill he had initially enjoyed as a World War II military icon.

The Ratification Problem and the War Criminals Issue

The war criminals issue came to a head in the summer of 1952, when it was caught in the parliamentary machinery of the Bundestag. Representatives of all parties made it clear that their consent to the General Treaty was contingent upon Germany's occupied status being reviewed and war criminals being released.[1] Against this background, Adenauer openly asked the Hankey circle to intercede with the British government. In this chapter, the focus of my analysis will be on the difficulties facing Adenauer in the Bundestag. I also hope to shed some light on the part played by Hankey and his associates and on the options open to them for exerting influence on the British government.

During a meeting with Liddell Hart on June 9, 1952, Adenauer indicated how inextricably the release of senior German military figures was bound up with ratification of the treaty. It would, he said, be of great assistance to the German government "if the Western Powers would demonstrate their goodwill by signal acts of clemency on their own initiative."[2] Speed was of the essence, according to Adenauer, because the first reading of the treaty text was scheduled for the beginning of July.

The mood in the Bundestag was tense. In a position paper, Erich Mende—founding member and chief whip of the FDP, who had served as an officer at the front—outlined the conditions that had to be met to ensure smooth parliamentary passage of the treaty. Mende's stance was unambiguous: "Despite being in fundamental agreement with the Federal Government's basic foreign policy, various coalition MPs from the war generation would have to refuse their consent [if] those former soldiers still in custody" were not released before the third reading of the treaty.[3] Mende argued that the participation of German soldiers in a defense alliance was associated with "psychological preconditions." After all, he said, an army needed to be animated by a spirit. "However," he added, "in the context of European solidarity and defense preparedness, this spirit cannot arise in any German division which knows that its former commanders or comrades are still in Allied prisons, despite the fact that there is no general belief in their guilt."[4] The ultimatum was addressed not only to the German government but also and especially to the Allies. Mende demanded that priority be given to releasing young, old, and sick prisoners.[5] The Deutsche Partei, which was laboring under the weight of enormous expectations from its constituency (specifically the Werl families), rejected this proposal. Hellwege feared that a "list of names would be viewed as analogous to a supplementary sentence by those left behind."[6] Nevertheless, Mende acceded to Adenauer's express wishes and prepared a list of over 140 prisoners who, in his view, could be released for health reasons.[7] The list had initially been compiled by experts from the Rechtsschutz-Stelle. Speaking on the record, Mende told reporters that he would have to "say no to the treaty if his own superior officers—Manstein, Kesselring and Hoth—remained in custody."[8]

There is no doubt that private interventions by members of Hankey's circle injected a new dynamic into the debate surrounding Kesselring's release. Liddell Hart attempted to mediate, and he intensified his efforts at Hankey's urging: in July, he met with the new British secretary of state for defense (and Kesselring's onetime opponent in Italy), Sir Harold Alexander.[9] According to Liddell Hart, Alexander had already raised the issue with the cabinet members and indicated that they would try to somehow accommodate Adenauer's wishes. The British and Americans were in agreement on this issue. At Alexander's request, the American ambassador to the Court of St. James, Julius Holmes, agreed to raise the matter with the State Department. For his part, Hankey held a confidential meeting with Gerald Isaacs, 2nd Marquess of

Reading, the minister of state for foreign affairs, during which he presented Adenauer's request for assistance and emphasized the urgent need for British concessions.[10] Although Hankey had found a reliable and powerful ally in Defense Secretary Alexander,[11] he still had not received any direct assurances from the government camp—in particular the prime minister.

In August, Lord Hankey met personally with Churchill to discuss those German war criminals still in custody.[12] During their meeting, Churchill is reputed to have said that a "signal should be sent," and the release of Field Marshals Kesselring and Manstein, both of whom were in very poor health due to their advanced years, was an opportunity to send such a signal.[13] Thanks to the prime minister's assent, the shift in British policy toward war criminals was now a done deal. In the Foreign Office, Hancock was under no illusions; writing to Herchenroder in Wahnerheide, he stated: "I think we all hope that Kesselring and Manstein will continue to enjoy ill-health for some time to come, so as to relieve us of the necessity of again accommodating them in Werl prison, at any rate before the ratification debate in the Bundestag."[14]

Immediately after the war, the British had undertaken an important mission in terms of the politics of memory—a mission to ensure that war crimes were expiated. That mission was now being downgraded in the face of new foreign policy considerations, in particular the aim of integrating Germany into a military alliance. They were therefore at pains to assist Adenauer's efforts to secure parliamentary ratification by pursuing a conciliatory war criminals policy. Admittedly, the Foreign Office recommended keeping a close watch on Manstein and Kesselring to be certain they did not receive too many hospital visits; the goal was to prevent them from "holding court" or intervening politically from their sickbeds, as had been the case in the past. Nevertheless, it was apparent that the British had very few sanctions at their disposal. The main thing now was to avoid losing face.

The *Neue Zeitung* was the first newspaper to detect this change of tack, warning of a "political deal." After all, readers were reminded, "during the Second World War certain events took place in the German Wehrmacht which, until then, had been unprecedented in the army of any civilized country."[15] With particular reference to the recurring justification advanced in defense of war criminals—that is, the alleged imperative to obey orders[16]—the *Neue Zeitung* noted that "the individual generals, officers and military figures were not convicted as a collective, but rather as individuals with personal responsibility because it was possible to prove that they were responsible for killing prisoners of war, for 'liquidating' Jews and other 'undesirable' population groups."[17] However, the paper's finding of guilt was not echoed elsewhere. The release of the putatively innocent field marshal had long become a symbol of a new and sovereign Germany, a country standing up for the rights of its veterans.

Kesselring's Cancer Operation, July 1952

All Kesselring's British advocates now needed was an event that could kick-start their campaign. And the field marshal's unexpected cancer diagnosis was tailor-made for the purpose. The first covert indication that Kesselring would soon be released came when he was operated on in a German hospital. The British authorities had started to wonder whether his diagnosis was genuine, and their suspicions were heightened by the fact that, following the operation, doctors at the Bochum hospital "Bergmannsheil" started lobbying on behalf of their patient. However, once British doctors had confirmed the diagnosis, it was up to the lawyers in Wahnerheide to come up with a carefully worded statement of reasons justifying Kesselring's release.

On July 8, after being examined by a German doctor attached to Werl Prison, Kesselring was admitted to the Bergmannsheil hospital with a suspected throat tumor;[18] an operation was scheduled for July 16. The operation was carried out by Kesselring's former military physician, Professor Hans Bürkle de la Camp, who had operated on Kesselring following his head injury on October 23, 1944. The fact that former Wehrmacht doctors not only diagnosed Kesselring but then proceeded to operate on him was an indication of the goodwill of the British—and of their hopes that they could soon wash their hands of the case. Nevertheless, the British continued to wonder whether Kesselring really did have cancer; they feared, with some justification, that his friends would stop at little to secure his release.

These fears were fueled by the nature of the German medical reports. In his surgical report, the assistant medical director, Dr. W. Jantke, diagnosed an "adenomatous cancer which had grown on the base of a salivary gland growth."[19] Following this report, the Werl Prison doctor, Dr. Busch, warned that in "view of the nature of the disease," no more time should be lost: Kesselring should be declared unfit for prison and released from Werl. The worry was that, like Mältzer in February 1952, Kesselring could die in prison, thus again generating "serious accusations leveled at the doctor and the English authorities."[20] The legal department (in particular, the secretary to the legal adviser in Wahnerheide, J. C. Piegrome) felt that it was "inappropriate of Dr. Busch to demand Kesselring's immediate release simply because another doctor had written a report, and both believe that Kesselring could die and we would be criticized if he dies while still serving his sentence."[21] For psychological reasons, the doctors had advised that Kesselring not be told the truth about his state of health so as to avoid delaying his recovery, and consequently, there could be no question of releasing him on health grounds. Weekly medical reports from Bochum were prepared to document further developments, and plans were made for Kesselring to undergo an independent examination by a British doctor within a few weeks.[22] Dr. Laternser took advantage of British indecision to submit another petition on behalf of Kesselring, noting "my client's serious illness."[23]

Kesselring was accommodated in a hospital room under guard. As in Werl, visitors were required to obtain a special permit issued by the prison management.[24] These measures were intended to prevent any contact between Kesselring and the press. The press, however, viewed the mere fact of Kesselring's admission to a normal German hospital as an initial victory,[25] heightening speculation that the former field marshal would be granted early release from Werl.[26] Rumor had it that Kesselring's most frequent visitor was Lieutenant Colonel Vickers, director of Werl Prison, who had allegedly visited Kesselring along with his wife and interpreter, bringing small gifts.[27] The longer Kesselring stayed in the hospital, the more the media frenzy grew.

At the beginning of August, Vickers had found Kesselring well on the way to recovery,[28] so the British were understandably surprised by a report issued by Dr. Bürkle de la Camp at the end of August arguing that Kesselring was no longer fit for prison.[29] He enclosed a diagnostic report by the specialist Dr. Beckmann stating that, in addition to cancer, Kesselring was suffering from a "cardiac valve defect and poor circulation of the peripheral cardiac vessels, as well as rheumatism."[30] Bürkle couched his cover note to Vickers diplomatically, writing that he was not stressing these symptoms "as a German, in order to provide the German field marshal Kesselring with disproportionate assistance vis-à-vis the English authorities."

However, in presenting this diagnosis, Bürkle was obviously acting primarily on behalf of his friend Albert Kesselring. He also contacted the British authorities in Wahnerheide directly, stating that he felt it would be appropriate to release Kesselring on health grounds. He stepped up the pressure on the British as well: speaking on radio, he asserted that, in his view, the patient was no longer fit for prison, even though he admitted that Kesselring's life was "not in acute danger." As he pointed out to Vickers, he viewed his radio interview as an opportunity to "calm the public."[31] Vickers passed on Bürkle's fears without further comment, stressing that Kesselring's recovery was being impeded by his impending return to Werl and noting that the doctor felt the "psychological effect" of being released would be "of very great benefit to the patient."[32] Vickers was thus taking Kesselring's side himself.

Obviously, getting a second opinion would be the simplest way of overcoming the British authorities' distrust of the German doctors—distrust caused by the Germans' unambiguous partisanship. The Foreign Office, in the person of Hancock, instructed the Legal Department in Wahnerheide to lose no time in instructing a British physician to examine Kesselring.[33] After all, the war criminals issue was due to be "decided in the next two months."

Kesselring's Honorary Presidency of Veterans' Associations: Symbolic Rehabilitation

Even though medical reasons were used to legitimate the release of the two military icons Kesselring and Manstein, the deciding factor proved to be the public pressure exerted on the British political establishment. As already outlined, the press played a crucial role in this regard. But the press was not responsible for the most recent campaign on behalf of Kesselring and Manstein, in the summer of 1952. That campaign was kick-started when the veterans' associations appointed the generals to honorary positions, thus rehabilitating them as soldierly role models and more or less erasing the war crimes from the public memory. Following the declarations of honor issued by General Eisenhower and Chancellor Adenauer, this acclamation was another key component bolstering the self-esteem of the Wehrmacht elite and restoring their public image.[34] Within a relatively short period, Kesselring had assumed the honorary presidency of three associations: the Luftwaffenring, the Stahlhelm, and the Verband deutsches Afrikakorps. At the end of July 1952, ten veterans' associations signed a joint manifesto demanding the release of all "so-called war criminals" as a precondition for German rearmament.[35] In this regard, the arguments for moral rehabilitation were based on a simple premise, as Kühne has shown: "Anyone who had suffered the martyrdom of being a prisoner of war could not be a murderer or war criminal; he had suffered, and those who had suffered were innocent."[36]

Plans by individual veterans' associations to appoint Kesselring as their honorary president had started to take shape in the spring of 1952. Such accolades had two goals. On the one hand, these moves were intended to reinforce demands for Kesselring, then still in custody, to be released. On the other hand, the associations felt that such appointments would increase their own public profile, thus helping them secure their pension demands.

Former members of the Luftwaffe were the first to adopt this course. On August 3, 1952, former Generalleutnant Martin Harlinghausen made contact with Kesselring to offer him the honorary chairmanship of the Luftwaffenring, established in May 1952.[37] Harlinghausen wrote that a decision had been made to "merge all the little Traditionsverbände in a spirit of comradeship," and a suitable leadership figure was required for this purpose; "during war and peace, Kesselring had been a model of selfless soldierly dutifulness and self-sacrifice" for them all. "No victor, no former enemy who accepts the ethos of honorable soldierhood, can deny you the respect due to a man of honor," he wrote the former field marshal, adding that this high regard also obliged former comrades in the Luftwaffenring to "stand up for your freedom and your rights." Harlinghausen went on to note that "the day is certainly not far off" when "we will be able to greet you in freedom and justice," for otherwise "we would have to doubt those who claim to stand for freedom and justice"—a clear swipe at the despised victors' justice.

The British viewed Harlinghausen's approach with mixed feelings. Since Kesselring was in the hospital, they had to question whether they were even in a position to prevent him from receiving such letters—or responding to them.[38] In addition, the Verband deutscher Soldaten had already announced its intention to award "various honorary positions to other war criminals from Werl."[39] Piegrome feared that similar offers would now be made to Erich von Manstein.[40] In the end, it was decided to deliver the letter, since, thanks to the fact that custody conditions were eased in the hospital, Kesselring would easily be able to make verbal contact with these correspondents.[41] As expected, he immediately accepted the honorary presidency: after all, it offered him the opportunity to take his first steps in freedom while holding a quasi-official position. He was also inducted into the Ordensgemeinschaft der Ritterkreuzträger des Eisernen Kreuzes e. V. (Order of the Knight's Cross). His membership significantly increased the association's prestige,[42] and it may have induced other senior officers holding the Knight's Cross grade of the Iron Cross to emulate Kesselring by joining, too.

Kesselring did not follow any systematic strategy when deciding which organizations to join, indicating that he was seeking the solidarity offered by these Traditionsverbände rather than pursuing any political ambitions. Judging by his reactions when offered the honorary presidency of various associations, it is evident that he took a certain naive pleasure in each appointment: as far as he was concerned, every one represented a continuing commitment to "his" soldiers. He did not realize that, by appointing him, the veterans' associations were simultaneously addressing unambiguous political demands to the Allies. It is also possible that personal vanity played some part in his decision to accept three honorary presidencies in quick succession without first gathering information on the aims of the associations in question.

Commenting on Kesselring's new appointments, the press seized on the opportunity to again assert demands for a "resolution to the war criminals issue" before the ratification debate, implicitly pressing for Kesselring's release.[43] The Communist *Tat* issued a prediction: "Given the current situation, it is now merely a technical question of when, and in which uniform, Mr. Kesselring will again be appointed a defender of Western culture."[44] The reaction in Italy, however, was rather more relaxed. Adopting a conciliatory tone in the conservative weekly *Libertas*, Lina Morino wrote that the veterans' associations could have appointed "a greater nationalist" than Kesselring. She came to the remarkable conclusion that the former field marshal was "anything but partisan or Nazi"—a conclusion that certainly helped influence the fundamentally (if temporarily) positive attitude in Italy.[45]

The approach adopted by the Luftwaffe veterans' association led the way for others to follow. Kesselring unofficially assumed the honorary presidency of the Verband deutsches Afrikakorps in August 1952; the appointment was formalized in October.[46] There is no doubt that this particular appointment had been a done deal for some time. As early as 1951, the war artist Hans Wessel, himself a veteran of the Africa campaign, had met Kesselring, who was undergoing dental treatment, in the British military hospital at Iserlohn. The encounter was prompted by the founding meeting of the Verband deutsches Afrikakorps. Wessel wanted to discuss plans (which were still quite vague) to create an "African Traditionsverband" with Kesselring and was interested in any suggestions the former field marshal might have.[47] Judging by the association's publications and the press reaction, this seems to have been Albert Kesselring's least noteworthy honorary presidency. All that has been preserved are a few welcoming words by Kesselring in the organization's journal, *Die Oase*.[48]

In August 1952, while still in the hospital, Kesselring accepted the honorary presidency of the Stahlhelm, which was established in the prior year.[49] In contrast to the general sense of fatigue in military circles at the time, the Stahlhelm managed to publish a regular eponymous monthly journal, but it needed a prestigious figurehead in order to recruit new members.[50] The association explained Kesselring's appointment by stating: "With this election, the Stahlhelm has embarked on a course to end the defamation of German soldiers in our *Volk*'s own self-image." The linkage with Kesselring's name, redolent of symbolism, was intended to allow veterans to see meaning in their wartime service once again, while also improving their social standing. With Kesselring, there would be a "genuine military contribution in the context of the Western world," to which "all our people would be prepared to give their assent." Not all assessments were as sanguine, however. Referring to an article in the *Schweizer Nationalzeitung*, the *Stimme des Friedens* asked whether Kesselring would even accept this offer. Both papers concurred that if he did, he would have joined the well-populated ranks of "those former German commanders who have still learnt nothing."[51] As it happened, assuming the presidency of the far right Stahlhelm certainly damaged rather than enhanced Kesselring's image.

Kesselring's election was facilitated by the fact that, in its first issue, the association's journal, *Der Stahlhelm*, cited Colonel Alexander Scotland—the British officer who had initially interrogated Kesselring and subsequently championed his cause—with words that could only be interpreted as a declaration of honor on the field marshal's behalf.[52] The article failed to mention Kesselring's past as a convicted war criminal,[53] and beyond that, his past as a whole was more or less reinterpreted. In certain circles, a conviction by Allied courts was considered a badge of honor, and many veterans' associations used the appointment of a convicted war criminal to their presidency to indicate they would no longer accept what they saw as the defamation of German soldiers. The Frankfurt-based *Neue Zeitung* was the only newspaper to cite an American High Commission staff member—one who was obviously not very familiar with the mentality of frontline veterans and their code of honor. He was quoted as saying that the veterans would have "displayed more courage had they appointed a survivor of the July 20th [attempt on Hitler's life in 1944] than, of all people, the war criminal Kesselring."[54]

Following Kesselring's appointment, numerous telegrams arrived from local and regional Stahlhelm chapters congratulating him on the successful outcome of his surgery.[55] The British considered the telegrams from veterans' associations "inappropriate," but they had no doubt that withholding them from Kesselring would cause a furor.[56] The secretary of the Legal Department, Bathurst, decided that all telegrams should be handed over to Kesselring on principle, as long as he did not intend to respond to them.[57] Once again, the British attempted to resolve their dilemma through compromise.

Kesselring also received felicitations from his "old comrades" in Italy. Now that he had been "appointed chairperson by the loyal veterans' associations," the Italian Fascist Rodolfo Graziani sent his best wishes to the "brave field marshal and loyal defender of European civilization."[58] The telegrams sent by Field Marshal Graziani and the "*camerati italiani*" (Italian comrades) were not handed over to Kesselring but were instead sent to Rome for the information of the British embassy,[59] so that officials there could take the steps deemed appropriate in circumstances where one war criminal was congratulating another.[60]

British sarcasm could not conceal the fact that Kesselring's image had been enhanced. Most people believed he was innocent, he was viewed in Germany as a soldierly icon, and three important veterans' associations had just appointed him as their honorary president. Sooner or later, the political establishment would have to acknowledge Kesselring's stature by releasing him.

The Grounds for Clemency

The verdict of the British physician examining Kesselring was clear: cancer.[61] In the Foreign Office, Frank Roberts displayed unconcealed delight when he wrote to Kirkpatrick that "we should be justified in recommending the exercise of clemency on medical grounds."[62] Although the authorities in London had initially considered paroling the former field marshal indefinitely, they felt that concrete evidence of clemency would be "more clear cut." It was considered that, with an eye on British public opinion, the best course would be to paint Kesselring's poor state of health in the blackest of colors. However, it was vital to avoid conveying a similar impression to the German media, since "it might not look very good if Kesselring's release could be painted as a last-moment effort to avoid his dying on our hands."

The news of Kesselring's release was received with equanimity in the American and British press. The public relations ground had been well laid, and the British public had been carefully prepared for the possible releases of German generals. The motto was "pardon without forgiveness," and the authorities took care to stress that they had not bowed to any concrete demands made by the nationalist camp in Germany but instead had wanted to extend a gesture of goodwill in a case that was less serious than certain others.[63] The press had already been speculating for some weeks that the ailing field marshal would never return to Werl. It is therefore unsurprising that Kesselring's release barely registered with the British press—and certainly not with the tabloids, which merely noted it in "other news." Kesselring himself had also never been the focus of the kind of public attention in England accorded to, for example, Erich von Manstein, who enjoyed a degree of fame as a result of the book by Reginald Paget. Just two questions were tabled in the British House of Commons regarding Kesselring's release.[64] Media coverage in the United States was much the same. In its report on October 24, the *New York Times* also stressed Kesselring's poor state of health.[65]

The decision to release Kesselring also decided Erich von Manstein's fate.[66] Although Roberts pointed out the possibility that a doctor might reach a different verdict in Manstein's case than in Kesselring's, he hoped that it would be possible to similarly justify releasing Manstein: "There is little to choose between their guilt and their names are generally coupled together."[67]

Kirkpatrick made every effort to resolve other contentious cases by taking the clemency route. It was important to ensure that the respect enjoyed by the British justice system was not damaged as a result of political pressure, which could lead to retrospective adjudication being taken to absurd lengths.

He stressed publicly that if leave was granted to appeal, any British court of appeal would have to set aside the verdicts imposed by individual military courts due to legal shortcomings. Such leave to appeal was, however, reserved for British subjects. He stated:

> I am sorry to harp so constantly on the shocking conduct of many of our war crime courts, but I feel it my duty to do so because we simply must not lull ourselves into believing that all is well here. It is not, and if we have any regard for justice we must take account of the fact. On purely political grounds also we must remember that we shall prejudice our chances of making Germany democratic and creating respect for the rule of law if our own conduct is vulnerable. Incidentally, I am not alone in my opinion of these trials.[68]

Kirkpatrick warned that the time would come when historians would research the war crimes issue, and he noted that it would reflect poorly on British justice if it were found that a shabby consideration of political expediency had been allowed to take the place of British legal traditions.[69]

Hancock explicitly pointed out that the British Foreign Office was anxious to avoid any impression that the British had bowed to German pressure in light of the ratification debate.[70] What written statement of grounds, then, should be provided to justify Kesselring's release? With the aid of the two medical reports, as well as the review report on Laternser's 1949 petition, Herchenroder drafted a final document.[71] His assessment of the legal situation was clear: Kesselring had been justly convicted; the facts spoke against him (at least in respect to the second count, on inciting the antipartisan war in Italy), and he had enjoyed a fair and exhaustive trial.[72] The medical reports, in particular, now justified releasing Kesselring.

It should be noted, despite a widespread view to the contrary, that the verdict imposed on Kesselring was never reviewed on the basis that he had not received a fair trial or because new evidence had come to light exonerating the former field marshal. In fact, after a careful legal review, Kesselring's guilt in connection with the death of Italian civilians (as specified by the second count of the indictment) remained beyond doubt. Even Basil Liddell Hart conceded as much in a letter to Hankey.[73] In view of the altered political relationship between Bonn and London (and also between Bonn and Rome) and considering the need to take into account the victims' suffering, the only option that appeared justifiable was to release Kesselring on health grounds.

Kesselring's Release

On October 22, 1952, the British high commissioner informed his Allied counterparts, William Donelly and André François-Poncet, that Queen Elizabeth II had pardoned Kesselring.[74] The Italians were notified even later than the Allied authorities. It was only on October 23 that Italy's ambassador to Bonn, reporting to the Foreign Ministry in Rome, noted that Kirkpatrick had asked him "what the attitude would be in Italy if Kesselring was now released."[75] Kirkpatrick had informed the ambassador of Kesselring's poor state of health and had also disclosed the political motives underlying the release; further, he assured him that Kesselring's release would be justified by his progressive cancer. The Italian ambassador, realizing that the decision had already been made, pointed out that the Italian public was likely to react negatively to the news.

The Italians must have felt duped when they learned that on the evening of the same day, Kesselring was officially released from Werl.[76] Initially, the Italian papers made an obvious effort to exercise restraint. However, after vehement protests in the Italian parliament by a few MPs, together with partisan associations and victims' groups, the situation escalated. Italy was buzzing with excitement. Kesselring only aggravated matters by the comments he made at a press conference, thus adding to the confusion. As well as polemical attacks on Kesselring himself, there were attacks on the German government, and these, in turn, prompted diplomatic reactions. The Rome and Bonn governments were faced with an uphill struggle in their attempts to regain control over the situation.

Reaction in Italy to Kesselring's Release

Criticism of the British government's decision was mixed with bitterness regarding the role played by Great Britain as the occupying power in Italy. Nevertheless, it had initially seemed that Kesselring's release would go more or less unnoticed in Italy, as had the Mackensen release earlier that month.[77] Thus, for example, the conservative *Corriere della Sera*, writing about Kesselring's crimes in Italy, concluded its piece with a detailed statement by his Bochum physician to the effect that "a second operation would probably prove necessary."[78] The intention may have been to create the impression that Kesselring was unlikely to live much longer and that there was no need for any agitation in view of his impending death. Striking a conciliatory note, the *Messaggero* editorialized that, although Kesselring's release would trigger protests, the decision to release him had been a humane gesture toward a sick man. Kesselring himself, the paper went on to say, had been "neither a Nazi nor a cannibal, but an honorable person" who was unequal to the responsibilities placed on his shoulders. His guilt lay in not having resigned once he learned of the massacres but instead tacitly tolerating the violence: "Within the literal meaning of the indictment, Kesselring was guilty. However, in a relative context—and especially when compared to other Wehrmacht army commanders—he was innocent." The paper went on to point out that Kesselring did not incite his troops to commit atrocities, and "without doubt this is one of the reasons why the English have now released him."[79] Even the Italian Communist *Unità* confined itself to a brief report, although it did express concern that Kesselring's release could be interpreted as a signal to resurgent Nazistic forces in Germany.[80] *Avanti!* recalled the Fosse Ardeatine massacre on March 24, 1944.[81] The reactions to Kesselring's release showed that, even in Italy, there were certain circles hoping to make a break with the past. A resolution protesting the release in Naples City Council was defeated by the votes of neo-Fascists and monarchists.[82]

As expected, the first critical voices were raised on the left. *La Stampa* felt that releasing the generals was tantamount to rehabilitation—and rehabilitation was an insult to the victims. Adopting a bitter tone, the editorial noted:

> They are not leaving prison with light hearts, in the hope of understanding the new world which has been built on the ruins of their old world, and in the hope of being of service to this new world. No, they are leaving prison as they always were, they carry with them the intact legacy of their past, all their miserable Nazistic concepts of honor, they are full of malevolence and pride, ready tomorrow to again attack with the same rage and, if so required, with the same efficiency.[83]

La Stampa drew parallels with other German war criminals and stressed the political bartering that formed the background to Kesselring's release. After all, the paper pointed out, Kappler's petition for clemency had been rejected in Italy at the same time, and his life sentence was now final.[84] The Italian news agency Roma described Kesselring's release as a "mine in the foundations of the still-fragile European union" and concluded that "cooperation with Germany is now impossible."[85]

The Communists, partisan associations, the peace movement, and the Camera del Lavoro (Chamber of Commerce) were the first groups to register their protests with the Italian government.[86] Italy's Jewish congregations lodged their objections directly with the ambassadors of Britain, the United States, and France. The Associazione Nazionale Partigiani d'Italia (Italian

Partisan Association, ANPI) issued a communiqué stating that "Italians will always view Kesselring as a war criminal, a murderer who had not yet expiated his guilt towards Italy and towards all of humanity. Releasing him was tantamount to not acknowledging the verdict of 1947, and means rehabilitating him."[87]

The initial press comments were followed by a parliamentary debate in Rome. Top officials of the Italian government had been informed of Kesselring's release only after the event, and it was later still when that news reached the Italian parliament. Italian MPs reacted with fury, demanding that their government lodge a protest with the British authorities. The MPs Sansone and Lizzadri, for instance, asked their government to "express the protest and objections of the Italian people to the release of Generaloberst von Mackensen," which had taken place—almost unnoticed—three weeks earlier.[88] Senator Lussu asked whether the Italian government had even been consulted before the British decision was made public. The responses provided by the Italian officials were as brief as they were illuminating, illustrating Italy's impotence when dealing with the British. They noted that "the British High Commissioner was under no obligation to consult the Italian government," although the British could have done so "had they wished." And the Italian government could only lodge an official protest with the government of another country, not with an occupying power. Senators Gasparotto, Sacco, and Fanfani had protested openly at Kesselring's release. Senator Fanfani was the minister for agriculture and, as presiding chairperson of the parliamentary session (the post was rotated), an official representative of the government. The president of the Italian parliament, Giovanni Gronchi, also registered his objections. It was suggested that Italy should seek Kesselring's extradition prior to retrying him in an Italian court.[89]

A damage-control exercise was obviously advisable, and elements within the Italian government jostled for position. The Foreign Ministry advised the president to avoid filing an official protest with the British government and thus annoying the Germans, since the German Liberal party, the FDP, which was part of the governing coalition, had explicitly included the early release of all war criminals in its program.[90] Instead, Italians should remember that it was only in June 1951 that their own government, over British protests, had used its newfound freedom to reduce sentences in order to pardon a war criminal convicted by a British court despite the fact that the British had previously refused to release this individual due to the gravity of the case. Striking a note of sarcasm, the Italian foreign minister suggested that when the opportunity arose, the British government should "examine the different treatment" meted out to an Italian war criminal who had murdered a British soldier and to a German war criminal who had "murdered hundreds of Italian civilians."[91] This remark revealed the true extent of the bitterness felt in Rome.

London hoped that it would be possible to somehow sugarcoat the bad news for the Italians. That is why, on October 27, the secretary of state for defense, Harold Alexander, speaking as a veteran of the Italian campaign, told the press that "Italian patriots must have a place in the heroic story of the British victory in Italy."[92] This declaration of honor on behalf of the Italian partisans is particularly remarkable when one considers that, just two years earlier, Alexander had made his poor opinion of Italian military capabilities clear.[93] The British view was that Alexander and Kesselring had been opponents of equal standing, whereas the Italians were deemed inferior soldiers. Therefore, Italians instantly recognized Alexander's hasty declaration for what it was: an attempt to render Kesselring's release more palatable.

Kesselring's Postrelease Press Conference

Kesselring's ill-considered remarks following his release inflicted damage on the new line adopted by the British in respect to war criminals. During a press conference, he made a number of revanchist statements that were eagerly transcribed by the assembled journalists. Kesselring's remarks on the war criminals issue seriously jeopardized British acceptance of Adenauer's security policy. Indeed, the authorities in London even started wondering whether it had been a mistake to release the former field marshal.

From his sickbed, one of Kesselring's first actions was to write a private round-robin to all his friends and fellow campaigners, as well as organizations that were close to him or had congratulated him on his release.[94] His rehabilitation had progressed to such an extent that even he himself saw no reason to make any mention of war crimes: "Even though my release was more than justified on health grounds, any pleasure is somewhat dampened by the fact that a legal consideration of my case was not taken into account at all. However, the times demand that we push aside resentments, making a break with a disastrous era in order to be able to work unencumbered for a better future."[95]

This letter of thanks *could* be benevolently interpreted as a private expression of opinion, but Kesselring was far more forthright at a hastily convened press conference held in the Bochum hospital on October 25. He persisted in embracing the concept of "justice, not clemency." Instead of thanking all the relevant authorities for their efforts, he criticized a declaration adopted by the German Bundestag to the effect that such releases would damage the standing of German soldiers: the releases were an act of "common sense," according to the convalescing field marshal. The assembled media agreed that he was in good spirits and clearly on the mend. Commenting on his imprisonment, Kesselring noted that it had been difficult "to overcome a sense of grievance" during the early years.[96] He then took the opportunity to advocate the cause of those still imprisoned, thus keeping his promise not to forget the "little people" in prison.[97]

Abandoning caution even further, Kesselring went on to demand that *all* those in custody be released, "without differentiating" between those who had and had not committed crimes. It was, he argued, "still better to commit an injustice in this manner" because "such an injustice will never be as great as the injustice inflicted on hundreds of other officers who were convicted and imprisoned for years for acts which they did not commit."[98] Obviously, Kesselring believed himself to be one of the innocently convicted. His demand for a general amnesty was naive, rooted in the conviction that he was indispensable to the planned rearmament. Echoing his friend Lord Hankey, he stated, "There are also enough war criminals around the world who have yet to be convicted by any court."[99] It is clear that the former field marshal was referring to Allied war criminals. He linked the amnesty demand with a warning that the European Defense Community treaties had to be ratified without delay.[100] Once former officers had been released from prison, their know-how could be used in the fight against the East, since a "future German army, which can depend on a core of soldiers with experience on the Eastern Front, will display the same determination to fight Bolshevism as the Wehrmacht."[101] He stressed, however, that he himself did not intend to play an active role in the rearmament negotiations. Ambiguously, he pronounced, "My future lies in my past."[102]

Kesselring's press conference provoked irritation in certain quarters, for a released war criminal was expected to adopt a more moderate tone. Yet some were prepared to benevolently minimize the import of his utterances: "The storm will pass, and within one or two weeks no one will be talking about the Kesselring case. That is, unless Kesselring himself—as unfortunately appears to be the case—mistakes his role and presents himself as a martyr to vengeful Allied justice."[103] Kesselring's ill-judged remarks at the press conference were reported extensively by the *Manchester Guardian* and the mass-circulation *Daily Express*. The *Guardian* was still able to find some sympathetic words of regret, noting that unjustified demands in Germany for war criminals to be released without distinction had succeeded in clouding an issue in respect to which West Germany, according to the *Guardian*, deserved the world's sympathy.[104]

German opponents of rearmament did not display similar restraint. Outraged, *Die Tat* noted:

> This serious illness, which could only be interpreted from the beginning as an appeal to our tear ducts, did not prevent him, a few days after he was "pardoned," from documenting his "willingness to defend Europe" in public, demanding the quickest possible ratification of the General Treaty. In this regard, it is apparent that he was referring to the same kind of "defense" which has made this general—in the eyes of various European nations—synonymous with terror, brutality and inhuman barbarity.[105]

The British embassy in Rome noted with some concern that, in contrast to the muted protests after Mackensen's release a few weeks earlier, Italy was now witnessing a veritable storm.[106] Nevertheless, Ambassador Sir Victor Mallet saw no cause for undue alarm: "I do not imagine that the Italian government will in fact make any official move on this subject." He predicted that the protests would not last for more than a week. The ambassador went on to note that the release of Kesselring and Mackensen had reminded the Italians of the trauma of the Fosse Ardeatine, "the worst atrocity which Italy suffered during the war," and he pointed out that the "modern nightmare of the Ardeatine caves" stirred up "atavistic phobias" in the Italian population. He warned that Kesselring's release could be interpreted to mean he had expiated his crimes. The ambassador's fears were justified. Kesselring's rehabilitation proceeded too rapidly. Broad swathes of the Italian public felt that too much was being asked of them: unaware of the Realpolitik constraints, they were unable to accept a mentality that appeared to just halt the consideration of the past at the expense of the victims.

The Italian media demanded that their government force the Bonn authorities to take action against those of Hitler's generals who refused to stay silent upon their release. Kesselring's comments were described as "a slap in the face of those who survived the assaults."[107] There was speculation that Germany might simply use the new European army as a smoke screen for its own ambitions to dominate Europe.[108]

Kesselring's remark that he would be required for a redeployment of German troops against the Soviet Union caused something of a stir,[109] especially in Italy, where his comments triggered significant unrest. There were demonstrations and strikes in a number of Italian cities.[110] The rumor that Kesselring was to play a significant role in a new German army caused members of partisan and victim organizations to carry their protests to the Italian parliament in person.[111] *Pravda* also reacted, albeit merely with propagandistic polemics. The Soviet newspaper cited *Avanti!* as saying that Kesselring's release, and his commission, merely reflected Washington's lack of trust in its own military. In any event, *Pravda* continued, the "butcher of Italy" was well qualified to establish German antipartisan brigades and, once again, to proceed against the "patriots of Italy, France, Belgium and Holland."[112] The Communist *Unità* announced that Adenauer had earmarked Kesselring for a senior position in the new German army,[113] and the East German *Berliner Zeitung* claimed to have information indicating that General Matthew Bunker Ridgway, the American officer who succeeded Eisenhower as supreme Allied commander Europe (SACEUR) and was involved in planning the new NATO troop deployments, had made provisions for Kesselring to occupy a "senior command position."[114] The president of East Germany, Wilhelm Pieck, therefore seized the opportunity to encourage Italian workers in their protests against the war criminal Kesselring, calling on citizens of the German Democratic Republic (GDR) to do likewise.[115] Elements within the German working class were also mobilized. The Europäische Arbeiterkommitee gegen die Remilitarisierung Deutschlands (European Workers' Committee against the Remilitarization of Germany) issued a leaflet protesting Kesselring's release, which it interpreted as a signal that "Adenauer's government wants war."[116]

Kesselring was astonished at the protests voiced by senators in the Italian parliament. As he saw it, he had saved the lives of "millions of Italians" by not following certain orders (such as Hitler's order to evacuate Rome), and in recognition of that fact, the "Italians should actually have erected a monument to him."[117] The Italian foreign minister, Count Zoppi, found this provocative argument particularly "hard to swallow." The result was a wave of further protests in Italy.[118] Meanwhile, in complacent contrast, the German press felt that Kesselring's remarks were "perfectly justified."[119] *La Stampa* was not alone in commenting that German media coverage was tantamount to a "victory parade," with no more mention being made of the crimes committed in Italy. There was a veritable "shower" of flowers and congratulatory telegrams.[120] "Does this reflect true public opinion in Germany?" *La Stampa* asked.[121]

It is noteworthy that the German press (with the exception of the Communist *Die Tat* newspaper) unanimously praised Kesselring's release as an act of political wisdom on the part of the British, while avoiding discussion of the crimes for which Kesselring had been convicted. At the most, it was noted (for example, in the *Rheinischer Post*) that he had "been charged with shooting partisans contrary to international law." Kesselring's innocence was, however, always stressed.[122] The *Hamburger Abendblatt* quoted his doctor, Professor

Bürkle de la Camp, on this point: "There can be no doubt that Kesselring is innocent; this must be said quite clearly."[123] The *Abendblatt* also found itself unable to accurately report either the year of Kesselring's conviction or the crime of which he had been convicted (giving the first as "1946" and the second as "alleged murder of hostages"). Criticism of the Allies was voiced from time to time by those who felt Kesselring's release had come "too late" for a man who was already "staring death in the face." FDP state chairperson Friedrich Middelhauve was quoted as saying that he expected a generous gesture "which would make a greater impression than if each individual German had to be wrested from Allied custody."[124] The German press cited Italian politicians of the "democratic center" (presumably referring to the governing party) as contending that, though they were completely opposed to Kesselring's release, "it would make no sense to further complicate the difficult situation in terms of European policy by, for example, filing extradition requests."[125]

However, the Italians did come up with a gesture to accommodate Kesselring. The MP Piero Calamandrei, rector of the Florentine University and one of those involved in planning the attack in the Via Rasella, reacted to Kesselring's desire for a monument by composing a striking poem about the German's activities as commander-in-chief, South-Western Command, on Italian soil.[126] The poem was inscribed in stone on the wall of the town hall on the piazza of the Lombardy town of Cuneo, and it was soon included in numerous school textbooks. The poem begins: "You will get it, Comrade Kesselring / the monument you demand from us Italians, / but it will be we who choose the stone to build it with, / [it will be built with] the silence of the tortured." In poignant language, the verses recall the atrocities committed against Italians by German soldiers during the war. The poem ends with a reference to the losses endured by the men of the Resistenza, who promised to again resist Kesselring in the event of another conflict: "Should you wish to return, / you will find us at our posts."[127] Although some passages in Calamandrei's poem—the cadence of which is reminiscent of a prayer—are no less polemical than Kesselring's own remarks, it must be viewed as an expression of protest at a time when, due to political considerations, the Italians were precluded from lodging an official objection. But in referencing the Resistenza, which had invested the new Italian state and the country's new government tradition with its foundation myth, Calamandrei was also signaling how times had changed. Given that Germany had yet to come to terms with its own past, the Italians were no longer prepared to ally themselves with the Germans at any cost. The German press initially took scant notice of this provocation.[128] It was only on February 7, 1953, that Bonn lodged an official protest with the

Italian Foreign Ministry through the German ambassador in Rome, asking that "demonstrations such as that in Cuneo cease in the future," even though "Kesselring's remark regarding the monument was undoubtedly inappropriate."[129] The message was that the focus should be on future commonalities, rather than reopening old wounds.

The dissenting voices went almost unnoticed amid the general euphoria in Germany surrounding Kesselring's release. As expected, most of the criticism came from papers operating under American license, as well as from socially liberal and communist newspapers. Thus, the pro-American *Neue Zeitung*, the SPD press service in Bonn, and the *Tägliche Rundschau* (published in East Berlin) all recalled that Kesselring had been found guilty of causing the deaths of 335 Italians in the Fosse Ardeatine.[130] The *Neue Mainzer Anzeiger* also warned that Kesselring could not "behave as though the German methods of warfare under Hitler had always been beyond reproach."[131]

Die Tat used Kesselring's release to voice general criticism of current Vergangenheitspolitik, and it deplored the continuity of the old elites: "Mr. Kesselring spent some years in gentlemanly imprisonment, allowed himself to be elected president of the Stahlhelm, became ill in time to give a 'European defense interview,' and is now considering settling in Bad Wiessee. The Adenauer government will grant him a decent pension from democratic tax monies."[132]

Two points should be noted in conclusion. Initially, the gratification surrounding Kesselring's release, achieved as a result of political pressure, generated an enthusiasm that sometimes gave way to reverence and veneration: for the first and last time since 1945, Kesselring was borne aloft on a wave of popularity. However, his press conference injected the first discordant notes into the euphoria. As a result of Kesselring's ill-considered remarks, the issue of war crimes resurfaced in the public discourse, even as old fears of a resurgent militarism were revived. Just a few days after his release, Kesselring ensured that the laboriously constructed image of the innocent general—an image constructed to facilitate his release—collapsed. Those who had helped him felt duped and realized they were now branded by the public as nationalists or (at the very least) as yesterday's men.

Limiting the Political Damage

In England, there were suspicions that the government had needlessly given in to the pressure exerted by old Nazis, thus aiding their resurgence in Germany. This belief gave credence to fears that had often been expressed during the war criminals debate: the desired positive political effect on the ratification debate did not materialize. Clearly, Kesselring's release was a triumph for the veterans' associations, and this, in turn, caused them to further lose touch with reality, leading to a continuing escalation in tensions. The soldiers' leaders continued to act as though "the fate of the nation depended on a few generals behind bars."[133] Adenauer now had to try to limit the damage.

The Ramcke Speech and Kirkpatrick's Reaction

Kesselring's performance after his release may have been an embarrassment that could be charitably dismissed, but the revanchist statements issued by Hermann Bernhard Ramcke, a former paratrooper general, tangibly aggravated the political situation. Ramcke's speech even cast a shadow on Kesselring's release. In view of their mutual demand for the release of all war criminals still in custody, Kesselring's and Ramcke's names were coupled in almost all the Italian press coverage, and even the *Neue Zeitung* commented that "the significance of the one event has been greatly increased by the other."[134]

Ramcke had been convicted as a war criminal in France and had escaped from custody under dramatic circumstances. On October 26, 1952, at the first major postwar meeting of Waffen SS members, held in Verden on the banks of the Aller River in Lower Saxony, he had demanded the immediate release of all German war criminals at home and abroad. Ramcke, who had not been a member of the SS himself, complained that "the true war criminals were those who caused the Versailles Treaty and dropped the atom bomb on Hiroshima."[135] His speech had a devastating effect in the UK, France, and the United States. Kirkpatrick was enraged:

> I am anxious to make Ramcke's name mud amongst all Germans. Consequently if any German mentions war criminals to me I shall say that I am always told in German quarters that relations with the West would be much improved if we took big-hearted action over war criminals. But the Ramcke episode demonstrates that this argument is quite fallacious and that the more of these lunatic war criminals we liberate the greater will be the volume of nonsense spoken and the greater the damage to Anglo-German, Franco-German, and American-German relations. As a result of Ramcke's action, therefore, I am resolved, in the interests of Anglo-German relations which I have much at heart, to keep these people in Werl as long as I can, provided I can do so without offending justice. I advise everyone else to take a similar line. But we should of course be careful not to use language which suggests that out of annoyance over Ramcke we intend to be unjust. The point we want to make is that as a result of Ramcke's behavior we are

> no longer led astray by the German argument that clemency improves relations.[136]

It seemed that even the Bundestag ratification debate could be in jeopardy. Adenauer felt constrained to ask the minister for justice whether Ramcke could be prosecuted for his remarks.[137] Unabashed, General Ramcke responded to Justice Minister Theodor Blank that such "nonsense" imperiled the release of his comrades.[138]

The extent to which the politics of memory was now dominated by the war criminals issue was illustrated by the "Christmas amnesty campaign" mounted by the *Offenbacher Abendpost*—and by Kirkpatrick's forceful response. Readers of the newspaper had declared their willingness to offer themselves as "hostages," going into prison over Christmas in place of the Werl prisoners. Asking Kirkpatrick to accept this "surety," the paper's editor said the effort would be "in the interests of Europe."[139] Kirkpatrick's reaction was highly indignant, and for the first time he appealed directly to the German public, whom he now assumed to be "victims of misinformation and confusion." Right at the start, Kirkpatrick made it clear that the authors of the letters were mistaken if they believed that those imprisoned in Werl could claim "with justification" to merely have "issued military orders which were only retrospectively deemed crimes by Allied courts."[140]

> Almost all the men and women in question were convicted of involvement in the killing of defenseless prisoners of war, or the murder or mistreatment of Allied citizens in forced labor camps or concentration camps. Unfortunately, I have to read the details of such cases, and even the evidentiary material disgusts me. . . . The brutality with which inmates of forced labor camps and concentration camps were treated was indescribable. In this regard, I can only say that any decent German would quite rightly be outraged and would demand punishment for a German treating a single dog in the manner that these millions of human beings were treated.[141]

Kirkpatrick came to the conclusion that "the release of a large part of the asocial elements in German society would truly do a disservice to Germany's image in the world." He refuted the argument that the clemency issue was poisoning German-British relations: "During the brief time I have been here 136 of 242 prisoners were released from Werl. During this period, however, the bitterness in our two countries regarding this issue has increased rather than decreased."[142] Under no circumstances would the so-called Christmas amnesty be entertained. Adenauer advised Kirkpatrick to exercise restraint in this issue. When viewed together with Ramcke's remarks, Kesselring's release suddenly appeared in a quite different light.

Those working on behalf of the war criminals remaining in custody—whether veterans' associations, Lord Hankey,[143] or even Dr. Ahrens[144]—were outraged at Ramcke's initiative, and they had no problem sympathizing with Kirkpatrick's anger. The resolution of the war criminals issue was now at stake. It became evident that, as feared, the politics of memory was exacting a high price. Large segments of the public were now confused about who exactly was a war criminal. And they were completely unaware of the crimes of which the war criminals were accused, demonstrating a diffuse repudiation of any German guilt.

Political Consequences for the Hankey Group

The initial enthusiasm surrounding Kesselring's release caused many to break cover and thank Lord Hankey directly for his work on the former field marshal's behalf. Now, however, many in England suspected Hankey of making common cause with the Germans, and as a result, his efforts to assist the German war criminals still in prison, including Field Marshal von Manstein, were stalled indefinitely.[145] Hankey's reputation was damaged by widespread press coverage of the telegrams he received from both Kesselring and the VdS thanking the British peer for his efforts.

While still in the hospital, Kesselring had sent a letter of thanks to his high-ranking champion.[146] Lord Hankey had previously sent him a visiting card with a note congratulating him on his release,[147] and he had promised to continue working to free all those remaining in custody. Now, Kesselring wrote, "I am happy to be traveling the same path as you, dear Lord Hankey, whom I admire as a courageous and successful pioneer in the war criminals issue, and in bringing our two peoples together in friendship." Kesselring promoted himself (and not only vis-à-vis Hankey) for a possible leadership position in a military umbrella organization. Kesselring's letter of thanks was accompanied by a bouquet of roses for Lady Hankey, a gesture that could be interpreted by critics as further proof of the close ties between Hankey and Kesselring.

In his reply to Kesselring, Hankey once again explained the motives that had led him and his associates to advocate the war criminals' cause. He explained that his method was to continuously press for a general review of the sentences coupled with indications of clemency, which could even include a general amnesty. This aspect is crucial, not only for legal or moral reasons but also because it was a vital component of the policy pursued by the North

Atlantic powers. That policy sought to persuade Germany to cooperate in order to achieve common goals, in hopes of creating peace on the basis of "friendship and security."[148] Hankey felt that he still had much to do to "bring influential people to realize how vital a factor the so-called War Criminals question is and must be on the German attitude towards cooperation with the rest of Europe and any real friendship which is the essential of cooperation and understanding."[149] Initially, however, he had to restrain himself in order to avoid jeopardizing what had already been achieved and adding fresh fuel to the rumors.

Gottfried Hansen, chairman of the German Soldiers' Association, sent Lord Hankey a telegram that openly thanked him for his work and also hinted at future areas of activity. The telegram blurred the lines between the war criminals issue and the fate of POWs still imprisoned in the Soviet Union.[150] The wording of the telegram was picked up and disseminated by Reuters and the *Manchester Guardian*. The *Guardian*'s correspondent, Terence Prittie, had been tipped off by Ahrens in Bonn, and the paper published a special report including an editorial comment. The German text of the telegram was released to the German press agency dpa in Düsseldorf.[151] In the United States, Fred Libby also distributed 30,000 copies of the text to media outlets as well as selected journalists, accompanied by a letter from Hansen to the chairpersons of American veterans' organizations.[152]

The outrage at Hankey's "treason" had severe repercussions. Critics felt that Duff Cooper, 1st Lord Norwich, had not been exaggerating when, speaking in the House of Lords following the Ramcke speech, he referred to a "generals' trade union" that—with the aid of influential British politicians—was in a position to exert political pressure. Hankey was provoked to abandon his restraint by a speech that Norwich gave, which he considered to be maliciously anti-German,[153] and he responded sharply in the House of Lords.

Hankey and his friends were not the only ones who were forced to exercise caution. Suddenly, all contacts with German bodies were viewed with suspicion in England. This aura of suspicion threatened, among other things, to thwart efforts at cooperation between the British Legion and the German veterans' association, the Verband deutscher Soldaten. Many had believed that such cooperation, geared toward international understanding, could play an important role in fostering a common war memory. Both sides felt that one of the primary purposes of such connections was to provide an assurance that they had fought chivalrously.[154] Members of the two veterans' associations, British and German, also felt that such contacts would raise the standing of soldiers in their former enemy's country. However, the saber rattling engaged in by Kesselring and Ramcke threatened to throw this delicate balance off kilter. The British Legion's press officer, Neill, let his German counterpart, Heinz Trettner, know that the cooperation negotiations would be postponed because "for tactical reasons, it is vital to avoid" the impression being created that "the establishment of contacts between German and English soldiers is interconnected with the war criminals issue."[155] There is no doubt that the politics of memory relating to war criminals reached its nadir following Kesselring's release and the Ramcke speech. Indeed, it threatened to grind things to a halt.

Adenauer Receives Kesselring

Following the press conference, German government representatives made it clear that they were shocked at Kesselring's naïveté, and they suggested that he should exercise considerable restraint in the future.[156] But it was not possible to simply ignore the former field marshal. Adenauer did all in his power to downplay the war criminals issue. While avoiding making public statements on the matter, he did receive prominent military figures in order to ensure that, through reference to the old elite, he took the wind out of the sails of political opponents to ratification.[157] As early as December 12, 1952, Adenauer granted Kesselring (accompanied by the federal government's security policy adviser, Herbert Blankenhorn) a half-hour audience.[158] After the meeting, Kesselring conferred with FDP chief whip Erich Mende. The topic of discussion was "the problems confronting soldierhood and the issue of those convicted in connection with the war."[159]

In Italy, even the governing party was baffled by the meeting. In holding it, Adenauer had shown "a low level of foreign policy finesse," according to politicians representing the ruling Democrazia Cristiana (Christian Democrats), and the Italian opposition detected "the true character of the Bonn government" and its "close relations with resistant Nazism."[160] Letters to the editor from some Germans also objected to Adenauer's decision to receive Kesselring.[161] However, Kesselring's supporters hoped to build on the rehabilitation achieved thus far, and they brokered further meetings with influential figures. In England, it was anticipated that Kesselring would "occupy a place of honor in the Germany of the future."[162]

Paratrooper Generalleutnant Heinz Trettner, who had served under Kesselring in Italy and was now active as deputy chair of the VdS, tried to persuade the former field marshal to seek the position of "authorized spokesman" for all German veterans' associations.[163] However, Kesselring refused, since he had already committed himself to the honorary presidency of the Stahlhelm, the Verband deutsches Afrikakorps, and the Luftwaffenring and thus felt unable to assume any further responsibilities.[164] As far as the veterans' associations were concerned, it was regrettable that Kesselring did not seize the opportunity to express himself politically, thus strengthening the VdS's position under his leadership.[165] The left-leaning *Stampa* also recognized the opportunity this would have presented, writing that "there is no doubt that Kesselring's word carries weight among Germany's veterans. . . . Were he to appear as spokesperson for the often divided Traditionsverbaende, he would also attain a political weight which no one could ignore when developing the new Wehrmacht."[166]

Despite eschewing any official function, Kesselring often acted as an unofficial spokesman on behalf of the VdS. In February 1953, for example, he was scheduled to meet the American secretary of state, John Foster Dulles, in order to explain the position of the VdS.[167] Kesselring was also credited with bringing about a meeting between the VdS chairman, Admiral Hansen, and the first commander-in-chief of NATO, General Lionel Ismay, 1st Baron Ismay, which he had asked Hankey to arrange.[168] He also wrote to Field Marshal Montgomery as well as the French marshal and designated NATO commander-in-chief, Alphonse Juin, hoping to use the "opportunities" offered by NATO to solve the war criminals issue.[169]

However, that issue lost much of its resonance once the General Treaty had been ratified.[170] The release of Erich von Manstein, in the spring of 1953, cleared the way—finally—for public discourse to start focusing on the substantive issues surrounding rearmament.[171] There is some speculation that it may also have been in British interests to largely center the war criminals debate on Kesselring and Manstein, in the hope that their release would offer the British authorities additional room for maneuver.

Foreign Policy Ramifications: Italy and the Attitude of NATO to the War Criminals Issue

Following the release of the two military icons Kesselring and Manstein, all sides initially avoided addressing the war criminals issue. However, secret contacts ensured that the final stage of the Allied war crimes policy was ultimately discussed at the highest level. There is strong evidence that after his appointment as first NATO general secretary on March 12, 1952, Lord Ismay used his position to advance the demands of German veterans' associations (specifically the VdS), which he had received via Lord Hankey. These demands included, as preconditions for a German defense contribution, both a general amnesty for remaining war criminals in the context of the alliance and the termination of the program of trials.[172] The speculation is that Ismay "recommended" acceptance of these demands to NATO. This assumption is based on a letter from Hankey asking Ahrens to inform Admiral Hansen (VdS chairman) that Lord Ismay would be prepared to meet Hansen in his Paris office in order to discuss the "VdS positions" regarding a general amnesty and an end to the program of trials.[173]

Ismay was both professionally and personally close to Hankey, having served as his deputy in the Committee of Imperial Defence, a position to which he had been appointed in 1936. There is no doubt that Ismay shared Hankey's reconciliatory views. During the war, he had acted as an adviser to all parties, and he was noted for his diplomatic skill and his role as a mediator between the political and military establishments.[174] It is therefore conceivable that the repeated appeals by Lord Hankey contributed to the unexpected decision to halt the Italian program of war crimes trials during the mid-1950s.[175]

Various facts argue in favor of this thesis, even though the records currently available do not offer incontrovertible evidence. Given this context, it is possible for the first time to explain why the Italian foreign minister, Gaetano Martino (a close friend of Ismay's and cofounder of the tripartite NATO council), wrote on October 10, 1956, to Defense Minister Paolo Emilio Taviani urging him to make sure the Italian military prosecutors ceased sending extradition requests to West Germany; his concern was that "the Bonn government could use [such requests] to prompt a debate regarding the behavior of German soldiers."[176] Taviani also viewed such a debate as undesirable given the nature of the problem then being confronted by the German government, which had to "overcome the resistance in its own camp to the development of a new German army, which NATO was impatiently urging." The letter from Martino amounted to nothing less than an official instruction by the Italian minister for foreign affairs to the minister for defense to halt the Italian program of trials for German war criminals (a program that had only just started) in order to avoid endangering German willingness vis-à-vis defense matters and the development of the Bundeswehr.[177]

Martino went on to couch his views in even more unambiguous terms. He had received an inquiry from the military prosecutor seeking the extradition of thirty German officers whose names had arisen in connection with the massacres on the Greek islands of Cephalonia and Corfu.[178] The minister conceded that "those who had taken part in such barbaric operations did not personally deserve any mercy." However, he noted with regret, the political situation had changed during the previous ten years: "As the person responsible for our country's foreign policy, I cannot deny that an extradition request filed today—a good 13 years after the painful events—would have a devastating effect on German and international public opinion, especially since many of the accused generals were convicted at the appropriate time (i.e., during the immediate postwar period) by Allied courts."[179] Taviani, who was a former Resistenza fighter and president of the partisan veterans' association (ANPI), appeared unperturbed by this expedient alliance. On October 20, 1956, writing in the margin of the ministerial letter, he noted: "I agree fully with Minister Martino."[180] On January 23, 1957, Martino again wrote to Taviani asking him to rein in an overzealous Italian military prosecutor who had already filed an extradition request. Martino let it be known that General Speidel, "whose name is on the extradition list," could become commander of NATO land forces in central Europe.[181]

Actually, Martino was wrong in this respect, for the name on the war criminals' list was that of Hans Speidel's brother, General der Flieger Wilhelm Speidel, who had also been convicted by the Americans following the Nuremberg Case 7 trial and who was being held in Landsberg. Nonetheless, it is remarkable that the Rome authorities were apparently prepared to accept a former war criminal in such a senior position as long as it served NATO's interests—even if such acceptance was diametrically opposed to Italy's own national interest. Although Taviani made his departmental colleagues aware of the fact that the names had been confused, he was party to the decision to cease importuning Bonn with extradition requests. It is thus unsurprising that by 1965, Italian military courts had tried just twenty-five defendants, handing down convictions in thirteen cases[182]—a meager balance sheet, albeit a predictable one in light of the directives received from Brussels and Rome.

Creating a New Narrative for Former Wehrmacht Members

To obtain the consent of the Bundestag—and thus of the electorate—to the planned rearmament, it was necessary to revise the negative image of all things military that had prevailed in German since 1945. The reformist concepts accompanying the development of the Bundeswehr questioned the validity of Germany's military inheritance. The debate surrounding the role of the military in the new German state was marked by a high degree of bitterness between the government and the veterans' associations. The veterans' culture was a major component of West German "civil society," organizing political, educational, and discussion events that often attracted guest speakers from all political parties.[183] The veterans' associations had a place in the "structure of the public memory of the war" and thus helped determine the public conception of the role played by the Wehrmacht in the war, especially during the first half of the 1950s.[184] Historian Jörg Echternkamp concluded as follows: "Even at an early stage, there were indications of exculpatory strategies which primarily utilized the myth of soldierhood and a recourse to secondary warrior virtues, leaving space for recognition of the soldier's achievements;

these strategies were aimed at wresting warfare away from its political context, covering the activity of the Wehrmacht with a veil of normality, and dissolving concrete personal responsibility in the mists of the past."[185]

In 1952, when three veterans' associations in succession appointed Kesselring as their honorary president, both soldiers' representatives and members of the political establishment hoped that he would act as the veterans' spokesman in the rearmament debate. The three associations had chosen Kesselring because a number of veterans believed he could play a bridging role between previous and future military generations. However, Kesselring was unable to perform this function for a variety of reasons. For one thing, he could not resolve the squabbles within the associations; these were particularly pronounced in the Stahlhelm, an association that, with its heavily conservative approach, was clearly located on the right side of the spectrum and thus represented a poor choice on the part of Kesselring himself. In addition, he managed to discredit the soldiers' concerns—concerns he symbolically represented—by making various ill-considered comments during his trip to Austria, in the course of a BBC interview, and as an expert witness in court.

The manner in which military icons positioned themselves publicly was vital to German public acceptance of rearmament.[186] However, within two years, Kesselring's reputation as an integrative figure in the rearmament debate had not only been exhausted but had actually been turned on its head. How can this phenomenon be explained? How could someone who enjoyed such a high degree of public support fall from grace so quickly? To what extent is it possible that Kesselring himself expedited his relegation to the "heroes' dungeon of oblivion"?[187]

After years of being shielded from the outside world, Kesselring was unable to adapt to the new political realities.[188] Years later, in a retrospective assessment of his involvement with the Stahlhelm, the *Frankfurter Rundschau* wrote that by assuming the honorary presidency of the organization, Kesselring had "walked onto the political stage, where he subsequently regularly tripped up."[189] It would appear that Kesselring himself frittered away his positive public image through a series of rather embarrassing public appearances around 1954. These incidents included his performance as an expert witness in the trials of Generals Berthold Ohm, Ferdinand Schörner, and Theodor Tolsdorff, which attracted considerable publicity. (The three generals had been indicted for shootings of German soldiers in the final days of the war.) The publication of his memoirs, *A Soldier to the End*, also helped foster a negative image of Kesselring, since he used his reminiscences to promulgate his own version of a "gentleman at war" and consistently ignored or retrospectively negated the involvement of the Wehrmacht and SS in war crimes.[190] Quite a few wished that the former field marshal had remained in custody.

Kesselring had enjoyed wide popularity in 1952, but his reputation plummeted rapidly thereafter, especially around 1954 and again during the 1957 Schörner trial. He then maintained a public silence during the final years of his life. The last section of this chapter will trace the story of his failure to carve out a positive postwar role for himself—a story marked by appearances at veterans' events and in court as an expert witness, as well as by the reaction his memoirs provoked.

Worthy of Tradition? Kesselring as a Military Role Model

Kesselring's release in October 1952 meant that the last of the main demands of the veterans' associations had been met. Consequently, there were no longer any major obstacles to the development of a new German army. In contrast to, for example, former General Staff officers Heusinger, de Maizière, and Speidel, Albert Kesselring played no active role in German rearmament plans. Though he was grateful for Theodor Heuss's unconditional support for the "reuse" of former Wehrmacht soldiers in the new army, he was rather disconcerted by the president's statement that "the bleeding to death of an over-extended army" could not create a tradition.[191] Kesselring believed that the Wehrmacht was the measure of all things, and he refused to subject his existing value system to the kind of revision demanded by Heuss. This view was buttressed by the continued existence of an anti-Communist concept of the enemy, and that notion served many soldiers as an "important bridge for the continuity" of military tradition and made it easier for them to join an army forming part of a Western alliance.[192] Many also succeeded in viewing the continuity of "structures, Wehrmacht personnel and everyday operations" as justification for clinging to a private moral narrative—a narrative recounting the "honorable nature of the Wehrmacht's behavior and fighting during the war."[193]

Kesselring viewed ideas of a substantively new order,[194] such as the concept of "self-guided leadership" or the "citizen in uniform," as a tacit reproach to the past, and accordingly, he dismissed such notions as "foreign to the German nature."[195] In 1957, his view was that the decisive factor governing whether to use Wehrmacht personnel in the new army was not the opinion of the personnel assessment board but rather a "soldier's battle value." This rejection can be traced back to the fact that "like many old soldiers, [Kesselring] did not understand the social, political and technical upheavals which had taken place since 1945 in the world and in West Germany, and which—according to the will of parliament—should also be reflected by the spirit of the Bundeswehr."[196] Indeed, he even categorically rejected the term *Bundeswehr*, since "the name of the Wehrmacht is entrenched both at home and abroad." He thus demonstrated his refusal to endorse a new beginning, even in conceptual terms.

This attitude was one of the factors underlying his decision to become involved in the so-called medals row. At the time, issues of external appearances such as uniforms and decorations, as well as formalities and conventions, "gave rise to heated debates, since many would still not accept that, during the Third Reich, military tradition as a whole had become fragile and questionable, since the military was barely in a position to counter an increasingly ideologized conduct of the war with resistance or protests."[197] Kesselring endorsed the demands of the veterans' associations, whose members were seeking to wear their war medals without any alterations.[198] His main argument in favor of this position was that the swastika was not a political symbol but rather had been the symbol of the state and accordingly could not be altered. Despite his dissenting views on this issue, his prominent position as honorary president of the Stahlhelm meant that Kesselring was appointed to the medals commission established by the federal president, Theodor Heuss.[199] The commission was presided over by Otto Gessler, who had served as defense minister (Reichswehr minister) during the Weimar Republic. Gessler ensured that the commission's members unanimously supported its concluding report, which recommended that the wearing of medals be permitted but without the swastika.[200] Kesselring was probably rather baffled by the final recommendation, which proposed that, in the future, decorations for courage be viewed solely as indications of personal merit, subject to an international code governing soldiers rather than to any state ideology.[201]

Kesselring's service on the medals commission was the sole official function performed by the former field marshal in connection with development of the Bundeswehr. He may have been disappointed that his expert advice was not sought to the extent he and his friends had anticipated given the initial resonance of his name and his importance to the rearmament debate while he was in prison. Only the Allies accorded him a little of the respect he sought as a soldierly icon: at the end of January 1954, he was invited to the U.S. military airfield at Fürstenfeldbruck, where he observed American jet fighter exercises from a helicopter. Indeed, he himself was reported to have boarded a jet fighter together with an American officer.[202] It should be noted, however, that this report was only carried by East German or Communist newspapers. Kesselring did not participate actively in the development of the West German air force, despite suggestions to the contrary by the East German paper *Neue Deutschland*, which even claimed: "Developments in Bonn indicate that, while Kesselring is not officially involved in the development of the new air force, the experience of the war criminal Kesselring is being utilized to a high degree."[203]

What narrative-forming role, even if only a symbolic one, could Kesselring have performed on behalf of his former soldiers? Given the paucity of sources and the fact that the Stahlhelm records have not been archived,[204] it is not easy to answer that question. But it does appear that, primarily due to naïveté and a lack of political instinct, Kesselring was unable to adapt to the changed realities of the postwar years. Neither the government nor the veterans' association members were able to understand the course taken by Kesselring or to foresee the arguments he would adopt. It is thus unsurprising that with each interview he granted or appearance he made, Kesselring became more and more marginalized within the Stahlhelm.

The dilemma was already foreshadowed by his first official actions in December 1952. At that time, striking a reconciliatory note, he called on all Stahlhelm members to work for a merger of German veterans' associations and to aim for an understanding with their counterparts in neighboring European countries. Such an understanding could, according to the former field marshal, "reduce the tensions remaining with the other nations."[205] This appeal may have been favorably received by the German government and the Allies, but it had certainly not been agreed to by the national leadership of the Stahlhelm. During the next few days, the Stahlhelm leaders denied that Kesselring "intended resigning from office"—a denial that can be interpreted as a shot across the former field marshal's bow.[206]

Kesselring did a complete about-face in his next appearance. In May 1953, speaking at the Stahlhelm national convention in Nuremberg, he was in tune with his traditionalist audience when he demanded that the "young German generation" be trained in "soldierly thinking in the best sense of the word." "Today, more than ever," he proclaimed, "value must be attached to a voluntary willingness to subordinate oneself and to obey."[207] The association's national director, Thomas Girgensohn, endorsed Kesselring's words, noting that young people deserved to be told "for what they might one day be expected to fight. . . . All of us, and especially the Stahlhelm as an association of frontline soldiers, must find an answer to that question."[208] However, Kesselring (and, with him, the entire board of the organization) failed to provide that answer. Instead, the honorary president resorted to dubious traditions and vague notions such as the "eternal values of soldierhood": Kesselring was trying to intellectually resume where he had left off in 1945.[209] He may also have unconsciously adopted a displacement mechanism in order to avoid more far-reaching criticism of events such as the collapse of discipline within the

Wehrmacht, which, in turn, had contributed to an escalation of the partisan war in Italy. In addition, he may have been trying to circumvent any debate regarding the role of the Wehrmacht as one of the three pillars of National Socialist ideology. At no time did Kesselring confront the notion that military concepts or fundamental virtues such as courage, dutifulness, and discipline could also be used to achieve immoral goals—nor did he confront the fact that the Germans had committed breaches of international law. Instead, he suppressed that fact just as he had suppressed the charges brought against him during his own trial.

Criticism was not long in coming, and it was particularly trenchant in the Communist press. Commenting on the Stahlhelm meeting, the Cologne-based *Volksstimme* scoffed that the "experienced murderer" was again intent on "preparing the ground for death and destruction." His appointment as Stahlhelm president was a "signal to the east," illustrating the "blitz-militarization and fascistization of the Adenauer state."[210] The East German radio service, commenting on Kesselring's demand for youth recruitment, noted that the militarists' efforts were doomed to failure since "the youth of West Germany is running away from them."[211]

Kesselring's honorary presidency of the Stahlhelm laid bare the dilemma facing the former field marshal. He attracted public notice by donning the Stahlhelm uniform and decorations in order to review a parade of member units and by demanding "social justice for old soldiers." From then on, he was exposed to heavy criticism. In letters-to-the-editor pages, irate citizens demanded that the prohibition on uniforms be extended to "Kesselring and his people."[212] Hans Flossdorf, a priest, represented the emerging pacifist school of thought in Germany when he demanded that Kesselring be officially silenced. He went on to say that the former field marshal left trouble in his wake wherever he appeared: "We want to hear no more of such questionable characters who are now everywhere creeping out of their mouseholes."[213]

Ironically, within the Stahlhelm, Kesselring was severely criticized for his alleged eagerness to conform to the new times. In July 1953, at the national Stahlhelm convention in Giessen, he proclaimed the so-called Giessen message,[214] to the "outrage of the staunchly conservative old *Stahlhelmers* from the WWI generation." He stated that though the old Stahlhelm had been a fighting organization, the new Stahlhelm was nonpartisan and supported the constitution and the state; after all, he continued, SPD members and Communists had also been "good soldiers" and could become members.[215] Kesselring's only concessions to the Stahlhelmers were rhetorical: "If we wish to overcome the growing materialism of today, we must again adopt the old but eternal values of soldierhood—indeed, we must fight fanatically for them."[216]

He again demanded “a merger of all veterans’ associations, release of war criminals, genuine and true equality for the German people and its new army, closer ties between free peoples, especially on European soil, and the reunification of Germany.” When asked by journalists whether he would be a candidate in the forthcoming Bundestag elections, Kesselring responded that he was not interested in playing an active political role. His negative response was something of an embarrassment to his former supporters in the FDP, who had discussed the possibility of his running for office.[217]

Speaking at the Stahlhelm convention held in Bremen on October 7, 1953, Kesselring presented his program to reform the organization, according to which: (1) the federal black-red-gold flag would be flown in place of the black-white-red emblems; (2) the old Stahlhelm greeting “*Front heil!*” would be abolished; and (3) SPD members would be accepted into the Stahlhelm, thus abandoning the “fight against Marxism” announced in the association’s relaunch program in 1951. He hoped to attract young members in particular and reaffirmed this aim at a Stahlhelm meeting in Nuremberg.[218] *Der Spiegel* praised this endeavor: the magazine noted that both Kesselring and the national director, Thomas Girgensohn, had exercised “forethought and a degree of skill” in keeping their promise to “renounce restorative Prussian ambitions.”[219] However, by pursuing this obviously progovernment course, Kesselring once again found himself at odds with his own supporters. There ensued a storm of protests, and Hamburg’s Stahlhelm leader, Walter Spohrmann, publicly accused Kesselring of turning frontline soldiers into a “Praetorian guard resembling the *Reichsbanner*” or a “social welfare organization”—or even a “trade union for generals.”[220] Those Stahlhelm members who believed that Kesselring was robbing them not only of their black-white-red national flag but also of their “*Front heil!*” salutation felt that their world had been turned upside-down. After all, had they not deliberately elected the field marshal as their honorary president in order to end the “defamation of German soldiers,” at least in their own self-perception?[221] Had not the use of Kesselring’s name, so redolent of symbolism, originally been intended to allow veterans to once again see meaning in their wartime service, while also improving their social standing? Now, their honorary president was showing himself willing to make concessions to a new era: indeed, he even seemed to be casting doubt on the warrior cult itself. The aging field marshal was unable to resolve the contradictions, and the Stahlhelm descended into political obscurity.

Kesselring’s dilemma was that he had no credibility either with the government or with Stahlhelm supporters. Some commentators have simply attributed the uncertain course he charted to ill-concealed National Socialist resentment. Admittedly, Kesselring had stated categorically that he would not participate in any event unless the West German colors (black-red-gold) were flown.[222] However, those writing letters to the editor—such as Otto Lehmann-Russbüldt, who had been active in the 1920s as a publicist for the peace movement—felt that this was merely a smoke screen, since Kesselring actually did represent the old black-white-red spirit. According to Lehmann, these were the colors "which, if otherwise arranged, produce the Swastika flag"—he had no doubt that Kesselring was merely using the new flag to mask the old one.[223] Nevertheless, Lehmann felt that Kesselring had a chance of becoming the next president of the Federal Republic. It was precisely this prospect that aroused considerable disquiet in Italy, as the East German *Neue Deutschland* reported. With a precision that appears astonishing today, the paper cited Kesselring's war crimes, specifying almost all the massacre sites.[224] Others also voiced their disapproval. Thus, Frankfurt reader Kurt Nurreck asked whether, when speaking of the ethical values of German soldierhood, Kesselring was referring to "those of the Waffen SS." His conclusion was that the former field marshal was "not a democrat by a long shot, simply because he appears under a democratic flag spreading his venom," and his letter culminated in the claim that "Kesselring and his consorts are the hereditary enemies of the German nation—not other nations."[225] Another Frankfurt reader, Georg Loh, was even more blunt. He noted that it would be "cheek on the part of such bankrupt individuals" if "fellows with no concept of honor" were to take the public for fools during the election campaign. "It revolts that, despite the penury of old people and the war injured, such people—people directly and indirectly responsible for this misery—are coming to the fore again."[226] Loh advised the Federal Republic to deny them their pensions: "Those who caused the misery should feel what it's like." Appealing to the generals to exercise restraint, the writer Benno Reifenberg criticized Kesselring's Giessen speech, noting that the former field marshal had "failed to distance himself sufficiently unambiguously from the regime which, since 1933, he served in a senior capacity, and to which he remained loyal until the end."[227] This impression was subsequently reinforced by the publication of Kesselring's memoirs and his various public appearances.

As early as October 1953, the Verfassungsschutz intelligence office issued the following confidential assessment of Kesselring's activities:

> After taking up office as President of the Stahlhelm, Kesselring attempted to enforce a new, moderate and loyal line within the Stahlhelm. He initiated his attempt to achieve acceptance of the black-red-gold flag, and to place the Stahlhelm's approach to the SPD on a new basis, in a manner which

> inevitably resulted in sharp contradictions. Kesselring overestimated the authority of his position, while underestimating the extent to which the old line was entrenched in respect of a large number of average Stahlhelm members. He thus misjudged the political situation within the Stahlhelm.[228]

One of the consequences of Kesselring's weak leadership was that the organization became split between traditionalist and more moderate tendencies. Admittedly, Kesselring did attempt to play a mediating role in the leadership of the fractured Stahlhelm.[229] But he found himself opening up a can of worms. In 1953, due to "personal differences among the leadership," the Stahlhelm split into two small organizations: the Stahlhelm and the Traditionsgemeinschaft der Stahlhelm (Association of Frontline Soldiers). Both groups subsequently sank into political obscurity.[230]

Kesselring's Public Appearances and Memoirs

Kesselring's reputation had already suffered as a result of his increasingly negative image as honorary president of the Stahlhelm, and his public appearances during 1954 merely served to compound the damage. These appearances involved an ostensibly private visit to Austria and an interview with the BBC. And they resulted in demands from commentators across the political spectrum for Kesselring to be "finally silenced in view of the difficult foreign policy conditions facing the Federal Republic." Ultimately, those demands signaled the end of Kesselring's public role.

On March 20, 1954, accompanied by his wife, Kesselring embarked on a two-week trip to Austria. Although ostensibly traveling as a private individual, he met with well-known representatives of aid organizations and veterans' associations, thus raising political concerns among the Austrian occupation authorities. After all, the Soviet foreign minister, Vyacheslav Molotov, speaking at the Berlin conference in January 1954, had already voiced concern that Germany could threaten Austrian independence. Thanks to his clumsy approach, Kesselring managed to symbolize all these concerns, unwittingly provoking a scandal with diplomatic ramifications.

Losing no time, Kesselring met with an official of the Soziales Friedenswerk foundation (an aid organization) on the day he arrived in Salzburg. They discussed assistance for relatives of Austrian Wehrmacht soldiers still being held as POWs by the Soviets.[231] The meeting was covered by the *Salzburger Nachrichten*, and, in conjunction with a press release issued by the Soviet Information Service in Austria, the coverage triggered a vigorous campaign against Kesselring's Austrian sojourn. The *Frankfurter Rundschau* reported that Kesselring was "greeted with marching tunes and bouquets" wherever he went.[232] Other articles bore headlines such as "Kesselring in Salzburg: Inspection Tour on Behalf of the West German Veterans' Association," "Official Reception for Wehrmacht Advocate," "War Criminal Kesselring Canvasses Freely in Austria," and "In 1933 It Was Frank, Now It Is Kesselring: Timely Memories of an Unwanted Visit."

The Austrian authorities reacted by asking Kesselring to leave. According to Interior Minister Oskar Helmer, he had conducted "political talks" in Austria, thus "abusing the country's hospitality."[233] By blithely continuing his visit and persisting in holding meetings, he had shown himself "unwilling to observe the democratic rules of the game," said Helmer in a sharply worded statement.[234] Kesselring was surprised that "the presence of a retired field marshal had become a political issue in Austria."[235] Notwithstanding the protests, he continued journeying into Styria, where he not only met former comrades-in-arms but also visited erstwhile prison-mates who had been interned in the British Wolfsberg camp, including a few SS members. The progovernment, Vienna-based newspaper *Neues Österreich* pointed out that "various categories of war criminals" had been interned in the Wolfsberg camp and, in view of this, wondered "what these gentlemen had to discuss with each other."[236] The West German press reported the demand for Kesselring to leave Austria as an "undesirable alien" with some consternation. The German chancellor's office issued a statement to the effect that "Kesselring would probably be deported by the police,"[237] thus ensuring that the scandal was widely covered by the German media.

The Austrian authorities ordered his deportation. However, Kesselring did not heed the official request to leave their country. Instead, he remained there until April 2, having stated that he "did not hold any official position in Germany" and was thus traveling in a purely private capacity. For the rest, he considered it his "duty to assist his former subordinates in the German Wehrmacht and camp comrades." In a defiant statement that was in marked contrast to his previous assurances, Kesselring asserted that this aim was "also supported by the Government of the Federal Republic of Germany." He stressed that he had been received as a "private individual" by the governor of Styria, Josef Krainer, in Graz.[238]

Kesselring made some poor choices in terms of the people he met with on this trip, and the images presented on the occasion of these meetings were rather unfortunate as well. In addition to meeting with "former national socialists who have been convicted pursuant to Austrian laws,"[239] as was pointed out by the Austrian Interior Ministry, he allowed himself to be filmed by the Austrian weekly newsreel service in front of his guest house in Aigen and while laying a wreath at the monument to fallen soldiers in Trautenfels. He then reacted to the growing debate in Austria by writing an "open letter" that was published on April 3 in *Der Obersteirer*, a weekly paper based in the Styrian town of Bruck. The letter was a response to a previous open letter from an Austrian frontline soldier, who described Kesselring's behavior as "inept." Kesselring wrote: "This poses a dilemma for me. If I have behaved incorrectly, it is because I have become a victim of my training."[240] He was still, he said, "to a greater extent than you believe, a comrade of my former soldiers." It was in this context that he wished his "chance meeting with old Styrian soldiers" to be viewed. Not without a touch of vanity, he added: "Unfortunately, however, it is a fact that—having attained a degree of popularity during the war—one becomes the centre of attention, whether or not one wants that." He had not been able to bring himself to reject his comrades "who, in Aigen, Graz and other places, pressed forward to express their joy at this reunion"; otherwise, he continued, they "could have been driven mad by [the sight of] their former commander-in-chief." Once again (and with considerable political ineptitude), Kesselring was disseminating his version of the unbreakable bonds of comradeship. In doing so, he was being quite sincere, revealing his naive and circumscribed perspective.

Kesselring's trip had direct political consequences, such as the Soviet decision to veto the planned lifting of visa requirements for West Germans visiting Austria; the veto was exercised at the meeting of the Allied council in Austria on April 30, 1954. The Soviet representative explained the decision by stating, among other things, that "war criminals such as Kesselring, Wittmann, and Rudel have recently undertaken unimpeded inspection tours of West Austria" in order to "establish nazistic-militaristic and veterans' associations of all kinds on Austrian territory, disseminate Greater German ideology among the members of these organizations and prepare the ground for a new *Anschluss* of Austria."[241]

The German government thus found itself facing diplomatic difficulties in respect to both the Soviet representatives and the Austrian authorities. The government publicly blamed Kesselring for the escalation of the situation. As a private visitor, according to the German government, there was no doubt that Kesselring should have avoided "wreath layings, receptions, open letters and similar."[242] Bonn's verdict on the former field marshal's tour was therefore clear: it was "embarrassing" and "ran counter to state interests."

It should be noted, however, that this was the official reaction to a mission that had proven highly unsuccessful. Yet it is extremely probable that the Bonn authorities had been notified of the trip in advance. After all, it took place shortly after a decision was made by the German government to grant pensions to former Wehrmacht soldiers living in Austria—a decision that prepared the ground for cooperation with such veterans. Kesselring's visit to Austria occurred in the context of German rearmament, and its purpose was to conduct initial soundings of former Wehrmacht soldiers in Austria,[243] in order to assess whether they might be interested in joining a new German army.[244] According to the Italian ambassador, the Americans viewed this development favorably, were given prior notice of the trip (as was the Austrian government), and had granted their approval.[245] It was only following the media furor that the Austrian government felt constrained to issue an official statement and deport Kesselring.

The *Frankfurter Allgemeine* noted that Kesselring had been the worst possible diplomat to dispatch on this mission, but it nevertheless excused the former field marshal on the grounds of boundless naïveté.[246] The *Westdeutsche Allgemeine* also struck a critical note: "His guest performance in Austria recently proved that the German military could almost be said to have a tradition of producing poor diplomats. It would be better for them to remain at home for the moment."[247] The conservative media were united in their dismay at the fact that the Soviets had been provided with an excuse to continue the occupation of Austria, given that Molotov seemed to be proven right in his claims that German militarism posed a threat to Austrian independence. "Even though Mr. Kesselring is not a politician, he should have seen that he was about to pursue a course which would damage his host country," admonished the *Frankfurter Allgemeine Zeitung*, which suspected that Kesselring's "sole intention was to provide new arguments," since "he even remained deaf" to the deportation order issued by the Austrian Interior Ministry.[248] The *Bonner Rundschau* was equally critical, noting that the field marshal "failed to take the hint."[249]

The *Deutsche Zeitung* was also struck by Kesselring's "thick skin," which it found particularly regrettable given the unpleasant fact that Austria, "due to its difficult political position between the former war Allies," saw itself constrained to "pre-empt any Soviet suspicions relating to its foreign policy by exercising scrupulous correctness."[250] The German government should also have used its channels to recall Kesselring so that he did not make the "problematic foreign policy situation" even more difficult as a result of further slip-ups. The conclusion was unambiguous: it should have been made clear to Kesselring "that the new German state expected him to exercise restraint."

Nevertheless, others welcomed Kesselring's visit. The *Abendpost* reported that the Austrian People's Party press office attacked Interior Minister Helmer for doing a disservice to the state by criticizing Kesselring.[251] The *Bonner Generalanzeiger* and *Welt* newspapers stressed that the Austrian security authorities had only acted as a result of pressure exerted by the "Communist and

Soviet press," which viewed the visit as an attempt to recruit former soldiers.[252] And *Die Welt* reported that the Austrian People's Party had come to Kesselring's defense. Noting that, in contrast to "dozens of foreigners from the Eastern states," Kesselring had "entered Austria with proper documentation," the paper claimed that the Austrian People's Party had defended the former field marshal against the "witch hunt" with which the authorities hoped to "do the East an obsequious favor."[253] Kesselring adopted this view following his return from Austria. Speaking at a meeting of the German Afrikakorps association, held in his honor in Bad Wiessee (where he was living), he stated that the "imputation that his aim was political or military agitation was a Communist slur."[254] His remarks indicate that, even in retrospect, he had blanked out the foreign policy ramifications and consequences of his trip.

In November 1954, Kesselring availed himself of another opportunity to make a significant gaffe. During a BBC interview with Aldan Crawley, broadcast as part of the *Opinion Formers* program, Kesselring told a startled British audience that German plans to invade England had failed only as a result of insufficient preparation, not as a result of the willingness of the British to defend their country. "Had [the invasion] succeeded, as I hoped," he added, "the war would have been over much sooner, which would after all have been a good thing for all of us."[255] To make matters worse, he made scandalous remarks "in a tone of regret, as one could clearly hear during the broadcast," reported the *Süddeutsche Zeitung*—for instance, observing, "Everyone knows that we cannot restore the Third Reich." Even in his choice of words, Kesselring manifested the spirit of the old Wehrmacht, stating that the new German army would "naturally" accept SS veterans because "Germany's best blood" ran in their veins. During this interview, Kesselring showed himself to be astonishingly unimpressed by the overall social developments in Germany following Nuremberg. The war crimes trials had illustrated the extent of dependence on Hitler and the impossibility of acting freely, yet Kesselring was now claiming in interviews (and later in his memoirs) that the Germans could have won the war with the aid of their own military skills. This view ignored the military reality of having a superior opponent on two fronts, while also completely disregarding the problems that a German victory would have posed for Europe.[256] When giving interviews or making other statements, the representatives of the old elite were concerned to ascribe retrospective meaning to the war and the millions of deaths it caused.

The East Berlin newspaper *Neues Deutschland* was happy at the turn of events, assessing Kesselring's presentations sharply: "It would be difficult to appear any more cynical, cheeky or unscrupulous. This is the language of the generals being let loose by Bonn on West German and West Berlin youth."[257]

By virtue of his position as Stahlhelm president, Kesselring was already predestined to be the focus of East German criticism. However, he significantly enhanced the potential for criticism with his inept appearances.

In the wake of the debate regarding West German rearmament, the GDR launched a propaganda campaign against former Wehrmacht generals who could be in line for new commands. In 1957, plans were made for a program utilizing the new medium, television. Entitled *Archive Testimony*, the program would portray Wehrmacht and Waffen SS figures examining their postwar careers in West Germany.[258] In addition to the piece on Kesselring, other episodes would deal with Generals Hasso von Manteuffel, Herbert Gille, Erhard Milch, and Dr. Hans Speidel as well as Admiral Helmuth Heye.[259] In 1959, the Telestudio West television service started a series on "people who have learned nothing from the past," to be titled *Teletribunal*. The aim was to hold a mock trial, for which the broadcaster was still seeking "witnesses" to the war crimes committed by "[Generals] Foertsch, Trautloft, Kesselring and Kielmannsegg."[260] It is striking that the generals selected were those holding senior positions in the Bundeswehr and NATO: in 1959, Count Johann-Adolf von Kielmannsegg was deputy commander of the 5th Armored Division, and Hermann Foertsch was deputy chief of staff at the European command headquarters of NATO. The propaganda dimension was obvious. In the end, however, the program researchers were unable to collect adequate persuasive information on Kesselring, with the result that even the editor in charge, Ewald Thomas, was forced to conclude with some disappointment that Kesselring's career did not offer sufficient material to hold the mock trial they had envisaged; it was therefore decided not to proceed with this piece. Yet despite the relative scarcity of actual facts on the basis of which the former field marshal could be attacked, Kesselring's own ill-considered appearances, such as his BBC interview, provided critics with plenty of ammunition.

Even in West Germany, he found himself subject to a storm of criticism. According to the *Süddeutsche Zeitung*, the BBC was overwhelmed by protests immediately after the broadcast. The *Frankfurter Neue Presse* was concerned that "Kesselring's personal opinion" could be viewed abroad as "the German people's opinion." Only the *Frankfurter Allgemeine Zeitung* argued that Kesselring's remarks were "fundamentally unsurprising": "One could have predicted to the BBC that the field marshal's hopeless ineptitude would lead to embarrassment. Once again, Kesselring did not pass up the opportunity to display a lack of political tact."[261]

Given this background, it was to be expected that Kesselring's memoirs would also meet with a critical reception. The problems posed by memoirs as historical source material are well known: after all, memory is extremely selective.[262] When examining memoirs by senior military figures, it is illuminating to probe the self-image that shines through the events being described and allows one to reach conclusions regarding the author. The purpose ascribed to the memoirs by the author himself becomes apparent.[263] Events gain acceptable meaning for the author by means of omission, additions, or embellishment, for the memory of war must be integrated into a more or less consistent self-image.[264] Therefore—especially in the case of officers who appeared before war crimes tribunals—the manner in which memoirists deal with the criminal reality of war is particularly instructive. Events that do not fit into the writer's self-image of a "good soldier" or a "fair war" are often omitted or briefly glossed over,[265] and Kesselring was no exception in this regard.

At the same time, however, one must take account of the expectations of fellow veterans that are bound up with such publications. In his memoirs, for example, Kesselring accommodated such expectations by always being positive in his remarks on others; in addition, his memoirs often claimed that actions that took place during the war—including some he had vigorously disagreed with at the time—had actually been the subject of consensus. Therefore, memoirs should never be used as historical sources in order to reconstruct the course of a war (even though the absence of other sources meant this was still the practice in the 1950s). Rather, memoirs should be viewed as apologias in the context of the period during which they were written.

Kesselring's memoirs, entitled *A Soldier to the End*, were published in May 1953. Despite enjoying brisk sales, the book received a guarded reception from German critics. Reviewing the book, the newsmagazine *Der Spiegel* concluded: "The title is deceptive. This is not a reader for air force comrades, but rather a remarkably meticulous contribution to war history which displays astounding authorial naiveté."[266] The *Süddeutsche Zeitung* also issued its verdict: "'*Soldat bis zum letzten Tag*' is both a defense and an attack. The intended meaning of 'soldier' is: nothing but a soldier, and responsible for nothing but the course of battle operations. 'Until the end' is a condemnation of all who 'gave up the ghost' before Kesselring's own final day, May 9th 1945."[267] The paper went on: "Based on his memoirs, however, one must also question the verdict issued by the Munich denazification court in 1951 to the effect that Kesselring was 'unaffected' by the law intended to free us from militarism." The *Stuttgarter Zeitung* felt that even the title reflected Kesselring's conflict, and it pointed out that people could not have been "mere soldiers."[268] Referring to Kesselring's dismissal of the officers who took part in the July 20, 1944, attempted assassination of Hitler as "oath-breakers," the paper described the book as "unsatisfactory" and went on to say that, as a "German and a humanist, not merely a soldier," Kesselring could have been expected to provide some intellectual stimulus in respect to the pressing issues of the day. The weekly newspaper *Die Zeit* was disappointed by the book's "questionable tendency" while at the same time "recognizing this man's ample professional qualities." The writer picked up on one of Kesselring's recurring themes: "An order is an order! This phrase, which is as pithy as it is stupid, echoes through all 475 pages—until the end."[269] The paper went on to say it was regrettable that, despite his competence, Kesselring "clearly never posed himself the question: Where does blind obedience end and a sense of responsibility start to take effect, if not at the highest levels of command?" A report by the Verfassungsschutz argued:

> As his book *Soldat bis zum letzten Tag* shows, Kesselring is a typical representative of those high-ranking military officers who reject any involvement with politics. The book has provoked severe criticism in the relevant circles, and not only because of its value in terms of war history. Thus, for example, the *Wehrwissenschaftliche Rundschau* wrote: In the mouth of one of the most senior military leaders—who, as he himself testifies, was able to exert influence on both Hitler and Göring—*Soldat bis zum letzten Tag* is a somewhat unsatisfactory response to the problem of mandatory obedience; a problem which became particularly urgent during the last war.[270]

In the view of the *Münchner Merkur*, the book made a major contribution to "German literature on the history of the war," serving to "further lift the cloud of fog surrounding German soldierhood after 1945."[271] However, future German soldiers would have to decide for themselves whether to adopt Kesselring's ideals or to "relegate the field marshal to the heroes' dungeon of oblivion."[272] The East Berlin *Tägliche Rundschau* used its review of the memoirs to launch a propaganda campaign: citing all Kesselring's war crimes, including those that did not come to trial (such as the bombing of Warsaw and Rotterdam), the paper renamed the book *Executioner until the End.*[273]

Kesselring's memoirs were first published in the United States in 1954. Despite the fact that, in 1947, a trial-weary American public had shown little interest in the crimes committed in Italy that were showcased at Nuremberg, there now was considerable interest in Albert Kesselring the man. The *Saturday Review* praised the memoirs (published in English using the eponymous title *Kesselring*) as the work of a "doorman of tragedy," an outlandish exaggeration.[274] The reviewer, Gordon Harrison, concluded that Kesselring "may not have been one of the greatest German generals, but he was certainly one of the stubbornest." His postwar fate, according to Harrison, was a "blot on the record" of Anglo-Saxon justice. However, Harrison noted that Kesselring's conviction could not be blamed on the English alone but was rather due to a "naïve post-war emotion" that poisoned the Nuremberg trials with the "spirit of revenge." He also agreed with Kesselring's view that he had been convicted in order to retrospectively glorify the battle waged by the Resistenza and generally discredit the German military. Harrison's article bordered on hagiography, and he concluded by appealing to readers to follow the route of "understanding and tolerance" mapped out by Kesselring in the book.

The review provoked severe criticism. New York reader Bruno Guarino concluded that Harrison had penned "an apology for a criminal," and he pointed out that Kesselring had been one of the "most powerful men in history," commanding "hordes of men" who, if he was guilty, had rendered themselves just as culpable.[275] Another reader wrote that Kesselring should be grateful to have escaped the gallows: "Grateful for having escaped the noose, the Field Marshal should have kept quiet."[276]

A three-page review in *Time* magazine also struck a critical note, pointing out that Kesselring was primarily rooted in the tradition of German generals who "agree that under twelve years of Hitler rule they saw no evil, spoke none and did none."[277] Loyally, he continued in his memoirs to express pleasure at Hitler's "unreserved confidence," and after the war, he good-naturedly assisted the Americans in writing the history of the war. According to *Time*, the style of the book was often reminiscent of a situation meeting in an operations center. For the rest, however, the magazine concluded that Kesselring displayed astonishing naïveté regarding the events prior to 1939. *Time* pointed out acerbically that whenever Kesselring did raise doubts about the Nazis, Göring managed to dispel them. In 1952, he finally "won his release" on the grounds of ill health. However, the *Time* article expressed no doubts regarding Kesselring's guilt as a war criminal, nor did it voice any criticism of the Allied military courts. Rather, the magazine concluded that Kesselring had remained a "Nazi in spirit" as honorary president of the Stahlhelm. The reviewer touched on Kesselring's statements as a court witness, as well as his unveiled threat to the Allies that there would be no German army while former comrades sat in prison. He also noted Kesselring's astonishment at the idea that people could require him to bow to democratic principles: "That is more than I can take." With that concluding statement, *Time* said it all: the aging field marshal was incorrigible.

The *New Yorker* summed up the view of most American critics, noting that Kesselring was a prime example of well-meaning German intelligence that used "technical capacity and incredible industry combined with obedience as a substitute for morality."[278] Nevertheless, Kesselring's version of a "soldier to the end" gained ground in the United States, underpinning his reputation as a congenial but powerless general—a reputation that still holds sway today.

Kesselring as an Expert Witness

Up to now, historians have paid limited attention to the war crimes trials held by West German courts between 1948 and 1960. However, they were a highly significant turning point in the history of the politics of memory. For the first time, German courts, unencumbered by the taint of victors' justice, addressed the crimes committed during the final phase of the war (such as the shooting of deserters or "traitors"), while also confronting the associated problem of the so-called imperative to obey orders. This process facilitated a critical examination of the behavior of senior Wehrmacht officers and their interpretation of the measures that were permitted to maintain military discipline. The nature of this critical examination was illustrated by the public reaction to the trials.[279] The trials were known publicly as the Generals' trials, a term that had less to do with the military rank of the accused than with the general view of (and contempt for) the crimes committed during the last stage of the war. The trials triggered a shift in public opinion in favor of the former military elite. There was growing disquiet and a sense that the crimes committed by high-ranking German officers could, after all, have been representative of more widespread Wehrmacht behavior than had initially been assumed.[280] One could only speculate as to the truth. Would an army that had executed its own members without trial have been likely to exercise restraint toward enemy soldiers or civilians? That was the question being posed by many.[281]

Kesselring, who testified as an expert witness and in other capacities during the trials of Generalleutnant Theodor Tolsdorff, Colonel Ohm, and Field Marshal Ferdinand Schörner, among others, increasingly found himself caught in the undertow of the negative publicity generated by the trials. There was an interplay of factors at work here: the damage to Kesselring's reputation was directly connected to the negative perception of his role as an expert witness, whereas his court appearances helped accelerate a process that was to end the veneration previously accorded to senior military figures.

Some trials, such as the Tolsdorff case, dragged on from appeal to appeal, in certain instances accompanied by a storm of media controversy. The alternating verdicts that were handed down—first guilty with life imprisonment, then not guilty, and finally guilty with twelve years in prison (all reached on the basis of the same legal material)—damaged the reputation of the justice system. Initially, German judicial sovereignty was confined to prosecuting crimes committed by the Wehrmacht against German civilians or soldiers (Control Council Law No. 4). From 1950, it was extended to cover war crimes in all occupied countries (Control Council Law No. 13). In 1958, it was therefore decided to establish a central office representing the state justice departments to prosecute Nazi war crimes—the Zentrale Stelle der Landesjustizverwaltung zur Aufklärung von NS-Gewaltverbrechen, known as the ZSL.[282] The office owed its origins to the difficulty of collecting evidence for war crimes trials and the realization that targeted investigations would be impossible without a central authority that could act as a repository for records and also have at its disposal specialized investigators.[283] (This need became particularly acute as a result of various appeals.) Following an extended lead-in period of collecting evidence, the office only started working on war crimes prosecutions in 1965. It still performs its functions today.[284]

In addition to the institutional framework, the year 1954 (in particular) witnessed changes to the political and psychological environment that facilitated a confrontation with the past. On August 30, 1954, the French National Assembly rejected the idea of a European defense community, triggering a wave of antimilitarism in West Germany and attracting plenty of new recruits to the ranks of those opposed to rearmament.[285] The reestablishment of German sovereignty, together with the increasing distance from events, triggered new interest in a confrontation with the past. The conviction of Wehrmacht generals by German courts thus marked a new phase, while also foreshadowing impending controversies. The veterans' associations especially never missed an opportunity to stress the negative impact of such verdicts on the prospects for the release of those German war criminals still in custody.[286] Nonetheless, there can be no doubt that the trials of Tolsdorff, Schörner, and Manteuffel, in particular, helped form the basis of a new, significantly more critical public attitude toward the Wehrmacht during the 1950s.[287]

Initially, little public notice was taken of Kesselring's attempts to secure the release of comrades still in prison. Following his own release, the former field marshal was obsessed with a desire to free all those still in custody—without exception. Indeed, he made this clear during his first postrelease interview. At first, he confined himself to working on behalf of former Werl prisonmates, acting as their spokesperson and contacting the Rechtsschutz-Stelle, which was attached to the German Foreign Office, to plead their case.[288] In 1954, he again championed the cause of the Werl inmates, forwarding letters he had received from prisoners complaining about a deterioration in their conditions.[289]

In April 1953, considerations of loyalty motivated Kesselring to issue an affidavit on behalf of his archenemy, Herbert Kappler, former head of the SS security office in Rome. He failed to take into account the inevitable damage to his reputation caused by this move.[290] Kappler, whose name was regularly mentioned by the Italian media in connection with the SD torture center in the Via Tasso, had "carried out good criminological work," had a "well-developed sense of responsibility," and possessed "personal courage," thanks to which he had "spared the civilian population in Rome incalculably greater suffering"—that was Kesselring's verdict, writing to the Italian prime minister, Alcide De Gasperi. One year later, Kesselring intervened personally with German foreign minister Clemens von Brentano,[291] and in 1956, he hoped that the pope would help secure the success of his clemency petition on Kappler's behalf.[292]

Afterward, Kesselring maintained close contact with the lawyer Dr. Rudolf Aschenauer, as well as with the campaign committee for Herbert Kappler administered by Princess Helene von Isenburg's Stille Hilfe prisoner aid organization.[293] In 1955, he contacted Adenauer and Undersecretary of State Walter Hallstein, backing a clemency petition for Kappler.[294] However, he did speak out against the historical distortions contained in the leaflets issued by the campaign committee: "In my last letter, I already mentioned that I am adopting the Kappler case. Nevertheless, I must point out that certain statements do not correspond with reality. This could turn into a fiasco if men like Moellhausen, officers on Mältzer's staff, get wind of it. The Jewish question, in respect of which I made the decision personally, also progressed in a rather different manner to that depicted."[295]

From 1953, after years of pursuing the war criminals issue through private interventions, Kesselring took on an official role, serving as an expert witness in various war crimes trials held in German courts. Most notable of these were the trial of Colonel Ohm and those of General Tolsdorff (1954) and Field Marshal Schörner (1957), known as the Generals' trials. His court appearances were highly significant in terms of the politics of memory. The wish to create a more positive image of the Wehrmacht in the context of the rearmament debate was jeopardized by the judicial confrontation with the crimes committed by so-called individual culprits.[296] The behavior of individuals during the final weeks of the war also had a significant bearing on potential recruitment to the new German army. Most officers working in the Blank Office, as well as those working in the military personnel assessment office (which supervised the recruitment of new officers), had never forgotten how various individuals had behaved during the final days of the war. Their perceptions helped shape what became official guidelines.[297] In this regard, there was a general consensus—in contrast to the view prevailing in 1945—that those who had displayed moral courage while preventing unnecessary destruction and sparing the lives of German soldiers should be considered exemplary officers.

The rigid attitude displayed by Kesselring during his first appearance as an expert military witness was particularly striking. The trial of Colonel Berthold Ohm was also known as the "Penzberg murder night trial." Ohm was accused of abetting the execution of seven Penzberg civilians during the night of April 28, 1945. He had ordered the village to be evacuated and blown up. However, this plan was obstructed by villagers: American troops were already in view, and villagers resisted the continuing defense of their village. Without further ado, Ohm ordered that they be summarily shot. The mayor of Penzberg was among the victims. Right at the start of his two-hour testimony, Kesselring openly coupled the issue of war crimes with that of rearmament, saying, "It will be impossible to find soldiers for the new army if one continues trying soldiers eight years after the end of the war."[298] He went on to defend Colonel Ohm's decision to shoot the allegedly "deviant" villagers, remarking that the decision was "well considered" because the local resistance posed a danger to the "orderly retreat of the unit."[299] There may be a deeper reason why Kesselring chose to champion the cause of a colonel who was a complete stranger to him. It is conceivable that the former field marshal's actions were motivated by his own trial trauma: he stereotypically repeated the arguments with which he was familiar from his own trial in Venice, failing to recognize that the case in question was completely different. In his view, another officer was again being subjected to an unjust tribunal. He therefore worked to mitigate crimes that he himself—if viewing them objectively—would never have approved of, as is clear from earlier entries in his private diaries.[300]

Press coverage of the trial fostered a broad-based condemnation of the generals as a group, and Kesselring was clearly caught in the undertow of this criticism.[301] *Der Mittag* asked: "Would Kesselring not have done better to remain silent and declare his bias?"[302] The media also probed the role he played in keeping the troops "up to the mark" during the final days of the war: "Is it right that an officer who himself played a dubious role in this regard should appear as an expert witness?"[303] The *Süddeutsche Zeitung* concluded that Kesselring was becoming "well-nigh a public annoyance."[304] And the paper went even further: "To cap it all, one would probably have to be called Albert Kesselring to dispute the fact that even in those final confused days of the war, and in the face of all the associated crises of conscience, there were people who acted with human dignity despite current orders—or to dispute that there were some who did not." Although the *Süddeutsche Zeitung*'s review of Kesselring's memoirs earlier that year had been moderately sympathetic, the paper now discredited him with a sarcastic declaration: "What an expert witness, what a justice fanatic, what an honorary president for veterans' association in our democratically governed state, this Albert Kesselring."

Readers' letters agreed with the paper's derisive conclusion.[305] The severity of the anti-Kesselring backlash is striking and can possibly be explained, at least in part, by his earlier popularity and the subsequent disenchantment and disappointment.

The Ohm case was clearly political dynamite, and it attracted even greater attention following Franz-Josef Strauss's reaction. Strauss was a minister without portfolio in the Bonn government at the time, although he later became prime minister of Bavaria and leader of the Christlich-Soziale Union (CSU), the Bavarian sister party of the CDU. He was designated the first federal defense minister once the new army had been fully established. Strauss was possibly one of the first to realize that public opinion had turned against the generals, and he now came out unambiguously against Kesselring. This confrontation was particularly significant because Strauss, as Germany's defense minister–designate, could not ignore Kesselring, who represented several veterans' associations. The minister's intervention put a premature end to any hopes the former field marshal may have harbored of a postwar career. As a member of the cabinet, Strauss demanded Kesselring's immediate dismissal from the medals commission,[306] and he was even clearer in his words to a district convention of the Mid-Franconia CSU held in Ansbach on November 29, 1953: "People of his stamp must never again hold defense authority or power."[307] Strauss noted that "much more would have been blown up had we all executed the senseless orders issued during the final days of the war."[308] He was also quoted as saying that "generals who supported the brown mobs in those days would be better advised to express remorse rather than to justify past events."[309]

According to the *Süddeutsche Zeitung*, Strauss also intended to ask the cabinet to assess whether it was "justifiable to pay substantial pensions to generals inflicting so much damage on the state."[310] The controversy caused by his comments on Kesselring reached its peak when the two men met in Bonn—a meeting that proved fruitless. In his memoirs, he stated that he and Kesselring were unable to agree on their view of the officer corps during the Third Reich.[311]

Strauss's remarks were cited more extensively in the two soldiers' newspapers, the *Deutsche Soldatenzeitung* and the *Demokratische Wehrpolitik—Kommentare und Informationen*, both of which explained why the minister disagreed with Kesselring's attitude and had questioned the approach taken by the commander-in-chief, Western Command during the final months. According to Strauss, "This is not about today seeking revenge on a man who viewed the life or death of six fellow human beings so lightly. But it is about ensuring that this act is not justified, but is rather deeply deplored for both political and humanitarian reasons."[312] It was incomprehensible that Kesselring, who had himself arranged for surrender soundings to be carried out in Switzerland, should now accuse "the men of Penzberg of high treason." Relatives of the Penzberg casualties charged Kesselring with "slandering the victims."[313]

Even within the ranks of the veterans' associations, there was an apparent mood shift. And for the first time, cautious criticism was voiced. The Stahlhelm's newspaper, *Der Stahlhelm*, published a New Year's message from the organization's president, Albert Kesselring, while also printing a critical open letter from a "former frontline soldier," Karl Weishäupl from Munich. Weishäupl was also an SPD member of the state parliament and state director of the German Association of War Victims.[314] His view was that by expressing approbation for a "frightful murder," Kesselring, as a senior commander in the former Wehrmacht, had provided "grist to the mill of our one-time enemies."[315] Moreover, Kesselring's activities as an expert witness represented a "disservice" to the ideals of true soldiers: "At home and abroad," he wrote, addressing the field marshal, "your expert opinions have given rise to the impression that you approve of the Nazistic criminal methods."[316] Weishäupl correctly concluded that Kesselring's reputation had suffered irreparable damage as a result of this trial—and in the long term, this would harm the former field marshal far more than his reputed stubbornness. He concluded: "Your aura has been heavily clouded by your behavior in court. That is bad in itself, but it is particularly bad for a man like you. Yours respectfully, Karl Weishäupl."[317] It is no longer possible to determine how many of Kesselring's former subordinates felt puzzled, or indeed embarrassed, at the naïveté displayed by a commander they had once venerated.

Kesselring was offered an opportunity to defend himself by responding directly to Weishäupl in the same issue of *Der Stahlhelm*. He wrote, "It never occurred to me to provide Ohm with legal backing in all respects. I merely attempted to show the court that Ohm had become a victim of circumstances."[318] Kesselring used the concept of duty to summarize his own motives for appearing in court as an expert witness.[319] Although the association's newsletter officially backed him as the organization's honorary president, his reputation had been damaged even among his supporters.[320]

During the Tolsdorff trial in Traunstein, Kesselring once again disseminated his thesis, already foreshadowed in his memoirs: fighting until the end had been "vital to the war" in order to provide "the armies in the east with an opportunity to penetrate the Allied combat zone."[321] On May 3, 1945, after a twenty-minute interrogation, the defendant, Generalleutnant Theodor Tolsdorff, had shot a sixty-year-old captain, Franz Holzhey, in the village of

Eisenärzt near Traunstein. The captain was shot because he had erected Red Cross signs in order to protect the village (home to a fully occupied auxiliary hospital) from enemy fire.[322] In court, Tolsdorff's defense was that he had received reports indicating Holzhey had flown surrender flags.[323]

Admittedly, Kesselring did make some attempt to condemn Holzhey's murder as such, but he then concluded that Tolsdorff had found himself in a difficult situation, since he would have been dismissed or court-martialed if he had surrendered together with his troops. According to Kesselring, it had been "legally possible and humanly understandable" in the circumstances to issue the execution order without first convening a court-martial,[324] and Tolsdorff was duty-bound to prevent the resistance from collapsing. For the rest, Kesselring remarked that "anyone could lose their nerve given the atmosphere at the time."[325] In addition, he noted, the continuation of the war until May 8 actually had allowed some troop units to retreat to the west, and "the hundreds of thousands of people who were thus saved disprove the widespread notion that further resistance was senseless during the final days of the war."[326] It was reasonable to hope that the Western Allies would make common cause with Germany against the Soviet Union, in accordance with the official offer made by Admiral Dönitz. "Even in retrospect, that would have been the best," concluded the witness.[327] He thus put forward one of his pet theses: the purported possibility, in 1945, that the Germans and the Western Allies would close ranks against the Soviet Union. In the end, Kesselring's testimony proved fruitless, for Tolsdorff was sentenced to three and a half years in prison.[328] The verdict was subsequently quashed, and two attempts were made to retry Tolsdorff, but Kesselring did not appear as an expert witness in the subsequent proceedings. It is no longer possible to determine whether this was on the advice of defense counsel or whether Kesselring himself had concluded that he should not appear.

By comparing the verdicts reached in, for example, the three trials of Tolsdorff, one can discern a clear evolution of social values in the wake of the rearmament debate. It is quite apparent that "the investigatory authorities did not operate in a socially neutral space," with the result that "social prejudices, concepts of historical facts, and thus the results of a collective retrospective re-working of the past, found expression."[329] Thus, over a period of less than ten years, the same facts gave rise to completely different conclusions.[330]

To avoid further fueling speculation regarding his own crimes, Kesselring refrained from any additional court appearances, as is evident from an examination of the preliminary investigations carried out by the Munich Regional Court into a case that owed its origins to Kesselring's orders. Captain Bartholomäus Rester was accused of summarily shooting three marauding soldiers whom he caught red-handed in the act of looting during the summer of 1944 in Italy. Kesselring was strikingly cautious in his written testimony. He speculated vaguely regarding the content of the order, which could "no longer be ascertained," and concluded on a conciliatory note: "In my view, to the extent that one can ascertain what happened 13 years ago, the defendant acted in the profound belief that he was performing a difficult soldierly duty."[331] The only explanation for this restraint is that Kesselring himself feared being brought to trial if events in the Italian theater again formed the subject of court proceedings.

In 1954, if only because of his military experience, Kesselring was still considered an acceptable expert witness during the Tolsdorff trial (even though Tolsdorff was convicted). Yet just three years later, he was being openly mocked for his testimony in the trial of Field Marshal Ferdinand Schörner. Immediately after being released from Soviet captivity in late 1956, Schörner had attracted attention because of his revisionist comments. He also repudiated charges that he had sacrificed his troops at the end of the war. Minister Franz-Josef Strauss once again exploited the negative potential represented by these comments to launch a general attack on the old Wehrmacht elite, echoing his earlier attacks on Kesselring. Strauss called the Bavarian Justice Ministry to ensure that Schörner would be served with a court summons upon his arrival in Munich.[332]

Even though preparations for Schörner's trial for alleged war crimes were quickly concluded, the trial itself did not start until October 1957. Schörner was accused of ordering the mass execution of soldiers under his command on charges of alleged defeatism and of fighting for Prague "until the last bullet" instead of declaring it a "hospital city." Finally, the former commander-in-chief was accused of donning civilian garb and fleeing in April 1945, abandoning his post and leaving his men to their fate as prisoners of the Soviet Union. During the preliminary investigation phase, the final charge was dropped due to lack of evidence. However, the real thrust of the trial was apparent: West Germany was distancing itself from Hitler's favorite general and thus also from the National Socialist heritage within the military elite. During this period, the debate regarding the extent to which the Wehrmacht leadership chose Hitler over the German people metamorphosed into questions regarding individual "soldierly honor."[333] Since Schörner was accused of committing war crimes against his own troops, there was substantial public interest in the trial. The "extent of the national trauma" was made manifest precisely because the victims were German soldiers or civilians.[334]

The shift in public opinion against the old generals becomes obvious if one examines the trial of Schörner, who was dubbed the "stay-the-course marshal." Even the German League of Veterans—the VdS—called on its members to testify against Schörner.[335] Only those officers working for the Blank Office, who had been personally requested by the interior minister to speak out against Schörner, initially decided to exercise official restraint in view of the anticipated negative debate surrounding the Wehrmacht's role during the final days of the war. Heusinger decreed that testifying officers should make it clear they were expressing their private opinions: he anticipated a propaganda move by the Soviet Union that "by repatriating Schörner had hoped to inject a note of agitation into the public debate surrounding the military legacy." It is quite possible that the veterans' associations had reached the same conclusion, which would explain why they also urged caution. Kesselring, however, seems to have read the signals too late. He kept his promise and appeared in court.

However, his role as an expert witness on behalf of Schörner was primarily confined to explaining the so-called catastrophe order issued by Hitler. On January 28, 1945, Hitler more or less set aside court-martial procedures, promising indemnity to all generals who resorted to severe measures "which go beyond the usual parameters" in order to maintain discipline. In this regard, the parallels with the charges laid against Kesselring himself (relating to the out-of-control partisan war in Italy) are particularly striking, since the orders in question were almost identical in their wording. This fact may help explain Kesselring's perfunctory testimony. He merely stated vaguely that Schörner had probably believed he was duty-bound to take a hard line. In any event, as commander-in-chief of the Southern Command, he was "unable to recall" any war crimes or victims of hanging. Kesselring was exposed to ridicule—and to severe media criticism.[336] In fact, the *Süddeutsche Zeitung* dubbed him the "catastrophe expert,"[337] apparently an indirect reference to Kesselring's own involvement in war crimes.

His role as an expert witness, as well as the role played by the various defendants in court—coupled with the media's use of the term *generals' trials*—gave rise to the impression that the Wehrmacht generals as a group were on trial.[338] Kesselring's reputation collapsed as rapidly as the image of the "good general" was dismantled. Suddenly, public debate focused on one issue: what distinguished a "Nazi general"?[339] After 1954, those who, like Kesselring, defended the hard line adopted during the final phase of the war were themselves viewed by the public as so-called Nazi generals. *Der Spiegel* quoted Kesselring as saying, "The only thing I really fear is being accused by history of having failed to exploit tactical options for our army because of excessive humanity."[340] Kesselring's reputation had reached its nadir.

The former field marshal had learned nothing from the criticism. As late as 1960, when Max Simon's trial for the murder of two civilians on April 7, 1945, in Brettheim near Ansbach went into its fourth appeal, Kesselring stated that Simon was an "honest man" and had acted with the best intentions.[341]

A memo jotted in the margins of German government correspondence illustrates how irrevocably Kesselring's reputation had been destroyed as a result of his appearances as an expert witness. Officials in the Chancellor's Office had asked the Rechtsschutz-Stelle how they should mark Kesselring's fiftieth anniversary of military service in 1954. It was agreed that Kesselring would "be received by the Minister in the near future, and on this occasion would be congratulated on his military anniversary," since "his activities as an expert witness during the two trials, which caused a great deal of public agitation, compel us to exercise restraint."[342] During that era, virtually every German officer holding the rank of general or above could expect to receive personal congratulations on his anniversary from a member of his troops, accompanied by a military band and culminating in the award of a medal of honor. Against that backdrop, the perfunctory recognition planned for Kesselring indicates how deeply disgraced he now was.

The press was even more restrained in its reaction to his anniversary. The *Soldat im Volk* journal carried a ten-line notice stating that Kesselring had celebrated his fiftieth year of military service on July 20, 1954, and promising to publish a longer article by a "competent" writer. As it turned out, the competent writer was none other than Siegfried Westphal, who—even after Kesselring's release—had continued to work tirelessly for his revered commander. In the Kesselring tribute, entitled "Story of a Soldier's Life," Westphal wrote about a "soldier's life which encompassed highs and lows, and which was out of the ordinary."[343] He concluded by noting that "few German army commanders" were given as "much respect among soldiers as Kesselring."

Just two years after his release, Kesselring's credit had been frittered away. The damage could not be repaired. The journal *Demokratische Wehrpolitik* even predicted repercussions in military circles: "One result of the confrontation between the minister and the marshal may be that those groups which had previously hoped to recruit Kesselring as a candidate for the chairpersonship of the intended umbrella group of veterans' associations will lose their interest."[344] The publication went on to note that "even in his book, *A Soldier to the End*, and with his assumption of the honorary Stahlhelm presidency," Kesselring had "demonstrated a tendency towards political blunders": "His arguments appear to render him unsuitable to become spokesperson of a veterans' association given the difficult circumstances in the Federal Republic."

The goodwill and enthusiasm with which the press had once championed Kesselring's cause—even putting a gloss on certain matters to avoid jeopardizing his release—had been replaced by deep disillusionment and criticism, reflecting a new and more self-confident phase in German attitudes toward the country's immediate military past. In addition, those who endorsed the criticism displayed political perspicacity. The *Süddeutsche Zeitung* praised Franz-Josef Strauss for finding "the courage to express words which may still ring uncomfortably in the ears of those veterans' association representatives who are caught up in old ideas" when he criticized "the increasingly embarrassing appearances by former Generalfeldmarschall Kesselring."[345] It was to be hoped that Strauss would "remember these words" in the future, when "the minister without portfolio may have become the Federal Defence Minister or Germany's EDC commissioner in Paris." The *Süddeutsche Zeitung* thus stressed the political advantages that could accrue, then and in the future, by turning against Germany's old elites.

Conclusion: Kesselring's Trial and Release in the Context of the Rearmament Debate

In writing this book, one of my primary aims was to shed light on the events that led to Kesselring's conviction and subsequent release. In view of the evidence that has come to light, it is impossible for the German debate on World War II to either ignore the facts surrounding the massacres of civilians during the Italian campaign or dismiss them as an "Italian invention."

The irony of the Kesselring case is that, some six decades after his trial, there is a widespread presumption of the former field marshal's guilt, largely due to his behavior following his release rather than to the evidence presented in Venice. However, there is an equally widespread and fallacious assumption, both in Germany and elsewhere, that the war in Italy was a "clean war" fought by "decent" soldiers on either side.

This book represents the first attempt to present and analyze the facts surrounding a case in which the politics of memory benefited a convicted war criminal. Kesselring was not released from prison in 1952 because he was innocent. Rather, he was released because the interplay of media management, political intervention, and domestic German imperatives had mushroomed into a unique campaign that, accompanied by the pressures of the rearmament debate, forced his release.

Admittedly, during the trial, the British achieved their aim of pinning the formal guilt for the Wehrmacht's crimes on Kesselring. However, the defense strategy of proving his personal innocence and fixing that innocence in the minds of trial observers and the press ensured that the British victory was a Pyrrhic one. The German lawyer Hans Laternser used the trial as a platform to rehabilitate the reputation of the Wehrmacht while justifying its military actions in the name of exigency. It became clear that international law was ambiguous on the permissibility of shooting hostages and reprisal killings, an ambiguity that benefited Kesselring. All these factors combined to form a fog of exculpation and obfuscation from which, just a short time later, the myth of the unjustly convicted field marshal was to emerge. His Venice trial was of particular importance to the subsequent rehabilitation strategy because it was in Venice that the first chapters in a positive narrative of Kesselring's military past were written.

Even if, in retrospect, no legally persuasive evidence has emerged of Kesselring's guilt in the murder of 335 civilians in the Fosse Ardeatine, since the order cannot be traced to him, the fact remains that neither he nor his officers attempted to stop the senseless killings—killings whose only effect was to further brutalize the Italian theater of war. Even sympathetic commentators, when discussing Kesselring's failure to halt the massacres, accused him of political shortsightedness and a lack of moral courage.[1] The second count of the indictment charged Kesselring with bearing the military responsibility for his troops' indiscipline because, as commander-in-chief, he had issued orders that could incite his soldiers to commit unwarranted acts of violence, rendering him complicit in the deaths of Italian civilians during the summer of 1944. This fact cannot be disputed, even though some of his troops either did not receive Kesselring's orders or only received them after the massacres. He bears particular blame for his failure to adequately monitor the actions of those military formations that, within the Wehrmacht, were known for their brutality. His guilt in this respect is not mitigated by the military argument that during the 1944 retreat, he was constrained to give the success and safety of his own soldiers in battle priority over the safety of the Italian civilian population.

Nevertheless, it is clear that, when compared with other, lower-ranking German officers, as well as those on the General Staff and the staff of the Wehrmacht High Command (not to mention the SS troops, who were particularly prominent in Italy), Kesselring bears a lesser guilt in the historical context of the German war of destruction. But he can be charged with having tolerated the war of terror against civilians even though—in contrast to other Wehrmacht officers of equal rank—he was not ideologically motivated to actively promote a war of destruction. There is thus an indisputable disparity between his moral guilt, on the one hand, and the absence of sufficient evidence to apportion legal blame, on the other. It is precisely this tension that many contemporaries seized on in their attempts to discredit the verdict. The same tension was to cause unease among his judges and finally to result in his swift release. As a symbol of the "war of destruction," Kesselring was ill chosen, and the British therefore played into the hands of those who still lived in denial. The name *Kesselring* soon came to symbolize two things: the guilty conscience of the victors and their erstwhile opponents' need for an icon who could be used to cast doubt on the entire concept of exacting legal retribution, through trials, for German war crimes. The Kesselring case plainly illustrates the limits to what is legally possible in war crimes trials.

The preceding pages clearly show that, until the end, British Vergangenheitspolitik remained full of contradictions in its approach to Kesselring.

Alexander Scotland, the British colonel who had interrogated Kesselring, once compared his trial and the charges against him—which Scotland viewed as "a German-Italian issue"—to a row the British were called on to mediate:

> Just why it was that Britain after the war concerned herself with the indictment of Germans in Italy is a mystery I have never been able to fathom. To this day I remain convinced that our intervention was unnecessary, unjust and wholly untenable. We were standing on the borderline between two European allies, Italy and Germany, striving to allocate the blame for a series of crimes committed by one nation against the other at a time when both were at war with Britain. Into the legal fray, nevertheless, we hurled our energies.[2]

Without wishing to endorse Scotland's controversial book, I would contend that the former interrogation officer did indirectly touch on Britain's main problem with the Kesselring trial: the British had no politically defined interest in a conviction. Although the position of the Allies was clear, there were deep divisions in London regarding the policy to be pursued. The Kesselring trial was not held out of conviction. Rather, it was held because the War Office and its military prosecutors in the judge advocate general's office felt politically obliged to try Kesselring in order to comply with the requirements of the 1943 Moscow Conference and because the British presided over the Allied military occupation of Italy. The deep unease felt by British judges and prosecutors was apparent in the inept manner in which the trial was conducted—in particular, the unsubstantiated allegation that Kesselring had called for a war against the Italian civilian population—and the immediate commutation of the sentence once it became clear that there was domestic British opposition to the verdict and that the Italians would refuse to execute the convicted officer.

The Kesselring case thus represents the first instance when the fundamental moral principle of retribution for war crimes was not just discredited but actually turned on its head from the victims' perspective. The trial shows that the British in Venice did not see themselves as advocates for the Italian victims. Rather, military judges who openly sympathized with the defendant adjudicated on the admissibility of military orders and operations. The Allied goal of making certain the trials would "ensure that justice is done," formulated in Moscow, was never met.

This study has shown how the complex tripartite relationship among Britain, Germany, and Italy was strained by the war crimes issue. British Vergangenheitspolitik was determined, in part, by different phases and varying positions within the government. But from the very beginning, it was also subject to two divergent streams of thought: the military line and the political line. The situation was further complicated by the military lawyers' strictures on the limits of legal possibility. The War Office—the arm of government charged with conducting the trials through the judge advocate general's office—was meticulous in its legal preparations for the proceedings, even as the Foreign Office was advising political caution as early as 1946. The primary concern of officials in the Foreign Office was the potential impact of the planned trials on the day-to-day occupation of Germany and on the country's stability, and they considered how the national government affected could be involved in the trials. The ranks of Foreign Office doubters were swelled by those who feared the trials would turn into a costly and labor-intensive debacle.

However, just when Foreign Office fears were being allayed by the military prosecutors' success in apportioning blame, as well as the successful conduct of the trials, opposition within the War Office to the war crimes trials was growing. Critics within the War Office started expressing reservations in 1947: they questioned whether one could convict an opponent whom the British themselves considered honorable and whose military logic—a logic of transmitting and obeying orders—would also have been binding on British officers. The reasons given by the British Mediterranean commander-in-chief, General Harding, when commuting Kesselring's sentence in 1947 illustrate this compromise between political requirements and military concepts of honor. When reading General Harding's statement of reasons, it also becomes clear that the military argument had prevailed.

In retrospect, the role played by Italy also remains ambiguous and inconsistent. Although the Italian government felt that the British war crimes trials had not taken sufficient account of Italian concerns, during subsequent trials (from 1948 to 1950), the Italian military courts consistently applied different legal standards, which one could argue were even more favorable to the defendants. The Italian approach put a severe strain on relations between London and Rome. For example, the Italians, unlike the British, accepted the "imperative of obeying orders" as a mitigating factor during the trial of Herbert Kappler.

British government officials found themselves faced with a dilemma as a result of Italian demands. They had to meet the Italian public's expectation that the German commander-in-chief would be punished while also taking account of the Italian legal position, which dictated that, on the basis of the evidence submitted, no Italian court could sentence Kesselring to death. After he had been sentenced in May 1947, the Italian government's refusal to carry out the execution put the ball firmly back in the British court. Confronted with unexpected public opposition at home, expertly steered by the group surrounding Winston Churchill, the British government was forced to address the broader question of British involvement in the prosecution of war crimes.

With the exception of trials already in preparation, the British series of trials ceased as a result of the domestic crisis in Britain triggered by the Kesselring proceedings. Given the decision to end the trials, the 1949 Manstein case gave rise to a heated debate that illustrated the sea change that had already occurred in British opinion. It is noteworthy that military arguments prevailed, clearly demonstrating not only the power relationships within Britain but also the manner in which the War Office's interests had come to supersede those of the Foreign Office. In terms of public opinion, "war criminals" were rehabilitated and transformed into "comrades." The possibility of Germany playing a military role was first mooted in the wake of this transformation, long before the threat within Europe—which became apparent as a result of the Korean War—made remilitarization a political reality, giving rise to a public debate on German rearmament. Having examined the debate within Britain, one must conclude that the British narrative of a clean Italian theater of war had been agreed upon as early as 1947 and that there was no interest in discussing issues such as whether British arms shipments and supplies had, in fact, escalated the partisan war in Italy.[3]

Following the establishment of the two German states in 1949, the business of government devolved to the first federal government under Konrad Adenauer. This development naturally impacted on the occupation policy of the Allies: Germany became a partner. The Allied high commissioners were appointed in rotation, and the appointment of the American John McCloy and the British Sir Ivone Kirkpatrick represented a political moderation that foreshadowed an end to the occupation policy and the start of cooperation with Germany. Although this was reflected in an end to the policy of dismantlement, it mainly reinforced German hopes for a review of war criminals' sentences. In this regard, it should be noted that each conciliatory step taken by the Allies reinforced the impression that victors' justice was now being rectified. Due to a unique interplay of media management, political self-interest, and the psychological need for a more positive evaluation of wartime events (particularly evident among soldiers' associations), German war crimes were retrospectively deleted from the collective West German memory or their perpetrators were reinvented as victims of a miscarriage of justice.

The campaign for Kesselring's release, a campaign of great symbolic value to all sides, demonstrated the close links between diverse interest groups inside and outside Germany. The efforts to secure his release went beyond personal intervention. While Kesselring's counsel was still trying to devise legal gimmicks with which to force a review and the field marshal's former subordinates were joining together in demonstrations of solidarity, a range of individuals representing churches, lawyers' groups, veterans' associations, and opponents of dismantlement were already active on Kesselring's behalf. They had recognized the symbolic value of the case and hoped to use it as a tool in their efforts to reclaim German sovereignty. In the summer of 1952, the German Liberal MP Erich Mende, speaking in the Bundestag, stated that Kesselring was serving his sentence "on behalf of us all." That statement shows how the Kesselring case had become a litmus test not only for British Vergangenheitspolitik but also for the politics of coming to terms with the past espoused by Adenauer.

This examination of the Kesselring case allows us, for the first time, to see how a powerful, closely interlinked war criminals' lobby added an international dimension to the politics of memory. After 1948, British policy on Germany was lastingly molded by the reconciliatory attitudes of Hankey, Liddell Hart, Bishop Bell, and Churchill. In this connection, it should be noted that very few of those involved in this campaign were interested in the release of the former German officer. Rather, many of those campaigning for his release felt that the case exemplified the continuing ambiguity of international law in respect to reprisal killings—an ambiguity that resurfaced in the Korean War. In their demands for Kesselring's release, British lobbyists consistently avoided advancing specific legal arguments.

Those lobbying outside Germany, specifically the British Hankey contingent and the group of U.S. senators together with the NCPW, had political motives that predated the official position adopted by the British government by several years. In advancing their conservative nationalist-militaristic arguments regarding what they viewed as the honorable war waged by the Wehrmacht, they also disseminated the idea of rapid German rearmament to help in the fight against the common (Bolshevik) enemy in the East. These "declarations of honor," which were well received by large sections of the public, helped advance the "real rehabilitation" demanded by the pro-German lobby. In the media battle being waged around the Kesselring case, such declarations guaranteed that the image of Kesselring's innocence became firmly embedded in public opinion. In this regard, it should not be forgotten that, even before the war, most of the British and American individuals who were subsequently prominent in the war criminals lobby were already inclined to be pro-German—or at least anticommunist.

In 1943, at the Moscow Conference, the Allies had made a political decision that German perpetrators should be punished. Following the disintegration of the alliance, it did not take long for efforts to be made in London to ensure that German officers, at least, were excluded from the denazification campaign. At the very minimum, the proponents of such a policy hoped to achieve a reduction in the officers' sentences. German arguments regarding the officers' personal integrity, the imperative of obeying orders, and errors made by the British during the trials were knitted together with the argument requiring a joint defense against the East. This process created the myth of a clean Wehrmacht that had become entrenched by the mid-1950s.[4]

Even Chancellor Adenauer, who had initially regarded the issue of war criminals as tangential to his policy of Western integration, quickly recognized the integrative power of the demand for the release of those officers still in custody and its potential to contribute to the republic's domestic stabilization. Adenauer's focus was not only on the pending elections but also—and primarily—on the manner in which his country's sovereignty might be regained in return for German rearmament. The establishment of a West German army presupposed national sovereignty, which, in turn, presupposed judicial sovereignty. Therefore, from a legal perspective, the debate also involved the war criminals sitting in Allied prisons on German soil, even though the main focus was on the demands being made by German veterans' associations for the release of *all* their former comrades as a precondition for rearmament. In the final analysis, the debate surrounding German rearmament provided the political impetus for a speedy and conciliatory resolution of the war criminals issue.

As well as casting a pall over Adenauer's government and the public debates in the Bundestag, the issue was omnipresent in the media between 1950 and 1952. The more concrete the negotiations regarding an end to occupation and the wording of the General Treaty became (which were premised on German rearmament), the more large sections of the population showed solidarity with what was actually a side issue: the demand for the last German war criminals still in custody to be released. In this way, the rearmament debate influenced and distorted the debate on German war crimes to such an extent that several issues became confused: the crimes committed during the war against civilians and POWs, the crimes committed by the National Socialists against concentration camp inmates, and the frequently arbitrary sentences imposed on POWs still in Soviet custody—the first to whom the term *so-called war criminals* was correctly applied.

One of the aims espoused by the campaign for clemency for the officers imprisoned in Germany, described as "so-called war criminals," was to achieve a shift in German public opinion and a more positive attitude toward the Wehrmacht's military legacy. It was hoped that the rehabilitative efforts made by, for instance, the Lutheran regional churches on Kesselring's behalf, as well as the fervent endorsement by the three veterans' associations that appointed him honorary chairperson and the pro-Kesselring press campaigns, would enable the German public—in particular, ordinary soldiers who had served in Italy—to attach retrospective purpose to his war service, thus helping foster public acceptance of German rearmament.

"Justice, not mercy" was the phrase used by the war criminals' lobbyists in their attempt to interpret Kesselring's release in 1952 as a landmark decision. However, the British authorities used medical and social reasons to explain their decision, citing the prisoner's poor health. The evidence shows that in the Kesselring case, the British avoided making a fundamental decision on the war criminals issue. Instead, their aim was to facilitate the pending submission of the treaties to the Bundestag. But the import in terms of Vergangenheitspolitik is clear. The Kesselring case shows plainly how the war criminals issue was linked with political demands. Adenauer attempted to use the General Treaty as a means of securing the release of German war criminals, thus regaining national honor as well as national sovereignty.

Four decades later, when a memorial event was held at the Bergfriedhof Cemetery in Bad Wiessee to mark the fortieth anniversary of Kesselring's death, representatives of the Bundeswehr declined to attend, stating that the former field marshal was "not worthy of being part of our tradition."[5] Kesselring's importance had diminished to such an extent that even the Nationaldemokratische Partei Deutschlands (NPD)—a neo-Nazi party—did not feel the need to attend the ceremonies. It was left to a small group of aging veterans representing the Deutsche Montecassino Vereinigung (German Montecassino Association) and the Bund Deutscher Fallschirmjäger (Association of German Paratroopers) to remember the past.[6] In one of the Bad Wiessee orations, it was stated that even as late as 1947, Kesselring "had been surprisingly sentenced to death by a military court in Venice of doubtful competence."[7] Today, as far as Kesselring's surviving troops are concerned—and thanks partly to British intervention—their former commander's reputation remains unsullied.

The symbolic nature of the Kesselring case has further implications. In the final analysis, it was precisely the ostensible defeat of British Vergangenheitspolitik and the concession of Kesselring's release that resulted in the collapse of the Kesselring myth. Due to the recovery of German sovereignty, the German public had become increasingly self-confident and critical and was no longer prepared to overlook the misconduct of Wehrmacht generals.

From the middle of the 1950s, Kesselring's popularity was in sharp decline as a result of adverse reviews of his memoirs, the former field marshal's speeches to veterans' gatherings, and his court appearances as an expert witness. By the time Kesselring died in 1960, eight years after the frenetic celebrations surrounding his release, his transformation from "innocent gentleman" to "Nazi general" was complete. The myth thus failed to survive the man.

NOTES

Introduction

1. Nikolaus Buschmann and Horst Carl, eds., *Die Erfahrung des Krieges: Erfahrungsgeschichtliche Perspektiven von der Französischen Revolution bis zum Zweiten Weltkrieg* (Paderborn 2001).

2. To cite just a selection, see Kai Ambos, *Der allgemeine Teil des Völkerstrafrechts: Ansätze einer Dogmatisierung* (Berlin 2002); Reinhard Merkel, "Nürnberg 1945: Militärtribunal—Grundlagen, Probleme, Folgen," *Merkur* 50 (1997): 918–936; Susanne Jung, *Die Rechtsprobleme der Nürnberger Prozesse, dargestellt am Verfahren gegen Friedrich Flick* (Tübingen 1992); and Rainer Huhle, ed., *Von Nürnberg nach Den Haag: Menschrechtsverbrechen vor Gericht—Zur Aktualität des Nürnberger Prozesses* (Hamburg 1996).

3. Two anthologies—Hannes Heer and Klaus Naumann, eds., *Vernichtungskrieg: Wehrmachtverbrechen 1941–1945* (Hamburg 1995), and Rolf-Dieter Müller and Hans-Erich Volkmann, eds., on behalf of the German Institute of Military History (hereafter cited as MGFA), *Die Wehrmacht: Mythos und Realität* (Munich 1999)—represent the two poles of current research trends when examining the history of the Wehrmacht during World War II.

4. See Ulrich Brochhagen, *Nach Nürnberg: Vergangenheitsbewältigung und Westintegration in der Ära Adenauer* (Hamburg 1994).

5. Norbert Frei, *Vergangenheitspolitik: Die Anfänge der Bundesrepublik und die NS-Vergangenheit* (Munich 1996), p. 13.

6. Ibid., p. 15.

7. Ibid., p. 16.

8. Alaric Searle, *Wehrmacht Generals, West German Society, and the Debate on Rearmament, 1949–1959* (Westport, CT, 2003).

9. Gerhard Schreiber, "Partisanenkrieg und Kriegsverbrechen der Wehrmacht in Italien 1943–1945," in Ahlrich Meyer, ed., *Repression und Kriegsverbrechen: Die Bekämpfung von Widerstands- und Partisanenbewegungen gegen die deutsche Besatzung in West- und Südeuropa* (Berlin 1997), pp. 93–129, at p. 99.

10. Kerstin von Lingen, ". . . wenn wir zum letzten Kampf in Italien antreten: Die Konstruktion von Kriegserinnerung am Beispiel des Kriegsverbrecherprozesses gegen Albert Kesselring," in Bruno Thoss and Hans-Erich Volkmann, eds., *Erster Weltkrieg–Zweiter Weltkrieg: Ein Vergleich—Krieg, Kriegserlebnis, Kriegserfahrung in Deutschland* (Paderborn 2002), pp. 687–710, at p. 690.

11. Peter Steinbach, *Nationalsozialistische Gewaltverbrechen: Die Diskussion in der deutschen Öffentlichkeit nach 1945* (Berlin 1981), pp. 28f.

12. For this reason, military titles were not only retained but also were even used without

the logical addition of "former." The old rank structures continued to live on in the minds of the Wehrmacht officers, who persisted in using them even after the Wehrmacht was dissolved.

13. Bundesarchiv-Militärarchiv (hereafter cited as BA-MA), N 431/936, Kesselring to Laternser, 29 August 1946.

14. Archivum Monacensum Societas Jesu (Archive of the Jesuit Order), Munich (hereafter cited as AMSJ Munich), Dept. 47, Hiemer Papers, Keller to Hiemer, 18 January 1947.

15. Norbert Frei, *Karrieren im Zwielicht: Hitlers Eliten nach 1945* (Frankfurt 2001), p. 318.

16. Jörg Echternkamp, "Mit dem Krieg seinen Frieden schliessen—Wehrmacht und Weltkrieg in der Veteranenkultur 1945–1960," in Thomas Kühne, ed., *Von der Kriegskultur zur Friedenskultur? Zum Mentalitätswandel in Deutschland seit 1945* (Münster 2000), pp. 78–93, at p. 79.

17. Ibid., p. 83.

18. Ibid., pp. 92f.

19. The so-called Heidelberger Juristenkreis (Heidelberg Lawyers' Circle), which has yet to be fully researched, played a major role in the rehabilitation of the generals. Initial information has been provided by Günther Buchstab, "Die Nürnberger Prozesse und der Heidelberger Kreis (1949–1955)," in Peter R. Weilemann, ed., *Macht und Zeitkritik: Festschrift für Hans-Peter Schwarz zum 65. Geburtstag* (Paderborn 1999), pp. 61–74.

20. Frei, *Karrieren*, p. 318.

21. Heribert Prantl, *Wehrmachtverbrechen: Eine deutsche Kontroverse* (Hamburg 1997).

22. As far back as the 1970s and early 1980s, the image of "the clean war waged by the Wehrmacht" had been refuted in works by Messerschmidt, Streit, and Krausnick; see Manfred Messerschmidt, *Die Wehrmacht im NS-Staat: Zeit der Indoktrination* (Hamburg 1969); Christian Streit, *Keine Kameraden: Die Wehrmacht und die sowjetischen Kriegsgefangenen 1941–1945*, 1st ed. (Stuttgart 1978), 2nd ed. (Bonn 1997); and Helmut Krausnick and Hans-Heinrich Wilhelm, *Die Truppe des Weltanschauungskrieges: Die Einsatzgruppen der Sicherheitspolizei und des SD 1938–1940* (Stuttgart 1978).

23. Christiane Nill-Theobald, *"Defences" bei Kriegsverbrechen am Beispiel Deutschlands und der USA: Zugleich ein Beitrag zu einem Allgemeinen Teil des Völkerstrafrechts* (Freiburg im Breisgau 1998); Peter Reichel, "Vergangenheitsbewältigung als Problem unserer politischen Kultur: Einstellungen zum Dritten Reich und seine Folgen," in Jürgen Weber and Peter Steinbach, eds., *Vergangenheitsbewältigung durch Strafverfahren? NS-Prozesse in der Bundesrepublik Deutschland* (Munich 1984), pp. 145–163; Peter Steinbach, "Zur Auseinandersetzung mit nationalsozialistischen Gewaltverbrechen in der Bundesrepublik Deutschland: Ein Beitrag zur deutschen politischen Kultur nach 1945," *Geschichte in Wissenschaft und Unterricht* (hereafter cited as *GWU*) 35 (1984): 65–85; Norman E. Tutorow, ed., *War Crimes, War Criminals and War Crimes Trials: An Annotated Bibliography and Source Book* (New York 1986); Wolfram Wette and Gerd R. Ueberschär, eds., *Kriegsverbrechen im 20. Jahrhundert* (Darmstadt 2001); and Alfred De Zayas, *Die Wehrmacht-Untersuchungsstelle* (Vienna 1980).

24. Roberto Battaglia, *Storia della Resistenza italiana*, 4th ed. (Turin 1979), p. 504.

25. An overview of the controversy is provided in Gian Enrico Rusconi, "Die italienische Resistenza auf dem Prüfstand," *Vierteljahreshefte für Zeitgeschichte* (hereafter cited as *VfZ*) 3, no. 42 (1994): 379–402.

26. Claudio Pavone, *Una guerra civile: Saggio sulla moralità nella Resistenza* (Turin 1991).

27. The obvious unwillingness of the Rome government to prosecute crimes legally was

also addressed, prompted by a newspaper article; see *L'Unità*, 1 October 2001, "Le stragi nazifasciste nascoste nell'Armadio della vergogna," by Franco Guistolisi. This topic has since been examined in Michele Battini, *Peccati di Memoria: La mancata Norimberga italiana* (Rome 2003).

28. Carlo Spartaco Capogreco, "Una storia rimossa dell'Italia Fascista: L'internamento dei civili jugoslawi (1941–1943)," *Studi Storici* 42, no. 1 (2001): 203–230; Filippo Focardi, "La questione della punizione die Criminali di Guerra in Italia," *Quellen und Forschungen aus italienischen Archiven und Bibliotheken* (hereafter cited as *QFIAB*) 80 (2000): 543–624.

29. Giorgio Rochat, *Guerre italiane in Libia e in Etiopia: Studi militari 1921–1939* (Treviso 1991).

30. *Corriere della Sera—Sette,* 28 July 2001, "Criminali di Guerra nostrani," by Ernesto Galli della Loggia; *La Stampa*, 27 July 2001, "Italiani bravi boia salvati da De Gasperi," by Alberto Papuzzi.

31. Erich Kuby, *Verrat auf Deutsch: Wie das deutsche Reich Italien ruinierte* (Hamburg 1982).

32. Gerhard Schreiber, *Die italienischen Militärinternierten im deutschen Machtbereich 1943–1945* (Munich 1990).

33. Lutz Klinkhammer, *Zwischen Bündnis und Besatzung: Das nationalsozialistische Deutschland und die Republik von Salò 1943–1945* (Tübingen 1993).

34. Gerhard Schreiber, *Deutsche Kriegsverbrechen in Italien: Täter, Opfer, Strafverfolgung* (Munich 1996); the expanded Italian edition also addressed the controversies surrounding the trial of the former Obersturmbannführer Erich Priebke from 1996 to 1998 in Rome; it was published under the title *La vendetta tedesca 1943–1945: Le rappresaglie naziste in Italia* (Milan 2000).

35. Michele Battini and Paolo Pezzino, *Guerra ai civili: Occupazione tedesca e politica del massacro, Toscana 1944* (Venice 1997); Giovanni Contini, *La memoria divisa* (Milan 1997); Paolo Pezzino, *Anatomia di un massacro: Controversia sopra una strage tedesca* (Bologna 1997); and Paolo Paoletti, *Sant'Anna di Stazzema 1944: La strage impunita* (Milan 1998).

36. For details on the issues surrounding the Fosse Ardeatine massacre and the perception of German war crimes against the background of the "Resistenza myth," see Joachim Staron, *Fosse Ardeatine und Marzabotto: Deutsche Kriegsverbrechen und Resistenza* (Paderborn 2002). Also see Steffen Prauser, "Rom in deutscher Hand: Die deutsche Besatzungszeit in der ewigen Stadt" (PhD diss., Florence European University Institute, 2005); Carlo Gentile's study on German massacres in Tuscany, entitled "Wehrmacht und SS im Kampf gegen Partisanen und Zivilbevölkerung in Italien 1943–1945," forthcoming 2009.

37. Friedrich Andrae, *Auch gegen Frauen und Kinder: Der Krieg der deutschen Wehrmacht gegen die Zivilbevölkerung in Italien 1943–1945* (Munich 1995).

38. Schreiber, *Deutsche Kriegsverbrechen,* p. 95.

39. Ibid., p. 582.

40. Ibid., p. 578.

41. Lutz Klinkhammer, "Grundlinien nationalsozialistischer Besatzungspolitik in Frankreich, Jugoslawien und Italien," in Christof Dipper, Rainer Hudemann, and Jens Petersen, eds., *Faschismus und Faschismen im Vergleich: Wolfgang Schieder zum 60. Geburtstag* (Cologne 1998), pp. 196–234, at p. 196.

42. Wolfram Wette and Gerd R. Ueberschär, eds., *Kriegsverbrechen im 20. Jahrhundert* (Darmstadt, 2001), pp. 11–17, at p. 14; Raymond Ruch, "Krieg gegen die Zivilbevölkerung: Die deutsche Partisanenbekämpfung in der Sowjetunion und in Italien 1941–1945" (master's thesis, University of Bern, 2003).

43. Since 2001, the universities of Pisa, Bari, Naples, and Florence have been involved in a cooperative program dedicated solely to researching war crimes. For this purpose, doctoral dissertations on the individual massacres were assigned, and several conferences on the topic have already been held with the aim of placing the German war crimes in an international context. See Luca Baldissara and Paolo Pezzino, eds., *Crimini e memorie di guerra: Violenze contro le popolazioni e politiche del ricordo* (Naples 2004). Further literature on this topic includes Paolo Pezzino, "Gli Alleati, l'Italia e i processi ai criminali nazisti," *Storia e Memoria* 10 (2001): 9–72; Mimmo Franzinelli, *Le Stragi Nascoste: L'armadio della vergogna—Impunità e rimzione dei crimini di guerra nazifascisti 1943–2001* (Milan 2002); Battini, *Peccati di Memoria*; Pier Paolo Rivello, "The Prosecution of War Crimes Committed by Nazi Forces in Italy," *Journal of International Criminal Justice* 3 (2005): 422–433; and Filippo Focardi, *La guerra della memoria: La Resistenza nel dibattito politico italiano dal 1945 a oggi* (Rome 2005).

44. It is not possible to refer to more than a small selection here—for example, Ludolf Herbst, *Option für den Westen: Vom Marshalplan bis zum deutsch-französischen Vertrag* (Munich 1989); Karlheinz Höfner, *Die Aufrüstung Westdeutschlands: Willensbildung, Entscheidungsprozesse und Spielräume westdeutscher Politik 1945 bis 1950* (Munich 1990); Wolfgang Krieger, *Adenauer und die Wiederbewaffnung* (Bonn 2000); Klaus v. Schubert, *Wiederbewaffnung und Westintegration: Die innere Auseinandersetzung um die militärische und aussenpolitische Orientierung der Bundesrepublik 1950–1954* (Stuttgart 1970); Rolf Steininger, *Wiederbewaffnung: Die Entscheidung für einen westdeutschen Verteidigungsbeitrag—Adenauer und die Westmächte 1950* (Erlangen 1989); Bruno Thoss and Hans-Erich Volkmann, eds., *Zwischen kaltem Krieg und Entspannung: Sicherheits- und Deutschlandpolitik der Bundesrepublik im Mächtesystem der Jahre 1953–1956* (Boppard 1988); Militärgerschichtliches Forschungsamt, ed., *Verteidigung im Bündnis: Planung, Aufbau und Bewährung der Bundeswehr 1950–1972* (Munich 1975); Hans-Erich Volkmann and Walter Schwengler, eds., *Die Europäische Verteidigungsgemeinschaft: Stand und Probleme der Forschung* (Boppard 1985); Gerhard Wettig, *Entmilitarisierung und Wiederbewaffnung in Deutschland 1943–1955* (Munich 1967); and Norbert Wiggershaus, "Die Entscheidung für einen westdeutschen Verteidigungsbeitrag 1950," in Roland G. Foerster, ed., *Anfänge westdeutscher Sicherheitspolitik*, vol. 1, *Von der Kapitulation zum Pleven-Plan* (Munich 1982), pp. 325–402.

45. A representative selection, with particular reference to the war crimes trials, includes Brochhagen, *Nach Nürnberg*; Frei, *Vergangenheitspolitik*; Eckhard Jesse, "'Vergangenheitsbewältigung' in der Bundesrepublik Deutschland," *Der Staat* 26 (1987): 539–565; Ulrich Herbert, *Best: Biographische Studien über Radikalismus, Weltanschauung und Vernunft 1903–1989* (Bonn 1996); Thomas Kühne, "Kameradschaft—'Das Beste im Leben des Mannes': Die deutschen Soldaten des Zweiten Weltkriegs in erfahrungs- und geschlechtergeschichtlicher Perspektive," *Geschichte und Gesellschaft* (hereafter cited as GG) 4, no. 22 (1996): 504–529; Adalbert Rückerl, ed., *NS-Prozesse: Nach 25 Jahren Strafverfolgung—Möglichkeiten, Grenzen, Ergebnisse* (Karlsruhe 1971); Rückerl, *NS-Verbrechen vor Gericht: Versuch einer Vergangenheitsbewältigung*, 2nd ed. (Heidelberg 1984); and Rückerl, *Strafverfolgung von NS-Verbrechen 1945–1978: Eine Dokumentation* (Heidelberg 1979).

46. Norbert Frei, Dirk van Laak, and Michael Stolleis, eds., *Geschichte vor Gericht: Historiker, Richter und die Suche nach Gerechtigkeit* (Munich 2000); Gerd R. Ueberschär, ed., *Der Nationalsozialismus vor Gericht: Die alliierten Prozesse gegen Kriegsverbrecher und Soldaten 1943–1952* (Frankfurt am Main 1999).

47. Robert Herde, *Command responsibility: Die Verfolgung der "Zweiten Garde" deutscher*

und japanischer Generäle im alliierten Prozessprogramm nach dem Zweiten Weltkrieg (Baden-Baden 2002).

48. Jörn Axel Kämmerer, "Kriegsrepressalie oder Kriegsverbrechen? Zur rechtlichen Beurteilung der Massenexekutionen von Zivilisten durch die deutsche Besatzungsmacht im Zweiten Weltkrieg," *Archiv des Völkerrechts* 37 (1999): 283–317.

49. Tom Bower, *Blind Eye to Murder: Britain, America and the Purging of Nazi Germany—A Pledge Betrayed*, 3rd ed. (London 1997).

50. The individual portrayals by Gerd F. Heuer do not meet scientific criteria: see his "Albert Kesselring," in Heuer, ed., *Die deutschen Generalfeldmarschälle und Grossadmirale 1939–1945*, 2nd ed. (Rastatt 1988), pp. 55–59; Franz Kurowski, *Generalfeldmarschall Albert Kesselring: Oberbefehlshaber an allen Fronten* (Berg am See 1985); and Otto E. Moll, "Albert Kesselring," in Heuer, ed., *Die deutschen Generalfeldmarschälle und Grossadmirale 1939–1945*, 2nd ed. (Rastatt 1988), pp. 61–71.

51. Shelford Bidwell, "Kesselring," in Corelli Barnett, ed., *Hitler's Generals* (London 1989), pp. 265–289; Peter Herde, "Albert Kesselring," Gesellschaft für Fränkische Geschichte (Franconian Historical Society), ed., *Fränkische Lebensbilder*, vol. 18 (Neustadt an der Aisch 2000), pp. 295–314; Elmar Krautkrämer, "Albert Kesselring," in Gerd R. Ueberschär, ed., *Hitlers militärische Elite*, vol. 1, *Von den Anfängen des Regimes bis Kriegsbeginn* (Darmstadt 1998), pp. 121–129; Samuel J. Lewis, "Albert Kesselring—Der Soldat als Manager," in Ronald Smelser and Enrico Syring, eds., *Die Militärelite des Dritten Reichs: 27 biographische Skizzen* (Berlin 1995), pp. 270–287; Kenneth Macksey, *Kesselring: The Making of the Luftwaffe* (London 1978) (new and revised edition entitled *Kesselring: German Master Strategist of the Second World War* [London 1996]).

52. Schreiber, *Partisanenkrieg*, p. 110.

53. Ivan Tognarini, *Kesselring e le stragi nazifasciste: 1944—Estate di sangue in Toscana* (Florence 2002).

54. Richard Raiber, "Generalfeldmarschall Kesselring, Via Rasella, and the 'Ginny Mission,'" *Militärgeschichtliche Mitteilungen* (hereafter cited as *MGM*) 56 (1997): 69–106. For a contrary view, see Staron, *Fosse Ardeatine*, pp. 52f., and Kerstin von Lingen, "Konstruktion von Kriegserinnerung: Der Prozess gegen Generalfeldmarschall Albert Kesselring vor einem britischen Militärgericht in Venedig (1947) und das Bild vom Krieg in Italien," *Militärgeschichtliche Zeitschrift* (hereafter cited as *MGZ*) 2, no. 59 (2000): 435–450, at p. 449.

55. Four major trials of German military commanders-in-chief took place between November 1946 and July 1947. The officers concerned were Field Marshal Albert Kesselring, Generaloberst Eberhard von Mackensen, and Generalleutnant Kurt Mältzer, as well as Waffen SS General Max Simon and Generalleutnant Eduard Crasemann. There were also several lesser British trials involving German war crimes in Italy. Those tried included SS Brigadeführer Willy Tensfeld and Kapitänleutnant Waldemar Krummhaar (charged with the shootings in Borgo Ticino) and Rittmeister Joseph Strauch (charged with the massacre of Fucecchio). Forty-nine trials were held in all. In this regard, see also Pezzino, "Gli Alleati," p. 21.

56. Paolo Pezzino, "Guerra ai Civili: Le stragi tra storia e memoria," in Luca Baldissara and Paolo Pezzino, eds., *Crimini e memorie di guerra: Violenze contro le popolazioni e politiche del ricordo* (Naples 2004), pp. 5–58, at p. 20; Pezzino, "Sui mancati processi in Italia ai criminali di guerra tedeschi," *Storia e Memoria* 10 (2001): 1–72.

57. The secret agreements between Karl Wolff and the Swiss middlemen Max Waibel and Max Husmann, acting on Allen W. Dulles's behalf, according to which SS massacres

would not form the subject of war crimes trials, may have played a role in this regard; see Public Records Office/The National Archives (hereafter cited as PRO/TNA), Kew, WO 310/123, statement by Heinrich Andergassen regarding the capitulation negotiations in Switzerland. Also see Kerstin von Lingen, "Conspiracy of Silence: How the Old Boys of American Intelligence Shielded Karl Wolff from Prosecution," *Holocaust and Genocide Studies* 22, no. 1 (2008): 74–109, and Georg Kreis, "Das Kriegsende in Norditalien," *Schweizer Monatshefte* 6, no. 65 (1985): 507–521, at pp. 509 and 520.

58. See, for example, *Süddeutsche Zeitung*, 20 April 2004, "Beweise aus dem Schrank der Schande: Sie wollen keine Rache, aber Gerechtigkeit—Wie die Überlebenden eines Massakers, das die Waffen-SS 1944 in einem toskanischen Bergdorf beging, den Prozess erwarten," by Christiane Kohl, p. 3.

59. Reinhard Stumpf, *Die Wehrmacht-Elite: Rang- und Herkunftsstruktur der deutschen Generale und Admirale 1933–1945* (Boppard 1982), p. 7.

60. BA-MA, N 750/1, private papers of Albert Kesselring.

61. Central State Archives of Bavaria—War Archives (Bayerisches Staatsarchiv Kriegsarchiv) (hereafter cited as KA Munich), Kesselring personnel file, OP 61536.

62. BA-MA, Pers. 6/6, supplemented by MSg. 109/1280.

63. BA-MA, C 32, sudy prepared by the Historical Division in 1951 entitled "The Army Historical Program in the European Theater and Command, 8 May 1943–31 December 1950," p. 50.

64. Bernd Wegner, "Erschriebene Siege: Franz Halder, die 'Historical Division' und die Rekonstruktion des Zweiten Weltkrieges im Geiste des deutschen Generalstabes," in Ernst Willi Hansen, ed., *Politischer Wandel, organisierte Gewalt und nationale Sicherheit: Beiträge zur neueren Geschichte Deutschlands und Frankreichs* (Munich 1995), pp. 287–302, at p. 294.

65. Echternkamp, "Mit dem Krieg," p. 82.

66. Gotthard Breit, *Das Staats- und Gesellschaftsbild deutscher Generale beider Weltkriege im Spiegel ihrer Memoiren* (Boppard 1973); Rolf Düsterberg, *Soldat und Kriegserlebnis: Deutsche militärische Erinnerungsliteratur (1945–1961) zum Zweiten Weltkrieg—Motive, Begriffe, Wertungen* (Paderborn 2000); Helmut Peitsch, *"Deutschlands Gedächtnis in seiner dunkelsten Zeit": Zur Frage der Autobiographie in den Westzonen Deutschlands und den Westsektoren von Berlin 1945 bis 1949* (Berlin 1990); and Hans Wagener, "Soldaten zwischen Gehorsam und Gewissen: Kriegsromane und Kriegstagebücher," in Hans Wagener, ed., *Gegenwartsliteratur und Drittes Reich: Deutsche Autoren in der Auseinandersetzung mit der Vergangenheit* (Stuttgart 1977), pp. 241–264.

67. Albert Kesselring, *Soldat bis zum letzten Tag* (Bonn 1953); Kesselring, *Gedanken zum Zweiten Weltkrieg* (Bonn 1955).

68. See Rainer Kesselring's preface to the second edition of the Kesselring memoirs, Albert Kesselring, *Soldat bis zum letzten Tag* (1999), p. i. Rainer Kesselring claimed that his mother, Irmgard Horn-Kesselring, had smuggled the memoirs out during a prison visit, typed them at home, and then submitted them to the publisher in accordance with Kesselring's instructions. Since Kesselring, as a convicted war criminal, was prohibited from publishing while in custody, his memoirs could only be issued following his release from detention in 1952.

69. Wegner, "Erschriebene Siege," p. 299.

70. PRO/TNA, Kew, WO 204/11005, WO 310/126–129, PREM 8/707, FO 1060/493–501, WO 311/28, WO 204/12798, FO 371/57557 and 51046, WO 235/438, FO 1005/1900.

71. Imperial War Museum Archives, London (hereafter cited as IWM), FO 642, vols. 1–6.

72. BA-MA, N 431. Part of the agreement I reached with the Bundesarchiv-Militärarchiv was that I would catalog the papers based on rough criteria, thus rendering them provisionally accessible.

73. In this regard, see Georg Meyer, "Zur Situation der deutschen militärischen Führungsschicht im Vorfeld des westdeutschen Verteidigungsbeitrages 1945–1950/51," in Roland G. Foerster, ed., *Anfänge westdeutscher Sicherheitspolitik*, vol. 1, *Von der Kapitulation zum Pleven-Plan* (Munich 1982), pp. 577–736.

74. AMSJ Munich, Dept. 47, Hiemer Papers.

75. National Archives, Washington (hereafter cited as NA), RG 338, File 000.5, Box 816.

76. Archivio Centrale dello Stato, Roma (Italian National Archives, Rome) (hereafter cited as ACS), and Archivio Storico-Diplomatico del Ministero degli Affari Esteri, Roma (Archives of the Italian Foreign Office, Rome) (hereafter cited as ASMAE).

77. BA-MA, BW 9/2127, confidential Verfassungsschutz report on the Stahlhelm, 20 October 1953.

78. Der Bundesbeauftragte für die Unterlagen des Staatssicherheitsdienstes der ehemaligen Deutschen Demokratischen Republik (Federal Commissioner for Documents of the State Security Service of the Former German Democratic Republic) (hereafter cited as BStU), HA IX/11; HA RHE; HA AF Pressemappe P.M-R; HA AF Pressemappe Objekt vor 1946.

Chapter 1: On the Italian Stage: Albert Kesselring

1. Albert Kesselring, *Soldat bis zum letzten Tag* (Bonn 1953), p. 11.

2. Kesselring traced his surname back to a minor Austrian aristocratic family Chezelrinch, whose members had "distinguished themselves as knights, patricians and priests in southern Germany and beyond, in Alsace and Switzerland"; see ibid. However, Peter Herde has so far been unable to verify the existence of this family in the course of his research; see Herde, "Albert Kesselring (1885–1960)," in Gesellschaft für Fränkische Geschichte (Franconian Historical Society), ed., *Fränkische Lebensbilder*, vol. 18 (Neustadt an der Aisch 2000), pp. 295–314, at p. 295.

3. Peter Herde, "Wolfgang Hagemann als Zeitzeuge und Zeuge im Kesselring-Prozess (April 25th, 1947)," in Hagen Keller, Werner Paravicini, and Wolfgang Schieder, eds., *Italia et Germania: Liber amicorum Arnold Esch* (Tübingen, Niethammer, 2001), pp. 51–112, at p. 55.

4. Herde, "Albert Kesselring," p. 295.

5. Ibid.

6. Kenneth Macksey, *Kesselring: The Making of the Luftwaffe* (London 1978), p. 18.

7. Herde, "Albert Kesselring," p. 296.

8. Archives of the Christian-Ernestinum-Gymnasium (secondary school) in Bayreuth, matriculation certificate for Albert Kesselring, 1904. My thanks to Professor Peter Herde and Dr. Rainer Trübsbach, Bayreuth, for referring me to this material.

9. Herde, "Albert Kesselring," p. 296.

10. Guido Kesselring studied medicine. The oldest brother, Georg, was of a "depressive constitution" and committed suicide at the age of twenty-one while studying law.

11. Macksey noted that, at the turn of the century, military or industrial careers were extremely popular for the sons of middle-class Bavarian families (see Macksey, *Kesselring*, p. 19), but he also claimed that Kesselring's parents were shocked by his choice of profession, since

they wanted him to pursue an academic career. However, given Kesselring's poor school reports, this assertion is questionable.

12. Kesselring, *Soldat*, p. 11. The latest edition of his memoirs includes a picture showing the four-year-old boy in uniform with a toy saber and fierce expression.

13. Munich War Archives, Kesselring personnel file No. OP 61536, application for leave submitted by Albert Kesselring, 1910.

14. Hans Rumschöttel, *Das bayerische Offizierskorps 1866–1914* (Berlin 1973), pp. 41ff.

15. Reinhard Stumpf, *Die Wehrmacht-Elite: Rang- und Herkunftsstruktur der deutschen Generale und Admirale 1933–1945* (Boppard 1982), p. xii.

16. Herde, "Albert Kesselring," p. 300.

17. Munich War Archives, personnel file, assessment dated 1 January 1909.

18. Munich War Archives, personnel file, assessment dated 1 January 1911: "He has great influence on his subordinates, and he is an understanding, calm and very successful instructor."

19. Herde, "Albert Kesselring," p. 298.

20. Munich War Archives, personnel file, assessment dated 1 January 1914.

21. Stumpf, *Wehrmacht-Elite*, p. 36. Three heavy artillery officers—Kesselring, Milch, and Robert Ritter v. Greim—switched to the Luftwaffe in 1933.

22. Macksey, *Kesselring*, p. 20.

23. Joachim Engelmann and Horst Scheibert, eds., *Deutsche Artillerie 1934–1945* (Limburg 1974), pp. 52f. However, see also Stumpf, *Wehrmacht-Elite*, p. 168n421.

24. Stumpf, *Wehrmacht-Elite*, p. 168.

25. Ibid., p. 12.

26. Herde, "Albert Kesselring," p. 296.

27. Alaric Searle, *Wehrmacht Generals, West German Society, and the Debate on Rearmament, 1949–1959* (Westport, CT, 2003), p. 19.

28. Munich War Archives, personnel file, assessments of Kesselring dated 1 January 1917 by Generalleutnant Kreppel, general in the heavy artillery. Also see Herde, "Albert Kesselring," p. 299.

29. Munich War Archives, personnel file, assessement dated 24 May 1917.

30. Macksey, *Kesselring*, p. 24.

31. Munich War Archives, personnel file, handwritten addendum to the assessment of Kesselring dated 24 May 1917, by Divisional Commander Wenninger, 29 May 1917.

32. Macksey, *Kesselring*, p. 25.

33. Herde, "Albert Kesselring," p. 299.

34. Franz Kurowski, *Generalfeldmarschall Albert Kesselring, Oberbefehlshaber an allen Fronten* (Berg am See 1985), p. 14.

35. Munich War Archives, personnel file, assessment by Seyler dated 10 August 1919.

36. Munich War Archives, personnel file, handwritten addendum by Brigade Commander von Zoellner dated 14 August 1919, to Seyler's assessment of Kesselring dated 10 August 1919.

37. Munich War Archives, personnel file, assessment by Seyler dated 10 August 1919.

38. Rudolf Absolon has calculated that the average time spent by an officer in a specific rank—for example, lieutenant colonel or colonel—was seven years. In Kesselring's case, this span was only two years: the rapidity of his advancement was thus above average. See Munich War Archives, service certificate for Albert Kesselring, 1 July 1952, and Absolon, *Die Wehrmacht im Dritten Reich*, vol. 6 (Boppard 1995), p. 481, diagram.

39. Kesselring, *Soldat*, pp. 18f.

40. Claus Guske, *Das politische Denken des Generals von Seeckt: Ein Beitrag zur Diskussion des Verhältnisses Seeckt—Reichswehr—Republik* (Berlin 1970), p. 270.

41. Ibid., p. 269.

42. Ibid., p. 270.

43. Ibid.

44. Ibid.

45. Kesselring, *Soldat*, p. 376.

46. Carl Dirks and Karl-Heinz Janssen, *Der Krieg der Generäle: Hitler als Werkzeug der Wehrmacht* (Berlin 1999), esp. pp. 11–33.

47. Staatsarchiv (State Archives) Nürnberg (hereafter cited as StA Nürnberg), IMT war crimes trial, A-310, interrogation of Kesselring by Kempner in front of the 1st Commission, dated 2 July 1946, p. 1763.

48. Dirks and Janssen, *Krieg*, p. 191.

49. Kesselring, *Soldat*, p. 19. In his 1952 memoirs, he painted a picture of a skeptic who was only convinced by the development of the military in his own professional area: "I avoided all personal contact with the National Socialist party until they became what you could call socially respectable in 1933. I was repelled by their behaviour on the street and their preference for march-pasts. . . . It was only when I assumed a leading position in the Aviation Ministry in October 1933 that I was impressed by the regime's single-minded approach, and the balance was tipped towards the more favorable impressions."

50. For a general perspective on this, see Searle, *Wehrmacht Generals*, p. 18.

51. Herde, "Albert Kesselring," p. 301.

52. Kesselring, *Soldat*, p. 27.

53. Ibid.

54. StA Nürnberg, IMT war crimes trials, A-310, interrogation of Kesselring by Kempner in front of the 1st Commission, dated 2 July 1947, p. 1774. A variation on this theme can also be found in his memoirs; see Kesselring, *Soldat*, p. 26.

55. The files on this are in the Bundesarchiv in Berlin-Lichterfelde, reference R 43 II (Reichskanzlei holdings, Dr. Lammers, grants), vols. 986a, 1092, 1565, and 1620. For general information, see Searle, *Wehrmacht Generals*, p. 19; Gerhard L. Weinberg, "Zur Dotation Hitlers an Generalfeldmarschall Ritter von Leeb," *MGM* 26 (1979): 97; and Gerd R. Ueberschär and Winfried Vogel, *Dienen und Verdienen: Hitlers Geschenke an seine Eliten* (Frankfurt 1999), p. 103.

56. StA Nürnberg, IMT war crimes trial, A-310, interrogation of Kesselring by Kempner in front of the 1st Commission, dated 2 July 1946, p. 1766.

57. Kesselring, *Soldat*, p. 27.

58. James S. Corum, "Stärken und Schwächen der Luftwaffe: Führungsqualitäten und Führung im Zweiten Weltkrieg," in Rolf-Dieter Müller and Hans-Erich Volkmann, eds., *Die Wehrmacht: Mythos und Realität* (Munich 1999), pp. 283–306, esp. pp. 284, 287, and 289.

59. Gerd F. Heuer, "Albert Kesselring: Luftflottenchef und Oberbefehlshaber an den grossen Fronten—Höchste Kommandostellen bis zum letzten Kriegstag," in Heuer, ed., *Die deutschen Generalfeldmarschälle und Grossadmirale 1939–1945*, 2nd ed. (Rastatt 1988), pp. 55–59, at p. 56.

60. The following passage was included in the first version of his 1953 memoirs, on p. 409 of the typescript. It was subsequently edited out, on the advice of former comrades (especially Röttiger): "Of far more concern than the successful Allied invasion was the

collapse of the German forces and civilians behind the battle lines in France. They proved by their actions and attitude that they had failed to understand the purpose of the war. They had neglected to prepare themselves for the impending battle for survival of the Volk." See BA-MA, Röttiger Papers N 422/4, p. 1.

61. Horst Boog, *Die deutsche Luftwaffenführung 1935–1945: Führungsprobleme, Spitzengliederung, Generalstabsausbildung* (Munich 1982), pp. 215 and 219.

62. Sam L. Lewis, "Albert Kesselring—Der Soldat als Manager," in Ronald Smelser and Enrico Syring, ed., *Die Militärelite des Dritten Reichs: 27 biographische Skizzen* (Berlin 1995), pp. 270–287, at p. 273. At that time, lighter aircraft were known colloquially as "flying Kesselrings."

63. Horst Boog, "Führungsdenken in der Luftwaffe im Zweiten Weltkrieg," in German Institute of Military History, ed., *Vorträge zur Militärgeschichte*, vol. 9 (Herford 1988), pp. 183–206, at p. 186.

64. Ibid., p. 183.

65. Horst Boog, "Der anglo-amerikanische strategische Luftkrieg über Europa und die deutsche Luftverteidigung," in Horst Boog, Werner Rahn, Reinhard Stumpf, and Bernd Wegner, eds., *Das deutsche Reich und der Zweite Weltkrieg*, vol. 6, *Der Globale Krieg: Die Ausweitung zum Weltkrieg und der Wechsel der Initiative 1941–1943* (Stuttgart 1990), pp. 429–565, at p. 437.

66. Jörg Friedrich, *Das Gesetz des Krieges: Das deutsche Heer in Russland 1941 bis 1945—Der Prozess gegen das Oberkommando der Wehrmacht* (Munich 1996), p. 720.

67. Kesselring, *Soldat*, p. 31.

68. Boog, "Führungsdenken," pp. 194 and 196.

69. Friedrich, *Gesetz*, p. 720.

70. Boog, *Deutsche Luftwaffenführung*, p. 516.

71. Kesselring, *Soldat*, p. 40.

72. Ibid., p. 219; Stumpf, *Wehrmacht-Elite*, p. 157. It appears that Milch attempted to expand his influence to the military arena following Wever's death. Stumpf pointed out that Milch's position was significantly stronger than Keitel's. One immediate consequence of Kesselring's resignation as chief of the General Staff was that the chief was no longer subordinate to the undersecretary of state.

73. Boog, *Deutsche Luftwaffenführung*, p. 512. Only Manfred v. Richthofen was credited with a similarly forceful leadership style.

74. Otto Ernst Moll, "Albert Kesselring, Soldat bis zum letzten Tag," in Gerd F. Heuer, ed., *Die deutschen Generalfeldmarschälle 1939–1945* (Rastatt 1988), pp. 61–71, at p. 64.

75. Herde, "Albert Kesselring," p. 297.

76. Stumpf, *Wehrmacht-Elite*, p. 65.

77. Ibid., p. 318.

78. Bibliothek für Zeitgeschichte (Library of Contemporary History) (hereafter cited as BfZ) Stuttgart, Sterz Collection, 59 160 A, Uffizi journal, Heinrich Voigtel of the staff of Observation Corps 71, entry dated 24 July 1944. The original telegram has not been preserved, since the war diaries for Army Group C are considered lost.

79. StA, IMT war crimes trial, A-310, interrogation of Kesselring by Kempner in front of the 1st Commission, dated 2 July 1946, p. 1775. Emphasis in the original.

80. Kesselring, *Soldat*, pp. 424f.

81. Friedrich Andrae, *Auch gegen Frauen und Kinder: Der Krieg der deutschen Wehrmacht gegen die Zivilbevölkerung in Italien 1943–1945* (Munich 1995), pp. 171f.; Gerhard

Schreiber, *Deutsche Kriegsverbrechen in Italien: Täter, Opfer, Strafverfolgung* (Munich 1996), pp. 164f.

82. Ulrich de Maizière, *In der Pflicht: Lebensbericht eines deutschen Soldaten im 20. Jahrhundert* (Herford 1989), pp. 105f.

83. Manfred Messerschmidt, "Die Wehrmacht: Vom Realitätsverlust zum Selbstbetrug," in Hans-Erich Volkmann, ed., *Ende des Dritten Reichs—Ende des Zweiten Weltkriegs* (Munich 1995), pp. 223–258, at p. 249.

84. Ernst August Bleibaum, Kesselring's ordnance officer, in the ARD (Arbeitsgemeinschaft der öffentlich-rechtlichen Rundfunkanstalten der Bundesrepublik Deutschland) documentary series "Soldaten für Hitler—Soldiers for Hitler," episode four, "Die Generäle—The Generals," first broadcast on 22 April 1998. I was involved in this television production and therefore had access to all the interviews in full. In the program's accompanying volume, Jürgen Engert, *Soldaten für Hitler* (Berlin 1998), see the chapter on Albert Kesselring, pp. 169–175. Surprisingly, this passage is missing from the interview with Bleibaum.

85. BA-MA, N 750/2, London Diary, p. 4. The so-called London Diary is not a real diary but a handwritten account composed by Kesselring during his detention in the London Cage prison in 1946. He himself referred to it as the "London Diary," and that term is used throughout the notes; there are no specific entry dates in the document.

86. Messerschmidt, "Wehrmacht," p. 254.

87. Wolfram Wette, *Die Wehrmacht: Feindbilder, Vernichtungskrieg, Legenden* (Darmstadt 2002), p. 192.

88. Dirks and Janssen, *Der Krieg der Generäle*, p. 191.

89. BA-MA, N 422/4, manuscript of Kesselring's memoirs, p. 410. In draft passages for the memoirs that were subsequently deleted, Kesselring wrote: "Once before (1918), as the English admitted, we gave up fighting one day too early, and thus had to accept the merciless dictates of Versailles."

90. Wette, *Wehrmacht*, p. 185.

91. BA-MA, RH 20-19/212, Supreme Army Command 19, appendixes to the War Journal, March 1945, Western Command, telegram to the Supreme Army Command 19, 22 March 1945.

92. Rudolf-Christoph Freiherr von Gersdorff, *Soldat im Untergang* (Frankfurt am Main 1977), pp. 176f. Gersdorff described the encounter as "the most shattering" he had ever had with a German field marshal, thus indicating that Kesselring's attitude was considered peculiar even in military circles.

93. Heinrich Schwendemann, "Strategie der Selbstvernichtung: Die Wehrmachtführung im 'Endkampf' um das 'Dritte Reich,'" in Rolf-Dieter Müller and Hans-Erich Volkmann, eds., *Die Wehrmacht: Mythos und Realität* (Munich 1999), pp. 224–244, at p. 243.

94. Wette, *Wehrmacht*, p. 192.

95. Herbert Kraus, "Karl Dönitz und das Ende des 'Dritten Reiches,'" in Hans-Erich Volkmann, ed., *Ende des Dritten Reichs—Ende des Zweiten Weltkriegs* (Munich 1995), pp. 1–24, at pp. 7f.

96. Georg Meyer, "Zur Situation der deutschen militärischen Führungsschicht im Vorfeld des westdeutschen Verteidigungsbeitrages 1945–1950/51," in Roland G. Foerster, ed., *Anfänge westdeutscher Sicherheitspolitik 1945–1956*, vol. 1, *Von der Kapitulation zum Pleven-Plan* (Munich 1982), pp. 577–736, at p. 581.

97. Ibid., p. 584.

98. Kesselring, *Soldat*, p. 300.

99. Georg Kreis, "Das Kriegsende in Norditalien 1945," *Schweizer Monatshefte* 65 (1985): 507–521, at p. 517; Bundesarchiv (Federal Archives at Koblenz) (hereafter cited as BA), Lindner Papers N 1245/45, typescript, "Das Kriegsende in Italien," by Heinrich von Vietinghoff-Scheel, 1950 (copy), 40 pages, at p. 24; and Peter Hattenkofer, "Das Kriegsende in Italien und seine historische Verarbeitung: Anmerkungen zu Kesselring, v. Vietinghoff und Röttiger," in Alessandro Massignani and Maurizio Dal Lago, eds., *La fine della guerra in Italia,* pp. 133–152, at p. 141.

100. BA-MA, Röttiger Papers N 422/4, letter from Kesselring to Röttiger, 24 March 1948: "I will not address the other issues; I have a firm view regarding certain matters, and even my current situation—which is more than lowly—has not changed that."

101. BA, Lindner Papers N 1245/45, typescript, "Das Kriegsende in Italien," p. 38.

102. BA-MA, N 750/2, London Diary, p. 3.

103. Ibid., p. 9.

104. BA-MA, N 750/3, Kesselring trial diary, entry dated 6 May 1947.

105. StA Nürnberg, IMT war crimes trials, A-333, examination of Kesselring by Kempner in front of the 1st Commission, dated 3 July 1946, pp. 2113 ("I regret every one of these incidents") and 2114.

106. Zentralen Stelle des Landesjustizverwaltungen zur Verfolgung von NS-Verbrechen in Ludwigsburg (hereafter cited as ZSL), JAG 260, statement by Kesselring in London dated 4 October 1946, report No. 1356 (b) (marked as Exhibit 3), 6 pages, at p. 6. (ZSL is the central office representing the state justice departments charged with prosecuting Nazi crimes; this archive recently became part of the Bundesarchiv and acquired a new "signature," BA-ZSL.)

107. Thomas Kühne, "Die Viktimisierungsfalle: Wehrmachtverbrechen, Geschichtswissenschaft und symbolische Ordnung des Militärs," in Michael Th. Greven and Oliver von Wrochem, eds., *Der Krieg in der Nachkriegszeit: Der Zweite Weltkrieg in Politik und Gesellschaft der Bundesrepublik* (Opladen 2000), pp. 183–196.

108. Ibid., p. 186.

109. Ibid.

110. Jörg Echternkamp, "Mit dem Krieg seinen Frieden schliessen—Wehrmacht und Weltkrieg in der Veteranenkultur 1945–1960," in Thomas Kühne, ed., *Von der Kriegskultur zur Friedenskultur? Zum Mentalitätswandel in Deutschland seit 1945* (Münster 2000), pp. 78–93, at p. 82.

111. Kühne, "Viktimisierungsfalle," p. 186.

112. Reinhard Stumpf, "Der Krieg im Mittelmeerraum 1942/1943: Die Operationen in Nordafrika und im mittleren Mittelmeer," in Horst Boog, Werner Rahn, Reinhard Stumpf, and Bernd Wegner, eds., *Das deutsche Reich und der Zweite Weltkrieg,* vol. 6, *Der Globale Krieg: Die Ausweitung zum Weltkrieg und der Wechsel der Initiative 1941–1943* (Stuttgart 1990), pp. 569–760, at p. 573.

113. Reinhard Stumpf, "Von der Achse Berlin–Rom zum Militärabkommen des Dreipaktes: Die Abfolge der Verträge 1936 bis 1942," in Horst Boog, Werner Rahn, Reinhard Stumpf, and Bernd Wegner, eds., *Das deutsche Reich und der Zweite Weltkrieg,* vol. 6, *Der Globale Krieg: Die Ausweitung zum Weltkrieg und der Wechsel der Initiative 1941–1943* (Stuttgart 1990), pp. 127–143. In this regard, see Kesselring's elucidations, in *Soldat,* pp. 140f.

114. German Federal Archives—Berlin Film Archives, Fehrbelliner Platz, *Wochenschau* reports on Kesselring, e.g., DW 618, DW 623, DW 688, and DW 708. During my research for the "Soldaten für Hitler" film project (episode 4, "Die Generäle—The Generals") for a television documentary, I was able to view *Wochenschau* reports on Kesselring.

115. The basic texts on the war in Italy are George F. Botjer, *Sideshow War: The Italian Campaign 1943–1945* (College Station, TX, 1996); Frederick William Deakin, *The Brutal Friendship: Hitler, Mussolini and the Fall of Italian Fascism* (London 1962); Lutz Klinkhammer, *Zwischen Bündnis und Besatzung: Das nationalsozialistische Deutschland und die Republik von Salò 1943–1945* (Tübingen 1993); Richard Lamb, *War in Italy 1943–1945: A Brutal Story* (New York 1994); Gerhard Schreiber, *Deutsche Kriegsverbrechen in Italien: Täter, Opfer, Strafverfolgung* (Munich 1996); and Michael Wedekind, *Nationalsozialistische Besatzungs- und Annexionspolitik in Norditaliern, 1943–1945* (Munich 2003).

116. Gerhard Schreiber, *Die italienischen Militärinternierte im deutschen Machtbereich 1943–1945* (Munich 1990), p. 91.

117. Josef Schröder, *Italiens Kriegsaustritt 1943: Die deutschen Gegenmassnahmen im italienischen Raum, Fall "Alarich" und "Achse,"* (Göttingen 1969), p. 11; Renzo DeFelice, *Mussolini L'Alleato,* (Rome 1995), vol. I, bk. 2, pp. 959–1089; Klinkhammer, *Zwischen Bündnis,* pp. 28f.; Erich Kuby, *Verrat auf Deutsch: Wie das deutsche Reich Italien ruinierte* (Hamburg 1982), pp. 165–179; Friedrich Karl von Plehwe, *Schicksalsstunden in Rom: Ende eines Bündnisses* (Berlin 1967), pp. 14–58; Jens Petersen, "Deutschland und der Zusammenbruch des Faschismus in Italien im Sommer 1943," in *MGM* 37 (1985): 51–69, at p. 51; and Schreiber, *Italienischen Militärinternierte,* pp. 38–45. For extensive information on the Axis alliance, see Jens Petersen, *Hitler–Mussolini: Die Entstehung der Achse Berlin–Rom 1933–1936* (Tübingen 1973).

118. Schreiber, *Deutsche Kriegsverbrechen,* p. 39.

119. Percy E. Schramm, ed., *War Journal of the Wehrmacht High Command, Wehrmacht General Staff,* vol. 3, *1 January 1943 to 31 December 1943,* compiled and annotated by Walther Hubatsch (Frankfurt am Main 1963), pp. 1460f., Führer's order dated 9 September 1943.

120. Wolfgang Schieder, "Das faschistische Italien," in Norbert Frei and Hermann Kling, eds., *Der Nationalsozialistische Krieg* (Frankfurt 1990), pp. 48–61, at p. 48.

121. Schreiber, *Deutsche Kriegsverbrechen,* p. 87.

122. Rudolf Rahn, *Ruheloses Leben: Aufzeichnungen und Erinnerungen* (Düsseldorf 1949), p. 234.

123. Cited in Schreiber, *Italienischen Militärinternierte,* p. 100.

124. B. H. Liddell Hart, ed., *The Rommel Papers* (London 1953), p. 445, Rommel's entry dated 9 September 1943; Schreiber, *Italienischen Militärinternierte,* p. 100.

125. Eugen Dollmann, *Dolmetscher der Diktatoren* (Bayreuth 1963), p. 187.

126. Pietro Torneer, "Le due faccie del Feldmaresciallo Albert Kesselring," *La Resistenza Breciana: Rassegna di studi e documenti* 31 (April 2000): 48–57, at p. 51.

127. Schreiber, *Deutsche Kriegsverbrechen,* p. 41.

128. Gerhard Schreiber, "Il settore occidentale della linea Gotica," *Storia e Memoria* 3, no. 1 (1994): 51–75, at p. 52.

129. Schreiber, *Deutsche Kriegsverbrechen,* pp. 41 and 43f.

130. Ibid., p. 100.

131. Ibid., p. 55.

132. Ibid., pp. 43f.

133. Gerhard Schreiber, *La vendetta tedesca, 1943–1945: Le rappresaglie naziste in Italia* (Milan 2000), pp. 72–82.

134. Gerhard Schreiber, "Deutsche Kriegsverbrechen gegenüber Italienern," in Wolfram Wette and Gerd R. Ueberschär, eds., *Kriegsverbrechen im 20. Jahrhundert* (Darmstadt 2001), pp. 222–234, at p. 223.

135. Torneer, "Le due faccie del Feldmaresciallo Albert Kesselring," p. 53.

136. Schreiber, *Deutsche Kriegsverbrechen*, pp. 48 and 61.

137. Ibid., p. 91.

138. See also Gabriele Hammermann, *Zwangsarbeit für den "Verbündeten": Die Arbeits- und Lebensbedingungen der italienischen Militärinternierten in Deutschland 1943–1945* (Tübingen 2002).

139. Bradley F. Smith and Elena Agarossi, *Unternehmen Sonnenaufgang: Das Kriegsende in Italien* (Cologne 1981), pp. 45ff.

140. Dickson concluded that "the Italian campaign was merely the latest lesson in the art of political and military compromise." See Paul D. Dickson, ed., *The Beginning of the End* (Waterloo, IA, 1995), p. 68.

141. Dominick Graham and Shelford Bidwell, *Coalitions, Politicians and Generals* (London 1993).

142. Katriel Ben Arie, *Die Schlacht bei Monte Cassino 1944* (Freiburg 1985), p. 13.

143. Ibid., p. 14.

144. Dickson, *Beginning of the End*, pp. 70f.

145. Nigel Nicolson, *Alex: The Life of Field Marshal Earl Alexander of Tunis* (London 1973), p. 255.

146. Shelford Bidwell, "Kesselring," in Corelli Barnett, ed., *Hitler's Generals* (London 1989), pp. 265–289, at p. 281.

147. This assessment can undoubtedly be traced back to the British field marshal Harold Alexander, Kesselring's opponent on the battlefield, who praised the German field marshal's crisis-management skills. Writing about Kesselring in 1943, Alexander had admiringly stated that the German was "always quicker" than the Allies—quicker in obtaining supplies, quicker in regrouping his troops, and quicker in reaching the correct decisions. Alexander's depiction was and is considered high praise in military circles (see Nicolson, *Alex*). A contemporaneous American secret service report also noted that Kesselring was a "competent expert" who deployed his staff well and "delegated responsibility correctly." The report stated that Kesselring was a "specialist" who seized on the great opportunity presented by the Africa campaign: "Certainly a ruthless man, with little doubt as to his ability" (see NA, Records of Army Staff, RG 319, Investigative Report Repository, Counter Intelligence file, XE 07 64 78, Albert Kesselring, probably 1944). See also Macksey, *Kesselring*, pp. 179ff.

148. The power struggle between the two rival field marshals, with both fighting for supreme command in Italy, was not without intrigue. Initially, it was planned that Rommel—who had more strategic experience—would assume supreme command in Italy. Kesselring, whom Hitler already considered suspect because of his allegedly pro-Italian attitude, was to be posted to Norway (see Torneer, "Le due faccie del Feldmaresciallo Albert Kesselring," p. 51). It has been said that Kesselring then sought to resign. Apparently, General Karl Wolff intervened with the Führer's headquarters at that point, stating that Kesselring had to remain in Italy to maintain control of the situation and ensure that Germany's former allies were not incited to revolt (see Dollmann, *Dolmetscher*, p. 187). Dollmann claimed that Wolff denigrated Rommel as "politically unreliable," thus ensuring that he was posted to the western front. This version is also confirmed by other sources to be found in the BA-MA, as Dr. Gerhard Schreiber confirmed in a telephone conversation with me on 27 July 2001.

149. Schreiber, *Deutsche Kriegsverbrechen*, p. 61.

150. Klinkhammer, *Zwischen Bündnis*, p. 69.

151. Danilo Veneruso, *L'Italia fascista 1922–1945* (Bologna 1981), p. 440.

152. Deakin, *Brutal Friendship*, p. 636.

153. Renzo DeFelice, *Breve Storia del Fascismo* (Milan 2000), p. 115.

154. Walter Rauscher, *Hitler und Mussolini: Macht, Krieg und Terror* (Graz 2001), pp. 533ff.

155. Giorgio Bocca, *La Repubblica di Mussolini* (Milan 1994), p. 42.

156. Lutz Klinkhammer, "Grundlinien nationalsozialistischer Besatzungspolitik in Frankreich, Jugoslawien und Italien," in Christof Dipper, Rainer Hudemann, and Jens Petersen, eds., *Faschismus und Faschismen im Vergleich: Wolfgang Schieder zum 60. Geburtstag* (Cologne 1998), pp. 196 and 204f.

157. Klinkhammer, *Zwischen Bündnis*, p. 69.

158. Deakin, *Brutal Friendship*, p. 746, quotes from BA-MA, RS 4/1121, papers on "Der deutsche General beim Hauptquartier der italienischen Wehrmacht," SS-Standarte Kurt Eggers, p. 322. Letter from the Obersturmführer to the SS Commandant of Görz Province dated 20 September 1944, regarding secondment of the Italian Lance Corporals P. P. and B. Z. to the SS, Reason: "Since these two Italians would immediately desert if one were to forcibly return them to the Italian division. . . . In the interests of the total war, it would be . . . better for them to serve in my unit, where their behaviour is beyond reproach."

159. Schreiber, *Deutsche Kriegsverbrechen*, p. 228.

160. Ibid.

161. Rauscher, *Hitler und Mussolini*, p. 537.

162. BA-MA, N 431/935, Friedrich-Constans Seifarth, "Die deutsche Militärverwaltung in (Mittel-)Italien," typescript, 1947.

163. Lutz Klinkhammer, "Die Abteilung 'Kunstschutz' der deutschen Militärverwaltung in Italien 1943–1945," *QFIAB* 72 (1992): 483–549, at p. 489.

164. Ernst Kubin, *Raub oder Schutz? Der deutsche militärische Kunstschutz in Italien* (Graz 1994), p. 103.

165. Ibid., p. 106.

166. Ibid., p. 108.

167. Rodolfo Siviero, *L'arte e il Nazismo: Esodo e ritorno delle opere d'arte italiane 1938–1963* (Florence 1984), pp. 28f.

168. Kubin, *Raub oder Schutz*, pp. 102f.; Klinkhammer, "Abteilung 'Kunstschutz,'" p. 592.

169. Klinkhammer, "Abteilung 'Kunstschutz,'" p. 542.

170. Ibid., p. 494. Among other incidents, marauding German soldiers burned down the State Archive stacks in Naples in 1943.

171. Kubin, *Raub oder Schutz*. On page 102, Kubin cited the U.S. "Report on German Kunstschutz (MFA&A) in Italy between 1943 and 1945," 30 June 1945.

172. Kubin, *Raub oder Schutz*, p. 111.

173. Herde, "Albert Kesselring," p. 53.

174. Kubin, *Raub oder Schutz*, p. 102.

175. Lutz Klinkhammer, *Stragi naziste in Italia* (Rome 1997), p. 8.

176. Giorgio Bocca, *Storia dell'Italia partigiana, Settembre 1943–Maggio 1945* (Bari 1966), pp. 17f. Although Bocca described the choice between rebellion and accommodation in emotional terms, he differentiated between young fighters and experienced anti-Fascists who were returning to Italy from exile in large numbers in order to fight in the Resistenza. This personal decision was described at length by Silvio Bertoldi, in *Salò: Vita e morte della RSI* (Milan 1976), pp. 77 f.; Veneruso, *L'Italia fascista*, pp. 435f., primarily addressed the decision by soldiers to join the partisans; and Klinkhammer, *Zwischen Bündnis*, p. 424, established

a connection between disarmament and capture of the Italian army, on the one hand, and the growth of the partisan movement in reaction to this, on the other hand.

177. Aurelio Lepre, *La Storia della repubblica di Mussolini: Salò—Il tempo dell'odio e della violenza* (Milan 1999), p. 311.

178. Cited in ibid., p. 3.

179. Gianni Oliva, *I vinti e i liberati: 8 Settembre 1943–25 Aprile 1945* (Milan 1994), p. 165.

180. The standard histories of the Resistenza were published as early as the 1970s, including Guido Quazza's *Resistenza e storia d' Italia: Problemi e ipotesi di ricerca,* 3rd ed. (Milan 1978), which traced the origins of Resistenza fighters and subsequent politicians, and Armando Vandagnini's *Gli anni della lotta: Guerra, Resistenza, Autonomia 1940–1948* (Trient 1978).

181. Bocca, *Storia dell'Italia partigiana,* p. 34.

182. Oliva, *Vinti,* pp. 161ff.

183. Bocca, *Storia dell'Italia partigiana,* p. 15. They included Ivanoe Bonomi, Alcide De Gasperi, Ettore Casati, Mauro Scoccimarro, Pietro Nenni, and Ugo La Malfa.

184. Ibid., p. 16.

185. Georg Kreis, "Das Kriegsende in Norditalien," *Schweizer Monatshefte* 6, no. 65 (1985): 514.

186. Gerhard Schreiber, "Die Irregulären: Guerilla, Partisanen und die Wandlungen des Krieges seit dem 18. Jahrhundert. Eine Einführung," in Bernd Bonwetsch, ed., *Partisanenkrieg und Volkskrieg: Zur Revolutionierung des Krieges im 20. Jahrhundert* (Göttingen 1985), pp. 9–35, at p. 25.

187. Schreiber, "Die Irregulären," p. 21.

188. Ibid., p. 23.

189. This term was first used by Claudio Pavone, in *Una guerra civile: Saggio sulla moralità nella Resistenza* (Turin 1991).

190. Klinkhammer, *Zwischen Bündnis,* p. 117.

191. Ibid., pp. 5–17.

192. See Kerstin Schmelzer, "Totaler Krieg auf italienisch? Die deutsche Auslandspropaganda in Italien 1943–1944" (master's thesis, University of Freiburg, 1995). Foreign propaganda was under the aegis of the Reich Foreign Office, rather than that of Joseph Goebbels's Propaganda Ministry. According to Joachim von Ribbentrop's instructions, the Italian people received filtered news, and they were notified of their German ally's friendly intentions through posters, brochures, and flyers that were encountered everywhere in daily life; moreoever, they were monitored by German spies. In addition to this foreign propaganda, the staff of the press attaché's office in the German embassy (which was charged with censoring the Fascist press), the Wehrmacht propaganda units, the Todt organization, the Sauckel staff, and the Italian Ministero per la Cultura Popolare (Ministry of Popular Culture, MINCULPOP) attempted to generate acceptance of the German measures (recruiting labor for Germany, compulsory armaments tasks, etc.) and to promote support for the various steps undertaken by the German military government in central Italy.

193. The best overview can be found in Ben Arie, *Schlacht bei Monte Cassino.* In all, 20,047 Germans are buried in the Cassino military cemetery alone. According to the German War Graves Commission, the Wehrmacht lost a total of 107,276 men in Italy between the summer of 1943 and the end of the war (quoted from *Der Neue Tag—Weiden,* 23–24 October 1993, "Montecassino, ein Symbol des Friedens, Bericht der deutschen Kriegsgräberfürsorge," by Gustav Kaiser).

194. Klinkhammer, *Stragi,* pp. 16f.

195. ZSL Ludwigsburg, JAG 260, Kesselring trial, Exhibit 2: "Voluntary statement by the Prisoner of War LD 1573 Generalfeldmarschall Albert Kesselring. Concerning the guerrilla warfare in Italy from 1943 to 1945," 4 October 1946, pp. 2f.

196. Ibid.

197. Gerhard Schreiber, "Partisanenkrieg und Kriegsverbrechen der Wehrmacht in Italien 1943–1945," in Ahlrich Meyer, ed., *Repression und Kriegsverbrechen: Die Bekämpfung von Widerstands- und Partisanenbewegungen gegen die deutsche Besatzung in West- und Südeuropa* (Berlin 1997), p. 114.

198. Ibid., p. 106.

199. Klinkhammer, *Stragi*, p. 21.

200. Walther Hubatsch, ed., *Hitler's Orders Governing the Conduct of War: Dokumente des Oberkommandos der Wehrmacht* (Koblenz 1983), pp. 201–206. "Operational areas" were always understood by the Wehrmacht to refer to a part of the war zone in which the army was operating. The operational areas were divided into "army areas," which in turn were divided into "combat zones" and "rear echelon army zones."

201. Schreiber, "Partisanenkrieg," p. 95.

202. Militärgeschichtliches Forschungsamt, ed., *Kriegstagebuch der Seekriegsleitung 1939–1945* [War Journal of the SKL—Marines Diary], vol. 53, ed. Werner Rahn and Gerhard Schreiber (Berlin 1994), January 1944, p. 330.

203. Percy Ernst Schramm, ed., *Kriegstagebuch des Oberkommandos der Wehrmacht* (Wehrmachtführungsstab) [War Journal of the Wehrmacht High Command], vol. 4 (Frankfurt am Main 1961), 1 January 1944 to 22 May 1945, p. 486.

204. BA-MA, C-032, Albert Kesselring, "Der Krieg hinter der Front: Der Bandenkrieg," a study written for the Historical Division around 1948, p. 16.

205. Schreiber, "Partisanenkreig," p. 98.

206. Carlo Gentile, "'Politische Soldaten': Die 16. SS-Panzer-Grenadier-Division 'Reichsführer-SS' in Italien 1944," *QFIAB* 81 (2001): 529–561, at p. 557.

207. See, for example, the daily report on the massacre of Sant'Anna di Stazzema, which spoke of 290 partisans killed in battle when, in fact, 560 women and children had been killed, in BA-MA, RH 20–14/46, Daily Report A.O.K. 14, Ia Nr. 4488/44 g.Kdos, 14 August 1944; also Schreiber, *Deutsche Kriegsverbrechen*, p. 203.

208. BA-MA, N 431/931, letter from Beelitz to Laternser, 23 January 1949.

209. Wette, *Wehrmacht*, p. 200.

210. BA-MA, RH 31 VI/8, Abt. Ia, AZ II/26, Nr. 6994/44, secret, p. 272, activity report by the First Officer of the General Staff (Ia) of the commander-in-chief, South-Western Command, 13 April 1944.

211. BA-MA, N 431/931, order governing responsibility for antipartisan warfare in Italy, 1 May 1944; also in N 422/15, p. 42, order issued by Kesselring governing responsibility for antipartisan warfare in Italy.

212. The Ic was the staff officer responsible for gathering intelligence and preparing a picture of the enemy's situation.

213. Charles F. Delzell, *Mussolini's Enemies: The Italian Anti-Fascist Resistance* (Princeton, NJ, 1961), p. 403.

214. BA-MA, N 422/15, p. 38, Kesselring's order dated 17 June 1944; also in BA-MA, RH 31 VI/10, commander-in-chief, South-Western Command/Ia T Nr. 0402/44gKdos dated 17 June 1944, Annex Z, War journal/plenipotentiary general 20 June 1944, cited and annotated in Schreiber, *Deutsche Kriegsverbrechen*, p. 102.

215. In this regard, Beelitz—at that time chief of operations on Kesselring's staff—noted

that he himself tried unsuccessfully to dissuade Kesselring from using this wording (my interview with Beelitz in Stuttgart on 29 October 1998). Beelitz explained that "it was in Kesselring's nature to always seek to assume responsibility for everything and everyone, so that his subordinates could execute their orders with as few restrictions as possible." In this case, however, Beelitz stated that "it was already clear then that Kesselring had exceeded the mark and thus rendered himself vulnerable to attack."

216. BA-MA, WFSt/Op (N), Head/Wehrmacht High Command No. 004879/42 gKdos, 16 December 1942.

217. Schreiber, *Deutsche Kriegsverbrechen,* p. 97.

218. Andrae, *Auch gegen Frauen und Kinder,* p. 157.

219. Gerhard Schreiber, "Deutsche Kriegsverbrechen in Italien," pp. 222–234, at p. 224.

220. See, for example, General Lemelsen's statement that he issued a supplementary order to mitigate that issued by Kesselring (BA-MA, N 431/305, affidavit by Lemelsen, 25 June 1946).

221. BA-MA, C-032, Albert Kesselring, "Der Krieg hinter der Front," p. 18.

222. BA-MA, N 422/15, S. 37, order issued by Kesselring on 1 July 1944.

223. In this regard, see Omer Bartov, *Hitler's Wehrmacht* (Hamburg 1995), pp. 94f.

224. PRO/TNA, Kew, WO 311/28, report from GHQ to the War Office regarding German war crimes in Italy, dated 5 October 1945, p. 11.

225. Ibid., p. 15.

226. Ibid.

227. BA-MA, N 431/305, affidavit by Lemelsen, 25 June 1946, p. 4.

228. BA-MA, N 431/870, statement by Major Josef Strauch, 21 August 1946, p. 12.

229. Schreiber, *Deutsche Kriegsverbrechen,* p. 98.

230. Ibid., p. 94.

231. Bartov, *Hitler's Wehrmacht,* p. 156.

232. Andrae, *Auch gegen Frauen und Kinder,* p. 158; Schreiber, *Deutsche Kriegsverbrechen,* p. 109.

233. BA-MA, N 422/15, pp. 35f., edict issued by Kesselring on 21 August 1944.

234. Bartov, *Hitler's Wehrmacht,* p. 97.

235. PRO/TNA, Kew, WO 311/28, report, p. 5.

236. BA-MA, N 422/15, p. 34, edict issued by Kesselring on 24 September 1944.

237. BA-MA, N 431/870, statement by Major Josef Strauch, 21 August 1946, p. 12. The military judges had merely conducted "friendly and superficial enquiries," as Major Strauch stated in court with regard to the inconclusive investigations into the massacre at Fucecchio (see Schreiber, *Deutsche Kriegsverbrechen,* p. 187).

238. This is also the view of Raymond Ruch, in "Krieg gegen die Zivilbevölkerung: Die deutsche Partisanenbekämpfung in der Sowjetunion und in Italien 1941–1945," manuscript, Bern 2003, p. 100.

239. For more on the partisan policy from the autumn of 1944, see Schreiber, "Partisanenkrieg," pp. 116ff. The files on Vietinghoff's partisan policy are available in PRO/TNA, Kew, WO 310/126.

240. Schreiber, *Deutsche Kriegsverbrechen,* p. 100.

241. Cited in Schreiber, "Partisanenkrieg," pp. 98f.

242. Schreiber, "Partisanenkrieg," p. 99.

243. Gentile, "Politische Soldaten," p. 353.

244. Joachim Staron, *Fosse Ardeatine und Marzabotto: Deutsche Kriegsverbrechen und Resistenza* (Paderborn 2002), p. 12. This circumstance is exemplified by the Marzabotto case, in respect to which the figure of 1,836 casualties was adjusted downward to 778.

245. Klinkhammer, *Stragi*, p. 15. The Italian literature assumes a figure of around 10,000 civilian casualties; see Enzo Colotti and Tristano Matta, "Rappresaglie, stragi, eccidi," in R. Sandri and F. Sassi, eds., *Dizionario della Resistenza: Storia e geografia della liberazione* (Turin 2000), pp. 254–267; Giorgio Rochat, "Una ricerca impossibile: Le perdite italiane nella seconda guerra mondiale," *Italia contemporanea* 201 (1995): pp. 688–700, at p. 697. Schreiber, *Deutsche Kriegsverbrechen*, p. 217, has put the number of civilian casualties at 16,000, including 7,400 Jews.

246. StA Nürnberg, IMT war crimes trials, A-333, examination of Kesselring, p. 2088.

247. Lutz Klinkhammer, "Der Partisanenkrieg der Wehrmacht 1941–1944," in Rolf-Dieter Müller and Hans-Erich Volkmann, eds., *Die Wehrmacht: Mythos und Realität* (Munich 1999), pp. 815–836, at p. 835.

248. Klinkhammer and Lingen are of this view, but Wette and Schreiber and most recently Ruch see the antipartisan war as a milder version of the war of destruction waged in the East.

249. Cited in Klinkhammer, *Stragi*, p. 20.

250. Ibid.

251. Klinkhammer, "Partisanenkrieg," p. 835.

252. Klinkhammer, *Stragi*, p. 97.

253. Ibid., pp. 73f.

254. Gentile, "Politische Soldaten," pp. 550f.

255. Ibid., p. 556.

256. Klinkhammer, *Stragi*, p. x.

257. Thomas Kühne, "Zwischen Vernichtungskrieg und Freizeitgesellschaft: Die Veteranenkultur in Deutschland (1945–1995)," in Klaus Naumann, ed., *Nachkrieg in Deutschland* (Hamburg 2001), pp. 90–113, at p. 101.

258. This development was also noted by Schreiber, in "Deutsche Kriegsverbrechen in Italien," p. 229.

259. Thomas Kühne, "Der nationalsozialistische Vernichtungskrieg und die 'ganz normalen' Deutschen: Forschungsprobleme und Forschungstendenzen der Gesellschaftsgeschichte des Zweiten Weltkriegs," pt. 1, *Archiv für Sozialgeschichte* 39 (1999): 580–663, 603–605.

260. Thomas Kühne, "Hitlers Soldaten und der Mythos der Kameradschaft," *Archiv für Sozialgeschichte* 38 (1998): 165–189, at p. 180.

261. Cited in ibid., p. 186.

262. The text is included in Gerd R. Ueberschär and Wolfram Wette, eds., *Der deutsche Überfall auf die Sowjetunion: "Unternehmen Barbarossa" 1941* (Frankfurt am Main 1991), pp. 251–254; Christian Streit, *Keine Kameraden: Die Wehrmacht und die sowjetischen Kriegsgefangenen 1941–1945* (Bonn 1997), pp. 33–44.

263. Andrae, *Auch gegen Frauen und Kinder*, p. 167.

264. Kühne, "Hitlers Soldaten," p. 186.

265. Ibid., p. 180.

266. Klaus Roghmann and Rolf Ziegler, "Militärsoziologie," in René König, ed., *Handbuch der empirischen Sozialforschung*, vol. 9, *Organisation Militär*, 2nd ed. (Stuttgart 1977), p. 174.

267. Kühne, "Hitlers Soldaten," p. 189.

268. Bartov, *Hitler's Wehrmacht*, p. 95.

269. Ibid., p. 112.

270. Andrae, in *Auch gegen Frauen und Kinder*, p. 158, cited examples of the increase in looting and rape during 1944.

271. Schreiber, *Deutsche Kriegsverbrechen*, p. 94.

272. BA-MA, RH 20–14/50, Army High Command 14, annexes to war journal No. 5, 1 October–31 December 1944, vol. 1, Annex 1033. The commander-in-chief of the Fourteenth Army, Lemelsen, Ia No. 6666/44 secret, A.H.Qu., 11 October 1944, ref. antipartisan warfare.

273. StA Nürnberg, IMT war crimes trials, A-333, examination of Kesselring, p. 2088.

274. Ibid., p. 2094.

275. Ibid., p. 2096.

276. Ibid., p. 2089.

277. Ibid., p. 2113.

278. Ibid., p. 2114.

279. ZSL, JAG 260, statement by Kesselring in London dated 4 October 1946, report no. 1351 (b), p. 16.

280. StA, IMT war crimes trials, A-333, examination of Kesselring, p. 2092.

281. ZSL, JAG 260, statement by Kesselring in London dated 4 October 1946, report no. 1351 (b) (marked as Exhibit 2), 17 pages, at p. 6.

282. Ibid., p. 2.

283. Ibid., p. 9.

284. BA-MA, N 431/890, proceedings of 17 February 1947, p. 20. The subsequent British trial prosecutor, Colonel Richard Halse, who used Kesselring's London statement as the basis for his opening address, commented on it by pointing out that these "few officers" had, after all, conjured up eighteen incidents forming the subject of the day's court proceedings, together with a further nine incidents complained of by Mussolini, which were therefore already known at the time, without the Germans launching any criminal prosecution.

285. ZSL, JAG 260, statement by Kesselring in London dated 4 October 1946, report no. 1356 (b) (marked as Exhibit 3), and report no. 1357 (b) (marked as Exhibit 4).

286. Ibid., p. 6; see also BA-MA, N 431/983, list prepared by Kesselring for Laternser, undated.

287. ZSL, JAG 260, statement by Kesselring in London dated 4 October 1946, report no. 1356 (b).

288. BA-MA, N 431/888, notes made by Kesselring for Laternser on Halse's opening statement, probably 17 February 1947.

289. BA-MA, N 431/878, notes by Kesselring regarding the cross-examination of Keller, 20–21 December 1947.

290. BA-MA, N 750/2, London Diary, p. 41.

291. Richard Raiber, "Generalfeldmarschall Kesselring, Via Rasella, and the 'Ginny Mission,'" *MGM* 56 (1997): 69–106.

292. Ibid., p. 101.

293. Ibid., p. 85. See also Kerstin von Lingen, "Partisanenkrieg und Wehrmachtjustiz am Beispiel: Italien 1943–1945," *Zeitschrift für Genozidforschung* 2 (2007): 8–40, at p. 40.

294. General Dostler was shot immediately following his trial in December 1945, which caused great consternation among German officers in the POW camps.

295. A detailed description of the command relationships in Rome and the different ver-

sions of the attack and subsequent punishment measures can be found in Steffen Prauser, "Mord in Rom? Der Anschlag in der via Rasella und die deutsche Vergeltung in den Fosse Ardeatine im März 1944," *VfZ* 50 (2002): 269–301; Staron, *Fosse Ardeatine*, pp. 35–70; Klinkhammer, *Stragi*, pp. 3–15; and Helmut Goetz, "Das Attentat in Rom und die Fosse Ardeatine (1944): Eine vorläufige Bilanz," *Innsbrucker Historische Studien* 6 (1983): 161–178. A more literary, but precise, description can be found in Robert Katz, *Mord in Rom* (Munich 1968), and Allessandro Portelli, *L'ordine è già stato eseguito* (Rome 1999).

296. Thus, for example, when reporting to Laternser about the events in the Fosse Ardeatine, Hans Eberhardt wrote—almost as an aside—that "the war journal, which at that time was kept by Lieutenant Klaus Kunkel, was lost as a result of enemy action during the retreat over the Po in April 1945. It can therefore no longer be used as evidence" (see BA-MA, N 431/931, Eberhardt to Laternser, 6 December 1948). In 1948, Laternser put all his faith in finding the missing war journals in order to verify the second command issued by Hitler; see chapter 3.

297. Giorgio Amendola, *Lettere a Milano* (Rome 1973); Rosario Bentivegna, *Achtung, Banditen!* (Milan 1983); Ivanoe Bonomi, *Diario di un anno: 2 giugnio 1943–10 giugnio 1944* (Milan 1947); Eugen Dollmann, *Roma nazista* (Milan 1951); Kesselring, *Soldat*; Eitel Friedrich Moellhausen, *Die gebrochene Achse* (Alfeld 1949); Rudolf Rahn, *Ruheloses Leben: Aufzeichnungen und Erinnerungen* (Düsseldorf 1949); and Siegfried Westphal, *Erinnerungen* (Mainz 1975).

298. The witness statements issued immediately after the individuals concerned were taken prisoner differ from those made specifically in preparation for the Rome trial of Mackensen and Mältzer, as well as those for the Kesselring trial. Therefore, the statements by Kesselring, Mackensen, Mältzer, and Kappler—all of whom were subsequently charged—are of particular interest.

299. The latest synthesis of all known witness statements and documents concerning the command sequence can be found in Prauser, "Mord," pp. 288f.

300. GAP and the Garibaldi formations were a Communist grouping assigned responsibility for carrying out particularly difficult resistance operations and attacks. There were fourteen central GAPs in Rome, commanded by nine men and five women, each of which could rely on a small group of helpers.

301. In his memoirs, Westphal mentioned a higher figure, but this has not been confirmed by historians (see Westphal, *Erinnerungen*, p. 257). He referred to 42 fatalities that had "deliberately" not been reported in order to avoid "further feeding the dictator's rage."

302. Laternser referred to 10 fatalities in his address to the court. See Hans Laternser, *Verteidigung deutscher Soldaten* (Bonn 1950), p. 52.

303. The different versions are specified by Staron, *Fosse Ardeatine*, p. 37.

304. Prauser, "Mord," pp. 279f.

305. Dollmann, *Roma nazista*, p. 241; Moellhausen, *Gebrochene Achse*, pp. 134f.

306. Prauser, "Mord," pp. 287f.

307. See Susanne Hein, "Der Fall Priebke und die italienische Strafjustiz," *Deutsche Richter-Zeitung* 479 (1996): 476–484; Walter Leszl, *Priebke: Anatomia di un processo* (Rome 1997).

308. Klinkhammer, *Stragi*, p. 9.

309. Ibid., p. 10.

310. ZSL, JAG 294, Rome trial, fifth trial day, testimony by Mackensen, p. 19; Dortmund Public Prosecutor's Office, Reg. 48360 d, Kappler's statement when examined on 21 July

1947 in Rome, p. 12 (I am indebted to Joachim Staron for referring me to this source); Laternser, *Verteidigung*, p. 56.

311. Manfred Bäumler's flight log, private papers of Peter Bäumler and family, Waiblingen, entry dated 22 March 1944: Munich (dep. 10.30 h) to Villafranca (arr. 11.23 h), Villafranca (dep. 17.15 h) to Novi Ligure (arr. 17.40 h). Bäumler's next entry regarding flights with the "*Feldm.*" was not made until 23 March, which buttresses the evidence provided by Raiber showing that Kesselring traveled between the different inspection points by car. Bäumler further noted: 25 March 1944: Florence (dep. 7.15 h) to Forlì (arr. 7.35 h) and Forlì (dep. 17.45 h) to Foligno (arr. 18.15 h). The files of Verona airbase (see BA-MA, RL 21/212) include an entry dated 22 March 1944 showing that Kesselring arrived from Munich at 11.25 and left for Foligno at 17.15. These flight times correspond precisely to the information provided by Bäumler. However, the war journal clerk in Villafranca (near Verona) stated that Kesselring had left for Foligno, the airport closest to the Monte Soratte command post. Given that the departure time corresponds precisely, this error could merely be due to inattention on the part of the journal clerk.

312. Westphal, *Erinnerungen*, p. 255, and Edmund Theil, *Kampf um Italien: Von Sizilien bis Tirol 1943–1945* (Munich 1983), p. 247.

313. Laternser, *Verteidigung*, p. 63.

314. Klinkhammer, *Stragi*, p. 10.

315. BA-MA, AOK 10, war journal—appendixes to war journal no. 5, telephone conversation between the head of the Tenth Army, Böhm, and Westphal on the evening of 23 March 1944.

316. During Kappler's trial, this assertion was also confirmed by witnesses who had worked closely with him, such as Carl Schütz, who was tasked with carrying out the execution; reproduced in Rudolf Aschenauer, *Der Fall Herbert Kappler: Ein Plädoyer für Recht, Wahrheit und Verstehen* (Munich 1967), p. 17, and the statement by *Kriminalrat* (police colonel) emeritus Carl Schütz dated 11 May 1951, reproduced on pp. 31f.

317. Klinkhammer, *Stragi*, p. 11.

318. Laternser, *Verteidigung*, p. 65.

319. Klinkhammer, *Stragi*, pp. 3f. The newly arrived group was forced to kneel on the bodies of those previously shot.

320. Schreiber, *Deutsche Kriegsverbrechen*, p. 125.

321. BA-MA, RL 21/212, logbook entry for the Villafranca airbase near Verona: "24.3.1944: at 17.40 h Waffen SS General Wolff departed for Foligno." (I am indebted to Carlo Gentile for referring me to this source.)

322. PRO/TNA, Kew, WO 235/438, affidavit by Georg Steigerthal, 22 November 1946.

323. BA-MA, N 431/872, Wehrmacht Investigation Office to the *Wehrmachtführungsstab*, 14 October 1944. The Investigation Office's inquiry related to an article about the massacre published in the *Neuen Züricher Zeitung* on 3 September 1944.

324. BA-MA, N 431/872, WFSt to Reichsführer SS, 6 November 1944.

325. BA-MA, N 431/872, RSHA to WFSt, 11 December 1944.

326. Alexander Fürst zu Dohna-Schlobitten, *Erinnerungen eines alten Ostpreussen* (Berlin 1999), p. 277. After this incident, Dohna received a punishment posting from Dostler because of insubordination. A note to the effect that Dohna was "politically unreliable" was entered in his personnel file. Dohna's statement in his memoirs therefore appears credible. Where possible, it has been verified using official army accounts.

327. Walther Hubatsch, *Hitlers Weisungen für die Kriegführung: Dokumente des Oberkommandos der Wehrmacht* (Koblenz 1983), Führer's order dated 18 October 1942, pp. 206–208.

328. Raiber, "Generalfeldmarschall Kesselring," p. 85. The witness statement regarding the destruction of the files was provided by Oberleutnant Hans-Georg Schultz, Colonel Kurt Almers's ordnance officer. Dohna (*Erinnerungen*, p. 275) merely stated that the "official activity report by the Chief Intelligence Officer" for March 1944 was "lost," and he based his presentation of events on private notes he made during 1946.

329. BA-MA, Gen.Kdo. LXXV A. K., volume of appendixes 7 in respect to war journal 1, activity report of the 3rd General Staff Officer's department dated 20 December 1943–30 April 1944; Dohna, *Erinnerungen*, p. 275.

330. Dohna, *Erinnerungen*, pp. 276f. Dohna pointed out that the shooting could have been avoided if the men had been sent immediately (without reporting to the Army High Command) to a POW camp. Dostler could also have exercised clemency and thus prevented the executions. The decision to eliminate the men may also have been influenced by the fact that they were not considered "genuine" Americans but rather American citizens of Italian descent who spoke fluent Italian and who—despite the fact that they did not disguise their uniforms—were seen as such and punished as "Italian traitors." According to Dohna, Dostler had demonstrated his scant regard for Italian lives on various occasions. Although Dohna believed that General Dostler bore the blame for the shootings, he wrote with hindsight after the war, "Had he disobeyed this order issued by the Führer, General Dostler would have been tried by court-martial and possibly condemned to death himself. That would not have helped the prisoners."

331. United Nations War Crimes Commission, ed., *Law-Reports of Trials of War Criminals*, vol. 1 (London, HMSO, 1949), Case No. 2 (Dostler), pp. 22–34.

332. NA, RG 153, entry 143, box 531, folder 16 115 3, bk. 1–2. Unfortunately, the document does not include the name of the soldier making the statement. (I am indebted to Richard Raiber for referring me to this source.)

333. NA, RG 153, entry 143, box 532, folder 16 115, bk. 1–2, statement by Albert Kesselring to Major Robert E. Haythorne, 6 October 1945. (I am indebted to Richard Raiber for referring me to this source.)

334. BA-MA, N 750/2, London Diary, p. 52: "Here, I also testified on behalf of Dostler, stating briefly that: I am unaware of this case; but if Generals Dostler and von Zangen wish to claim that they sought my decision, I will naturally assume responsibility without probing further! There was no more I could do for Dostler."

335. Westphal, *Erinnerungen*, p. 378.

336. NA, RG 153, entry 143, box 532, folder 16b115, bk. 1–2, statement by Siegfried Westphal to Major Robert E. Haythorne, 4 October 1945. (I am indebted to Richard Raiber for referring me to this source.)

337. Westphal, *Erinnerungen*, p. 356.

338. BA-MA, N 750/2, London Diary, p. 5.

339. Dohna, *Erinnerungen*, p. 274; Westphal, *Erinnerungen*, p. 364; my interview with Beelitz, 4 December 1998.

340. BA-MA, N 750/2, London Diary, p. 14.

341. Meyer, "Zur Situation," p. 657.

342. Kesselring, *Soldat*, p. 422.

343. BA-MA, N 750/2, London Diary, p. 47: "The main interest was in my Field Marshal's baton. I removed my medals for the last time that day."

344. Siegfried Westphal, *Der deutsche Generalstab auf der Anklagebank: Nürnberg 1945–48* (Mainz 1978), p. 92.

345. BA-MA, N 750/2, London Diary, pp. 10f.

346. Kesselring complained to General Dwight Eisenhower about the conditions of internment and—pointing to his serious head injury dating back to the late autumn of 1944—requested a bed. However, he received no concessions. See Burton C. Andrus, *I Was the Nuremberg Jailer* (New York 1969), pp. 44f.

347. BA-MA, N 750/2, London Diary, pp. 49f.

348. Westphal, *Der deutsche Generalstab*, pp. 131f.

349. BA-MA, N 750/2, London Diary, pp. 30f.

350. BA-MA, N 750/2, London Diary, p. 16.

351. Meyer, "Zur Situation," p. 658.

352. The relevant correspondence and notes can be found in BA-MA, N 431/828, questions put to Röttiger. On 8 December 1945, during the main Nuremberg war crimes trial, Hans Röttiger issued a declaration in lieu of oath (Affidavit No. 15, Reg. No. USA 559), which severely incriminated his superior during his period as general chief of staff of the Fourth Army. This Affidavit No. 15 concerned antipartisan warfare in Russia and the activities of the SD behind the front in the central section. In his affidavit, Röttiger noted that the troops had been ordered by the highest authorities—the Wehrmacht High Command—to use the most ruthless means in combating partisans. In a subsequent affidavit, cited as Affidavit No. 16, Röttiger described the "excesses of SD unit committed by shooting Jews and other persons, thus agitating the civilian population." He remarked that, in his view, these "excesses" and the resultant public outrage posed a risk to the army's safety. His commander-in-chief had, at that time, sought the removal of the SD. Röttiger also stated for the record that "despite general awareness of the SD's special duties, and the fact that these duties were apparently performed with the knowledge of the highest Wehrmacht authorities, we resisted their methods as far as possible, since they posed a risk to our own troops." During the court proceedings against the General Staff and the Wehrmacht High Command, this statement was viewed as particularly incriminating. Defense counsel for the General Staff, Hans Laternser, together with a military advisory group comprising Field Marshal von Manstein, General Westphal, General Walter Warlimont, and Generaloberst Franz Halder, placed great emphasis on demolishing these statements by attacking the credibility of Röttiger as a witness, as evidenced by document N 431/829.

353. BA-MA, N 750/2, London Diary, p. 14.

354. The so-called bunker was a low-lying punishment cell measuring 2.25 by 2.40 meters, intended for one prisoner. It had an open latrine and a ventilation slit in the wall. See David Irving, *Die Tragödie der deutschen Luftwaffe: Aus den Akten und Erinnerungen von Feldmarschall Milch* (Frankfurt am Main 1970), p. 380: "Milch was led into a dark, tiny cell in which he could . . . see five other inmates. He recognized Field Marshal Kesselring, Field Marshal von Brauchitsch and three other men by their voices. . . . There was only space for four camp beds in Milch's cell; the other two prisoners had to sleep on the floor."

355. BA-MA, N 750/new acquisition 2000, serial number 6, letter from Kesselring to his wife, 21 April 1946.

356. BA-MA, N 750/2, London Diary, p. 57.

Chapter 2: Allied Politics of Memory: The War Crimes Trials

1. BA-MA, N 431/872, appeal issued by General Alexander to German troops in Italy, 20 October 1944: "The officers and men carrying out such orders are war criminals." He cited the villages of Stia, Camerino, Civitella, and Roncastaldo by name. According to Alexander, soldiers from the Hermann Göring Division were responsible for two of these incidents; the other two were ascribed to army units.

2. Cited in Gerhard Schreiber, "Deutsche Kriegsverbrechen in Italien," in Wolfram Wette and Gerd R. Ueberschär, eds., *Kriegsverbrechen im 20. Jahrhundert* (Darmstadt 2001), pp. 222–234, at p. 228.

3. Robert Herde, *Command Responsibility: Die Verfolgung der "Zweiten Garde" deutscher und japanischer Generäle im alliierten Prozessprogramm nach dem Zweiten Weltkrieg* (Baden-Baden 2001), p. 98. Herde provided a comprehensive survey of the Allied plans for war crimes trials and, in particular, offered illuminating details illustrating the American position.

4. Tom Bower, *Blind Eye to Murder: Britain, America and the Purging of Nazi Germany—A Pledge Betrayed*, 2nd ed. (London 1997), p. 39.

5. Martin Broszat, "Siegerjustiz oder strafrechtliche 'Selbstreinigung'? Aspekte der Vergangenheitsbewältigung der deutschen Justiz während des Besatzungszeit 1945–1949," *VfZ* 4, no. 29 (1981): 477–544, at p. 478. The commission was first headed by Sir Cecil Hurst, who was then succeeded by the Australian Lord Wright. The files of the UNWCC were published in 1948 by the War Crimes Commission, in London, in a publication entitled *History of the United Nations War Crimes Commission and the Development of the Laws of War.*

6. Donald Bloxham, *Genocide on Trial: War Crime Trials and the Formation of Holocaust History and Memory* (Oxford 2001), p. 7.

7. Herde, *Command Responsibility*, p. 96.

8. Lothar Kettenacker, "Die Behandlung der Kriegsverbrecher als anglo-amerikanisches Rechtsproblem," in Gerd R. Ueberschär, ed., *Der Nationalsozialismus vor Gericht: Die alliierten Prozesse gegen Kriegsverbrecher und Soldaten 1943–1952* (Frankfurt am Main 1999), pp. 17–31, at p. 22.

9. Bower, *Blind Eye to Murder*, p. 43.

10. Bloxham, *Genocide*, p. 9.

11. Peter Steinbach, *Nationalsozialistische Gewaltverbrechen: Die Diskussion in der deutschen Öffentlichkeit nach 1945* (Berlin 1981), p. 22.

12. Ibid. Churchill deliberately neglected to inform Stalin of the establishment of the UNWCC, and Stalin then refused to join the commission retrospectively.

13. Herde, *Command Responsibility*, p. 105.

14. Bower, *Blind Eye to Murder*, p. 55.

15. The American secret service—the OSS—gathered information but never made it available for trial purposes. See Herde, *Command Responsibility*, p. 119.

16. Ibid., p. 122.

17. Cited in *Foreign Relations of the United States (FRUS)*, Diplomatic Papers 1943, vol. 1, General (Washington, DC, 1963), Moscow Conference, pp. 749–773, Annex 10, Declaration of German Atrocities, pp. 768–769, at p. 769.

18. Herde, *Command Responsibility*, p. 111.

19. Wolfram Wette, *Die Wehrmacht: Feindbilder, Vernichtungskrieg, Legenden* (Darmstadt 2002), p. 208.

20. Sheldon Glueck, *The Nuremberg Trial and Aggressive War* (New York 1946), p. 102.

21. Steinbach, *Nationalsozialistische Gewaltverbrechen*, p. 23.

22. Bloxham, *Genocide*, p. 17.

23. Steinbach, *Nationalsozialistische Gewaltverbrechen*, p. 23.

24. Ibid., p. 36.

25. Wolfram Wette, "Das Bild der Wehrmacht-Elite nach 1945," in Gerd R. Ueberschär, ed., *Hitlers militärische Elite*, vol. 2 (Darmstadt 1998), pp. 293–308, at p. 297.

26. *Der Prozess gegen die Hauptkriegsverbrecher vor dem Internationalen Militärgerichtshof (IMT), Nürnberg, 14. November 1945–1. Oktober 1946* (Gemäss den Weisungen des Internationalen Militärgerichtshofes vom Sekretariat des Gerichtshofes unter der Autorität des Obersten Kontrollrats für Deutschland veröffentlicht), 41 vols., ed. Lawrence D. Egbert and Paul A. Joosten (Nuremberg 1947), 1:313.

27. There were trials of doctors (Case 1), Generalfeldmarschall Erhard Milch (Case 2), selected jurists (Case 3), the SS Main Economic Administration Office (Case 4), Friedrich Flick (Case 5), IG Farben (Case 6), the "South-Eastern Generals" for "hostage murders" (Case 7), members of the Race and Settlement Office (RuSHA) (Case 8), and the SD Einsatzgruppen leader Otto Ohlendorf and others (Case 9). There were also trials of German arms manufacturers, especially the Krupp family (Case 10), diplomats in the German Foreign Office (the so-called Wilhelmstrasse trial) (Case 11), and army commanders-in-chief (the so-called Wehrmacht High Command trial, involving especially Field Marshal von List and others) (Case 12). In all, 185 high-ranking individuals were charged. See Bengt von zur Mühlen, ed., *Die zwölf Nürnberger Nachfolgeprozesse* (Berlin 2000).

28. Bower, *Blind Eye to Murder*, p. 30. See also Robert Morgan, *The United States and West Germany 1945–1973: A Study in Alliance Politics* (Oxford 1973).

29. Bower, *Blind Eye to Murder*, p. 42.

30. Reinhard Stumpf, *Die Wehrmacht-Elite: Rang- und Herkunftsstruktur der deutschen Generale und Admirale 1933–1945* (Boppard 1982), p. 298.

31. John Alan Appleman, *Military Tribunals and International Crimes* (Indianapolis, IN, 1954); Steinbach, *Nationalsozialistische Gewaltverbrechen*, p. 29.

32. Steinbach, *Nationalsozialistische Gewaltverbrechen*, p. 29.

33. Robert K. Woetzel, *The Nuremberg Trials in International Law* (London and New York 1960), p. 218.

34. Ulrich Brochhagen, *Nach Nürnberg: Vergangenheitsbewältigung und Westintegration in der Ära Adenauer* (Hamburg 1994), pp. 24f. Brochhagen stated that 1,672 individuals were convicted by American courts, 1,085 by British courts, and 2,107 by French courts.

35. Gerd R. Ueberschär, "Sowjetische Prozesse gegen deutsche Kriegsgefangene," in Gerd R. Ueberschär, ed., *Der Nationalsozialismus vor Gericht: Die alliierten Prozesse gegen Kriegsverbrecher und Soldaten 1943–1952* (Frankfurt am Main 1999), pp. 240–261, at p. 249. Because of the "simplified rules of procedure" that, in 80 percent of cases, denied German defendants the services of defense counsel or an interpreter, the Soviet trial program remained highly controversial and primarily served propaganda purposes.

36. Telford Taylor, *Die Nürnberger Prozesse: Hintergründe, Analysen und Erkenntnisse aus heutiger Sicht*, 2nd ed. (Munich 1994), pp. 103ff; Bower, *Blind Eye to Murder*, p. 40.

37. Bower, *Blind Eye to Murder*, p. 244. Telford Taylor suspected racial reasons, as well as solidarity between "northern" armed forces (see Taylor, *Nürnberger Prozesse*, p. 285). J. W. Dower also referred to the racial aspect involved in the far more severe treatment meted out to Japanese generals in his study *War without Mercy: Race and Power in the Pacific War* (New York 1993).

38. Bower, *Blind Eye to Murder*, p. 30.

39. Herde, *Command Responsibility*, p. 97.

40. Bloxham, *Genocide*, p. 25.

41. United Nations War Crimes Commission, Report No. 44, p. 2. BA-ZSL Ludwigsburg, JAG 260, Strafverfahren gegen Kesselring, Albert, document "Minutes of Pretrial Advice," Judge Advocate General to Commanding General Central Mediterranean Forces Harding, 7 January 1947.

42. PRO/TNA, Kew, WO 310/127, memorandum JAG, 13 January 1946, p. 11.

43. "War Crimes Report of the War Crimes Inquiry Staff," presented to Parliament by the secretary of state for the Home Department by command of Her Majesty, ed. Sir Thomas Hetherington and William Chalmers, London 1989, p. 55.

44. Erich Schwinge, author of the military penal code promulgated in 1936 who later acted as an expert witness for the defense in the Kesselring trial, stated in §158 V, paragraph 1 of the 1936 German military penal code that German soldiers in occupied countries were extraterritorial and could thus not fall within the jurisdiction of foreign courts. See Herde, *Command Responsibility*, p. 131.

45. Herde, *Command Responsibility*, p. 128.

46. Gerd Hankel, *Die Leipziger Prozesse: Deutsche Kriegsverbrechen und ihre strafrechtliche Verfolgung nach dem ersten Weltkrieg* (Hamburg 2003); Hankel, "Deutsche Kriegsverbrechen des Weltkriegs 1914–18 vor deutschen Gerichten," in Wolfram Wette and Gerd R. Ueberschär, eds., *Kriegsverbrechen im 20. Jahrhundert* (Darmstadt 2001), pp. 85–98; Walter Schwengler, *Völkerrecht, Versailler Vertrag und Auslieferungsfrage: Die Strafverfolgung wegen Kriegsverbrechen als Problem des Friedensschlusses 1919/1920* (Stuttgart 1982); and Herde, *Command Responsibility*, pp. 37–62.

47. Herde, *Command Responsibility*, p. 133.

48. *British Manual of Military Law* (1936), §366, and the *American Rules of Land Warfare*, FM 27-10 (1940), §366.

49. IWM, Papers of Lieutenant Colonel P. M. Marjoribanks-Egerton, PMME 4. On p. 86 of the *Manual of Military Law* (on reprisals and shooting of hostages), a section has been struck through in red and a new typewritten passage dated April 1944 has been pasted over it.

50. Bower, *Blind Eye to Murder*, p. 298.

51. The British started their program of trials on 17 September 1945, with the "Bergen-Belsen trial" of camp personnel from Bergen-Belsen and other concentration camps, held in Lüneburg. Bergen-Belsen concentration camp had been liberated by the British in March 1945.

52. Herde, *Command Responsibility*, p. 22.

53. Brochhagen, *Nach Nürnberg*, p. 24. (The figures are not completely accurate, since Manstein had not yet received his eighteen-year custodial sentence at this point.)

54. Ibid., p. 26.

55. See, for example, BA-MA, N. Seeger, the trial of Lieutenant General Willy Seeger in Wuppertal in the autumn of 1946.

56. Bloxham, *Genocide*, p. 25. See also Annie Deighton, *The Impossible Peace: Britain, the Division of Germany and the Origins of the Cold War* (Oxford 1990), p. 78.

57. Bloxham, *Genocide*, p. 97.

58. Ibid., p. 27.

59. Brochhagen, *Nach Nürnberg*, p. 31.

60. Ibid., p. 53.

61. NA, RG 338, file 000.5, box 816, Records and Reports of War Crime Trial of Albert

Kesselring to the Commanding General Mediterranean Theatre of Operations, undated, probably June 1947.

62. PRO/TNA, Kew, WO 219/ 3585, UNWCC, C. 135, 16 July 1945. Wolff appears as No. 346 on "list 7 of UN War Crimes Commission's list of accused persons detained by the Allied Forces HQ, Mediterranean theatre," a list that also includes the last commanders-in-chief of the Wehrmacht in Italy, Field Marshal Albert Kesselring and Generaloberst Heinrich von Vietinghoff-Scheel, and the head of the SD in Italy, Wilhelm Harster.

63. PRO/TNA, Kew, WO 311/28, report from GHQ to the War Office regarding German war crimes in Italy, 5 October 1945.

64. Bloxham, *Genocide*, p. 25.

65. PRO/TNA, Kew, WO 310/123, letter from Shapcott, JAG London, to AG3 (War Crimes Branch, CMF), 15 March 1946.

66. PRO/TNA, Kew, WO 311/28, report from GHQ to the War Office regarding German war crimes in Italy, 5 October 1945, p. 1.

67. PRO/TNA, Kew, WO 310/123, handwritten letter from King to Passingham, 14 August 1945.

68. PRO/TNA, Kew, WO 310/127, JAG memorandum, 13 January 1946, p. 1.

69. Ibid., p. 10.

70. PRO/TNA, Kew, WO 310/127, minute from JAG to HQ CMF, 25 July 1946: "in connection with war crimes committed by the Wehrmacht in Italy against Italian civilians as a result of Anti-Partisan measures."

71. ASMAE, AP 1946, Germania, b. 1, report, 27 September 1946, p. 6.

72. BA-MA, N 431/934, article manuscript (German translation) for the *Gazzettino—Sera*, Venice, ca. 8 May 1947, by Guido Polacco, editor-in-chief, 15 pages, at p. 1.

73. Paolo Pezzino, "Sui mancati processi in Italia ai criminali di guerra tedeschi," in *Storia e Memoria* 10 (2001): 1–72, at p. 16.

74. Ibid., p. 12.

75. ASMAE Rome, b. 176, IV/10, "Eccidio delle Fosse Ardeatine," Ministero degli Affari Esteri, Ufficio Collegamento, Appunto per la Direzione Gen. Affari Politici, 10 October 1945. This source relates to a summary of the interrogations of Dollmann, Kappler, and Wolff.

76. ASMAE, AP 1952, b. 173, London Embassy to the Foreign Ministry in Rome, 15 November 1945.

77. An indirect reference to this can be found in PRO/TNA, Kew, WO 204/12798, Kappler file, in a message dated 5 July 1947, from the British HQ to the War Crimes Group in Italy, referring to this list, Signature HQ USFET, AG0000.5GAP-AGO.

78. ASMAE, AP 1952, b. 173, London Embassy to the Foreign Ministry in Rome, 15 November 1945. However, during the initial phase of Italian planning, the term *war crimes* primarily referred to "art theft in Italy."

79. ASMAE, AP 1946, Germania, b. 1, Riunione del 7 ottobre (1946), ogetto: Criminali nazisti "Fosse Ardeatine," three-page report, p. 1. The text refers to "una ragione politica più che militare" (a political matter rather than a military one).

80. ASMAE, AP 1946, Germania, b. 1, memorandum for the Allied Commission, Rome, 9 April 1946.

81. ASMAE, AP 1952, b. 174, Criminali di Guerra, Procura generale Militare (Borsari) a Ministero degli Affari Esteri, 28 March 1946.

82. ASMAE, AP 1946, Germania, b. 1, Ministero degli Affari Esteri, Appunto per l'Ufficio di Collegamento, undated (probably 28 May 1946). Three pages, at p. 2.

83. ASMAE, AP 1946, Germania, b.1, Ministero degli Affari Esteri, Ufficio

Collegamento, Appunto per la Direzione Generale Affari Politici, ogetto: Criminali di Guerra, Rome, 28 May 1946. The German massacres of Italian soldiers on Corfu and Cephalonia were a particular focus in this regard.

84. PRO/TNA, Kew, WO 310/127, HQ (A-Branch) to ALCOM, 8 February 1946.

85. Ibid., p. 31.

86. Only a small group of General Staff officers were involved, namely, the relevant chiefs of the General Staffs. These included Kesselring's two chiefs of staff, Westphal (until June 1944) and Röttiger (from 10 June 1944); the chief of staff of the Tenth Army, Fritz Wentzell; the chief of staff of the Fourteenth Army, Wolf-Rüdiger Hauser; and the chiefs of staff of army group Liguria, Nagel, and Pemsel.

87. One may assume that the decision not to prosecute members of the General Staffs was taken because of the effort involved and because it would be very difficult to prove that they had "motivated the perpetrators." However, when questioning General Staff officers, the practice was to leave them in the dark regarding their eventual fate. Thus, when interrogated in London as late as November 1946, Colonel Beelitz was threatened by Colonel Scotland: "You will be next." (My interview with Beelitz on 29 October 1998, in Stuttgart.)

88. Appleman, *Military Tribunals*, p. 301.

89. ASMAE, AP 1946, Germania, b. 1, Comissione alleata, ogetto: Processi per delitti di guerra, al Ministero per Grazia e Giustizia, 29 June 1946.

90. PRO/TNA, Kew, WO 311/28, report, War Crimes Group to Judge Advocate, 5 October 1945, p. 32.

91. ASMAE, AP 1946, Germania, b. 1, Ministero degli Affari Esteri, Appunto per il Ministro Zoppi, 27 September 1946, six pages.

92. ASMAE, AP 1946, Germania, b. 1, Ministero degli Affari Esteri, Appunto per l'Ufficio di Collegamento, undated (probably 28 May 1946), p. 2.

93. PRO/TNA, Kew, WO 310/123, handwritten letter from King to Passingham, 14 August 1945.

94. PRO/TNA, Kew, WO 311/28, report, p. 4. According to this report, a substantial number of German documents seized in Italy were already lost en route to the Allied headquarters, and others arrived unsorted with numerous other documents, so it was impossible to track them down using systematic criteria. These documents were thus unavailable to the people preparing the planned trials.

95. Ibid., p. 3.

96. In this regard, see Michele Battini, *Peccati di Memoria: La mancata Norimberga italiana* (Rome 2003).

97. A research group from Pisa University, headed by Paolo Pezzino, was commissioned by the Italian government to prepare an investigative report on the so-called cabinet of shame. (The "armadio della vergogna" was a file cabinet in the cellars of the Roman military prosecutor's office. In the summer of 1994, in the wake of investigations carried out by the Italian military prosecutor Antonio Intelisano into the activities of SS officers Erich Priebke and Karl Hass, American investigation files regarding German war crimes in Italy were "rediscovered" in this file cabinet, causing a scandal in Italy.) See Paolo Pezzino, "Gli Alleati, l'Italia e i processi ai criminali nazisti," *Storia e Memoria* 10 (2001): 9–72, and Mimmo Franzinelli, *Le Stragi Nascoste: L'armadio della vergogna—Impunità e rimzione dei crimini di guerra nazifascisti 1943–2001* (Milan 2002).

98. See Franco Giustolisi, "Gli scheletri dell'Armadio," in *Micromega* 1 (2000): 345–355, at p. 347.

99. PRO/TNA, Kew, WO 311/28, report, p. 30.

100. Ibid.

101. PRO/TNA, Kew, FO 371/51046, Foreign Office memo dated 14 November 1945.

102. PRO/TNA, Kew, FO 371/51046, Foreign Office telegram to the War Office, 24 November 1945.

103. Ibid.

104. On 14 November 1946, the victors finally made it clear to the Italians that their request for an Italian assessor to be included would not be granted. (ASMAE, b. 176, IV 1/10 "Eccidio delle Fosse Ardeatine," Headquarters Allied Commission to the Italian Foreign Ministry, 14 November 1946.)

105. Hans Woller, "'Ausgebliebene Säuberung'? Die Abrechnung mit dem Faschismus in Italien," in Klaus-Dietmar Henke and Hans Woller, eds., *Politische Säuberung in Europa: Die Abrechnung mit Faschismus und Kollaboration nach dem Zweiten Weltkrieg* (Munich 1991), pp. 148–191, at 153.

106. Thus, an urgent letter from the Italian minister of war to the foreign minister stated that the Italians had to be involved in the Fosse Ardeatine trial "at all costs," in order to restore Italian prestige and avoid domestic unrest. (ASMAE, b. 176, IV 1/10 "Eccidio delle Fosse Ardeatine," Ministero della Guerra, ogetto: Crimini di guerra, 27 September 1946.)

107. PRO/TNA, Kew, FO 371/51046, letter from Colonel Isham, War Office, to the Foreign Office, 19 December 1945.

108. PRO/TNA, Kew, FO 371/57557, letter from Colonel Halse to the Judge Advocate General, London, 30 October 1946.

109. Charles F. Delzell, ed., *Mediterranean Fascism 1919–1945* (New York 1970), p. 228.

110. ACS, PCM (Presidenza del Consiglio dei Ministri), Gabinetto 1944–47, b. 1.2.2., n. 15626, letter from the Italian Foreign Minister to the Defence Minister, telespresso N.1., Segr. Pol., Rome, 2 January 1947.

111. As early as 4 October 1946, the Italian Foreign Ministry had asked for a place on the judges' bench "because of the special nature of the case." (See ASMAE, b. 176, IV 1/10 "Eccidio delle Fosse Ardeatine," Ministero degli Affari Esteri [Zoppi], telespresso dated 6 October 1946.)

112. Filippo Focardi, "La questione della punizione die Criminali di Guerra in Italia," *QFIAB* 80 (2000): 543–624, at p. 605. Following the Italian Peace Treaty in February 1947, the Italian government received extradition requests relating to Italian citizens accused of war crimes; most of these came from Yugoslavia. They can be broken down as follows: Yugoslavia, 729 requests; Greece, 111; Soviet Union, 12; France, 30; and Albania, 3. The Allied lists of war criminals included 833 individuals, of whom around 600 had been brought to trial by 1948. Italian war crimes committed during the Abyssinian and Libyan wars in the 1930s, however, remained almost completely exempt from prosecution; see Giorgio Rochat, *Guerre italiane in Libia e in Etiopia: Studi militari 1921–1939* (Treviso 1991).

113. This wrangling becomes apparent if one looks at file notes in the British Foreign Office, according to which Yugoslavia complained that Italy was not extraditing the war criminals being sought, whereas the British, in contrast, were arresting Italians within Italy for their own purposes. In this regard, Ambassador Ward noted that the Italians were dragging out extradition proceedings by pointing to the fact that Yugoslavia had not yet established diplomatic relations with Italy. In addition, the Italians attempted to protect their POWs by arresting them themselves if the persons involved were being sought by the British jurisdiction (PRO/TNA, Kew, FO 371/57557, letter from Ward to Attlee, 11 December 1946, and associated memos).

114. PRO/TNA, Kew, FO 371/57557, register of telephone calls and telegrams, sheet dated 4 November 1946.

115. PRO/TNA, FO 371/ 57557, telegram FO to Embassy, 11 December 1946.

116. PRO/TNA, Kew, FO 371/57557, telegram from Ward to the Foreign Office, 1 November 1946.

117. PRO/TNA, Kew, FO 371/57557, Foreign Office to War Office (Isham), 19 December 1945.

118. NA, RG 338, United States Command, Mediterranean Theater of Operations U.S. Army (hereafter cited as MTOUSA), Records of the Special Staff, AG HQ, Decimal Correspondence File, 000.5, Reports and Records of War Crimes Trial of Albert Kesselring, Location: 290:53/32/06/box 816, report by Captain Murphy (hereafter cited as NA, Report).

119. PRO/TNA, Kew, WO 310/127, JAG to British Rhine Army HQ, 3 April 1946. The officers involved were Generalmajor Eduard Crasemann for the Italian theater, Generalmajor Alexander Bourquin for war crimes in Italy and in Greece, Major General Hans Ehlert (for Italy), and Generalleutnant Richard Heidrich (for Italy).

120. BA-MA, N 431/936, Kesselring to Laternser, 31 December 1946. He wrote that Potter could not guarantee being able to keep Kesselring in the Historical Division Group until January 1947 "in order to thus delay the trial." Nevertheless, Potter clearly was successful until January 1947.

121. PRO/TNA, Kew, WO 310/127, JAG (Shapcott) to Colonel H. Potter, 15 October 1946.

122. Peter Herde, "Wolfgang Hagemann als Zeitzeuge und Zeuge im Kesselring-Prozess (April 25th 1947)," in Hagen Keller, Werner Paravicini, and Wolfgang Schieder, eds., *Italia et Germania: Liber amicorum Arnold Esch* (Tübingen, Niethammer, 2001), p. 53, has also made reference to this. An American interrogation group not only had comprehensively documented the massacre in Sant'Anna and questioned witnesses but also had captured the deserter Willi Haase, who had taken part in the massacre and was able to name the perpetrator unit (NA, RG 153, 5th Army Report War Crimes, German atrocities, investigation, file no. 000.5–570 JA-0). It was only in the summer of 1999 that the files were made available for historical research again after being released in Washington.

123. Marzabotto was within the operational territory of the II U.S. Corps, Sant'Anna, part of the U.S. Fifth Army.

124. However, in order to facilitate "delayed punishment," the Italian military prosecutor at La Spezia commenced preliminary investigations in January 2001 involving three SS *Unterscharführer* (junior squad leaders) charged with participation in the Sant'Anna di Stazzema massacres; the trial opened on 20 April 2004 (see *Die Woche*, 16 February 2001, "Delayed Punishment: Italy Is at the Brink of a New Wave of War Crimes Trials—Some Suspects, Former Members of the Waffen SS, Are Still Living in Germany," by Udo Gümpel, p. 11; *Süddeutsche Zeitung*, 20 April 2004, "Evidence from the Cabinet of Shame," by Christiane Kohl, p. 3).

125. Peter Herde shares this view: see Herde, "Wolfgang Hagemann," p. 53.

126. PRO/TNA, Kew, WO 310/127, JAG memorandum, p. 5.

127. PRO/TNA, WO 310/123, brief Napier, War Crimes Commission CMF to War Office, 9 April 1946.

128. PRO/TNA, Kew, WO 311/28, report, p. 14.

129. Ibid.

130. Ibid., p. 26.

131. PRO/TNA, Kew, WO 310/127, JAG memorandum, p. 2.

132. PRO/TNA, Kew, WO 311/28, report, 5 October 1945, p. 30. For this reason, the author of the report at least (Mitchell) felt morally bound to devote all his energies to investigating the atrocities: "The matter is one in which we should interest ourselves since we played a major part in fostering the very partisan warfare which led to the reprisals."

133. PRO/TNA, Kew, WO 311/28, report, p. 18.

134. PRO/TNA, Kew, WO 310/127, telegram, 3 July 1946. In return, Rigney visited the JAG CMF at Naples in July 1946 for information available about German atrocities in Italy; see PRO/TNA, Kew, WO 310/123, message from Chief of Counsel Nuremberg to JAG CMF, 18 July 1946 and 25 July 1946.

135. PRO/TNA, Kew, WO 310/123, message from Chief of Counsel Nuremberg to JAG CMF, 21 August 1946.

136. PRO/TNA, Kew, WO 310/127, telegram from GHQ to JAG London, 10 January 1947. Both trials were now set to continue until the end of February 1947. PRO/TNA, Kew, WO 310/129, Special trial instructions, 7 February 1947.

137. PRO/TNA, Kew, WO 310/127, JAG memorandum, p. 5. As early as 1945, British investigators had found that the SS forces were not the only ones to get their hands dirty in the fight against the partisans; individual Wehrmacht units had also been involved in massacres. For example, it had initially been planned to try Generalleutnant Kurt Mältzer not only for the massacre in the Fosse Ardeatine but also for the massacre in Palazzo del Pero on 24 June 1944. Plans were also made to try Generalmajor Paul Steinbach for a similar incident. Steinbach's area around Bologna had been the scene of numerous lesser incidents, which leads to the conclusion that soldiers were "encouraged" (and covered) from above to adopt a harsh approach. However, these trials never took place because Steinbach succumbed in March 1945 and Mältzer was already sentenced to death.

138. PRO/TNA, Kew, WO 310/127, Judge Advocate Halse to the War Crimes Group Caserta, Major McKee, 1 January 1947. Colonel Halse had indicated confidentially, as early as 1 January 1947, that no concrete charges could be lodged against SS Obergruppenführer Karl Wolff. Not even the interrogation of SS Generals Willy Tensfeld, Karl Brunner, and Karl Buerger in the London District Cage had thrown up any incriminating evidence.

139. Since it was known that SS Obergruppenführer Hans Adolf Prützmann had assumed Wolff's duties in July 1944 when Wolff fell ill, the British feared that Prützmann would "presumably take over Wolff's responsibility for any crimes committed by the SS and the Police during that period" (PRO/TNA, Kew, WO 310/127, JAG memorandum, p. 7).

140. Thus, Dollmann escaped custody several times with the aid of the American secret service and was provided with false papers (see PRO/TNA, Kew, FO 371/57557, HQ Caserta to Foreign Office, 5 December 1946). Kappler was also initially interrograted separately by the CIC, although he was then transferred to a normal POW camp.

141. Christian Vordemann, *Deutschland—Italien 1949–1961: Die diplomatischen Beziehungen* (Frankfurt am Main 1994), at p. 65.

142. PRO/TNA, Kew, FO 371/57557, HQ Caserta to Foreign Office, 27 November 1946: Dollmann "did not participate in negotiations which led to the German Surrender, and was given no promise of special immunity by anyone having authority to do so. The Allied Force Headquarters has put out a press statement to this effect."

143. Also reporting in this context was the German newsweekly *Der Spiegel*, 31 (1948): 13f., "A Semi-trial: Martyrs Were Needed." Twice—in an article on the Kappler trial in 1948 and in a 1962 article about "*Wölffchen*'s" rise from Himmler's personal adjutant to supreme SS and police commander in Italy—*Der Spiegel* attributed Wolff's exemption from

prosecution after 1945 to a "secret episode" during the surrender negotiations with Allen Dulles, who had "assured the capitulator Wolff of indemnity." Himmler's shadow, Karl Wolff, had "not been brought to book by any Allied court" but was "merely called as a witness by the Nuremberg Tribunal, was allowed to appear wearing full insignia," and was "sentenced to a mere four years imprisonment by the Hamburg-Bergedorf court in 1949," of which "he served just one week." Wolff now benefited from his role as the driving force behind the German surrender negotiations in Italy. After 1945, he always held better cards than Kesselring, who had long argued against a premature capitulation in Italy. For this reason, the Bergedorf court found: "As a human being, it must be certified that, with his honest nature, Wolff was a foreign body in the SS." In 1964, Wolff was sentenced to fifteen years' imprisonment for his role in the deportation of Jews "as an accessory to murder in at least 300,000 cases," despite the fact that, in interviews such as that with the *Neue Illustrierte,* he claimed until the end that he had heard nothing of this while working at Himmler's side and had never attended the major "final solution" conferences. In this regard, *Der Spiegel* quoted Adolf Eichmann as saying that "Wolff, as a drawing room officer, was always at pains to keep his white gloves clean."

144. PRO/TNA, Kew, WO 310/123, voluntary statement by SS Sturmbannführer Heinrich Andergassen, 21 February 1946. Friedrich Pfrommer, who kept the war journal for the South-Western Command, expressed himself similarly in his private notes on the end of the war in Italy (private paper of Professor Edelgard Pfrommer, Bammental, donation to the BA-MA Freiburg planned).

145. PRO/TNA, Kew, WO 311/28, report, p. 31.

146. Michael Salter, *Nazi War Crimes, US Intelligence and Selective Prosecution at Nuremberg: Controversies Regarding the Role of the Office of Strategic Services* (London 2007); Kerstin von Lingen, *Verschwörung des Schweigens: SS und Secret Service—Die Akte Karl Wolff* (Paderborn: Schoeningh, forthcoming).

147. PRO/TNA, Kew, WO 310/123, telegram from JAG to CMF, 28 May 1946, and PRO/TNA, Kew, WO 310/127, letter JAG to HQ, 25 July 1946. It was probably decided to try Kesselring individually in May 1946.

148. PRO/TNA, Kew, WO 310/127, War Crimes Group to JAG, 1 October 1947.

149. PRO/TNA, Kew, WO 310/127. Telegram from GHQ to the Judge Advocate, 10 January 1947. On 10 January 1947, the British judge advocate general received a recommendation from Allied GHQ in Caserta suggesting that the Kesselring trial start on 10 February 1947. It was to be followed immediately by Wolff's trial. It was explicitly stated that both trials should not extend beyond 28 February 1947.

150. PRO/TNA, Kew, WO 310/127, Memorandum, Halse, to War Crimes Group, Caserta, Major McKee, 1 January 1947.

151. PRO/TNA, Kew, WO 310/127, telegram from JAG to the War Crimes Group/South-East Europe, 19 February 1948.

152. PRO/TNA, Kew, WO 310/127, JAG to War Crimes Group, 28 October 1947.

153. PRO/TNA, Kew, WO 310/127, JAG to War Crimes Group, 31 October 1947. With had been released to Germany, and his whereabouts were now unknown, as the Americans regretfully informed the British authorities.

154. Regarding Fossoli, see Richard Lamb, *War in Italy 1943–1945: A Brutal Story* (New York 1994).

155. PRO/TNA, Kew, WO 310/127, War Crimes Group to Major Marshal, JAG, 9 September 1947; Lamb, *War,* p. 50.

156. One of the most renowned postwar Italian writers, Primo Levi, provided a literary

description of the route from Rome to Auschwitz via Fossoli in his autobiographical work *If This Is a Man—Survival at Auschwitz* (London 1958).

157. PRO/TNA, Kew, WO 310/127, JAG to War Crimes Group, 15 September 1947: "With so little evidence to go upon there is no doubt whatever that he would deny all knowledge of the incident. As you know, Wolff was fully interrogated both in CMF [Central Mediterranean Forces] and later at London District Cage concerning atrocities in Italy but it was found impossible to obtain any incriminating admissions of any kind from him."

158. Battini, *Peccati*, p. 156.

159. For more on the specific plans and the details of the Rome trial, see Joachim Staron, *Fosse Ardeatine und Marzabotto: Deutsche Kriegsverbrechen und Resistenza* (Paderborn 2002), pp. 132–148.

160. ACS, PCM, Gabinetto 1948–1950, b. 305, cat. 14-6, n. 10268, "Onoranze ai 320 caduti alle Cave Ardeatine," letter from relatives of the Fosse Ardeatine massacre to Allied headquarters, a copy of which was sent to the Italian Justice Ministry for reference, 19 July 1946. The relatives demanded that the "hateful war criminals Mältzer and Kesserling [*sic*] should be brought before an Italian military court without delay, so that they could be tried and convicted in Rome, together with the war criminals Dollmann and Kappler, who were still in Allied hands."

161. PRO/TNA, Kew, FO 371/51046, telegram from Caserta to Rome, 3 August 1946.

162. Regarding the trial planning process, see ASMAE, b. 176, IV 1/10, Quartier generale Comissione Alleata, ogetto: Processi per delitti di guerra, massacro Fosse Ardeatine, al ministero di Grazia e Giustizia, 30 September 1946; ASMAE, b. 176, IV 1/10, Quartier generale Comissione Alleata, ogetto: Processi per delitti di guerra, massacro Fosse Ardeatine, al Ministero di Grazia e Giustizia, 14 October 1946; and ASMAE, AP 1946, Germania, b. 1, gabinetto del Ministro Ufficio di Collegamento, al Ministero della Guerra, Col. Sormanti, 16 October 1946.

163. PRO/TNA, Kew, WO 310/128, guidelines issued by Caserta HQ on the Rome trial, undated.

164. Herde, *Command responsibility*, p. 300. In terms of criminal law, according to Herde, the execution of the 330 people was not illegal in itself—what was illegal was the execution of the 5 additional individuals, since this act was not covered by an order from above. Another problematic issue was the fact that the hostages had not been selected in accordance with international legal conventions, which dictated that they should have been chosen as potential victims even before the event.

165. PRO/TNA, Kew, WO 235/438, transcripts of the trial of Mackensen et al., 18 November 1946, p. 17.

166. Ibid., p. 7.

167. BA-MA, N 431/578, Rome trial transcripts, second day (20 November 1946), examination of Kappler by Christ, p. 9.

168. Herde, *Command Responsibility*, p. 303.

169. PRO/TNA, Kew, proceedings, address by Keller, 28 November 1946, p. 5. Kesselring was the supreme commander in the combat zone, which included Rome after the Allied landings at Anzio and Nettuno, and he was thus in command of all units, including SS and SD troops.

170. Staron, *Fosse Ardeatine*, p. 141.

171. PRO/TNA, Kew, WO 310/128, JAG to Caserta HQ, undated. The charge that the accused were unable to follow English trial law had "no basis."

172. At this time, there were fears in Allied headquarters—and elsewhere—that the Communists could gain power by democratic means. Ward reported to Attlee that the Communist press had taken no notice at all of the trial until the prosecutor described the attack in the Via Rasella—which had been carried out by Communists—as a crime: that triggered stormy protests in the Communist newspaper *L'Unità*.

173. ASMAE, AP 1946, Germania, b. 1, Ministero degli Affari Esteri, processo per l'eccidio delle Fosse Ardeatine, nota del ministero della guerra, 8 November 1946.

174. *Time*, 9 December 1946, "War Crimes."

175. PRO/TNA, Kew, FO 371/57557, Ward to Attlee, 4 December 1946.

176. PRO/TNA, Kew, FO 371/57557, telegram from Ward to the Foreign Office, 4 December 1946. He therefore felt it would be preferable not to issue any explanation in this matter. Rather, he recommended that an explanation be published quickly, according to which Dollmann would be tried together with Kappler in regard to the massacre: "Italians rightly or wrongly consider Dollmann to be a very big criminal and they will certainly not forget about him."

177. BA-MA, N 750/2, London Diary, p. 73.

178. PRO/TNA, Kew, WO 310/128, Playfair to Harding, 1 December 1946.

179. PRO/TNA, Kew, WO 310/128, Grant (AAG A3) to Colonel A, November 1946.

180. PRO/TNA, Kew, WO 310/128, communication from Caserta HQ to the War Office, 11 December 1946.

181. PRO/TNA, Kew, FO 371/57557, telegram from the Vatican to Caserta, 6 December 1946 (petition on behalf of Mackensen). D'Arcy Godolphin Osborne, British envoy to the Vatican, informed Caserta HQ on 6 December 1946 that the pope had been requested by Mrs. von Mackensen and Mrs. Mältzer personally to intervene to have the death sentences commuted. The pope would be happy to do this "for humanitarian reasons," it was reported, but he wanted to know what the prospects for success were in GHQ. A few years later, the pope intervened in London quite openly on Kesselring's behalf (see PRO/TNA, Kew, FO 1060/493, Minute Sheet, Principal Legal Adviser, Petition War Criminals, G. Ingham, 10 February 1950, petition from the pope on Kesselring's behalf based on the "sparing of Rome").

182. Ibid. Osborne contacted the military authorities to confirm that he had acted correctly by informing the undersecretary of state that an intervention would be futile and could possibly be used as ammunition for Communist propaganda in Rome.

183. Generalmajor Wolf Hauser informed Laternser that Dr. Fabian von Schlabrendorff was prepared to defend Generaloberst von Mackensen in the Rome case (BA-MA, N 431/932, Hauser to Laternser, 6 October 1946).

184. PRO/TNA, Kew, WO 310/128, Rome to Caserta, top secret, 5 December 1946.

185. PRO/TNA, Kew, WO 310/128, message from HQ Caserta to A-Branch (Grant), undated. Kesselring was formally still in U.S. custody, and he was returned by an American escort to Allendorf immediately after the Rome trial. He was only transferred to British custody once his own trial was pending.

186. PRO/TNA, Kew, FO 371/57557, Foreign Office memo, 6 December 1946.

187. PRO/TNA, Kew, FO 371/57557, telegram from Foreign Office to Ward, 11 December 1946. In the summer of 1946, during the trial of the Rome police director, Pietro Caruso, the director of "Regina Coeli" Prison had been lynched on the street en route to the courthouse.

188. PRO/TNA, Kew, FO 371/57557, telegram, Embassy to Foreign Office, 24 December 1946, p. 1.

189. Bloxham, *Genocide*, p. 27.

190. ZSL, JAG 260, criminal proceedings against Albert Kesselring, "Minutes of Pretrial Advice," JAG to Harding, 7 January 1947.

191. PRO/TNA, Kew, FO 310/128, Caserta HQ to Stirling, 17 March 1947.

192. PRO/TNA, Kew, WO 310/129, Robertson to Harding, 7 April 1947.

193. PRO/TNA, Kew, WO 310/129, Grant to Harding, 9 April 1947.

194. PRO/TNA, Kew, WO 310/129, Robertson to Harding, 18 April 1947. According to this communication, there was a possibility that Mältzer would again be called as a witness when it came to the closing statement.

195. PRO/TNA, Kew, WO 310/128, Rhine Army HQ to Caserta HQ, 19 April 1947.

196. PRO/TNA, Kew, PREM 8/707, message from Harding to War Office, 29 June 1947.

197. BA-MA, N 431/934, article manuscript (German translation) for the *Gazzettino—Sera*, Venice, ca. 8 May 1947, by Guido Polacco, editor-in-chief, 15 pages, at p. 1.

198. *Omnibus*, 12 May 1947, p. 1: "Tremavano le mani a Kesselring": "Many guarantee that the Field Marshal will be acquitted." Some speculations voiced in private were cited as representative of several other similar assessments (see AMSJ, Abt. 47, Hiemer Papers, letter from Kesselring to the von Hoermann family in Brazil, dated "end of April, 1947").

199. In a press release issued after the trial, Laternser emphasized that Kesselring had not been concerned for himself; rather, he had been concerned "for his honor and the honor of German soldiers and the German military leadership. Kesselring is convinced that he conducted the war in Italy as decently and humanely as possible" (BA-MA, N 431/932, Laternser to Hamsher, 9 June 1947). In his final address to the court, Laternser stressed that Kesselring had "not defended himself" but had defended "the ideals he represented" (PRO/TNA, Kew, FO 642 [preserved in IWM], vol. 5, 59th day, 6 May 1947).

200. BA-MA, N 750/7, reactions to the death sentence, including Beelitz's and Röttiger's. This theme resurfaced in 1951 when Albrecht Böhme offered himself as a witness for Kesselring's denazification proceedings, giving as his reason: "The defense of the Field Marshal is a defense of the honor of non-Nazi German soldiers who only knew their duty to the Fatherland, and it is one of our most honorable concerns to do the best that we can!" (letter from Böhme to Laternser, 27 April 1951, in BA-MA, N 750/6).

201. AMSJ, Dept. 47, Hiemer Papers, Keller to Hiemer, 18 January 1947.

202. BA-MA, N 431/932, Luise Jodl to Laternser, 27 December 1946. Luise Jodl wrote of "the honest hope for a victorious battle." Before her marriage, Luise Jodl, née von Benda, had worked, inter alia, as secretary to Wehrmacht General Enno von Rintelen in Rome, and she was personally familiar with conditions in Italy up to 1944. She advised Laternser when selecting witnesses. See Luise Jodl, *Jenseits des Endes: Leben und Sterben des Generalobersten Alfred Jodl* (Vienna 1976).

203. BA-MA, N 750/3, Kesselring trial diary, entry dated 9 February 1947: "The battle commences!"

204. AMSJ, Dept. 47, Hiemer Papers, letter from Generalrichter Keller to Hiemer, 18 January 1947.

205. BA-MA, N 431/932, Laternser to Hiemer, 25 December 1947: Case 7 (trial of the "South-East Generals"), where he defended Field Marshals Wilhelm List and Maximilian Weichs, and Case 12 (Wehrmacht High Command trial), where he appeared for Field Marshal Wilhelm Ritter von Leeb.

206. Field Marshal von Leeb was sentenced to three years' imprisonment, which he had already served by the time the verdict was announced. He was thus effectively sentenced to

time served, which was interpreted as "an acquittal due to proven innocence" (see, for example, Siegfried Westphal, *Der deutsche Generalstab auf der Anklagebank: Nürnberg 1945–48* [Mainz 1978], p. 141).

207. BA-MA, N 431/978, denazification indictment against Hans Laternser, 11 May 1948. On 1 May 1933, he was admitted to the National Socialist Party with membership number 2,100,161.

208. Ibid. Since Laternser had never "provided the photograph required for a membership card to be issued," he officially remained a probationary member without a membership card, which later allowed him to be classified as a "follower" when he appeared before the Denazification Commission. Nevertheless, he contested this finding, seeking classification in group V ("discharged") in order to avoid paying the RM 2,000 fine (see BA-MA, N 431/978, denazification decision regarding Laternser, 9 July 1948).

209. NA, Report, folder 3, American Assessment of the Kesselring Trial, Annex B, Defense Counsel (short biographies).

210. Information from the German Federal Archives, Central Verification Office, BA Aachen-Kornelimünster, Zentralnachweisstelle, Laternser personnel file, 22 August 2000. On 1 December 1939, Laternser joined the 3rd Landesschützenzug Regiment, 5/XII Corps and, after one month's basic training, was transferred to the Wiesbaden airbase company as early as 28 December 1939. He was thus a member of the Luftwaffe ground staff. He took part in several training courses and was promoted to sergeant on 1 April 1941. He then trained Luftwaffe recruits in Mainz-Finthen. Having applied for a field commission in 1940, he was promoted to first lieutenant on 1 October 1943. From November 1942, Laternser was a staff officer with the 8th Luftwaffe Field Division. Originally, this division was to be deployed in the relief of Stalingrad, but in fact it was posted to the great bend of the Don River from the end of 1942 to the summer of 1943.

211. Information provided by the German Office for Notifying Close Relatives of Fallen Soldiers in the Former German Wehrmacht (WASt), Berlin, regarding Hans Laternser, 10 October 2000. In his memoirs, Westphal stated that Laternser had "led a company in the East" (see Siegfried Westphal, *Erinnerungen* [Mainz 1975], p. 367).

212. Information provided by the Catholic Parish Office of Schlangenbad on 21 February 2001; Laternser had lived in Schlangenbad since 1957.

213. BA-MA, N 431/933, Laternser to Kesselring, 29 November 1946.

214. BA-MA, N 431/936, Kesselring to Laternser, 26 October 1946. Following the Nuremberg trial of major war criminals, he wrote: "Through the Nuremberg trial, you conquered our hearts as someone the Wehrmacht can have faith in."

215. The preparations were undertaken by Field Marshal von Manstein, Field Marshal Kesselring, Generaloberst Halder, and General Westphal. These preparations were closely associated with the "Memorandum on the Army," which had been prepared as early as November 1945 under the guidance of Manstein, von Halder, Brauchitsch, Warlimont, and Westphal (Westphal, *Erinnerungen*, pp. 366 and 372).

216. One slight pointer in this regard is provided by a letter from Laternser to Oberregierungsrat Dr. Seifarth (erroneously spelled Seyffarth) dated 25 June 1946, in which Laternser requested a memorandum prepared by Seifarth on the German military administration in Italy; in Kesselring's view, this memorandum would assist his defense, and moreover, it also contained "a great deal of useful material" for the defense of the General Staff and the Wehrmacht High Command (see BA-MA, N 431/935, Laternser to Seifarth [Seyffarth], 25 June 1946).

217. Information provided by the German Federal Archives, Central Verification Office, Aachen, 22 August 2000.

218. BA-MA, N 431/936, Kesselring to Laternser, 26 October 1946: "I appreciate your interest in the cause of soldiers."

219. BA-MA, N 431/935, Westphal to Laternser, 12 August 1946.

220. Hoermann warned that the Brazilian funds should not be sent to a consulate or embassy ("experience has shown that such transfers . . . do not serve their purpose") but should rather be transferred directly via the Vatican. Handling the funds through the Vatican was an obvious choice, since Brazil was "very Catholic" and maintained better relations with the Vatican than with Italy (BA-MA, N 431/932, undated letter from Hoermann, handwritten, probably autumn 1946). Hoermann made sure Laternser "knew that his costs etc. would be paid sooner or later from Brazil" (letters from Hoermann's niece, Alda Niemeyer, Brazil, to the author, 6 May 2000 and 26 January 2001).

221. At the end of June, Mrs. Kesselring received a letter from Brazil accusing Laternser himself of causing the plan to fail. Due to the "declaration which he issued in Venice stating that he was being financed from Brazil," the letter said, "Laternser has caused quite a fuss in the press here" (BA-MA, N 431/937, letter extract, Hans von Hoermann to Liny Kesselring, June 1947). Because foreign currency transactions by the Banco do Brasil—even those going to the Vatican—had to be checked and approved, it was "impossible for Dona Margarida and her family to help, much as they would have liked to do so." Some "grass had to grow" over the matter first. "Albert" and "Wiesbaden" should draw lessons from the affair and learn not to talk so much about things. Liny Kesselring's view was that the Vatican representatives were responsible for the plan failing, since they had not "acted in the manner discussed" (BA-MA, N 431/937, Liny Kesselring to Laternser, 16 June 1947).

222. However, they did not have to starve, for they were well fed in the German Franciscan convent in Venice. During the trial, each member of Laternser's team received £1 in pocket money per week from the British, although this was in the form of a loan repayable following the trial (BA-MA, N 431/935, Laternser to Dalrymple, 11 April 1947).

223. BA-MA, N 431/933, Laternser to Moellhausen, 23 February 1950: "Due to the fact that I spent years away from my practice, and certainly did not get rich during the trials I was involved in, I now have to start from the beginning again in Wiesbaden. It will take some time before I can live free of cares again. The ongoing overheads are extraordinarily high."

224. BA-MA, N 431/932, letter from Hiemer to Laternser, 2 July 1947: "As the result of a letter from the Casa Fontana, dated 23 June 1947, Dr. Frohwein is now in a very happy financial situation, thanks to friends here and across the ocean. Dr. Stück has also received donations from across the ocean."

225. On 5 November 1947, the fee of RM 17,000 was transferred to Laternser by Kesselring's brother, Guido, and his nephew, Kurt Himmel, a brewery owner (BA-MA, N 431/933, bank slip dated 5 November 1947 for RM 7,000 in the name of Dr. Guido Kesselring, Bayreuth, and bank slip dated 11 November 1947 for RM 10,000 in the name of Kurt Himmel, Marktsteft). Laternser had the money deposited in an escrow account.

226. However, it may be that Kesselring's request was not granted for pragmatic reasons: Generalrichter Hans Keller, who was interned in the Bellaria-Rimini generals' camp, was permanently available, whereas Laternser was in the American zone in Germany and was thus too far away from the War Crimes Group preparing the trial on site in Italy.

227. BA-MA, N 431/936, Kesselring to Laternser, 31 December 1946.

228. AMSJ, Dept. 47, Hiemer Papers, Keller to Hiemer, 18 January 1947.

229. BA-MA, N 750/2, London Diary, p. 63: "However, one had to accept the possibility that, even if the London jurists do not consider legal proceedings necessary, a trial will be held because so much has been written and said about the Kesselring case around the world. In addition, the English Army in Italy, which is much more heavily subject to the pressure of Italian opinion, may have formed a rather more negative opinion."

230. BA-MA, N 750/2, London Diary, p. 78: "Since I was informed on January 7th by a Major attached to the Historical Division that I must hold myself in readiness after Friday January 10th, I know that my trial will take place. On the radio, I heard directly that the trial will take place in Venice in the middle of February, or during the second half of February. In front of an Allied court? Is this word a 'mistake,' or is this really the case? Will the trial then be extended to the states bringing charges?"

231. BA-MA, N 750/2, London Diary, p. 69: "If, for example, generals refuse to sign clemency petitions on behalf of Jodl and Keitel (e.g., Halder), or are only prepared to sign a clemency petition for Falkenhorst at my urging, having first deleted the words 'comradely solidarity,' then I feel emotionally separated from these men. I have also told various generals, and Büchs, that if a petition is not spontaneously prepared after my conviction, I don't want them to prepare one at all. Mine is not a beggar's nature!"

232. BA-MA, N 750/2, London Diary, p. 78: "Which means: Venice? World interest declines further away from Rome; the 'Street' is also not as vocal. Two positive factors! On the other hand, however, Venice is close to the Monte Grappa antipartisan police operations. These events will probably be addressed during the proceedings."

233. In 1963, Richard Halse wrote a report on his forty years in the JAG department, in which he also briefly dealt with the Kesselring trial. This source is of inestimable value, since it offers an inside view by a British participant, and I am indebted to Tom Bower (London) for providing me with a copy of this report from his private papers. In 1980, shortly before Halse's death, Bower was able to interview the colonel during his research for *Blind Eye to Murder.* Halse, "40 Years On," unpublished memoirs, probably written in 1963, 96 pages, at p. 45: "Jim Hamilton took me over to Venice and I at once decided that if there was to be a trial of Kesselring that would be the place. We selected a court between the Rialto bridge and the market."

234. BA-MA, N 431/936, Kesselring to Laternser, 29 August 1946. This letter included two drafts, one a draft letter to the Italian witness Marchich, who was asked to recruit other Italians as witnesses, and the other a draft letter to the German camp leader General Hartmann in Rimini-Miramare.

235. BA-MA, N 431/935, Laternser to Weizsäcker, 21 September 1946.

236. For example, Kesselring drafted a letter to Vice Admiral Loewisch that included a positive affidavit for Loewisch to sign in favor of Kesselring and his manner of dealing with Hitler's destruction order in Italy. He requested confirmation that even though Kesselring had retained the Wehrmacht High Command plans for the destruction of Italian ports, he only did so "to ensure that they would be fully dropped in the event" (BA-MA, N 431/933, Kesselring to Loewisch, 21 October 1946, Laternser's copy).

237. BA-MA, N 431/932, Laternser to Ingelheim, 30 August 1946.

238. Alexander P. Scotland, *The London Cage* (London 1957), p. 180.

239. BA-MA, N 431/874, voluntary statement made by Kesselring to Lieutenant Nicholson, British Rhine Army, Allendorf, 13 November 1944. That Kesselring made this statement with the impending Rome trial in mind is also indicated by the fact that he testified to the outstanding personal qualities of Mackensen and Mältzer. Given General Mältzer's famous rages

directed at his subordinates, not to mention his problems with alcohol, one can only interpret this statement as an obliging favor on Kesselring's part.

240. Ibid., p. 2. In addition, a reduction in the "shooting ratio" would have been impossible without entailing personal disadvantages or risks for the public. When Kesselring was informed by Ernst von Weizsäcker after the event that the Vatican had criticized the killing of innocent people, he ordered his intelligence officer (Ic), Zolling, to investigate the matter; Zolling found at the time that the only victims were convicted criminals.

241. BA-MA, N 750/2, London Diary, pp. 42f.: "I want to place myself in front of my subordinates. This means that there are some things I cannot write down to avoid incriminating them. But there is one thing I can confide in these pages: I am truly shaken by how little my closest subordinates have been proactive, and how heavily they have incriminated me, because they have simply not made the effort to probe the real reasons for my actions, and have merely let matters take their course with a flick of the hand."

242. BA-MA, N 431/888, notes made by Kesselring for Laternser on Halse's opening statement, probably 17 February 1947, 14 loose sheets, at sheet 6.

243. Ibid., sheet 7.

244. Beelitz's most recent reference to this egocentric, self-sacrificial motivation occurred when I interviewed him in Stuttgart on 14 February 2001; he died in September 2001.

245. Erich Schwinge, *Militärstrafgesetzbuch* [Military Penal Code] (Berlin 1936). The code went through six editions by 1944. Schwinge was not only a theoretician but also, as an army judge, a practitioner of a rigorous deterrent justice system—a system to which, especially in the final months of the war, many soldiers fell victim. See the biographical study by Detlef Garbe, *"In jedem Einzelfall . . . bis zur Todesstrafe": Der Militärstrafrechtler Erich Schwinge—Ein deutsches Juristenleben* (Hamburg 1989), and also Manfred Messerschmidt and Fritz Wüllner, *Die Wehrmachtjustiz im Dienste des Nationalsozialismus: Zerstörung einer Legende* (Baden-Baden 1987); in contrast, see Erich Schwinge's apologia, *Verfälschung und Wahrheit: Das Bild der Wehrmachtgerichtsbarkeit* (Tübingen 1988), and Schwinge, *Bilanz der Kriegsgeneration: Ein Beitrag zur Geschichte unserer Zeit* (Marburg 1978).

246. BA-MA, N 431/931, Frohwein to Laternser, 5 November 1946.

247. PRO/TNA, Kew, FO 642, vol. 5, 54th day (25 April 1947). In February 1944, Schütze served as judge with the Tenth Army; from March 1944 to 15 May 1944, he served as assistant to the divisional judge in Italy (334th Division), and then he was again sent to serve as judge with the Tenth Army. As an army judge, he was cognizant of events surrounding the punishment operation in the Fosse Ardeatine, which took place in his immediate area of work. He also would have been aware of the Bandenbefehle, and their effects, in the course of his work as a judge.

248. As the best-known German professor of military law—Schwinge was a permanent contributor to the *Zeitschrift für Wehrrecht*, the main journal for military jurists during the National Socialist era—he was superbly qualified to contribute to a successful defense in the Kesselring case. Laternser had previously asked Professor Wolgast in Würzburg for assistance (BA-MA, N 431/935, Laternser to Wolgast, 30 October 1946).

249. ZSL, JAG, criminal proceedings against Albert Kesselring, index of witness statements, section 5, "Schwinge."

250. Erich Schwinge and Otto Peter Schwelling, *Die deutsche Militärjustiz in der Zeit des Nationalsozialismus* (Marburg 1977).

251. Ibid. Thus, Laternser already knew Erich Schwinge and Friedrich Frohwein from Marburg, where the two men held academic positions. It is therefore possible that Laternser

had studied under Schwinge. In 1931, Frohwein moved to Kassel, where he was appointed to a senior civil service position. Albrecht Schütze, who was two years his senior, took his exams with Laternser in 1934 in Berlin and subsequently worked as a public prosecutor attached to the Berlin Regional Court.

252. Hiemer was initially employed as an announcer with Vatican Radio, before being appointed professor of holy scripture at the Pontifical College in Anagni; he held this post from 1943 to 1946. In January 1944, he handed Kesselring a memorandum from the bishops of Anagni, Alatri, Ferentino, and Veroli, demanding that church property be protected and that monasteries in the front area remain undamaged. The memorandum also demanded that the civilian population be spared and sought an end to the deportations of Italian civilians to work in the Reich. During the meeting at Rocca di Mezzo on 3 January 1944, Kesselring guaranteed this protection. He was subsequently held in high esteem by both Hiemer and the Italian bishops who were involved. Thereafter, Hiemer had liaised—at Kesselring's request—between the field marshal and the Vatican and Italian bishops.

253. Wette, "Bild der Wehrmacht-Elite," p. 296.

254. Günter Buchstab, "Die Nürnberger Prozesse und der 'Heidelberger Kreis' (1949–1955)," in Peter R. Weilemann, ed., *Macht und Zeitkritik: Festschrift für Hans-Peter Schwarz zum 65. Geburtstag* (Paderborn 1999), pp. 61–74.

255. The Röttiger Papers (BA-MA, N 422/12) include a handwritten appeal to "use all contacts" to ensure a successful defense of accused comrades and also to awaken foreign media interest in the cases.

256. BA-MA, N 431/936, Kesselring to Laternser, 29 August 1946.

257. See the speeches and addresses of welcome at the memorial event commemorating the fortieth anniversary of Kesselring's death in Wiessee, 20 September 2000, Archives of the German Montecassino Association.

258. BA-MA, N 431/933, Laternser to the camp commandants of Dachau, Garmisch, Bridgend, and Rimini and Field Marshal von Manstein, 21 September 1946: "Possible charges include command orders, the antipartisan war in Italy, bombing raids (Warsaw, Rotterdam and Coventry)."

259. BA-MA, N 431/931, Fähndrich to Laternser, 28 October 1946, from the Gmunden/Upper Austria camp, seven affidavits; BA-MA, N 431/931, Doerstling to Laternser, 26 October and 15 November 1946, from the Garmisch camp (PWE 8), thirty-seven affidavits.

260. Thus, writing from Dachau camp, Walter Hutmacher told Laternser that he could expect "the most important exculpatory statements on Field Marshal Kesselring's behalf" from Rimini-Bellaria camp. He provided further information regarding witnesses' names and addresses and promised that more addresses would be collected (BA-MA, N 431/931, Hutmacher to Laternser, 1 October 1946). Erich von Manstein wrote from the Special German POW Camp 11 in Bridgend, England, sending nineteen affidavits in Kesselring's favor; see BA-MA, N 431/933, accompanying letter from the Bridgend camp command in Manstein's name to Laternser, 10 December 1946, and BA-MA, N 431/931, Laternser to Bridgend, 27 December 1946.

261. The affidavits mentioned were given to the attorney Dr. von Rohrscheidt to take to Laternser in Nuremberg, rather than being entrusted to the postal service.

262. Kesselring's statements to the "Great Court" in London (February 1946), his statement to the "Commission" (July 1946), Westphal's statement to the "Commission" (June 1946), and the interrogations of Kesselring, Westphal, and Zollings by American prosecutor Colonel Williams were also considered important to Mackensen and Kesselring (BA-MA, N 431/932, Hauser to Laternser, 6 October 1946).

263. BA-MA, N 431/935, Röttiger to Laternser, 7 October 1946.

264. Ibid. With regard to Röttiger's witness list, it is noteworthy that Laternser did not avail himself of all the suggestions.

265. Ibid. The following witnesses were earmarked in respect to Rotterdam: "General d. Fl. Helm, Speidel (Dachau or Garmisch), General d. Fl. Seidemann (Munster camp), Generalleutnant Trettner (Munster camp), the latter also in respect to Italy, Speidel also in respect to Warsaw."

266. Ibid. The following witnesses were earmarked in respect to Coventry: "General d. Fl. Bülovius, Lt. General Plocher, Lt. General Korte (all in Allendorf Camp)."

267. Ibid. The following were to testify in respect to Italy (antipartisan warfare): "General v. Senger und Etterlin (England), Colonel i. G. v.d. Knesebeck, Colonel i. G. Fähndrich and Lt. Colonel i. G. Eggert (Dachau), Colonel Heggenreiner (German adjutant to Graziani), Marshal Graziani, Cardinal Schuster (previously Milan), Prof. Bruhns and Reidemeister in respect to art treasures (whereabouts unknown), General Dr. Meinardus in respect to field hospitals sites (Rimini)."

268. BA-MA, N 431/936, Kesselring to Laternser, 29 August 1946. From January 1942 until November 1944, Buttlar was the First Army General Staff officer and chief of operations (army) in the Wehrmacht High Command. According to rumors in Allendorf, Buttlar was preparing a new affidavit for Mackensen that would precisely delineate the events leading to 335 Italians being shot in the Fosse Ardeatine, with particular regard to the chain of command.

269. Thus, Generalmajor Wolf Hauser—former chief of General Staff of the Fourteenth Army—asked Laternser, then still involved in the Nuremberg IMT trial, to take custody of the affidavits he had gathered on behalf of Kesselring and von Mackensen (BA-MA, N 431/932, letter from Hauser to Laternser, 29 August 1946).

270. Despite the fact that he also testified at Nuremberg, Beelitz did not encounter his former commanding officer, Kesselring, there, since he only testified on the issue of antipartisan warfare in the "Small Court," where he spent no more than two days (my interview with Beelitz in Stuttgart on 14 February 2001). As already mentioned, after testifying on Göring's behalf, Kesselring did not stay in the witnesses' wing—where Beelitz was accommodated—but was held in solitary confinement like the other defendants.

271. BA-MA, N 431/931, Beelitz to Laternser, 22 October 1946. The circumspection displayed by Kesselring's former chief of operations is striking: he had retained copies of the affidavits and reports on partisan activity so that he could hand them to Laternser personally if the latter was already in Italy and could no longer be reached by mail in Germany. He also told witnesses that they should send a copy of their affidavit to Father Dahlgruen, Via Toscana 7, Rome, "requesting that he pass them to the German defense at the start of the trial" (PRO/TNA, Kew, WO 310/129, Beelitz, model for witnesses, undated). This circumspection is particularly noteworthy when one considers the circumstances under which the officers were detained and the difficulties attendant on making copies of affidavits that often ran to several pages, notwithstanding the fact that Bellaria camp had an office at the inmates' disposal.

272. BA-MA, N 431/931, Beelitz to Laternser, 22 October 1946. Beelitz established contact with Mr. Wolfgang Hagemann, who had borne responsibility for "art protection" in Italy from 1944 to 1945. Kesselring hoped that Hagemann's testimony would prove exculpatory and would strengthen the idea of Kesselring as a "friend of Italy." It was also intended that Hagemann would provide documents or letters of gratitude from Italian authorities or churches, thus further buttressing the idea that Kesselring had spared Italy's cultural treasures.

273. BA-MA, N 431/932, Ingelheim to Laternser, 23 September 1946.

274. Seifarth wrote that he "honored the Field Marshal as a man" but could "now no longer conceal" the fact that he was "resolutely politically opposed" to Kesselring and had been part of the "movement of July 20th 1944 associated with Regierungspräsident Graf von der Schulenbrug, Breslau" (BA-MA, N 431/935, Seifarth to Laternser, 4 October 1946). Laternser exploited this loyalty, writing to Seifarth that he needed witnesses to testify in the same manner about Kesselring's attitude to Florence; he also asked him to describe "the results of his pro-Italian policy," referring to disadvantages vis-à-vis Hitler (BA-MA, N 431/935, Laternser to Seifarth, 30 October 1946).

275. BA-MA, N 431/305, folder, "Unused affidavits."

276. BA-MA, N 431/932, appendix to letter from Hasche, 6 February 1947, p. 1.

277. BA-MA, N 431/932, letter from Hasche to Laternser, 6 February 1947. Knesebeck's statements related to the command situation in the antipartisan war, in particular the blurred lines of command between the SS and Luftwaffe.

278. BA-MA, N 431/935, Scotland to Laternser, 30 November 1946.

279. I was able to trace Eduard Spitzeder's whereabouts in later years, but he died in 1992. His son, Edmund Spitzeder of Peiting, kindly examined the family papers but was unable to find any notes made by his father regarding the wartime period.

280. BA-MA, N 431/936, Kesselring to Laternser, 29 August 1946, item 3.

281. BA-MA, N 750/2, London Diary, p. 74.

282. BA-MA, N 431/933, Laternser to Manstein, 30 October 1946.

283. BA-MA, N 431/935, draft letter from Laternser to the German camp commandants, 30 October 1946.

284. Ibid.

285. On 4 October 1946, when being interrogated by Colonel Scotland, Kesselring provided written statements on each specific case. ZSL, JAG 260, Exhibit 3, voluntary statement by POW Albert Kesselring regarding the atrocities committed within the operational area of Army Group C during the fight against Italian partisans from 1943 to 1945.

286. He was probably referring to the supreme SS and police commander, Karl Wolff.

287. BA-MA, N 431/878, memo by Kesselring for Laternser regarding antipartisan orders, undated.

288. Ibid.

289. He probably knew quite a lot, judging by his Nuremberg and London statements, as well as the memos he prepared at Laternser's request following the prosecution's opening statement (BA-MA, N 431/873). Kesselring's trial diary (BA-MA, N 750/3) includes a note to the effect that he dictated this "questionnaire" on 22 February. On 23 February, he held a "long questionnaire discussion with Laternser."

290. BA-MA, N 431/878, memo by Kesselring for Laternser regarding antipartisan orders, undated.

291. Ibid. These would include, for example, Sia and Partina (April 1944), Civitella (29 June 1944), Guardistallo (29 June 1944), Montemignaio (29 June 1944), Palazzo del Pero (24 June 1944), Gubbio (20–23 July 1944), Caprane (23 September 1944), Bussano (26 September 1944), and Villa del'Albero (27 November 1944).

292. Ibid., Padulivo, p. 3.

293. PRO/TNA, Kew, WO 310/127, confidential inquiry by Colonel Halse to the Judge Advocate General's Office, 25 July 1946.

294. Beelitz—then a colonel and encouraged to record his affidavit somewhat later than

Kesselring—gave me an interview in Stuttgart on 29 October 1998. He stated that when he was in the London Cage during December 1946, the cells were very cramped; there were no tables, and the bunks were folded up during the day. The guards indicated their disdain by placing the prisoners' food on the cell floors. He and the prisoner in the next cell, Field Marshal Gerd von Rundstedt, froze because there was practically no heating.

295. Scotland, *London Cage,* p. 178.

296. Kesselring paid particular attention to whatever radio and press coverage he could access. Thus, on 26 October 1946, he sent Laternser a "really nice" article from the U.S. military paper *Stars and Stripes,* which he had been given surreptitiously (BA-MA, N 431/936, Kesselring to Laternser, 26 October 1946).

297. Scotland, *London Cage,* pp. 12 and 178.

298. BA-MA, N 750/2, London Diary, p. 61.

299. Ibid., pp. 61—63.

300. BA-MA, N 431/935, Laternser to Scotland, 16 November 1946. Here, Laternser referred to a letter dated 16 November 1946, in which he asked Scotland for copies of seized German records relating to the antipartisan war.

301. BA-MA, N 431/931, War Crimes Commission to Laternser, 5 September 1946.

302. BA-MA, N 431/305, unused affidavits, Allen Dulles, 1 August 1946. Dulles referred to the agreements between himself and Wolff not to allow any further destruction in Italy during the German retreat; otherwise, the surrender negotiations would have been terminated. Both Wolff and the commander-in-chief in Italy at the time, Generaloberst von Vietinghoff-Scheel, had agreed to this.

303. BA-MA, N 431/931, Laternser to Field Marshal Alexander, 16 November 1946.

304. BA-MA, N 431/931, Office of the Governor-General of Canada, General Alexander, to Laternser, 22 March 1947. Nigel Nicolson stressed that Alexander regretted not being able to go out on a limb in this matter for political reasons; see Nicolson, *Alex: The Life of Field Marshal Earl Alexander of Tunis* (London 1973), p. 296.

305. BA-MA, N 431/935, Laternser to Zolling, 21 September 1946. As early as 21 September 1946, even before the end of the Nuremberg trial, he had written to the German commandant of Dachau camp seeking defense witnesses and affidavits. He also wrote to Colonel Zolling (Kesselring's former chief of intelligence, who had already been released) and to the former German ambassador to the Vatican, Ernst von Weizsäcker, as well as to Manstein, who was interned in Bridgend camp in England. Zolling was a particularly problematic witness, but his evidence would be crucial when it came to the selection of candidates for execution in the Fosse Ardeatine massacre. On 21 October and again on 21 December 1946, Laternser reiterated his plea to Zolling to have his statements certified. However, by then, Zolling had been moved to Dachau camp, where he was unable to meet Laternser's requests. The matter was only resolved during the trial. On 21 February 1947, Laternser received a letter from Westphal explaining that during the summer of 1946, Zolling had been involved in a serious road accident while traveling in an open-backed truck during a prisoner transport. He had been hospitalized for several months with serious head injuries before being interned in Dachau camp. It was only in the middle of January 1947 that he, Westphal, had succeeded in obtaining Zolling's release from Dachau, since he required him for the Historical Division in Allendorf. Zolling was a "shadow of himself." Westphal advised calling him as a witness toward the beginning of the trial in order to spare this "badly beaten man" further suffering (BA-MA, N 431/935, Westphal to Laternser, 21 February 1947).

306. BA-MA, N 431/936, Kesselring to Laternser, 26 October 1946, item 1. At the end of

October, Kesselring had finished "the written work for Frohwein or Schütze," thus forming—as he wrote hopefully to Laternser—the basis for the "success to which they aspired" during the forthcoming visit to Rimini camp.

307. Ibid., item 3. During this third phase, Laternser deliberately sought witnesses who could reinforce the picture drawn by Kesselring, as well as Westphal, of the war in Italy. In this regard, he tried to personally visit the men in question to discuss the required statements; such precautions made sense in a time of postal disruptions and possible phone taps.

308. BA-MA, N 431/932, letter from Laternser to General Jordan (general commanding Panzer troops), 7 January 1947, enclosing a handwritten draft by Kesselring on the antipartisan war in Italy, the "police operation in the Bassano del Grappa and Caprane area." The letter illustrates the importance of this inquiry. Laternser wrote: "Field Marshal Kesselring states that he primarily requested the cleansing of the Grappa mountain range in order to finally facilitate reconnaissance and development of the position intended for this area." Jordan accepted all the wording in the letter.

309. BA-MA, N 431/931, Laternser to the specified camp commandants, 7 January 1947. The camps in question were Munsterlager (Sub-Camp C), Garmisch-Partenkirchen, Bridgend/Glamorgan (POW Camp 11) in South Wales, the 1st SEP Center CMF in Rimini-Riccione, Gmunden Camp in Upper Austria, and Allendorf Quarry Camp near Marburg. Those individuals who were specified by name included Commanding Generals Feuerstein, Herr, Hauck, and Schlemm, as well as Divisional Commanders von Rohr, Graeser, Dr. Pollack, Jost, Ehlert, Schrank, Heidrich, Pfeiffer, Raepke, Steinmetz, Reinhardt, von Heygendorff, Trompeter, Boelcke, and Schmalz. Laternser was rather circumspect in making his request: "Which of the gentlemen specified is aware of details regarding the events listed below, which involved acts against partisans and associated measures against partisan groups [*Bandengruppen*]?" Once again, Laternser's detailed knowledge is remarkable. He specified the locations classified by month: Partina and Stia, Civitella, Guardistallo, Palazzo del Pero, Montemignaio, Cavriglia, Padulivo, Valdarno, San Polo, Fibocchi (Castiglione), Cucchio, Quota, Bucine, Rifredo Castello, Apuaner Alpen, Fuccecchio, Borgo Ticino, Bochoia, Pasino, Torlano, Valli di Pasubio, Crecentino, Montecchio di Crossara, Vercelli, San Stefano Magra, Verucchio, Caprano, Bassano, Sarsina, San Martino, and Villa dell'Albero.

310. Ibid. At the same time, he tried to obtain information regarding other commanders under Kesselring's authority. He was particularly anxious to discover the names of the commanders of the Secret Field Police in the South-West Army Group and Luftflotte 2 (Airfleet 2)—probably in order to be able to identify those directly responsible for the "events."

311. BA-MA, N 431/935, Vietinghoff to Laternser, 21 June 1946, report, 8 pages, at p. 6. On learning of the massacre at San Polo from an Allied radio broadcast on 14 July 1944, Vietinghoff initiated court-martial inquiries, as did General Herr, who immediately relieved the commander responsible, Colonel Wolf Evert, of his duties. Regarding the destruction of Italian industrial facilities ordered by the Wehrmacht High Command, which Vietinghoff successfully resisted, he stated that he had not wanted to plunge the Italian people into misery and long-term unemployment, since he "still viewed them as friends"—probably a dig at Kesselring's well-known statement that he "could now only hate" the Italians.

312. Kesselring had himself suggested SS and police commanders as potential witnesses to antipartisan operations, since they were extremely well informed regarding the war waged on the partisans and in some cases had carried out the so-called actions themselves. Laternser initially advised against seeking statements from SS witnesses (BA-MA, N 431/936, Kesselring to Laternser, 26 October 1946, 12 items, item 3; thus, it was intended that Laternser should

approach former Gauleiter Hofer and SS Commander Brunner, seeking statements on the Caprane and Bassano case).

313. BA-MA, N 431/935, Laternser to von Seidel in Bridgend, 21 December 1946. Laternser's wording was ambiguous: "Simon, . . . Brunner, . . . Tensfeld . . . should be aware of events in . . . " In his letter, he wrote that Simon was in the best position to issue a statement on events in Apuana (this probably referred to the Appuanian Coast near Pietrasanta, especially the reprisal at Sant'Anna di Stazzema), whereas Brunner would be best informed regarding Caprane, Bassano, and Sassina; further, he said that Tensfeld would be able to provide information on Vercelli and Crescentino and that General Roth should issue statements on Valdarno and Fibocchi.

314. BA-MA, N 431/935, Röttiger to Laternser, 7 October 1946. Ekkehardt Albert was also interned in Allendorf, where he was unable to withstand the pressure exerted by the "defense staff" under Westphal's command.

315. Carlo Gentile, "'Politische Soldaten': Die 16. SS-Panzer-Grenadier-Division 'Reichsführer-SS' in Italien 1944," *QFIAB* 81 (2001): 540, and BA-MA, RH 20-14/41, AOK 14, War Journal No. 4, 30 September 1944, p. 377.

316. During the war, Kesselring attached particular value to maintaining good contacts with the Italian clergy. He stated he was willing to spare works of art or even entire cities (such as Rome, Florence, and Siena), and in specific cases, he secured the release of Italian internees following interventions by the bishops of Florence and Bologna (see Eugen Dollmann, *Dolmetscher der Diktatoren* [Bayreuth 1963], p. 183). In return, however, Kesselring expected the princes of the church to appeal to the public for calm and to use their sermons to exhort Italians to obey their German occupiers.

317. The letters were taken to Italy by church couriers thanks to the good offices of Cardinal Frings, the archbishop of Cologne, and the Missione Pontefica, the Vatican embassy in Germany (BA-MA, N 431/934, 6 February 1947).

318. BA-MA, N 431/931, Laternser to the Archbishop of Florence, 20 January 1947.

319. BA-MA, N 431/931, Laternser to Berndorff, 20 January 1947.

320. For more on the role played by the pope in this issue, see Giovanni Miccoli, *I dilemmi e i silenzi di Pio XII: Vaticano, Seconda Guerra Mondiale e Shoah* (Milan 2000), and Robert Katz, *Fatal Silence: The Pope, the Resistance and the German Occupation of Rome* (London 2003). There probably were unofficial contacts between German ambassador Ernst von Weizsäcker and Pope Pius XII relating to the Via Rasella attack (Katz, *Fatal Silence*, p. 257). Also see Pierre Blet, *Pie XII et la Seconde Guerre Mondiale d'après les archives du Vatican* (Paris 1997), p. 250. John Cornwell, *Pius XII: Der Papst, der geschwiegen hat* (Munich 1999), p. 374, noted that the *Osservatore Romano*, in its issue published on 26 March 1944, expressed sympathy with the relatives of the murdered soldiers and with the "320 people sacrificed in place of the guilty parties." This piece in the Vatican newspaper antagonized both sides: the Germans angrily pointed out that all those killed had already been condemned, and the partisans accused the pope of betraying Italy's interests and taking the side of the occupiers. This allegation had also been made in another context. In an article in *Osservatore Romano* dated 30 October 1943, the Vatican took the Germans' side, praising the humanity displayed by the German occupiers and their efforts to protect cultural treasures (see BA-MA, N 431/935, letter from Ernst von Weizsäcker to Laternser, 24 June 1946; regarding the date of the article, it should probably read 1944).

321. Simon Wiesenthal, *Recht, nicht Rache: Erinnerungen* (Frankfurt 1988); Cornwell, *Pius XII*, p. 375.

322. The letter in which Oberstleutnant Dietrich offered himself to the pope (!) as a defense witness for Kesselring was transmitted to Laternser by the Vatican secretariat (!) and can be found in BA-MA, N 431/865.

323. AMSJ Munich, Dept. 47, Hiemer Papers, letter from Hiemer to Montini, Vatican, 14 February 1947.

324. Laternser and the former German ambassador to the Vatican, Ernst von Weizsäcker, briefly discussed a plan to call a witness from the Vatican to attest to Kesselring's benevolence and his efforts to protect Italian cultural treasures. However, this plan was abandoned due to time constraints, and a corresponding request was never submitted to the Holy See (BA-MA, N 431/935, Laternser to Weizsäcker, 30 October 1946, and Weizsäcker's response, 22 November 1946).

325. This statement refers particularly to an essay by Cambridge professor H. Lauterpacht entitled "The Law of Nations and the Punishment of War Crimes," published in the 1944 *Yearbook of International Law.* Schwinge ordered twenty copies of the essay for use in the trial (BA-MA, N 431/935, Schwinge to Brother Vögele, 14 March 1947). Laternser's files also contain a note of thanks from Professor Schwinge to the rector of the German-Hungarian seminary in Rome, dated March 1947. Schwinge expressed his gratitude not only for the rector's hospitality but also for "valuable bibliographical references" that had helped prepare the defense case. Rector Brust had apparently drawn Schwinge's attention to the article (BA-MA, N 431/931, Schwinge to Rector Father Carlo Brust, Rome, 20 March 1947).

326. BA-MA, N 431/862, affidavit issued by the bishops of Alatri, Ferentino, and Veroli, 25 July 1946.

327. BA-MA, N 431/864, Archbishop of Florence to Laternser, 24 February 1947.

328. BA-MA, N 431/864, Archbishop of Siena to Laternser, 24 February 1947.

329. BA-MA, N 431/935, telegram from Venturi to Laternser, 24 February 1947.

330. BA-MA, N 750/3, Kesselring's trial diary, entry dated 26 April 1947. "Read by the judge without inflection" was Kesselring's assessment.

331. BA-MA, N 431/931, examination permit for Laternser regarding Kesselring dated 31 December 1946; BA-MA, N 431/931, examination permit for Laternser regarding Kesselring dated 2 January 1946 (this should probably read 2 January 1947).

332. BA-MA, N 431/933, Laternser to the Secretary General of the Nuremberg IMT enclosing camp mail for Rimini and Bridgend, 21 September 1946.

333. BA-MA, N 431/866, Laternser's witness list for the Kesselring trial, sorted according to the items regarding which testimony had been submitted.

334. See also the 6 May 1947 letter of farewell to Kesselring from British soldiers serving in the guard detachments, praising him for setting an outstanding soldierly example (BA-MA, N 431/935).

335. BA-MA, N 431/935, Röttiger to Laternser, 27 April 1947.

336. Jürgen Engert, *Soldaten für Hitler* (Berlin 1998), interview with Hans Engelhardt, p. 175. While still in Allendorf camp, before being transferred to British custody in Venice, Kesselring allegedly told his guard, Engelhardt, that "if they find me guilty, I will simply have to bite the bullet and bear the consequences, possibly even forfeiting my life. However, if I am found innocent they will have to release me. Whatever the outcome, I must accept it."

337. NA, RG 338, file 000.5, box 816, Report of War Crimes Trial against Albert Kesselring.

338. "Bombardamento di luci," reported the *Gazzettino—Sera* on 10 February 1947, "Dopo rapide battute iniziali rinviato di otto giorni il processo," by Guido Polacco.

339. BA-MA, N 750/3, Kesselring trial diary, entry dated 10 February 1947.

340. ASMAE, AP 1952, Criminali di Guerra, b. 176, report by the Italian Press Agency ANSA, 10 February 1947.

341. NA, RG 338, file 000.5, box 816, Report of War Crimes Trial against Albert Kesselring.

342. Halse, "40 Years On," p. 47, referred to bored American officers in the courtroom.

343. A letter from Röttiger to Laternser included a sentence mentioning "American witnesses" who were due to travel to the court on 28 April 1947 to testify on Kesselring's behalf. However, no verification of this could be found in the trial records (BA-MA, N 431/935, Röttiger to Laternser, 27 April 1947).

344. Thus, Colonel Notestein gave Laternser his copy of the unamended 1940 edition of the American *Rules of Land Warfare* for the defense presentation on 18 March 1947. Notestein wanted to draw Laternser's attention to the fact that American trial law had been retrospectively changed and that the American military legal code actually allowed reprisals against noncombatants. Laternser made use of it; see Richard Raiber, "Generalfeldmarschall Kesselring, Via Rasella, and the 'Ginny Mission,'" *MGM* 56 (1997): 100, and the court transcript of the 24th day (18 March 1947), NA, RG 338, United States Command, MTOUSA, Records of the Special Staff, AG HQ, General Correspondence File 000.5, box 817. I am indebted to Dr. Richard Raiber for this reference.

345. Robert Herde, *Command Responsibility*, p. 304, and BA-MA, N 431/935, opening speech by Laternser, 10 February 1947, p. 3.

346. When questioned in London, Kesselring was only asked about his Bandenbefehle; none of the four statements he made there addressed the shootings in the Fosse Ardeatine. Kesselring could therefore assume that he was primarily charged with issuing orders that facilitated the Apennine bloodbath and was unlikely to be tried for the events in Rome. It is also apparent that Kesselring was unaware his statements could be used against him in court. At the start of the trial, with his own peculiar logic, he stated rather naively that he had learned his London statements by heart "to avoid making any errors now," but at the time, he said, they had "not seemed important to him" (ZSL, JAG 260/1, cross-examination of Kesselring, day 17 [10 March 1947], p. 3).

347. PRO/TNA, Kew, WO 310/127, JAG memorandum.

348. PRO/TNA, Kew, WO 311/28, report, p. 28.

349. Ibid.

350. PRO/TNA, Kew, WO 310/127, JAG memorandum.

351. Ibid.

352. Halse, "40 Years On," p. 47.

353. When interviewed on 4 December 1998 in Stuttgart, Beelitz commented that Halse shook hands with the German accused and witnesses but never with his interpreter. Forrest was greatly hurt by this and apparently told Beelitz, "As far as the English are concerned, we German Jews are dirt."

354. BA-MA, N 431/934, article manuscript (German translation) for the *Gazzettino—Sera*, Venice, ca. 8 May 1947, by Guido Polacco, editor-in-chief, 15 pages, at p. 1.

355. *Cronaca Versilia*, 4 March 1947, "L'autodifesa di Kesselring."

356. BA-MA, N 431/934, article manuscript, p.1.

357. BA-MA, N 750/3, Kesselring trial diary, entry dated 3 March 1947.

358. Halse, "40 Years On," p. 45. On page 46, he wrote: "One could not help to like Kesselring as a man and there was no doubt that he was a good commander."

359. Ibid., p. 46.

360. Ibid., p. 45.

361. Ibid., p. 47: "During the trial, I entertained the defence to dinner, and despite the language barrier it was a very successful evening." In his diary entry on 14 February 1947, Kesselring noted that Laternser and Schwinge had been invited to dinner by Halse and Scotland.

362. BA-MA, N 750/5, reports of proceedings of war crimes trials, copy, p. 13.

363. BA-MA, N 431/935, opening speech by Laternser, 10 February 1947, p. 2.

364. Ibid.

365. Ibid., p. 5.

366. BA-MA, N 431/931, Buerkner to Laternser, 8 January 1947. Laternser had requested an opinion from Leopold Buerkner. Vice Admiral Buerkner, formerly head of the Foreign Section in the office of Admiral Wilhelm Canaris at the Wehrmacht High Command, was in charge of an "international law group." However, Buerkner regretfully noted that this group did not itself investigate breaches of international law but merely issued opinions on international law for the Wehrmacht General Staff. Buerkner's statement was therefore of no use to Kesselring, since he would have been unable to obtain an opinion from Buerkner's department before issuing the Bandenbefehle.

367. BA-MA, N 431/890, proceedings of 17 February 1947, p. 4. When outlining the aims of a British war crimes trial, Halse stated that his duty as prosecution counsel was to convince the court of the defendant's guilt in respect to the two charges constituting the indictment. If Halse was unable to outline the facts of the matter and present a convincing case for Kesselring's guilt, the defendant would have to be acquitted. In legal terms, this allowed Laternser to influence the verdict by challenging the evidence offered by the prosecution.

368. Generalrichter Keller had not been consulted and had thus not eliminated potentially explosive wordings such as "I will indemnify any commander who exceeds our normal restraint" (BA-MA, N 431/890, proceedings of 17 February 1947, opening speech by Halse, p. 13).

369. Ibid., p. 15: "He gave to the troops and the police under his command licence and liberty to do whatever they wanted."

370. Herde, *Command Responsibility*, p. 305.

371. BA-MA, N 750/3, Kesselring trial diary, entry dated 18 February 1947.

372. BA-MA, N 431/886, notes by Kesselring for Laternser, undated but before 30 April 1947.

373. BA-MA, N 750/3, Kesselring trial diary, entry dated 26 February 1947: "An Italian witness had brought terrible photos."

374. BA-MA, N 750/5, reports of proceedings of war crimes trials, selected and edited by the United Nations War Crimes Commission, vol. 8, case no. 44, "The Trial of Albert Kesselring," copy, 17 typewritten pages, at p. 3.

375. BA-MA, N 431/890, proceedings dated 17 February 1947, opening speech by Halse, p. 11.

376. Ibid.: "The German Army, with all their method, made no provisions to ensure that the right number of people were killed, made no enquiries to see how the execution was to be carried out."

377. Ibid.: "It was done completely recklessly."

378. Ibid., p. 21.

379. Ibid., p. 12.

380. BA-MA, N 431/873, exhibits relating to antipartisan operations (so-called sergeant affidavits).

381. IWM, FO 642, vol. 1, 2nd day, 17 February 1947, p. 5. Laternser referred to obvious translation errors that had apparently passed unnoticed. Thus, he based one objection on the death of an 84-year-old woman and her 14-year-old nephew, since such a statement "was highly implausible given the relationship stated." The Italian word *nipote* may refer either to a nephew or a grandson. None of the court interpreters had corrected the error, and Laternser's objection was sustained.

382. BA-MA, N 431/680, Laternser's objection to the "sergeant affidavits," 17 February 1947, 3 pages, at p. 2.

383. Much later, Laternser was to prove himself a true master when it came to discrediting witness statements. He thus attracted attention during the Frankfurt Auschwitz trial through his attempts to brand concentration camp witnesses as unreliable by claiming that their memories had been impaired by their harrowing experiences (see Christian Dirks, "Selekteure als Lebensretter: Die Verteidigungsstrategie des Rechtsanwalts Dr. Hans Laternser," in Irmtrud Wojak, ed., *"Gerichtstag halten über uns selbst": Geschichte und Wirkung des ersten Frankfurter Auschwitz-Prozesses* [Frankfurt 2001], pp. 163–192, at p. 172).

384. Ibid.

385. Ibid., p. 4: "He carried out the instructions thus received as humanely as possible."

386. The examination of witnesses often degenerated into pure hair-splitting, as shown by the following example (BA-MA, N 431/893, 21 March 1947, cross-examination of Beelitz, p. 2): Halse (regarding the Rome transcript): "Are you telling us that you made an error, or the stenographer?" Beelitz: "I certainly never said that either the stenographer or the interpreter made a mistake; after all the field marshal wasn't there. The discussion was also transcribed in German, so that Generalrichter Keller could access the text." Judge: "Let's drop this matter, I don't see any contradictions in the witness's statements."

387. Raiber, "Generalfeldmarschall Kesselring," p. 76.

388. BA-MA, N 431/874, transcript of Rome trial, cross-examination of Kesselring, 25 November 1946, p. 7. During the Rome trial, Mackensen had stated for the record that the order he received through Kesselring's headquarters already bore an addendum to the effect that the reprisal was to be carried out by the SD. Following Mackensen's statement, Kesselring changed his testimony, stating that this addendum had come personally from Hitler and that he had transmitted both orders to Mackensen in the form of a single order.

389. ZSL, JAG 260, trial transcripts, 16th day (7 March 1947), Kesselring cross-examination, p. 7. This sentence was cited by, among others, the *New York Times*, 8 March 1947, "Kesselring Takes Blame," p. 7, col. 3; *Time*, 19 May 1947, "War Crimes," p. 29; and *Time*, 19 April 1954, "Kesselring."

390. BA-MA, N 431/893, transcript of 14 March 1947 (German), examination of Kesselring, p. 16. He was thus asked by Halse: "Is it or is it not a fact, that you left your headquarters on March 24th 1944, and your chief did not notify you of the matter at all?" K.: "I can no longer recall this."

391. ZSL, JAG 260, trial transcripts, 16th day (7 March 1947), Kesselring cross-examination, pp. 7 and 10. Halse asked Westphal: "Did you call Field Marshal Kesselring?" Westphal responded: "No. After I was told that he was . . . that one could not reach him, I did not even try."

392. ZSL, JAG 260/2, Westphal cross-examination, 35th day (31 March 1947), p. 16. Though it is not improbable that Kesselring's car accident and the resulting triple skull fracture affected his memory, such impairment is unlikely to have been as selective as claimed here by Westphal.

393. ZSL, JAG 260/2, Zolling cross-examination, 38th day (3 April 1947), p. 16.

394. ZSL, JAG 260, trial transcripts, 16th day (7 March 1947), Kesselring cross-examination, p. 7.

395. Halse, "40 Years On," p. 46.

396. Ibid.: "I always thought he [Beelitz] was the nigger in the woodpile and that it was probably he and not Kesselring who passed on the order for the Rome massacre for I had a sneaking feeling that Kesselring was not at his headquarters at the time the order came through."

397. Thomas Kühne, "Kameradschaft—'das Beste im Leben eines Mannes,'" GG 22 (1996): 504–529, at p. 519.

398. Friedrich Andrae, *Auch gegen Frauen und Kinder: Der Krieg der deutschen Wehrmacht gegen die Zivilbevölkerung in Italien 1943–1945* (Munich 1995), p. 107. Hitler citation included in Kühne, "Kameradschaft," p. 518.

399. ZSL, JAG 260/2, Zolling cross-examination, 35th day (31 March 1947), p. 31.

400. Scared by Italian newspaper reports that all noncommissioned officers (NCOs) and other ranks suspected of war crimes were to be extradited to Italy, Kesselring formally appealed to the president of the court, Hakewell-Smith, asking him to prevent such extraditions (PRO/TNA, Kew, WO 310/129, Kesselring to Hakewell-Smith, 11 April 1947). Hakewell-Smith passed Kesselring's appeal on to GHQ in Padova (PRO/TNA, Kew, WO 310/129, Hakewell-Smith to GHQ Padova, 13 April 1947).

401. Herde, *Command Responsibility*, p. 310. In this regard, issues relating to the convening of courts-martial, the proportionality of punishment actions against civilians, and the prior threat of such actions using wall posters or radio announcements were repeatedly probed.

402. BA-MA, N 431/934, article manuscript (German translation) for the *Gazzettino—Sera*, Venice, ca. 8 May 1947, by Guido Polacco, editor-in-chief, 15 pages, at p. 6.

403. BA-MA, N 750/3, Kesselring trial diary, entry dated 26 February 1947.

404. *Cronaca Versilia*, 29 February 1947, "Non ci sono prove delle atrocità tedesche," and *Cronaca Versilia*, 4 March 1947, "L'autodifesa di Kesselring."

405. *Süddeutsche Zeitung*, 4 March 1947, "Military Imperatives," p. 2; *Time*, 19 May 1947, "War Crimes," p. 29.

406. BA-MA, N 431/886, Kesselring's notes for Laternser, pt. 3, undated, probably relating to Lemelsen's testimony during cross-examination, 16–17 April 1947.

407. Kesselring was mistaken. The bloody massacre at Bardine San Terenzo was committed by the 16th Panzer Grenadier Division "Das Reich" under the command of Major Walter Reder. See Schreiber, "Deutsche Kriegsverbrechen," p. 183.

408. ZSL, JAG 260/2, Zolling cross-examination, 36th day (1 April 1947), p. 2.

409. BA-MA, N 750/3, Kesselring trial diary, entry dated 8 April 1947.

410. BA-MA, N 431/305, Lemelsen, copy of a deposition written on 22 February 1946 in London for the War Office (Italian Theatre of War, pt. 2), p. 2.

411. Cited in Omer Bartov, *Hitler's Wehrmacht* (Hamburg 1995), p. 132.

412. ZSL, JAG 260/3, trial transcripts, 46th day (16 April 1947), p. 21.

413. Ibid., p. 22.

414. Cited in Lutz Klinkhammer, *Zwischen Bündnis und Besatzung: Das nationalsozialistische Deutschland und die Republik von Salò 1943–1945* (Tübingen 1993), p. 479: "Furthermore, anyone aiding the criminal and perfidious bands (partisans) must be shot immediately: [whether such aid consists of] providing food or accommodation, or transmitting military intelligence." Theoretically, this meant that even children were fair game.

415. BA-MA, N 431/933, Lemelsen to Laternser, 12 May 1947. General Lemelsen believed that the media coverage of the trial would expose him to the charge of having incriminated the field marshal. He feared that this view could, "if spread at home," show him in a bad light "vis-à-vis his comrades."

416. ZSL, JAG 260/2, trial transcripts, 23rd day (17 March 1947), p. 15.

417. BA-MA, N 431/886, Kesselring's notes for Laternser, pt. 3, undated, probably relating to Lemelson's testimony under cross-examination, 16–17 April 1947.

418. Ibid.

419. ZSL, JAG 260, trial transcripts, 17th day (10 March 1947), p. 29.

420. *Times*, 11 March 1947, "German 'Softness' to Partisans: Kesselring's Claim," p. 3.

421. Herde, *Command Responsibility*, p. 312.

422. BA-MA, N 431/887, closing speech by Laternser, 30 April 1947, printed in Hans Laternser, *Verteidigung deutscher Soldaten* (Bonn 1950), pp. 51–108, at p. 51.

423. BA-MA, N 431/936, Kesselring to Laternser, undated, probably 29 April 1947.

424. BA-MA, N 431/936, Kesselring to Hilde Laternser, 1 May 1947.

425. His notes on the prosecutor's closing speech make it clear that Kesselring was deeply annoyed by the charge that he had failed in his supervisory duties: "Even supervision has its limits." Referring to the chain of command in Rome, he also asked: "I'd like to know why I bothered to talk for so long?! The order was not crystal clear!" (BA-MA, N 431/877, Kesselring memo regarding Halse's closing speech; these notes are unsorted and undated but probably are from 1 May 1947.

426. Herde, *Command Responsibility*, p. 314.

427. This issue continues to be the subject of controversy today; see William A. Schabas, *Genozid im Völkerrecht* (Hamburg 2003). The laws of war applicable at the time were vague on the legality of reprisal killings and on the ratio to be used if they were legal. The view was that, even though reprisal killing constituted coercion that breached international law, it could—pursuant to customary law—be used in reaction to breaches of international law by the other side. (For a summary, see Steffen Prauser, "Mord in Rom? Der Anschlag in der via Rasella und die deutsche Vergeltung in den Fosse Ardeatine im März 1944," in *VfZ* 50 [2002]: 295 and 301.) The 1907 Hague Land War Regulations only devoted fifteen articles to the issue of "military force in occupied territories," but it did not deal with reprisals. For a more detailed treatment, see Jost Dülfers, "Regeln im Krieg? Kriegsverbrechen und die Haager Friedenskonferenzen," in Wolfram Wette and Gerd R. Ueberschär, eds., *Kriegsverbrechen im 20. Jahrhundert* (Darmstadt 2001), pp. 35–49, esp. pp. 44ff.; Peter Cornelius Mayer-Tasch, *Guerrillakrieg und Völkerrecht: Essay, Bibliographie und Dokumentation* (Baden-Baden 1972), pp. 37ff.; Schabas, *Genozid im Völkerrecht*, esp. pp. 699ff.; and Gerhard Werle, *Völkerstrafrecht* (Tübingen 2003). For more on the view disseminated during the National Socialist period, see Alfred Waltzog, *Recht der Landkriegführung: Die wichtigsten Abkommen des Landkriegsrechts* (Berlin 1942).

428. United Nations War Crimes Commission, ed., *Law-Reports of Trials of War Criminals*, vol. 1 (London, HMSO, 1949), Case No. 44, pp. 10–14, at p. 14.

429. Ibid.

430. Ibid.

431. Legal studies of this issue were only carried out during the trial of List et al. (Case 12—Wehrmacht High Command trial), as the law report on Kesselring's trial pointed out on p. 4: "This distinction was also made in the judgment of the American Military Government Court in the United States v. List and others. See BA-MA, N 431/792, Prosecution's

Memorandum of Law, Theodore Fenstermacher, in Case 7, the trial of Feldmarschall List et al., 19 November 1947, p. 44. For the purpose of this opinion, the term 'hostages' will be considered as those persons of the civilian population who are taken into custody for the purpose of guaranteeing with their lives the future good conduct of the population of the community from which they were taken. The term 'reprisal prisoners' will be considered as those individuals who are taken from the civilian population to be killed in retaliation for any offence committed by unknown persons within the occupied area . . . where innocent individuals are seized and punished for a violation of the laws of war which has already occurred, no question of hostages is involved. It is nothing more than an infliction of a reprisal. . . . Throughout the evidence in the present case we find the term 'hostages' applied where a 'reprisal' only was involved."

432. Herde, *Command Responsibility*, p. 317.

433. NA, Report, p. 4. Murphy reported that the court had been unable to resolve the legally vital issue relating to the legal position in respect to reprisals.

434. Ibid., p. 5. This assertion is in marked contrast to the defense's claim that Kesselring was denied an opportunity to respond to the verdict or give a final speech from the dock. Although Laternser could have responded to the verdict on Kesselring's behalf, he waived this option—but not without referring to Kesselring's historical role during the trial in fighting to defend the honor of his former soldiers: "The Feldmarschall asks me quite definitely, that at this stage of the proceedings he does not wish that I should address the court any more. It was his idea when deciding to defend himself, to defend the ideas for which he stood and not his own person." PRO/TNA, Kew, FO 642, vol. 5, 58th day (6 May 1947).

435. *Omnibus*, 12 May 1947, "Tremavano le mani a Kesselring," p. 2.

436. *Avanti!*, 7 May 1947, "Kesselring condannato a morte."

437. BA-MA, N 750/3, Kesselring trial diary, entry dated 6 March 1947.

438. BA-MA, N 431/886, summary by Kesselring for Laternser, undated but before 30 April 1947.

439. Ibid.

440. Ibid.

441. Ibid., p. 3; Scotland, *London Cage*, p. 179.

442. Ibid.

443. BA-MA, N 750/11, Kesselring to Liny, 4 May 1947.

444. BA-MA, N 431/877, Kesselring memo regarding Halse's closing speech, undated but probably 1 May 1947.

445. If one accepts that Hitler's order would have to be mentioned in all four war journals kept by the units involved (the South-Western Command's war journal, the Rome city commandant's war journal, the Tenth Army's war journal, and the Fourteenth Army's war journal), it seems strange that not a single copy was thought to have survived the war.

446. BA-MA, N 431/935, Laternser to Westphal, 23 February 1948.

447. BA-MA, N 431/896, memo by Laternser, undated. There may have subsequently been good reasons for not using the war journal, for example, to avoid documenting Kesselring's absence from headquarters and Westphal's involvement in the shootings.

448. My own research indicates that at the end of April 1945, the officer charged with keeping the war journal for the South-Western Command/Army Group C, Lieutenant Fritz Pfrommer, ordered Lieutenant Contzen to pack the war journals (comprising around twenty volumes on which Pfrommer had worked since January 1944) in a wooden crate; they were to be wrapped in a Nazi flag and buried in a brickworks between Bozen and Meran to protect

them from advancing American troops. This conversation was witnessed by Kapitänleutnant Wilfried von Selzam, adjutant to the navy liaison officer on Kesselring's staff, Kapitän von Kutzleben (confirmed in my telephone conversations with Dr. Wilfried von Selzam, Garmisch-Partenkirchen, 10 September 2001, and Mrs. Elfriede Pfrommer and Dr. Wilhelm Pfrommer, 6 September 2001). In September 2001, I discussed this discovery with personnel at the German Military Archives, and the archive director thereupon wrote to Italy requesting permission to excavate. We are still awaiting the final conclusion to these investigations.

449. My transcript of 13 September 2001 telephone message from Dr. Gerd R. Ueberschär relating to the transfer in Freiburg BA-MA.

450. This is the assumption put forward by Sacha Zala in *Geschichte unter der Schere politischer Zensur: Amtliche Aktensammlungen im internationalen Vergleich* (Munich 2001), p. 246.

451. BA-MA, N 431/934, Laternser to Pfrommer, 23 December 1948.

452. BA-MA, N 431/934, Pfrommer to Laternser, 27 December 1948. The war journal had also included an "extensive report from Rome concerning the attack of the German police company."

453. BA-MA, N 431/934, Pfrommer to Laternser, 9 March 1949.

454. He regretted that the war journal for the period in question maintained by the city commandant of Rome and kept by Lieutenant Nicolaus Kunkel had disappeared "as a result of enemy action during the retreat across the Po in April 1945." (BA-MA, N 431/931, Eberhardt to Laternser, 6 December 1948; a copy is also available in N 431/896.) The loss of the diary has also been confirmed by Dr. Nikolaus Kunkel himself (BA-MA, N 431/933, Kunkel to Laternser, 9 January 1949, and my interview with him on 14 June 2002 in Stuttgart).

455. BA-MA, N 431/896, report by Dr. Hans Eberhardt, 3 December 1948.

456. BA-MA, N 431/933, Laternser to Kunkel, 24 December 1948.

457. BA-MA, N 431/933, affidavit by Kunkel, 9 January 1949.

458. BA-MA, N 431/931, affidavit by Buttlar, draft dated February 1949, p. 1.

459. BA-MA, N 431/931, Buttlar to Laternser, 3 April 1949.

460. BA-MA, N 431/931, Beelitz to Laternser, 23 May 1949.

461. My assumption in this regard is shared by Dr. Nikolaus Kunkel, whom I interviewed on 14 June 2002 in Stuttgart. Based on their research, Klinkhammer and Prauser have come to the same conclusion.

462. BA-MA, N 431/932, Laternser to Hamsher, 9 June 1947, 6 pages.

463. BA-MA, N 431/933, Kesselring's "closing words," draft dated 4 May 1947, 3 pages.

464. Ibid., p. 2.

465. Ibid.

466. Albert Kesselring, *Soldat bis zum letzten Tag* (Bonn 1953), p. 444.

467. Ibid.

468. This is also indicated by the fact that this closing statement is included in Laternser, *Verteidigung*, pp. 108ff., but does not appear anywhere in Kesselring's memoirs.

469. Ibid., p. 109.

470. NA, Report, p. 5.

471. Ibid.

472. Ibid.

473. BA-MA, N 431/934, letter from O'Perry to Murphy, 22 August 1947.

474. Ibid.

475. BA-MA, N 431/792, Prosecution's Memorandum of Law, Theodore Fenstermacher,

in Case 7, the trial of Feldmarschall List et al., 19 November 1947, p. 44. Italics are the author's own.

476. Jörg Echternkamp, "Wut auf die Wehrmacht? Vom Bild der deutschen Soldaten in der unmittelbaren Nachkriegszeit," in Rolf-Dieter Müller and Hans-Erich Volkmann, eds., *Die Wehrmacht: Mythos und Realität* (Munich 1999), pp. 1058–1080, at p. 1062.

477. Ibid., p. 1066.

478. *Tagesspiegel,* 19 February 1947, "The Case against Kesselring," p. 3; *Süddeutsche Zeitung,* 15 February 1947, "Kesselring and the Open City," p. 3; *Tagesspiegel,* 26 February 1947, "New Details in the Kesselring Trial," p. 2; *Süddeutsche Zeitung,* 4 March 1947, "Military Imperatives," p. 2 (this was the first mention in the German media of executed children and infant victims); and *Süddeutsche Zeitung,* 10 May 1947, "Kesselring Sentenced to death," p. 3.

479. *Süddeutsche Zeitung,* 21 February 1947, "Kesselring Ordered Hostage Murders: Responsibility of Senior Military Personnel for War Crimes," p. 2; *Süddeutsche Zeitung,* 22 February 1947, "The 'Saviour' of Italian Culture," p. 3.

480. *Il Nuovo Corriere della Sera,* 9 February 1947, "La Guerra in Italia si chiamò Kesselring," by Indro Montanelli, p. 1; *Cronaca Versilia,* 19 February 1947, "Sant'Anna capo d'accusa contro i criminali di guerra."

481. Echternkamp, "Wut auf die Wehrmacht," p. 1065.

482. See, for example, *New York Herald Tribune,* "Kesselring Considered the Italian Partisans to Be War Criminals," 21 February 1947; *New York Times,* 4 March 1947, "Kesselring Cites Italian Betrayal: Also Says British Military Law Permits Reprisals against Innocent Hostages," p. 12, col. 3; and *New York Herald Tribune,* "Kesselring Says He Spared Tiber Bridges," 22 February 1947.

483. In this regard, see Alaric Searle, *Wehrmacht Generals, West German Society, and the Debate on Rearmament, 1949–1959* (Westport, CT, 2003), p. 6.

484. *Neue Zeitung,* 9 May 1947, "Death Sentence for Kesselring."

485. *Gazzettino—Sera,* 17 February 1947, "Nuove accuse e nuove difese," by Guido Polacco, p. 1.

486. *Gazzetino—Sera,* 15 February 1947, "Sarà contestato a Kesselring l'eccidio di Sant'Agata Torricella?" p. 1.

487. The author of the article also criticized the "hapless conduct of the war" by the Allies who had "turned the country into a battlefield for a further two years by landing much too far to the south," instead of landing farther north and putting an end to the (German) "spook." The author may have been a military observer.

488. BA-MA, N 431/931, anonymous author to Laternser, enclosing a newspaper cutting from Reggio Emilia, 4 March 1947.

489. BA-MA, N 431/934, letter from Asti to Kesselring, 7 March 1947. This letter—the only one from former Italian soldiers to be signed in full—is representative of those letters from former soldiers whose primary argument was that "following the lost war, the vanquished should not be additionally humiliated by holding trials" and that "genuine soldiers shared Kesselring's view that he was only performing his duty, which was to protect his own soldiers." The letter ends with the hope that Kesselring would be "fully acquitted," the wish of all "reasonable Italians," and was signed by Capitano Pilota Magagnoli, Tenente Pilota Luigi Raspo, and Sergente Pilota Mario Borsanis from Asti, who extended the "hand of comradeship" to Kesselring.

490. BA-MA, N 431/931, letter from Contini to Laternser, 10 March 1947. Contini wrote

that it was a pity millions of Kesselring's victims were not alive to see how the former field marshal was "convicted by an entire people." Unfortunately, he went on, Kesselring still had traitors at his disposal who took his side in affidavits: it was too bad that it had not been possible to eliminate them all and complete the cleansing operation with machine-gun salvos. Contini expressed anger at Kesselring's constant attempts to defend himself: he should at least await his hanging in silence; as he saw it, the "hysterical fuss being made of the Field Marshal and his duplicity" was inappropriate. Millions of women and children, according to Contini, had been gutlessly slaughtered because "you were not soldiers, *criminale* Kesselring, you were murderers." In Contini's view, it would have been appropriate if Kesselring had shared Mussolini's fate so that "the Italian people would not have to continue suffering" through this trial.

491. Herde, *Command Responsibility*, p. 321.

492. Bloxham, *Genocide*, p. vii. Based on this, the foundations for subsequent clemency were laid during the trial itself, to the extent that the court adopted a benevolent approach to the defendant.

493. Even today, the fact that Albert Kesselring—of all people—was brought to trial occasions some surprise. This surprise had been voiced not only in publications issued by veterans' associations but even in encyclopedia articles. See, for example, the article "Albert Keßelring" [*sic*] by Thilo Vogelsang, in *Neue Deutsche Biographie*, vol. 11 (Berlin 1977), pp. 542–543; Hans-Dietrich Ahrens, "Albert Kesselring," in *Alte Kameraden* 48, no. 552, journals 7 and 8 (2000): 8–9; and Deutsche Montecassino Vereinigung, Rede-Manuskript "Gedenkfeier zum 40. Todestag des GFM Kesselring," report by Karl-Heinz Meissner, September 2000, in author's private collection.

Chapter 3: In Search of a New British Politics of Memory

1. However, Bellenger's importance should not be exaggerated. The army, navy, and air force ministries lost their place in the cabinet after October 1946, when the position of secretary of state for defense was inaugurated. Although the positions of first lord of the Admiralty (the navy minister) and secretary of state for war (the army minister, Frederick Bellenger) were continued, these officials only had the rank of undersecretaries of state. The main powers that they retained related to administration of their particular military arm and to the right of pardon.

2. PRO/TNA, Kew, PREM 8/707, discussion memo for Attlee concerning Churchill's call, 6 May 1947.

3. BA-MA, N 431/934, copy from the *Daily Telegraph*, probably 12 May 1947.

4. Otto Kranzbühler, "Wert und Unwert historischer Strafprozesse—Erörtert am Nürnberger Beispiel," in Karl Foster, ed., *Möglichkeiten und Grenzen für die Bewältigung von historischer und politischer Schuld in Strafprozessen* (Würzburg 1962), pp. 15–36, at p. 36; see also Georg Meyer, "Zur Situation der deutschen militärischen Führungsschicht im Vorfeld des westdeutschen Verteidigungsbeitrages 1945–1950/51," in Roland G. Foerster, Christian Greiner, Georg Meyer, Hans-Jürgen Rautenberg, and Norbert Wiggershaus, eds., *Von der Kapitulation zum Pleven-Plan: Anfänge westdeutscher Sicherheitspolitik*, vol. 1 (Munich 1982), pp. 577–735, at p. 624.

5. PRO/TNA, Kew, PREM 8/707, letter from Churchill to Attlee, 13 May 1947.

6. *Sunday Pictorial*, 11 May 1947, interview with General Leese, reports by Major Redman.

7. *Stars and Stripes: The Rome Daily American*, 13 May 1947, "Briton Praises Kesselring:

General Says Sentence 'Sad'—Leese: 'If things had gone the other way, the man sentenced to death might have been me.'"

8. In this regard, see the extensive archives held in Churchill College, Cambridge (primarily the exchange of letters with Lord Hankey).

9. Nigel Nicolson, *Alex: The Life of Field Marshal Earl Alexander of Tunis* (London 1973), p. 296. Churchill had asked Alexander to intervene, and Alexander discussed all further measures with Churchill. Nicolson wrote that the telegram had doubtless contributed to commuting the death sentence to imprisonment.

10. PRO/TNA, Kew, PREM 8/707, telegram, 8 May 1947: "I am unhappy over Kesselring's sentence and hope that it will be commuted. Personally, as his old opponent on the battlefield, I have no complaints against him. Kesselring and his soldiers fought against us hard but clean. Alexander, Field Marshal."

11. Although direct verification of this intervention has not yet been possible, more work could be done on this using the Hankey-Churchill correspondence that is preserved in Churchill College, Cambridge. The fact is that Churchill was part of Lord Maurice Hankey's circle of friends, a group that met at irregular intervals at Limpsfield, Hankey's Surrey country house, to discuss political issues. This group also included Lord de L'Isle and Dudley.

12. Lord de L'Isle and Dudley was himself a veteran of the Italian campaign and was awarded the Victoria Cross for his part in the landing at Anzio.

13. Hansard, Parliamentary Debates, Lords, 13 May 1947, col. 657.

14. PRO/TNA, Kew, PREM 8/707, 7 May 1947, memo.

15. PRO/TNA, Kew, PREM 8/707, letter from Drew to Rowan, 13 May 1947.

16. ASMAE, AP 1952, b. 176, Criminali di Guerra tedeschi, draft of a final Foreign Office memorandum on the abolition of the death penalty, Borsari opinion, 24 September 1947

17. In this regard, see the surprised reaction in London, documented in PRO/TNA, PREM 8/707, letter from Bellenger to Bevin, 8 May 1947, as well as the Italian statement in ASMAE Rome, AP 1952, b. 176, Criminali di Guerra tedeschi, final Foreign Ministry memorandum on the abolition of the death penalty, 13 October 1947.

18. *New York Times*, 16 May 1947, "Britains Score Sentence: Rally to Aid Kesselring, Whose Lawyer Files Appeal," p. 6, col. 3.

19. Due to the supposed risk of impending suicide, all personal items of clothing—as well as cutlery, towels, and a lamp—were removed from Kesselring's cell on the day the verdict was announced. In response, Laternser felt constrained to state that Kesselring had promised "under oath" that he "would not commit suicide" (BA-MA, N 431/934, statement by Kesselring that he would not commit suicide, 7 May 1947; BA-MA, N 431/934, Laternser to Commanding Officer 86 Area, Venice, 7 May 1947). This situation triggered newspaper reports to the effect that Kesselring intended to take his own life or that he was to be kidnapped by his former comrades-in-arms. On 22 June 1947, the *Sunday Empire News* claimed to have uncovered a plan to liberate Kesselring from his captivity and thereby save him from the death sentence. The newspaper claimed that this action would be motivated by a recognition of "an inappropriate verdict." The paper reported that Allied soldiers and Germans disguised as Allied forces had been unmasked as accomplices. Now, special forces had been assigned to guard duty, and the paper claimed that they kept watch over Kesselring around the clock to prevent poison from being smuggled in to him and thus allowing him to commit suicide and evade justice (translation, included in BA-MA, N 750/14).

20. *Continental Daily Mail*, 30 May 1947, "The Reign of Law—or Just 'Vae victis'? Will It Help to Shoot Kesselring?" At the same time, the *Daily Mail* in Britain published an article

entitled "Will It Help to Shoot Kesselring?" The introduction to the first article is noteworthy: "The *Continental Daily Mail*, while not necessarily agreeing with the views expressed below, publishes the article because it undoubtedly represents the opinion of a wide section of the public." The introduction went on to comment that the Kesselring case "is attracting a good deal of uneasy attention."

21. *Sunday Chronicle*, 8 June 1947, "The Moral Conscience of a General: Problem behind the Kesselring case," by Milton Shulman (a copy of the article is preserved in BA-MA, N 431/935).

22. *Times*, 16 May 1947, letter to the editor from D. Johnston.

23. *Times*, 21 May 1947, letter to the editor from J. H. Whitfield.

24. *Daily Telegraph*, 15 May 1947, letter to the editor from J. Turnbright.

25. *Daily Telegraph*, 15 May 1947, letter to the editor, "Kesselring's Fate: Need Mercy Be Denied?" by Randolph Churchill.

26. Kesselring's German advocates could scarcely believe their luck in attracting support from such a prominent quarter. Writing to Laternser, Schwinge exulted: "Isn't Randolph Churchill's letter marvellous? The *Daily Telegraph* is one of the most widely read English dailies" (BA-MA, N 431/935, Schwinge to Laternser, 20 May 1947, handwritten postscript).

27. *Daily Telegraph*, 16 May 1947, letter to the editor from P. Poole.

28. *Daily Telegraph*, 20 May 1947, letter to the editor from S. Moore. Moore argued that, faced with such a conflict of conscience, an honorable soldier would either resign or commit suicide rather than lay a hand on innocent civilians.

29. *Times*, 19 May 1947, letter to the editor from Maurice Share.

30. *Daily Telegraph*, 22 May 1947, letter to the editor from Randolph S. Churchill.

31. The JAG found that no new evidence had surfaced during the trial that would exonerate Kesselring or even prevent his execution (PRO/TNA, Kew, WO 310/129, JAG to Harding, 22 May 1947, and PRO/TNA, Kew, PREM 8/707, memorandum for the Prime Minister, 25 June 1947).

32. PRO/TNA, Kew, PREM 8/707, letter from Shawcross to Bellenger, 15 May 1947, p. 1: "I have not the slightest doubt that if Mr. Churchill or any other British subject desired to petition the King in regard to Kesselring, such a petition would have to be considered on the advice of the responsible Minister."

33. PRO/TNA, Kew, PREM 8/707, letter from Shawcross to Bellenger, 15 May 1947: "I am not suggesting in any way that Kesselring ought to be reprieved: that is not a matter for me and my only desire is that we should not again make an unnecessary mistake about the legal position."

34. PRO/TNA, Kew, PREM 8/707, letter from Bellenger to Bevin, 8 May 1947.

35. Some notes on the options for granting a pardon may be helpful. The secretary of state for war was not directly involved in the procedure for confirming disputed verdicts. Rather, this was a matter for the Mediterranean commander-in-chief and the judge advocate general. The latter would carefully reexamine the conduct of the trial and then advise General Harding, the commander-in-chief. Once the verdict was announced by General Harding, the accused still had a short grace period because Bellenger would have to be notified of the decision before it was executed. Kesselring could only have been executed once the secretary of state for war had confirmed Harding's decision. Bellenger thus constituted the court of final appeal, with the power to confirm or set aside sentences.

36. PRO/TNA, Kew, PREM 8/707, letter from Bellenger to Bevin, 8 May 1947, p. 6.

37. PRO/TNA, Kew, WO 310/129, secret, War Office to CMF (20?) May 1947.

38. PRO/TNA, Kew, PREM 8/707, telegram from Harding to the War Office, 29 June 1947.

39. Harding was referring to the amendment of the manual in 1944. Harding stated that the Bandenbefehle for which Kesselring was charged had only been in force for a comparatively short time and that they had been immediately rescinded once the military became aware of grievances.

40. PRO/TNA, Kew, PREM 8/707, telegram from Harding to the War Office, 29 June 1947, p. 2.

41. Harding requested permission to confine any public announcement to a bald statement of his decision, without elucidation. He proposed the following text: "General Harding in his capacity as GOC in C CMF has confirmed the findings of guilty as in the cases of Kesselring, Mackensen and Mältzer. However, having regard to the circumstances in which the war crimes in question were committed, the otherwise clean war record of the individuals concerned, and especially since the fate of the individual directly and personally responsible for the killings in the Ardeatine caves is undecided and uncertain, General Harding has decided to commute the sentences in all three cases to imprisonment for life." PRO/TNA, Kew, PREM 8/707, Harding to War Office, 29 June 1947, p. 3.

42. Extracts printed in, for example, the *New York Times*, 5 July 1947, p. 2, col. 7.

43. PRO/TNA, Kew, WO 310/129, Associazione Nazionale Partigiani d'Italia, Comitato Provinciale di Brescia, to Comando Forze Armate Alleate, Padova, 7 July 1947: "This decision insults the entire Italian nation which suffered German wrath for so long, and it debases the sacrifice of those who died, and those who fought and suffered for freedom." During the last days of the war, many partisans and Germans died in battle, especially in the region around Brescia, but no massacres occurred.

44. *Il Tempo*, 5 July 1947, "Kesselring graziato."

45. *New York Times*, 6 July 1947, "Kesselring," p. 40, col. 2.

46. PRO/TNA, Kew, WO 310/127, telegram from JAG to the War Crimes Group/South-East Europe, 26 January 1948.

47. PRO/TNA, Kew, WO 310/127, telegram from JAG to the War Crimes Group/South-East Europe, 19 February 1948.

48. J. H. Hoffmann, "German Field Marshals as War Criminals? A British Embarrassment," *Journal of Contemporary History* 23 (1988): 17–35, at p. 17.

49. Ibid., p. 18.

50. PRO/TNA, Kew, FO 371/64475, C-in-C Lübeck to Foreign Office, 23 October 1947, cited in ibid., p. 20.

51. Hoffmann, "German Field Marshals," p. 20.

52. Ibid.

53. PRO/TNA, Kew, FO 371/70798, memo from Smedley (FO, German Section), 24 April 1948, cited in ibid., p. 23.

54. Ibid.

55. PRO/TNA, Kew, FO 371/ 77045, letter FO to Robertson, 11 January 1949.

56. Hoffmann, "German Field Marshals," p. 25.

57. PRO/TNA, Kew, CAB 129/34, CP (49) 90, memorandum issued by War Secretary Shinwell, 19 April 1949, cited in ibid., pp. 27f.

58. Hansard, Parliamentary Debate, Commons, 28 October 1948, col. 256.

59. House of Commons exchange between Bevin and Churchill, 22 September 1948, cited in Hoffman, "German Field Marshals," p. 26, and in Meyer, "Situation der deutschen militärischen Führungsschicht," p. 624.

60. In a headline replete with Cold War language, *Pravda* noted that "Winston Churchill Races to Free Hitler Disciple and Murderer Manstein," cited in Ulrich Brochhagen, *Nach Nürnberg: Vergangenheitsbewältigung und Westintegration in der Ära Adenauer* (Hamburg 1994), p. 29.

61. Hoffmann, "German Field Marshals," p. 28.

62. Heinrich Senfft, "Lauter feine Herren: Deutsche Kriegsverbreher, einige Lords und die Wiederbewaffnung," *Blätter für deutsche und internationale Politik* 8 (2001): 995–1004, at p. 995.

63. Hoffmann, "German Field Marshals," p. 29.

64. Ibid., p. 30.

65. Oliver von Wrochem, "Die Auseinandersetzung mit Wehrmachtverbrechen im Prozess gegen den Generalfeldmarschall Erich von Manstein 1949," *Zeitschrift für Geschichtswissenschaft* (hereafter cited as *ZfG*) 4 (1998): 329–353; also Wrochem, "Rehabilitation oder Strafverfolgung: Kriegsverbrecherprozess gegen Generalfeldmarschall Erich von Manstein im Widerstreit britischer Interessen," *Mittelweg* 6, no. 3 (1997): 26–36.

66. Hoffmann, "German Field Marshals," p. 30.

67. BA-MA, N 431/936, Dalrymple to Laternser, 13 June 1949.

68. Despite being sentenced to twelve years' imprisonment, he spent just three years in custody. Like Kesselring in 1952, he was released due to ill health in 1953.

69. Rüdiger von Manstein and Theodor Fuchs, *Manstein: Soldat im 20. Jahrhundert—Militärisch-Politische Nachlese* (Munich 1981), p. 302; Meyer, "Situation der deutschen militärischen Führungsschicht," p. 628.

70. Hoffmann, "German Field Marshals," p. 31.

71. Brochhagen, *Nach Nürnberg*, p. 30.

72. Ibid., p. 31.

73. Meyer, "Situation der deutschen militärischen Führungsschicht," p. 628, and Brochhagen, *Nach Nürnberg*, p. 31.

74. Brochhagen, *Nach Nürnberg*, p. 26.

75. PRO FO 371/85913, Robertson to Kirkpatrick, 9 January 1950.

76. PRO/TNA, Kew, FO 1060/499, Vickers to legal department, Herford, 22 February 1949. Written notes by Kesselring were enclosed, presumably regarding his custody conditions and his trial.

77. Churchill College, Cambridge, HNKY 18/5, Liddell Hart to Hankey, 4 May 1950. Liddell Hart wrote: "General Wade, who reviewed the case, told me himself that he had come to the conclusion that in reality Kesselring was innocent of the charge on which he was convicted."

78. PRO/TNA, Kew, FO 1060/493, Deputy Legal Adviser, Moller, to Chief Legal Officer, Land Commissioner's Office, Düsseldorf, 5 April 1950.

79. Reginald T. Paget, *Manstein: His Campaigns and His Trial* (London 1951), p. 191.

80. Hoffmann, "German Field Marshals," p. 31.

81. Hans-Peter Schwarz, *Die Ära Adenauer 1949–1957*, vol. 1, *Gründerjahre der Republik* (Stuttgart 1981), p. 290.

82. PRO/TNA, Kew, PREM 8/707, Private Secretary of the Prime Minister (T. L. Rowan) to the War Office (A. C. W. Drew), 13 May 1947: "[A debate] . . . would involve making the matter public."

83. BA-MA, N 431/936, Kesselring to Laternser, 23 October 1947.

84. BA-MA, N 431/936, Kesselring to Laternser, 18 September 1948. During this period,

Laternser was initially involved in defending the so-called South-Eastern Generals in Nuremberg, former field marshals Wilhelm List and Maximilian Freiherr von Weichs. Known as Case 7 ("the hostage murder case"), this trial involved the murder of partisans in the Balkans, and it prepared the ground for the Wehrmacht High Command trial (Case 12), which opened in February 1948, during which Laternser acted as defense counsel for former field marshal von Leeb. Kesselring and Laternser also planned to publish a "Wehrmacht white book," which would detail war crimes committed by the other side.

85. Thus, for example, as early as October 1948, the attorneys representing General Curt Gallenkamp (also being held in Werl) approached Laternser to discuss a "common approach to the sentence reviews expected in the near future" (BA-MA, N 431/933, Lüdecke to Laternser, 18 October 1948). Laternser responded that, according to information received from the War Office in London, a sentence review was not expected until after 1 November 1948 (BA-MA, N 431/933, Laternser to Lüdecke, 9 November 1948). Such initial uncoordinated contacts subsequently resulted in the formation of the Heidelberg Lawyers' Circle, which focused on developing appeal strategies. This topic will be examined in some depth later in this volume.

86. BA-MA, N 431/936, Kesselring to Laternser, 30 July 1947.

87. Following his trial, General Max Simon was also held in Wolfsberg and Werl, occupying a cell next to Kesselring, so there was plenty of opportunity for the two men to discuss various matters. Kesselring was outraged that the Bandenbefehl he had issued on 17 June 1944—which had helped secure his own conviction—had not been viewed by prosecutors in the Simon trial as having led to the massacres of civilians. In Kesselring's opinion, this fact confirmed that he had been caught in the mill of an all-powerful victors' justice—an arbitrary and inconsistent justice in which the same orders could be interpreted in varying ways: "Sometimes I really feel disgusted" (BA-MA, N 431/936, Kesselring to Laternser, 12 September 1947).

88. BA-MA, N 431/896, Kesselring to Laternser, 2 November 1947.

89. BA-MA, N 431/896, brief entitled "War Crimes Trials," 23 pages, apparently written by Kesselring in autumn 1947 and also issued in the names of Mackensen and Mältzer. The document revisited all the disputed aspects of the trial and ended by stressing the illegality of the verdict: "One should not mistake the fact that permanent war crimes trials constitute a permanent state of war, precluding any mutual rapprochement, nor should one mistake the fact, however, that permanent war crimes trials have a dubious basis in terms of national and international law, and constitute illegal warfare, as we can see in the despicable Bandenkrieg and all its violent consequences today" (p. 23).

90. BA-MA, N 431/896, declaration by Mackensen, Wolfsberg, 7 July 1947, 6 pages, at p. 6. Mackensen wrote: "It is particularly difficult to bear the loss of liberty, since I cannot even give my life a meaning through penance, for I am not conscious of any guilt. I cannot attach guilt to the fact that my attempt to cleanly dispose of an unpleasant matter failed, as I have discovered after 2¼ years. I could not act differently today than I did at the time."

91. Ibid., p. 5. Stirling had "from the very beginning openly displayed such a hostile and hate-filled attitude towards all German officers that I must object to him on the grounds of excessive bias."

92. BA-MA, N 431/896, memo by Laternser on his meeting with Field Marshal Kesselring, Generaloberst von Mackensen, and Generalleutnant Mältzer, 30 January 1948, 3 pages.

93. Although Field Marshal von List had been sentenced to life in prison, he was released on health grounds at the end of 1952. The charges against Laternser's second client, Field

Marshal von Weichs, were dropped, since he was deemed unfit to stand trial (see Thomas A. Schwartz, "Die Begnadigung deutscher Kriegsverbrecher," *VfZ* 38 [1990]: 375–414, at p. 409).

94. He stressed that Generaloberst von Mackensen had been absolved of "all responsibility" as a result of Hitler's second order tasking the SD with execution of the operation. The same also applied to Generalleutnant Mältzer, who in any event could not be held responsible for the reprisal given the competency of his superior, Mackensen. Furthermore, according to Kesselring, the charge of "transmitting orders" was not punishable under Italian military law (BA-MA, N 431/938, Kesselring to Laternser, 17 March 1949).

95. He wrote to Laternser that in September 1947, it had seemed possible that Hildemann's case would be reopened (BA-MA, N 431/931, Kesselring to Laternser, enclosing a copy of a letter from Gallenkamp concerning the Hildemann case, 24 April 1948). The commander-in-chief of British forces in Europe, Sholto Douglas, had ordered a review of Hildemann's sentence. Hildemann claimed that his attorney, Dr. Lüdecke, had told him that the result of the review was positive (BA-MA, N 431/936, Lüdecke to Hildemann, copy sent to Laternser by Gallenkamp, 24 April 1948). However, rumors had reached Lüdecke to the effect that even if the Hildemann case had resulted in a miscarriage of justice, the verdict could not be set aside because British investigations had shown that there had been around 100 such wrongful convictions, including "people who have already been hanged." The British commander-in-chief was loath to create a precedent, since numerous other defendants would then appeal on the basis of this case.

96. There are indications pointing to a highly efficient network of former Wehrmacht officers, including veterans of the Italian campaign. For example, when seeking witnesses, Laternser was able to rely unquestioningly on General Theodor Busse's list of contacts: the general collected addresses on behalf of Laternser and his colleagues, making them available in order to help coordinate defense strategies. Busse sent Buttlar's address with a note: "I believe that one can now await events with equanimity" (BA-MA, N 431/931, Busse to Laternser, 1 January 1949).

97. BA-MA, N 431/931, Beelitz to Laternser, 8 May 1947.

98. Two days after the verdict was announced in London, Beelitz wrote to London that he had anticipated the outcome "merely for political reasons" (see ibid.).

99. BA-MA, N 431/935, Westphal to Laternser, 29 May 1947. Now that the court battle had been lost, Westphal was planning the "campaign at home." He asked Laternser to send him his closing speech, since there was "great" interest in Kesselring's fate, and he wanted to "talk about it" in Germany.

100. BA-MA, N 782, clemency petitions for Kesselring, 8 May 1947, and PRO/TNA, Kew, WO 310/129, English version. Copies were sent to Field Marshal Alexander (whom Kesselring had fought in Italy), Field Marshal Montgomery (Kesselring's adversary in North Africa), and General Harding, who had served as commander-in-chief of Allied forces in the Mediterranean during 1947. This information points to an almost military planning of Kesselring's defense: nothing was left to chance, and all avenues of intervention that could lead to the former field marshal's case being reopened were explored.

101. BA-MA, N 431/933, clemency petition from Generals Lemelsen and Herr on behalf of Kesselring, English, 8 May 1947.

102. BA-MA, N 782, clemency petitions for Kesselring, 8 May 1947.

103. BA-MA, N 431/931, Franz to Laternser, 15 May 1947.

104. BA-MA, N 431/935, Seidemann to Laternser, 15 May 1947. In an accompanying

note, Seidemann wrote to Laternser that "Field Marshal Kesselring should know that he is not alone during these dark days, that we know and respect him, and hope that the verdict will be favorably amended."

105. PRO/TNA, Kew, PREM 8/707, message to the military attaché, 11 May 1947: "We ask that the life of this brave man be spared."

106. BA-MA, N 431/937, Liny Kesselring to Laternser enclosing a draft of her petition to Queen Elizabeth, 29 May 1947. Queen Elizabeth, who died in 2002, was the mother of the present British queen, Elizabeth II.

107. BA-MA, N 431/934, Hiemer's draft appeal to Pius XII, 8 May 1947, 3 pages.

108. BA-MA, N 431/934, Laternser to Pius XII, 10 May 1947. The trial was important in order to "re-establish good relations between Italy and Germany, and in general for the victory of what is good and just over the destructive forces of our age."

109. Ibid.

110. BA-MA, N 431/936, Laternser to Kesselring, 16 June 1947. There is no concrete evidence of this intervention in the British records I consulted. It is, unfortunately, not possible to access the relevant section of the Vatican archives.

111. BA-MA, N 431/937, Liny Kesselring to Laternser, 19 February 1951. In February 1951, a cousin of Kesselring's contacted the Papal Nuncio in Kronberg seeking an intervention on Kesselring's behalf. In response, he was told that—at the "request of His Holiness's State Secretariat"—the Vatican had contacted the relevant British authorities. The Vatican was informed that although Kesselring's release was not being considered, the case was due for review.

112. PRO/TNA, Kew, FO 1060/493, Haritz to the High Commissioner, 14 December 1950.

113. PRO/TNA, Kew, FO 1060/495, Knapp to the British High Commissioner, 4 December 1951. Paul Knapp offered to spend Christmas and New Year's Day in prison in place of Kesselring, and he explained his request by saying that he would consider it an "honor" to perform such a service for his former commanding officer. In 1951, Mrs. Wever (widow of General Walter Wever, Kesselring's predecessor as Luftwaffe chief of General Staff) offered to spend Christmas in prison in Kesselring's place (PRO/TNA, Kew, FO 1060/493, Wever to the High Commissioner, December 1951).

114. PRO/TNA, Kew, FO 1060/493, memo from Roots to Passmore, 20 December 1950.

115. PRO/TNA, Kew, FO 1060/493, Roots, office of the Principal Legal Adviser, to Haritz, 21 December 1950.

116. The papers left by the former pilot Manfred Bäumler (private papers, Peter Bäumler, Waiblingen) include descriptions of camp conditions in Wolfsberg, "Notes on the last six months, winter 1947/48, by Field Marshal Kesselring, Werl."

117. BA-MA, N 431/936, Kesselring to Laternser, 22 May 1947. Kesselring noted with some satisfaction that he had received a "brief and friendly" greeting from a British colonel in Wolfsberg camp. British guards had also told him that they were amazed at the sentence and would plead his case. On a personal level, the guards attempted to entertain the prisoners; see BA-MA, N 750/3, entry dated 12 June 1947, in which Kesselring reported that a cricket match was held in the camp.

118. Albert Kesselring, *Soldat bis zum letzten Tag* (Bonn 1953), p. 451. Writing in his diary, he described short, unsupervised strolls (BA-MA, N 750/3, e.g., entries dated 26 June 1947, 1 July 1947, and 3 July 1947). A photograph survives of one of these strolls, showing Kesselring, Mackensen, and Mältzer dressed in hiking gear. The photo was reprinted in Kesselring's memoirs, *Soldat,* facing p. 299.

119. BA-MA, N 431/936, Kesselring to Laternser, 22 May 1947; BA-MA, N 750/3, journal, entry dated 10 June 1947. According to his diary, he attended a cabaret performance in the camp on 1 July 1947.

120. BA-MA, N 431/936, Kesselring to Laternser, 7 June 1947. The local villagers were also friendly, sending him gifts and flowers via the camp staff (kitchen assistants, see entry dated 5 July 1947) or the local priest, Father Schreiber (BA-MA, N 750/3, entry dated 12 June 1947). Kesselring also frequently visited the "nurses in the military hospital," who plied him with coffee (e.g., BA-MA, N 750/3, journal, entries dated 22 June 1947 and 29 June 1947).

121. Kesselring's American friends in the Historical Division—impervious to events—were eager to resume working with him. Thus, as early as 20 June 1947, Colonel Potter of the Allendorf Historical Division sought leave to bring Kesselring to Allendorf for an extended interview from 1 July to 15 July (PRO/TNA, Kew, WO 310/129, staff message Control GHQ CMF, 20 June 1947; also in BA-MA, N 431/937, Liny Kesselring to Laternser, undated but after 2 July 1947).

122. In his memoirs, Kesselring noted that a "former SS major" had told him that "everything had been prepared for my escape." Kesselring claimed to have "firmly" rejected this rescue attempt, since he did not want to "by escaping, reinforce my enemies' (and I can only view the court thus) belief in the rightness of their actions, thus issuing a confession of guilt" (Kesselring, *Soldat*, p. 451). This encounter cannot be verified using either Kesselring's diaries or letters, but it is not improbable given similar events. Several senior Nazis had been helped to abscond from Wolfsberg camp to South America or Syria, thanks to the escape aid organization sponsored by the Graz industrialist Theodor Soucek (this reference can be found in Simon Wiesenthal, *Recht, nicht Rache: Erinnerungen* [Frankfurt 1988], p. 64).

123. The relevant files are in PRO/TNA, Kew, FO 1060/499, Kesselring registration form, Werl Prison, 22 October 1947.

124. BA-MA, N 431/896, memo by Laternser on his meeting with Field Marshal Kesselring, Generaloberst von Mackensen, and Generalleutnant Mältzer, 30 January 1948, 3 pages.

125. Prisoners were allowed to keep the lights on until 10 P.M. in order to do such written work (otherwise, lights-out was at 8 P.M.), and cells were also equipped with "desks and suitable lighting" (PRO/TNA, Kew, FO 1060/499, note on the committal of Kesselring, Mackensen, and Mältzer, and the work of prisoners in Werl, 22 November 1947).

126. Theoretically, prisoners were allowed one visit by a relative each month. However, given Liny Kesselring's difficulty in obtaining permits to travel from the American to the British zone, as well as her financial circumstances, she only saw her husband around every three months for an hour.

127. PRO/TNA, Kew, FO 1060/499, Kesselring prison conditions, signed by Morgan, 17 February 1948.

128. BA-MA, N 750/5, Bäumler to Superintendent Kleyer, 26 November 1948.

129. PRO/TNA, Kew, FO 1060/499, Kesselring to the public prosecutor, 31 May 1948, request for English lessons to be held three times a week (also in PRO/TNA, Kew, FO 1060/499, Kesselring to the prison director, 13 July 1948). See also *Essener Kurier*, 29 November 1951, "Panzer-Meyer: I Am Being Treated Fairly." During this interview, another Werl inmate—former Waffen SS General Kurt Meyer—admitted that language lessons were the imprisoned generals' "favorite passtime":"[Meyer] studies English every day with Manstein and Kesselring."

130. For example, Laternser's book *Defending German Soldiers* was passed to Kesselring by Kleyer (BA-MA, N 431/936, Kesselring to Laternser, 8 November 1950).

131. Money transfers were also clearly handled through Kleyer. However, correspondence with Laternser dated 21 May 1949 (in BA-MA, N 431/933) indicates that Kleyer was apparently unwilling or unable to pass on the money. Money intended for General Willy Seeger was also not received. Nonetheless, suspicions of embezzlement were never substantiated. (My interview with Dr. Wolfgang Seeger, 28 December 1998, in Stuttgart.)

132. BA-MA, N 431/936, Kesselring to Laternser, 16 November 1950.

133. BA-MA, N 431/933, Laternser to Kleyer on Kesselring's behalf, enclosing a letter from Scotland, 13 May 1950.

134. BA-MA, N 431/933, Laternser to Kleyer on Kesselring's behalf, enclosing a letter from Scotland, 7 November 1950.

135. BA-MA, N 431/933, Laternser to Kleyer with enclosure, 8 February 1951.

136. Like Mackensen and Mältzer, Kesselring still declined to submit a clemency petition. He was, however, considering requesting a "transfer to an English camp" in the hope of receiving better food. However, he did not pursue this plan because he feared it could spell an end to visits from relatives.

137. BA-MA, N 431/932, Laternser to Halse, draft dated 30 March 1948.

138. BA-MA, N 431/935, Westphal to Kleyer for Kesselring, 13 May 1948.

139. BA-MA, N 431/932, Westphal to Liddell Hart, 6 August 1948.

140. BA-MA, N 431/936, Kesselring to Laternser, 29 October 1948, 4 pages, at p. 4.

141. Kesselring on the arrival of General Schmidt, the attorney Frohwein's former superior.

142. Kesselring was glad that the new wing was no longer located to the southwest, since their former cells had been drafty.

143. Kesselring, *Soldat*, p. 452. Later, Vickers spent some time as director of Spandau Prison, which was under the jurisdiction of the four Allied powers.

144. PRO/TNA, Kew, FO 1060/499, Vickers to the Zonal Office of the Legal Adviser, 27 October 1948. Vickers found that the German guards were all "Kesselring's former subordinates" and therefore treated him with great respect, passing him forbidden messages from outside and themselves informing the outside world of Kesselring's state of health and conditions of imprisonment.

145. BA-MA, N 750/new acquisition 2000, serial no. 15, rhyming card congratulating him on his birthday on 30 November 1948: "And one more thing—for in all the days / which we've experienced in misery and ignominy / you carried us along / and your heart never faltered. / Continue setting an example, that for which we aim / continue to be a luminous banner! / then these hours will not have been in vain / Field Marshal, this is our wish."

146. BA-MA, N 431/936, Kesselring to Laternser, 11 January 1950. Kesselring also informed Monsieur Favre of the Red Cross accordingly, during his visit to Werl in July 1950 (BA-MA, N 431/936, Kesselring to Laternser, 9 July 1950).

147. *Dithmarscher Landeszeitung*, 24 June 1950, "First Visit to Manstein and Kesselring."

148. *Der Spiegel* 51 (18 December 1948): 21.

149. *Deutsche Woche*, Munich, 2 January 1952, "General Staff in Jail."

150. Thus, following a visit to Werl, the journalist Sefton Delmer wrote an article stating that Kesselring continually received packages and that—thanks to British food—the German prisoners were far better fed than the average German at the time. In the wake of this article, the prison director, Lieutenant Colonel H. C. Morgan, was replaced and the number of guards increased, and packages were prohibited. See BA-MA, N 431/937, Liny Kesselring to Laternser, 11 June 1948; Kesselring, *Soldat*, p. 453.

151. Although the studies were originally intended for internal U.S. Army use, they were

subsequently published. See Donald S. Detwiler, ed., *German World War II Military Studies*, 24 vols. (New York 1971). Volume 14 includes a few studies by Kesselring of the Africa campaign and Italy. The full manuscripts are in BA-MA Freiburg.

152. At the end of the war, American staffs were primarily seeking German intelligence documents, files for the planned war crimes trial, and material regarding German weapons technology (especially aeronautical and missile engineering). Although American military historians hoped to obtain the documentary records required to construct an operational history of World War II, this goal was initially regarded as secondary. See Christian Greiner, "'Operational History (German) Section' und 'Naval Historical Team': Deutsches militärstrategisches Denken im Dienst der amerikanischen Streitkräfte von 1946 bis 1950," in Manfred Messerschmidt, Klaus A. Maier, Werner Rahn, and Bruno Thoss, eds., *Militärgeschichte. Probleme, Thesen, Wege* (Stuttgart 1982), pp. 409–435, at p. 412.

153. University of Virginia, Alderman Library, Oron Hale Papers, RG 21/98.911, group 3, box 18, folder 5; Government Service War Department, Historical (Shuster) Commission, Interrogation of Former German Officers, Assorted Correspondence, Interview notes and report drafts, 1945 (this document was kindly sent to me by Dr. Astrid Eckert, DHI Washington). Kesselring voluntarily made himself available even for this preliminary historiographical phase. On 17 July 1945, members of the so-called Shuster Commission—under the direction of George Shuster, president of Hunter College—traveled from Paris to the American VIP camp in Mondorf, Luxembourg. Kesselring was one of the first officers to be questioned. His responses to Shuster's questions regarding troop morale, the mood among the soldiers, and Wehrmacht ardor are illuminating documents of their time, especially when compared with subsequent studies of military operations. Thus, Albert Kesselring's satisfaction with his own career shone through when he wrote that "all combat troops" displayed enthusiasm and when he commented on the "deeply entrenched sense of duty" that he considered formed the basis for "staying the course for six years"—a sense of duty that, as a commander, he had found "useful." See the aforementioned Shuster Commission papers and the entry referring to Kesselring and his response to Question 1 regarding "Enthusiasm or a sense of duty in the German Wehrmacht."

154. Gerd R. Ueberschär, *Generaloberst Franz Halder: Generalstabschef, Gegner und Gefangener Hitlers* (Göttingen 1991), p. 92.

155. Meyer, "Situation der deutschen militärischen Führungsschicht," p. 605.

156. Ibid., and study prepared by the Historical Division in 1951 entitled "The Army Historical Program in the European Theater and Command, 8 May 1943–31 December 1950," p. 69: "The homeworkers received normal German housing, pay at the rate of RM 400 to 600 monthly, and the equivalent of the prisoner of war noon meal and amenity supplies" (p. 89). I am indebted to Dr. Bruce Siemon, American Headquarters Europe, Heidelberg, for this reference.

157. BA-MA, N 750/2, London Diary, pp. 44–46: "I have been involved and will be involved. As far as I am concerned, there are pressing reasons for this. 1.) I am a fanatical supporter of a Western orientation. This is my political creed. 2.) This includes allowing the Western powers to access all those experiences which they did not gain themselves. These experiences are most easily conveyed in the context of a war history and they can then be . . . evaluated in terms of organisation, technology and tactics. 3.) Our adversary is entitled to receive a truthful portrayal of the war events, and this affords us the opportunity of writing a German history which will be a monument to the names of our soldiers. So I will become—which I never believed I would have to—a temporary historian!"

158. Based on the surviving correspondence, it seems that the Franciscan sisters offered a well-organized prisoner care system for German officers being held in Italy. According to Kesselring's correspondence, the sisters were in contact with the prisoners Simon, Krummhaar, Strauch, and Reder, whom they provided with food in prison while also bringing them letters from their relatives and attorneys (BA-MA, N 750/acquisition 2000, serial number 45, letter from Mother Alfonsa, Venice, to Kesselring, Werl, 4 January 1948).

159. Ibid.

160. In this, he was in agreement with his superior, Franz Halder, and the section head of the Garmisch working group, former Field Marshal Georg von Küchler: "The German actions, viewed from a German perspective, will be set down, thus erecting a monument to our troops" (cited in Bernd Wegner, "Erschriebene Siege: Franz Halder, die 'Historical Division' und die Rekonstruktion des Zweiten Weltkrieges im Geiste des deutschen Generalstabes," in Ernst Willi Hansen, ed., *Politischer Wandel, organisierte Gewalt und nationale Sicherheit: Beiträge zur neueren Geschichte Deutschlands und Frankreichs* [Munich 1995], pp. 287–302, at p. 294).

161. BA-MA, N 431/936, Kesselring to Laternser, 30 July 1950. Writing to Laternser, Kesselring spoke of himself and his team for the first time.

162. Charles B. Burdick, "Vom Schwert zur Feder: Deutsche Kriegsgefangene im Dienst der Vorbereitung der amerikanischen Kriegsgeschichtsschreibung über den zweiten Weltkrieg—Die organisatorische Entwicklung der Operational History (German) Section," *MGM* 10 (1971): 69–80, at p. 72.

163. Detlev Bald, "Alte Kameraden: Offizierskader in der Bundeswehr," in Ursula Breymayer, ed., *Willensmenschen: Über deutsche Offiziere* (Frankfurt 1999), pp. 50–64, at p. 62.

164. Wegner, "Erschriebene Siege," p. 291.

165. BA-MA, N 750/2, London Diary, p. 33. Kesselring also seems to have been wavering, as shown by his journal entry: "It is clear that one could no longer cooperate if the General Staff were deemed to have been a 'criminal organisation.' This danger has been dispelled, not because of our beautiful eyes but because of the general consequences."

166. Ibid. Kesselring believed that cooperation was a prerequisite for subsequent close collaboration with the Allies against the Soviet Union. Franz Halder succeeded in obtaining constant improvements to privileges such as mail services, visiting times, and remuneration, thus ensuring that the German officers enjoyed significant advantages.

167. Charles B. Burdick, "Deutschland und die Entwicklung der amtlichen amerikanischen Militärgeschichtsforschung (1920–1960)," in Karl Dietrich Bracher, ed., *Deutschland zwischen Krieg und Frieden: Beiträge zur Politik und Kultur im 20. Jahrhundert—Festschrift für Hans-Adolf Jacobsen* (Düsseldorf 1991), pp. 99–107, at p. 103.

168. Bald, "Alte Kameraden," p. 62.

169. Ueberschär, *Generaloberst Franz Halder*, p. 95. The statement by Geyr von Schweppenburg is part of the collection of records held by the Institute for Contemporary History in Munich. I am indebted to Professor Ueberschär for kindly notifying me of this matter.

170. As head of the OSS, Donovan had maintained a friendly relationship with General Walter Warlimont since the end of the war. As early as autumn 1945, he encouraged Warlimont to convene a small group of like-minded officers in order to prepare documents that, if necessary, could be read out in court in the form of witness testimony, thus laying down the general line to be adopted by others. The so-called Generals' Memorandum should also be viewed in this context. The memorandum, entitled "Das deutsche Heer von 1920–1945" [The Germany Army from 1920 to 1945], was prepared under the supervision of Erich von

Manstein with the reported involvement of Halder, General Siegfried Westphal, and Kesselring (Westphal, *Erinnerungen* [Mainz 1975], p. 372). Speaking in 1945 to Fabian von Schlabrendorff, who had been considered as defense attorney for the Wehrmacht High Command and General Staff before Laternser was awarded the mandate, Donovan said he believed the Nuremberg trials to be "unwise" for both legal and political reasons (Fabian von Schlabrendorff, *Begegnungen in fünf Jahrzehnten* [Tübingen 1979], p. 348).

171. Meyer, "Situation der deutschen militärischen Führungsschicht," p. 680.

172. BA-MA, N 750/2, London Diary, p. 23.

173. PRO/TNA, Kew, FO 1060/500, Ward to Kesselring, 10 January 1952.

174. BA-MA, N 431/937, Liny Kesselring to Laternser, undated but probably after 2 July 1947.

175. PRO/TNA, Kew, FO 1060/499, Kesselring to the Werl Prison directorate, 23 October 1947. Losing no time, he wrote to Potter the next day, asking him to dispatch a delegation of American officers with new material and for the purposes of a meeting. PRO/TNA, Kew, FO 1060/499, Kesselring to Potter, 23 October 1947.

176. PRO/TNA, Kew, FO 1060/499, Harry C. Larter, Chief Historian, to the Werl Prison directorate, 1 April 1948.

177. BA-MA, N 431/937, Kesselring to Laternser, 11 June 1948.

178. SS Major Reder—charged in Italy with the massacres in Marzabotto, Sant'Anna di Stazzema, and San Terenzo—had issued an extensive affidavit regarding the massacres in question.

179. Generalmajor Wilhelm Schmalz had served in Italy as the senior regimental commander of the Hermann Göring Panzer Division from 1 June 1944. I am indebted to Gerhard Schreiber for his letter of 26 June 2001 providing me with this information.

180. BA-MA, N 431/936, Kesselring to Laternser, 10 March 1950.

181. BA-MA, N 431/936, Kesselring to Laternser, 23 May 1949. In addition, it had not been possible "to find a witness who could offer evidence that the leadership could be held responsible for alleged excesses against the partisans."

182. Kerstin von Lingen, "Partisanenkrieg und Wehrmachtjustiz am Beispiel: Italien 1943–1945," *Zeitschrift für Genozidforschung* 2 (2007): 8–40, at p. 38.

183. BA-MA, N 431/936, Kesselring to Laternser, 25 September 1950. Kesselring was glad that the eighty-five witnesses for the prosecution had, in effect, been "witnesses for the defence, since they had only good to say about the division."

184. Ibid.

185. BA-MA, N 431/931, Laternser to Frohwein, 21 February 1949.

186. Norbert Frei, *Vergangenheitspolitik: Die Anfänge der Bundesrepublik und die NS-Vergangenheit* (Munich 1996), p. 21.

187. Ibid., p. 134.

188. BA-MA, N 431/936, secretariat of Regional Bishop Meiser (Rusam) to Laternser, 22 March 1951. Acting through a consistory member named Rusam, Meiser had contacted Laternser seeking information on the Kesselring family's financial circumstances and the prisoners' state of health. Rusam wrote that in his clemency petition, Bishop Meiser would focus on the "personal circumstances" of the prisoner and his family, rather than on legal issues. The bishop had sounded out the church authorities in Rhineland-Westphalia (which included Werl) to find out more about the prison (see also BA-MA, N 431/936, Laternser to Kesselring, 27 April 1951).

189. BA-MA, N 431/933, Schwarzhaupt to Laternser, 27 March 1951. Thus, Dr.

Schwarzhaupt—of the Lutheran Church's External Affairs Office, which was directed by Consistory President Martin Niemöller—asked for documentation regarding other Werl cases. This documentation was to be submitted to the bishop of Chichester to "make it clear to him that the English military courts did not address [these cases] with the requisite thoroughness and objectivity."

190. Frei, *Vergangenheitspolitik*, p. 163.

191. Neuhäusler also received a copy of the petition; see BA-MA, N 431/934, Laternser to Neuhäusler, 13 March 1951.

192. In the Kesselring case, for example, Irmgard Horn-Kesselring directed requests to Bishops Neuhäusler (Munich) and Jäger (Paderborn), whereas Laternser appealed to Cardinal Josef Frings of Cologne.

193. PRO/TNA, Kew, FO 1060/494, clemency appeal from Archbishop Jäger to the High Commissioner, 18 May 1951, three appendixes: Freytag-Loringhoven clemency appeal, Horn-Kesselring clemency appeal, and "Kesselring's intended closing words in Venice," taken from Jäger's letter.

194. Ibid.

195. During the war, Hudal had acted as a liaison between the Vatican and Kesselring. He had also protested on behalf of the Vatican against the deportation of Italian Jews from Rome during the autumn of 1943 (John Cornwell, *Pius XII: Der Papst, der geschwiegen hat* [Munich 1999], p. 359).

196. Wiesenthal, *Recht*, p. 79. Hudal has long been the subject of controversy among historians, primarily because of his role as a prominent advocate for German POWs and his role in helping well-known Nazi perpetrators, such as the camp commandant of Treblinka, Franz Stangl, to escape to South America.

197. Clemens Vollnhals, *Evangelische Kirche und Entnazifizierung 1945–1949: Die Last der nationalsozialistischen Vergangenheit* (Munich 1989), p. 20.

198. Ibid., p. 21.

199. Clemens Vollnhals, "Die Hypothek des Nationalprotestantismus: Entnazifizierung und Strafverfolgung von NS-Verbrechen nach 1945," *GG* 18 (1992): 51–69, at p. 51.

200. BA-MA, N 431/931, Dibelius secretariat to Laternser, 25 May 1949. After the war, Otto Dibelius was appointed bishop of Berlin-Brandenburg. In 1926, he had drafted the famous program entitled "The Century of the Church." After the war, he stressed the church's willingness to purify itself of "*deutschchristlichen* influences" (the Nazis' church movement), but he opposed the introduction of democracy, which he termed an "alien ideology" that Germans associated with unemployment and an inefficient foreign policy due to their experience during the Weimar period. See Vollnhals, *Evangelische Kirche und Entnazifizierung*, p. 19.

201. BA-MA, N 431/933, Laternser to Meiser, 13 March 1951.

202. Martin Niemöller, held in Dachau from 1941 to 1945 as one of the leading thinkers of the Confessing Church, had served as a naval officer in the Weimar Reichswehr and was one of the leaders of the Freikorps. As such, he could certainly identify with the demands for "honorable" military officers to be released. Niemöller was disappointed by the policy pursued by the Allies toward Germany, in particular the policy of dismantlement, which, in his view, deprived the country of the means for reconstruction.

203. Frei, *Vergangenheitspolitik*, p. 137. For more detail, see Vollnhals, *Evangelische Kirche und Entnazifizierung*, pp. 51–69.

204. Allegedly, Dibelius said about Niemöller, "No one but he could represent our church abroad, since there was still bitter enmity towards all things German." Cited in Otto

Dibelius, *Ein Christ ist immer im Dienst: Erlebnisse und Erfahrungen in einer Zeitenwende* (Stuttgart 1961), p. 260.

205. Asmussen to bishops and senior officials, 29 November 1946. Cited in Vollnhals, *Evangelische Kirche und Entnazifizierung*, p. 40.

206. BA-MA, N 431/936, Laternser to Kesselring, 19 July 1949.

207. Frei, *Vergangenheitspolitik*, p. 139.

208. BA-MA, N 431/936, Kesselring to Laternser, 12 August 1947.

209. Ibid. The Württemberg regional bishop, Theophil Wurm, had suggested to Mackensen's son, Klaus von Mackensen, that he provide the bishop with material on the Mackensen case. Mackensen himself had suggested that Kesselring should piggyback on this, since their cases were "more or less of a piece."

210. BA-MA, N 431/931, Asmussen to Laternser, 18 August 1949. Using Gollancz as a conduit proved to be very beneficial, since he had the greater influence.

211. BA-MA, N 431/933, Lukowicz to Laternser, 10 July 1950.

212. BA-MA, N 431/936, Laternser to Kesselring, 19 January 1949.

213. BA-MA, N 431/896, Kesselring to Laternser, 2 November 1947: "It is important that effective newspaper editorials are sent to foreign government and party functionaries, as well as Wehrmacht personalities, so that these ideas are also disseminated abroad."

214. BA-MA, N 431/934, distribution list, Kesselring plea. Thirty-four copies were sent out between 16 July and 22 August 1947.

215. Ibid. Father Hiemer assumed responsibility for distributing the documents among church circles.

216. BA-MA, N 431/935, Schweinitz to Laternser, 17 July 1947. Oberstleutnant Viktor von Schweinitz had conducted the capitulation negotiations in Switzerland as the authorized representative of the commander-in-chief, South-Western Command, Heinrich von Vietinghoff-Scheel, and he signed the surrender document on 29 April 1945, in Caserta.

217. General der Flieger Wilhelm Speidel had been sentenced to 5¾ years of imprisonment in Nuremberg, where he was a defendant in the trial dealing with partisan warfare, case 7. He was being held in Landsberg. Laternser was personally acquainted with Wilhelm Speidel, since he had defended Field Marshals List and von Weichs during the same trial.

218. BA-MA, N 431/935, Speidel to Laternser, 21 July 1947.

219. "M." may have been George C. Marshall, former U.S. army chief of General Staff and secretary of state from 1947 to 1949. The official contact person for clemency issues, John McCloy, was only appointed Allied high commissioner for Germany in 1949.

220. See the statement by Heinrich Andergassen (PRO/TNA, Kew, WO 310/123) regarding the surrender negotiations in Switzerland, which involved a secret agreement between Waffen SS General and Supreme SS and Police Commander Karl Wolff and Allen Dulles on behalf of the Allies. They agreed that SS massacres would not be the subject of war crimes trials.

221. Research on this topic is still in its early stages. For an initial overview, see Richard Breitman, Norman J. W. Goda, Timothy Naftali, and Robert Wolfe, *U.S. Intelligence and the Nazis* (Cambridge 2005). For further information on the protection afforded to Wolff by Dulles and Donovan, see Michael Salter and Suzanne Ost, "War Crimes and Legal Immunities—The Complicities of Waffen-SS General Karl Wolff in Nazi Medical Experiments," *Rutgers Journal of Law and Religion* 4, no. 1 (2003): 12–26; Kerstin von Lingen and Michael Salter, "Contrasting Strategies within the War Crimes Trials of Kesselring and Wolff," *Liverpool Law Review* 26, no. 3 (2005): 225–266; and Michael Salter, *Nazi War Crimes, US Intelligence and Selective Prosecution at Nuremberg: Controversies Regarding the Role of the Office of Strategic Services* (London 2007).

222. BA-MA, N 431/935, Laternser to Speidel, 15 July 1947.

223. BA-MA, N 431/936, Laternser to Kesselring, 22 April 1950.

224. BA-MA, N 431/931, Laternser to Cavallero, 22 April 1950.

225. BA-MA, N 431/931, Cavallero to Laternser, 3 May 1950.

226. Ibid.

227. BA-MA, N 431/936, Laternser to Kesselring, 23 June 1947.

228. *Die Zeit*, 22 May 1947, "Kesselring and Schacht," p. 1.

229. BA-MA, N 431/935, Schweinitz to Laternser, 17 July 1947. Schweinitz promised to use the petition in accordance with the agreement reached at Wiesbaden in January 1947; i.e., he would make contact with supporters he knew. For this purpose, he also requested the petition drafted by Otto Kranzbühler on behalf of Admiral Karl Dönitz (see also BA-MA, N 431/935, Laternser to Speidel, 29 September 1947).

230. BA-MA, N 431/936, distribution list, and Laternser to Kesselring, 4 May 1949.

231. BA-MA, N 431/936, Laternser to Kesselring, 11 June 1949.

232. One copy was sent to the *Zeit* weekly newspaper and another to the *Kieler Nachrichten*. It is not clear how Laternser chose these publications, but one can assume that journalists writing for them had come to his attention as a result of critical articles, leading Laternser to hope for "pro-Kesselring" coverage in these papers.

233. BA-MA, N 431/938, address distribution list.

234. *Der Spiegel*, "Trial by Half: Martyrs Were Needed" 31 (1948): 13–14, available at http://wissen.spiegel.de/wissen/dokument/dokument.html?id=44418558&top=SPIEGEL. Even the subtitle—"Martyrs Were Needed"—supports this thesis. Undated proofs for the article can be found in BA-MA, N 431/933, but without Laternser's handwritten annotations. It is thus not clear whether Laternser saw the proofs before they went to print and was able to comment orally on them or whether he simply received the manuscript for his information.

235. Frederick J. Libby, *To End War: The Story of the National Council for Prevention of War* (New York 1969).

236. Freda Utley, *The High Cost of Vengeance* (Chicago 1949). The German translation, *Kostspielige Rache*, was published in Hamburg in 1950. The book was a best seller both in the United States and in Germany.

237. Wolfgang Krieger, "Die amerikanische Deutschlandplanung: Hypotheken und Chancen für einen Neuanfang," in Hans-Erich Volkmann, ed., *Ende des Dritten Reichs—Ende des Zweiten Weltkriegs* (Munich 1995), pp. 25—50, at pp. 28f.

238. Lothar Kettenacker, "Der britische Rahmenplan für die Besetzung Deutschlands und seine unerwarteten Folgen," in Hans-Erich Volkmann, ed., *Ende des Dritten Reichs—Ende des Zweiten Weltkriegs* (Munich 1995), pp. 51–74, at p. 52.

239. Tom Bower, *Blind Eye to Murder: Britain, America and the Purging of Nazi Germany—A Pledge Betrayed* (London 1995), pp. 245f. Although Bower touched on the pressure groups, he did not examine the significance of Lord Hankey or his coordinating role.

240. Stephen Wentworth Roskill, *Hankey: Man of Secrets* (London 1974), p. 644.

241. In this regard, see Maurice Hankey, *Diplomacy on Conference: Studies in Public Affairs 1920–1946* (London 1946).

242. For details of Hankey's life, see his entry, written by George Mallaby, in the *Dictionary of National Biography* (Oxford 1981), pp. 485–487.

243. Lord Maurice Hankey, *Politics, Trials and Errors* (Oxford 1950). Even the title is a giveaway, illustrating Hankey's attitude to the official policy of the British government and the Allied program of war crimes trials.

244. My research developed from an orientation sketch that depicted Lord Hankey and

his campaign group, in Ahrens's private archives. I am indebted to Dr. Hanns-Dietrich Ahrens, Essen, for the breakdown of Lord Hankey's circle, shown here for the first time. The links between these men would have remained concealed without the assistance of Dr. Ahrens, who died in 2005.

245. Maugham had also distinguished himself as a critic of the war crimes trials: see Viscount Maugham, *U.N.O. and War Crimes,* postscript by Lord Hankey (London 1951).

246. Hanns-Dietrich Ahrens, *Demontage: Nachkriegspolitik der Alliierten* (Munich 1982), p. 72.

247. Russell Grenfell was the author of several books (translated into German) on the navy during World War II. The most important of these in the present context is Grenfell, *Bedingungsloser Hass? Die deutsche Kriegsschuld und Europas Zukunft* (Tübingen 1974).

248. Churchill College, Cambridge, Hankey to the Bishop of Chichester, George Bell, 11 December 1951.

249. Victor Gollancz, pacifist and socialist, led the camp of British opponents to the war crimes trials, which he termed a "repellant mixture of hypocrisy and self-justification, coupled with a thirst for revenge." In this regard, see Gollancz, *Stimme aus dem Chaos* (Nuremberg 1948), pp. 242ff. In 1947, in his polemic "In Darkest Germany," Gollancz had drawn attention to the catastrophic food shortages and the consequences of the Allied dismantlement policy, but he was later criticized as having used exaggerated numbers of references. See John Farquharson, "'Emotional but Influential': Victor Gollancz, Richard Stokes and the British Zone of Germany, 1945–9," *Journal of Contemporary History* 22 (1987): 501–519.

250. Paget, *Manstein,* p. 3.

251. Veale wrote several books dealing with the war crimes issue. The best known are *Advance to Barbarism* (London 1951; German edition, 1954), and *War Crimes Discreetly Veiled* (New York 1959).

252. Fuller had been politically active in the 1930s, serving as an MP for the British Union of Fascists. He was considered an important British military theoretician. See Anthony John Trythall, *"Boney" Fuller: The Intellectual General 1878–1966* (London 1977), pp. 240–275; Brian Holden Reid, *J. F. C. Fuller: Military Thinker* (London 1987), pp. 195–216; Alaric Searle, "Was There a 'Boney' Fuller after the Second World War? Major-General J. F. C. Fuller as Military Theorist and Commentator, 1945–1966," *War in History* 11, no. 3 (2004): 327–357.

253. Ahrens, *Demontage,* p. 51.

254. Churchill College, Cambridge, Bell to Hankey, 29 April 1949. Bell used this letter to set the next targets for the Bell-Hankey team: an end to the war crimes trials, no further deportations (to Russia), a review or reversal of the war crimes sentences already issued, and improvements to the "really bad" imprisonment conditions in Spandau.

255. The diplomats were Robert Craigie (British ambassador in Tokyo), F. Piggot (diplomat), and B. Blakeney.

256. For details of Ismay's career, see his entry, written by Ronald Lewin, in *Dictionary of National Biography* (Oxford 1981), pp. 570–572. For details of Ismay's diplomatic skill during the establishment of NATO, see Winfried Heinemann, "1956 als das Krisenjahr der NATO," in Norbert Wiggershaus, ed., *Das internationale Krisenjahr 1956: Polen, Ungarn, Suez* (Munich 1999), pp. 615–637, at p. 616. Heinemann expressed this view of Ismay: "He undoubtedly saw his office as a political one."

257. The German press was captivated by the idea of a pro-German British interrogation officer, which gave rise to the wildest speculations. Thus, in April 1949, Viktor Freiherr

von der Lippe wrote to Laternser saying that, while in Paris, he had read an article about the Kesselring trial and Scotland's positive comments. According to von der Lippe, the article claimed that Scotland had served in World War II as a double agent on behalf of Britain and Germany and that he was, in fact, a German divisional commander. Kurt Kramm, from Friedrichshafen, wrote to Laternser claiming to have served with Scotland in German South-West Africa, where Scotland had been recruited as an interpreter for the Schutztruppe (a German colonial militia) (BA-MA, N 431/936, Laternser to Kesselring, 27 October 1949; BA-MA, N 431/935, Scotland to Laternser, 31 December 1949; BA-MA, N 431/936, Laternser to Kesselring, 6 January 1950).

258. Alexander P. Scotland, *The London Cage* (London 1957), pp. 87, 178, 182, 183, 186.

259. BA-MA, N 431/935, Scotland to Laternser, 31 December 1949. On New Year's Day 1949, Scotland wrote to Laternser—whom he had met several times in Wiesbaden—stating that he had now completed his record of the Kesselring trial and would soon be in a position to submit a petition on Kesselring's behalf. He also wished Laternser success in his efforts to secure "more reasonable conditions of life for the mis-named war criminals." This communication was the first time that terms such as *mis-named* and *so-called* war criminal had been used by a British player in connection with Kesselring.

260. BA-MA, N 431/935, Scotland to Laternser, 30 October 1950. Thus, Scotland asked Laternser for details of the case in order to "fire another shot at the Foreign Office."

261. BA-MA, N 431/935, Laternser to Scotland, 22 April 1950.

262. BA-MA, N 431/935, Scotland to Laternser, 7 May 1950.

263. BA-MA, N 431/933, Laternser to Father Kleyer on Kesselring's behalf, enclosing a letter from Scotland, 13 May 1950.

264. BA-MA, N 431/936, Kesselring to Laternser, elucidations regarding the order issued on 29 March 1944, 11 January 1950.

265. BA-MA, N 431/935, Scotland to Laternser, 6 February 1950.

266. PRO/TNA, Kew, FO 1060/493, Petition from Scotland to the Foreign Office, 8 May 1950; also BA-MA, N 431/935, Petition from Scotland to the Foreign Office, 8 May 1950, 3 pages.

267. BA-MA, N 431/935, Petition from Scotland to the Foreign Office, 8 May 1950, Point 13. Scotland claimed it had "been made quite clear" that Kesselring spent the night at his battle headquarters, and he did not address this crucial issue further.

268. However, the discovery of the flight logs maintained by Kesselring's former pilot, Manfred Bäumler, has since clarified the field marshal's itinerary beyond doubt. The logs prove, at a minimum, that Kesselring could not have been personally involved in the Fosse Ardeatine massacre, since he was in Liguria on that date. (BA-MA, N 431/931, Laternser to Bäumler, 27 January 1948, Return of Flight Logs IX and X. Today, they are in the possession of Peter Bäumler's family, which is where I discovered and inspected them.)

269. BA-MA, N 431/935, Petition from Scotland to the Foreign Office, 8 May 1950: "a feature our ordered military minds could not then grasp or believe."

270. Ibid. Scotland wrote: "That Kesselring is convinced that he was pre-judged in Venice in the Spring of 1947 is also no doubt on record in your Department." He noted that there was a deep feeling of resentment in Germany "caused by the handling of the charges against these accused in the Courts at Rome and Venice, and their retention in prison." Pointedly, Scotland also commented that public opinion associated the death sentences imposed on Kesselring, Mackensen, and Mältzer primarily with Stirling, the judge advocate general involved in both instances.

271. Ibid., distribution list on p. 3.

272. BA-MA, N 431/935, Scotland to Laternser, 15 June 1950.

273. *Dithmarscher Landeszeitung*, 24 June 1950, "A First Visit to Werl," by Sefton Delmer. Delmer wrote about the prisoners' daily lives, emphasizing their work in the garden and their historical studies. He alleged that the sole aim of these studies was to "remain in contact with their colleagues on the outside. They are at the end of a secret line of communication which today again links the staff officers of Hitler's former Wehrmacht."

274. *Der Spiegel* 24 (15 June 1950): Panorama section.

275. BA-MA, N 431/936, Kesselring writing on Mackensen's behalf to Laternser, 11 July 1950. Kesselring's comment related to the restrictions imposed as a result of the article, which became apparent a few days later.

276. BA-MA, N 431/935, Scotland to Laternser, 15 June 1950. Scotland assumed that the Foreign Office had been unable to "stomach" his petition.

277. PRO/TNA, Kew, FO 1060/493, letter drafted by Douglas Passmore, Wahnerheide, to Scotland, 23 June 1950.

278. PRO/TNA, Kew, FO 1060/493, letter drafted by Douglas Passmore, Wahnerheide, to Scotland, 23 June 1950, including handwritten annotation by Alfred Brown dated 26 June 1950.

279. PRO/TNA, Kew, FO 1060/493, Brown, Wahnerheide, to Marsden-Smedley, Foreign Office, 27 June 1950.

280. In this respect, Britain faced some enormous obstacles. For example, the Italian authorities demanded a fee for the files of the Kappler trial. Since this fee could only be paid in Italian lire, the Treasury had to be involved, significantly delaying the entire process. Therefore, Basil Marsden-Smedley of the Foreign Office decided not to pursue the Kappler trail, and he passed the Kesselring case back to the high commissioner for Germany and his legal advisers for a decision (PRO/TNA, Kew, FO 1060/493, Foreign Office to Office of the Legal Adviser, Moller, 13 June 1950).

281. BA-MA, N 431/936, Kesselring to Laternser, 21 February 1949. He wrote to Laternser that he had presented his "well-known wishes regarding M. and M." While in custody, Kesselring was always concerned with securing the release of Mackensen and Mältzer, whom he considered innocent, and he always stated that as the former commander-in-chief, he was the only officer who should be imprisoned for the Fosse Ardeatine massacre.

282. Ibid.

283. *Der Abend*, East Berlin, 14 March 1950, "Prison Visit: Meeting between General Bishop and Kesselring, Topic: Airforce." This was clearly part of a communist campaign against West German rearmament, depicting Kesselring as an expert-in-waiting ready to serve in the next war.

284. BA-MA, N 431/935, Laternser to Scotland, 29 January 1951. Laternser by now had full confidence in his British correspondent and wrote quite bluntly. He stated that another of the men convicted in Italy, General Eduard Peter Crasemann, had "been found guilty of alleged participation in the Fuccechio Swamp cases and sentenced to 10 years' imprisonment." Crasemann began serving his sentence in Werl. Shortly before Laternser wrote this letter to Scotland, Crasemann had died there, since "he could not accept his fate," which "killed him."

285. BA-MA, N 431/936, Laternser to Kesselring, 30 January 1951.

286. BA-MA, N 431/933, Laternser to Kesselring, enclosing a copy of a letter from Scotland, 9 February 1951.

287. BA-MA, N 431/935, Scotland to Laternser, 15 June 1950.

288. Alexander Preston Scotland, *Fall Kesselring—The Kesselring Case* (Bonn 1952).

289. BA-MA, N 431/936, Kesselring to Laternser on behalf of Mackensen, 11 July 1950. The following statement by Kesselring illustrates his entire worldview: he sat innocently in prison, having been convicted on "flimsy evidence." Immediately after the war, Kesselring at least hinted at having scruples, but he relinquished these again in favor of a monolithic war memory in which the overarching picture of a clean German Wehrmacht in Italy left no room for the massacres and their Italian victims.

290. BA-MA, N 431/936, Kesselring to Laternser, 27 October 1950. Thus, on 29 October 1950, the *Sunday Express* published a letter from one Peterpaul von Donat demanding Kesselring's release. Lieutenant Colonel von Donat had already advocated Kesselring's case in September, in the *Daily Express*—as von Donat, writing to Laternser, noted with some satisfaction.

291. For details of Liddell Hart's career, see his entry in *Dictionary of National Biography* (Oxford 1981).

292. Alaric Searle, "A Very Special Relationship: Basil Liddell Hart, Wehrmacht Generals and the Debate on West German Rearmament, 1945–1953," *War in History* 5, no. 3 (1998): 327–357, at p. 328. In this regard, see the different motivations attributed to Liddell Hart for his contact with German generals (idealism or a sense of fair play versus egotism and an instinct for maintaining power) in two biographies, the first by B. Bond, *Liddell Hart: A Study of His Military Thought* (London 1977), and the second by J. J. Mearsheimer, *Liddell Hart and the Weight of History* (London 1988).

293. Liddell Hart, *The Other Side of the Hill* (London 1948).

294. Searle, "A Very Special Relationship," p. 337.

295. Ibid., p. 331.

296. Basil Liddell Hart, with the help of Lucie Marie Rommel, *The Rommel Papers* (London 1953).

297. Searle, "A Very Special Relationship," p. 354. He collaborated in the first biography ever written on Rommel—Desmond Young, *Rommel* (London 1950).

298. This fact is indicated by the large number of English-language biographies of Rommel, all of which emphasize his military skill, and by a range of Web sites. The interest has not waned over the decades; see David Fraser, *Knight's Cross: A Life of Field Marshal Erwin Rommel* (London 1993); Ronald Lewin, *Rommel as Military Commander* (London 1969); Samuel W. Mitcham, *Rommel's Desert War: The Life and Death of the Afrika Korps* (New York 1982); and also by Mitcham, *Rommel's Last Battle: The Desert Fox and the Normandy Campaign* (New York 1983).

299. Searle, "A Very Special Relationship," p. 356.

300. Ibid., p. 333n26, including a reference to archive material in the Liddell Hart Centre for Military Archives, King's College, London (hereafter cited as LHCMA), especially Liddell Hart Papers, 9/24/155.

301. Searle, "A Very Special Relationship," p. 338.

302. Ibid., p. 334.

303. BA-MA, N 431/932, Westphal to Laternser, 25 August 1948. Unaware of the political aims of the Hankey group, Westphal wrote to Laternser that Liddell Hart seemed to be "truly well-disposed to us" and that he would "sincerely try" to do something for Kesselring.

304. BA-MA, N 431/932, Liddell Hart to Laternser, 3 June 1949, in which Liddell Hart expressed his thanks for a copy of the petition.

305. BA-MA, N 431/932, Liddell Hart to Westphal, 16 August 1948.

306. Searle, "A Very Special Relationship," p. 338.

307. Kesselring, *Soldat,* p. 452.

308. Searle, "A Very Special Relationship," p. 338.

309. Ibid., pp. 335 and 346.

310. Ibid., p. 341.

311. Ahrens, *Demontage,* pp. 183f. The Essen-based PR consultant Ahrens played a key role in these efforts, and he performed a bridging function between the United States and Germany, as well as subsequently providing a link to the Hankey circle. According to Ahrens, the aim was to "unsettle the enemy by making him doubt the justice of his cause and the fairness of his methods."

312. Ibid., p. 85.

313. Letter from Ahrens to the author, 14 December 2000.

314. Ahrens, *Demontage,* p. 89.

315. Ibid., p. 240. Even at an advanced age, Hoover expressed opposition to the Morgenthau plan. See ibid., p. 42.

316. David A. Horowitz, *Beyond Left and Right: Insurgency and the Establishment* (Illinois 1997). I would like to thank Professor Michael Hochgeschwender, Munich University, for his help in the political categorization of the American senators in question.

317. Cited in Ross A. Kennedy, "The Ideology of American Isolationism 1931–1939," *Cercles* 5 (2002): 59.

318. Ibid. Kennedy also pointed out that during the 1930s, the isolationists had pioneered the use of media outlets—primarily the *New Republic*—as a means of mobilizing public opinion in their favor.

319. Because of their guiding principles, the Quakers were one of the first groups to provide aid not only to concentration camp victims but also to German internees and POWs. Later, their efforts metamorphosed into a commitment to convicted war criminals, who received prison visits and packages. See Richenda Scott, ed., *Die Quäker* (Stuttgart 1974), p. 200; Heinrich Otto, *Werden und Wesen des Quäkertums und seine Entwicklung in Deutschland* (Vienna 1972), pp. 367f. and 373.

320. The NCPW was established in 1921 in connection with the Washington Naval Conference. The organization's primary aim was to "educate the American public towards peace," particularly through an educational program combating "hate and intolerance" via press and print publications as well as broadcasts. Between 1921 and 1941, almost US$2 million were spent on these efforts. At the same time, the NCPW acted as an umbrella association for over thirty other American pacifist groups, which attracted particular support during the war (see Libby, *To End War*). During the war, the NCPW strategy changed, and its leaders argued that the debate should no longer focus on preventing war but rather on accelerating an acceptable negotiated peace. Thus, in the spring of 1943, NCPW president Libby gave a radio interview in which he recommended striving for a negotiated peace as soon as possible. He used a slogan that was to become popular: "If we don't negotiate, Stalin will win the war." Incidentally, the organization thus demonstrated that it was no longer simply strictly pacifist but primarily anticommunist (see letter from National Council for Prevention of War, Deputy Secretary James Finucane, to Ahrens, 23 May 1950, Ahrens Papers, private collection, Essen). James Finucane succeeded the organizer of the famous CARE packages, Al Beverage (see Libby, *To End War,* p. 181). In this letter, Finucane distinguished the aims of his organization from those of Morgenthau, who chaired the Society for the Prevention of World War III, which was often confused with the NCPW.

321. Ahrens, *Demontage*, p. 43. Thirty-four senators had signed a corresponding petition by Libby in the summer of 1945; their initiative did not succeed.

322. Ibid., p. 51. Hoover was also a Quaker.

323. Horowitz, *Beyond Left and Right*, p. 234.

324. Libby, *To End War*, p. 180. In 1947, he even succeeded, through Senators Langer, Eastland, and Bridges, in having an amendment to the Trade with the Enemy Act passed, which was intended to legalize private food packages (see Ahrens, *Demontage*, p. 44).

325. On the complex issue of Allied dismantlement policy, see Werner Abelshauser, "Wirtschaft und Rüstung in den fünfziger Jahren," in Werner Abelshauser and Walter Schwengler, eds., *Anfänge westdeutscher Sicherheitspolitik*, vol. 4, *Wirtschaft und Rüstung, Souveränität und Sicherheit* (Munich 1997), pp. 1–186, particularly pp. 48ff.

326. This was partially successful—for example, in saving the Salzgitter iron and steel works from removal (see ibid., p. 181).

327. Ahrens Papers, private collection, Essen, note on visit with Finucane to Werl, 8 October 1951.

328. Ibid., pp. 66 and 82.

329. Ibid., p. 74.

330. Libby, *To End War*, p. 181. Here, Libby's account became nebulous, which indicates that—contrary to the official Allied retribution line—procedures for intervening on behalf of German war criminals had been endorsed at the highest levels of government and therefore remained classified: "This story would occupy another book."

331. These would "bear any comparison with the sadistic barbarities carried out in German concentration camps," according to Meyer, "Situation der deutschen militärischen Führungsschicht," p. 633.

332. Congress Report, 1st session, debates of the 81st Congress, 27 January 1949; included in BA-MA, N 524 (Schulze-Gaevernitz), p. 48.

333. Letter from Ahrens to the author, 14 December 2000. Ahrens had to, for example, prepare reports on the "calories provided to the Ruhr population" and "ill-treatment of prisoners in Landsberg." Ahrens himself was in the United States from May 1947 to April 1948, where he collaborated with Libby to initiate a campaign in the United States seeking an end to the dismantlement policy (see Ahrens, *Demontage*, pp. 58 and 88f.).

334. Libby, *To End War*, p. 181.

335. Ahrens, *Demontage*, p. 271.

336. As in the battle that had just been fought to prevent dismantlement, those engaged in the current battle for public opinion included the Essen-based Ahrens PR consultancy and Franz-Josef Müser, the director general of the Bochum Verein (a steel mill forming part of the German United Steelworks Association) (see ibid., p. 144).

Chapter 4: The Politicization of the War Crimes Issue

1. Klaus A. Maier, "Die internationalen Auseinandersetzungen um die Westintegration der Bundesrepublik Deutschland und um ihre Bewaffnung im Rahmen der europäischen Verteidigungsgemeinschaft," in Lutz Köllner, Klaus A. Maier, Wilhelm Meier-Dörnberg, and Hans-Erich Volkmann, eds., *Anfänge westdeutscher Sicherheitspolitik*, vol. 2, *Die EVG-Phase* (Munich 1990), pt. 1, pp. 1–234, at p. 1.

2. Norbert Wiggershaus, "Die Entscheidung für einen westdeutschen Verteidigungs-

beitrag 1950," in Roland G. Foerster, Christian Greiner, Georg Meyer, Hans-Jürgen Rautenberg, and Norbert Wiggershaus, eds., *Anfänge westdeutscher Sicherheitspolitik 1945–1956*, vol. 1, *Von der Kapitulation zum Pleven-Plan* (Munich 1982), pt. 3, pp. 325–402, a: p. 347.

3. There is extensive literature on this issue in Germany. Currently, the most in-depth summary of the various currents in the debate can be found in the anthology published by the Hamburg Institute for Social Research and edited by Klaus Naumann, *Nachkrieg in Deutschland* (Hamburg 2001). The most important book on the era is still Hans-Peter Schwarz's *Die Ära Adenauer: Gründerjahre der Republik 1949–1957* (Stuttgart and Wiesbaden 1981). Other selected overviews of the topic include Martin Broszat, Klaus-Dietmar Henke, and Hans Woller, eds., *Von Stalingrad zur Währungsreform: Zur Sozialgeschichte des Umbruchs in Deutschland* (Munich 1988); Anselm Doering-Manteuffel, *Die Bundesrepublik Deutschland in der Ära Adenauer: Aussenpolitik und innere Entwicklung 1949–1963* (Darmstadt 1983); Christoph Klessmann, *Die doppelte Staatsgründung: Deutsche Geschichte 1945–1955* (Bonn 1982); Rudolf Morsey, *Die Bundesrepublik Deutschland: Entstehung und Entwicklung bis 1969*, 2nd ed. (Munich 2002); Axel Schildt and Arnold Sywottek, eds., *Modernisierung im Wiederaufbau: Die westdeutsche Gesellschaft der 50er Jahre* (Bonn 1993); Hans-Peter Schwarz, "Die ausgebliebene Katastrophe: Eine Problemskizze zur Geschichte der Bundesrepublik," in Hermann Rudolph, ed., *Den Staat denken* (Berlin 1990), pp. 151–174; and Kurt Sontheimer, *Die Adenauer-Ära: Grundlegung der Bundesrepublik* (Munich 1991).

4. *Picture Post*, 24 July 1948, "Will There Be War?" by Basil Liddell Hart. See also Alaric Searle, "A Very Special Relationship: Basil Liddell Hart, Wehrmacht Generals and the Debate on West German Rearmament, 1945–1953," *War in History* 5, no. 3 (1998): 341 and 344.

5. Searle, "A Very Special Relationship," p. 357.

6. Hanns-Dietrich Ahrens, *Demontage: Nachkriegspolitik der Alliierten* (Munich 1982), p. 154. Cameron was writing about Franz-Josef Müser, the managing director of an iron- and steelworks called the Bochumer Verein. Questioning the actions of Müser, who had incited workers to ignore a British military order, and of Hans Kallen, Cameron noted that the two men in question were at liberty and claimed—writing with some disgust—that they would be happy to watch the Allies preparing to try men such as Generals Rundstedt and Manstein.

7. Ibid., p. 261.

8. Basil Liddell Hart, *Gedanken zur Verteidigung Europas* (Coburg 1951).

9. Wilhelm Meier-Dörnberg, "Die Planung des Verteidigungsbeitrags der Bundesrepublik Deutschland im Rahmen der EVG," in Lutz Köllner, Klaus A. Maier, Wilhelm Meier-Dörnberg, and Hans-Erich Volkmann, eds., *Anfänge westdeutscher Sicherheitspolitik*, vol. 2, *Die EVG-Phase* (Munich 1990), pp. 605–756, at pp. 607f.

10. Wolfram Wette, *Die Wehrmacht: Feindbilder, Vernichtungskrieg, Legenden* (Darmstadt 2002), p. 234.

11. Maier, "Internationalen Auseinandersetzungen," p. 59.

12. Ibid., p. 117.

13. Wiggershaus, "Entscheidung," p. 367.

14. Dieter Krüger, *Das Amt Blank: Die schwierige Gründung des Bundesministeriums für Verteidigung* (Freiburg 1993).

15. Ibid., p. 337.

16. Maier, "Internationalen Auseinandersetzungen," p. 15.

17. Ibid., pp. 5ff.

18. Ibid., pp. 12ff.

19. Ibid., p. 21.

20. Wiggershaus, "Entscheidung," p. 402.

21. Klaus-Dietmar Henke, "Die Trennung vom Nationalsozialismus: Selbstzerstörung, politische Säuberung, 'Entnazifizierung,' Strafverfolgung," in Klaus-Dietmar Henke and Hans Woller, eds., *Politische Säuberung in Europa: Die Abrechnung mit Faschismus und Kollaboration nach dem Zweiten Weltkrieg* (Munich 1991), pp. 21–83, at p. 77.

22. See Detlef Bald, *Militär und Gesellschaft 1945–1990: Die Bundeswehr der Bonner Republik* (Baden-Baden 1994), p. 16.

23. Wiggershaus, "Entscheidung," pp. 333f.

24. Roland G. Foerster, "Innenpolitische Aspekte der Sicherheit Westdeutschlands 1947–1950," in Roland G. Foerster, Christian Greiner, Georg Meyer, Hans-Jürgen Rautenberg, and Norbert Wiggershaus, eds., *Anfänge westdeutscher Sicherheitspolitik 1945–1956*, vol. 1, *Von der Kapitulation zum Pleven-Plan* (Munich 1982), pt. 3, pp. 403–576, at p. 572.

25. Ibid., p. 573.

26. Hans-Erich Volkmann, "Die innenpolitische Dimension Adenauerscher Sicherheitspolitik in der EVG-Phase," in Lutz Köllner, Klaus A. Maier, Wilhelm Meier-Dörnberg, and Hans-Erich Volkmann, eds., *Anfänge westdeutscher Sicherheitspolitik*, vol. 2, *Die EVG-Phase* (Munich 1990), pp. 235–604, at pp. 463ff.

27. Norbert Frei, *Vergangenheitspolitik: Die Anfänge der Bundesrepublik und die NS-Vergangenheit* (Munich 1996), p. 189. Thus, writing in the *Süddeutsche Zeitung* on the occasion of the amnesty law's enactment and the impending end of the denazification process, Ernst Müller-Meiningen created a direct link with the war criminals issue and demanded that the amnesty should now apply to all "Germans convicted by Allied courts." See Frei, *Vergangenheitspolitik*, and *Süddeutsche Zeitung*, 16 December 1949, "Schlussstrich," by Ernst Müller-Meiningen, p. 3.

28. Frei, *Vergangenheitspolitik*, p. 187.

29. Henke, "Trennung," p. 78. Ironically, the phrase "for a better Germany" has its origins in the final words of Colonel Claus Schenk Graf von Stauffenberg, just before being shot for his attempt on Hitler's life on 20 July 1944. During the early 1950s, Stauffenberg's plot was still seen as high treason; today, his actions are considered heroic.

30. Proceedings of the German Bundestag, transcripts, 1st legislative period, 1949, vol. 1, p. 27.

31. Thus, for example, he asked McCloy to cancel the planned executions in Landsberg, since the death penalty had been abolished in Germany and the German people "would consider it a particular hardship if, almost five years after the end of the war, the American occupying power was still carrying out executions on German soil." Cited in Ulrich Brochhagen, *Nach Nürnberg. Vergangenheitsbewältigung und Westintegration in der Ära Adenauer* (Hamburg 1994), p. 39.

32. Frei, *Vergangenheitspolitik*, p. 197. This is also apparent from the fact that he did not mention the word once in the "security memorandum"; see Klaus v. Schubert, ed., *Sicherheitspolitik der Bundesrepublik Deutschland: Dokumentation 1945–1977*, 2 vols. (Cologne 1978–1979), 1: 79–83, for the wording of the security memorandum.

33. Proceedings of the German Bundestag, 1st legislative period, 8 November 1950, p. 3614.

34. Frei, *Vergangenheitspolitik*, p. 196.

35. Alaric Searle, *Wehrmacht Generals, West German Society, and the Debate on Rearmament, 1949–1959* (Westport, CT, 2003), pp. 49ff.

36. See, for example, the demand by VdS chairman Gottfried Hansen for a "Christmas amnesty," 1950, in *FAZ*, 27 December 1950, "Allgemeine Amnestie," and *Times*, 28 December 1950; also in PRO/TNA FO 1060/53, Verband deutscher Soldaten, Hansen, to McCloy, 4 February 1951, and PRO/TNA FO 1060/454, Hansen to McCloy, 25 March 1951.

37. Michael Geyer, "Der kalte Krieg, die Deutschen und die Angst: Die westdeutsche Opposition gegen Wiederbewaffnung und Kernwaffen," in Klaus Naumann, ed., *Nachkrieg in Deutschland* (Hamburg 2001), pp. 267–318, at pp. 296f.

38. Georg Meyer, "Zur Situation der deutschen militärischen Führungsschicht im Vorfeld des westdeutschen Verteidigungsbeitrages 1945–1950/51," in Roland G. Foerster, Christian Greiner, Georg Meyer, Hans-Jürgen Rautenberg, and Norbert Wiggershaus, eds., *Von der Kapitulation zum Pleven-Plan: Anfänge westdeutscher Sicherheitspolitik*, vol. 1 (Munich 1982), p. 652.

39. Krafft Freiherr Schenck zu Schweinsberg, "Die Soldatenverbände in der Bundesrepublik," in Georg Picht, ed., *Studien zur politischen und gesellschaftlichen Situation der Bundeswehr*, vol. 1 (Witten 1965), pp. 96–177, at p. 116.

40. Ibid.

41. Frei, *Vergangenheitspolitik*, p. 195. The humiliation of professional officers by Hitler was never decried, even in retrospect. The extent of that humiliation is indicated by the fact that at the end of the war, just 7 of 23 field marshals still occupied their posts without measures having been taken against them, 22 generals and admirals had been sentenced to death, and 110 generals and admirals had chosen suicide instead of dishonor ("more than in any other army in the world"). These statistics are contained in Gert Buchheit, *Soldatentum und Rebellion: Die Tragödie der deutschen Wehrmacht* (Rastatt 1961), p. 297.

42. Searle, "A Very Special Relationship," p. 345.

43. For an extensive discussion of this issue, see Foerster, "Innenpolitische Aspekte der Sicherheit Westdeutschlands," 1: 403–576.

44. Henke, "Trennung," p. 76.

45. The difficult path toward collaboration with former enemies becomes particularly clear if one reads the memoirs of those involved, such as Herbert Blankenhorn, *Verständnis und Verständigung: Blätter eines politischen Tagebuchs 1949–1979* (Frankfurt am Main 1980); Gerd Kobe, *Der Wind kam von Westen: Ein fast schon historischer Bericht* (Würzburg 1974); Ulrich de Maizière, *In der Pflicht: Lebensbericht eines deutschen Soldaten im 20. Jahrhundert* (Herford and Bonn 1989); and Hans Speidel, *Aus unserer Zeit: Erinnerungen* (Berlin 1977).

46. Meyer, "Situation der deutschen militärischen Führungsschicht," p. 623.

47. BA-MA, N 431/936, Laternser to Kesselring, 30 January 1951.

48. Klaus Naumann, "Integration und Eigensinn: Die Sicherheitseliten der frühen Bundesrepublik zwischen Kriegs- und Friedenskultur," in Thomas Kühne, ed., *Von der Kriegskultur zur Friedenskultur? Zum Mentalitätswandel in Deutschland seit 1945* (Münster 2000), pp. 202–218, at p. 214.

49. Georg Meyer, *Adolf Heusinger: Dienst eines deutschen Soldaten 1915 bis 1964* (Hamburg 2001), pp. 345ff.

50. Searle, "A Very Special Relationship," p. 342.

51. Meyer, "Situation der deutschen militärischen Führungsschicht," p. 641.

52. BA-MA, N 431/933, Speidel to Laternser, 1 January 1949. Speidel wrote to Laternser that he had again contacted Truman Smith and was now considering approaching Clay directly.

53. Regarding Schwerin's role in establishing the Federal Ministry of Defense, see Krüger, *Amt Blank*.

54. BA-MA, N 431/931, Buss to Laternser, 3 June 1950.

55. BA-MA, N 431/933, Schwerin to Laternser via Buss, 15 June 1950: "Given the current stage of development, it seems to me that any attempt to challenge the verdict will be stillborne. Von Manstein must also know and assume this, even if he finds it difficult."

56. Hans-Jürgen Rautenberg and Norbert Wiggershaus, "Die 'Himmeroder Denkschrift' vom Oktober 1950: Politische und militärische Überlegungen für einen Beitrag der Bundesrepublik Deutschland zur westeuropäischen Verteidigung," *MGM* 21 (1977): 135–206, at p. 169. See also Wette, *Wehrmacht,* p. 233.

57. Rautenberg and Wiggershaus, "'Himmeroder Denkschrift,'" p. 169.

58. Ibid., p. 189.

59. Meyer, "Situation der deutschen militärischen Führungsschicht," p. 622n101.

60. Frei, *Vergangenheitspolitik,* p. 16.

61. Peter Steinbach, "Nationalsozialistische Gewaltverbrechen in der deutschen Öffentlichkeit nach 1945," in Jürgen Weber and Peter Steinbach, eds., *Vergangenheitsbewältigung durch Strafverfahren? NS-Prozesse in der Bundesrepublik Deutschland* (Munich 1984), pp. 13–39, at p. 14.

62. Meyer, "Situation der deutschen militärischen Führungsschicht," p. 619.

63. Wette, *Wehrmacht,* p. 192.

64. Steinbach, "Nationalsozialistische Gewaltverbrechen," p. 18.

65. Schenck zu Schweinsberg, "Soldatenverbände," p. 118.

66. Frei, *Vergangenheitspolitik,* p. 170.

67. Henke, "Trennung," p. 77; Frei, *Vergangenheitspolitik,* p. 192.

68. PRO/TNA, Kew, FO 1060/493, clemency document commuting the sentence to twenty-one years' imprisonment, 3 February 1950. Other custodial sentences were also commuted: Crasemann's sentence was reduced to seven years and Gallenkamp's to ten years.

69. The British only considered a "real" pardon in the case of Mackensen (PRO/TNA, Kew, FO 1060/493, Minute Sheet, Deputy Legal Adviser, Petition for War Criminals, 13 February 1950). The Rome trial was open to challenge, since "there [was] a suggestion" that Mackensen's counsel "did not have a full opportunity to prepare their defence being treated as POWs throughout, as they were." Interventions on behalf of Mackensen never constituted a concerted campaign such as that waged on Kesselring's behalf, perhaps because he never occupied a particularly prominent position in the Wehrmacht; also, as early as 1950, there were already indications that he might be released for health reasons.

70. PRO/TNA, Kew, FO 1060/493, Minute Sheet, Principal Legal Adviser, Petition for War Criminals, G. Ingham, 10 February 1950. They were still expecting to receive a petition from the Vatican on Kesselring's behalf, relating to Rome having been declared an open city. It is impossible to determine from the surviving files whether this petition ever reached London.

71. PRO/TNA, Kew, FO 1060/493, Legal Adviser, Moller, to Laternser, 28 March 1950. Laternser was informed that the sentence had been "commuted" to twenty-one years—which was in no way equivalent to a pardon. He was also informed that Kesselring's case would be up for review on 1 January 1953 and Mältzer's on 1 January 1952. Eberhard von Mackensen's case was the only one to be reviewed separately, since the prison doctor had recommended that he be spared imprisonment.

72. Frei, *Vergangenheitspolitik,* p. 161.

73. As part of my special agreement with the BA-MA (Dr. Günther Fetzer), I agreed to catalog Laternser's papers (N 431) in return for being able to use them in my research for this study. This cataloging work was carried out in the summer of 1998, and it came about as a

result of the kind recommendation of Professor Gerhard Weinberg of the University of North Carolina at Chapel Hill.

74. Peter Maguire, *Law and War: An American Story* (New York 2001), p. 225.

75. Frei, *Vergangenheitspolitik*, p. 165.

76. Ibid., p. 163.

77. Dr. Gawlik, of the Zentrale Rechtsschutz-Stelle, was well known to Laternser from their days in Nuremberg, where he had defended General Dehner during the course of Case 7. See BA-MA, N 431/150, Memorandum by Dr. Hans Gawlik in the proceedings against List et al. regarding the admissibility of rebuttals of evidence.

78. Frei, *Vergangenheitspolitik*, p. 164.

79. BA-MA, N 431/936, Laternser to Kesselring, 27 April 1951.

80. BA-MA, N 431/935, Schwinge to Laternser, 23 September 1950.

81. BA-MA, N 431/935, Schwinge to Laternser, 25 November 1950.

82. Frei, *Vergangenheitspolitik*, p. 166.

83. Since 1945, Höfler had played a leading role in the development of the Caritas aid agency, and he displayed a particular commitment to Germans imprisoned abroad. In 1952, he was appointed a delegate to the UN Special Commission on War Criminals' Issues; see the official guide to the Bundestag, 2nd legislative period, p. 368.

84. Meyer, "Situation der deutschen militärischen Führungsschicht," p. 631.

85. Frei, *Vergangenheitspolitik*, p. 186.

86. Ibid.

87. Frei, *Vergangenheitspolitik*, p. 184.

88. Ibid., p. 188. Laternser did inform Kesselring that he had never received funding from the German government for his services in Italy (BA-MA, N 431/936, Laternser to Kesselring, 5 July 1950). However, Kesselring stuck to his version of events, insisting that he knew "for a fact" that the "lawyers had received subsidies from the Federal Government, for example up to 100,000 Lire for Italy" (BA-MA, N 431/936, Kesselring on behalf of Mackensen to Laternser, 11 July 1950).

89. BA-MA, N 431/936, Laternser to Kesselring, 30 January 1951. Laternser wrote reassuringly that he would happily waive any fees, but he nonetheless submitted a bill to Gawlik.

90. BA-MA, N 431/936, Laternser to Kesselring, 27 April 1951.

91. BA-MA, N 431/936, Kesselring to Laternser, 30 April 1950. Thus, Kesselring advised his attorney to make direct contact with the federal prosecutor, Dr. Wahl, in the ministry, since Wahl was dealing with the war crimes trials. One could also seek funding from the ministry or attempt to obtain information regarding the status of the Reder and Strauch trials. According to Kesselring, German attorneys could earn fees of up to 10,000 lire during the course of these Italian proceedings. He wrote, "It is my conviction that the German government must represent our interests, since it seems that nothing can be achieved purely through the trial process."

92. BA-MA, N 431/936, Kesselring on behalf of Mackensen to Laternser, 11 July 1950.

93. Frei, *Vergangenheitspolitik*, pp. 185f.

94. Ibid., p. 229.

95. BA-MA, N 431/936, Laternser to Kesselring, 1 August 1950. Laternser informed Kesselring that he had already spoken once with Dehler, who "made a good impression," but added that he would shortly approach him again on Kesselring's behalf.

96. Schenck to Schweinsberg, "Soldatenverbände," p. 106.

97. Regarding what follows, see also Georg Meyer, "Soldaten ohne Armee: Berufssoldaten

im Kampf um Standesehre und Versorgung," in M. Broszat, K.-D. Henke, and H. Woller, eds., *Von Stalingrad zur Währungsreform* (Munich 1988), pp. 651–682; Meyer, "Soldaten wie andere auch? Zur Einstellung ehemaliger Angehöriger der Waffen-SS in die Bundeswehr," in Harald Dickerhof, ed., *Festgabe Heinz Hürten zum 60. Geburtstag* (Frankfurt am Main 1988), pp. 545–594, and specifically on the Hilfsgemeinschaft auf Gegenseitigkeit (HIAG, the SS veterans' aid organization), pp. 554ff.; Klaus Peter Tauber, *Beyond Eagle and Swastika: German Nationalism since 1945* (Middleton 1965); D. Clay Large, "Reckoning without the Past: The HIAG of the Waffen-SS and the Politics of Rehabilitation in the Bonn Republic, 1950–1961," *Journal of Modern History* 59 (1987): 79–113; and Jay Lockenour, *Soldiers as Citizens: Former Wehrmacht Officers in the Federal Republic of Germany 1945–1955* (Lincoln, NE, 2001).

98. Alaric Searle, "Veterans' Associations and Political Radicalism in West Germany, 1951–1954: A Case Study of the Traditionsgemeinschaft Grossdeutschland," *Canadian Journal of History* 34 (August 1999): 221–248, at p. 223.

99. Kesselring assumed the honorary presidency of three of these associations: the Stahlhelm, the Luftwaffenring, and the Verband deutsches Afrikakorps.

100. Schenck zu Schweinsberg, "Soldatenverbände," p. 103. The organization's first Executive Committee included Generals Crüwell, Heinz Guderian, Bernhard Ramcke, Gottfried Hansen, Krakau, Hasso von Manteuffel, and Student, as well as Generals Herbert Gille and Paul Hausser (formerly of the Waffen SS).

101. Searle, "Veterans' Associations," p. 222.

102. Schenck to Schweinsberg, "Soldatenverbände," p. 105.

103. Ibid., p. 127.

104. Dietrich Wagner, *FDP und Wiederbewaffnung: Die wehrpolitische Orientierung der Liberalen in der Bundesrepublik Deutschland 1949–1955* (Boppard 1978), pp. 38f.

105. James M. Diehl, *The Thanks of the Fatherland: German Veterans after the Second World War* (London 1993), p. 223.

106. Ibid., p. 226.

107. Thus wrote Ahrens when first making contact with Lord Hankey; see Churchill College, Cambridge, Maurice Hankey Papers, HNKY 13/3; also see Heinrich Senfft, "Lauter feine Herren: Deutsche Kriegsverbrecher, einige Lords und die Wiederbewaffnung," *Blätter für deutsche und internationale Politik* 8 (2001): 995–1004, at p. 998.

108. *Stuttgarter Zeitung*, 17 March 1953, "Wiedergutmachung."

109. Schenck zu Schweinsberg, "Soldatenverbände," p. 138.

110. Detlev Bald, *Militär und Gesellschaft 1945–1990: Die Bundeswehr der Bonner Republik* (Baden-Baden 1994), pp. 32f.

111. Henke, "Trennung," p. 40.

112. BA-MA, N 431/936, Aschenauer to Kesselring, 19 October 1950.

113. BA-MA, N 431/936, Laternser to Kesselring, 30 October 1950.

114. BA-MA, N 431/931, Friesner to Laternser, 3 November 1950. Friessner was also affected by the denazification process, and he had "asked the gentlemen in Munich, including Dr. Aschenauer, to address this important issue of denazification for all comrades without distinction, and to pursue it in such a manner that no delays would arise under any circumstances."

115. BA-MA, N 431/931, Laternser to Aschenauer, 3 November 1950. Laternser pointed out that, as a Bavarian, Kesselring would have to be denazified in Bavaria.

116. BA-MA, N 431/931, Aschenauer to Kesselring, 8 November 1950. Hanns-Dietrich

Ahrens accompanied Aschenauer to Werl in the guise of his assistant (letter from Ahrens to the author, 17 December 2000). He stated that during the visit, they also discussed further steps to secure Kesselring's release. Ahrens wrote a poem about this first meeting with Kesselring; the poem, entitled "*Besuch in Werl*" [Visit to Werl], was reprinted in several veterans' journals. In Werl, Ahrens's primary impression of Kesselring was of a soldier; he noted: "A meditative man at the window bars, still wearing a soldier's uniform: tattered, darned and with sleeves ripped. He remained an officer—even in Werl, even under these circumstances."

117. Thomas Alan Schwartz, "Die Begnadigung deutscher Kriegsverbrecher: John J. McCloy und die Häftlinge von Landsberg," *VfZ* 38 (1990): 375–414, at p. 396; Henke, "Trennung," p. 78.

118. For further information, see Clemens Vollnhals, ed., *Entnazifizierung: Politische Säuberung und Rehabilitierung in den vier Besatzungszonen* (Munich 1991). The concept of "bystander-fabrication" was used to ironically describe the procedures; see Lutz Niethammer, *Die Mitläuferfabrik: Die Entnazifizierung am Beispiel Bayerns* (Bonn 1982). The U.S. directives on denazification are also available at http://digital.library.wisc.edu/1711.dl/History.Denazi.

119. BA-MA, N 422/15, p. 7, denazification indictment against Albert Kesselring, 22 November 1951.

120. PRO/TNA, Kew, FO 1060/500, Aschenauer application for a visit permit, 10 March 1952.

121. BA-MA, N 422/15, p. 1, Kesselring to Röttiger, 16 February 1951.

122. PRO/TNA, Kew, FO 1060/499, combined identification and registration form for those released from internment, 2 May 1949.

123. *Die Welt*, 3 April 1952, "Kesselring Prosecution Collapses."

124. PRO/TNA, Kew, FO 1060/495, Vickers to legal department, Wahnerheide, 11 January 1952.

125. Once the verdict had been announced, Aschenauer helped Kesselring sort out his pension entitlements (PRO/TNA, Kew, FO 1060/500, Aschenauer to Vickers, 15 April 1952). After all, one of the purposes of the denazification process—which should not be overlooked—was to enable relatives of convicted war criminals to receive a pension. (See also BA-MA, N 431/933, Laternser to the consistor Rusam, 13 April 1951. In 1951, following the enactment of the Pensions Act in 1950, Liny Kesselring was awarded "bridging assistance" of just DM 180 per month and DM 80 maintenance for her elderly mother.) That is why, during a visit to the Allied commission in Werl, Kesselring repeatedly brought the conversation back to his pension entitlements. (PRO/TNA, Kew, FO 1060/493, Pensions of Ex-Wehrmacht members and their families, Petition of Field Marshal Kesselring, by Alfred Brown, Office of the Legal Adviser, Control Commission Germany, Wahnerheide, 14 February 1950, and PRO/TNA, Kew, FO 1060/493, Legal Department, Land Commissioner's Office, Düsseldorf, G. B. Summers, 24 March 1950.)

126. Niethammer, *Die Mitläuferfabrik*, p. 653.

127. *Neue Zeitung*, 3 April 1952, "Civilian Court Proceedings against Kesselring Discontinued."

128. *Die Welt*, 3 April 1952, "Kesselring Prosecution Collapses."

129. *Der Mittag*, Düsseldorf, 3 April 1952, "Moral Acquittal for Kesselring."

130. Frei, *Vergangenheitspolitik*, p. 178.

131. BA-MA, N 431/936, Laternser to Kesselring, 3 August 1949.

132. Thus, after this report, Laternser received calls from Reuters and other news agencies seeking information on the current status of the Kesselring case and the substance of the petition.

133. BA-MA, N 431/931, Dix to Laternser, 2 May 1950. According to this letter, Riess had approached Dr. Dix because he was interested "in Marshal Kesselring as a person," whom he considered to be a "perfect gentleman."

134. BA-MA, N 431/936, Laternser to Kesselring, 5 July 1950.

135. BA-MA, N 431/936, Kesselring to Laternser, 9 July 1950.

136. BA-MA, N 431/935, telegram from Riess to Laternser, 6 May 1950.

137. N 431/935 includes a note by Laternser that probably referenced his discussion, since it was captioned "Curt Riess," the "first Allied correspondent in the Hotel Berchtesgadener Hof." (This referred to the interview that Kesselring gave to American journalists on 9 May 1945, after being taken prisoner.) Laternser's trial assessment was supposed to comprise "three type-written pages" and indicate who, from the Allied side, had spoken in Kesselring's favor in court or on his behalf following the verdict (in his memo, Laternser noted, "General Leese, America, France, Switzerland and Germany").

138. Riess attached particular value to Laternser's statement that after the attack on the police company, the SS had demanded that all Rome be evacuated as punishment, which Kesselring forbade, citing the risk posed by "congested roads" to military mobility.

139. BA-MA, N 431/935, telegram from Riess to Laternser, 1 June 1950.

140. BA-MA, N 431/935, telegram from Riess to Laternser, 16 June 1950, p. 1 of 4.

141. Journalist Curt Riess developed a suitable defense for Kesselring by pointing out that he also allowed himself to note that "this [the selection of candidates for execution] was intended to ensure that the hostage shootings were a pure enforcement of sentence within legal limits." Therefore, one could not "accuse the Field Marshal of having breached his supervisory duty," since he would not have been able to control the SD. Regarding the accusations relating to antipartisan warfare and the large-scale killing of civilians pursuant to Kesselring's orders, Laternser prefaced his remarks by saying that Kesselring had done "everything humanly possible" to ensure that the "illegal partisan war did not even arise," and once it had arisen, he had combatted it in a "limited and localised manner" to keep it within "acceptable limits." He had attempted to monitor the war against the partisans "in order to incrementally normalise it in accordance with the situation" and to ensure that attacks "did not remain unpunished." Laternser's arguments were couched in military terms, and he seemed quite unaware that Kesselring's "humane" manner of conducting the antipartisan war ("cleansing," "normalising," etc.) actually constituted the substance of the charges: the killing of Italian civilians. As an example of Kesselring's pro-Italian approach, Laternser noted that the SS had immediately demanded the evacuation of Rome following the attack, which Kesselring refused for military reasons. He also stressed in his draft that Kesselring had declared Rome an open city, contrary to Hitler's wishes, although Hitler had subsequently notified Kesselring that he himself had made such a decision. (Ibid., p. 3.)

142. Ibid.

143. Ibid., p. 4.

144. BA-MA, N 431/935, Riess to Laternser, 26 June 1950.

145. BA-MA, N 431/935, Riess to Laternser, 23 June 1950. Riess was particularly critical of the manner in which Laternser stressed Kesselring's good relationship with Mussolini and Hitler—this would, he said, "have the opposite effect to that intended . . . on all decent people." Riess concluded his criticism of Laternser by saying, "If you are able to recall the article, please do so."

146. BA-MA, N 431/935, Riess to Laternser, 26 June 1950.

147. Outraged, Laternser rejected any suggestion that Kesselring should be described as being of low intelligence; see BA-MA, N 431/935, Laternser to Riess, 26 June 1950.

148. BA-MA, N 431/935, Riess to Laternser, 23 June 1950.

149. BA-MA, N 431/936, Laternser to Kesselring, 1 August 1950. Praising the article, he said that though he did not agree with all of it, he could "only appreciate its general tenor."

150. BA-MA, N 750/14, Curt Riess, "Freedom for Kesselring!" *Quick* 30 (23 July 1950): 1004–1010. Riess illustrated the article with a picture showing his first encounter with Kesselring during the tea party held on the occasion of his capitulation in Berchtesgaden.

151. BA-MA, N 431/936, Kesselring to Laternser, 30 July 1950. Kesselring asked Laternser to tell Riess he found that the "elaboration" was as "rich in content as it is manly."

152. This is a striking illustration of how the campaign groups working on behalf of war criminals were interlinked. Following an inquiry, the paper received Laternser's address from the Justice Ministry's Rechtsschutz-Stelle. Thus, the Federal Ministry of Justice not only was aware of the planned media campaigns but also seemed to approve them.

153. BA-MA, N 431/931, Brüning, *Christ und Welt* editorial team, to Laternser, 31 October 1950.

154. The Italian relatives argued that the reprisal in the Fosse Ardeatine could have been predicted and that since the German occupation forces had threatened such measures in the event of attacks, those committing the attack should therefore have surrendered. Kesselring was amazed at this turn of events because the relatives' claim verified his own (false) testimony about appealing to the attackers to give themselves up.

155. BA-MA, N 431/936, Kesselring to Laternser, 10 May 1950, 4 pages. The main items noted by Kesselring were the "lack of preparation time" for defense counsel; the "ignorance of English court proceedings" (Keller); the inadequate consultation with Keller at the start of the trial; the "actual threat posed by the public in Rome"; the "anomalous composition of the court"; the "inadequate indictment comprising just a few sentences"; the fact that the opening speech in Rome was only in English; "no conclusion, no statement of reasons for the verdict"; and "no statement of reasons with respect to the Review Board proceedings."

156. Ibid. Kesselring made the following criticisms of the conduct of the trial: "sole recognition of the Anglo-Saxon view of international law, completely ignoring the continental view which is equally legitimate and binding on German soldiers"; "not an English trial, but rather a trial with an English basis, according importance to the Nuremberg principles which had been formulated specifically for the Germans"; "*ex post facto* law—expedient amendment of the *Manual of Military Law*"; "the principle of *in dubio pro reo,* which is also accepted in England, was not taken into account; all officers' testimony was completely ignored, the general behaviour of the accused was not taken into account, despite the dubious gathering of evidence"; and "items of evidence and the fact that they were clearly open to challenge."

157. Ibid.

158. *Christ und Welt,* 2 August 1951, "Kesselring, the Italians and the British: An Attack in Rome and Its Bewildering Consequences—Appeal in Werl?"

159. Ibid. There *was* a pathetic comment by a British officer cited in the article. Following Kesselring's conviction, the officer was quoted as saying that he "blushed with shame to think that Field Marshal Kesselring had been treated in such a manner by a so-called British military court. This type of procedure is inhumane."

160. BA-MA, N 431/936, Laternser to Kesselring, 15 May 1950. A journalist from *Der Spiegel* had approached him, saying that he wanted to write an article the tenor of which

would be "completely in Kesselring's favor." As he had previously done for *Christ und Welt,* Kesselring provided Laternser with his notes. Laternser sent his petition to the *Der Spiegel* journalist, and the article was published on 25 April 1951.

161. *Christ und Welt,* 2 August 1951, "Kesselring, the Italians and the British."

162. *Essener Kurier,* 24 September 1951, "A Knight in Prison Garb: Case against Kesselring to Be Re-opened? Exonerating Files Are Piling Up in Bonn."

163. *Neue Ruhr Zeitung,* 24 April 1951, "Imprisoned Generals Hope for an Appeal."

164. *Hamburger Allgemeine Zeitung,* 23 February 1950, "Renaissance of a Friendship," by Will-Werner von Bergen.

165. BA-MA, N 431/936, Kesselring to Laternser, 21 November 1949. Kesselring also felt this was important to "show the public how the Germans conducted the war in Italy, and what they did for the Italians."

166. BA-MA, N 431/936, Laternser to Kesselring, 1 August 1950.

167. BA-MA, N 431/933, Meyer to Laternser, 21 February 1951.

168. Meyer served as an officer during the Wilhelmine era, and he took his pilot's exam in 1911. Since the Luftwaffe had not yet been established, he can only have served with the field artillery, with which Kesselring also served. The field artillery worked with barrage balloons and focused on enemy observation.

169. BA-MA, N 431/933, Meyer to Kesselring, 21 February 1951.

170. Ibid. The English would certainly not sit down at a table with the Germans as long as one English general was "held in custody on the basis of revolutionary law."

171. PRO/TNA, Kew, FO 1060/494, Albert Willy Meyer, Berlin, to the High Commissioner, 10 August 1951; enclosed translated cuttings from the *Steglitzer Anzeiger* newspaper dated 5–6 May 1951 and *Sie* magazine dated 29 July 1951. On 10 August 1951, he wrote to the British high commissioner, Kirkpatrick, asking that Kesselring be released because—"according to my conscientious examination of the case"—he had been wrongfully imprisoned. Meyer enclosed a newspaper cutting in which he demanded that an appeal be allowed in the Kesselring case and described the verdict as "destructive" and "incomprehensible."

172. PRO/TNA, Kew, FO 1060/494, Albert Willy Meyer, Berlin, to the High Commissioner, 10 August 1951.

173. BA-MA, N 431/933, Meyer to Kesselring, 21 February 1951. Meyer was working as a "correspondent for West German newspapers," and he wrote to Kesselring that he was trying to "play his part in ensuring that the nature of Bolshevism is better understood in the Republic."

174. Frei, *Vergangenheitspolitik,* p. 239.

175. *Westdeutsches Tageblatt,* 14 October 1950, "'War Criminals' without Power or Rights." To illustrate its story, the paper used the Manstein and Rome cases and also cited a critical editorial from the independent Brussels daily *La Lanterne,* according to which the trial of Ernst von Falkenhausen had been held too late.

176. *Dithmarscher Landeszeitung,* 24 June 1950, "First Visit to Manstein and Kesselring."

177. *Frankfurter Allgemeine Zeitung,* 14 December 1950, p. 2.

178. Reginald T. Paget, *Manstein: His Campaigns and His Trial* (London 1951).

179. "Wäre Manstein ein Engländer gewesen . . . Paget und Lord Hankey fordern Revision," German translation of article in *Picture Post,* 24 September 1951

180. Statements made by Ahrens indicate that the correspondent, Terence Prittie, was close to him; Ahrens supplied him with information. This fact becomes apparent if one reads the coverage of Kesselring's release.

181. *Manchester Guardian*, 23 April 1951, "Ex-Generals in British Gaol: Sentences for War Crimes Disputed." The article quoted Kesselring as saying that escape would be tantamount to a confession of guilt.

182. *Frankfurter Allgemeine Zeitung*, 24 April 1951, "Und Werl?" The *FAZ* writer did not mince words: "It is a peculiarity of all courts established on the basis of special laws that their creators consider them—in contrast to any ordinary courts—to be infallible, and that . . . there is no possibility of appeal." An appeal was also to be used to harmonize international military law in this respect: "Then German soldiers before court would have to accept that which was fair to the British as justice."

183. *Die Zeit*, 24 October 1951, "Werl in the British Election Campaign," by Countess Marion Dönhoff.

184. *Rheinischen Post*, 7 July 1951, "Werl," by Paul Leverkuehn: "At that time, the Allies stated that international law was at a stage of development which allowed them to disregard treaties such as the Geneva Convention regarding the treatment of prisoners of war. They formed a court of victors."

185. "Werl: The Stain Remains," *Der Spiegel* 27 (4 July 1951): 13–14. In January 1943, an execution unit comprising German policemen shot six British soldiers in Trandum Forest. The British soldiers were in civilian clothes, and the shooting had been "ordered by the Führer." The nine policemen demanded that they be retried by a German court.

186. *Essener Allgemeine Zeitung*, 19 July 1951, "Kesselring: Collaboration with the West."

187. The "Justice, Not Clemency" *Der Stern* series started on 5 August 1951, pp. 11–23, and concluded on 19 August 1951, pp. 11–13. A bon mot by Kesselring was quoted as a headline: "'I sit as ordered by law!'"

188. Ibid.

189. *Die Welt*, 2 October 1951, "Justice for Werl."

190. *Deutsches Allgemeines Sonntagsblatt*, Hamburg, 25 November 1951, "Why Not Finally Get to the Root of the Evil?"

191. *La Stampa*, 13 July 1952 (translation), "The Comfortable Prison" (in Auswärtiges Amt der Bundesrepublik Deutschland—Politisches Archiv, Berlin [hereafter cited as AA-PA], Abt. 2/2109).

192. PRO/TNA, Kew, FO 1060/499, Liny Kesselring to Vickers, 14 February 1952. Liny's application, in February 1952, for her husband to be granted leave "on his word of honor" to celebrate the ninety-fifth birthday of her mother, Luise Keyssler, at the end of March 1952 had been granted.

193. PRO/TNA, Kew, FO 1060/500, "Ticket of leave" for Albert Kesselring, 31 May 1952. He was in Wiessee from 31 May to 6 June 1952, and the formalities had a distinct military tinge: he was no longer a prisoner but a soldier on leave, and he was accordingly granted a ticket of leave.

194. Klaus Bloemer and Hellmut Prinz, "Generalfeldmarschall Kesselring: Urlaub auf Ehrenwort," *Schwäbische Illustrierte* 25 (21 June 1952): 690–691 and cover page with Kesselring sitting on a bank on Lake Tegern, Bavaria.

195. *Der Spiegel* 26 (1952), People section, p. 3.

196. PRO/TNA, Kew, FO 1060/496, memo by Roots, legal department, Wahnerheide, 2 May 1952. In this regard, J. C. Piegrome wrote that there was no legal reason to refuse a visit.

197. PRO/TNA, Kew, FO 1060/496, Herchenroder, Wahnerheide, to Kirkpatrick, 3 May 1952, and handwritten memo by Kirkpatrick to the effect that the Foreign Office should be asked to resolve the problem.

198. PRO/TNA, Kew, FO 1060/496, Foreign Office to legal department, Wahnerheide, 9 May 1952.

199. PRO/TNA, Kew, FO 1060/496, Vickers to legal department, Wahnerheide, 20 June 1952.

200. PRO/TNA, Kew, FO 1060/496, Hoppe to Kesselring, English translation, 31 May 1952.

201. PRO/TNA, Kew, FO 1060/496, handwritten note by J. G. Ward on a memo from Bathurst to Kirkpatrick, 14 June 1952.

202. PRO/TNA, Kew, FO 1060/500, Vickers to legal department, Wahnerheide, 15 July 1952.

203. *Essener Kurier*, 29 November 1951, "Panzer-Meyer: I Am Being Treated Fairly."

204. The biggest media storm erupted in September 1951, when it was reported that Kesselring had been liberated from prison by "his" paratroopers. Toward midnight on 18 September, the prison director, E. R. Vickers, received several calls asking whether it was true that Kesselring had escaped. The callers included the local police station and the United Press agency in Frankfurt. During that night alone, Vickers received around ten calls from a range of newspapers seeking information (PRO/TNA, Kew, FO 1060/495, report from Vickers to the Office of the Legal Adviser, Wahnerheide, 19 September 1951). Even the federal government inquired about Kesselring's whereabouts the following day.

205. BA-MA, N 431/936, Kesselring to Laternser, 8 November 1950.

206. PRO/TNA, Kew, FO 1060/493, Kesselring to Adenauer, 27 November 1950, three pages, at p. 1. Kesselring feared that "the many defects which have become apparent both in the investigatory and in the court proceedings will continue, with the result that the special justice, which is today not only disputed but rejected by all sides, will become the permanent legal basis."

207. Ibid. The letter dealt with three issues: the "Rome case" (Fosse Ardeatine), "antipartisan warfare," and the "Simon/Reder" case. Kesselring focused heavily on Laternser's arguments regarding procedural defects and legal technicalities. He also insisted that the second Hitler order had relieved the Wehrmacht (and thus Kesselring himself) of any responsibility for the massacre—a version that had meanwhile been documented not only by the petition but also through the Kappler trial. In particular, he referred to Hitler's style of leadership, which the judge advocate general had found incomprehensible, questioning the second Hitler order because it had not been issued in writing. In addition, he referred to the charge that he had not fulfilled his duty of supervision: this charge, he felt, was refuted merely by the fact that the SD had been responsible for carrying out the reprisal, independent of the Wehrmacht. What is striking about the arguments put forward in this letter (as was the case in the petition) is that Kesselring only touched incidentally on the whole issue of antipartisan warfare in Italy. Thus, in seeking to justify himself, he noted that twelve incidents had occurred before or after he had issued the orders in question, so he could therefore not be viewed as the originator of all violence against the Italian civilian population. In particular, he said, such an interpretation could not be put on the wording of his orders, which had also been wrongly translated in court.

208. PRO/TNA, Kew, FO 1060/493, Kesselring to Brown, 2 January 1951, six pages, at p. 3; also BA-MA, N 431/936, Kesselring to Sir Alfred Brown, 2 January 1951.

209. PRO/TNA, Kew, FO 1060/493, Kesselring to Brown, 2 January 1951, p. 5. When describing the Simon case for Brown and explaining the role of the prosecution witness Major Reder, commander of the 16th SS Panzer Grenadier Division, which had carried out most of the massacres, Kesselring also stressed that "Reder always stated that he was unaware of the orders issued by the Field Marshal."

210. Ibid. This attitude is noteworthy since—both during the trial and in the petition—it had been stressed that the army authorities were extremely relieved not to have anything more to do with the Rome case. This relief was now transmuted into regret, culminating in the claim that the army would have executed the reprisals, at the very least, without "irregularities" and thus "better" than the SD.

211. PRO/TNA, Kew, FO 1060/493, Kesselring to Brown, 2 January 1951, p. 4.

212. Ibid.

213. BA-MA, N 431/936, Laternser to Kesselring, 30 January 1951.

214. Ibid., p. 6. Operating from prison, where "all comrades" were, Kesselring repeatedly made the mistake of putting his own prospects at risk for the sake of comradeship because he wanted to bring the others along with him. By doing so, however, he breached an unwritten postwar code by publicly defending Waffen SS members.

215. PRO/TNA, Kew, FO 1060/495, Kesselring to Adenauer, 4 January 1952. He concluded his letter with the hope that "your current all-embracing political efforts will be crowned with success."

216. PRO/TNA, Kew, FO 1060/495, Bathurst, Wahnerheide, memo dated 8 January 1952.

217. PRO/TNA, Kew, FO 1060/495, Foreign Office to Kirkpatrick, 29 January 1952.

218. PRO/TNA, Kew, FO 1060/496, Hallstein to Bathurst, Wahnerheide, 31 March 1952.

219. PRO/TNA, Kew, FO 1060/495, report by Passmore to the Foreign Office, 15 December 1951.

220. "Justice, Not Clemency: The Enemy's Voice Penetrates the Prison Walls of Werl," *Der Stern* 32 (12 August 1951): 11–14.

221. PRO/TNA, Kew, FO 1060/495, report on "The Kesselring case," typewritten with corrections, nine pages, 1951. According to this report, the British prosecution's aim in respect to the first count was to prove that Kesselring had ordered a reprisal using a ration of ten to one, which was "excessive," and that, by transmitting his order down the ranks, he was responsible for the manner in which the order was executed. The judge advocate was quoted as saying during the trial, "The Field Marshal's real defence is: 'I never carried out any orders at all, all I did was to pass along the chain of communication, a message to the SD'" (p. 2). With regard to the second count, the prosecutor had stated that the wording of Kesselring's orders issued on 17 June and 1 July 1944 ran counter to the customs of war. The order on 17 June had constituted an incitement to the troops to commit excesses. Furthermore, according to the prosecutor, the order issued on 1 July aggravated the previous one, since in this order, Kesselring had definitely given notice of reprisals. He had not revoked this instruction until September. "That is the gravamen of this charge" (p. 4).

222. Ibid., p. 6.

223. Ibid., p. 7.

224. Ibid.

225. Lassa Oppenheim and Hersh Lauterpacht, *International Law,* vol. 2, *Disputes, War, Neutrality* (London 1947), p. 460. Also see United Nations War Crimes Commission, *Law-Reports of Trials of War Criminals,* vol. 1 (London, HMSO, 1949), Case No. 44, p. 4.

226. In this regard, see the elucidations provided by Gerhard Schreiber in "Deutsche Kriegsverbrechen in Italien," in Wolfram Wette and Gerd R. Ueberschär, eds., *Kriegsverbrechen im 20. Jahrhundert* (Darmstadt 2001), pp. 222–234, at pp. 226ff.

227. In the past, Stirling had attracted some attention as the officer responsible for dismantlement. See Ahrens, *Demontage,* p. 147.

228. PRO/TNA, Kew, FO 1060/494, Hughes to Kirkpatrick regarding his rescue by Kesselring, 27 March 1950. In his statement, Hughes described how Kesselring had personally arranged for him to be transferred to a British POW camp, from which he had subsequently escaped. Kesselring intervened on Hughes's behalf after a German attending physician drew his attention to Hughes's status as a "political prisoner" and his threatened execution by the Gestapo pursuant to Hitler's "commando order." The document is noteworthy for two reasons in particular. First, it is remarkable that a British soldier should intervene on behalf of a senior German commander in prison. And second, given Kesselring's possible involvement in the shooting of the American Ginny commando unit near Genoa in March 1944, it suggests that Kesselring was not a "hardliner" but rather that he had attempted to circumvent the commando order and conceal it from the relevant SD and Gestapo offices.

229. PRO/TNA, Kew, FO 1060/494, D. A. Stirling to Sir Brian Robertson, 1 April 1950. Stirling was clearly greatly affected by Kesselring's fate, since he wrote, "I should like to help him in any way I can. Perhaps this evidence might make it possible for you to get his sentence reduced. Anyhow, I felt it my duty to send it to you for what it's worth."

230. Brochhagen, *Nach Nürnberg*, p. 26.

231. PRO/TNA, Kew, FO 1060/494, T. G. Coverdale to Alfred Brown, 12 April 1950.

232. PRO/TNA, Kew, FO 1060/494, Alfred Brown to T. G. Coverdale, 15 April 1950.

233. Ibid. Thus, according to the interpretation of the American military jurists, no one could be held solely culpable for having transmitted an order within that individual's chain of command. This interpretation would have been crucial to an acquittal in, for example, the 1946 Mackensen und Mältzer cases.

234. PRO/TNA, Kew, FO 1060/494, B. H. Robertson to D. A. Stirling, 18 April 1950. Brown then met with General Robertson, who appeared to share his views, to tell him more about the matter in person.

235. Frei, *Vergangenheitspolitik*, p. 223.

236. Wette, *Wehrmacht*, p. 232.

237. Thomas Kühne, "Zwischen Vernichtungskrieg und Freizeitgesellschaft: Die Veteranenkultur in Deutschland (1945–1995)," in Klaus Naumann, ed., *Nachkrieg in Deutschland* (Hamburg 2001), pp. 90–113, at p. 93.

238. Georg Meyer, *Adolf Heusinger: Dienst eines deutschen Soldaten 1915–1964* (Hamburg 2001), pp. 435ff.

239. Meyer, "Situation der deutschen militärischen Führungsschicht," p. 622.

240. Cited in Brochhagen, *Nach Nürnberg*, p. 49.

241. Cited in Frei, *Vergangenheitspolitik*, p. 205.

242. Brochhagen, *Nach Nürnberg*, p. 43.

243. Wolfram Wette, "Das Bild der Wehrmacht-Elite nach 1945," in Gerd R. Ueberschär, ed., *Hitlers militärische Elite*, vol. 2 (Darmstadt 1998), p. 301; Wette, *Wehrmacht*, p. 233.

244. Proceedings of the German Bundestag, 1st legislative period, 1951, p. 4984; German Bundestag debate on 5 April 1951 regarding Art. 131 of the German Basic Law, "declaration of honor" issued by Chancellor Adenauer.

245. PRO FO 371/93535, Kirkpatrick speaking in the British Press Club, 16 January 1951.

246. Brochhagen, *Nach Nürnberg*, p. 61.

247. Ivone Kirkpatrick, *The Inner Circle* (London 1959), p. 251.

248. Brochhagen, *Nach Nürnberg*, p. 58.

249. PRO FO 371/93536, Kirkpatrick to Foreign Office, Gainer, 3 February 1951, translation cited in Brochhagen, *Nach Nürnberg*, p. 57.

250. See Axel Christian Azzola, *Die Diskussion um die Aufrüstung der BRD im Unterhaus und in der Presse Grossbritanniens: November 1949–Juli 1952* (Meisenheim am Glan 1971).

251. Brochhagen, *Nach Nürnberg*, p. 58.

252. Ibid., p. 60.

253. PRO/TNA, Kew, FO 371/93541, speech by Attlee in the House of Commons, 12 February 1951.

254. See, for example, *Times*, 29 March 1951.

255. PRO/TNA, Kew, FO 800/520, notes by Attlee for Bevin, 18 February 1951.

256. PRO/TNA, Kew, CAB 128/19, minutes of the cabinet meeting on 31 May 1951.

257. Stephen Wentworth Roskill, *Hankey: Man of Secrets* (London 1974), p. 644.

258. Tom Bower, *Blind Eye to Murder: Britain, America and the Purging of Nazi Germany—A Pledge Betrayed* (London 1981, 1995).

259. PRO/TNA, Kew, FO 1060/495, Schumacher to Stokes, 9 November 1951, 3 pages, at p. 2.

260. PRO/TNA, Kew, FO 1060/495, Stokes to Schumacher, 19 November 1951.

261. PRO/TNA, Kew, FO 371/93553, Dönhoff to Stokes, 10 July 1951. Countess Marion Dönhoff, a member of the *Zeit* editorial team, had spontaneously offered to take "steps" on behalf of Kesselring, Mackensen, and Mälzer. Contact had been made through Mackensen's son, Klaus von Mackensen. Information provided to me by Richard von Mackensen, 29 August 1998.

262. PRO/TNA, Kew, FO 371/85899, Vatican to the British mission to the Holy See, 18 February 1950.

263. PRO/TNA, Kew, FO 1060/495, Hancock, German Political Department, London, to Bathurst, Legal Department, Wahnerheide, 26 November 1951.

264. PRO/TNA, Kew, FO 1060/495, Letter to Stokes drafted by Hancock, November 1951.

265. Ibid., handwritten note by Kirkpatrick.

266. PRO/TNA, Kew, FO 1060/495, Kirkpatrick to Roberts, Foreign Office, 29 November 1951.

267. PRO/TNA, Kew, FO 1060/495, Bathurst, Wahnerheide, to Hancock, German Political Department, London, 3 December 1951.

268. Roskill, *Hankey*, p. 644.

269. Brochhagen, *Nach Nürnberg*, p. 66.

270. Paget, *Manstein*. In its report entitled "The Ghost of Saporoshje," issued on 2 April 1952, *Der Spiegel* magazine also defended Manstein, unexpectedly joining the ranks of those praising the former field marshal.

271. Brochhagen, *Nach Nürnberg*, p. 69.

272. Ibid., p. 76.

273. Frei, *Vergangenheitspolitik*, p. 245n53.

274. Ahrens Papers, private collection, Hankey to Ahrens, December 1951.

275. Frei, *Vergangenheitspolitik*, p. 245.

276. Ibid., p. 246.

277. The British were referring to cases where Italian civilians had killed British pilots. In October 1946, the Italians assumed responsibility for Italian war criminals previously in British custody. However, the end of the 1940s saw repeated media campaigns seeking the war criminals' release. In 1949, London granted the Rome government authority to issue pardons (see the whole development in correspondence at PRO/TNA, Kew, WO 310/4). Just two years

later, all but two of the Italian war criminals had been released. See Brochhagen, *Nach Nürnberg*, p. 65.

278. Brochhagen, *Nach Nürnberg*, p. 71.

279. Ibid., p. 81.

280. Frei, *Vergangenheitspolitik*, p. 246.

281. *Neue Volkszeitung*, Essen, 1 March 1952, "Nazi Generals to Be Released." The most prominent prisoner in this group was General Gallenkamp.

282. *Kölnische Rundschau*, 18 December 1951, "Werl Prison Empty in Two Years."

283. *Hamburger Freie Presse*, 10 December 1951, "Gille to Churchill."

284. *Neue Zeitung*, 29 December 1951, "British Review War Crimes Trial Files."

285. *Deutsche Woche*, Munich, 2 January 1952, "General Staff in Jail: Kesselring Office Continues Its Work—Officers' Club Manners in Prison."

286. *Der Heimkehrer*, Göppingen, January 1952, "Now What's Missing in Werl Is Action."

287. *Deutscher Kurier*, Frankfurt, 1 May 1952, "Kesselring, Too, Is Waiting for Justice: Ambush Warfare," by Kurt Neher.

288. Benno Wundshammer, "The Last Men of Werl," *Revue* 14 (5 April 1952): 8. The article included a facsimile of an entry made by Kesselring in an autograph book that, despite its clumsiness, undoubtedly had the intended effect on a sympathetic readership and would have been widely viewed as an attack on victors' justice: "There is no virtue in never erring, but there is virtue in desisting from error as soon as possible."

289. *Picture Post*, 24 December 1951, "Christmas Light in Werl."

290. *FAZ*, 7 January 1952, "The War Criminals' Glorioles," by Thilo Bode, p. 1.

291. Ibid.

292. Frei, *Vergangenheitspolitik*, p. 247.

293. Ibid.

294. *Friedenspost*, East Berlin, 21 October 1951, "Pilgrimage to Werl."

295. The manner in which rumors regarding a redeployment of the war criminals (who just a short while earlier had been vilified) took root is also illustrated by an article in the *Neue Münchner Illustrierte* regarding Waffen SS General Kurt Meyer, known as "Panzer-Meyer." According to the article, Meyer's prosecutor had said: "If, however, it is expedient for the West to employ Meyer, it would be foolish to let him rust in jail." (*Neue Münchner Illustrierte*, 22 December 1951, "The Alienated General.")

296. *Die Tat*, 22 December 1951, "'Probation Unit' for War Criminals."

297. Ibid.

298. *L'Unità*, 23 December 1951, "Gli Occupanti inglesi in Germania liberano altri 42 criminali di guerra."

299. PRO/TNA, Kew, FO 1060/495, translation of an article in *Der Mittag* dated 2 January 1952.

300. BA-MA, N 750/new acquisition 2000, serial number 8, letter from von Donat to Kesselring, 29 July 1951.

301. Frei, *Vergangenheitspolitik*, p. 248.

302. Ibid., p. 249.

303. Volkmann, "Innenpolitische Dimension," pp. 291ff.

304. Frei, *Vergangenheitspolitik*, p. 249.

305. "We demand reparations for the injustice created by National Socialism and denazification. We distance ourselves from the victors' verdicts, which were intended to discriminate

against our people and, in particular, our soldiers." See Dr. Friedrich Middelhauve, *Das Deutsche Programm* [The German Program], *fdk* (*frei demokratische korrespondenz [Free Democrats' Correspondence]*), year 3, 29 July 1952, cited in Wagner, *FDP*, p. 51.

306. Bundestag debate on 7 February 1952, proceedings of the German Bundestag, 1st legislative period, p. 8132 C, speech by Euler.

307. Ibid.

308. Ibid.

309. Frei, *Vergangenheitspolitik*, p. 250.

310. Ibid.

311. Ibid., p. 251.

312. Ibid.

313. The draft stated that (1) death sentences would no longer be executed; (2) convicted prisoners who had served a third of their sentences would be released; and (3) the remaining prisoners would be reviewed by commissions with a mixed membership, presided over by a neutral chairperson. The penal system was to be governed by the following guidelines: (1) prisoners whose sentences were subject to review by the mixed-membership commission should be held separately from other types of prisoners in Germany, and (2) the prison director should be from a neutral country. Cited in Brochhagen, *Nach Nürnberg*, pp. 76f.

314. Frei, *Vergangenheitspolitik*, p. 252.

315. Brochhagen, *Nach Nürnberg*, p. 72.

316. Ibid.

317. Frei, *Vergangenheitspolitik*, p. 255.

318. Roskill, *Hankey*, p. 650.

319. Churchill College, Cambridge, HNKY 18/4, Notes by Lord Hankey, Dr. Bell and War Criminals, 2 February 1959. In this memorandum, Hankey extensively described his work on behalf of war criminals and their release from prison, while also stressing that he played an alternating role with the bishop of Chichester, George Bell, with whom he consulted regarding any initiatives.

320. Searle, "A Very Special Relationship," p. 346.

321. Searle, *Wehrmacht Generals*, p. 166. See also the nonacademic description in Hanns-Dietrich Ahrens, "Feldmarschall Albert Kesselring," *Luftwaffenrevue* 48 (March 2000): 67–70, at 68.

322. For an extensive treatment of what follows, see Frei, *Vergangenheitspolitik*, pp. 258–261.

323. Ibid., p. 259.

324. Ibid., p. 260.

325. Ibid., p. 264.

326. Roskill, *Hankey*, p. 650.

327. Konrad Adenauer, *Teegespräche 1950–1954*, ed. Hanns Jürgen Küsters (Berlin: Stiftung Bundeskanzler Adenauer Haus, 1984), p. 466: "Churchill spoke very openly about it, about Manstein, Kesselring etc., this isn't a problem for him at all, so in general I can say that we were very well-received by Parliament, we were very well-received by the British public, by Churchill and by the other prominent members of the British cabinet, by Butler, Lord Alexander etc."

328. Brochhagen, *Nach Nürnberg*, p. 78.

329. Frei, *Vergangenheitspolitik*, p. 264.

330. Ibid., p. 266.

331. Ibid.

332. Volkmann, "Innenpolitische Dimension," pp. 235–604, at p. 245.

333. PRO/TNA, Kew, FO 1060/496, Hellwege to Kesselring, 18 April 1952. Although the letter was translated into English by the prison authorities, it was then handed over to Kesselring.

334. PRO/TNA, Kew, FO 1060/496, Herchenroder, Wahnerheide, to Kirkpatrick, 30 April 1952; handwritten note by Kirkpatrick in the margin, 30 April 1952. Kirkpatrick suggested making inquiries in the Foreign Office.

335. PRO/TNA, Kew, FO 1060/496, memo from Herchenroder, Wahnerheide, to Kirkpatrick, 28 May 1952.

336. PRO/TNA, Kew, FO 1060/496, memo from Bathurst, Wahnerheide, to Kirkpatrick, 13 June 1952.

337. PRO/TNA, Kew, FO 1060/496, Foreign Office to Wahnerheide, 27 May 1952.

338. PRO/TNA, Kew, FO 1060/496, memo from Herchenroder, Wahnerheide, to Kirkpatrick, 28 May 1952; handwritten note by Kirkpatrick on the memo, 3 June 1952.

339. PRO FO 371/97979, notes by Churchill, June 1952. During that month, he wrote: "I certainly had hoped that they would be let out as soon as we got back to power but eight months have passed and they are still in prison. This depresses me very much and is contrary to all my instincts of dealing with the vanquished and especially with the Germans."

340. PRO FO 371/97985, Churchill to the Minister of State, 23 August 1952.

341. PRO FO 371/97985, notes by Roberts, 27 August 1952.

342. PRO FO 371/97985, Eden to Churchill, 29 August 1952.

343. Frei, *Vergangenheitspolitik*, p. 270.

344. Adenauer, *Teegespräche*, pp. 219f.: "I always feel sorry for the NCO whom nobody cares about, and who is therefore just sitting there. On several occasions, I have explicitly told Allied representatives that I am not pleading for the generals, but for the other people, since they also have families and are just as human as the others."

345. Frei, *Vergangenheitspolitik*, p. 268.

346. Ibid., p. 271.

347. AA-PA, Abt. 2/2098, Übersicht über die Entwicklung des Kriegsverurteiltenproblems in den westlichen Ländern 1950–1955, statistics for 1955.

348. Elisabeth Noelle and Peter Neumann, eds., *Jahrbuch der öffentlichen Meinung* (Allensbach 1952), p. 202.

Chapter 5: Kesselring's Release

1. Walter Schwengler, "Der doppelte Anspruch: Souveränität und Sicherheit—Zur Entwicklung des völkerrechtlichen Status der Bundesrepublik Deutschland 1949 bis 1955," in Werner Abelshauser and Walter Schwengler, eds., *Anfänge westdeutscher Sicherheitspolitik*, vol. 4, *Wirtschaft und Rüstung, Souveränität und Sicherheit* (Munich 1997), pp. 187–566, at pp. 277ff.

2. Churchill College, Cambridge, HNKY 18/5, Liddell Hart to Hankey, 10 June 1952.

3. See *fdk* (*Freie Demokratische Korrespondenz*), 19 June 1952, pp. 2–6, cited in Norbert Frei, *Vergangenheitspolitik: Die Anfänge der Bundesrepublik und die NS-Vergangenheit* (Munich 1996), p. 268.

4. Frei, *Vergangenheitspolitik*, p. 268.

5. Ibid., p. 269.

6. Ibid., p. 272.

7. Ibid., p. 273.

8. Ibid. See *Frankfurter Allgemeine Zeitung*, 25 July 1952.

9. Churchill College, Cambridge, HNKY 18/5, Liddell Hart to Hankey, 5 July 1952. In his letter, Liddell Hart criticized the fact that although a British doctor had been sent to assess Manstein's health, he "had not been given a definite hint, as should have been done, that he should try to provide medical grounds for Manstein's release." Accordingly, no medical recommendation for early release had been issued.

10. Stephen Wentworth Roskill, *Hankey: Man of Secrets* (London 1974), p. 651.

11. Later, long after Kesselring had been released, Alexander continued to champion the cause of those German war criminals still in custody. In addition, he forcefully advocated a German contribution to Western defense in the context of NATO and had thus been helping to drive forward preparations for rearmament since 1953 (see Hans Speidel, *Aus unserer Zeit: Erinnerungen* [Berlin 1977], p. 316).

12. Hanns-Dietrich Ahrens, "Ein Stück Verbandsgeschichte—Schlagzeilen für den VdS," *Soldat im Volk* 4 (July-August 2003): 161–162. According to Ahrens, when he met with Hankey at the latter's Surrey country house, Limpsfield, in late autumn of 1952, he was "made privy to the strategy aimed at securing the release of irreproachable officers from the prisons in Werl, Wittlich and Landsberg."

13. Hanns-Dietrich Ahrens, "Feldmarschall Albert Kesselring," *Luftwaffenrevue* 48 (March 2000): 67–70, at p. 68.

14. PRO/TNA, Kew, FO 1060/497, Hancock, Foreign Office, to Herchenroder, Wahnerheide, 28 August 1952.

15. Frei, *Vergangenheitspolitik*, p. 276. In this regard, see *Neue Zeitung*, 9–10 August, 1952, "Notwendige Klärung."

16. See Wolfram Wette, ed., *Retter in Uniform: Handlungsspielräume im Vernichtungskrieg der Wehrmacht* (Frankfurt 2002).

17. Ibid.

18. Franzjosef Müser, head of the Bochumer Verein iron- and steelworks, which also included the hospital, granted Kesselring free hospital accommodations and assured him that he could remain until fully recovered (letter from Ahrens to the author, 18 January 2001).

19. PRO/TNA, Kew, FO 1060/497, report by Jantke on Kesselring's surgery, 2 August 1952.

20. PRO/TNA, Kew, FO 1060/497, report by Busch to Vickers, 22 July 1952.

21. PRO/TNA, Kew, FO 1060/497, memo by Piegrome, 30 July 1952.

22. Ibid. If the doctor also insisted that Kesselring was unfit for prison, Piegrome would himself talk to the doctor about releasing Kesselring as long as the doctor agreed to inform the field marshal of the reason for his release, i.e., that he was unlikely to live much longer due to the cancer.

23. BA Koblenz, B 305/7060, Laternser's petition for a renewed review and reversal of the sentence imposed on Albert Kesselring, 23 August 1952.

24. PRO/TNA, Kew, FO 1060/501, letter from Vickers to Bürkle de la Camp, 16 September 1952. Visit permits were issued to Mrs. Kesselring; Kesselring's nephew and owner of the Marktsteft Kesselring brewery, Kurt Himmel and his wife; Pastor Dietrich Schüttler and his wife; the former general Dransfeld; and the former colonel von Below.

25. Although Kesselring had been hospitalized several times while in prison, he had always been admitted to the British military hospital in Iserlohn, most recently in 1951. Even then, there had been attempts to transfer him out of the British sphere of influence and have

him admitted to a German hospital, which has given rise to speculation that long-term preparations had been made not only for his release but also for the ostensible medical grounds for that release. See PRO/TNA, Kew, FO 1060/493, report by Dr. Busch on Kesselring's dental treatment, 24 January 1951. In 1951, Dr. Busch, the prison doctor at Werl, had argued that Kesselring's various medical complaints (gall bladder trouble, high blood pressure, neuralgia, and rheumatism) could be due to "metastases originating from the teeth," and he recommended transferring Kesselring to the Bochum hospital "Bergmannsheil" so that he could undergo dental operations and be fitted with dental prostheses. Dr. Busch's advice was rejected, and Kesselring instead underwent an operation in the British military hospital in Iserlohn in March 1951.

26. *Picture Post*, 15 July 1952, "Acquitted."

27. *Neue Zeitung*, 3 September 1952, "Cheerful Hours for Kesselring: Werl Commandant Frequent Guest in the Former Field Marshal's Sickroom."

28. PRO/TNA, Kew, FO 1060/501, report from Vickers to the Legal Adviser, Wahnerheide, 5 August 1952. On 5 August 1952, he also asked that the attending doctor issue weekly reports on Kesselring's state of health and prognosis.

29. PRO/TNA, Kew, FO 1060/497, Bürkle de la Camp to Vickers, 29 August 1952.

30. PRO/TNA, Kew, FO 1060/497, Beckmann's diagnosis, 25 August 1952.

31. PRO/TNA, Kew, FO 1060/501, report by Vickers to the Legal Adviser, Wahnerheide, 16 October 1952.

32. PRO/TNA, Kew, FO 1060/501, report by Vickers to the Legal Adviser, Wahnerheide, 2 September 52.

33. PRO/TNA, Kew, FO 1060/497, memo of a telephone call by Hancock, 3 September 1952. Manstein was also to be examined, even though his case was "not so urgent." However, the "Foreign Office would find themselves in difficulty if they had to release Kesselring while retaining Manstein," since Manstein enjoyed a "better press" in England and there was more public sympathy with his fate than with Kesselring's.

34. Wolfram Wette, *Die Wehrmacht: Feindbilder, Vernichtungskrieg, Legenden* (Darmstadt 2002), p. 232.

35. Alaric Searle, *Wehrmacht Generals, West German Society, and the Debate on Rearmament, 1949–1959* (Westport, CT, 2003), p. 167.

36. Thomas Kühne, "Zwischen Vernichtungskrieg und Freizeitgesellschaft: Die Veteranenkultur in Deutschland (1945–1995)," in Klaus Naumann, ed., *Nachkrieg in Deutschland* (Hamburg 2001), pp. 90–113, at p. 101.

37. PRO/TNA, Kew, FO 1005/1900, letter from Harlinghaus to Kesselring, 3 August 1952.

38. PRO/TNA, Kew, FO 1060/497, memo by J. G. Ward regarding Harlinghausen's letter, 18 August 1952.

39. PRO/TNA, Kew, FO 1060/497, memo by Paton regarding Harlinghausen's letter, 15 August 1952.

40. PRO/TNA, Kew, FO 1060/497, memo by Piegrome regarding Harlinghausen's letter, 31 July 1952 (the date may be a typing error; it was more likely 31 August 1952).

41. PRO/TNA, Kew, FO 1060/497, memo regarding Harlinghausen's letter, 19 August 1952.

42. According to information provided to me on 17 December 2000 by Jürgen Heinze, director of the Ordensgemeinschaft der Ritterkreuzträger und des Eisernen Kreuzes e. V., Kesselring was a member of the association from December 1956 until his death in 1960. His membership number was 550. The association was established in 1953; after 1955, its director was former Generaloberst Alfred Keller. When Kesselring joined, the association already had

about 1,000 members. Around half of the 7,318 holders of the Knight's Cross did not survive the war. Around a quarter organized themselves within the Ordensgemeinschaft (information provided by Jürgen Heinze on 11 January 2001). These figures refer to December 2000, when the association had a total of 2,300 members, primarily from the army. Membership was open to all ranks. (See also Krafft Freiherr Schenck zu Schweinsberg, "Die Soldatenverbände in der Bundesrepublik," in Georg Picht, ed., *Studien zur politischen und gesellschaftlichen Situation der Bundeswehr*, vol. 1 (Witten 1965), p. 175.

43. Thus, for example, in July 1952, the Bund deutscher Fallschirmjäger (Association of German Paratroopers), in its monthly journal *Die grünen Teufel*, demanded "Justice for Field Marshal Kesselring." See also "Paratroopers Very Popular Again," *Der Spiegel* 30 (25 July 1951): 10f.

44. *Die Tat*, 16 August 1952, "War Criminal Kesselring Elected President of the *Stahlhelm*."

45. *Libertas*, 16 October 1952, "German Militarism and Decision-Making Freedom," by Lina Morino (annotated by the German government's press and information service, in the files of AA-PA).

46. Information provided to me on 15 December 2000 by Heinz Becker, director of the Verband deutsches Afrikakorps.

47. *Die Oase*, 2001, "The Origins of Our Association," p. 3.

48. The archives of the Verband deutscher Afrikakorps e.V. are held by Hans-Günther Stark, Wessling. I would like to thank him for kindly allowing me to inspect them.

49. The Stahlhelm, which had been established in 1919, was originally politically nonpartisan. However, in 1931, it united with the National Socialists and the German Nationalists to form the Harzburg Front. It won fifty-two seats in the March 1933 Reichstag elections, running under the banner of the Black-White-Red Battle Front, together with the nationalist Volkspartei (People's Party). As early as September 1933, the predecessor organization Wehrstahlhelm was transferred to the SA (Sturmabteilung). The final *Gleichschaltung* (consolidation) took place in March 1934 with the establishment of the Nationalsozialistischer deutscher Frontkämpferbund (Stahlhelm); that entity was, however, dissolved in 1935. The Stahlhelm–Bund der Frontsoldaten was relaunched at a meeting on 24 February 1951. As a result, the association could anticipate the return of substantial assets that had been confiscated by the National Socialists. However, old and new differences soon became apparent between the association's director (Karl Simon), his deputy (Dr. Lehmann), and the association's organizer (Thomas Girgensohn). As a result, several so-called honor court proceedings were held at the beginning of 1953. The feud between Simon and the association's "captain," Girgensohn, reached such proportions that an honor court was convened in April 1953. Kesselring presided over the proceedings, and Simon was excluded from the Stahlhelm for two years. Simon had disclosed Girgensohn's previous activities in the SA leadership to Home Affairs Minister Lehr (see "*Stahlhelm*: Dueling Challenges Issued," *Der Spiegel* 26 [1953]: 10f.), and he was accused of denouncing former comrades to denazification committees. In contrast, Girgensohn—whom Simon suspected of allowing prominent Nazis to infiltrate the Stahlhelm—was acquitted. Although the Stahlhelm, as a political association, claimed to be rooted in democracy, the organization's publications were openly contemptuous of the political parties operating in the Federal Republic. Nonetheless, representatives of right-wing parties in particular used the annual Stahlhelm conventions as a platform for their ideas. In 1955, the SPD tabled a parliamentary question in the Bundestag regarding breaches of the uniform prohibition at the national Stahlhelm convention in Goslar. Stahlhelm members

had appeared publicly at the convention wearing their specific association uniforms. During the debate, CDU parliamentarians warned the Stahlhelm to exercise more restraint in the future, and others tried to downplay the incidents in view of the association's small following (see Schenck to Schweinsberg, "Soldatenverbände," p. 131).

50. *Stimme des Friedens*, 20 October 1952, "*Front Heil* with Kesselring!" The citation appointing Kesselring to the honorary presidency, issued by the Stahlhelm's leadership, stated: "We pledge ourselves to loyally follow our elected president, because we place rock-solid faith in this man, who has spent an entire lifetime providing that he put the wellbeing of the *Volk* above all personal considerations. . . . We call on our Stahlhelmcomrades: All for Germany with Kesselring! Naught for ourselves! *Front Heil!*"

51. Cited in ibid.

52. "They Fought Decently," *Der Stahlhelm* 1 (October 1951). Scotland had said: "Since leaving the Army, I have fought for Field Marshal Kesselring, von Mackensen and Mältzer to be freed and pardoned. I have tried to convince the Foreign Office and the Control Commission that these men are innocent of the charges laid against them. I have no doubt that their conviction was a grave miscarriage of justice, and that their continuing detention in prison is a serious political error."

53. Cited in *Stimme des Friedens*, 20 October 1952, "*Front Heil* with Kesselring!" *Der Stahlhelm* continued: "The hour has come when our *Volk* will, of its own volition, declare that the cleanliness and decent attitude of the German soldier are beyond any doubt, and that it rejects any defamation as unjustified slander. The fact that German committed crimes does not change anything in this regard. All nations have their criminal elements."

54. Cited in *Corriere della Sera*, 10 August 1952, "Aspro ammonimento americano per la tentata riabilitazione die Kesselring," by Giorgio Sansa.

55. PRO/TNA, Kew, FO 1060/497, memo by Warr regarding Stahlhelm telegram, 20 August 1952.

56. PRO/TNA, Kew, FO 1060/497, memo by Paton regarding Graziani's telegram, 19 August 1952.

57. PRO/TNA, Kew, FO 1060/497, memo by Bathurst regarding telegrams, 27 August 1952. The authorities in Wahnerheide realized that similar protestations of affection could be directed to Manstein, who was then undergoing cataract surgery in Kiel, and they had decided to cover their backs by seeking instructions from the Foreign Office. (See PRO/TNA, Kew, FO 1060/497, memo by Herchenroder regarding telegrams, 21 August 1952, handwritten memo by Kirkpatrick: "Ask FO.")

58. PRO/TNA, Kew, FO 1060/497, telegram from Graziani, 12 August 1952.

59. PRO/TNA, Kew, FO 1060/497, Chancellory of the High Commissioner in Germany to the British Embassy in Rome, 10 September 1952. It was only on 19 January 1953 that the embassy realized what it termed "ammunition in the battle against the MSI" (the Fascist Italian Party after the war) had landed in its lap, following which it passed the telegram to De Gasperi, who received it with pleasure (see also FO 1060/498, British Embassy in Rome to Ward, Wahnerheide, 20 March 1953).

60. PRO/TNA, Kew, FO 1060/497, memo by Herchenroder on the telegram from Graziani and the camerati italiani, 15 August 1952.

61. PRO/TNA, Kew, FO 1060/497, memo by Herchenroder for Kirkpatrick, 5 September 1952. Since Manstein was due to undergo surgery on 6 September and was not permitted to receive visitors, Kesselring's examination was also postponed. He had originally been due to be examined by a British military doctor on 8 September.

62. PRO/TNA, Kew, FO 1060/497, Roberts to Kirkpatrick, 13 September 1952.

63. *Economist*, 17 October 1952, "Pardon without Forgiveness."

64. In a parliamentary question answered by Undersecretary of State for Foreign Affairs Anthony Nutting on 12 November, MP Hamilton voiced the suspicion that Lord Alexander had adopted an excessively benevolent approach to his respected former enemy; a remark made by Kesselring following his release had given rise to this assumption. He was assured that, as secretary of state for defense, Alexander reviewed each case and would not comment on his decisions (see PRO/TNA, Kew, FO 1060/497, Parliamentary Question, 12 November 1952, Ex-Field Marshal Kesselring). On 24 November, MP Arthur Lewis asked with some concern whether it was intended that the British would pay Kesselring compensation for his years of imprisonment: this was denied (see PRO/TNA, Kew, FO 1060/497, Parliamentary Question, 24 November 1952, Field Marshal Kesselring [release]).

65. *New York Times*, 24 October 1952, "British Formally Release Kesselring, War Criminal."

66. Herchenroder noted that, in his view, it would not be possible to release Kesselring without extending the same clemency to Manstein (see PRO/TNA, Kew, FO 1060/497, Herchenroder to Hancock, 3 September 1952).

67. The German media speculated along similar lines—for example, the *Westdeutsche Allgemeine Zeitung*, 2 October 1952, "Impending Release of Manstein, List and Kesselring."

68. PRO/TNA, Kew, FO 371/97989, Kirkpatrick to Foreign Office, 20 October 1952.

69. Ulrich Brochhagen, *Nach Nürnberg: Vergangenheitsbewältigung und Westintegration in der Ära Adenauer* (Hamburg 1994), p. 86.

70. PRO/TNA, Kew, FO 1060/497, Hancock to Herchenroder, 3 September 1952.

71. PRO/TNA, Kew, FO 1060/497, 1952 Review of Sentences of War Criminals, Case of Kesselring, Albert, by M. F. P. Herchenroder, September 1952, twelve pages. He noted that, given the similar charges but different sentences, a review of the Kesselring case could have justified a reduction to twelve years' imprisonment in the Manstein case (p. 9).

72. Ibid., pp. 8f.

73. Churchill College, Cambridge, HNKY 18/5, Liddell Hart to Hankey, 4 May 1950.

74. PRO/TNA, Kew, FO 1060/497, pardon for Kesselring, to Donelly and Poncet, from Kirkpatrick, 22 October 1952.

75. ASMAE, AP 1952, Germania, b. 95,53/1, Telespresso No. 12604/246, Italian Embassy in Bonn to the Foreign Ministry in Rome, 23 October 1952.

76. PRO/TNA, Kew, FO 1060/501, Kesselring's release ticket (with his room inventory attached), 5 November 1952. He never returned to the prison: his discharge papers were sent to his sickroom in Bochum.

77. *L'Unità*, 3 October 1952, "Il Criminale nazista von Mackensen ha lasciato ieri il carcere di Werl," by Sergio Segre.

78. *Corriere della Sera*, 24 October 1952, "Kesselring liberato definitiovamente dagli Inglesi."

79. *Messaggero*, 24 October 1952, "Kesselring graziato dalle autorità brittaniche," p. 5.

80. *L'Unità*, 24 October 1952, "Rimesso in Libertà il criminale Kesselring," by Sergio Segre.

81. *Avanti!* 26 October 1952, "Kesselring si offre per commandare l'esercito europeo contro L'URSS."

82. *Die Welt*, 17 November 1952, "No Protest against Kesselring."

83. *La Stampa*, 25 October 1952, "La liberazione di Kesselring: Politica pericolosa."

84. *La Stampa*, 24 October 1952, "Kesselring graziato dal ministro Eden: Kappler ricorre di nuovo contro la condanna al ergastolo."

85. *Die Tat*, 1 November 1952, "On Kesselring's Release: A General Who Committed War Crimes in Return for a General Treaty."

86. PRO/TNA, Kew, FO 1060/497, report by Mallet, British Embassy in Rome, to Eden, London, 29 October 1952.

87. *L'Avanti!* 26 October 1952, "Il boia Kappler ricacciato nell'ergastolo mentre gli italiani maledicono Kesselring." The document continued: "This is rejected by the Resistenza, in the name of the 130 martyrs of Marzabotto, in the name of the 345 martyrs of the Fosse Ardeatine, in the name of the 560 martyrs of Sant'Anna, the 200 martyrs of Vinca, the 122 martyrs of Pietransieri, the 109 martyrs of Valia, and in the name of all victims of Nazi barbarity. In the name of the Italian martyrs, we demand that our government use diplomatic channels to protest energetically to the British government. Our protest is a hopeful gesture to the dignity of our Foreign Ministers for this insulting repudiation of all the principles which governed our battle, and which are now again in danger as a result of the resurgent German Nazi militarism."

88. ASMAE, AP 1952, Germania, b. 95, 53/1, Appunto per il Presidente del Consiglio, 26 October 1952, four pages, at p. 1. This document is a comprehensive report prepared for the Italian president regarding parliamentary reactions to the release of Kesselring and to the release of Eberhard von Mackensen.

89. The Communist *L'Unità* had expressed similar views, thus significantly increasing tensions. See *L'Unità*, 25 October 1952, "Il governo deve chiedere la consegna del boia Kesselring."

90. Ibid., p. 3. On 21 October 1952, *La Stampa* published an identical article headlined "Heuss chiede la liberazione di tutti i criminali di guerra."

91. ASMAE, AP 1952, Germania, b. 95, 53/1, letter from Foreign Minister Zoppi to Ambassador Brosio, London, 29 October 1952. Foreign Minister Zoppi instructed Manlio Brosio, ambassador to London, to press for the release of Maria Pasquinelli, who had murdered the British general De Winton in the Free Territory of Trieste, citing the fact that Kesselring was, after all, responsible for far more murders. Maria Pasquinelli was considered a national hero, since she had pointed out during the trial that the general was shot because the British had "betrayed the Italian people" by giving the territory of Istria to the Yugoslavs after the war.

92. *Messaggero*, 28 October 1952, "Il contributo italiano alla vittoria degli alleati."

93. In 1950, writing for a special issue of the *London Gazette*, Alexander had described his experiences in the Italian theater of war. He wrote that the partisans had not presented a serious military problem for the Germans and that Badoglio's allied troops were all inadequate soldiers who constantly had to be prevented from deserting: according to Alexander, they would seize any opportunity to position themselves on the side of the victors. This derisive view had been fully shared by the British Army, the Wehrmacht, and the U.S. Army during the war, and it survived the war with the stubbornness of prejudice. By contrast, he magnified the stature of his partner Kesselring. On 19 April 1947, during Kesselring's trial, Alexander had sent the report to the British War Office, where it subsequently gathered dust. See "Italy: the Usual Apathy," *Der Spiegel* 29 (20 July 1950): 17f.; *La Stampa*, 15 June 1950, "Alexander e la veritá"; *La Stampa*, 16 June 1950, "La cattiva memoria del maresciallo Alexander," p. 1.

94. BA-MA, N 750/new acquisition 2000, sheet 79. In the letter, after thanking people for their good wishes and stating, "I am conscious of the obligation this constitutes, and will attempt to prove myself worthy of your comradeship," Kesselring wrote that old grudges had to

be put aside: "I would not do justice to the present and its demands if I continued to harbour resentments. We must push aside that which divides us if we are to grow closer within a small Europe."

95. *Soester Beobachter/Werler Anzeiger*, 12 December 1952, "Kesselring Thanks Paratroopers."

96. *Süddeutsche Zeitung*, 26 October 1952, "'My Future Lies in the Past.'"

97. Ahrens Papers, private collection, letter from Kesselring to Ahrens, 15 September 1952.

98. *Manchester Guardian*, 26 October 1952, "Kesselring Demands Release of His Comrades"; *La Stampa*, 26 October 1952, "Avrei meritato."

99. *New York Herald Tribune*, 25 October 1952, "Kesselring for Liberating All War Criminals."

100. *Die Welt*, 25 October 1952, "Do Not Delay for Even a Day! Kesselring Endorses the Defense Community"; *Frankfurter Allgemeine Zeitung*, 25 October 1952, "Kesselring: Do Not Delay! 'If it was up to us soldiers, we would long since have had a united Europe.'"

101. *Manchester Guardian*, 26 October 1952, "Kesselring Demands Release of His Comrades"; *New York Herald Tribune*, 25 October 1952, "Kesselring for Liberating All War Criminals"; *L'Unità*, 25 October 1952, "L'alfiere nazista della guerra al bolscevismo: Impudenti dichiarazioni del criminale."

102. *New York Herald Tribune*, 25 October 1952, "Kesselring for Liberating All War Criminals."

103. SPD press service, 7 November 1952, "Italy and Kesselring."

104. Cited in *Welt am Sonntag*, 26 October 1952, "England's Echo Following Kesselring's Release."

105. *Die Tat*, 1 November 1952, "On Kesselring's Release."

106. PRO/TNA, Kew, FO 1060/497, report by Mallet, British Embassy in Rome, to Eden, London, 29 October 1952.

107. *L'Avanti!* 30 October 1952, "Il popolo ed il parlamento francese insorgono contro la nuova minaccia nazista all'Europa."

108. Ibid.

109. *L'Avanti!* 25 October 1952, "Kesselring si offre per commandare."

110. *Neue Zeitung Frankfurt*, 26 October 1952, "Strikes in Protest at Kesselring's Release."

111. *Corriere della Sera*, 26 October 1952, "Continuano le proteste per la scarcerazione di Kesselring"; *Cronaca Versilia*, 29 October 1952, "Le famiglie die Martiri dal Presidente della Camera"; *Neue Zeitung Frankfurt*, 27 October 1952, "Protests in Italy against Kesselring's Release."

112. *L'Avanti!* 28 October 1952, "Un commento della Pravda: Kesselring destinato all'impiego contro i partigiani antiatlantici."

113. *L'Unità*, 24 October 1952, "Rimesso in Libertà il criminale Kesselring."

114. *Berliner Zeitung*, East Berlin, 26 October 1952, "War Criminal Kesselring Walks Free."

115. *L'Unità*, 2 November 1952, "Wilhelm Pieck ai lavoratori italiani: Siamo con voi contro Kesselring," by Sergio Segre.

116. Europäische Arbeiterkommitee gegen die Remilitarisierung Deutschlands (European Workers' Committee against the Remilitarization of Germany), "Kesselring Released from Werl Prison," October 1952, pamphlet, twelve pages, at p. 11.

117. *La Stampa*, 26 October 1952, "Avrei meritato che gli italiani mi erigessero un monumento."

118. ASMAE, AP 1952, Germania, b. 95, 53/1, letter from Foreign Minister Zoppi to Ambassador Brosio, London, 29 October 1952.

119. *Hannoversche Allgemeine Zeitung*, 27 October 1952, "Kesselring Answers Italy."

120. *Berliner Zeitung*, East Berlin, 26 October 1952, "War Criminal Kesselring."

121. *La Stampa*, 26 October 1952, "Avrei meritato che gli italiani mi erigessero un monumento."

122. *Rheinische Post*, 24 October 1952, "Kesselring frei." Kesselring, so the headline said, was looking forward, "in the knowledge that he was innocent," to his life as a "free man."

123. *Hamburger Abendblatt*, 24 October 1952, "Colonel Vickers Brought the News."

124. *Abendpost*, Frankfurt, 24 October 1952, "Echo in Respect of Kesselring: Why Released So Late?"

125. *Frankfurter Rundschau*, 1 November 1952, "Italy Will Not Demand Kesselring's Extradition."

126. Reprinted in ASMAE, AP 1952, Germania, b. 95, 53/1, newspaper cutting. Calamandrei's monument is located on the piazza in Cuneo; a stone copy is on the wall next to the church in Sant'Anna di Stazzema. The text is tantamount to a statement of the Resistenza's creed and that of the villages affected by the massacres, and the monument is always decorated with fresh flowers.

127. The full text is as follows: "Lo avrai, camerata Kesserling [*sic*], il monumento che pretendi da noi Italiani, ma con che pietra si costruirà, a deciderlo tocca a noi. Non coi sassi affumicati dei borghi inermi straziati dal tuo sterminio, non colla terra dei cimitieri, dove i nostri compagni giovinetti riposano in serenità, non colla neve inviolata delle montagne che per due inverni ti sfidarono, non colla primavera di queste valli che ti videro sfuggire. Ma soltanto col silenzio dei torturati. Più duro di ogni macigno, soltanto con la roccia di questo patto, giurato fra uomini liberi, che volontari si adunarono, per dignità, non per odio, decisi a riscattare la vergogna e il terrore del mondo. Su queste strade, se vorrei tornare, ai nostri posti ci ritroverai, morti e vivi collo stesso impegno, popolo serrato intorno al monumento che si chiama ora e sempre: Resistenza." (Piero Calamandrei.)

The text translates roughly as: "You will get it, Comrade Kesselring, the monument you demand from us Italians, but it will be we who choose the stone to build it with: Not with the smoke-blackened stones of the harmless suburbs lacerated by your extermination, nor with the soil of the cemeteries where our young companions rest peacefully, not with the inviolate snow of the mountains that challenged you for two winters nor with the snow of these valleys that witnessed your flight. But only with the silence of the tortured. Only with the rock of this pact, harder than any boulder, sworn by free men who willingly assemble out of dignity not hate, determined to redeem the world from shame and terror. Should you wish to return you will find us at our posts on these roads, the dead and the living with the same commitment, a people serried [assembled] around the monument to be called now and forever: Resistance." (I am indebted to Michael Friel for this translation.)

128. *Deutsche Zeitung und Wirtschaftszeitung*, 31 December 1952, "A Monument for Kesselring."

129. ASMAE, AP 1950–57, Germania, b. 189, 53/1, Promemoria by the Embassy of the Federal Republic of Germany in Rome, 7 February 1953.

130. *Neue Zeitung Frankfurt*, 27 October 1952, "Protests in Italy against Kesselring's Release"; SPD press service, 7 November 1952, "Italien und Kesselring"; *Tägliche Rundschau*, 1 November 1952, "Italy's Mass Protests against Kesselring."

131. *Neuer Mainzer Anzeiger*, 3 November 1952, "Outrage Surrounding Kesselring."

132. *Die Tat*, 1 November 1952, "On Kesselring's Release."

133. Frei, *Vergangenheitspolitik*, p. 280.

134. *Neue Zeitung Frankfurt*, 29 October 1952, "Debate Continues to Rage in Italy Concerning Kesselring's Release," by Louis Barcata.

135. Ahrens Papers, private collection, manuscript of speech by former paratrooper General Ramcke, meeting of the Waffen SS in Verden/Aller, 26 October 1952 (copy). Playing on the fact that SS members were ostracized as "criminals" and could not be employed in the public service, Ramcke said that they should count themselves lucky to be blacklisted, since one day the blacklists would be "lists of honor."

136. PRO FO 371/97991, Kirkpatrick, 5 November 1952.

137. Frei, *Vergangenheitspolitik*, p. 283n67.

138. Ibid., and pp. 76f.

139. AA-PA, col. 2/2109, pp. 1f. of the letter.

140. Ibid., p. 3.

141. Ibid., pp. 1f.

142. Ibid., p. 3.

143. Ahrens Papers, private collection, Hankey to Ahrens, 27 October 1952: "It would be absolutely useless to approach the British Legion in present circumstances. It would take weeks, maybe months, to live down von Ramcke."

144. Churchill College, Cambridge, HNKY 18/3, Ahrens to Hankey, 1 November 1952.

145. Churchill College, Cambridge, HNKY 18/3, Ahrens to Hankey, 9 November 1952.

146. Churchill College, Cambridge, HNKY 18/2, Kesselring to Hankey, 6 November 1952. "My thanks are multiplied by the knowledge of your devoted efforts to achieve a sensible solution to the war criminals issue." Kesselring took the opportunity to once again make his position clear to Hankey, stressing that he had been harshly dealt with by a victors' justice that was not open to sensible arguments: "I spoke of a sensible solution because, as someone who is quite familiar with the situation, and as a 'victim,' I cannot see a solution based on law. It is only for that reason that I accepted being released on the grounds of health without resentment." He continued in a fighting tone: "I also believe that, as a 'free man,' I will be able to do more for my comrades in misfortune still sitting in prison, and for better relations between our peoples, than as a 'repining prisoner'!"

147. Ahrens Papers, private collection, Hankey to Ahrens, 27 October 1952.

148. Churchill College, Cambridge, HNKY 18/2, Hankey to Kesselring, 18 November 1952.

149. Ahrens Papers, private collection, Hankey to Ahrens, 29 October 1952.

150. He cabled: "Release of Field Marshal Kesselring represents great step forward in English-German understanding. Former German soldiers congratulate you on making decisive advances in obtaining justice for former foes. Solution of so-called war criminals problem will increase possibility of releasing Germans held in Soviet camps. Admiral Hansen." Ahrens Papers, private collection, draft article and collection of material for the VdS, spring 2000.

151. Archives of the VdS, Bonn, Kesselring dossier, letter from Ahrens to Trettner, VdS, 27 October 1952.

152. As well as Kesselring's letter to British Foreign Secretary Eden, Libby had (as early as November) sent letters to the American generals Matthew Ridgway and Thomas Handy, after first contacting Sir Harold Alexander. Ahrens Papers, private collection, Finucane to Ahrens, 13 December 1952, and letter from Kesselring to Ahrens enclosing letters to Eden, Lord Alexander, General Ridgway, General Handy, 5 November 1952; also Hanns-Dietrich Ahrens, "Field Marshal Albert Kesselring," *Luftwaffenrevue* 48 (March 2000): 67–70, at p. 68.

153. Ahrens Papers, private collection, Hankey to Ahrens, 7 November 1952.

154. Kühne, "Zwischen Vernichtungskrieg und Freizeitgesellschaft," p. 106.

155. Ahrens Papers, private collection, Ahrens to Trettner, 24 November 1952.

156. Searle, *Wehrmacht Generals,* p. 168.

157. Frei, *Vergangenheitspolitik,* p. 288.

158. Stiftung Bundeskanzler Adenauer Haus, archives, I 04.03, Adenauer date book, entry dated 12 December 1952, 6 P.M. to 6:30 P.M.

159. *Frankfurter Rundschau,* 15 December 1952: "Kesselring Visits the Chancellor"; *Frankfurter Allgemeine Zeitung,* 15 December 1952: "Kesselring Visits the Chancellor."

160. *Frankfurter Rundschau,* 17 December 1952: "Annoyance in Rome at Kesselring-Adenauer Contact."

161. *Süddeutsche Zeitung,* letter to the editor from Franz Bernhard, Munich, 23 December 1952, "Mr. Kesselring of All People."

162. *DIPLO (Diplomatische Industrie-Korrespondenz Ahrens),* dated 8 November 1952. *DIPLO*—Ahrens's newsletter, a press digest with news of political and economic interest—was circulated at a subscription price to industrial clients of Ahrens's PR agency; it was also sent on request to interested parties in the media and VdS, as well as to lawyers. Letter from Ahrens to the author, 5 November 2001.

163. Telephone conversation between Heinz Trettner and the author, 18 June 2001.

164. *Die Welt,* 28 October 52: "Stahlhelm President Kesselring." Nevertheless, during his first meeting with the national Stahlhelm leaders Simon and Lehmann, he made it clear that cooperation between all veterans' associations was a matter of particular concern to him.

165. The integrative effect of his name, with its potential to unite the fractured and often jealous rivals among the Traditionsverbände, probably reached its zenith shortly after his release.

166. *La Stampa,* 26 October 1952, "Avrei meritato."

167. Ahrens Papers, private collection, Ahrens to Kesselring, 1 February 1953.

168. Ahrens Papers, private collection, Ahrens to Trettner, 24 November 1952.

169. Ahrens Papers, private collection, Kesselring to Ahrens, end of December 1952.

170. Frei, *Vergangenheitspolitik,* p. 282.

171. Searle, *Wehrmacht Generals,* p. 168.

172. Kühne, "Zwischen Vernichtungskrieg und Freizeitgesellschaft," p.112, mentioned that appeals for the release of Walter Reder continued into the 1980s.

173. Ahrens Papers, private collection, letter from Hankey to Ahrens, 14 December 1952.

174. "Ismay" entry, written by Ronald Lewin, in *Dictionary of National Biography* (Oxford 1981), pp. 570–572.

175. This commitment continued. Shortly before his death in 1963, Lord Hankey was still campaigning on behalf of Major Walter Reder, unsuccessfully seeking his release; see F. J. P. Veale, "Lord Hankey: The Greatest British Public Servant of the Age," *Social Justice Review* (April 1963): 12–15, at p. 15.

176. Franco Giustolisi, "Gli scheletri dell'Armadio" [Skeletons in the Closet], *Micromega* 1 (2000): 345–355, at p. 350. The letters were quoted verbatim. In 1999, Giustolisi, a journalist and publisher of the weekly magazine *L'Espresso,* uncovered the scandal of the missing investigation files in Italy; that, in turn, is currently the subject of the investigation by the parliamentary commission of inquiry, which has been issuing ongoing reports on its findings. Unfortunately, the originals are unavailable for inspection, since an Italian commission of inquiry is currently dealing with them. In the German press, the matter was revisited in Christiane Kohl, "Cabinet of Shame," *Der Spiegel* 17 (2001): 56–58.

177. *Süddeutsche Zeitung*, 29 October 1999, "Italy Shields German War Criminals: In Deference to Its NATO Partner, Rome Has Waived Prosecution," by Christiane Kohl, p. 1.

178. The massacres on Cephalonia and Corfu, during which around 5,000 Italian POWs from the Acqui were murdered despite having surrendered, have yet to be the subject of court proceedings. The commander who executed the massacre, Harald von Hirschfeld, fell during the final months of the war (see Gerhard Schreiber, *La vendetta tedesca, 1943–1945: Le rapressaglie naziste in Italia* [Milan 2000], pp. 83f.).

179. Giustolisi, "Scheletri," p. 351. Martino was referring to the conviction of those responsible for the massacres in Cephalonia and Corfu, Generals Alexander Löhr and Hubert Lanz, following the Nuremberg Case 7 trial, which dealt with hostage murders.

180. Ibid., p. 352.

181. Ibid., p. 353.

182. Ibid.

183. Kühne, "Zwischen Vernichtungskrieg und Freizeitgesellschaft," p. 93.

184. Ibid., p. 95.

185. Jörg Echternkamp, "Wut auf die Wehrmacht? Vom Bild der deutschen Soldaten in der unmittelbaren Nachkriegszeit," in Rolf-Dieter Müller and Hans-Erich Volkmann, eds., *Die Wehrmacht: Mythos und Realität* (Munich 1999), p. 1080.

186. Klaus Naumann, "Integration und Eigensinn. Die Sicherheitseliten der frühen Bundesrepublik zwischen Kriegs- und Friedenskultur," in Thomas Kühne, ed., *Von der Kriegskultur zur Friedenskultur? Zum Mentalitätswandel in Deutschland seit 1945* (Münster 2000), pp. 202–218, at p. 214.

187. The quotation is from an article in the *Münchner Merkur*, 1 April 1953, "The Field Marshal," by Werner Runge.

188. Searle, *Wehrmacht Generals*, p. 277.

189. *Frankfurter Rundschau*, 22 September 55, "A Field Marshal Reflects."

190. The recent discovery of publishing contracts between Kesselring and the Athenäum publishing house in Bonn indicates for the first time that the former field marshal had signed a preliminary contract with Gerhard von Reutern, the head of the publishing house, on 22 September 1950 while he was still held in Werl. In February 2000, I managed to acquire these documents, together with other letters, for the BA-MA during an auction held by the Historica firm of auctioneers in Munich. The documents have since been included in the Kesselring Papers, N 750, in Freiburg. In the preface to a new edition of his father's memoirs published by Schnellbach in 2000, Kesselring's adopted son, Rainer, confirmed that the book was written in custody, partly in the hope of paying off remaining legal debts: "My father wrote them in Werl Prison shortly before his release in 1952, and my mother, Irmgard Horn-Kesselring (who died in 1982) smuggled the manuscript out of Werl during a visit, and then typed it up."

191. In clear contrast to the prevailing view in military circles, Heuss believed that tradition could only stem from moral courage and resistance: "This army found its martyrs in the soldiers of July 20th, who rose up in the hope of sparing the Fatherland total devastation—in their failure, in their end, was also the destruction of a core value of the army's decent tradition: chivalry towards the vanquished." See "Soldierhood in Our Time," speech given on 12 March 1959, in Theodor Heuss, *Politiker und Publizist: Aufsätze und Reden* (a collection of essays and speeches by Heuss), commentary and annotation by Martin Vogt (Tübingen 1984), pp. 488–499, at p. 495.

192. Detlev Bald, "Alte Kameraden: Offizierskader in der Bundeswehr," in Ursula Breymayer, ed., *Willensmenschen: Über deutsche Offiziere* (Frankfurt 1999).

193. Martin Kutz, "Militär und Gesellschaft im Deutschland der Nachkriegszeit (1946–1995)," in Ute Frevert, ed., *Militär und Gesellschaft im 19. und 20. Jahrhundert* (Stuttgart 1997), pp. 277–313, at p. 283.

194. Ulrich de Maizière, "Die Bundeswehr—Neuschöpfung oder Fortsetzung der Wehrmacht?" in Rolf-Dieter Müller and Hans-Erich Volkmann, eds., *Die Wehrmacht: Mythos und Realität* (Munich 1999), pp. 1171–1183, at p. 1182.

195. *Der Stahhelm*, information bulletin no. 77, November 1957.

196. Bald, "Alte Kameraden," p. 141.

197. Hans-Jürgen Rautenberg, "Zur Standortbestimmung der künftigen deutschen Streitkräfte," in Roland G. Foerster, ed., *Anfänge westdeutscher Sicherheitspolitik 1945–1956*, vol. 1, *Von der Kapitulation bis zum Pleven-Plan* (Munich 1982), p. 830.

198. In common with many other soldiers' representatives, he believed that the uniform of the Bundeswehr differed too greatly from that of the Wehrmacht. Writing in the association newsletter, *Der Stahlhelm*, he demanded: "Give our young soldiers a uniform that leads them towards the tradition of German frontline soldiers in uniform; a uniform in which they feel comfortable and of which they can be proud." See *Der Stahlhelm*, October 1956.

199. Heuss, *Politiker*, p. 500.

200. Otto Gessler, *Reichswehrpolitik in der Weimarer Zeit*, ed. Kurt Sendtner (Stuttgart 1958), p. 94.

201. Rautenberg, "Standortbestimmung," p. 833.

202. *Hamburger Volkszeitung* (Kommunistische Partei Deutschlands, KPD, the Communist Party of Germany), 13 February 1954, "US Ignominy."

203. *Neues Deutschland*, 31 January 1954, "Kesselring: The Extended Arm of Politics." In his theoretical writings, Kesselring had emphasized the significance of the Luftwaffe, stressing that an air force should always occupy a "prime position in a nation's arsenal." Kesselring had good contacts with the head of personnel in the Luftwaffe Section of the Blank Office, where the former commander of fighter pilots in Italy, Colonel Günther Freiherr von Maltzahn, acted as his inside man. Further research along these lines will be published in the series of documents being issued by the German Institute of Military History.

204. It was possible to locate a manuscript for a speech on "The German Defense Concept" in the Munich War Archives, Waldenfels Papers, vol. 5; the speech is accompanied by a few photos showing Kesselring at Stahlhelm meetings and bears a handwritten annotation by Waldenfels: "by General Kesselring." Since the manuscript reflects the well-known conservative nature of Kesselring's defense policy approach and thus offers nothing new, it will not be discussed further.

205. *Frankfurter Rundschau*, 15 December 1952, "Kesselring Visits the Chancellor."

206. *Generalanzeiger für Bonn und Umgebung*, 15 December 1952, "Stahlhelm Denial."

207. *Nürnberger Nachrichten*, 11 May 1953, "Kesselring Takes over Stahlhelm."

208. Ibid.

209. Schenck zu Schweinsberg, "Soldatenverbände," p. 141.

210. *Volksstimme*, Cologne, 29 May 1953, "War Criminal Kesselring: For Me the Future Lies in the Past."

211. Rundfunk-Dienst, Ost-Information (an information service for broadcasting), 8 February 1955, "Kesselring's Statements in the Journal *Der Stahlhelm*."

212. "Stahlhelm," *Der Spiegel* 33 (1953): 34, reader's letter from A. Wagner, Frankfurt: "It appears that the Neo-Stahlhelmers are able to flout the uniform prohibition, which has now once again been explicitly confirmed in the Public Order Act. Led by retired Field Marshal Kesselring, who (despite having lost two wars, and despite his experiences following the

collapse, failed to seize the opportunity to lead a life of civilian reflection) now, as Stahlhelm president, holds his speeches in a voice accustomed to command or—clad in leather coat, with a sword belt and peaked cap—reviews, just as in the past, parades of men whom he has infected with his enthusiasm for steel helmets, the Reich flag of war and runic insignia."

213. *Neue Ruhr Zeitung*, 22 September 1954, "He Should Be Silent!" reader's letter from Father Flossdorf, Mülheim: "Today Kesselring speaks beneath the 'celebrated Reich banner of war,' while drawing pensions from the German people on whom they want to once again bestow a glorious past. We are grateful for such gentlemen, who served Hitler 'loyally' until the end. When will the Federal Home Affairs Minister intervene?" Flossdorf felt that "Hitler appears to live on in Kesselring," and he suggested that Kesselring should "rather become a navvy [an unskilled worker] to clear away the wreckage which he helped create."

214. Bruno W. Reimann, *Aufarbeitung der Vergangenheit in Giessen: Die NS-Geschichte als soziales Tabu*, 2nd ed. (Giessen: Institute for Sociology, 1993), pp. 23f.

215. "Stahlhelm: The Kesselring Problem," *Der Spiegel* 8 (1954): 8–10, at p. 9.

216. *Frankfurter Neue Presse*, 13 July 1953, "Stahlhelm Issues New 'Message': Kesselring Justifies the Demands of Former Frontline Soldiers."

217. N. Bäumler Papers, private collection, letter from Liny Kesselring to Bäumler, 19 July 1953.

218. *Telegraf*, 23 July 1954, "Notice."

219. Ibid., p. 10.

220. "Stahlhelm: The Kesselring Problem," *Der Spiegel*.

221. Cited in *Stimme des Friedens*, 20 October 1952, "*Front Heil* with Kesselring!"

222. *Der Spiegel* 30 (1953), People section, p. 3.

223. *Frankfurter Rundschau*, 20 July 1953, Letters page, "Obsession Following Giessen Stahlhelm Meeting," from Otto Lehmann-Russbüldt, Berlin.

224. *Neues Deutschland*, East Berlin, 14 January 1954, "What the Italian People Think of Kesselring."

225. *Frankfurter Rundschau*, 21 July 1953, Letters page, "Hereditary Enemies of the German People," from Kurt Neurreck, Frankfurt.

226. *Frankfurter Rundschau*, 21 July 1953, Letters page, "Does the General Also Want to Be a Politician?" from Georg Loh, Frankfurt.

227. *Süddeutsche Zeitung*, 8 August 1953, "Kesselring—'Not Affected.'"

228. Ibid., p. 208.

229. BA-MA, BW 9/2127, Confidential Verfassungsschutz report on the "Stahlhelm," 20 October 1953, pp. 191–225, at p. 208. The German Bundesministerium für Verfassungsschutz (BfV) is an intelligence agency similar in function to the Federal Bureau of Investigation (FBI).

230. Ibid., pp. 194f.

231. BA Koblenz, B 106/15456, report by the Federal Interior Ministry on Kesselring's Austrian trip, March–April 1954.

232. *Frankfurter Rundschau*, 30 March 1954, "What Does Kesselring Want in Austria?"

233. *Westdeutsche Allgemeine Zeitung*, 5 April 1954, "Kesselring: Charges Unfounded"; *Bonner Rundschau*, 5 April 1954, "Kesselring Regrets"; *Mannheimer Morgen*, 5 April 1954, "Unfounded."

234. *Frankfurter Allgemeine Zeitung*, 31 March 1954, "Abuse of the Right to Hospitality." Helmer's statement continued: "He caused the country which, in accordance with the principles of democracy, was prepared to grant even him the opportunity to recuperate,

unprecedented annoyance, offering cheap propaganda material to Austria's enemies. A man like Kesselring should have realised that, by such behaviour, he delighted our enemies and played into their hands."

235. *Düsseldorfer Nachrichten*, 5 April 1954, "Generalfeldmarschall Kesselring"; *Westdeutsche Allgemeine Zeitung*, 5 April 1954, "Kesselring: Charges Unfounded"; *Bonner Rundschau*, 5 April 1954, "Kesselring Regrets"; *Mannheimer Morgen*, 5 April 1954, "Unfounded."

236. Cited in the *Frankfurter Rundschau*, 30 March 1954, "What Does Kesselring Want in Austria?"

237. *Süddeutsche Zeitung*, 25 March 1954, "Kesselring Visit Unwanted."

238. *Die Welt*, 27 March 1954, "Kesselring in Graz."

239. Ibid.

240. Cited in BA Koblenz, B 106/15456, report by the German Interior Ministry on Kesselring's Austrian trip, March–April 1954.

241. Ibid.

242. Ibid.

243. Ibid. Similar visits to the Salzburg region had already been made by former Generaloberst Lothar Rendulic (himself an Austrian) and Major Ulrich Rudel. The latter was a prominent opponent of Austrian contingents participating in rearmament.

244. ASMAE, AP 1951–1955, Germania, b. 29, report by the Italian Foreign Office on Kesselring's visit to Austria, 22 April 1954.

245. Ibid.

246. *Frankfurter Allgemeine Zeitung*, 29 March 1954, "No Finesse." Kesselring was "probably unaware that he had thus supplied valuable propaganda material against Austria to the Communist and Soviet press which had been lying in wait."

247. *Westdeutsche Allgemeine Zeitung*, 1 April 1954, "A Lack of Finesse."

248. *Frankfurter Allgemeine Zeitung*, 29 March 1954, "No Finesse."

249. *Frankfurter Rundschau*, 29 March 1954, "Kesselring Not Wanted in Austria."

250. *Deutsche Zeitung*, 3 April 1954, "Insensitive": "Mr. Kesselring would have been well-advised, both for personal reasons and for reasons of political tact, to heed the clear signal given by the Austrian government and leave immediately."

251. *Abendpost*, 1 April 1954, "Disservice": It was "questionable whether a tourism destination could afford subjecting prominent guests who are out of favor with the Communist '*Österreichischer Volksstimme*' to abuse and turning them into the focus of media debate."

252. *Generalanzeiger*, 25 March 1954, "Kesselring's 'Visit' Unwanted"; *Die Welt*, 25 March 1954, "Vienna Reservations Concerning Kesselring Trip."

253. *Die Welt*, 30 March 1954, "Austrian People's Party Defends Kesselring"; BA Koblenz, B 106/15456, extracts from the press and information digest issued by the Federal Office for the Protection of the Constitution, dated 30 March 1954, p. 7.

254. BA Koblenz, B 106/15456, extracts from the press and information digest.

255. Cited in the *Süddeutsche Zeitung*, 17 November 1954, "So Kesselring Spoke to the English . . . The BBC Program Presented 'Average' German Opinions: A Storm of Outrage," by Curt Geyer; *Frankfurter Neue Presse*, 20 November 1954, "Seeking German Opinion: The Kesselring Interview Opened Up a Can of Worms," by Geyer; *Die Welt*, 12 November 1954, "Kesselring Provokes Indignation."

256. Friedrich Gerstenberger, "Strategische Erinnerungen: Die Memoiren deutscher Offiziere," in Hannes Heer and Klaus Naumann, eds., *Vernichtungskrieg: Verbrechen der Wehrmacht 1941–1944* (Hamburg 1995), pp. 620–633, at p. 627.

257. *Neues Deutschland*, East Berlin, 13 November 1954, "So Kesselring, Former Nazi General, Spoke on British Radio on November 10th."

258. "Soviet Zone: Vacation on Sylt," *Der Spiegel* 50 (1957): 54–56, at p. 56. The director, Andrew Thorndike, noted: "We want to show what those people who were always around Hitler, and who were never mentioned by name, are doing today."

259. Unfortunately, I have been unable to find this material, despite searching the records of the Ministry for State Security in the Berlin-Hoppegarten Federal Archives. However, the files of the Ministry for State Security do indicate that the Interior Ministry in Czechoslovakia was provided with a "cassette containing seven films of original documents from the RSHA, Section VI," in which Kesselring is also supposed to be mentioned. The material is thought to be in Prague. See BStU Berlin, RHE 22a–66 CSSR, letter from HV A Section X71 to Central Department IX711, Gen. Oberstltn. Stolze, 9 December 1966.

260. It remains an idea, however; see the files in BstU Berlin, RHE 18-66, re: *Neues Deutschland*, East Berlin, 1959.

261. *Frankfurter Allgemeine Zeitung*, 20 November 1954, "Kesselring."

262. Gerstenberger, "Strategische Erinnerungen"; Gotthard Breit, *Das Staats- und Gesellschaftsbild deutscher Generale beider Weltkriege im Spiegel ihrer Memoiren* (Boppard 1973); Rolf Düsterberg, *Soldat und Kriegserlebnis: Deutsche militärische Erinnerungsliteratur (1945–1961) zum Zweiten Weltkrieg—Motive, Begriffe, Wertungen* (Paderborn 2000); Helmut Peitsch, *"Deutschlands Gedächtnis in seiner dunkelsten Zeit": Zur Frage der Autobiographie in den Westzonen Deutschlands und den Westsektoren von Berlin 1945 bis 1949* (Berlin 1990); Hans Wagener, "Soldaten zwischen Gehorsam und Gewissen: Kriegsromane und Kriegstagebücher," in Hans Wagener, ed., *Gegenwartsliteratur und Drittes Reich: Deutsche Autoren in der Auseinandersetzung mit der Vergangenheit* (Stuttgart 1977), pp. 241–264.

263. Gerstenberger, "Strategische Erinnerungen," p. 623.

264. Ibid., p. 622.

265. Ibid.

266. "Books," *Der Spiegel* 46 (1953): 35.

267. *Süddeutsche Zeitung*, 8 August 1953, "Kesselring—'Not Affected,'" by Robert Borchardt. Borchardt was himself a former officer and holder of the Knight's Cross. Of partial Jewish descent, he became a journalist after the war and subsequently worked as a diplomat (press attaché) in Washington. After holding a senior position in the German Foreign Office, he ended his career as head of the Assessment Section in the BND (Bundesnachrichtendienst, the German intelligence service).

268. *Stuttgarter Zeitung*, 11 May 1953, "A Soldier until the End," by Paul Mahlmann: "This soldier portrayed by Kesselring lacks a sense of belonging to the Western culture, a willingness to defend that culture and the associated insight that any totalitarianism threatening that culture—whether National Socialist or Communist—must be viewed as 'Enemy No. 1.' Thus, what is lacking is the spiritual foundation which must be intrinsic to the *Volk*, and accordingly to the soldiers who come from the *Volk*'s ranks."

269. *Die Zeit*, 4 June 1953, "An Order Is an Order! The Memoirs of Field Marshal Kesselring," by Heinz Hell.

270. BA-MA, BW 9/2127, confidential report by the Federal Office for the Protection of the Constitution, *Der Stahlhelm*, 20 October 1953, pp. 191–225, at pp. 207f.

271. *Münchner Merkur*, 1 April 1953, "The Field Marshal," by Werner Runge.

272. Ibid.

273. *Tägliche Rundschau*, East Berlin, 6 March 1954, "War Criminal Albert Kesselring in the Past and Present," by Zeiger.

274. *Saturday Review*, 17 April 1954, "Doorman of Tragedy," by Gordon Harrison, p. 13.

275. *Saturday Review*, letter to the editor from Bruno Guarino, 8 May 1954, p. 26.

276. *Saturday Review*, letter to the editor from Alfred Werner, 8 May 1954.

277. *Time*, 19 April 1954, book review, "Smiling Al," pp. 106–110.

278. *New Yorker*, 26 March 1955, book review by A. J. Liebling, pp. 124–134, at p. 125.

279. Alaric Searle, "Revising the Myth of a 'Clean *Wehrmacht*': Generals' Trials, Public Opinion, and the Dynamics of *Vergangenheitsbewältigung* in West Germany, 1948–1960," *Bulletin of the German Historical Institute* (London) 25, no. 2 (November 2003): 17–48, at p. 26.

280. Ibid., p. 38.

281. Searle, "Revising the Myth," p. 45.

282. Ruth Bettina Birn, "Wehrmacht und Wehrmachtangehörige in den deutschen Nachkriegsprozessen," in Rolf-Dieter Müller and Hans-Erich Volkmann, eds., *Die Wehrmacht: Mythos und Realität* (Munich 1999), pp. 1081–1099, at p. 1081; in this regard, see also Adalbert Rückerl, ed., *Strafverfolgung von NS-Verbrechen 1945–1978: Eine Dokumentation* (Heidelberg 1979).

283. Birn, "Wehrmacht und Wehrmachtangehörige," p. 1085.

284. Ibid., p. 1081; in this regard, see also Rückerl, *Strafverfolgung von NS-Verbrechen*. The ZSL collections have been archived and are accessible in situ in Ludwigsburg.

285. Hans Ehlert, "Innenpolitische Auseinandersetzungen um die Pariser Verträge und die Wehrverfassung 1954 bis 1956," in Hans Ehlert, Christian Greiner, Georg Meyer, and Bruno Thoss, eds., *Anfänge westdeutscher Sicherheitspolitik 1945–1956*, vol. 3, *Die NATO-Option* (Munich: German Institute of Military History, 1993), pp. 235–560, at pp. 321ff.; Searle, "Revising the Myth," p. 31; Michael Geyer, "Der kalte Krieg, die Deutschen und die Angst: Die westdeutsche Opposition gegen Wiederbewaffnung und Kernwaffen," in Klaus Naumann, ed., *Nachkrieg in Deutschland* (Hamburg 2001), pp. 267–318.

286. Searle, "Revising the Myth," p. 30.

287. Ibid., p. 39.

288. AA-PA, B 10 (Sect. 2), vol. 2109, notes made for a presentation by Dr. Born on behalf of Trützschler, 28 January 1953. In January 1953, Kesselring met with the section head, von Trützschler, and reported on the deteriorating prison conditions in Werl following the escape of seven prisoners from the Breda fortress in Italy.

289. AA-PA, B 10 (Sect. 2), vol. 2110, letter from Trützschler to Kesselring, 9 November 1954.

290. BA-MA, N 642 (Aschenauer), box 15, affidavit issued by Albert Kesselring on behalf of Herbert Kappler, 10 April 1953. Kesselring concluded that, like himself, Kappler had found his name caught up in "atrocity propaganda," and this had prompted him to write to the Italian prime minister "to help disseminate the historical truth." In contrast to his testimony during his own trial, as well as the 1949 petition, Kesselring now stated for the record that even Kappler bore no guilt for the shooting of 335 Italians. Kappler had merely followed "orders from on high entrusting the SD with the whole operation" and had believed himself constrained to follow Hitler's order to the letter.

291. BA-MA, N 642/15, Kesselring to Aschenauer (the Stille Hilfe prisoner aid organization), 4 February 1956.

292. BA-MA, N 642/15, Kesselring to Aschenauer (the Stille Hilfe prisoner aid organization), 11 June 1956.

293. AMSJ Munich, Hiemer Papers. Some sheets are contained in BA-MA, N 642/15. It is no longer possible to inspect all the leaflets issued by the aid committee and to analyze

them in the light of Kesselring's statements; only a few have been found in Hiemer's papers in Munich and in Aschenauer's papers in Freiburg.

294. AA-PA, B 10 (Sect. 2), p. 255, Kesselring to Permanent Secretary Hallstein, 27 May 1955; a reference to his intervention can also be found in BA-MA, N 642/15, Kesselring to the Stille Hilfe aid organization ("Princess Isenburg"), 3 March 1955. On 31 July 1955, this was followed by a note from the German government seeking Kappler's release. However, there was no response. Kesselring's naïveté was apparent when he stated: "I fear that the period which would have been favorable for Kappler's release by the Italian government has already expired, and I particularly regret this since, while Kappler was not a friend, I got to know him as an official who saved the lives of hundreds, if not thousands, of German soldiers from the partisans in Italy."

295. BA-MA, N 642/15, Kesselring to Aschenauer or the Stille Hilfe aid organization, 15 July 1958. Here, Kesselring was referring to his claim that, in October 1943, he had decided not to become involved in the deportation of Roman Jews. Whether or not this was the case, it is certain that Himmler dispatched SS men from Berlin to Rome to carry out the deportation.

296. Searle, "Revising the Myth," pp. 27f.

297. Peter Steinbach, "Widerstand und Wehrmacht," in Rolf-Dieter Müller and Hans-Erich Volkmann, ed., *Die Wehrmacht: Mythos und Realität* (Munich 1999), pp. 1150–1170, at pp.1150ff.

298. BA Koblenz, B 106/15456, dpa report dated 19 November 1953.

299. *Der Mittag*, 26 November 1953, "Expert Military Testimony."

300. See chapter 1.

301. Searle, "Revising the Myth," p. 39.

302. *Der Mittag*, 26 November 1953, "Expert Military Testimony."

303. Ibid.

304. *Süddeutsche Zeitung*, 21 November 1953, "Kesselring the Expert Witness," by Robert Borchardt. Paraphrasing a few particularly striking passages in Kesselring's testimony, the *Süddeutsche Zeitung* asked angrily: "What does he mean by saying that a 'little colonel' simply did not understand the military criminal code and, as a soldier, saw 'red'? Does one really have to be a 'fiddly lawyer behind a secure desk' to know that one cannot simply murder people with impunity, as happened in Penzberg?"

305. Writing from Mittenwald, reader Max Schollinger concluded that the generals should "finally shut up," given that they had once before got away with it, and should "disappear into the furthest corners of the country, in the knowledge that they bear an enormous share of responsibility for that criminal period," instead of "continuing today to approve of clear Nazi crimes and murders in their role as expert court witnesses." See *Süddeutsche Zeitung*, 28 November 1953, Letters to the *Süddeutsche Zeitung*, "The Generals' War Balance Sheet," by Max Schollinger, from Mittenwald. Walburg von Szily, writing from Kassel, even feared that "through such statements, General Kesselring has clumsily destroyed all the laborious work done to achieve Germany's resurgence." See *Hessische Nachrichten*, 1 December 1953, Letters, "For and Against Kesselring," by Walburg v. Szily, from Kassel. Another Kassel reader, Heinz Schütz, was the sole writer to find words of understanding—words written by a loyal follower that probably most closely approximated Kesselring's own ill-considered views: "Field Marshal Kesselring made his statements during the trial of his comrade Ohm as a soldier, and we soldiers will defend our comrade Kesselring!" See *Hessische Nachrichten*, 1 December 1953, Letters, "For and Against Kesselring," by Heinz Schütz, from Kassel.

306. Kabinettsprotokolle der Bundesregierung (Federal government cabinet minutes), ed. Friedrich P. Kahlenberg (Munich 1989), vol. 6, meeting dated 24 November 1953, p. 532.

307. *Bonner Rundschau*, 30 November 1953, "Franz-Josef Strauss Criticizes Kesselring"; *Frankfurter Rundschau*, 30 November 1953: "Strauss against Kesselring."

308. *Frankfurter Rundschau*, 30 November 1953, "Strauss against Kesselring." There had been "an obligation to restrain as quickly as possible the criminal activities of a clique intent on prolonging its existence at the people's expense."

309. *Bonner Rundschau*, 30 November 1953, "Franz-Josef Strauss Criticizes Kesselring."

310. Ibid.

311. Franz-Josef Strauss, *Die Erinnerungen* (Berlin 1989), p. 28. Kesselring's "received concept of comradeship" prevented him even tolerating sharp criticism of officers, whereas Strauss himself had still been "full of rage at the generals" who had been unable to "put an end to Hitler." I believe that Strauss got his dates wrong: he wrote of a meeting in December 1952, rather than 1953 as here. However, Strauss was only appointed a minister in October 1953. There is no record of a meeting between Strauss and Kesselring immediately following the latter's release (in 1952) either in the relevant diaries or elsewhere.

312. "Minister Strauss against Marshal Kesselring," *Demokratische Wehrpolitik* 2, no. 3 (1954): 1.

313. *Norddeutsches Echo* (KPD), 2 March 1954, "Charges Filed against Kesselring: Relatives Will Not Silently Accept His Impudence."

314. MP Karl Weishäupl, "Expertise," *Der Stahlhelm* 1 (1954): 1: "Your arrogant question regarding whether a court with lay judges would be in a position to clarify this complex matter, as well as your conclusion that the lay judges would find it very difficult to adjudicate, not to mention your egotistical remark that you are a justice fanatic, your comment that a 'soldier who can only see red will react differently from a fiddly lawyer behind a secure desk,' and your curious proposal that, at the time, skin was sold for the highest price possible—and not least your deliberate attack on the honor of decent Penzberg citizens whom you accused of high treason."

315. Ibid.

316. Ibid.

317. An abbreviated version of the letter by Weishäupl was printed in the *Süddeutsche Zeitung* on 5 December 1953, headed "Questions for Kesselring."

318. "Expertise," *Der Stahlhelm* 1 (1954): 2, open letter from Kesselring to Weishäupl, 12 December 1953. He wrote: "If even I found it upsetting to listen to witness statements, given their meagre and conditional nature, it must have been an almost unbearable burden for the lay judges to have to adjudicate in this case. As one who fought at the front until the final day, was personally familiar with the development, course and interplay of circumstances, and felt the atmosphere, I believe that my primary duty is to provide enlightenment in this regard." The *Stahlhelm* then printed an abbreviated version of Kesselring's expert testimony. In this regard, it should be noted that this involved a retrospective version, since Kesselring spoke extemporaneously in court and injected his words with the excitement peculiar to him when speaking in a courtroom. As a result, any objectionable wordings were not included in the written version. See also "Albert Kesselring Responds to Karl Weishäupl," *Münchner Merkur*, 15 January 1954.

319. "Albert Kesselring Responds to Karl Weishäupl," *Münchner Merkur*, 15 January 1954: "I felt it to be my duty, under oath, in accordance with the law applicable at the time, and after examining my own conscience and taking into account the circumstances at the

time, to voice my conclusion without regard to prevailing trends. It would not have been consistent with my duty as an expert witness to respond emotionally to the questions asked of me."

320. "Expertise," *Der Stahlhelm* 1 (1954), p. 3. The editorial office questioned "whom it would actually serve" if every opportunity continued to be taken to "denigrate soldierly attitudes and statements." The summary memo prepared by the *Stahlhelm* editorial office, known by the abbreviation HOG (ibid., "The Expert and the Babbler"), finally concluded that the trial had paid homage to the *Zeitgeist* but had not served to probe the motives leading soldiers to commit disputed acts.

321. *Die Welt*, 23 June 1954, "Kesselring on the Order to Shoot."

322. *Bild*, 23 June 1954, "The Marshal Provides the General with Cover: Kesselring as a Witness."

323. *Die Welt*, 24 June 1954, "Former General Tolsdorff Was Sentenced to Three and a Half Years in Prison."

324. *Frankfurter Rundschau*, 23 June 1954, "General Had Captain Shot"; *Bild*, 23 June 1954, "The Marshal Provides the General with Cover: Kesselring as a Witness."

325. *Frankfurter Rundschau*, 23 June 1954, "General Has Captain Shot."

326. *Die Welt*, 23 June 1954, "Kesselring on the Order to Shoot"; dpa report dated 22 June 1954, in BA Koblenz, B 106/15456.

327. *Westfälische Allgemeine*, 23 June 1954, "Kesselring: 'Resistance Was Not Senseless.'"

328. BA Koblenz, B 106/15456, press digest issued by the Verfassungsschutz, 30 September 1958.

329. Birn, "Wehrmacht und Wehrmachtangehörige," p. 1083.

330. Ibid., p. 1099.

331. BA-MA, N 422 (Röttiger)/15, affidavit by Albert Kesselring regarding the order to shoot, 12 June 1957, pagination of private papers, p. 45 (reverse).

332. Searle, *Wehrmacht Generals*, p. 247.

333. Echternkamp, "Wut," p. 1073.

334. Searle, "Revising the Myth," p. 25.

335. Searle, *Wehrmacht Generals*, p. 247.

336. Searle, "Revising the Myth," p. 33.

337. Searle, *Wehrmacht Generals*, p. 254.

338. Searle, "Revising the Myth," p. 42.

339. Ibid., pp. 38 and 41.

340. "Kesselring Speaks to Stahlhelm Members," *Der Spiegel* 37 (1954): 4.

341. "War Crimes: Brettheim—'Hang the Fellows!'" *Der Spiegel* 32 (1960): 17ff. Kesselring agreed with Simon's statement: "We believed that we could still save something if we lost the war respectably."

342. BA Koblenz, B 106/15456, Section VI A 3 to Principal Officer Dr. Schmidt, Bonn, 12 July 1954.

343. Siegfried Westphal, "Story of a Soldier's Life," *Deutsche Soldatenzeitung* (August 1954). Westphal described the war crimes trial, having himself been involved in preparing the defense concept, rather cryptically: "Following the collapse, like so many other German soldiers, he learnt to drain the cup of defeat to its dregs. At the beginning of 1947, he was brought to court as a war criminal in Venice. Here, too, he always covered for the actions of his subordinates, even if they were not directly attributable to his orders. The British court had to pay respect to the defendant as a man." Westphal's personal entanglement in those events in Italy that led to Kesselring's trial shines through in this excerpt.

344. *Demokratische Wehrpolitik Hamburg* (press information service), "Minister Strauss against Marshal Kesselring," two-page leaflet in BA Koblenz, ZSg 120, box 253 "Kesselring."

345. *Süddeutsche Zeitung*, 1 December 1953, "Strauss against Kesselring."

Conclusion: Kesselring's Trial and Release in the Context of the Rearmament Debate

1. *Neuer Mainzer Anzeiger*, 3 November 1952, "Outrage Surrounding Kesselring."

2. Alexander Preston Scotland, *Fall Kesselring—The Kesselring Case* (Bonn 1952), p. 182.

3. Wolfram Wette, *Die Wehrmacht: Feindbilder, Vernichtungskrieg, Legenden* (Darmstadt 2002), p. 223. Wette correctly pointed out that there was great interest outside Germany in promoting the image of a clean Wehrmacht. For the first time, concrete evidence to support Wette's contention has been provided in this study.

4. Alaric Searle, "Revising the Myth of a 'Clean Wehrmacht': Generals' Trials, Public Opinion, and the Dynamics of *Vergangenheitsbewältigung* in West Germany, 1948–1960," in *Bulletin of the German Historical Institute* (London) 25, no. 2 (November 2003): 46.

5. Following an inquiry by Hanns-Dietrich Ahrens, the Bundeswehr's Institute of Military History stated: "Certainly nobody would dream of including Kesselring in the history and traditions maintained by the Bundeswehr." Cited in Hanns Dietrich Ahrens, "Albert Kesselring," *Alte Kameraden* 48, no. 7–8 (July–August 2000): 8–9, at p. 8.

6. Archives of the Deutsche Montecassino Vereinigung, manuscript "Gedenkfeier zum 40. Todestag des GFM Kesselring," report by Karl-Heinz Meissner on the memorial event, private archive.

7. Ahrens, "Albert Kesselring," p. 8.

BIBLIOGRAPHY

List of Abbreviations

AA	German Foreign Office
ACS	Archivio Centrale dello Stato
AFHQ	Allied Force Headquarters
ANFIM	Assoziazione Nazionale tra le Famiglie Italiane dei Martiri
ANPI	Assoziazione Nazionale Partigiani d'Italia
ASMAE	Archivio storico-diplomatico del MAE
BA	German Federal Archives
BA-MA	German Federal Military Archives
BfZ	Bibliothek für Zeitgeschichte
CLN	Comitato di Liberazione Nazionale
DC	Democrazia Christiana
DGAP	Direzione Generale Affari Politici
FO	Foreign Office
GAP	Gruppo d'Azione Patriottico
GHQ CMF	General Headquarters Central Mediterranean Forces
HIAG	Hilfsgemeinschaft auf Gegenseitigkeit
HPFSS	Höherer Polizeiführer
IWM	Imperial War Museum
JAG	Judge Advocate General
KA	*Alte Kameraden*
MAE	Ministerio degli Affari Esteri
MGM	*Militärgeschichtliche Mitteilungen*
MGZ	*Militärgeschichtliche Zeitschrift*
NA	National Archives
OBSW	Commander-in-Chief, South-Western Command
OKW	Wehrmacht High Command
PA-AA	Politisches Archiv des Auswärtigen Amtes
PCI	Partito Comunista Italiano
PGM	Procura Generale Militare
PRO/TNA	Public Record Office, now known as the National Archives, in Kew
QFIAB	*Quellen und Forschungen aus italienischen Archiven und Bibliotheken*
RSI	Repubblica Sociale Italiana
SD	Sicherheitsdienst—Security Service
SHAEF	Supreme Headquarters Allied Expeditionary Forces
TMR	Tribunale Militare territoriale di Roma
VdK	Verband der Kriegsopfer und Hinterbliebenen

WO	War Office
ZfG	*Zeitschrift für Geschichtswissenschaft*
ZSL	Zentrale Stelle der Landesjustizverwaltung zur Verfolgung von NS-Verbrechen

Archival Sources

Archivio Centrale Dello Stato, Roma (Acs)
Presidenza del Consiglio dei Ministri
- PCM 1944–1947
- PCM 1948–1950
- PCM 1962–1964

Archivio Storico-Diplomatico Del Ministero Degli Affari Esteri, Roma (ASMAE)
- Amb. Parigi 1861–1950, b. 408
- DGAP 1946, Germania, b. 1
- DGAP 1946–1950, Germania, b. 5

Public Record Office, London (PRO)
- FO 371/51046
- FO 371/57557
- FO 371/93547
- FO 371/97986
- FO 1060/455 and 470
- PREM 8/707
- WO 204/12798
- WO 235/438 (Trial of Eberhard von Mackensen and Kurt Mältzer)
- WO 235/584 (Trial of Max Simon)
- WO 310/127 and 128
- WO 311/28

Imperial War Museum, London (IWM)
- FO 642 (Kesselring Trial Proceedings)
- PMME (Majoribanks-Egerton Papers)

Churchill College, Cambridge
- HNKY 18/2, 3, 4, 5 (Lord Maurice Hankey Papers, correspondence with Bell, Liddell Hart, Ahrens, Kesselring)

National Archives, Washington, D.C. (NA)
- RG 338, File 000.5, Box 816, Reports and Records of War Crimes Trial of Albert Kesselring, report by Captain Murphy
- XE 07 64 78, Albert Kesselring file, assessments from 1944 and 1945

Bundesarchiv Berlin-Lichterfelde
- R 43 II (Reichskanzlei holdings, Dr. Lammers, donations), Vols. 986a, 1092, 1565, 1620
- Former BDC, Research: 0.914, *Wehrmacht* folder
- Former BDC, RKK, Kesselring
- Press clipping collection, former BDC, various, *Wehrmacht*, Kesselring; Mackensen

Bundesarchiv Koblenz
- All. Proz. 21/174 (Allied trials, Laternser speech in Venice)
- B 106/15456 (intelligence service reports on Kesselring after 1952)
- B 305/397, 401, 403 (Zentrale Rechtsschutz-Stelle, Italy)

NL 1245 (August Lindner)
ZSg 120 (press clipping collection relating to Kesselring, 1949–1954)
Bundesarchiv-Militärarchiv, Freiburg
BW 9, BW 48
C-032 (study from the "Historical Division" holdings, author Albert Kesselring: "Der Krieg hinter der Front: Der Bandenkrieg")
MSg 109/1280 (Kesselring's military career)
N 318 (Friedrich Schulz Papers)
N 422 (Hans Röttiger Papers), Vol. 4
N 431 (Hans Laternser Papers), Vols. 305, 578, 680, 860, 863, 870, 876, 880, 881, 882, 886, 888, 890, 899, 931, 932, 935, 936
N 524 (Gero von Schulze-Gaevernitz Papers)
N 581 (Eberhard von Mackensen Papers), Vols. 24, 26–30
N 642 (Rudolf Aschenauer Papers), Box 3, Box 15
N 750 (Albert Kesselring Papers), Vols. 2, 3, 5, 6
N 782 (Dietrich Beelitz Papers), Vols. 2, 3, 8, 15, 20–23, 27
RH 20–10 (AOK 10), Vol. 106
RH 20–14 (AOK 14), Vols. 41, 50, 54, 121
Bayerisches Hauptstaatsarchiv–Kriegsarchiv, München (KA München)
OP 61536 (Kesselring personnel file)
Politisches Archiv des Auswärtigen Amtes, Berlin (PA-AA)
B 10 (Section 2), Vols. 2098, 2093, 2109, 2110, 2111
B 24, Bd. 261, 503 (Ref. V 4) Legal Section
Staatsarchiv Nürnberg (Nuremberg State Archives) (STA Nürnberg)
War Crimes Trials (IMT), Commission minutes, A-310, A-333
Zentrale Stelle der Landesjustizverwaltungen zur Verfolgung von NS-Verbrechen, Bundesarchiv Ludwigsburg (ZSL)
JAG 260 (Kesselring trial)
JAG 294 (Trial of Mackensen and Mältzer)
Der Bundesbeauftragte für die Unterlagen des Staatssicherheitsdienstes der Ehemaligen Deutschen Demokratischen Republik (BSTU)
HA AF Press folder, p. 120
HA AF Press folder, items prior to 1946, pp. 2, 28
HA IX Index card
HA RHE 18–66 to 22a–66, pp. 39–41
Stiftung Bundeskanzler-Adenauer-Haus, Röndorf/Bonn
I 04.03 (Adenauer visitor lists, 1952)
Archivum Monacense Societatis Jesu, Munich (AMSJ)
Sect. 47, Father Alfons Hiemer Papers
Deutschen Dienststelle für die Benachrichtigung der Nächsten Angehörigen von Gefallenen der Ehemaligen Deutschen Wehrmacht (WAST), Berlin
Research on Laternser and Spitzeder
Bundesarchiv–Zentralnachweisstelle, Aachen-Kornelimünster
Eduard Spitzeder personnel file
Hans Laternser personnel file
Bibliothek für Zeitgeschichte, Stuttgart
Sterz Collection, 59 160 A, Diary of Uffz. Heinrich Voigtel

Family Archives
Manfred Bäumler, held by Peter Bäumler, Waiblingen
Fritz Pfrommer, held by Professor Edelgard Pfister-Pfrommer, Bammental
Victor von Schweinitz, held by Yvonne v. Schweinitz, Essen
Vietinghoff-Scheel family archives, held by Lonny Hechler, Bayreuth
Private Archives
Bund deutscher Fallschirmjäger, Professor Heinz Bliss, Witzenhausen
Ordensgemeinschaft der Ritterkreuzträger des Eisernen Kreuzes e.V., Jürgen Heinze, Berlin
Private papers, Dr. Hanns-Dietrich Ahrens, Essen
School archives of the Christian-Ernestinum-Gymnasium, Bayreuth
Verband deutscher Soldaten (VdS), Bonn (partially transferred to Freiburg, BA-MA, BW 48, in the form of the Gottfried Hansen Papers)
Verband deutsches Afrikakorps, Hans-Günther Stark, Wessling
Deutsche Monte Cassino Vereinigung, Joseph Klein, Wolfsburg
Contemporary Witnesses
Dr. Hanns-Dietrich Ahrens, Essen
Dietrich Beelitz, Stuttgart
Dr. Nikolaus Kunkel, Munich
Albert Schnez, Bonn
Dr. Winfried v. Selzam, Garmisch-Partenkirchen
Heinz Trettner, Mönchengladbach
Other Interviewees
Dr. Rainer Kesselring, Berg
Alda Niemeyer, Blumenau (Brazil)
Prof. Elfriede Pfisterer-Pfrommer, Bammental
Dr. Kurt Rupprecht, Coburg
Yvonne v. Schweinitz, Essen
Dr. Wolfgang Seeger, Stuttgart
Dr. Bruce Siemon, Heidelberg
Dr. Edmund Spitzeder, Peiting
Siegfried Westphal jun., Munich

Printed Primary Sources

Detwiler, Donald S., ed. *German World War II Military Studies*, 24 vols. New York, 1971.

Foreign Relations of the United States. *Diplomatic Papers 1943*, Vol. I, General, Washington, D.C., 1963.

Hetherington, Sir Thomas, and William Chalmers, eds. *War Crimes: Report of the War Crimes Inquiry: Presented to Parliament by the Secretary of State for the Home Department by Command of Her Majesty*. July 1989.

Heuss, Theodor. "Pensionen für Offiziere?" (paper dated 1948). In *Theodor Heuss, Politiker und Publizist: Aufsätze und Reden*, annotated by Martin Vogt. Tübingen, 1984, 346–349.

———. "Soldatentum in unserer Zeit" (speech made on March 12th 1959). In *Theodor Heuss, Politiker und Publizist: Aufsätze und Reden*; annotated by Martin Vogt. Tübingen, 1984, 488–499.

Hubatsch Walther, ed. *Hitlers Weisungen für die Kriegführung: Dokumente des Oberkommandos der Wehrmacht*. Koblenz, 1983.

——, comp. "Kriegstagebuch des Oberkommandos der Wehrmacht (KTB des OKW)." *War Journal of the Wehrmacht High Command, Wehrmachtführungsstab, Vol. III: January 1st to December 31st 1943*. Frankfurt/Main, 1963.

Ipsen, Knut. *Völkerrecht*. Munich, 1990.

"Kriegstagebuch der Seekriegsleitung (KTB der SKL)." *War Journal of the Naval War Command, 1939–1945, Part A, Vol 53. January, 1944*, ed. Werner Rahn and Gerhard Schreiber with the assistance of Hansjoseph Maierhöfer. Berlin, 1995.

Küsters, Hanns Jürgen, ed. *Adenauer: Teegespräche 1950–1954*. Berlin, 1984.

Lauterpacht, Hersh, and Lassa Oppenheim. *International Law*. London, 1948.

Law Reports of Trials of War Criminals, The United Nations War Crimes Commission, Vol. I, London, HMSO, 1949, Cases No. 2 (Dostler), No. 43 (Mackensen/Mältzer), and No. 44 (Kesselring).

Middelhauve, Friedrich. "Das Deutsche Programm." In *fdk (freie demokratische korrespondenz)*, Year 3, 29 July 1952.

Der Prozess gegen die Hauptkriegsverbrecher vor dem Internationalen Militärgerichtshof (IMT). Nürnberg, 14.11.1945–01.10.1946, 41 vols. Nuremberg, 1947.

Schubert, Klaus v., ed. *Sicherheitspolitik der Bundesrepublik Deutschland: Dokumentation 1945–1977*. 2 vols. Cologne, 1978–1979.

Schwinge, Erich. *Militärstrafgesetzbuch*. Berlin, 1936.

Seckendorf, Martin, ed. "Die Okkupationspolitik des deutschen Faschismus in Jugoslawien, Griechenland, Albanien, Italien und Ungarn (1941–1945)." In *Dokumentensammlung Europa unterm Hakenkreuz 1938–1945*. 8 vols. Vol. 6. Berlin/Heidelberg, 1992.

Die Sowjetunion auf internationalen Konferenzen während des Grossen Vaterländischen Krieges 1941 bis 1945, Vol. 1, Die Moskauer Konferenz der Aussenminister der UdSSR, der USA und Grossbritanniens (October 19th–30th 1943). Moskau/Berlin, 1988.

Memoirs

Ahrens, Hanns-Dietrich. *Demontage: Nachkriegspolitik der Alliierten*. Munich, 1982.

Andrus, Burton. *I Was the Nuremberg Jailer*. New York, 1969.

Below, Nicolaus V. *Als Hitlers Adjutant 1937–45*. Mainz, 1980.

Bentivegna, Rosario. *Achtung, Banditen! Roma 1944*. Milan, 1983.

Blankenhorn, Herbert. *Verständnis und Verständigung: Blätter eines politischen Tagebuchs 1949–1979*. Frankfurt/Main, 1980.

Bonomi, Ivanoe. *Diario di un anno: 2 giugnio 1943–10 giugnio 1944*. Milan, 1947.

Dibelius, Otto. *Ein Christ ist immer im Dienst: Erlebnisse und Erfahrungen in einer Zeitenwende*. Stuttgart, 1961.

Dohna-Schlobitten, Alexander Fürst zu. *Erinnerungen eines alten Ostpreussen*. Berlin, 1999.

Dollmann, Eugen. *Dolmetscher der Diktatoren*. Bayreuth, 1963.

——. *Roma nazista*. Milan, 1951.

Dulles, Allan. *Verschwörung in Deutschland*. Kassel, 1949.

Dulles, Allan, and Gero von Gaevernitz. *Unternehmen sunrise—Die geheime Geschichte des Kriegsendes in Italien*. Düsseldorf, 1967.

Gersdorff, Rudolf-Christoph Frhr. von. *Soldat im Untergang*. Frankfurt/Main, 1977.

Gollancz, Victor. *Stimme aus dem Chaos*. Nuremberg, 1948.

Jodl, Luise. *Jenseits des Endes: Leben und Sterben des Generalobersten Alfred Jodl*. Vienna, 1976.

Kesselring, Albert. *Gedanken zum Zweiten Weltkrieg*. Bonn, 1955.

——. *Soldat bis zum letzten Tag*. Bonn, 1953.
Kirkpatrick, Ivone. *The Inner Circle*. London, 1959.
Kobe, Gerd. *Der Wind kam vom Westen: Ein fast schon historischer Bericht*. Würzburg, 1974.
Laternser, Hans. *Verteidigung deutscher Soldaten: Plädoyers vor alliierten Gerichten*. Bonn, 1950.
Libby, Frederick. *To End War: The Story of the National Council for Prevention of War*. New York, 1969.
Mackensen, Eberhard von. *Über den Tag hinaus: Gedichte*. Wuppertal, 1981.
Maizière, Ulrich de. *In der Pflicht: Lebensbericht eines deutschen Soldaten im 20. Jahrhundert*. Herford/Bonn, 1989.
Moellhausen, Eitel Friedrich. *Die gebrochene Achse*. Alfeld, 1949.
Plehwe, Friedrich Karl von. *Schicksalsstunden in Rom: Ende eines Bündnisses*. Berlin, 1967.
Portelli, Allessandro. *L'ordine è già stato eseguito*. Rome, 1999.
Rahn, Rudolf. *Ruheloses Leben. Aufzeichnungen und Erinnerungen*. Düsseldorf, 1949.
Schlabrendorff, Fabian von. *Begegnungen in fünf Jahrzehnten*. Tübingen, 1979.
Schwinge, Erich. *Bilanz der Kriegsgeneration: Ein Beitrag zur Geschichte unserer Zeit*. Marburg, 1980.
——. *Verfälschung und Wahrheit: Das Bild der Wehrmachtgerichtsbarkeit*. Tübingen, 1988.
Schwinge, Erich, and Otto Peter Schwelling. *Die deutsche Militärjustiz in der Zeit des Nationalsozialismus*. Marburg, 1977.
Scotland, Alexander Preston. *Der Fall Kesselring—The Kesselring Case*. Bonn, 1952.
Speer, Albert. *Erinnerungen*. Frankfurt, 1969.
Speidel, Hans. *Aus unserer Zeit: Erinnerungen*. Berlin, 1977.
Strauss, Franz Josef. *Die Erinnerungen*. Berlin, 1989.
Theil, Edmund. *Kampf um Italien: Von Sizilien bis Tirol, 1943–1945*. Munich, 1983.
Utley, Freda. *The High Cost of Vengeance*. Chicago, 1949.
Vietinghoff-Scheel, Heinrich von. *La fine della Guerra in Italia: Appunti dell'ultimo comandante in capo tedesco in Italia (Recoaro, ottobre 1944–aprile 1945), a cura di Peter Hattenkofer, Alessandro Massignani e Maurizio Dal Lago*. Valdagno, 1997.
Wessel, Wilhelm. *Umkämpftes römisches Land: Das Erlebnisbuch vom Kriege in Italien, das Erlebnisbuch aus den Kämpfen um Cassino und Nettuno*. N.p., 1944.
Westphal, Siegfried. *Der deutsche Generalstab auf der Anklagebank: Nuremberg 1945–1948*. Mainz, 1978.
——. *Erinnerungen*. Mainz, 1975.
Wiesenthal, Simon. *Recht, nicht Rache: Erinnerungen*. Frankfurt/Main, 1988.

Unpublished Memoirs

Halse, Richard. *40 Years On*. Unpublished memoirs, typescript, 96 pages, ca. 1963.
Pfrommer, Friedrich. *Erlebnisbericht über die Vorgänge um die Kapitulation in Norditalien, 30.04.–02.05.1945*, ca. 1960.

Secondary Sources

Abelshauser, Werner. "Wirtschaft und Rüstung in den fünfziger Jahren." In *Anfänge westdeutscher Sicherheitspolitik, Vol. 4, Wirtschaft und Rüstung, Souveränität und Sicherheit*, ed. idem. Munich, 1997, 1–186.

Absolon, Rudolf. *Die Wehrmacht im Dritten Reich*. Boppard, 1995.
Agarossi, Elena, and Bradley Smith. *Unternehmen Sonnenaufgang: Das Kriegsende in Italien*. Cologne, 1981.
Ahrens, Hanns-Dietrich. "Albert Kesselring." *KA*, Nr. 7/8, Year 48 Vol. 552 (July/August 2000): 8–9.
Algardi, Zara. *Processo ai fascisti*. Rome, 1973.
Amendola, Giorgio. *Lettere a Milano*. Rome, 1973.
Andrae, Friedrich. *Auch gegen Frauen und Kinder: Der Krieg der deutschen Wehrmacht gegen die Zivilbevölkerung in Italien, 1943–1945*. Munich, 1995.
Appleman, John Alan. *Military Tribunals and International Crimes*. Indianapolis, 1954.
Aschenauer, Rudolf. *Der Fall Herbert Kappler: Ein Plädoyer für Recht, Wahrheit und Verstehen*. Munich, 1967.
Aspekte der deutschen Wiederbewaffnung bis 1955. Boppard, 1975.
Azzola, Axel Christian. *Die Diskussion um die Aufrüstung der BRD im Unterhaus und in der Presse Grossbritanniens: November 1949–Juli 1952*. Meisenheim am Glan, 1971.
Bald, Detlef. "Alte Kameraden: Offizierskader in der Bundeswehr." In *Willensmenschen: Über deutsche Offiziere*, ed. Ursula Breymayer. Frankfurt, 1999, 50–64.
———. *Militär und Gesellschaft 1945–1990: Die Bundeswehr der Bonner Republik*. Baden-Baden, 1994.
Baring, Arnulf. *Aussenpolitik in Adenauers Kanzlerdemokratie: Bonns Beitrag zur Europäischen Verteidigungsgemeinschaft*. Munich/Vienna, 1969.
Bartov, Omer. *Hitlers Wehrmacht: Soldaten, Fanatismus und die Brutalisierung des Krieges*. Hamburg, 1995.
Battaglia, Roberto. *Storia della Resistenza italiana*. Torino, 1979.
Battaglia, Roberto, and Giuseppe Garritano. *Der italienische Widerstandskampf 1943 bis 1945*. East Berlin, 1970.
Battini, Michele. *Peccati di Memoria: La mancata Norimberga italiana*. Rome, 2003.
Battini, Michele, and Paolo Pezzino. *Guerra ai civili: Occupazione tedesca e politica del massacro, Toscana 1944*. Venice, 1997.
Ben Arie, Katriel. *Die Schlacht bei Monte Cassino 1944*. Freiburg, 1985.
Bertoldi, Silvio. *Salò: Vita e morte della RSI*. Milan, 1976.
Bidwell, Shelford. "Kesselring." In *Hitler's Generals*, ed. Corelli Barnett. London, 1989, 265–289.
Birn, Ruth Bettina. "Wehrmacht und Wehrmachtangehörige in den deutschen Nachkriegsprozessen." In *Die Wehrmacht: Mythos und Realität*, ed. Rolf-Dieter Müller and Hans-Erich Volkmann. Munich 1999, 1081–1099.
Blet, Pierre. *Pie XII et la Seconde Guerre Mondiale d'après les archives du Vatican*. Paris, 1997.
Bloxham, Donald. *Genocide on Trial: War Crime Trials and the Formation of Holocaust History and Memory*. Oxford, 2001.
———. "Punishing German Soldiers During the Cold War: The Case of Erich von Manstein." *Patterns of Prejudice* 33, 4 (1999): 25–45.
Bocca, Giorgio. *La Repubblica di Mussolini*. Milan, 1994.
———. *Storia dell' Italia partigiana, Settembre 1943–Maggio 1945*. Bari, 1966.
Boog, Horst. "Der anglo-amerikanische strategische Luftkrieg über Europa und die deutsche Luftverteidigung." In *Das deutsche Reich und der Zweite Weltkrieg, Vol. 6, Der Globale Krieg: Die Ausweitung zum Weltkrieg und der Wechsel der Initiative 1941–1943*, ed. idem, Werner Rahn, Reinhard Stumpf, and Bernd Wegner. Stuttgart, 1990, 429–565.

———. *Die deutsche Luftwaffenführung 1935–1945: Führungsprobleme, Spitzengliederung, Generalstabsausbildung.* Munich, 1982.

———. "Führungsdenken in der Luftwaffe im Zweiten Weltkrieg." In *Vorträge zur Militärgeschichte,* Vol. 9. Herford, 1988, 183–206.

———, ed. *Luftkriegführung im Zweiten Weltkrieg: Ein internationaler Vergleich.* Bonn, 1993.

Borgert, Heinz-Ludger, Walter Stürm, and Norbert Wiggershaus. *Dienstgruppen und westdeutscher Verteidigungsbeitrag: Vorüberlegungen zur Bewaffnung der Bundesrepublik Deutschland.* Boppard, 1982.

Botjer, George F. *Sideshow War: The Italian Campaign, 1943–1945.* College Station, TX, 1996.

Bower, Tom. *Blind Eye to Murder: Britain, America and the Purging of Nazi Germany—A Pledge Betrayed.* London, 1997.

Bradley, Dermot, ed. *Die Generale des Heeres, 1921–1945.* Osnabrück, 1999.

Breit, Gotthard. *Das Staats- und Gesellschaftsbild deutscher Generale beider Weltkriege im Spiegel ihrer Memoiren.* Boppard, 1973.

Brill, Heinz. *Bogislaw von Bonin im Spannungsfeld zwischen Wiederbewaffnung–Westintegration–Wiedervereinigung: Ein Beitrag zur Entstehungsgeschichte der Bundeswehr 1952–1955.* Baden-Baden, 1987.

Brochhagen, Ulrich. *Nach Nürnberg: Vergangenheitsbewältigung und Westintegration in der Ära Adenauer.* Hamburg, 1994.

Broszat, Martin, Klaus Dietmar Henke, and Hans Woller, eds. *Von Stalingrad zur Währungsreform: Zur Sozialgeschichte des Umbruchs in Deutschland.* Munich, 1988.

Buchheit, Gert. *Soldatentum und Rebellion: Die Tragödie der deutschen Wehrmacht.* Rastatt, 1961.

Buchstab, Günter. "Die Nürnberger Prozesse und der 'Heidelberger Kreis' (1949–1955)." In *Macht und Zeitkritik: Festschrift für Hans-Peter Schwarz zum 65. Geburtstag,* ed. Peter Weilmann, Hanns Jürgen Küsters, and idem. Paderborn, 1999, 61–74.

Burdick, Charles B. "Deutschland und die Entwicklung der amtlichen amerikanischen Militärgeschichtsforschung (1920–1960)." In *Deutschland zwischen Krieg und Frieden: Beiträge zur Politik und Kultur im 20. Jahrhundert, Festschrift für Hans-Adolf Jacobsen,* ed. Karl Dietrich Bracher. Düsseldorf, 1991, 99–107.

———. "Vom Schwert zur Feder: Deutsche Kriegsgefangene im Dienst der Vorbereitung der amerikanischen Kriegsgeschichtsschreibung über den zweiten Weltkrieg: Die organisatorische Entwicklung der Operational History (German) Section." *MGM* 10 (1971): 69–80.

Buschmann, Nikolaus, and Horst Carl. *Die Erfahrung des Krieges: Erfahrungsgeschichtliche Perspektiven von der Französischen Revolution bis zum Zweiten Weltkrieg.* Paderborn, 2001.

Colotti, Enzo, and Tristano Matta. "Rappresaglie, stragi, eccidi." In *Dizionario della Resistenza, Storia e geografia della liberazione, Band eins,* ed. idem, R. Sandri, and F. Sassi. Turin, 2000, 254–267.

Contini, Giovanni. *La memoria divisa.* Milan, 1997.

Cornwell, John. *Pius XII. Der Papst, der geschwiegen hat.* Munich, 1999.

Corum, James S. "Stärken und Schwächen der Luftwaffe: Führungsqualitäten und Führung im Zweiten Weltkrieg." In *Die Wehrmacht: Mythos und Realität,* ed. Rolf-Dieter Müller and Hans-Erich Volkmann. Munich, 1999, 283–306.

Deakin, Frederick William. *The Brutal Friendship: Hitler, Mussolini and the Fall of Italian Fascism*. London, 1962.

DeFelice, Renzo. *Breve Storia del Fascismo*. Milan, 2000.

———. *Mussolini L'Alleato*. Rome, 1995.

Deighton, Annie. *The Impossible Peace: Britain, the Division of Germany and the Origins of the Cold War*. Oxford, 1990.

Delzell, Charles F., ed. *Mediterranean Fascism 1919–1945*. New York, 1970.

———. *Mussolini's Enemies: The Italian Anti-Fascist Resistance*. Princeton, N.J., 1961.

Dickson, Paul D., ed. *The Beginning of the End*. Waterloo, 1995.

Diehl, James M. *The Thanks of the Fatherland: German Veterans after the Second World War*. London/Chapel Hill, 1993.

Dirks, Carl, and Karl-Heinz Janssen. *Der Krieg der Generäle: Hitler als Werkzeug der Wehrmacht*. Berlin, 1999.

Dirks, Christian. "Selekteure als Lebensretter: Die Verteidigungsstrategie des Rechtsanwalts Dr. Hans Laternser." In *"Gerichtstag halten über uns selbst": Geschichte und Wirkung des ersten Frankfurter Auschwitz-Prozesses*, ed. Irmtrud Wojak. Frankfurt, 2001, 163–192.

Doering-Manteuffel, Anselm. *Die Bundesrepublik Deutschland in der Ära Adenauer: Aussenpolitik und innere Entwicklung 1949–1963*. Darmstadt, 1983.

Dower, J. W. *War without Mercy: Race and Power in the Pacific War*. New York, 1993.

Dülfer, Jost. "Regeln im Krieg? Kriegsverbrechen und die Haager Friedenskonferenzen." In *Kriegsverbrechen im 20. Jahrhundert*, ed. Wolfram Wette and Gerd R. Ueberschär. Darmstadt, 2001, 35–49.

Düsterberg, Rolf. *Soldat und Kriegserlebnis: Deutsche militärische Erinnerungsliteratur (1945–1961) zum Zweiten Weltkrieg: Motive, Begriffe, Wertungen*. Paderborn, 2000.

Echternkamp, Jörg. "Mit dem Krieg seinen Frieden schliessen—Wehrmacht und Weltkrieg in der Veteranenkultur 1945–1960." In *Von der Kriegskultur zur Friedenskultur? Zum Mentalitätswandel in Deutschland seit 1945*, ed. Thomas Kühne. Münster, 2000, 78–93.

———. "Wut auf die Wehrmacht? Vom Bild der deutschen Soldaten in der unmittelbaren Nachkriegszeit." In *Die Wehrmacht: Mythos und Realität*, ed. Rolf-Dieter Müller and Hans-Erich Volkmann. Munich, 1999, 1058–1080.

Ehlert, Hans. "Innenpolitische Auseinandersetzungen um die Pariser Verträge und die Wehrverfassung 1954 bis 1956." In *Anfänge westdeutscher Sicherheitspolitik 1945–1956*, Vol. 3, *Die NATO-Option*. Munich, 1993, 235–560.

Engelmann, Bernd. *Wie wir wurden, was wir sind: Von der bedingungslosen Kapitulation bis zur unbedingten Wiederbewaffnung*. Munich, 1980.

Engelmann, Joachim, and Horst Scheibert, eds. *Deutsche Artillerie 1934–1945*. Limburg, 1974.

Engert, Jürgen. *Soldaten für Hitler, Begleitband zur gleichnamigen ARD-Sendereihe*. Berlin, 1998.

Erdmann, Karl Dietrich. *Das Ende des Reiches und die Neubildung deutscher Staaten*. Munich, 1984.

Fischer, Alexander, ed. *Wiederbewaffnung in Deutschland nach 1945: Referate einer Tagung der Fachgruppe Geschichtswissenschaft der Gesellschaft für Deutschlandforschung, Vol. 27–29: Febr. 1984 in Vlotho/Weser*. Berlin, 1986.

Focardi, Filippo. "La questione della punizione dei Criminali di Guerra in Italia." QFIAB 80 (2000): 543–624.

Foerster, Roland G. "Innenpolitische Aspekte der Sicherheit Westdeutschlands 1947–1950." In *Anfänge westdeutscher Sicherheitspolitik 1945–1956, Vol. 1, Von der Kapitulation bis zum Pleven-Plan, Part 4,* ed. Roland G. Foerster et al. Munich, 1982, 403–576.

Franzinelli, Mimmo. *Le Stragi Nascoste: L'armadio della vergogna: Impunità e rimzione dei crimini di guerra nazifascisti 1943–2001*. Milan, 2002.

Frei, Norbert. *Karrieren im Zwielicht: Hitlers Eliten nach 1945*. Frankfurt, 2001.

———. *Vergangenheitspolitik: Die Anfänge der Bundesrepublik und die NS-Vergangenheit*. Munich, 1996.

Frei, Norbert, Dirk van Laak, and Michael Stolleis, eds. *Geschichte vor Gericht: Historiker, Richter und die Suche nach Gerechtigkeit*. Munich, 2000.

Friedrich, Jörg. *Das Gesetz des Krieges. Das deutsche Heer in Russland 1941 bis 1945. Der Prozess gegen das Oberkommando der Wehrmacht*. Munich, 1996.

———. *Die kalte Amnestie: NS-Täter in der Bundesrepublik*. Frankfurt/Main, 1994.

———. *Freispruch für die Nazi-Justiz: Die Urteile gegen NS-Richter*. Berlin, 1998.

Garbe, Detlef. "In jedem Einzelfall . . . bis zur Todesstrafe." In *Der Militärstrafrechtler Erich Schwinge: Ein deutsches Juristenleben*. Hamburg, 1989.

Gentile, Carlo. "'Politische Soldaten.' Die 16. SS-Panzer-Grenadier-Division 'Reichsführer-SS' in Italien." *QFIAB* 81 (2001): 529–561.

Gerstenberger, Friedrich. "Strategische Erinnerungen: Die Memoiren deutscher Offiziere." In *Vernichtungskrieg: Verbrechen der Wehrmacht 1941–1944*, ed. Hannes Heer and Klaus Naumann. Hamburg, 1995, 620–633.

Gessler, Otto. *Reichswehrpolitik in der Weimarer Zeit*. Stuttgart, 1958.

Geyer, Michael. "Der kalte Krieg, die Deutschen und die Angst: Die westdeutsche Opposition gegen Wiederbewaffnung und Kernwaffen." In *Nachkrieg in Deutschland*, ed. Klaus Naumann. Hamburg, 2001, 267–318.

Giustolisi, Franco. "Gli scheletri dell'Armadio." *Micromega* 1 (2000): 345–355.

Glueck, Sheldon. *The Nuremberg Trial and Aggressive War*. New York, 1946.

Goetz, Helmut. "Das Attentat in Rom und die Fosse Ardeatine (1944): Eine vorläufige Bilanz." *Innsbrucker Historische Studien* 6 (1983): 161–178.

Graham, Dominick, and Shelford Bidwell. *Coalitions, Politicians and Generals*. London, 1993.

Greiner, Christian. "'Operational History (German) Section' und 'Naval Historical Team': Deutsches militärstrategisches Denken im Dienst der amerikanischen Streitkräfte von 1946 bis 1950." In *Militärgeschichte: Probleme, Thesen, Wege*, ed. Manfred Messerschmidt. Stuttgart, 1982, 409–435.

Grenfell, Russell. *Bedingungsloser Hass? Die deutsche Kriegsschuld und Europas Zukunft*. Tübingen, 1974.

Guske, Claus. *Das politische Denken des Generals von Seeckt: Ein Beitrag zur Diskussion des Verhältnisses Seeckt–Reichswehr–Republik*. Berlin, 1970.

Hammermann, Gabriele. *Zwangsarbeit für den "Verbündeten": Die Arbeits- und Lebensbedingungen der italienischen Militärinternierten in Deutschland 1943–1945*. Tübingen, 2002.

Hankel, Gerd. "Deutsche Kriegsverbrechen des Weltkriegs 1914–18 vor deutschen Gerichten." In *Krigsverbrechen im 20. Jahrhundert*, ed. Wolfram Wette and Gerd R. Ueberschär. Darmstadt, 2001, 85–98.

———. *Die Leipziger Prozesse: Deutsche Kriegsverbrechen und ihre strafrechtliche Verfolgung nach dem ersten Weltkrieg*. Hamburg, 2003.

Hankey, Lord Maurice. *Politics, Trials and Errors*. Oxford, 1950.

Hattenkofer, Peter. "Das Kriegsende in Italien und seine historische Verarbeitung: Anmerkungen zu Kesselring v. Vietinghoff und Röttiger." In *La fine della guerra in Italia*, ed. idem, Alessandro Massignani, and Maurizio Dal Lago Valdagno, 1997, 133–152.

Heer, Hannes, and Klaus Naumann, eds. *Vernichtungskrieg: Verbrechen der Wehrmacht 1941–1945*. Hamburg, 1995.

Hein, Susanne. "Der Fall Priebke und die italienische Strafjustiz." In *Deutsche Richter-Zeitung* (December 1996): 476–484.

Heinemann, Winfried. "1956 als das Krisenjahr der NATO." In *Das internationale Krisenjahr 1956: Polen, Ungarn, Suez*, ed. idem and Norbert Wiggershaus. Munich, 1999, 615–637.

Henke, Klaus-Dietmar. "Die Trennung vom Nationalsozialismus: Selbstzerstörung, politische Säuberung, 'Entnazifizierung,' Strafverfolgung." In *Politische Säuberung in Europa: Die Abrechnung mit Faschismus und Kollaboration nach dem Zweiten Weltkrieg*, ed. idem and Hans Woller. Munich, 1991, 21–83.

Herbert, Ulrich. *Best: Biographische Studien über Radikalismus, Weltanschauung und Vernunft 1903–1989*. Bonn, 1996.

Herbst, Ludolf. *Option für den Westen: Vom Marshalplan bis zum deutsch-französischen Vertrag*. Munich, 1989.

Herde, Peter. "Albert Kesselring (1885–1960)." *Fränkische Lebensbilder*, Vol. 18, *Neustadt an der Aisch* (2000): 295–314.

———. "Wolfgang Hagemann als Zeitzeuge und Zeuge im Kesselring-Prozess (25 April 1947)." In *Italia et Germania: Liber amicorum Arnold Esch*, ed. Hagen Keller, Werner Paravicini, and Wolfgang Schieder. Tübingen, 2001, 51–112.

Herde, Robert. *Command Responsibility: Die Verfolgung der "Zweiten Garde" deutscher und japanischer Generäle im alliierten Prozessprogramm nach dem Zweiten Weltkrieg*. Baden-Baden, 2001.

Heuer, Gerd. "Albert Kesselring: Luftflottenchef und Oberbefehlshaber an den grossen Fronten–Höchste Kommandostellen bis zum letzten Kriegstag." In *Die deutschen Generalfeldmarschälle und Grossadmirale 1939–1945*, ed. idem. Rastatt, 1988, 55–59.

Hildebrand, Karl F. *Die Generäle der deutschen Luftwaffe 1935–1945*. Osnabrück, 1991.

Hoffman, J. H. "German Field Marshals as War Criminals? A British Embarassment," *Journal of Contemporary History* 23 (1988): 17–35.

Höfner, Karlheinz. *Die Aufrüstung Westdeutschlands: Willensbildung, Entscheidungsprozesse und Spielräume westdeutscher Politik 1945 bis 1950*. Munich, 1990.

Holden Reid, Brian. *J. F. C. Fuller: Military Thinker*. London, 1987, 195–216.

Horowitz, David A. *Beyond Left and Right: Insurgency and the Establishment*. Illinois, 1997.

Irving, David. *Die Tragödie der deutschen Luftwaffe: Aus den Akten und Erinnerungen von Feldmarschall Milch*. Frankfurt/Main, 1970.

Jesse, Eckhard. "'Vergangenheitsbewältigung' in der Bundesrepublik Deutschland." *Der Staat* 26 (1987): 539–565.

Jung, Susanne. *Die Rechtsprobleme der Nürnberger Prozesse, dargestellt am Verfahren gegen Friedrich Flick*. Tübingen, 1992.

Kämmerer, Jörn Axel. "Kriegsrepressalie oder Kriegsverbrechen? Zur rechtlichen Beurteilung der Massenexekutionen von Zivilisten durch die deutsche Besatzungsmacht im Zweiten Weltkrieg." *Archiv des Völkerrechts* 37 (1999): 283–317.

Katz, Robert. *Fatal Silence: The Pope, the Resistance and the German Occupation of Rome*. London, 2003.

———. *Mord in Rom*. Munich, 1968.

Kettenacker, Lothar. "Der britische Rahmenplan für die Besetzung Deutschlands." In *Ende des Dritten Reiches–Ende des Zweiten Weltkriegs: Eine perspektivische Rückschau*, ed. Hans Erich Volkmann. Munich, 1995, 51–74.

———. "Die Behandlung der Kriegsverbrecher als anglo-amerikanisches Rechtsproblem." In *Der Nationalsozialismus vor Gericht: Die alliierten Prozesse gegen Kriegsverbrecher und Soldaten 1943–1952*, ed. Gerd R. Ueberschär. Frankfurt/Main, 1999, 17–31.

Klessmann, Christoph. *Die doppelte Staatsgründung: Deutsche Geschichte 1945–1955*. Bonn, 1982.

Klinkhammer, Lutz. "Der Partisanenkrieg der Wehrmacht 1941–1944." In *Die Wehrmacht: Mythos und Realität*, ed. Rolf-Dieter Müller and Hans-Erich Volkmann. Munich, 1999, 815–836.

———. "Der *Resistenza*-Mythos und Italiens faschistische Vergangenheit." In *Sieger und Besiegte: Materielle und ideelle Neuorientierung nach 1945*, ed. Holger Afflerbach. Tübingen, 1997, 119–139.

———. "Die Abteilung 'Kunstschutz' der deutschen Militärverwaltung in Italien 1943–1945." *QFIAB* 72 (1992): 483–549.

———. "Grundlinien nationalsozialistischer Besatzungspolitik in Frankreich, Jugoslawien und Italien." In *Faschismus und Faschismen im Vergleich: Wolfgang Schieder zum 60. Geburtstag*, ed. Christof Dipper, Rainer Hudemann, and Jens Petersen. Cologne, 1998, 183–213.

———. *Stragi naziste in Italia*. Rome, 1997.

———. *Zwischen Bündnis und Besatzung: Das nationalsozialistische Deutschland und die Republik von Salò 1943–1945*. Tübingen, 1993.

Kranzbühler, Otto. "Wert und Unwert historischer Strafprozesse–erörtert am Nürnberger Beispiel." In *Möglichkeiten und Grenzen für die Bewältigung von historischer und politischer Schuld in Strafprozessen*, ed. Karl Foster. Würzburg, 1962, 15–36.

Kraus, Herbert. "Karl Dönitz und das Ende des 'Dritten Reiches.'" In *Ende des Dritten Reiches–Ende des Zweiten Weltkriegs: Eine perspektivische Rückschau*, ed. Hans-Erich Volkmann. Munich, 1995, 1–24.

Krausnick, Helmut, and Hans-Heinrich Wilhelm. *Die Truppe des Weltanschauungskrieges: Die Einsatzgruppen der Sicherheitspolizei und des SD 1938–1940*. Stuttgart, 1978.

Krautkrämer, Elmar. "Generalfeldmarschall Albert Kesselring." In *Hitlers militärische Elite, Vol. 1, Von den Anfängen des Regimes bis Kriegsbeginn*, ed. Gerd. R. Ueberschär. Darmstadt, 1998, 121–129.

Kreis, Georg. "Das Kriegsende in Norditalien 1945." *Schweizer Monatshefte* 65, 6 (1985): 507–521.

Krieger, Wolfgang, ed. *Adenauer und die Wiederbewaffnung*. Bonn, 2000.

———. "Die amerikanische Deutschlandplanung: Hypotheken und Chancen für einen Neuanfang." In *Ende des Dritten Reichs–Ende des Zweiten Weltkriegs: Eine perspektivische Rückschau*, ed. Hans-Erich Volkmann. Munich, 1995, 25–50.

Kroener, Bernhard R. "Strukturelle Veränderungen in der militärischen Gesellschaft des Dritten Reiches." In *Nationalsozialismus und Modernisierung*, ed. Michael Prinz and Rainer Zitelmann. Darmstadt, 1991, 267–296.

Krüger, Dieter. *Das Amt Blank: Die schwierige Gründung des Bundesministeriums für Verteidigung*. Freiburg, 1993.

Kubin, Ernst. *Raub oder Schutz? Der deutsche militärische Kunstschutz in Italien*. Graz, 1994.

Kuby, Erich. *Verrat auf Deutsch: Wie das deutsche Reich Italien ruinierte*. Hamburg, 1982.

Kühne, Thomas. "Der nationalsozialistische Vernichtungskrieg und die 'ganz normalen' Deutschen: Forschungsprobleme und Forschungstendenzen der Gesellschaftsgeschichte des Zweiten Weltkriegs, Erster Teil." *Archiv für Sozialgeschichte* 39 (1999): 580–663.

———. "Die Viktimisierungsfalle: Wehrmachtverbrechen, Geschichtswissenschaft und symbolische Ordnung des Militärs." In *Der Krieg in der Nachkriegszeit: Der Zweite Weltkrieg in Politik und Gesellschaft der Bundesrepublik*, ed. Michael Greven and Oliver von Wrochem. Opladen, 2000, 183–196.

———. "Hitlers Soldaten und der Mythos der Kameradschaft." *Archiv für Sozialgeschichte* 38 (1998): 165–189.

———. "Kameradschaft—'Das Beste im Leben des Mannes': Die deutschen Soldaten des Zweiten Weltkriegs in erfahrungs- und geschlechtergeschichtlicher Perspektive." *Geschichte und Gesellschaft* 22, 4 (1996): 504–529.

———. "Zwischen Vernichtungskrieg und Freizeitgesellschaft: Die Veteranenkultur in Deutschland (1945–1995)." In *Nachkrieg in Deutschland*, ed. Klaus Naumann. Hamburg, 2001, 90–113.

Kurowski, Franz. *Generalfeldmarschall Albert Kesselring: Oberbefehlshaber an allen Fronten*. Berg am See, 1985.

Kutz, Martin. "Militär und Gesellschaft im Deutschland der Nachkriegszeit (1946–1995)." In *Militär und Gesellschaft im 19. und 20. Jahrhundert*, ed. Ute Frevert. Stuttgart, 1997, 277–313.

Lamb, Richard. *War in Italy 1943–1945: A Brutal Story*. New York, 1994.

Lang, Jochen von. *Der Adjutant: Karl Wolff: Der Mann zwischen Hitler und Himmler*. Munich, 1985.

Large, D. Clay. "Reckoning without the Past: The HIAG of the Waffen-SS and the Politics of Rehabilitation in the Bonn Republic, 1950–1961." *Journal of Modern History* 59 (1987): 79–113.

Lepre, Aurelio. *La Storia della repubblica di Mussolini: Salò: il tempo dell'odio e della violenza*. Milan, 1999.

Leszl, Walter. Priebke. *Anatomia di un processo*. Rome, 1997.

Lewis, Sam L. "Albert Kesselring—Der Soldat als Manager." In *Die Militärelite des Dritten Reichs: 27 biographische Skizzen*, ed. Ronald Smelser and Enrico Syring. Berlin, 1995, 270–287.

Liddell Hart, B. H., ed. *The Rommel Papers: With the Assistance of Lucie-Marie Rommel, Manfred Rommel and General Fritz Beyerlein*. London, 1953.

Liddell Hart, Basil. *The Other Side of the Hill: Germany's Generals, Their Rise and Fall, with Their Own Account of Military Events, 1939–1945*. London, 1948.

Lingen, Kerstin von. "Konstruktion von Kriegserinnerung: Der Prozess gegen Generalfeldmarschall Albert Kesselring vor einem britischen Militärgericht in Venedig (1947) und das Bild vom Krieg in Italien." *MGZ* 59, 2 (2000): 435–450.

Lockenour, Jay. *Soldiers as Citizens: Former Wehrmacht Officers in the Federal Republic of Germany, 1945–1955*. Lincoln, NE, 1995.

Loth, Wilfried. *Die Teilung der Welt: Geschichte des Kalten Krieges 1941–1955*. Munich, 1980.

Macksey, Kenneth. *Kesselring: The Making of the Luftwaffe*. London, 1978.

Maguire, Peter. *Law and War: An American Story*. New York, 2001.

Maier, Klaus A. "Die internationalen Auseinandersetzungen um die Westintegration der Bundesrepublik Deutschland und um ihre Bewaffnung im Rahmen der europäischen

Verteidigungsgemeinschaft." In *Anfänge westdeutscher Sicherheitspolitik. Vol. 2, Part 1 Die EVG-Phase*, ed. Lutz Köllner, Klaus A. Maier, Wilhelm Meier-Dörnberg, and Hans-Erich Volkmann. Munich, 1990, 1–234.

Maizière, Ulrich de. "Die Bundeswehr—Neuschöpfung oder Fortsetzung der Wehrmacht?" In *Die Wehrmacht: Mythos und Realität*, ed. Rolf-Dieter Müller and Hans-Erich Volkmann. Munich, 1999, 1171–1183.

Manstein, Rüdiger von, and Theodor Fuchs. *Manstein: Soldat im 20. Jahrhundert: Militärisch-politische Nachlese*. Munich, 1981.

Maugham, Viscount. *U.N.O. and War Crimes*. London, 1951.

Mayer-Tasch, Peter Cornelius. *Guerrillakrieg und Völkerrecht: Essay, Bibliographie und Dokumentation*. Baden-Baden, 1972.

Meier-Dörnberg, Wilhelm. "Die Planung des Verteidigungsbeitrags der Bundesrepublik Deutschland im Rahmen der EVG." In *Anfänge westdeutscher Sicherheitspolitik, Vol. 2, Die EVG-Phase*, ed. Lutz Köllner et al. Munich, 1990, 605–756.

Merkel, Reinhard. "Nürnberg 1945: Militärtribunal, Grundlagen, Probleme, Folgen." *Merkur* 50 (1997): 918–936.

Messerschmidt, Manfred. "Die Wehrmacht: Vom Realitätsverlust zum Selbstbetrug." In *Ende des Dritten Reiches–Ende des Zweiten Weltkriegs: Eine perspektivische Rückschau*, ed. Hans-Erich Volkmann. Munich, 1995, 223–258.

———. *Die Wehrmacht im NS-Staat: Zeit der Indoktrination*. Hamburg, 1969.

———. "Vorwärtsverteidigung: Die 'Denkschrift der Generale' für den Nürnberger Gerichtshof." In *Vernichtungskrieg: Verbrechen der Wehrmacht 1941 bis 1945*, ed. Hannes Heer and Klaus Naumann. Hamburg, 1995, 531–550.

Messerschmidt, Manfred, and Fritz Wüllner. *Die Wehrmachtjustiz im Dienste des Nationalsozialismus: Zerstörung einer Legende*. Baden-Baden, 1987.

Meyer, Georg. *Adolf Heusinger: Dienst eines deutschen Soldaten 1915–1964*. Hamburg, 2001.

———. "Soldaten ohne Armee: Berufssoldaten im Kampf um Standesehre und Versorgung." In *Von Stalingrad zur Währungsreform, Zur Sozialgeschichte des Umbruchs in Deutschland*, ed. Martin Broszat, Klaus-Dietmar Henke, and Hans Woller. Munich, 1988, 651–682.

———. "Soldaten wie andere auch? Zur Einstellung ehemaliger Angehöriger der Waffen-SS in die Bundeswehr." In *Festgabe Heinz Hürten zum 60. Geburtstag*, ed. Harald Dicherhof. Frankfurt/Main, 1988, 545–594.

———. "Zur Situation der deutschen militärischen Führungsschicht im Vorfeld des westdeutschen Verteidigungsbeitrages 1945–1950/51." In *Anfänge westdeutscher Sicherheitspolitik 1945–1956, Vol. 1. Von der Kapitulation bis zum Pleven-Plan*, ed. Roland G. Foerster et al. Munich, 1982, 577–736.

Miccoli, Giovanni. *I dilemmi e i silenzi di Pio XII: Vaticano, Seconda Guerra Mondiale e Shoah*. Milan, 2000.

Mitscherlich, Alexander, and Margarete Mitscherlich. *Die Unfähigkeit zu trauern: Vom Umgang der Deutschen mit ihrer Vergangenheit*. Munich, 1967.

Moll, Otto E. "Albert Kesselring, Soldat bis zum letzten Tag." In *Die deutschen Generalfeldmarschälle 1939–1945*, ed. idem. Rastatt, 1988, 61–71.

Morgan, Robert. *The United States and West Germany 1945–1973: A Study in Alliance Politics*. Oxford, 1973.

Morsey, Rudolf. *Die Bundesrepublik Deutschland: Entstehung und Entwicklung bis 1969*. Munich, 1987.

Mühlen, Bengt von zur, ed. *Die zwölf Nürnberger Nachfolgeprozesse*. Berlin, 2000.

Müller, Rolf-Dieter, and Hans-Erich Volkmann, eds. *Die Wehrmacht: Mythos und Realität.* Munich, 1999.

Naumann, Klaus. "Integration und Eigensinn: Die Sicherheitseliten der frühen Bundesrepublik zwischen Kriegs- und Friedenskultur." In *Von der Kriegskultur zur Friedenskultur? Zum Mentalitätswandel in Deutschland seit 1945*, ed. Thomas Kühne. Münster, 2000, 202–218.

——, ed. *Nachkrieg in Deutschland.* Hamburg, 2001.

Neumann, Peter, and Elisabeth Noelle, eds. *Jahrbuch der öffentlichen Meinung.* Allensbach, 1952.

Nicolson, Nigel. *Alex: The Life of Fieldmarshal Earl Alexander of Tunis.* London, 1973.

Niethammer, Lutz. *Die Mitläuferfabrik: Die Entnazifizierung am Beispiel Bayerns.* Berlin, 1982.

Nietzsche, Friedrich. *Sämtliche Werke: Kritische Studienausgabe in 15 Bänden, hrsg. von Giorgio Colli und Mazzino Montinari, Vol. 5. Jenseits von Gut und Böse, Abschnitt 68.* Munich, 1980.

Nill-Theobald, Christiane. *"Defences" bei Kriegsverbrechen am Beispiel Deutschlands und der USA: Zugleich ein Beitrag zu einem Allgemeinen Teil des Völkerstrafrechts.* Freiburg im Breisgau, 1998.

Oliva, Gianni. *I vinti e i liberati: 8 Settembre 1943–25 aprile 1945.* Milan, 1994.

Otto, Heinrich. *Werden und Wesen des Quäkertums und seine Entwicklung in Deutschland.* Vienna, 1972.

Paget, Reginald Thomas. *Manstein: Seine Feldzüge und sein Prozess.* Wiesbaden, 1952.

Palmer Domenico, Roy. *Processo ai fascisti.* Milan, 1996.

Paoletti, Paolo. *La strage del 23 Agosto 1944.* Firenze, 1994.

——. *Sant'Anna di Stazzema 1944: La strage impunita.* Milan, 1998.

Pavone, Claudio. *Una guerra civile: Saggio sulla moralità nella Resistenza.* Turin, 1991.

Peitsch, Helmut. *"Deutschlands Gedächtnis in seiner dunkelsten Zeit": Zur Frage der Autobiographie in den Westzonen Deutschlands und den Westsektoren von Berlin 1945 bis 1949.* Berlin, 1990.

Petersen, Jens. "Der Ort der Resistenza in Geschichte und Gegenwart." *QFIAB* 72 (1992): 550–571.

——. "Deutschland und der Zusammenbruch des Faschismus in Italien im Sommer 1943." *MGM* 37 (1985): 51–69.

——. *Hitler–Mussolini: Die Entstehung der Achse Berlin–Rom, 1933–1936.* Tübingen, 1973.

Pezzino, Paolo. *Anatomia di un massacro: Controversia sopra una strage tedesca.* Bologna, 1997.

——. "Sui mancati processi in Italia ai criminali di guerra tedeschi." *Storia e Memoria* 10 (2001): 1–72.

Prantl, Heribert. *Wehrmachtverbrechen: Eine deutsche Kontroverse.* Hamburg, 1997.

Prauser, Steffen. "Mord in Rom? Der Anschlag in der Via Rasella und die deutsche Vergeltung in den Fosse Ardeatine im März 1944." *Vierteljahreshefte für Zeitgeschichte* 50 (2002): 269–301.

Quazza, Guido. *Resistenza e storia d' Italia: Problemi e ipotesi di ricerca.* Milan, 1978.

Raiber, Richard. "Generalfeldmarschall Kesselring, Via Rasella, and the 'Ginny Mission.'" *MGM* 56 (1997): 69–106.

Rauscher, Walter. *Hitler und Mussolini: Macht, Krieg und Terror.* Graz, 2001.

Rautenberg, Hans-Jürgen. "Zur Standortbestimmung der künftigen deutschen Streitkräfte." In

Anfänge westdeutscher Sicherheitspolitik 1945–1956, Vol. 1. Von der Kapitulation bis zum Pleven-Plan, ed. Roland G. Foerster et al. Munich, 1982, 737–879.

Rautenberg, Hans-Jürgen, and Norbert Wiggershaus. "Die 'Himmeroder Denkschrift' vom Oktober 1950: Politische und militärische Überlegungen für einen Beitrag der Bundesrepublik Deutschland zur westeuropäischen Verteidigung." *MGM* 21 (1977): 135–206.

Reichel, Peter. "Vergangenheitsbewältigung als Problem unserer politischen Kultur: Einstellungen zum Dritten Reich und seine Folgen." In *Vergangenheitsbewältigung durch Strafverfahren? NS-Prozesse in der Bundesrepublik Deutschland*, ed. Jürgen Weber and Peter Steinbach. Munich, 1984, 145–163.

Reimann, Bruno W. *Aufarbeitung der Vergangenheit in Giessen: Die NS-Geschichte als soziales Tabu*. Giessen, 1993.

Rochat, Giorgio. *Guerre italiane in Libia e in Etiopia: Studi militari 1921–1939*. Treviso, 1991.

———. "Una ricerca impossibile: Le perdite italiane nella seconda guerra mondiale." *Italia contemporanea* 201 (1995): 688–700.

Roghmann, Klaus, and Rolf Ziegler. "Militärsoziologie." In *Handbuch der empirischen Sozialforschung, Vol. 9, Organisation Militär*, ed. René König. Stuttgart, 1977.

Roskill, Stephen Wentworth. *Hankey: Man of Secrets*. London, 1974.

Ruch, Raymond. "Krieg gegen die Zivilbevölkerung: Die deutsche Partisanenbekämpfung in der Sowjetunion und in Italien 1941–1945." Master's thesis, Bern, 2003.

Rückerl, Adalbert, ed. *NS-Prozesse: Nach 25 Jahren Strafverfolgung: Möglichkeiten, Grenzen, Ergebnisse*. Karlsruhe, 1971.

———, ed. *NS-Verbrechen vor Gericht: Versuch einer Vergangenheitsbewältigung*. Heidelberg, 1984.

———. "Staatsanwaltschaftliche Ermittlung der NS-Verbrechen–Schwierigkeiten und Ergebnisse." In *Vergangenheitsbewältigung durch Strafverfahren? NS-Prozesse in der Bundesrepublik Deutschland*, ed. Jürgen Weber and Peter Steinbach. Munich, 1984, 71–83.

———, ed. *Strafverfolgung von NS-Verbrechen 1945–1978: Eine Dokumentation*. Heidelberg, 1979.

Rumschöttel, Hans. *Das bayerische Offizierskorps 1866–1914*. Berlin, 1973.

Rusconi, Gian Enrico. "Die italienische Resistenza auf dem Prüfstand." *VfZ* 42, 3 (1994): 379–402.

Salter, Michael, and S. Ost. "War Crimes and Legal Immunities: The Complicities of Waffen-SS General Karl Wolff in Nazi Medical Experiments." *Rutgers Journal of Law and Religion* 4, 1 (2003): 12–26.

Schabas, William A. *Genozid im Völkerrecht*. Hamburg, 2003.

Schenck zu Schweinsberg, Krafft Freiherr. "Die Soldatenverbände in der Bundesrepublik." In *Studien zur politischen und gesellschaftlichen Situation der Bundeswehr*, ed. Georg Picht. Vol. 1. Witten, 1965, 96–177.

Schick, Christa. "Die Internierungslager." In *Von Stalingrad zur Währungsreform: Zur Sozialgeschichte des Umbruchs in Deutschland*, ed. Martin Broszat, Klaus-Dietmar Henke, and Hans Woller. Munich, 1988, 301–326.

Schieder, Wolfgang. "Das faschistische Italien." In *Der Nationalsozialistische Krieg*, ed. Norbert Frei and Hermann Kling. Frankfurt, 1990, 48–61.

Schildt, Axel, and Arnold Sywottek, eds. *Modernisierung im Wiederaufbau: Die westdeutsche Gesellschaft der 50er Jahre*. Bonn, 1993.

Schmelzer, Kerstin. "Totaler Krieg auf italienisch? Die deutsche Auslandspropaganda in Italien 1943–1944." Master's thesis, Freiburg, 1995.

Schreiber, Gerhard. "Deutsche Kriegsverbrechen in Italien." In *Kriegsverbrechen im 20. Jahrhundert*, ed. Wolfram Wette and Gerd R. Ueberschär. Darmstadt, 2001, 222–234.

———. *Deutsche Kriegsverbrechen in Italien: Täter, Opfer, Strafverfolgung*. Munich, 1996.

———. *Die italienischen Militärinternierten im deutschen Machtbereich 1943–1945: Verraten, verachtet, vergessen*. Munich, 1990.

———. "Il settore occidentale della linea Gotica." *Storia e Memoria* 3, 1 (1994): 51–75.

———. *La vendetta tedesca: 1943–1945: Le rappresaglie naziste in Italia*. Milan, 2000.

———. "L'eccidio di Caiazzo e le miserie della giustizia tedesca." *Italia Contemporanea* 201 (1995): 661–685.

———. "Partisanenkrieg und Kriegsverbrechen der Wehrmacht in Italien 1943 bis 1945." In *Repression und Kriegsverbrechen: Die Bekämpfung von Widerstands- und Partisanenbewegungen gegen die deutsche Besatzung in West- und Südeuropa*. Berlin, 1997, 93–129.

Schröder, Josef. *Italiens Kriegsaustritt 1943: Die deutschen Gegenmassnahmen im italienischen Raum, Fall "Alarich" und "Achse."* Göttingen, 1969.

Schubert, Klaus V. *Wiederbewaffnung und Westintegration: Die innere Auseinandersetzung um die militärische und aussenpolitische Orientierung der Bundesrepublik 1950–1954*. Stuttgart, 1970.

Schulz, Gerhard. "Die Irregulären: Guerilla, Partisanen und die Wandlungen des Krieges seit dem 18. Jahrhundert. Eine Einführung." In *Partisanenkrieg und Volkskrieg: Zur Revolutionierung des Krieges im 20. Jahrhundert*, ed. Gerhard Schulz and Bernd Bonwetsch. Göttingen, 1985, 9–35.

Schwarz, Hans-Peter. *Die Ära Adenauer: Gründerjahre der Republik 1949–1957*. Stuttgart/Wiesbaden, 1981.

———. "Die ausgebliebene Katastrophe: Eine Problemskizze zur Geschichte der Bundesrepublik." In *Den Staat denken*, ed. Hermann Rudolph. Berlin, 1990, 151–174.

Schwartz, Thomas Alan. "Die Begnadigung deutscher Kriegsverbrecher: John J. McCloy und die Häftlinge von Landsberg." *VfZ* 38 (1990): 375–414.

Schwendemann, Heinrich. "Strategie der Selbstvernichtung: Die Wehrmachtführung im 'Endkampf' um das 'Dritte Reich.'" In *Die Wehrmacht: Mythos und Realität*, ed. Rolf-Dieter Müller and Hans-Erich Volkmann. Munich, 1999, 224–244.

Schwengler, Walter. "Der doppelte Anspruch: Souveränität und Sicherheit: Zur Entwicklung des völkerrechtlichen Status der Bundesrepublik Deutschland 1949 bis 1955." In *Anfänge westdeutscher Sicherheitspolitik, Vol. 4, Wirtschaft und Rüstung, Souveränität und Sicherheit*, ed. Werner Abelshauser. Munich, 1997, 187–566.

———. *Völkerrecht, Versailler Vertrag und Auslieferungsfrage: Die Strafverfolgung wegen Kriegsverbrechen als Problem des Friedensschlusses 1919/1920*. Stuttgart, 1982.

Schwengler, Walter, and Hans-Erich Volkmann, eds. *Die Europäische Verteidigungsgemeinschaft: Stand und Probleme der Forschung*. Boppard, 1985.

Scott, Richenda, ed. *Die Quäker*. Stuttgart, 1974.

Searle, Alaric. "A Very Special Relationship: Basil Liddell Hart, Wehrmacht Generals and the Debate on West German Rearmament, 1945–1953." *War in History 1998*, 5: 327–357.

———. "Revising the Myth of a Clean Wehrmacht: Generals' Trials, Public Opinion, and the Dynamics of Vergangenheitsbewältigung in West Germany, 1948–1960." *German Historical Institute London, Bulletin* 25, 2 (Nov. 2003): 17–48.

———. "Veterans' Associations and Political Radicalism in West Germany, 1951–1954: A Case Study of the Traditionsgemeinschaft Grossdeutschland." *Canadian Journal of History* 39 (August 1999): 221–248.

———. "Was There a 'Boney' Fuller after the Second World War? Major-General J. F. C. Fuller as Military Theorist and Commentator, 1945–1966." *War in History* 11, 3 (2004): 327–357.

———. *Wehrmacht Generals, West German Society, and the Debate on Rearmament 1949–1959*. Westport, 2003.

Senfft, Heinrich. "Lauter feine Herren: Deutsche Kriegsverbrecher, einige Lords und die Wiederbewaffnung." *Blätter für deutsche und internationale Politik* (August 2001): 995–1004.

Siviero, Rodolfo. *L'arte e il Nazismo: Esodo e ritorno delle opere d'arte italiane 1938–1963*. Firenze, 1984.

Sloterdijk, Peter. *Literatur und Organisation von Lebenserfahrung: Autobiographien der zwanziger Jahre*. Munich, 1978.

Sontheimer, Kurt. *Die Adenauer-Ära: Grundlegung der Bundesrepublik*. Munich, 1991.

Staron, Joachim. *Fosse Ardeatine und Marzabotto: Deutsche Kriegsverbrechen und Resistenza*. Paderborn, 2002.

Steinbach, Peter. "Der Nürnberger Prozess gegen die Hauptkriegsverbrecher." In *Der Nationalsozialismus vor Gericht: Die alliierten Prozesse gegen Kriegsverbrecher und Soldaten 1943–1952*, ed. Gerd R. Ueberschär. Frankfurt/Main, 1999, 32–44.

———. *Nationalsozialistische Gewaltverbrechen: Die Diskussion in der deutschen Öffentlichkeit nach 1945*. Berlin, 1981.

———. "Nationalsozialistische Gewaltverbrechen in der deutschen Öffentlichkeit nach 1945." In *Vergangenheitsbewältigung durch Strafverfahren? NS-Prozesse in der Bundesrepublik Deutschland*, ed. Jürgen Weber and Peter Steinbach. Munich, 1984, 13–39.

———. "Widerstand und Wehrmacht." In *Die Wehrmacht: Mythos und Realität*, ed. Rolf-Dieter Müller and Hans-Erich Volkmann. Munich, 1999, 1150–1170.

———. "Zur Auseinandersetzung mit nationalsozialistischen Gewaltverbrechen in der Bundesrepublik Deutschland: Ein Beitrag zur deutschen politischen Kultur nach 1945." *Geschichte in Wissenschaft und Unterricht* 35 (1984): 65–85.

Steininger, Rolf. *Wiederbewaffnung: Die Entscheidung für einen westdeutschen Verteidigungsbeitrag: Adenauer und die Westmächte 1950*. Erlangen, 1989.

Streit, Christian. *Keine Kameraden: Die Wehrmacht und die sowjetischen Kriegsgefangenen 1941–1945*. Bonn, 1997.

Stumpf, Reinhard. "Der Krieg im Mittelmeerraum 1942/1943: Die Operationen in Nordafrika und im mittleren Mittelmeer." In *Das deutsche Reich und der Zweite Weltkrieg, Vol. 6, Der Globale Krieg: Die Ausweitung zum Weltkrieg und der Wechsel der Initiative 1941–1943*, ed. Horst Boog, Werner Rahn, Reinhard Stumpf, and Bernd Wegner. Stuttgart, 1990, 569–760.

———. *Die Wehrmacht-Elite: Rang- und Herkunftsstruktur der deutschen Generale und Admirale 1933–1945*. Boppard, 1982, 7.

———. "Von der Achse Berlin–Rom zum Militärabkommen des Dreipaktes: Die Abfolge der Verträge 1936 bis 1942." In *Das deutsche Reich und der Zweite Weltkrieg, Band 6. Der Globale Krieg: Die Ausweitung zum Weltkrieg und der Wechsel der Initiative 1941–1943*, ed. Horst Boog, Werner Rahn, Reinhard Stumpf, and Bernd Wegner. Stuttgart, 1990, 127–143.

Tauber, Klaus Peter. *Beyond Eagle and Swastika: German Nationalism since 1945*. Middletown, CT, 1965.

Taylor, Telford. *Die Nürnberger Prozesse: Hintergründe, Analysen und Erkenntnisse aus heutiger Sicht*. Munich, 1994.

Thoss, Bruno, and Hans-Erich Volkmann, eds. *Zwischen kaltem Krieg und Entspannung:*

Sicherheits- und Deutschlandpolitik der Bundesrepublik im Mächtesystem der Jahre 1953–1956. Boppard, 1988.

Tognarini, Ivan. *Kesselring e le stragi nazifasciste: 1944: Estate di sangue in Toscana*. Firenze, 2002.

Torneer, Pietro. "Le due faccie del Feldmaresciallo Albert Kesselring." *La Resistenza Breciana: Rassegna di studi e documenti* 31 (April 2000): 48–57.

Trythall, Anthony John. *Boney Fuller: The Intellectual General 1878–1966*. London, 1977, 240–275.

Tutorow, Norman E., ed. *War Crimes, War Criminals and War Crimes Trials: An Annotated Bibliography and Source Book*. New York, 1986.

Ueberschär, Gerd R. *Generaloberst Franz Halder: Generalstabschef, Gegner und Gefangener Hitlers*. Göttingen, 1991.

———. "Sowjetische Prozesse gegen deutsche Kriegsgefangene." In *Der Nationalsozialismus vor Gericht: Die alliierten Prozesse gegen Kriegsverbrecher und Soldaten 1943–1952*, ed. idem. Frankfurt/Main, 1999, 240–261.

Ueberschär, Gerd R., and Winfried Vogel. *Dienen und Verdienen: Hitlers Geschenke an seine Eliten*. Frankfurt/Main, 1999.

Vandagnini, Armando. *Gli anni della lotta: Guerra, Resistenza, Autonomia 1940–1948*. Trient, 1978.

Veale, F. J. P. *Der Barbarei entgegen: Wie der Rückfall in die Barbarei durch Kriegführung und Kriegsverbrecherprozesse unsere Zukunft bedroht*. Hamburg, 1954.

———. "Lord Hankey: The Greatest British Public Servant of the Age." *Social Justice Review* (April 1963): 12–15.

———. *War Crimes Discreetly Veiled*. New York, 1959.

Veneruso, Danilo. *L'Italia fascista 1922–1945*. Bologna, 1981.

Verteidigung im Bündnis: Planung, Aufbau und Bewährung der Bundeswehr 1950–1972, ed. Militärgeschichtliches Forschungsamt. Munich, 1975.

Vogelsang, Thilo. "Albert Keßelring." *Neue Deutsche Biographie* 11 (1977): 542–543.

Volkmann, Hans-Erich. "Die innenpolitische Dimension Adenauerscher Sicherheitspolitik in der EVG-Phase." In *Anfänge westdeutscher Sicherheitspolitik, Band 2: Die EVG-Phase*, ed. Lutz Köllner, Klaus A. Maier, Wilhelm Meier-Dörnberg, and Hans-Erich Volkmann. Munich, 1990, 235–604.

Volkmann, Hans-Erich, and Walter Schwengler, eds. *Die Europäische Verteidigungsgemeinschaft: Stand und Probleme der Forschung*. Boppard, 1985.

Vollnhals, Clemens. "Die Hypothek des Nationalprotestantismus: Entnazifizierung und Strafverfolgung von NS-Verbrechen nach 1945." GG 18 (1992): 51–69.

———. *Evangelische Kirche und Entnazifizierung: 1945–1949: Die Last der nationalsozialistischen Vergangenheit*. Munich, 1989.

Von Lingen, Kerstin. "'Condannato al silenzio.' Governi alleati e crimini nazisti in Italia: I condizionamenti politici sulla ricerca della verità." In *12 agosto 1944: La strage di Sant'Anna di Stazzema*, ed. Marco Palla. Florence 2003, 153–162.

———. "Conspiracy of Silence: How the 'Old Boys' of American Intelligence Shielded SS-General Karl Wolff from Prosecution," *Holocaust and Genocide Studies* 22, no. 1 (2008): 74–109.

———. "Der Fall Kesselring: Britische Vergangenheitspolitik und die Kriegsverbrecherlobby." In *Historische Dimensionen von Kriegsverbrecherprozessen nach dem Zweiten Weltkrieg*, ed. H. Radtke, D. Rössner, T. Schiller, and W. Form. Baden-Baden 2007, 137–158.

———. "Eine Frage der Ehre: Die Legendenkonstruktion der Offiziere vom 'Sauberen Krieg' an der Italienfront." In *Vom Umgang mit der Vergangenheit—ein deutsch-italienischer Vergleich, ed.* Christiane Liermann, Martha Margotti, and Bernd Sösemann. Tübingen, 2007, 91–120.

———. "Generalfeldmarschall Albert Kesselring—Soldat bis zum letzten Tag?" In *Karrieren im Nationalsozialismus,* ed. Gerhard Hirschfeld. Frankfurt, 2004, 205–224.

———. "La lunga via verso la pace: Retroscena e interessi attorno all' 'Operation Sunrise.'" *Storia e Regione* 17, no. 1 (2008): 159–178.

———. "Partisanenkrieg und Wehrmachtjustiz: Italien 1943–1945." *Zeitschrift für Genozidforschung* 8, no. 2 (2007): 8–40.

———. "'Resistenza-Mythos'" und die Legende vom 'Sauberen Krieg an der Südfront.' Konstruktion von Kriegserinnerung in Italien und Deutschland 1945–2005." In *"Transformationen" der Erinnerungskulturen in Europa nach 1989,* ed. Bernd Faulenbach and Franz-Josef Jelich. Essen, 2006, 329–364.

———. "Soldiers into Citizens. 'Wehrmacht' officers in the Federal Republic of Germany (1945–1960)," review article. *Bulletin of the German Historical Institute London* 27, no. 2 (November 2005): 45–67.

———. "'. . . wenn wir zum letzten Kampf in Italien antreten.' Die Konstruktion von Kriegserinnerung am Beispiel des Kriegsverbrecherprozesses gegen Albert Kesselring." In *Erster Weltkrieg—Zweiter Weltkrieg. Ein Vergleich,* ed. Bruno Thos and Hans-Erich Volkmann. Paderborn, 2002, 687–709.

Von Lingen, Kerstin, and Michael Salter. "Contrasting Strategies within the War Crimes Trials of Kesselring and Wolff." *Liverpool Law Review* 26, no.3 (2005): 225–266.

Von Nürnberg nach Den Haag. *Menschrechtsverbrechen vor Gericht: Zur Aktualität des Nürnberger Prozesses*. Hamburg, 1996.

Vordemann, Christian. *Deutschland–Italien 1949–1961: Die diplomatischen Beziehungen.* Frankfurt, 1994.

Wagener, Hans, ed. "Soldaten zwischen Gehorsam und Gewissen: Kriegsromane und Kriegstagebücher." In *Gegenwartsliteratur und Drittes Reich: Deutsche Autoren in der Auseinandersetzung mit der Vergangenheit.* Stuttgart, 1977, 241–264.

Wagner, Dietrich. *FDP und Wiederbewaffnung: Die wehrpolitische Orientierung der Liberalen in der Bundesrepublik Deutschland 1949–1955*. Boppard, 1978.

Weber, Jürgen. *Die Bundesrepublik wird souverän 1950–1955*. Munich, 1986.

———. *Gründung eines neuen Staates 1949*. Munich, 1981.

Wedekind, Michael. *Nationalsozialistische Besatzungs- und Annexionspolitik in Norditalien, 1943–1945*. Munich, 2003.

Wegner, Bernd. "Erschriebene Siege: Franz Halder, die 'Historical Division' und die Rekonstruktion des Zweiten Weltkrieges im Geiste des deutschen Generalstabes." In *Politischer Wandel, organisierte Gewalt und nationale Sicherheit: Beiträge zur neueren Geschichte Deutschlands und Frankreichs,* ed. Ernst Willi Hansen. Munich, 1995, 287–302.

——— "Hitlers zweiter Feldzug gegen die Sowjetunion: Strategische Grundlagen und historische Bedeutung." In *Der Zweite Weltkrieg: Analysen–Grundzüge–Forschungsbilanz,* ed. Wolfgang Michalka. Munich, 1990, 652–666.

Weinberg, Gerhard L. "Zur Dotation Hitlers an Generalfeldmarschall Ritter von Leeb." *Militärgeschichtliche Mitteilungen* (*MGM*) 26 (1979): 97.

Werle, Gerhard. *Völkerstrafrecht*. Tübingen, 2003.

Wette, Wolfram. "Das Bild der Wehrmacht-Elite nach 1945." In *Hitlers militärische Elite*, ed. Gerd R. Ueberschär. Vol. 2. Darmstadt, 1998, 293–308.

———. *Die Wehrmacht: Feindbilder, Vernichtungskrieg, Legenden*. Darmstadt, 2002.

———. "Fall 12: Der OKW-Prozess." In *Der Nationalsozialismus vor Gericht: Die alliierten Prozesse gegen Kriegsverbrecher und Soldaten 1943–1952*, ed. Gerd R. Ueberschär. Frankfurt, 1999, 199–216.

———, ed. *Retter in Uniform: Handlungsspielräume im Vernichtungskrieg der Wehrmacht*. Frankfurt, 2002.

Wette, Wolfram, and Gerd R. Ueberschär, eds. *Kriegsverbrechen im 20. Jahrhundert*. Darmstadt, 2001.

Wettig, Gerhard. *Entmilitarisierung und Wiederbewaffnung in Deutschland 1943–1955*. Munich, 1967.

Wiggershaus, Norbert. "Die Entscheidung für einen westdeutschen Verteidigungsbeitrag 1950." In *Anfänge westdeutscher Sicherheitspolitik 1945–1956, Vol. 1, Von der Kapitulation bis zum Pleven-Plan*, ed. Roland G. Foerster. Munich, 1982, 325–402.

Woetzel, Robert K. *The Nuremberg Trials in the International Law*. London/New York, 1960.

Woller, Hans. "'Ausgebliebene Säuberung?' Die Abrechnung mit dem Faschismus in Italien." In *Politische Säuberung in Europa: Die Abrechnung mit Faschismus und Kollaboration nach dem Zweiten Weltkrieg*, ed. Henke Klaus-Dietmar and Hans Woller. Munich, 1991, 148–191.

———. *Die Abrechnung mit dem Faschismus in Italien 1943 bis 1948*. Munich, 1996.

Woodward, Llewellyn. *British Foreign Policy in the Second World War*. London, 1962.

Wrochem, Oliver von. "Die Auseinandersetzung mit Wehrmachtverbrechen im Prozess gegen den Generalfeldmarschall Erich von Manstein 1949." *ZfG* 4 (1998): 329–353.

———. "Rehabilitation oder Strafverfolgung: Kriegsverbrecherprozess gegen Generalfeldmarschall Erich von Manstein im Widerstreit britischer Interessen." *Mittelweg* 36, no. 3 (1997): 26–36.

Wüllner, Fritz. *Die NS-Militärjustiz und das Elend der Geschichtsschreibung: Ein grundlegender Forschungsbericht*. Baden-Baden, 1991.

Zala, Sacha. *Geschichte unter der Schere politischer Zensur: Amtliche Aktensammlungen im internationalen Vergleich*. Munich, 2001.

Zayas, Alfred De. *Die Wehrmacht-Untersuchungsstelle*. Vienna, 1980.

INDEX

www.ingramcontent.com/pod-product-compliance
Ingram Content Group UK Ltd.
Pitfield, Milton Keynes, MK11 3LW, UK
UKHW041854031026
15587UKWH00006B/1233/J

9 780700 616411